Published by NCVO
Society Building
8 All Saints Street
London N1 9RL

First published in 1928 as the Voluntary
Services Handbook and Directory

This edition published February 2017

Copyright NCVO 2017

Registered charity number 225922

Designed by Steers McGillan Eves

Printed by Pureprint

British Library Cataloguing in Public Data

A catalogue record for this book is available
from the British Library

Every effort has been made to ensure the
accuracy of the information contained within
this publication.

ISBN: 978-0-7199-0025-9

THE VOLUNTARY AGENCIES DIRECTORY 2017

NCVO

CHAMPIONING VOLUNTARY ACTION

# ABOUT THE DIRECTORY

### How to use this directory

Entries are arranged alphabetically and provide contact details for each organisation. There is a brief description of the aims and activities, together with a broad summary of the types of services offered.

 Provides grants

 Membership scheme

 Information or advisory service

 Undertakes research

 Umbrella or resource body

The index at the back provides broad categorisations for each organisation.

### Criteria for inclusion

'Voluntary agency' is broadly interpreted as a self-governing body of people who have joined together to take action for the betterment (as they see it) of the community, not for financial gain. Organisations affiliated to any political party are not eligible for inclusion. Limitations on space make it impossible to include every voluntary agency, so, as far as possible, organisations need to meet the following criteria:

- have a nationwide, rather than local, remit

- be a leading body in their field

- have headquarters in the UK.

Organisations not included in the directory are welcome to apply for inclusion, free of charge, in the next edition. Email publications@ncvo. org.uk for more details.

Inclusion in the directory does not constitute an endorsement by NCVO.

### Accuracy of contents

NCVO accepts no liability for the accuracy of the information. All organisations listed in the directory were contacted directly by NCVO and given the opportunity to update the details of their entry. NCVO reserves the right to include or exclude entries as part of the publishing process, and to edit all details supplied.

# A-Z
## OF VOLUNTARY AGENCIES

## 10:10

8 Delancey Passage, London NW1 7NN
T: 020 7388 6688
E: hello@1010uk.org
www.1010global.org
**Executive Director: Heidi Proven**
We're on the way to a cleaner, cleverer, low-carbon world and everyone deserves a chance to help build it. 10:10 creates these chances and brings people together to make the most of them. 10:10ers work together to: celebrate the good stuff already happening, and help it spread; save energy at home, work and locally; light up our best-loved places with crowdfunded clean energy; and convince people in power to tackle the stuff we don't control.
**Employees: 13**
**Regional offices: 1**

## 25% ME Group – Support for Severe ME Sufferers

21 Church Street, Troon,
Ayrshire KA10 6HT
T: 01292 318611
E: enquiry@25megroup.org
www.25megroup.org
The 25% ME Group is a unique nationwide charitable organisation managed entirely by volunteers (most of whom are severely affected by ME) and was set up to offer support services to those severely affected by ME (myalgic encephalomyelitis) and their carers.
**Employees: 2**
**Volunteers: 12**

## 3 Villages Youth Project

2 Elms Close Terrace, Newlyn, Penzance,
Cornwall TR18 5AU
T: 01736 364707
E: julyan.drew@gmail.com
3villagesyouthproject.org.uk
**Chair of Trustees: Julyan Drew**
Working with and for children and young people in Newlyn, Mousehole and Paul in Cornwall.
**Employees: 1**
**Volunteers: 11**
**Regional offices: 1**

## 3H Fund (Helping Hands for Holidays)

B2 Speldhurst Business Park, Langton Road,
Speldhurst, Tunbridge Wells,
Kent TN3 0AQ
T: 01892 860207
E: info@3hfund.org.uk
www.3hfund.org.uk
**Charity Manager: Lynne Loving**

3H Fund organises subsidised group holidays for physically disabled children (aged 13+) and adults with the support of volunteer helpers, so that family carers can have a separate and much-needed period of respite.
**Employees: 6**
**Volunteers: 60+**
**Income: £235,000 (2015–16)**

## 4Children

City Reach, 5 Greenwich View Place,
London E14 9NN
T: 020 7512 2112
F: 020 7512 2010
E: info@4children.org.uk
www.4children.org.uk
**Chief Executive: Anne Longfield**
4Children is a national children's charity that aims to place children and young people at the centre of policy development and service delivery, creating and supporting opportunities that enable all children to fulfil their potential and all parents to access the support they need. The organisation has led the lobbying for, and development of, childcare and out-of-school activities over the last 20 years whilst supporting a major growth in childcare places.
**Employees: 80**
**Regional offices: 1**

## A Rocha UK

13 Avenue Road, Southall,
Middlesex UB1 3BL
T: 020 8574 5935 (also fax)
E: uk@arocha.org
www.arocha.org
The advancement of the Christian faith and understanding of its relevance to the environment.
**Employees: 13**
**Volunteers: 30**

## Abbeyfield Society

Abbeyfield House, 53 Victoria Street,
St Albans AL1 3UW
T: 01727 857536
F: 01727 846168
E: post@abbeyfield.com
www.abbeyfield.com
Abbeyfield is one of the largest voluntary sector providers of housing and care for older people in the UK. Abbeyfield believes older people should be able to obtain the support and care they need to remain independent and involved in life. Founded in 1956 by Richard Carr-Gomm, Abbeyfield has grown to include about 700 houses throughout the UK providing accommodation and support for around 7,500 older people, run by professional staff and more than 7,500 volunteers.

## AbilityNet

PO Box 94, Birmingham Road, Warwick,
Warwickshire CV34 5WS
T: 0870 240 4455
Helpline: 0800 269545
E: enquiries@abilitynet.org.uk
www.abilitynet.org.uk
A national charity helping disabled adults and children use computers and the internet by adapting and adjusting their technology.

## AbleChildAfrica

Unit 3, Graphite Square, Vauxhall Walk,
London SE11 5EE
T: 020 7793 4144
E: info@ablechildafrica.org.uk
www.ablechildafrica.org.uk
**Executive Director: Jane Anthony**
AbleChildAfrica specialises in advocating for and supporting disabled children and young people in Africa. In order to achieve this we support partner organisations to carry out life-changing work with disabled children and young people and work alongside them to use their experiences and learning to campaign for more widespread change in attitudes and practice.
**Employees: 7**
**Volunteers: 2**

## Academy of Youth Limited

University of The First Age, The Toll House,
180–182 Fazeley Street, Digbeth,
Birmingham B5 5SE
T: 0121 766 8077
E: info@ufa.org.uk
www.aoy.org.uk
Advances the education of children, young people and adults through an institution that is committed to: raising educational achievement; preparing children and young people for the challenge of adult life; transforming educational opportunities.

## Access Community Trust

114 High Street, Lowestoft NR32 1HN
T: 01502 527200
E: julie.gordon@accessct.org
www.accessct.org
Chief Executive: Emma Ratzer
To promote social inclusion, reducing vulnerability and homelessness by providing accommodation, education, training and practical support tailored to individual needs. We offer mental health and wellbeing services, have two recruitment mentors and a youth-led project addressing social issues faced by young people who are vulnerable, socially excluded and isolated. It is our mission to provide our clients and local community with unrivalled services.
Employees: 130
Volunteers: 30
Regional offices: 1

## ACCURO (Care Services)

South Side Suite 5 (North), Level 11, Terminus House, Terminus Street, Harlow CM20 1XA
T: 01279 433667 (also fax)
E: alison@accuro.org.uk
www.accuro.org.uk
CEO: Arthur Steward
Accuro provides a range of services for children, young people and adults with a disability resident in West Essex. Services include youth groups, a Saturday play club, an adult friendship scheme, etc.
Employees: 75
Volunteers: 80
Income: £530,000 (2014–15)

## Achieve Lifestyle

Egham Leisure Centre, Vicarage Road
T: 01784 437695
E: admin@achievelifestyle.co.uk
www.achievelifestyle.co.uk
Central Services Manager: Debbie Wilmott

## Action Against Allergy

PO Box 278, Twickenham TW1 4QQ
T: 020 8892 4949
Helpline: 020 8892 2711
E: aaa@actionagainstallergy.freeserve.co.uk
www.actionagainstallergy.co.uk
Executive Director: Patricia Schooling
Advances understanding, awareness and recognition of allergic medical conditions and allergy-related illness and the actions needed for research, diagnosis and treatment.
Employees: 3
Volunteers: 3

## Action Against Hunger UK

1st Floor, Rear Premises, 161–153 Greenwich High Road, London SE10 9JA
T: 020 8293 6190
E: m.eaton@actionagainsthunger.org.uk
www.actionagainsthunger.org.uk
Executive Director: Jean-Michel Grand
Action Against Hunger is an international humanitarian organisation committed to ending child hunger. Recognised as a leader in the fight against malnutrition, ACF works to save the lives of malnourished children while providing communities with sustainable access to safe water and long-term solutions to hunger.
Employees: 163
Volunteers: 25
Income: £16,902,000 (2015–16)

## Action Against Medical Accidents

Christopher Wren Yard, 117 High Street, Croydon, Surrey CR0 1QG
T: 020 8688 9555
Helpline: 0845 123 2352
F: 020 8667 9065
E: support@avma.org.uk
www.avma.org.uk
Chief Executive: Peter Walsh
Action against Medical Accidents (AvMA) is an independent UK charity that works for better patient safety and justice for people who have been affected by a medical accident.
Employees: 22
Volunteers: 70

## Action for Blind People

c/o RNIB office, 105 Judd Street, London WC1H 9NE
T: 020 7388 1266
Helpline: 0303 123 9999
E: info@actionforblindpeople.org.uk
www.actionforblindpeople.org.uk
Chief Executive: Miriam Martin
Action for Blind People provides practical and emotional advice and support across England to people who are blind or partially sighted and their friends and family.
Employees: 365
Volunteers: 573
Regional offices: 16
Income: £20,530,000 (2013–14)

## Action for Children

Action for Children, 3 The Boulevard, Ascot Road, Watford, Hertfordshire WD18 8AG
T: 01923 361500
Helpline: 0300 123 2112
E: ask.us@actionforchildren.org.uk
www.actionforchildren.org.uk
Chief Executive: Sir Tony Hawkhead
Action for Children exists to help the most vulnerable children and young people break through injustice, deprivation and inequality so they can achieve their full potential. We work across the UK, Northern Ireland and internationally. Action for Children works directly with more than 300,000 children, young people, parents and carers each year and runs more than 650 services.

## Action for ME

42 Temple Street, Keynsham, Bristol BS31 1EH
T: 0117 927 9551
F: 0117 986 1152
E: admin@actionforme.org.uk
www.actionforme.org.uk
Chief Executive: Sonya Chowdhury
At Action for ME we provide information and support for people affected by Myalgic Encephalomyelitis (ME), and work collaboratively to raise awareness, campaign for better services and fund vital research. People affected by ME can access support and information through our publications, Welfare Rights Line and online Services Directory, available via our Online ME Centre at www.actionforme.org.uk.
Employees: 19
Regional offices: 1

## Action for Prisoners' Families

15–17 The Broadway, Hatfield, Hertfordshire AL9 5HZ
T: 020 7553 3080
E: luke.evans@prisonersfamilies.org.uk
www.prisonersfamilies.org.uk
Director: Deborah Cowley
Membership organisation for prisoners' and offenders' families and those who work with them. Works for the benefit of prisoners' and offenders' families by: providing advice, information and training; providing opportunities for members to share experiences, concerns and successes; listening to prisoners' families and promoting, developing and supporting services and resources that they need or would like; lobbying for improved structures, procedures, conditions and services to promote the wellbeing of prisoners' and offenders' families.
Employees: 7

## Action for Sick Children

10 Ravenoak Road, Cheald Hulme,
Stockport SK8 7DL
T: 0161 486 6788
Helpline: 0800 074 4519
E: enquiries@actionforsickchildren.org
www.actionforsickchildren.org
CEO: Val Jackson
We join parents and professionals in
promoting high-quality healthcare for
children in hospital and at home.
Employees: 10
Volunteers: 6
Regional offices: 1

## Action Medical Research

Vincent House, North Parade, Horsham,
West Sussex RH12 2DP
T: 01403 210406
F: 01403 210541
E: info@action.org.uk
www.action.org.uk
Chief Executive: Julie Buckler
Action Medical Research is the leading
UK-wide medical research charity saving
and changing children's lives. Since we
began in 1952, we've been funding medical
breakthroughs that have helped save
thousands of children's lives and changed
many more. We want to make a difference in:
tackling premature birth and treating sick and
vulnerable babies; helping children affected by
disability, disabling conditions and infections;
targeting rare diseases that together severely
affect many forgotten children.
Employees: 51
Volunteers: 1050
Regional offices: 1
Income: £7,500 (2013–14)

## Action on Addiction

Head Office, East Knoyle, Salisbury,
Wiltshire SP3 6BE
T: 0300 330 0659
F: 01747 832028
E: admin@actiononaddiction.org.uk
www.actiononaddiction.org.uk
Chief Executive: Graham Beech
The charity Action on Addiction takes action
to disarm addiction in all its forms through
a uniquely comprehensive approach that
encompasses research, treatment (both
residential and non-residential), rehabilitation,
family support, education, training and
campaigning. Our vision is to see people
free from addiction and its effects.
Employees: 145
Regional offices: 5

## Action on Disability and Work UK

The Vassall Centre, Gill Avenue, Fishponds,
Bristol BS16 2QQ
T: 0117 961 7900
E: andy.rickell@adwuk.org
www.adwuk.org
Chief Executive Officer: Andy Rickell
Action on Disability and Work UK (ADWUK)
is a disabled people's user-led organisation
that supports disabled people to have
successful working lives. Our national advice
service provides advice on work-related
issues to disabled people, employers and
professionals. We run a local work club
supporting disabled people looking for
work, volunteering opportunities or self-
employment. We provide consultancy and
training for employers on any disability issue.
Employees: 10
Volunteers: 12
Regional offices: 1

## Action on Elder Abuse

PO Box 60001, London SW16 9BY
T: 020 8835 9280
Helpline: 0808 808 8141
F: 020 8696 9328
E: enquiries@elderabuse.org.uk
www.elderabuse.org.uk
Chief Executive: Gary FitzGerald
Aims to prevent abuse in old age through
raising awareness, education, promoting
research and the collection and dissemination
of information.

## Action on Hearing Loss (the new name for RNID)

19–23 Featherstone Street,
London EC1Y 8SL
T: 020 7296 8000
F: 020 7296 8199
E: informationline@hearingloss.org.uk
www.actiononhearingloss.org.uk
We aim to make daily life better for deaf and
hard of hearing people. Our campaigns,
information, services and support of scientific
and technological research are some of the
ways we're trying to help. We also support
other organisations in their aim to provide
better services to their deaf and hard of
hearing employees and customers.
Employees: 1400
Volunteers: 200
Regional offices: 7

## Action on Smoking and Health

Suites 59–63, 6th Floor, New House,
67–68 Hatton Garden, London EC1N 8JY
T: 020 7404 0242
F: 020 7404 0850
E: phil.rimmer@ash.org.uk
www.ash.org.uk
Chief Executive: Deborah Arnott
ASH is an organisation that provides
information on all aspects of tobacco and
works to advance policies and measures that
will help to prevent the addiction, disease and
unnecessary premature death caused by
smoking. ASH was established in 1971 by the
Royal College of Physicians.
Employees: 8

## Action to Regenerate Community Trust

67 Market Place, Warminster,
Wiltshire BA12 9AZ
T: 01225 290595
E: nicholas.gardham@regeneratetrust.org
www.rslm.org
Chief Executive Officer: Stephen Kearney
RE:generate is an enterprising social action
charity and grant-making trust. Our mission
is to tackle poverty and the root causes of
poverty and disadvantage. We work with
people to encourage them to: develop local
enterprising solutions to problems, participate
in public life and wake up to their potential
to make change in their lives and their
community. We aim to transform the
relationship between communities, agencies,
organisations and the state.
Employees: 6
Volunteers: 103
Regional offices: 1

## Action with Communities in Rural England

Suite 109, Unit 9, Cirencester Office Park,
Tetbury Road, Cirencester,
Gloucestershire GL7 6JJ
T: 01285 653477
F: 01285 654537
E: acre@acre.org.uk
www.acre.org.uk
Chief Executive: Sylvia Brown
Action with Communities in Rural England
is the national umbrella body of the Rural
Community Action Network (RCAN),
which operates at national, regional and local
level in support of rural communities across
the country. We aim to promote a healthy,
vibrant and sustainable rural community
sector that is well connected to policy and

decision-makers who play a part in delivering this aim.
**Employees: 16**

## ActionAid

33–39 Bowling Green Lane,
London EC1R 0BJ
T: 020 3122 0561
F: 020 7278 5667
E: rachel.leonard@actionaid.org
www.actionaid.org
Working in partnership with poor people to eradicate poverty by overcoming the injustice and inequity that cause it.
**Employees: 244**
**Volunteers: 7500**
**Regional offices: 3**

## Active Training and Education Trust

8 St Ann's Road, Malvern,
Worcestershire WR14 4RG
T: 01684 562400
Helpline: 0845 456 1205
F: 01684 562716
E: info@ate.org.uk
www.ate.org.uk
**Director of Operations: Liz Macartney**
The trust runs and promotes educational residential experiences for children and young people, through a programme of imaginative and creative summer camps, and through weekend and weekday sessions for schools, as well as FunDays in schools. It also runs training, INSET, conferences, etc, on the subject of fun and imagination in education.
**Employees: 3**
**Volunteers: 200**

## Actors Benevolent Fund

E: willie.bicket@abf.org.uk

## ADD Information Services

5th Floor Premier House, 112 Station Road,
Edgware, Middlesex HA8 7BJ
T: 020 8952 1515
E: info@addiss.co.uk
www.addiss.co.uk
The object of the charity is to relieve children and those persons suffering from attention deficit hyperactivity disorder (ADHD) and to advance the education of the public about the disorder.
**Employees: 3**

## ADD International (Action on Disability and Development)

ADD International, The Foundry,
17–19 Oval Way, London SE11 5RR
T: 0300 303 8835
F: 01373 473064
E: supportercare@add.org.uk
www.addinternational.org
ADD International is a disability rights organisation. We support disability activists who are fighting for independence, equality and opportunity for disabled people living in poverty in Africa and Asia.
**Employees: 100**
**Volunteers: 5**
**Regional offices: 5**

## Addaction

67–69 Cowcross Street,
London EC1M 6PU
T: 020 7251 5860
F: 020 7251 5890
E: info@addaction.org.uk
www.addaction.org.uk
**Chief Executive: Simon Antrobus**
Addaction reduces both the use of, and the harm caused by, drugs and alcohol.
**Employees: 640**
**Volunteers: 100**
**Regional offices: 2**

## Addiction Recovery Agency

King's Court, King Street, Bristol BS1 4EE
T: 0117 930 0282
E: info@addictionrecovery.org.uk
www.addictionrecovery.org.uk
Aims to support those who are affected by addiction to drugs, alcohol and gambling. We provide accommodation to clients in Bristol and engage in treatment to address their addiction. We also provide counselling to clients affected by gambling addiction. A newly developed service Connect Psychology is part of the Increasing Access to Psychological Therapies services in Bristol.

## Adfam

25 Corsham Street, 1st Floor,
London N1 6DR
T: 020 7553 7640
F: 020 7253 7991
E: admin@adfam.org.uk
www.adfam.org.uk
**Chief Executive: Vivienne Evans**
Adfam is a registered charity working with families affected by drugs and alcohol. Adfam provides accessible, clear and accurate information via their website and publications for families affected by drug and alcohol, including good practice guides and training

manuals for professionals working with family members. We challenge and influence policy makers, planners and the media to understand and represent more accurately the issues affecting families of drug and alcohol users.
**Employees: 13**
**Regional offices: 2**

## Adhar Project

E: admin.box@adharproject.org

## ADHD Solutions CIC

St Gabriel's Community Centre,
Kerrysdale Avenue, Leicester,
St Gabriel's Community Centre,
Kerrysdale Avenue, Leicestershire LE4 7GH
T: 0116 261 0711
E: info@adhdsolutions.org
www.adhdsolutions.org
**Director/CEO: Christine Jarvis**
ADHD Solutions aims to improve the life chances of people with Attention Deficit Hyperactivity Disorder (ADHD) by: delivering a quality service that supports and empowers children/young people, adults and their families to develop strategies for use at home, school and the work place; identifying critical times and triggers, preventing crises occurring; reducing social isolation and the risk of adverse outcomes, including antisocial behaviour, long-term mental health problems, educational underachievement, worklessness, family breakdown and social exclusion.
**Employees: 12**
**Volunteers: 35**
**Regional offices: 1**
**Income: £301,104 (2014–15)**

## Adoption UK

Linden House, 55 The Green,
South Bar Street, Banbury,
Oxfordshire OX16 9AB
T: 01295 752240
F: 01295 752241
E: press@adoptionuk.org.uk
www.adoptionuk.org.uk
Adoption UK helps to make adoptions work and promotes loving and supportive relationships between children and their adoptive families. It provides independent support and advice to all concerned with adoption, offering a wealth of relevant experience from generations of adoptive families to prospective and established adopters and those who work with them.
**Employees: 28**
**Volunteers: 130**
**Regional offices: 50**

## Adullam Homes Housing Association

Walter Moore House, 34 Dudley Street,
West Bromwich, West Midlands B70 9LS
T: 0121 500 2828
F: 01250 02824
E: info@adullam.org.uk
www.adullam.uk.net
**Chief Executive: Trevor Palfreyman**
Adullam Homes is a specialist provider in quality housing and support services and was founded in 1972. Adullam Homes now houses and supports 1,200 people at any one time, throughout the North West and the Midlands. The Association is renowned for its expertise in supporting and developing vulnerable and excluded people in addition to integrating service users and residents into the world of work.
**Employees: 220**
**Volunteers: 30**
**Regional offices: 2**

## Adventist Special Needs Association (ASNA)

ASNA, Howbery Park, Suite W-05,
Windrush Innovation Centre,
Wallingford, Oxon, Oxfordshire OX10 8BA
T: 01491 821104
Helpline: 01491 833395
E: info@asna.info
www.asna.info
**Honorary Secretary/Development Director: Sophia Nicholls**
Supporting people living with special needs and disabilities by providing respite care – residential short breaks, family fun days, resources, volunteer carers, advice and information. We also support professionals and other people working with people living with disabilities and special needs by providing advice, information, resources, disability training and awareness programmes.
**Employees: 1**
**Volunteers: 30**

## Adventure Service Challenge Scheme

East Lynn, Lansdown Lane, Bath BA1 4NB
T: 01225 329838 (also fax)
E: asc@asc-scheme.org.uk
www.asc-scheme.org.uk
**Chair: Roger Crocker**
ASC Scheme is a nationally available, structured, flexible scheme of activities for children aged eight to 14 and over. It is used by schools, youth clubs, uniformed organisations, special needs groups, etc. It offers young people adventure, the chance to give service to their community and a challenge. It is a three-fold programme helping young people develop in today's world, achieve their potential and prepare for a fulfilling and responsible adult life.
**Volunteers: 15**
**Regional offices: 7**

## Adventure Unlimited

64 Edward Street, Brighton,
East Sussex BN2 0JR
T: 01273 681058
E: info@aultd.org
www.aultd.org
**Director: Louise Stone**
Adventure Unlimited is a registered charity based in Brighton and Hove. Its aim is to enrich the lives of disadvantaged young people through outdoor education events run by formerly unemployed adults. We run adventure activity and climbing events for groups and individuals of all ages. For more information about its work, please go to the website.
**Employees: 10**
**Volunteers: 30**
**Regional offices: 1**

## Adverse Psychiatric Reactions Information Link (APRIL)

Room 311, Linen Hall,
162–168 Regent Street, London W1B 5TD
T: 020 7998 1561
E: info@april.org.uk
www.april.org.uk
**Chair: Millie Kieve**
The objective of APRIL is to promote greater awareness, recognition and safe treatment of adverse psychiatric reactions and withdrawal symptoms that may be caused by prescribed and over-the-counter medicines and anaesthetics.
**Employees: 1**
**Volunteers: 5**

## Advice on Individual Rights in Europe

3rd Floor, 17 Red Lion Square,
London WC1R 4QH
T: 020 7831 4276
F: 020 7404 7760
E: info@airecentre.org
www.airecentre.org
Operates a law centre specialising in European Union law and international human rights law, in particular, the European Convention on Human Rights.

## Advice Services Alliance

7th Floor, Tavis House, Tavistock Square,
London WC1H 9NA
T: 07904 377460
E: info@asauk.org.uk
www.asauk.org.uk
**Director: Lindsey Poole**
ASA is the umbrella body for the independent not-for-profit advice sector. It aims to: promote collaboration between advice agencies; provide a voice for the sector; analyse advice needs and provision; support the development of high-quality independent advice services; encourage better information on and public awareness of the rights of the citizen.
**Employees: 1**
**Income: £80,000 (2013–14)**

## AdviceUK

PO Box 70716, London EC1P 1GQ
T: 0300 777 0107
E: mail@adviceuk.org.uk
www.adviceuk.org.uk
**Chief Executive: Steve Johnson**
AdviceUK promotes the provision of independent advice services across the UK; supports centres delivering independent advice to the public; acts as a coordinating network and voice for centres; provides a discussion forum on issues of concern to centres and their clients and helps formulate and promote policies with regard to advice work.
**Employees: 17**
**Regional offices: 2**

## Advisory Centre for Education (ACE) Ltd

ACE Education Advice & Training,
72 Durnsford Road, London N11 2EJ
T: 020 8888 3377
Helpline: 0300 011 5142
F: 020 7354 9069
E: enquiries@ace-ed.org.uk
www.ace-ed.org.uk
ACE provides a free advice service for parents of children in state-maintained schools. It advocates changes in state schools to help them to become more responsive to the needs of parents and children. It offers training in specialist areas of education and supports local organisations giving advice on education.
**Employees: 18**
**Volunteers: 2**
**Regional offices: 1**

## Advisory Committee on the Protection of the Sea

Anne-Laure Riber,
Trinity College (Julian Hunt),
Saint Johns Street, Cambridge  CB2 1TQ
T: 01223 746918
E: info@acops.org
www.acops.org.uk
The Committee exists to: promote the preservation of the seas of the world from pollution by human activities; promote and conduct research into the causes and effects of pollution of the seas; advance public education by the study of the impact of human activities upon the natural resources of the sea.

## Advisory Council for the Education of Romany and Other Travellers

ACERT, C/O 12 Leinster Road,
London  N10 3AN
T: 020 8374 1286
E: info@acert.org.uk
www.acert.org.uk
Chair: Rosemarie McCarthy
ACERT campaigns for: equal access and opportunities in education; safe and secure accommodation; equal access to health and other community services; good community relations; an end to discrimination for all Gypsy, Roma and Traveller families.
Volunteers: 15
Regional offices: 1
Income: £13,000 (2014–15)

## Afasic

20 Bowling Green Lane,
London  EC1R 0BD
T: 020 7490 9410
Helpline: 0845 355 5577
F: 020 7251 2834
E: info@afasic.org.uk
www.afasic.org.uk
Chief Executive: Linda Lascelles
Afasic is a UK-wide charity that helps children and young people with speech, language and communication impairments and their families. Afasic operates a helpline for parents and a website, produces information and literature, is a membership organisation and has local groups across the country. Afasic runs training events and conferences for parents and professionals and activities for children and young people.
Employees: 21
Volunteers: 150
Regional offices: 2

## African Caribbean Leukaemia Trust (ACLT)

2A Garnet Road, (Off Gillett Road),
Thornton Heath, Surrey  CR7 8RD
T: 020 3757 7700
E: info@aclt.org
www.aclt.org
Chief Executive: Orin Lewis
ACLT is a UK charity established in 1996 with the aim of raising awareness and registering potential lifesaving donors onto the stem cell (bone marrow), blood and organ donor registers. We have a particular focus on black, Asian and mixed race communities due to the severe lack of representation on the registers from individuals in these communities. To date ACLT have signed up approximately 70,000 people of all ethnicities to the stem cell register.
Employees: 4
Volunteers: 110
Regional offices: 1
Income: £194,083 (2014–15)

## African Community Involvement Association

Justin Plaza 3, Viceroy Suite 1,
341 London Road, Croydon  CR4 4BE
T: 020 8687 2400
F: 020 8646 4363
E: membership@acia.org.uk
www.acia-uk.org
Works towards the relief of sickness among persons with AIDS or HIV infection, particularly by the provision of culturally appropriate care and support services for people from the African community.

## African Community Partnership

Barnes Wallis Community Centre,
74 Wild Goose Drive, New Cross,
London  SE14 5LL
T: 020 7635 9000
F: 020 7635 9600
E: africap@btconnect.com
Employees: 2
Volunteers: 12

## African Health Policy Network

107–109 The Grove, Stratford,
London E15 1HP
T: 020 8555 5778
F: 020 7017 8919
E: info@ahpn.org.uk
www.ahpn.org
CEO: Francis Kaikumba
The principal object of the network is to alleviate the suffering of persons subject to or affected by HIV and to promote sexual health amongst African communities in the UK and elsewhere by providing training, support, research and information and increasing public awareness of effective policies and good practice.
Employees: 7
Volunteers: 14

## African Pastors Fellowship

Station House, Station Approach, Adisham,
Canterbury, Kent  CT3 3JE
T: 01227 812021
E: admin@africanpastors.org
africanpastors.org
CEO: Revd David Stedman
African Pastors Fellowship is a UK charity working alongside church and community leaders in East Africa: training, equipping and resourcing so communities might be transformed.
Employees: 3
Income: £100,000 (2014–15)

## AFTAID – Aid for the Aged in Distress

Epworth House, 25 City Road,
London  EC1Y 1AA
T: 0870 803 1950
F: 0870 803 2128
E: info@aftaid.org.uk
www.aftaid.org.uk
Chair: Susan Elson
AFTAID makes grants for the purchase of essential items to enable older people in need of vital financial assistance maintain independent living in the familiar surroundings of their home. AFTAID provides a safety net when distressed elderly people cannot obtain the help they require from social services, caring agencies or their own family.

## After Adoption

Unit 5 Citygate, 5 Blantyre Street,
Manchester, Lancashire  M15 4JJ
T: 0161 839 4932
Helpline: 0800 056 8578
F: 0161 832 2242
E: information@afteradoption.org.uk
www.afteradoption.org.uk
Chief Executive: Lynn Charlton
After Adoption is a Voluntary Adoption Agency and the leading provider of adoption support services within the UK. We specialise in finding families for children with complex needs and deliver a full range of adoption services from our seven regional offices across England and Wales.
Employees: 126
Volunteers: 99
Regional offices: 7

## Aftermath Support

Aftermath Support, c/o Merseyside Police, Bromborough Village Road, Bromborough, Wirral, Merseyside CH62 7JG
T: 0845 634 4273
F: 0151 777 2583
E: support@aftermathsupport.org.uk
www.aftermathsupport.org.uk
**Manager: Jackie Briscoe**
Aftermath Support provides emotional and practical help to all victims of road collisions, including families and witnesses. Help is available for those who have been bereaved as well as those sustaining injury. We offer a choice of face-to-face and/or telephone support in Merseyside, Cheshire and Lancashire (where we have support workers) or telephone support in other areas.
**Employees: 3**
**Volunteers: 36**
**Regional offices: 1**

## AGCAS

Millenium House, 30 Junction Road, Sheffield S11 8XB
T: 0114 251 5750
F: 0114 251 5751
E: sarah.nichols@agcas.org.uk
www.agcas.org.uk
AGCAS has established an enviable position within the UK and beyond as a strong, collaborative body for HE careers professionals. Our primary aim is to help our members improve the accessibility and quality of careers information, advice and guidance. We work in partnership with organisations not only across the UK and Ireland but also with careers practitioners throughout the world.
**Employees: 5**
**Volunteers: 1000**

## Age Concern Central Lancashire

Arkwright House, Stoneygate, Preston, Lancashire PR1 3XT
T: 01772 552850
E: help@55plus.org.uk
www.55plus.org.uk
**Chief Executive: Linda Chivers**
Age Concern Central Lancashire is a well-established charity delivering services and support to meet the needs of local people who are over 55 and their carers primarily in Preston and South Rabble. Our aim is to support individuals to maintain and

re-establish daily living skills, promoting independence and encouraging physical and mental wellbeing.
**Employees: 120**
**Volunteers: 250+**
**Regional offices: 1**
**Income: £2,500,000 (2015–16)**

## Age Concern Eastbourne

William and Patricia Venton Centre, Junction Road, Eastbourne, East Sussex BN21 3QY
T: 01323 638474
E: john.trainor@ageconcerneastbourne.co.uk
www.ageconcerneastbourne.or.uk
**Chief Executive: John Trainor**
To enhance and improve the experience in later life of people in Eastbourne and the surrounding area through the delivery of first-class activities, services, information and advice designed to promote wellbeing for all.
**Employees: 31**
**Volunteers: 200**
**Regional offices: 1**
**Income: £700,000 (2015–16)**

## Age Concern Hassocks and District

Pauline Thaw Centre, Dale Avenue, Hassocks, West Sussex BN6 8LW
T: 01273 844461
E: enquiries@achassocks.co.uk
www.achassocks.co.uk
**Chairman: John Rose**
We operate a social day centre offering a freshly cooked, three-course meal every weekday (costs £5 at October 2015). Minibus transport is available. Coffee shop and charity shop open weekdays and Saturday mornings. Chiropody and hairdressing available on site. Regular outings, events and entertainment. Pre-lunch, chair-based exercises. Wheelchairs for hire. Monthly hearing aid maintenance. Membership is free but registration is required after the first visit. New volunteers are always welcome.
**Employees: 9**
**Volunteers: 70+**
**Income: £200,000 (2014–15)**

## Age UK

Tavis House, 1–6 Tavistock Square, London WC1H 9NA
T: 0800 169 6565
E: contactageuk@ageuk.org.uk
www.ageuk.org.uk

## Age UK Portsmouth

The Bradbury Centre, 16–18 Kingston Road, Portsmouth PO1 5RZ
T: 023 9286 2121
F: 023 9288 3523
E: kathy.kay@ageukportsmouth.org.uk
www.ageukportsmouth.org.uk
**Chief Executive Officer: Dianne Sherlock**
Mission: To help adults in Portsmouth and south east Hampshire enjoy a better quality of life, with a specific focus on all aspects of getting older. We assist older people to live independently and exercise choice. We are dynamic and driven by results and constantly deliver for older people. We are passionate about what we do and care about each individual. We are experts, authoritative and quality orientated.
**Employees: 80**
**Volunteers: 40**

## AgeCare

Head Office, High Broom, Stone Cross, Crowborough, East Sussex TN6 3SL
T: 01892 611542
E: enquiries@agecare.org.uk
www.agecare.org.uk
AgeCare establishes and supports residential care homes for older people and promotes education and training of staff employed to care for older people.

## AIESEC (UK) Ltd

29–31 Cowper Street, London EC2A 4AT
T: 020 7549 1800
E: mae@aiesec.co.uk
www.aiesec.co.uk
**President: Lubka Mieresova**
AIESEC is a 65-year-old global organisation that develops students into leaders by running and participating in an international exchange programme. We are present in 125 countries and send more than 600 students from the UK abroad every year.
**Employees: 11**
**Volunteers: 987**
**Regional offices: 22**

## Air Cadets

Headquarters Air Cadets, Royal Air Force, Cranwell, Sleaford, Lincolnshire NG34 8HB
T: 01400 267632
E: acfo@atc.raf.mod.uk
www.raf.mod.uk/aircadets
Promotes and encourages among young people a practical interest in aviation and in the Royal Air Force; provides training which will be useful both in the services and civil life; fosters the spirit of adventure and develops

the qualities of leadership and good citizenship.

## Airey Neave Trust

The Airey Neave Trust, PO Box 111, Leominster HR6 6BP
T: 020 7833 4440
E: aireyneavetrust@gmail.com
www.aireyneavetrust.org.uk
The advancement of education by the furtherance of research into personal freedom under the law of any nation in the world and the dissemination of the useful results of such research.

## Al-Anon Family Groups UK and Eire

Family Groups Limited,
57B Great Suffolk Street, London SE1 0BB
T: 020 7593 2070
Helpline: 020 7403 0888
E: enquiries@al-anonuk.org.uk
www.al-anonuk.org.uk
Al-Anon Family Groups provide support to anyone whose life is, or has been, affected by someone else's drinking, regardless of whether that person is still drinking or not.

## Albany Trust

239A Balham High Rd, London SW17 7BE
T: 020 8767 1827
E: practicemanager@albanytrust.org
www.albanytrust.org.uk
The Trust provides counselling and psychotherapy, which aim to create a better climate for more honest and open relationships. We work with couples and individuals experiencing difficulties in their relationship or with their sexuality.
Employees: 1

## Albert Kennedy Trust

Unit 112, Cremer Business Centre,
37 Cremer Street, London E2 8HD
T: 020 7831 6562
F: 020 7405 6929
E: admin@akt.org.uk
www.akt.org.uk
Chief Executive: Tim Sigsworth
The Trust's aim is to ensure that all lesbian, gay and bisexual young people are able to live in accepting, supportive and caring homes by providing a range of services to meet the individual needs of those who would otherwise be homeless or in a hostile environment.
Employees: 22
Volunteers: 200
Regional offices: 3

## Albrighton Moat and Gardens

Albrighton Moat and Gardens,
Blue House Lane, Albrighton,
Near Wolverhampton WV3 3FL
T: 01902 372441
E: moat@albrightontrust.org.uk
www.albrightontrust.org.uk
Operations Manager: Sandie Jackson
The Trust is dedicated to providing sports, arts, training and recreational activities for people of all ages who have disabilities or are disadvantaged, it enables and empowers them, regardless of disabilities, to participate in and enjoy activities that they are otherwise denied.
Employees: 5
Volunteers: 20
Income: £120,000 (2014–15)

## Alcohol Concern

Alcohol Concern, 25 Corsham Street,
London N1 6DR
T: 020 7566 9800
Helpline: 0300 123 1110
F: 020 7488 9213
E: contact@alcoholconcern.org.uk
www.alcoholconcern.org.uk
Chief Executive: Don Shenker
Alcohol Concern is the national agency on alcohol misuse campaigning for effective alcohol policy and improved services for people whose lives are affected by alcohol-related problems.
Employees: 20
Volunteers: 1
Regional offices: 1

## Alcohol Research UK

Room 178, Queen Anne Business Centre,
28 Broadway, London SW1H 9JX
T: 020 7340 9502
F: 020 7340 9505
E: andrea.tilouche@alcoholresearchuk.org
www.aerc.org.uk
The Council administers a charitable foundation, the Alcohol Education and Research Fund, which finances projects within the UK for education and research and for novel forms of help for people with drinking problems, including offenders.
Employees: 3
Volunteers: 15

## Alcoholics Anonymous

PO Box 1, 10 Toft Green, York YO1 7NJ
T: 01904 644026
F: 01904 629091
E: aainformation@gsogb.org.uk
www.alcoholics-anonymous.org.uk
To stay sober and to help other alcoholics to achieve sobriety. A fellowship of men and women who share their experience, strength

and hope with each other so that they may solve their common problem and help others to recover from alcoholism. The only requirement for membership is a desire to stop drinking. AA has no dues or fees.
Employees: 10
Regional offices: 3

## Alexandra Rose Day

5 Mead Lane, Farnham, Surrey GU9 7DY
T: 01252 726171
F: 01252 727559
E: ahampton@alexandraroseday.org.uk
www.alexandraroseday.org.uk
Chief Executive: Diana le Clercq
Alexandra Rose Day is an umbrella organisation that helps small and local charities across England and Wales raise funds. Any charity that helps children, young people, disabled people and the elderly can apply to take part in a Rose Day collection or Rose Charities Raffle. Participating charities can also apply for a grant from our Special Appeal Fund.
Employees: 3
Volunteers: 2

## Alington House Community Association

4 North Bailey, Durham, Durham DH1 3ET
T: 0191 386 4088
E: abpegasus553@gmail.com
www.alingtonhouse.org.uk
Co-ordinator: Alan Barnett
Alington House Community Centre is situated in historical Durham city close to the cathedral. An ideal venue for conferences, seminars, meetings and parties. We have a number of different size rooms to hire and free wifi available. Parts of the centre are from the 17th century, it is a grade 2* listed building and with views of Durham city this makes a fantastic place to hire.
Employees: 3
Volunteers: 20
Income: £90,000 (2015–16)

## Alkaptonuria Society

66 Devonshire Road, Cambridge CB1 2BL
T: 01223 322897
E: oliver@akusociety.org
www.akusociety.org
CEO: Oliver Timmis
Advances the education of the public into all matters relating to Alkaptonuria disease and its causes.
Employees: 5
Regional offices: 1
Income: £300,000 (2015–16)

## Allergy UK

Planwell House, LEFA Business Park,
Edington Way, Sidcup, Kent DA14 5BH
T: 01322 619898
E: info@allergyuk.org
www.allergyuk.org
Allergy UK is the country's leading national
patient information charity dealing with
allergy. We provide up-to-date information
on all aspects of allergy and food intolerance.
Our fully trained helpline staff guide callers to
the appropriate allergy specialist.
Employees: 11
Volunteers: 12

## Alliance of Healing Associations

Secretary's Office, 21 Mitchell Road,
St Austell, Cornwall PL25 3AX
T: 01726 74843
F: 01726 67148
E: secretaryforbaha@gmail.com
britishalliancehealingassociations.com
President: Ken Baker
The Alliance consists of over 43 different
organisations to date. This covers nearly
4,000 accredited spiritual healers and in the
region of 1,000 student healers. Our object
is the promotion and advancement of spiritual
healing. The Alliance was formed in 1976,
acquiring charitable status in 1982.
Employees: 1
Volunteers: 3
Regional offices: 4

## Almshouse Association

Billingbear Lodge, Maidenhead Road,
Wokingham, Berkshire RG40 5RU
T: 01344 452922
F: 01344 862062
E: naa@almshouses.org
www.almshouses.org
The Association: advises members on any
matters concerning almshouses and the
welfare of the elderly; promotes improvements
in almshouses and studies and research into
all matters concerning them; makes grants
and loans to members; keeps under review
existing and proposed legislation affecting
almshouses and when necessary takes action;
encourages the provision of almshouses.
Employees: 8

## Alone in London

Unit 6, 48 Provost Street, London N1 7SU
T: 020 7278 4224
F: 020 7837 7943
E: yvonne.jones@depaulcharity.org.uk
www.als.org.uk
Aims to: relieve the homelessness of young
people aged under 26; enable young people
to live as independently as possible; provide
practical and emotional support for young
people at risk of homelessness; bring young
people's homelessness to public attention.
Employees: 39
Volunteers: 40

## Alopecia UK

39 Wykeham Drive, Basingstoke,
Hampshire RG23 8HW
T: 07763 293687
E: info@alopeciaonline.org.uk
www.alopeciaonline.org.uk
Charity Manager: Jen Chambers
Alopecia UK works to improve the lives of
those affected by alopecia. The work of the
charity is focused around its three aims:
support – to provide impartial information,
advice and support to help people feel less
isolated; awareness – to raise awareness to the
general public and healthcare professionals
about alopecia and its psychological impact;
research – to support medical and
psychological researchers who aim to find
effective treatments.
Employees: 1
Volunteers: 30

## Alternatives to Violence Project, Britain

The Grayston Centre, 28 Charles Square,
London N1 6HT
T: 020 7324 4755
E: info@avpbritain.org.uk
www.avpbritain.org.uk
Chair of Trustees: Anne Martin
The Alternatives to Violence Project (AVP)
provides workshops in prisons and in the
general community for anyone who wants to
learn how to handle conflict without resorting
to, or becoming subject to, violence of any
kind. AVP also runs a distance learning course
for prisoners throughout Britain.
Employees: 5
Volunteers: 75
Regional offices: 6

## Alzheimer's Society

43-44 Crutched Friars, London EC3N 2AE
T: 0330 333 0804
Helpline: 0300 222 1122
F: 020 7423 3501
E: enquiries@alzheimers.org.uk
www.alzheimers.org.uk
The Society's principal objectives are the
provision of practical support, information
and advice to people with Alzheimer's disease
and other dementias and those who care for
them, and the promotion of research into the
disease and other dementias.
Employees: 1200
Regional offices: 260

## Amal Trust

15h Bourne House,
Westbourne Grove W2 4UA
T: 020 7727 5882
F: 020 7727 5859
E: info@amaltrust.co.uk
www.amaltrust.org
Chairman: Hashim Charif
The object of the charity is to propagate Islam
to young Muslims and non-Muslims through
classes, lectures and seminars; to guide the
youth of today away from bad street culture
through Light of the Youth social activities like
summer camps, sporting competitions and
other social activities.
Employees: 3
Volunteers: 12
Regional offices: 2

## Ambition

371 Kennington Lane, London SE11 5QY
T: 020 7793 0787
E: info@ambitionuk.org
www.ambitionuk.org
Chief Executive: Helen Marshall
Ambition is the UK's leading youth club
charity. Our members work with over 3,500
youth clubs and youth community projects
across the UK, supporting more than
350,000 young people. We develop the
services our members need and use our
influence to open up exciting opportunities
for them.
Employees: 13

## Amnesty International Secretariat

1 Easton Street, London WC1X 0DW
T: 020 7413 5500
F: 020 7956 1157
E: amnestyis@amnesty.org
www.amnesty.org
Amnesty International is a worldwide
campaigning movement that works to
promote all human rights enshrined in the
Universal Declaration of Human Rights and
other international standards.
Employees: 469
Volunteers: 86
Regional offices: 12

## Amnesty International United Kingdom

The Human Rights Action Centre,
17–25 New Inn Yard, London EC2A 3EA
T: 020 7033 1500
F: 020 7033 1503
E: sct@amnesty.org.uk
www.amnesty.org.uk
Campaigns within Britain about Amnesty
International's (AI) worldwide concerns.

AI is a worldwide human rights movement independent of any government, political faction, ideology, economic interest or religious creed. It works for the: release of people imprisoned for their ethnic origin, sex, colour or beliefs, provided they have neither used nor advocated violence; abolition of torture and the death penalty; fair and early trial of all political prisoners; end to extra-judicial executions and 'disappearances'; observance of the UN Universal Declaration of Human Rights.
**Employees: 120**
**Volunteers: 80**
**Regional offices: 3**

## Amphibian and Reptile Conservation

655A Christchurch Road, Boscombe, Bournemouth, Dorset BH1 4AP
T: 01202 391319
E: angela.reynolds@arc-trust.org
www.arc-trust.org
Co-ordinates and implements conservation efforts for threatened amphibians and reptiles, particularly in the UK and Europe, and promotes research.

## Amref Health Africa

15–18 Lower Ground Floor, White Lion Street, London N1 9PD
T: 020 7269 5520
E: info@amrefuk.org
www.amrefuk.org
**CEO: Samara Hammond**
Amref Health Africa is an international African organisation. AMREF was founded in Kenya in 1957 as the Flying Doctors of East Africa; we are now Africa's largest health NGO with programmes in Ethiopia, Kenya, Senegal, South Sudan, South Africa, Tanzania and Uganda. Last year we brought better health to over 12 million people across Africa.
**Employees: 18**

## AMSPAR

Tavistock House North, Tavistock Square, London WC1H 9LN
T: 020 7387 6005
F: 020 7388 2648
E: info@amspar.co.uk
www.amspar.com
**CEO: Thomas Brownlie**
AMSPAR promotes quality and coherence in the delivery of vocational qualifications aimed at medical secretaries, practice managers, administrators and receptionists, and encourages and supports standards of excellence in the pursuit of continuous professional development and lifelong learning.
**Employees: 3**

## Anaphylaxis Campaign

PO Box 275, Farnborough, Hampshire GU14 6XS
T: 01252 546100
Helpline: 01252 542029
F: 01252 377140
E: info@anaphylaxis.org.uk
www.anaphylaxis.org.uk
**Chief Executive: Lynne Regent**
The campaign fights for people with life-threatening allergies by providing education, information and support, campaigning on their behalf and promoting research.
**Employees: 13**
**Volunteers: 75**

## Anchor Trust

1st Floor, 408 Strand, London WC2R 0NE
T: 020 7759 9107
E: office.support-lon@anchor.org.uk
www.anchor.org.uk
The Anchor Trust offers relief to older people, together with those in need by reason of physical or mental frailty, illness or disability, through the provision of housing, amenities and services for their accommodation, care, support, relief and treatment.

## Ancient Monuments Society

St Ann's Vestry Hall, 2 Church Entry, London EC4V 5HB
T: 020 7236 3934
E: office@ancientmonumentssociety.org.uk
www.ancientmonumentssociety.org.uk
**Secretary: Matthew Saunders**
Founded in 1924 to campaign for historic buildings of all ages and all types.
**Employees: 2**
**Volunteers: 30**

## Andover Neighbourcare

14 Union St, Andover, Hampshire SP10 1PA
T: 01264 351579
E: neighbourcare3@andover.co.uk
andoverneighboucare.co.uk
**General Manager: Pam Delderfield**
Remit of Andover Neighbourcare: To relieve persons resident in area of benefit who are in need by reason of age, disability, sickness or poverty by the provision of such voluntary care work as may be charitable. Andover Neighbourcare offers many services to predominantly older people in Andover and surrounding villages. Services include: transport to doctors, hospitals and clubs; cleaning; gardening; shopping; lunch club; drop-in centre; health and general

information; minibus hire; outings and computer lessons.
**Employees: 6**
**Volunteers: 120**
**Regional offices: 1**

## Angel Foundation

Angel House, Borough Road, Sunderland, Tyne and Wear SR1 1HW
T: 0191 568 0800
E: info.uk@god.tv
www.god.tv
**Head of Network Development: Tevon Jordan**
**Employees: 72**
**Volunteers: 30**

## Anglo Jewish Association

28 Queen Street, London EC4R 1BB
T: 020 7449 0909
E: info@anglojewish.org.uk
www.anglojewish.org.uk
The Association promotes the education of Jews and other persons in Jewish matters. Membership of the Association is open to all British citizens who wish to retain their Jewishness and comprises a representative cross-section of the Anglo-Jewish community.

## Angolan Civic Communities Alliance (ACCA)

C/O Sangat Advice Centre, Sancroft Road, Harrow, Middlesex HA3 7NS
T: 020 8423 3003
Helpline: 07940 556897
F: 020 8864 8881
E: acca.enquiries@gmail.com
**Executive Director: Alex da Costa**
The Angolan Civic Communities Alliance (ACCA) is one of the main drop-in centres for Angolan refugees and migrants and for other refugees and migrants from the Portuguese-speaking communities in Britain.
**Employees: 2**
**Volunteers: 25**

## Animal Rescue Charity

Foxdells Sanctuary, Foxdells Lane,
Rye Street, Bishop's Stortford,
Hertfordshire CM23 2JG
T: 01279 501547
E: cbmitchell@animalrescue.org.uk
www.animalrescuecharity.org.uk
The charity provides a safe and caring
environment for neglected and unwanted
domestic animals and helps and rehabilitates
wildlife wherever possible.
Employees: 10
Volunteers: 50
Regional offices: 1

## Animal Welfare Foundation

7 Mansfield Street, London W1G 9NQ
T: 020 7908 6375
E: erikas@bva.co.uk
www.bva-awf.org.uk
Chairman: Tiffany Hemming
The Animal Welfare Foundation is committed
to improving the welfare of animals through
veterinary science, education and debate.
We apply the knowledge, skill and compassion
of veterinary professionals in effective and
practical ways. We fund scientific research
that impacts the welfare of animals, encourage
debate, produce evidence-based guidance
for owners and vets and manage projects
that tackle issues such as puppy farming and
non-accidental injury to pets.
Employees: 2
Volunteers: 20
Income: £216,995 (2014–15)

## Ann Craft Trust

University of Nottingham, University Park,
Nottingham NG7 2RD
T: 0115 951 5400
F: 0115 951 5232
E: ann-craft-trust@nottingham.ac.uk
www.anncrafttrust.org
CEO: Deborah Kitson
The Trust responds nationally to the needs
and concerns of staff working in the statutory,
voluntary and independent sectors in the
interests of adults and children with learning
disabilities who may be at risk of abuse. It
improves working practices through research,
training, publications, information and advice.

## Anna Freud Centre

12 Maresfield Gardens, London NW3 5SU
T: 020 7794 2313
F: 020 7794 6506
E: rose.palmer@annafreud.org
www.annafreud.org
Chief Executive: Professor Peter Fonagy

The Anna Freud Centre is committed to
developing innovative methods of prevention
and treatment for children and young people
with emotional and behavioural difficulties.
We provide a vital lifeline for families under
pressure and are the UK's only children's
mental health organisation to combine
practice, training and world-class research,
with a focus on family wellbeing. We provide
specialist help, we train others and we carry
out innovative research.
Employees: 170
Volunteers: 1

## Anne Frank Trust UK

Star House, 104–108 Grafton Road,
London NW5 4BA
T: 020 7284 5858
E: info@annefrank.org.uk
www.annefrank.org.uk
Drawing on the power of Anne Frank's
diary, we aim to inspire and educate a new
generation to build a world of mutual respect,
compassion and social justice.

## Anthony Nolan Trust

2 Heathgate Place, 75–87 Agincourt Road,
London NW3 2NU
T: 0303 303 0303
E: info@anthonynolan.org
www.anthonynolan.org.uk
The Trust maintains a register of 350,000
volunteer bone marrow donors who are
prepared to give some of their marrow to save
the life of another person, irrespective of
country, colour, race or creed. It carries out
research into the causes of failure in bone
marrow transplants when donor and recipient
appear to be matched.

## Anti-Slavery International

Thomas Clarkson House,
Unit 4 The Stableyard, Broomgrove Road,
London SW9 9TL
T: 020 7501 8920
F: 020 7738 4110
E: info@antislavery.org
www.antislavery.org
Director: Aidan McQuade
Anti-Slavery International, founded in 1839,
is committed to eliminating all forms of
slavery throughout the world. Slavery,
servitude and forced labour deny basic dignity
and fundamental human rights. Anti-Slavery
International works to end these abuses
by campaigning for slavery's eradication,
exposing current cases, supporting the
initiatives of local organisations to release
people and pressing for more effective

implementation of international laws
against slavery.
Employees: 24
Volunteers: 10

## Antiquarian Horological Society

New House, High Street, Ticehurst,
East Sussex TN5 7AL
T: 01580 200155
E: secretary@ahsoc.org
www.ahsoc.org
Chairman: David Thompson
A learned Society founded to encourage
the study and conservation of timepieces.
Employees: 2

## Anxiety Care UK

8 Nicholas Court, 3 Wallwood Road,
London E11 1DQ
T: 07552 877219
E: admin@anxietycare.org.uk
www.anxietycare.org.uk
Anxiety Care UK works with clients towards
recovery from anxiety and provides cognitive
behavioural therapy (CBT), together with
support, information and encouragement
while undergoing this therapy. It promotes
the reality of anxiety disorders, and
encourages those affected to use their
strengths to work towards recovery and
to maintain it.

## Anxiety UK (formerly National Phobics Society)

c/o Zion Community Resource Centre,
339 Stretford Road, Hulme,
Manchester M15 4ZY
T: 0844 477 5774
F: 0161 226 7727
E: info@anxietyuk.org.uk
www.anxietyuk.org.uk
Chief Executive: Nicky Lidbetter
Anxiety UK works to relieve and support
those living with anxiety and anxiety-based
depression by providing information, support
and understanding via an extensive range
of services, including 1:1 therapy. We work
with external agencies and healthcare
professionals to improve services for those
living with anxiety and anxiety-based
depression and also campaign to raise
awareness of the conditions.
Employees: 6
Volunteers: 500
Regional offices: 1

## Apex Charitable Trust Limited

Tontine House, 24 Church Street,
St Helens, Merseyside WA10 1BD
T: 01744 612898
E: sthelens@apextrust.com
www.apextrust.com
CEO: Kim Hughes
The Trust aims to help people with criminal
records obtain appropriate employment by
providing them with employability skills they
need to compete in the labour market, advice
and guidance support around disclosure of
their conviction(s) and a holistic approach in
supporting our service users. North West,
Merseyside provision only.
Employees: 5
Volunteers: 10
Regional offices: 1
Income: £150,000 (2014–15)

## Apostleship of the Sea

National Headquarters, Stella Maris,
Herald House, Lamb's Passage, Bunhill Row,
London EC1Y 8LE
T: 020 7588 8285
F: 020 7588 8280
E: salvina@apostleshipofthesea.org.uk
www.aos-usa.org
Promotes the spiritual and material welfare
of seafarers and their families.
Employees: 15
Volunteers: 30

## Aquaterra Leisure

Suite 1.40 Millbank Tower, 21–24 Millbank,
London SW1P 4QP
T: 020 3474 0552
E: laura.gray@aquaterra.org
www.aquaterra.org

## Arbours Association Limited

6 Church Lane, London N8 7BU
T: 020 8340 7646
E: info@arboursassociation.org
www.arboursassociation.org
Director: T.J.Ryan
The Arbours Association provides
long-term residential accommodation and
psychotherapeutic support for those in
emotional distress. It also offers a low-to-
high cost psychotherapy service for members
of the public. It also runs the Arbours
Association Training Programme for those
wishing to qualify as psychoanalytic
psychotherapists, with a postgraduate
professional support organisation (AAP).
Employees: 20
Volunteers: 1

## ARC

ARC House, Marsden Street, Chesterfield,
Derbyshire S40 1JY
T: 01246 555043
F: 01246 555045
E: contact.us@arcuk.org.uk
www.arcuk.org.uk
ARC is a UK-wide umbrella body for
providers of services to people with a learning
disability. We promote best practice and
support good-quality provision by training,
projects and partnerships between providers.
We represent providers' views at local,
regional, national and European levels. We
have a large training consortium and hold UK
and national conferences to bring providers
together to promote best practice and share
problems and solutions.
Employees: 55
Regional offices: 4

## ARC (Antenatal Results and Choices)

345 City Road, London EC1V 1LR
T: 020 7713 7356
Helpline: 0845 077 2290
E: info@arc-uk.org
www.arc-uk.org
Director: Jane Fisher
ARC offers information and support to
parents who are: making decisions before,
during and after the antenatal testing
process; told that their unborn baby has
an abnormality; having to make difficult
decisions about continuing the pregnancy;
having to make difficult decisions about
ending the pregnancy; dealing with the
consequences of their decisions. ARC also
works with health professionals, providing
training, support and publications.
Volunteers: 43

## Architects Benevolent Society

43 Portland Place, London W1B 1QH
T: 020 7580 2823
E: help@absnet.org.uk
www.absnet.org.uk
The Society relieves persons engaged or
formerly engaged in the practice of
architecture, and the wives, widows, children
and other dependants of such persons being
in necessitous circumstances.

## Architectural Heritage Fund

The Architectural Heritage Fund,
3 Spital Yard, Spitalfields E1 6AQ
T: 020 7925 0199
F: 020 7930 0295
E: diane.kendal@ahfund.org.uk
www.ahfund.org.uk

Promotes the permanent preservation of
historic buildings in the UK by providing
advice, information and financial assistance
in the form of grants and loans for projects
undertaken by building preservation trusts
and other charities.

## Army Cadet Force Association

Holderness House, 51–61 Clifton Street,
London EC2A 4DW
T: 020 7426 8370
E: exec-asst@armycadets.com
www.armycadets.com
The Association develops among its members
the qualities of good citizenship and the spirit
of service to Queen, country and local
community, and gives encouragement and
training to those considering a career in the
regular army or service in the reserve forces.
The ACF is a voluntary youth movement,
sponsored principally by the army, and takes
part in both military and community activities.

## Army Families Federation

IDL 414, Floor 2, Zone 3, Ramilies Building,
Marlborough Lines,
Monxton Road SP11 8HJ
T: 01264 382326
F: 01264 382327
E: us@aff.org.uk
www.aff.org.uk
The AFF is a unique, two-way communications
link between the British Army and its families.
As a registered charity with branches in
Northern Ireland, Germany and Cyprus, its
objectives are to voice the views and concerns
of army families about their way of life,
helping to get things changed for the better.
Employees: 54
Regional offices: 3

## ARNI Institute

PO Box 68, Lingfield, Surrey RH7 6QQ
Helpline: 07712 211378
E: tom@arni.uk.com
www.arni.uk.com
Secretary: Dr Tom Balchin
The Institute aims to encourage and advance
the rehabilitation of those suffering from the
effects of stroke and other brain injuries that
have resulted in partial paralysis.
Volunteers: 43
Regional offices: 1

## Arthritis Action

Arthritis Action, 64 Victoria Street,
9th Floor, London, Central SW1E 6QP
T: 020 3781 7120
Helpline: 01323 408617
E: info@arthritisaction.org.uk
www.arthritisaction.org.uk
**Chief Executive: Shantel Irwin**
Arthritis Action's vision is for people to live active lives, free from arthritis pain. Our aim is to empower people with arthritis to take control of their lives, manage their condition and reduce the need for medical intervention. Working in partnership with members, health professionals, other charities, researchers, arthritis experts and corporates is very important to us.
**Employees: 13**
**Regional offices: 2**
**Income: £376,000 (2013–14)**

## Arthritis and Musculoskeletal Alliance

Bride House, 18–20 Bride Lane,
London EC4Y 8EE
T: 020 7842 0910
F: 020 7842 0901
E: lynnlevi@arma.uk.net
arma.uk.net
The Arthritis and Musculoskeletal Alliance (ARMA) is the UK umbrella association bringing together support groups, professional bodies and research organisations in the field of arthritis and other musculoskeletal conditions.
**Employees: 2**
**Volunteers: 45**

## Arthritis Care

Floor 4, Linen Court, 10 East Road,
London N1 6AD
T: 020 7380 6540
Helpline: 0808 800 4050
F: 020 7380 6502
E: peter@arthritiscare.org.uk
www.arthritiscare.org.uk
**Chief Executive: Neil Betteridge**
Arthritis Care is a user-centred and user-led charity, with people with all types of arthritis at the heart of what we do. We are the voice of people with arthritis and their families, providing high-quality information and support to enable people living with arthritis to make positive and practical changes to their lives.
**Employees: 120**
**Volunteers: 200**
**Regional offices: 5**

## Arthritis Research UK

Copeman House, St Mary's Court,
St Mary's Gate, Chesterfield,
Derbyshire S41 7TD
T: 0300 790 0400
F: 01246 558007
E: enquiries@arthritisresearchuk.org
www.arthritisresearchuk.org
Raises funds and finances research into the causes and cure of the rheumatic diseases; encourages the teaching of rheumatology to medical and paramedical under- and postgraduates; stimulates public authorities to provide better treatment facilities.
**Employees: 150**
**Volunteers: 5000**
**Regional offices: 4**

## Arthur McDougall Fund

McDougall Trust Unit W219,
Second Floor, West Building,
Westminster Business Square 1–45,
Durham Street, London SE11 5JH
T: 020 7620 1080
F: 020 7928 1258
E: admin@mcdougall.org.uk
www.mcdougall.org.uk
Aims to advance knowledge and encourage study and research in: political and economic science, the functions of government and the services provided to the community by public and voluntary organisations; methods of election of, and the selection and government of, representative organisations, whether national, civic, commercial, industrial or social.
**Employees: 1**
**Volunteers: 10**

## Arthur Rank Centre

Stoneleigh Park, Kenilworth,
Warwickshire CV8 2LG
T: 024 7685 3060
F: 024 7641 4808
E: info@germinate.net
www.germinate.net
**CEO: Jerry Marshall**
The ARC is committed to helping create sustainable vibrant rural communities and has a particular concern for the 900,000 rural households living in poverty, those who feel isolated and families experiencing difficulties. We offer support directly and work to equip the UK's 13,000 rural churches to bring physical, social and spiritual transformation to communities.
**Employees: 7**
**Volunteers: 2**

## Article 19

Free Word Centre, 60 Farringdon Road,
London EC1R 3GA
T: 020 7324 2500
E: renato@article19.org
www.article19.org
**Executive Director: Thomas Hughes**
Article 19 is an international human rights organisation that works to promote, protect and develop freedom of expression, including access to information and the means of communication.

## Arts Council England

14 Great Peter Street, London SW1P 3NQ
T: 0845 300 6200
F: 0161 934 4426
E: enquiries@artscouncil.org.uk
www.artscouncil.org.uk
Arts Council England is the national development agency for the arts in England, distributing public money from government and the National Lottery. We believe in the transforming power of the arts – power to change the lives of people throughout the country. Our ambition is to place the arts at the heart of national life, reflecting the country's rich and diverse cultural identity as only the arts can. We want people throughout England to experience arts activities of the highest quality. We believe that access to the arts goes hand in hand with excellence.

## Artswork

Second Floor, Cadogan House,
37 Commercial Road, Southampton,
Hampshire SO15 1GG
T: 023 8033 2491
E: alice@artswork.org.uk
www.artswork.org.uk
**Chief Executive: Jane Bryant**
Artswork is the national, independent youth arts development agency, committed to making a difference to the lives of children and young people.
**Employees: 26**

## Arun Co-ordinated Community Transport

Unit S3, Rudford Industrial Estate,
Ford Road, Arundel,
West Sussex BN18 0BD
T: 01903 723584
F: 01903 718631
E: manager@arun-cct.org
www.arun-cct.org
**Chairman of Trustees: Graham Paull**
Arun Co-Ordinated Community Transport is a registered not-for-profit, charity based in Littlehampton that offers a range of transport solutions for the residents of the local

community within the Arun area who have difficulty using public transport due to a mobility or visual disability, illness, frailty, age or other impairment.
**Employees: 5**
**Volunteers: 35**
**Regional offices: 1**
**Income: £153,678 (2014–15)**

## ARVAC Association for Research in the Voluntary and Community Sector

School of Health Sciences,
University of East Anglia,
Norwich Research Park, Earlham Road,
Norwich, Norfolk NR4 7TJ
E: info@arvac.org.uk
www.arvac.org.uk
Chair: Prof John Diamond
ARVAC promotes effective community action through research by bringing together university-based researchers and community-based practitioners. ARVAC supports community research though networking, training and events. ARVAC networks members online, sharing resources and information. A regular online bulletin and social media keep members in touch with community research developments. An annual lecture (spring in London) and an annual conference and AGM (autumn, regional city) are opportunities for members to meet and network face to face.
**Volunteers: 10**
**Income: £1,000 (2015–16)**

## ASDAN

Wainbrook House, Huddsvale Road,
St George, Bristol BS5 7HY
T: 0117 941 1126
F: 0117 935 1112
E: sallyfinn@asdan.org.uk
www.asdan.co.uk
ASDAN's aim is the advancement of education, by providing opportunities for all learners to develop their personal and social attributes and levels of achievement through the use and attainment of ASDAN resources and awards, and the relief of poverty, where poverty inhabits such opportunities for learners.
**Employees: 40**

## Asha Projects

13 Shrubbery Road, London SW16 2AS
T: 07870 570861
Helpline: 020 8696 0023
F: 020 8677 9920
E: admin@asha.org.uk
www.ashaprojects.org.uk
Asha means 'hope'. Our mission is to empower Asian women to live independently and achieve the goals that they have set for themselves.
**Employees: 9**
**Volunteers: 2**

## Ashoka (UK) Trust

15 Old Ford Road, Bethnal Green,
London E2 9PJ
T: 020 8980 9416
E: ppelimanni@ashoka.org
www.ashoka.org
UK Director: Mark Cheng
Ashoka contributes to the social progress of developing countries by encouraging and empowering outstanding individuals in those countries who have shown they have the capacity and character to achieve substantial change, in a wide variety of fields, through the organisations they lead.

## Asian Family Counselling Service

Suite 51, The Lodge, Windmill Place,
2–4 Windmill Lane, Southall UB2 4NJ
T: 020 8571 3933 (also fax)
E: afcs@btconnect.com
www.asianfamilycounselling.org
Director: Kulbir Randhawa
Asian Family Counselling Service provides family, marital and individual counselling for the Asian community resident in the UK. Counsellors offer caring, personal and confidential counselling in the client's language with an awareness of their cultural and ethnic backgrounds.
**Employees: 6**
**Volunteers: 6**
**Regional offices: 2**
**Income: £139,790 (2013–14)**

## Asian Foundation for Help

BIA House, 116 Ealing Road, Wembley,
Middlesex HA0 4TH
T: 020 8903 3019
E: ketan@asianfoundation.org.uk
www.asianfoundation.org.uk
Chairman: Hitesh Popat
A voluntary organisation raising funds to help the poor and needy.
**Volunteers: 20**
**Regional offices: 3**
**Income: £125,000 (2014–15)**

## Asian People's Disability Alliance Ltd

Daycare And Development Centre,
Alric Avenue, off Bruce Road, Harlesden,
London NW10 8RA
T: 020 8830 4220
F: 020 8830 3890
E: apdmcha@aol.com
www.apda.org.uk
CEO Joint: Zeenat Jeewa
Aims to ensure that Asian people with disabilities are accorded full status, rights and facilities to enable them to participate fully and represent their own interests in all areas of society.
**Employees: 15**
**Volunteers: 10**
**Regional offices: 1**

## Aspire

Aspire Leisure Centre, Wood Lane,
Stanmore HA7 4AP
T: 020 8954 5759
E: info@aspire.org.uk
www.aspire.org.uk
Aspire is a national charity that provides practical help to people who have been paralysed by Spinal Cord Injury, helping them move from injury to independence. Every eight hours in the UK someone is paralysed by a spinal cord injury; it can happen to anyone at any time and no one is prepared for how it will change their life. Our services include: Aspire Grants, Aspire Housing, independent living, assistive technology, campaigning and research.
**Employees: 80**
**Volunteers: 20**

## ASSERT

PO Box 4962, Nuneaton CV11 9FD
Helpline: 0300 999 0102
F: 01268 415940
E: assert@angelmanuk.org
www.angelmanuk.org
Aims to relieve the need of those with Angelman Syndrome and their families, to advance the education of the public in Angelman Syndrome and to promote research into Angelman Syndrome.
**Volunteers: 10**

## Assist UK

Redbank House, 4 St Chad's Street,
Manchester M8 8QA
T: 0161 832 9757
E: admin@assist-uk.org
www.assist-uk.org
CEO: Alan Norton
Assist UK is an umbrella organisation for a
UK-wide network of locally situated disabled/
independent living centres. Most centres
include a permanent exhibition of products
and equipment that provide people with
opportunities to see and try products and
equipment and get information and advice
from professional staff about what might suit
them best.
Employees: 5
Volunteers: 18
Regional offices: 41

## Associated Board of the Royal Schools of Music

24 Portland Place, London W1B 1LU
T: 020 7636 5400
F: 020 7467 8223
E: abrsm@abrsm.ac.uk
www.abrsm.ac.uk
Aims to advance the arts, science and skills of
music, speech and drama throughout the UK
and overseas.
Employees: 95
Volunteers: 250

## Associated Country Women of the World

Mary Sumner House, 24 Tufton Street,
London SW1P 3RB
T: 020 7799 3875
F: 020 7340 9950
E: info@acww.org.uk
www.acww.org.uk
Operations Manager: Tish Collins
An international membership organisation
that aims to raise the standard of living of
rural women and their families through
education, training, support and community
development programmes. It gives women
a voice at international level through its links
with United Nations agencies and liaises with
other NGOs. It has an administrative office
in London and organises a world conference
every three years. ACWW connects and
supports women and communities worldwide.
Employees: 8
Volunteers: 50

## Association for Child and Adolescent Mental Health

St Saviour's House, 39–41 Union Street,
London SE1 1SD
T: 020 7403 7458
F: 020 7403 7081
E: martin.pratt@acamh.org
www.acamh.org
The Association undertakes the scientific
study of all matters concerning the mental
health and development of children, young
people and their families.
Employees: 7

## Association for Continence Advice

Fitwise Management Ltd, Blackburn House,
Redhouse Road, Bathgate EH47 7AQ
T: 01506 811077
E: aca@fitwise.co.uk
www.aca.uk.com
The Association acts as a multidisciplinary
forum for healthcare professionals with
a special interest in the promotion of
continence and the management of
incontinence and educates professionals
about the prevention and treatment of
incontinence.

## Association for Family Therapy

7 Executive Suite, St James Court,
Wilderspool Causeway,
Warrington WA4 6PS
T: 01925 444414
E: s.kennedy@aft.org.uk
www.aft.org.uk
Chair: Jeanette Neden
AFT's key aim is to benefit the public by
working to continually improve standards
of professional family therapy and systemic
practice. Members promote family therapy
through practice, training, management and
research. AFT provides the Journal and
Context magazine for its members and a
number of conferences.
Employees: 4
Volunteers: 30

## Association for Glycogen Storage Disease (UK)

Old Hambledon Racecourse,
Sheardley Lane, Droxford,
Hampshire SO32 3QY
T: 0300 123 2790
E: allan.muir@agsd.org.uk
www.agsd.org.uk
Chairman: Andrew Wakelin
The Association is a contact and support
group for all persons affected by some form
of glycogen storage disease. It also creates
public awareness of GSD and acts as a focus

for educational, scientific and charitable
activities related to this disorder.
Employees: 2
Regional offices: 1

## Association for Humanistic Psychology

BM Box 3582, London WC1N 3XX
T: 0845 707 8506
E: admin@ahpb.org
www.ahpb.org
The Association educates the public about
humanistic psychology, disseminates
alternative ways of dealing with human
problems, both personal and societal, and
encourages the development of the individual
to his/her full potential.
Volunteers: 6

## Association for Language Learning

University of Leicester, University Road,
Leicestershire LE1 7RH
T: 0116 229 7600
F: 0116 223 1488
E: info@all-languages.org.uk
www.all-languages.org.uk
Director: Linda Parker
The aims of the Association are: to
support members' professional work and
development; to develop policies that reflect
views and interests of members; to promote
improved standards of language teaching and
learning; to encourage understanding of the
importance of languages, communication
and cultural issues.
Employees: 4
Volunteers: 50+

## Association for Learning Technology

Gipsy Lane, Headington, Oxford OX3 0BP
T: 01865 484125
F: 01865 484165
E: thomas.palmer@alt.ac.uk
www.alt.ac.uk
Chief Executive: Maren Deepwell
ALT is a professional and scholarly association
that seeks to bring together all those with an
interest in the use of learning technology.
We represent and support our members
and provide services for them; facilitate
collaboration between practitioners,
researchers and policy makers; spread
good practice in the use of learning
technology; raise the profile of research

in learning technology and support the professionalisation of learning technologists.
**Employees: 5**
**Volunteers: 42**
**Regional offices: 1**
**Income: £423,950 (2015–16)**

## Association for Multiple Endocrine Neoplasia Disorder

The Warehouse, Draper Street,
Southborough, Tunbridge Wells,
Kent TN4 0PG
T: 01892 516076
E: jo.grey@amend.org.uk
www.amend.org.uk
CEO: Jo Grey

AMEND provides information and support services to families affected by multiple endocrine neoplasia (MEN) disorders and associated endocrine tumours and syndromes. We produce patient information with the help of our expert medical advisory team, run a professional counselling helpline and hold patient educational events. Membership is free and open to all via our HONCode certified website at www.amend.org.uk.
**Volunteers: 20**
**Income: £92,991 (2015–16)**

## Association for Perioperative Practice

Daisy Ayris House, 42 Freemans Way,
Harrogate, North Yorkshire HG3 1DH
T: 01423 881300
Helpline: 01423 880997
E: stephanie.oates@afpp.org.uk
www.afpp.org.uk
Chief Executive Officer: Dawn Stott

Improving patient care in perioperative practice.
**Employees: 22**

## Association for Physical Education

Room 17, Bredon, University of Worcester,
Henwick Grove, Worcester WR2 6AJ
T: 01905 855584
E: enquiries@afpe.org.uk
www.afpe.org.uk

The Association for Physical Education (afPE) is committed to being the UK representative organisation of choice for people and agencies delivering or supporting the delivery of physical education in schools and in the wider community.
**Employees: 10**

## Association for Project Management

Ibis House, Regent Park, Summerleys Road,
Princes Risborough,
Buckinghamshire HP27 9LE
T: 0845 458 1944
F: 0845 458 8807
E: mike.robinson@apm.org.uk
www.apm.org.uk
Chief Executive: Andrew Bragg

Association for Project Management (APM) is the largest independent body of its kind in Europe, a professional membership association with the mission to develop and promote the professional disciplines of project and programme management for the public benefit. APM currently forms a community of around 19,500 individual and 500 corporate members in all sectors and industries, including public sector, civil engineering, financial services, retail, logistics, science and arts.
**Employees: 60**
**Volunteers: 400**

## Association for Science Education

College Lane, Hatfield AL10 9AA
T: 01707 283000
F: 01707 266532
E: info@ase.org.uk
www.ase.org.uk
Chief Executive: Shaun Reason

ASE is the largest subject association in the UK. As the professional body for all those involved in science education from pre-school to higher education, the ASE provides a national network supported by a dedicated staff team. Members enjoy benefits such as journals, book sales service, publishing and Public Liability insurance.
**Employees: 20**
**Volunteers: 50**

## Association for the Study of Obesity

PO Box 410, Deal, Kent CT14 4AL
T: 01304 367788
E: asooffice@aso.org.uk
www.aso.org.uk

Promotes medical research into the causes, prevention and treatment of obesity. It facilitates contact between individuals and organisations interested in any aspect of the problem of obesity and body weight regulation. An organisation for health professionals.

## Association for the Teaching of the Social Sciences

Bailey Suite, Palatine House,
Belmont Business Park, Durham,
County Durham DH1 1TW
T: 0191 383 0839
Helpline: 0191 383 0782
E: enquiries@britsoc.org.uk
www.atss.org.uk

Provides opportunities for those teaching and researching in the social sciences to meet so that they may develop and share ideas and strategies for the promotion and delivery of the teaching of social sciences.
**Employees: 2**
**Volunteers: 30**

## Association of Blind and Partially Sighted Teachers and Students

BM Box 6727, London WC1N 3XX
T: 0117 966 4839
E: e.standen@btinternet.com
www.abapstas.org.uk

Provides support to visually impaired teachers and students and those with an interest in education or training and campaigns on their behalf.

## Association of Blind Piano Tuners

31 Wyre Crescent, Darwen,
Lancashire BB3 0JG
T: 0844 736 1976
E: abpt@uk-piano.org
www.uk-piano.org

The aims of the association are to further the interests and raise the status of blind and partially sighted piano tuners, give them all possible assistance in their work and maintain or raise the standard of service given by blind piano tuners.

## Association of Breastfeeding Mothers

PO Box 207, Bridgwater,
Somerset TA6 7YT
T: 0844 412 2948
Helpline: 0300 330 5453
E: admin@abm.me.uk
www.abm.me.uk

We offer mother-to-mother breastfeeding support and up-to-date breastfeeding information.
**Volunteers: 100**

## Association of British Credit Unions

T: 0161 832 3694
E: info@abcul.org
www.abcul.org/home

## Association of Charitable Foundations

314–320 Acorn House,
14 Upper Woburn Place, Gray's Inn Road,
London WC1X 8DP
T: 020 7255 4499
F: 020 7255 4496
E: charlotte@acf.org.uk
www.acf.org.uk
Chief Executive: David Emerson
The Association of Charitable Foundations
(ACF) is the membership association for
foundations and grant-making charities in the
UK. For 25 years we have supported trusts
and foundations, respecting and safeguarding
their independence, and helping them to be
effective in the many ways that they use their
resources. www.acf.org.uk
Employees: 6

## Association of Charitable Organisations

Acorn House, 314–320 Gray's Inn Road,
London WC1X 8DP
T: 020 7255 4480
F: 020 7255 4496
E: info@aco.uk.net
www.aco.uk.net
Chief Executive: Dominic Fox
The Association of Charitable Organisations
(ACO) is the national UK umbrella body for
charities that give grants and welfare support
to individuals in need. ACO provides support
to its members through networking, raising
standards, promoting good practice, lobbying
and campaigning, information, advice and
online services.
Employees: 2

## Association of Charity Independent Examiners

The Gatehouse, White Cross, South Road,
Lancaster, Lancashire LA1 4XQ
T: 01524 34892
E: info@acie.org.uk
www.acie.org.uk
Chair: Chris Smith
Promotes the greater effectiveness of
charities in the UK in the achievement of their
charitable objectives by: providing advice,
support and training to any person acting or
wishing to act as an independent examiner of
charity accounts; promoting and maintaining
high standards of practice and professional
conduct; providing charity trustees with

information in connection with the selection
and appointment of independent examiners.
Employees: 2
Volunteers: 500
Income: £50,809 (2015–16)

## Association of Chief Executives of Voluntary Organisations

Regents Wharf, 8 All Saints Street,
London N1 9RL
T: 020 7014 4600
E: marketing@acevo.org.uk
www.acevo.org.uk
Interim Chief Executive: Asheem Singh
ACEVO is the only professional association
for voluntary sector CEOs in England and
Wales. We connect, develop, support and
represent over 2,000 members. Over the
last 20 years, our aim has been to increase
the professionalism of our members and raise
standards across the voluntary sector.
Employees: 15
Regional offices: 1

## Association of Community Based Business Advice

2nd Floor, 200A Pentonville Road,
London N1 9JP
T: 020 7832 5842
E: info@acbba.org.uk
www.acbba.org.uk
Executive Director: Armando Pardo
We provide business training, advice and
mentoring support to people interested
in small business with a focus on self-
employment. Our aim is to promote
viable, income generating, enterprises that
enable people to make a living out of their
business activities.
Employees: 3

## Association of Dance Therapists (International)

Flat 1, Penlee, Lindridge Road,
Babbacombe, Torquay, Devon TQ1 3SD
T: 01803 314366
E: deniseputtock@yahoo.co.uk
www.schoolofdancetherapy.com
Director of Studies: Denise Puttock
We are a small, non-profit-making
organisation.
Volunteers: 6

## Association of Disabled Professionals

The Vassall Centre, Gill Avenue,
Gill Avenue, Bristol BS16 2QQ
T: 0844 445 7123
E: advice@adwuk.org
www.adwuk.org
Chief executive: Andy Rickell
ADP exists to improve the educational/
employment opportunities available to
disabled people, allowing disabled people to
retain employment commensurate with their
abilities and to participate fully in the everyday
life of society. It aims to improve public
knowledge of the capabilities and needs of
disabled people. ADP provides employment
advice, information and peer support to
disabled people. It operates the Disabled
Entrepreneurs' Network, providing advice
and support to self-employed disabled people
www.disabled-entrepreneurs.net. It is part of
ADWUK.

## Association of Governing Bodies of Independent Schools

3 Codicote Road, Welwyn,
Hertfordshire AL6 9LY
T: 01438 840730
F: 05603 432632
E: comms@agbis.org.uk
www.agbis.org.uk
General Secretary: Stuart Westley
The Association of Governing Bodies of
Independent Schools supports and advises
governing bodies of schools in the
independent sector under the umbrella of
ISC. The objectives of the Association are the
advancement of education in independent
schools and the promotion of good
governance in such schools.
Employees: 3

## Association of Interchurch Families

6th Floor, 10 Aldersgate Street,
London EC1A 4HJ
T: 020 3384 2947
E: info@interchurchfamilies.org.uk
www.interchurchfamilies.org.uk
Executive Development Officer: Doral Hayes
The Association is a focus for all concerned
with marriages between committed
Christians of different church allegiances,
and more widely with 'mixed marriages'. It
promotes Christian unity and offers a support
network for interchurch families (usually
where one partner is Roman Catholic) and
a voice for such families in the churches.
Employees: 1
Volunteers: 50
Income: £35,000 (2014–15)

## Association of Jewish Ex-Servicemen and Women

Shield House, Harmony Way, Hendon, London NW4 2BZ
T: 020 8202 2323
E: headoffice@ajex.org.uk
www.ajex.org.uk
AJEX is the only UK Jewish charity totally devoted to the care and welfare of Jewish ex-service personnel and their dependants in need. The Association provides practical support in assisting with mobility equipment, household emergency repairs, respite breaks and general wellbeing.

## Association of Jewish Refugees in Great Britain

Jubilee House, Merrion Avenue, Stanmore, Middlesex HA7 4RL
T: 020 8385 3070
E: carolhart@ajr.org.uk
www.ajr.org.uk
The Association aims to assist Jewish refugees from Nazi oppression and their families, primarily from Central Europe, by providing a wide range of services.

## Association of Medical Research Charities

Charles Darwin House, 12 Roger Street, London WC1N 2JU
T: 020 7685 2620
F: 020 7685 2621
E: ceoffice@amrc.org.uk
www.amrc.org.uk
Chief Executive: Aisling Burnand
The Association of Medical Research Charities (AMRC) is a membership organisation of the leading medical and health research charities in the UK. Working with our member charities and partners, we aim to support the sector's effectiveness and advance medical research by developing best practice, providing information and guidance, improving public dialogue about research and science, and influencing government.
Employees: 10
Volunteers: 1

## Association of Natural Burial Grounds

Natural Death Centre, In The Hill House, Watley Lane, Twyford, Winchester SO21 1QX
T: 01962 712690
E: contact@naturaldeath.org.uk
www.naturaldeath.org.uk
Manager: Rosie Inman-Cook

Run by the Natural Death Centre charity.
Volunteers: 5

## Association of Radical Midwives

West Greenridge Farmhouse, Lowgate, Hexham, Northumberland NE46 2NX
T: 07810 665733
E: rothleylakehouse@gmail.com
www.midwifery.org.uk
Administration Secretary: Katherine Hales
The aims of the Association are: to improve maternity services, especially within the NHS; to preserve and enhance choices in childbirth for all women; to re-establish the full role of the midwife; to encourage the evaluation of maternity care; to encourage research.
Employees: 3
Volunteers: 12

## Association of Reflexologists

Victoria House, Victoria Street, Taunton, Somerset TA1 3FA
T: 01823 351010
E: info@aor.org.uk
www.aor.org.uk
Chief Executive: Carolyn Story
The Association was set up to create an independent, fully democratic network of professional reflexologists, providing them with support and ongoing education through seminars and workshops.
Employees: 11

## Association of Research Ethics Committees

AREC Office 13, Cherry Drive, Durham DH6 2BG
T: 0845 604 5466
E: jackiemaull@arec.org.uk
www.arec.org.uk
Chief Executive: Jackie Maull
AREC is an independent, voluntary organisation established to set standards within the field of research ethics. AREC is the voice of research ethics within the UK.
Employees: 2
Volunteers: 16

## Association of Therapeutic Communities

Waterfront, Kingsdown Road, Walmer, Kent CT14 7LL
T: 01242 620077
E: post@therapeuticcommunities.org
www.therapeuticcommunities.org

The Association acts as a focus for information, debate, training and support for people who work in therapeutic communities, or who are interested in this way of working. Members are drawn from all sectors of the healthcare and social-work professions and share a belief in the importance of participation by both staff and patients in creating and maintaining a therapeutic environment.

## Association of Volunteer Managers

PO Box 1449, Bedford, Bedfordshire MK44 5AN
E: info@volunteermanagers.org.uk
www.volunteermanagers.org.uk
Chair: Debbie Usiskin
The Association of Volunteer Managers is an independent body that aims to support, represent and champion people who manage volunteers in England regardless of field, discipline or sector. It has been set up by and for people who manage volunteers.
Employees: 1
Volunteers: 30
Income: £20,000 (2013–14)

## Association of Young People with ME

10 Vermont Palce, Tongwell, Milton Keynes MK12 8JA
T: 01908 379737
Helpline: 0845 123 2389
E: info@ayme.org.uk
www.ayme.org.uk
Chief Executive: Mary-Jane Willows
AYME is a national service for young people suffering from the condition known as ME/CFS. It works on behalf of those young people whose lives are affected, through media coverage, representations to government and other agencies, and through talks and presentations. It provides advice, guidance, information and support for young people and their families. It promotes campaigns for the recognition, diagnosis, treatment and acceptance of ME/CFS.
Employees: 6
Volunteers: 45
Regional offices: 1
Income: £20,000 (2013–14)

## Asthma UK

Summit House, 70 Wilson Street,
London EC2A 2DB
T: 020 7786 4900
F: 020 7256 6075
E: reception@asthma.org.uk
www.asthma.org.uk
Asthma UK aims to help and advise people
with asthma to understand and control their
condition so that they may live healthier and
more active lives. It promotes research into
asthma, its causes, treatments and cure.
Employees: 90
Regional offices: 75

## Asylum Aid

Asylum Aid, Club Union House,
253–254 Upper Street, London N1 1RY
T: 020 7354 9631
Helpline: 020 7354 9264
F: 020 7354 5620
E: jessicac@asylumaid.org.uk
www.asylumaid.org.uk
Chief Executive: Wayne Myslik
Provides advice and representation to
refugees and asylum seekers in the UK.
Employees: 14
Volunteers: 5
Regional offices: 1

## Ataxia UK

12 Broadbent Close, London N6 5JW
T: 020 7582 1444
Helpline: 0845 644 0606
E: smillman@ataxia.org.uk
www.ataxia.org.uk
CEO: Sue Millman
Ataxia UK raises money for research into
ataxia and provides information, advice and
support to people affected by ataxia.
Employees: 12
Volunteers: 100
Income: £1,000,000 (2015–16)

## Ataxia-Telangiectasia Society (A–T Society)

Rothamsted, Harpenden,
Hertfordshire AL5 2JQ
T: 01582 760733
F: 01582 760162
E: info@atsociety.org.uk
www.atsociety.org.uk
Chief Executive: William Davis
The A-T Society provides information and
practical support to people with A–T and
their families to enable them to live their lives
to the full. It also funds bio-medical and
clinical research to improve treatments and
find a cure. The Society provides advocacy,
counselling and financial grants. It provides

opportunities for people living with A–T to
meet and organises activity breaks. It has
established two national specialist clinics and
works to raise standards of care locally.
Employees: 3
Volunteers: 18

## ATD Fourth World UK Ltd

48 Addington Square, London SE5 7LB
T: 020 7703 3231
F: 020 7252 4276
E: atd@atd-uk.org
www.atd-uk.org
ATD Fourth World is an anti-poverty
organisation committed to ending extreme
poverty by working in partnership with those
living in and experiencing poverty. We regard
the existence of poverty as a denial of human
rights and work to enable people living in
poverty to take on active roles within their
communities. We believe that people in
poverty are the real experts on poverty issues
and should become the key partners in all
anti-poverty projects.
Employees: 10
Volunteers: 30
Regional offices: 2

## ATTEND

11–13 Cavendish Square, London W1G 0AN
T: 020 7307 2570 (also fax)
E: info@attend.org.uk
www.attend.org.uk
Chief Executive: David Wood
ATTEND aims to relieve patients and former
patients of hospitals in the UK and other
persons in the community who are sick,
convalescent, disabled, handicapped, infirm,
socially isolated or in need of financial
assistance. It supports the work of health
bodies and those who care for people using
healthcare services, courts or the prison
services.
Employees: 18
Volunteers: 31000
Regional offices: 1

## Attlee Foundation

5 Thrawl Street, London E1 6RT
T: 020 7375 3212
Helpline: 020 7183 0093
E: tania.shaikh@attleeycc.org.uk
www.attlee.org.uk
The Foundation honours the memory of
Clement Richard Attlee, Prime Minister
1945–51, by initiating projects for young
people and for the alleviation of poverty and
hardship.
Employees: 4
Volunteers: 10

## Aurora Health Foundation

Head Office, 4 Ebor Cottages,
Kingston Vale, London SW15 3RT
T: 020 8541 1951
E: info@aurorafoundation.org.uk
www.aurorahealthfoundation.org.uk
Chief Executive Officer: Susannah Faithfull
Aurora is a charity that provides specialist
counselling, support and complementary
therapies to people abused in childhood.
Employees: 12
Volunteers: 4
Regional offices: 1

## Autism Independent UK

199–203 Blandford Ave, Kettering,
Northamptonshire NN16 9AT
T: 01536 523274
E: autism@autismuk.com
www.autismuk.com
Director: Keith Lovett
The Autism Society exists to increase
awareness of autism, together with well-
established and newly developed approaches
in the diagnosis, assessment, education and
treatment. The main goal is to improve the
quality of life for persons with autism.

## Autism Plus

The Exchange Brewery, 2 Bridge Street,
Sheffield, South Yorkshire S3 8NS
T: 0114 384 0284
F: 0114 384 0292
E: melanie.russell@autismplus.co.uk
www.autismplus.org
Managing Director: Glynis Davidson
The Charity aims to provide innovative and
person-centred solutions for people with
ASD and other disabilities, irrespective of
where and how they live. It aims to improve
their quality of life and to extend and exercise
their rights to access more control over
their lives.
Employees: 346
Volunteers: 87
Regional offices: 2

## Autism Research Ltd

49 Orchard Avenue, Shirley,
Croydon CR0 7NE
T: 020 8777 0095
E: iaro@autismresearch.wanadoo.co.uk
www.iaro.org.uk
Director/Secretary: Gerda McCarthy
Autism Research carries out and encourages
research into the mental and emotional
condition of autism and any other conditions
that might be associated with autism. It
disseminates the results of such research.
Volunteers: 4

## AVERT

4 Brighton Road, Horsham,
West Sussex RH13 5BA
T: 01403 210202
E: info@avert.org
www.avert.org
Chief Executive: Sarah Hand
AVERT is an international HIV and AIDS charity based in the UK. Through our HIV/AIDS information website community projects in sub-Saharan Africa and information and advocacy service, we provide education, treatment and care to avert the spread of AIDS.
Regional offices: 1

## Aviation Environment Federation

Broken Wharf House, 2 Broken Wharf,
London EC4V 3DT
T: 020 7248 2223
F: 020 7329 8160
E: info@aef.org.uk
www.aef.org.uk
Director: Tim Johnson
The AEF is the principal UK non-profit-making environmental association concerned with the environmental effects of aviation, ranging from aircraft noise issues associated with small airstrips or helipads, to the contribution of airline emissions to climate change. The AEF was established in 1975 and now has over 120 affiliated members comprising community and environmental groups, local authorities, parish councils, businesses and consultancies. Individual and student members are also welcomed.
Employees: 3
Volunteers: 3
Regional offices: 1

## AVID (Association of Visitors to Immigration Detainees)

Archway Resource Centre,
1b Waterlow Road, London N19 5NJ
T: 020 7281 0533
E: enquiries@aviddetention.org.uk
www.aviddetention.org.uk
Director: Ali McGinley
National network of volunteer visitors to immigration detainees. We support those held under immigration acts in the UK with our network of 17 voluntary groups and over 650 visitors.

## AVIF (Able Volunteers International Fund)

Flat 1, 13 Cheltenham Parade, Harrogate,
North Yorkshire HG1 1DD
E: alowndes@avif.org.uk
www.avif.org.uk
Founder Trustee: Alison Lowndes
AVIF is an innovative online charity, assisting with sustainable development via online and onsite volunteering in rural Kenya, East Africa. AVIF does not charge fees.
Volunteers: 200
Regional offices: 2

## Avocet Trust

Clarence House, 60–62 Clarence Street,
Hull, Humberside HU9 1DN
T: 01482 329226
E: info@avocettrust.co.uk
www.avocettrust.co.uk
Chief Executive: LC Howell
Avocet provides lifetime support to vulnerable people to enable them to live valued lives. Avocet provides a range of services including 24-hour support in clients' homes, as well as short-stay care and through-the-door domiciliary services. Going forward the Trust plans to provide employment training services as well as employment placement services.
Employees: 300

## Aylesham Neighbourhood Project

Ackholt Road, Aylesham, Canterbury,
Kent CT3 3AJ
T: 01304 840134
E: office@aylesham-np.org.uk
aylesham-np.org.uk
Chief Executive: Kathryn Rogers
Aylesham Neighbourhood Project (the Project) is a charitable company that works in local communities to inspire children and families to recognise potential, make positive change and achieve bright futures. The Project delivers community-based services across Dover District that are person centred and give positive opportunities for children and families.
Employees: 22
Volunteers: 9

## Back Up (transforming lives after spinal cord injury)

Jessica House, Red Lion Square,
191 Wandsworth High Street,
London SW18 4LS
T: 020 8875 1805
E: admin@backuptrust.org.uk
www.backuptrust.org.uk
Chief Executive: Louise Wright
Our vision is a world where people with a spinal cord injury can realise their full potential. Our mission is to: inspire people affected by spinal cord injury to transform their lives; challenge perceptions of disability; deliver services that build confidence and independence and offer a supportive network.
Employees: 30
Volunteers: 400
Regional offices: 1
Income: £1,500,000 (2015–16)

## BackCare

16 Elmtree Road, Teddington,
Middlesex TW11 8ST
T: 020 8977 5474
F: 020 8943 5318
E: info@backcare.org.uk
www.backcare.org.uk
BackCare helps people manage and prevent back pain by providing advice, promoting self-help, encouraging debate and funding scientific research into back care.
Employees: 8
Volunteers: 180
Regional offices: 30

## Bank Workers Charity

E: jenna.southgate@bwcharity.org.uk

## Bar Pro Bono Unit

289–293 High Holborn,
London WC1V 7HZ
T: 020 7092 3960
E: enquiries@barprobono.org.uk
www.barprobono.org.uk
The unit provides free legal advice and
representation for deserving cases where
Legal Aid is not available and where the
applicant is unable to afford legal assistance.
Applicants are strongly encouraged to
approach an advice agency or solicitor before
applying to the unit.

## Barnardo's

Tanners Lane, Barkingside, Ilford,
Essex IG6 1QG
T: 020 8550 8822
F: 020 8551 6870
E: supportercare@barnardos.org.uk
www.barnardos.org.uk
Chief Executive: Javed Khan
As one of the UK's leading children's
charities, Barnardo's believes in children
regardless of their circumstances, gender,
race, disability or behaviour. We believe in the
abused, the vulnerable, the forgotten and the
neglected. We will support them, stand up for
them and bring out the best in each and every
child. We do this because we believe in
children.
Employees: 6800
Volunteers: 12000
Regional offices: 9

## Barnsley Hospice

104–106 Church Street, Gawber, Barnsley,
South Yorkshire S75 2RL
T: 01226 244244
E: enquiries@barnsley-hospice.org
www.barnsleyhospice.org
Chief Executive/Chair: Julie Ferry
Barnsley Hospice is a charity dedicated to
providing quality, specialist, palliative and
end-of-life care to all adults in Barnsley, as
well as their family and friends. The Hospice's
vision is to: be the first choice for patients,
referrers, customers and donors of all our
services; provide more services to more
people; strive to be one of the best hospices
in England.
Employees: 120
Volunteers: 350
Income: £3,900,000 (2014–15)

## BASIC

The Brain And Spinal Injury Centre,
554 Eccles New Road, Salford M5 5AP
T: 0161 707 6441
Helpline: 0870 750 0000
E: enquiries@basiccharity.org.uk
www.basiccharity.org.uk
CEO: Wendy Edge
The Brain And Spinal Injury Centre – or
BASIC – provides community rehabilitation
and support services to help people rebuild
their lives following acquired brain injury and
neurological illness.
Employees: 14
Volunteers: 35
Regional offices: 1
Income: £435,000 (2014–15)

## BasicNeeds UK

158a Parade, Leamington Spa,
Warwickshire CV32 4AE
T: 01926 330101
E: jess.mcquail@basicneeds.org
www.basicneeds.org
Executive Director: Jess McQuail
BasicNeeds is an international non-
governmental organisation working to
improve the lives of people living with mental
illness and epilepsy. Predominantly focused
on low and middle income countries, we work
right across the system with individuals and
communities, local and national governments
and international organisations. To date, over
640,700 people have benefitted from our
programmes in Africa and Asia.
Employees: 7

## BBC Children in Need Appeal

PO Box 1000, London W12 7WJ
T: 020 8576 7788
F: 020 8576 8887
E: pudsey@bbc.co.uk
www.bbc.co.uk/pudsey
Chief Executive: David Ramsden
The Children in Need appeal provides grants
to properly constituted organisations working
with children and young people aged 18 and
under, who: may have experienced mental,
physical or sensory disabilities; have
behavioural or psychological disorders;
are living in poverty or situations of
deprivation; are suffering through distress,
abuse or neglect.
Employees: 43
Regional offices: 12

## BCS

First Floor, Block D, North Star House,
North Star Avenue, Swindon,
Wiltshire SN2 1FA
T: 01793 417417
F: 01793 480270
E: customerservice@hq.bcs.org.uk
www.bcs.org
CEO: David Clarke
Professional membership association
representing over 70,000 people worldwide
working in IT and computing. We promote
wider social and economic progress through
the advancement of information technology
science and practice. We bring together
industry, academics, practitioners and
government to share knowledge, promote
new thinking, influence the development of
computing education, shape public policy and
inform the public.
Employees: 220
Regional offices: 2

## Be Your Best Foundation

Portsmouth Guildhall, Guildhall Square,
Portsmouth, Hampshire PO1 2AB
T: 023 9298 5716
E: dan@rockchallenge.co.uk
www.rockchallenge.co.uk
Chairman of the Board of Directors:
Juno Hollyhock
The Foundation aims to improve quality of
life by encouraging young people to take
an active role in building safe and healthy
communities. The primary aim of the
Foundation is to raise funds to stage Rock
Challenge events across the UK, an anti-drug
and crime initiative that takes the form of a
friendly performing arts competition for 11 to
18 year olds. Rock Challenge encourages
a natural high through live performance.
Employees: 3
Volunteers: 100
Regional offices: 1

## Beacon Awards

12 Angel Gate, 320–326 City Road,
London EC1V 2PT
T: 020 7713 9326
E: contact@beaconfellowship.org.uk
www.beaconawards.org.uk
The Beacon Awards were established in
2003 with the aim of promoting effective
philanthropic giving through the creation
of a nationally recognised awards scheme
to highlight best practice and innovation
in philanthropy. In addition to the biennial
awards ceremony, Beacon also runs a
programme of roundtables that offer
opportunities for philanthropists to connect
with each other in order to share best

practice and learn about the best philanthropic work in the UK today.

**Employees: 1**
**Volunteers: 6**

## Beanstalk

6 Middle Street, London EC1A 7JA
T: 020 7729 4087
E: info@beanstalkcharity.org.uk
www.beanstalkcharity.org.uk
Chief Executive: Ginny Lunn
Beanstalk is a national literacy charity that recruits, vets, trains and supports volunteers to work in primary schools with children who have fallen behind with their reading. Our vision is that all children and young people will have the essential skills they need to grow up and lead successful lives.

**Employees: 115**
**Volunteers: 3000**
**Regional offices: 17**

## Beat

2nd Floor, Wensum House,
103 Prince of Wales Road, Norwich,
Norfolk NR1 1DW
T: 0300 123 3355
Helpline: 0345 634 1414
F: 01603 664915
E: info@b-eat.co.uk
www.b-eat.co.uk
Chief Executive: Andrew Radford
Beat is the leading UK-wide charity providing information, help and support for people affected by eating disorders – anorexia, bulimia nervosa and binge eating disorder through helplines, online services and emails.

**Employees: 30**
**Volunteers: 850**

## Behçet's Syndrome Society

Kemp House, 152–160 City Road,
London EC1V 2NX
T: 0345 130 7328
Helpline: 0345 130 7329
E: info@behcetsdisease.org.uk
www.behcets.org.uk
Chairman: Alan Booth
Behçet's (pronounced Betjets) is a rare, complex and life-long condition caused by disturbances in the body's immune system. It causes inflammation in many parts of the body. Behçet's can affect people of any age, but it most commonly affects those between the ages of 20 and 40. The Behçet's Syndrome Society runs a helpline, funds

research and offers financial support for patients in need.

**Employees: 1**
**Volunteers: 15**
**Income: £45,000 (2015–16)**

## Beth Johnson Foundation

Parkfield House, 64 Princes Road, Hartshill,
Stoke-on-Trent, Staffordshire ST4 7JL
T: 01782 844036
F: 01782 746940
E: debbie.everden@bjf.org.uk
www.bjf.org.uk
Chief Executive: Steve Robinson
The Foundation undertakes innovative work to develop evidence-based approaches to the social aspects of ageing. Currently we have UK programmes in intergenerational work, positive ageing and advocacy. Our work is approached from a life course perspective and we provide resources, training and consultancy in support of our aims.

**Employees: 24**
**Volunteers: 40**
**Regional offices: 1**

## Bethany Children's Trust

Office 211, 22 Eden Street,
Kingston Upon Thames, Surrey KT1 1DN
T: 020 8977 7571
E: admin@bethanychildrenstrust.org.uk
www.bethanychildrenstrust.org.uk
Director: Susie Howe
The Bethany Children's Trust's vision is to see every child in the world loved, safe, nurtured and free to reach their God-given potential. We are strengthening churches and Christian projects that care for vulnerable children throughout the world, with training workshops, prayer and financial support. BCT also works with other Christian organisations worldwide, to speak out with, and for, children at risk and challenge the Church, local communities and world leaders to address their needs.

**Employees: 3**
**Volunteers: 2**
**Regional offices: 1**
**Income: £180,000 (2013–14)**

## Bexley Snap

Thames Innovation Centre, 2 Veridion Way,
Erith, Kent DA18 4AL
T: 020 8320 1488
E: ceo@bexleysnap.org.uk
www.bexleysnap.org.uk
Chief Executive: Carol Penny
Our vision is that disabled children have choices and a right to a fulfilling life. We aim

to increase choice of services and activities available to children and young people while reducing the isolation and frustration experienced by their families. We offer a range of weekend, evening and school holiday play and leisure activities for disabled children, a pre-school programme for disabled babies and toddlers, and a comprehensive support programme for parents/carers.

**Employees: 42**
**Volunteers: 23**

## BHA

Democracy House, 609 Stretford Road,
Old Trafford, Manchester M16 0QA
T: 0845 450 4247
F: 0845 450 3247
E: info@thebha.org.uk
www.thebha.org.uk
Chief Executive: Priscilla Nkwenti
BHA challenges health inequalities for disadvantaged and marginalised communities. We make a positive contribution in health provision and service delivery. Using expertise in the field of health, social care policy and service development, we provide efficient and appropriate advice and services to communities at grass-root level. We take a strategic and consultative role by working with policy makers and legislators to ensure effective service development and delivery to people from disadvantaged and marginalised communities.

**Employees: 36**
**Volunteers: 33**
**Regional offices: 2**
**Income: £1,700,000 (2014–15)**

## BIBIC

Knowle Hall, Knowle, Bridgwater,
Somerset TA7 8PJ
T: 01278 684060
F: 01278 685703
E: info@bibic.org.uk
www.bibic.org.uk
BIBIC exists to maximise the potential of children with sensory, social, communication, motor and learning difficulties. We work with parents and carers, offering a valuable support system that offers time to talk, expert advice and practical help.

**Employees: 39**
**Volunteers: 8**

## Bible Society

Stonehill Green, Westlea,
Swindon SN5 7DG
T: 01793 418100
E: contactus@biblesociety.org.uk
www.biblesociety.org.uk
Chief Executive: James Catford
Employees: 105
Volunteers: 700

## Big Issue Foundation

1–5 Wandsworth Road, London SW8 2LN
T: 020 7526 3200
F: 020 7526 3401
E: foundation@bigissue.com
www.bigissue.org.uk
CEO: Stephen Robertson
The Big Issue Foundation is a national charity
that connects vendors with the vital support
and solutions that enable them to rebuild
their lives and journey away from
homelessness.
Employees: 23
Volunteers: 15
Regional offices: 7

## Big Society Capital

Chronicle House, 72–78 Fleet Street,
London EC4Y 1HY
T: 020 7186 2500
E: enquiries@bigsocietycapital.com
www.bigsocietycapital.com
Chief Executive: Cliff Prior
Big Society Capital is an organisation set up
to help grow the social investment market, so
that charities and social enterprises who want
to borrow money can access the finance they
need to maintain and increase their support
for people in need in the UK. Since 2012, we
have committed £140 million in investments
to specialist organisations who lend to
charities and social enterprises.

## Bipolar UK

11 Belgrave Road, London SW1V 1RB
T: 020 7931 6480
F: 020 7931 6481
E: info@bipolaruk.org.uk
wwww.bipolaruk.org.uk
Bipolar UK is the national charity dedicated
to supporting individuals with the much
misunderstood and devastating condition of
bipolar, their families and carers.
Regional offices: 3

## BirdLife International

Wellbrook Court, Girton Road,
Cambridge CB3 0NA
T: 01223 277318
F: 01223 277200
E: tracy.spraggon@birdlife.org
www.birdlife.org
BirdLife International is a partnership of
people for birds and the environment. Over
10 million people worldwide support the
BirdLife Partnership of national NGO
conservation organisations and local
networks. BirdLife's vision is of a world rich in
biodiversity, with people and nature living in
harmony, equitably and sustainably. BirdLife's
aim is to conserve wild birds, their habitats
and global biodiversity by working with people
towards sustainability in the use of natural
resources.
Employees: 65
Volunteers: 8
Regional offices: 6

## Birth Companions

PO Box 64597, London SW17 1DR
T: 07855 725097
Helpline: 020 7117 0037
E: info@birthcompanions.org.uk
www.birthcompanions.org.uk
Director: Annabel Kennedy
Our overall aim is to improve the wellbeing
of pregnant women and new mothers who
are, have been or are at risk of being detained.
We do this by improving their mental health,
reducing isolation, enabling them to give
their babies the best possible start in life
and improving their conditions. We work in
HMP Holloway as well as in the community
supporting women antenatally, during birth
and postnatally.
Employees: 5
Volunteers: 34

## Black and Ethnic Minority Diabetes Association

c/o One Westminster, 37 Chapel Street,
London NW1 5DP
T: 07401 097733
Helpline: 07831 046824
E: info@bemda.org
www.bemda.org
Executive Director: Aderonke Kuti
BEMDA, founded in 1995, is a user-led,
health-focused organisation that was
established to promote the health of diabetics
in the community and reduce the impact of
diabetes-related health problems in black and
ethnic minority communities in particular,

without excluding diabetics and their carers
from other communities from our services.
Employees: 2
Volunteers: 8
Income: £25,007,000 (2013–14)

## Black Environment Network

UK Office, 268 Bannerdale Road,
Sheffield S11 9FE
E: ukoffice@ben-network.org.uk
www.ben-network.org.uk
Development Manager: Max Ghani
BEN works for full ethnic participation in the
built and natural environment. BEN uses the
word 'black' symbolically recognising that the
black communities are the most visible of all
ethnic communities. We work with black,
white and other ethnic communities.
Volunteers: 2

## Black Training and Enterprise Group

2nd Floor, 200A Pentonville Road,
London N1 9JP
T: 020 7832 5800
F: 020 7832 5829
E: jeremy@bteg.co.uk
www.bteg.co.uk
The group aims to ensure fair access and
outcomes for black communities in
employment, training and enterprise and
to help black organisations to play an active
role in the economic regeneration of local
communities through partnership with others.
Employees: 5
Volunteers: 2

## Bladder and Bowel Foundation

SATRA Innovation Park, Rockingham Road,
Kettering, Northamptonshire NN16 9JH
T: 01536 533255
Helpline: 0845 345 0165
F: 01536 533240
E: heather.ellison@
bladderandbowelfoundation.org
www.bladderandbowelfoundation.org
Executive Director: Robert Dixon
B&BF is now the UK's largest advocacy
charity providing information and support
for all types of bladder and bowel-related
problems, including incontinence, prostate
problems, constipation and diverticular
disease, for patients, their families, carers
and healthcare professionals.
Employees: 3
Volunteers: 1
Regional offices: 1

## Blesma, The Limbless Veterans

**Frankland Moore House,
185–187 High Road, Chadwell Heath,
Romford, Essex RM6 6NA
T: 020 8590 1124
F: 020 8599 2932
E: chadwellheath@blesma.org
www.blesma.org
Chief Executive: Barry Le Grys**
Blesma, The Limbless Veterans is the national charity for all limbless serving and ex-service men and women, their widows and dependants. It is a membership organisation which helps wounded service men and women rebuild their lives by providing rehabilitation activities and welfare support. Their membership includes those who have lost the use of a limb, an eye or the sight of an eye.
**Employees: 62
Volunteers: 28
Income: £4,000,000 (2013–14)**

## Blind Children UK

**Hillfields, Reading Road, Burfield Common,
Reading, Berkshire RG7 3YG
T: 0800 781 1444
E: enquiries@blindchildrenuk.org
www.blindchildrenuk.org
Chief Executive: Richard Leaman**
Blind Children UK provides services for the families of children and young people with a visual impairment from birth to 25 years. Our services include family support, educational advocacy, IT advice, activities and CustomEyes large-print children's books and as part of Guide Dogs we can also provide Habilitation and Mobility support. Subject to criteria grants may be given for computers for home use.

## Blind Veterans UK

**12–14 Harcourt Street, London W1H 4HD
T: 020 7723 5021
Helpline: 0800 389 7979
F: 020 7262 6199
E: info@blindveterans.org.uk
www.blindveterans.org.uk
Chief Executive: Nick Caplin CB**
Blind Veterans UK, formerly St Dunstan's, believe that no one who's served our country should battle blindness alone. We're here to help with a lifetime's practical and emotional support, regardless of when people served or how they lost their sight. We get our members back on their feet, recovering their

independence and discovering a life beyond sight loss.
**Employees: 380
Volunteers: 349
Regional offices: 12**

## Blindaid Africa

**Prospect Cottage, Wells Road, Radstock,
Avon BA3 3RP
T: 01761 434385
E: peter@blindaid.org
www.blindaid.org
Director: Rosalie Lees**
The provision of tools for learning and living for blind young people in Africa – that is our motto and objective. We provide minimal cost (mostly pre-used) materials and equipment to enable blind students to participate and compete effectively in their national education systems and to integrate effectively in the school and community social environments.
**Employees: 2
Volunteers: 10
Regional offices: 2
Income: £2,500 (2011–12)**

## Bliss

**2nd and 3rd Floors, 9 Holyrood Street,
London SE1 2EL
T: 020 7378 1122
F: 020 7403 0673
E: josiea@bliss.org.uk
www.bliss.org.uk**
Bliss, the premature baby charity, is dedicated to making sure that more babies born prematurely or sick in the UK survive and that each one has the best quality of life.
**Employees: 21
Volunteers: 250
Regional offices: 25**

## Blond McIndoe Research Foundation

**E: maxine.smeaton@blondmcindoe.org
www.blondmcindoe.org**

## Blood Pressure UK

**60 Cranmer Terrace, London SW17 0QS
T: 020 8772 4994
F: 020 8772 4999
E: info@bloodpressureuk.org
www.bloodpressureuk.org**
The BPA aims to significantly improve the prevention, diagnosis and treatment of high

blood pressure in order to prevent death and disability from stroke and heart disease.
**Employees: 6
Volunteers: 2
Regional offices: 1**

## Bloodwise

**43 Great Ormond Street,
London WC1N 3JJ
T: 020 7405 0101
E: info@lrf.org.uk
bloodwise.org.uk**
Works to defeat leukemia and related blood diseases (lymphomas, myeloma, myelodysplasia, myeloproliferative disorders, aplastic anaemia).

## Blue Cross

**Shilton Road, Burford,
Oxfordshire OX18 4PF
T: 0300 777 1897
E: kerry.lane@bluecross.org.uk
www.bluecross.org.uk
CEO : Sally de la Bedoyere**
Blue Cross has been dedicated to the health and happiness of pets since 1897. Abandoned or unwanted, ill or injured – we do what's needed to give every pet a healthy life in a happy home. We're a charity, so the more help you give us, the more help we can give pets.
**Employees: 650
Regional offices: 16**

## BMS World Mission

**PO Box 49, 129 Broadway,
Didcot OX11 8XA
T: 01235 517700
F: 01235 517601
E: mail@bmsworldmission.org
www.bmsworldmission.org
General Director: David Kerrigan**
The purpose of the Society is to enable Baptist churches to respond to the call of God throughout the world by pursuing the following objectives: to make known the Gospel of Jesus Christ; to prevent and relieve poverty; to relieve sickness and promote and protect health; to advance education; to alleviate human suffering caused by disaster overseas.
**Employees: 180
Volunteers: 186
Regional offices: 1**

## Board of Deputies of British Jews

6 Bloomsbury Square, London WC1A 2LP
T: 020 7543 5400
E: info@bod.org.uk
www.bod.org.uk
The Board acts as the representative body of the UK Jewish community, composed of some 330 deputies elected by synagogues and by certain national communal bodies. It is the voice of the Jewish community and protects the rights and interests of Jews in the UK. It monitors legislation and any discriminatory measures, legal or social, affecting the Jewish community and watches over the interests of co-religionists in countries where they are oppressed and persecuted.

## Boaz Trust

First Floor, 110 Oldham Road, Manchester, Greater Manchester M4 6AG
T: 0161 202 1056
F: 0161 228 7332
E: info@boaztrust.org.uk
boaztrust.org.uk
Chief Executive: Ros Holland
*Referrals only* Boaz Shared Houses and Hosting scheme provides accommodation for asylum seekers who have been refused and are destitute and also for homeless refugees. Referrals are accepted via our online forms at http://boaztrust.org.uk/referral. Practical and pastoral support is available for our clients when they are staying in Boaz accommodation. The Boaz Night Shelter is available through the winter months from October to April.
Employees: 10
Volunteers: 250
Income: £310,000 (2012-13)

## Bobath Centre for Children with Cerebral Palsy

Bradbury House, 250 East End Road, London N2 8AU
T: 020 8444 3355
E: enquiries@bobath.org.uk
www.bobath.org.uk
Centre Director: Christine Barber MSc MCSP DSA(CSP)
We provide specialist physio, occupational and speech and language therapy for children with cerebral palsy and allied neurological conditions. We also provide training in Bobath theory and practice for health professionals in the UK and abroad.
Employees: 20
Volunteers: 4
Income: £1,000 (2015-16)

## Body and Soul

99–119 Rosebery Avenue, London EC1R 4RE
T: 020 7923 6880
E: info@bodyandsoulcharity.org
www.bodyandsoulcharity.org
Director: Emma Colyer
A charity supporting children, teenagers and adults who are living with and closely affected by HIV in the UK. Our strategy aims to impact five key areas of member wellbeing: physical health, mental health, psychosocial wellbeing, practical support and maximising productivity.
Employees: 12
Volunteers: 200+
Regional offices: 1

## Body Shop Foundation

Watersmead, Littlehampton, West Sussex BN17 6LS
T: 01903 844039
F: 01903 844202
E: bodyshopfoundation@thebodyshop.com
www.thebodyshopfoundation.org
CEO: Lisa Jackson
The Body Shop Foundation funds projects across the globe. The groups we support address human and civil rights and animal and environmental protection issues.
Employees: 8
Volunteers: 150

## Bond

Regents Wharf, 8 All Saints Street, London N1 9RL
T: 020 7837 8344
F: 020 7837 4220
E: mwright@bond.org.uk
www.bond.org.uk
Chief Executive: Ben Jackson
Bond is the network of UK-based voluntary organisations working in international development and development education. Bond members aim to improve the extent and quality of the UK and Europe's contribution to international development, the eradication of global poverty and the upholding of human rights.
Employees: 35
Income: £3,000,000 (2013–14)

## Book Aid International

39–41 Coldharbour Lane, Camberwell, London SE5 9NR
T: 020 7733 3577
F: 020 7978 8006
E: info@bookaid.org
www.bookaid.org
Director: Alison Hubert
Book Aid International works in partnership with libraries in Africa, providing books, resources and training to support an environment in which reading for pleasure, study and life-long learning can flourish.
Employees: 20
Volunteers: 50

## Booktrust

Book House, 45 East Hill, London
T: 020 8875 4584
E: trudi.kent@booktrust.org.uk
www.booktrust.org.uk/
PA To Chief Executive: Trudi Kent

## Bore Place

Bore Place Road, Chiddingstone, Edenbridge, Kent TN8 7AR
T: 01732 463255
E: hello@boreplace.org
www.boreplace.org
Director: Caroline Arnold
Commonwork's vision is of a fairer world in which people work together and with nature, recognising that all are interconnected. We work towards this vision in practical ways, through our study centre and education programmes on an organic farm in Kent. We: offer hands-on activities in food, farming, sustainable development, global citizenship, climate change, renewable energy; offer CPD for teachers and school leaders; share the lessons from our practical work locally, regionally and nationally.
Employees: 26
Volunteers: 26
Regional offices: 1

## Born Free Foundation

3 Grove House, Foundry Lane, Horsham, West Sussex RH13 5PL
T: 01403 240170
E: info@bornfree.org.uk
www.bornfree.org.uk
The Foundation works to investigate, expose and alleviate animal suffering in zoos and to promote the protection of wildlife in its natural habitat.

## Bowel Cancer UK

9 Rickett Street, London SW6 1RU
T: 020 7381 9711
F: 020 7381 5752
E: admin@bowelcanceruk.org.uk
www.bowelcanceruk.org.uk
The principal objectives of the Charity are to help all people concerned about colorectal cancer by: providing authoritative information, support and advice for those affected by the disease, their carers and their families; raising awareness of the disease to increase knowledge and understanding of the symptoms; educating the public and healthcare professionals about methods of prevention and treatments; campaigning for improved choice, equality of access to treatments and best care.
Employees: 13
Volunteers: 20

## Boys' Brigade

Felden Lodge, Felden,
Hemel Hempstead HP3 0BL
T: 01442 231681
F: 01442 235391
E: enquiries@boys-brigade.org.uk
www.boys-brigade.org.uk
Brigade Secretary: Steve Dickinson
Christian Youth Organisation for children and young people of all faiths and none, from 4–8 years. Through its activity programme and resources, the Boys' Brigade partners churches and communities to care for and challenge young people for life by a programme of informal education underpinned by the Christian faith.
Employees: 40
Volunteers: 15000
Regional offices: 3

## Brain and Spine Foundation

3.36 Canterbury Court, Kennington Park,
1–3 Brixton Road, London SW9 6DE
T: 020 7793 5900
Helpline: 0808 808 1000
F: 020 7793 5939
E: emma@brainandspine.org.uk
www.brainandspine.org.uk
CEO: Ken Walker
The Brain and Spine Foundation is a national charity that aims to improve the care, treatment and prevention of neurological disorders through patient and carer information programmes.
Employees: 8
Volunteers: 100

## Brain Research Trust

Dutch House, 307–308 High Holborn,
London WC1V 7LL
T: 020 7404 9982
E: info@brt.org.uk
www.brt.org.uk
The Brain Research Trust was founded as an independent medical charity, not part of the NHS, with the aim of supporting research at the Institute of Neurology, London, into diseases of the brain and nervous system.

## Braintree District Voluntary Support Agency

Braintree Community Centre,
19–21 Bocking End, Braintree,
Essex CM7 9AH
T: 01376 550507
E: bdvsa@bdvsa.org
www.bdvsa.org.uk
Chief Officer: Rachel Fahie
BDVSA's mission is to empower communities in Braintree District through the promotion and development of local voluntary and community action. We deliver our mission by supporting voluntary and community organisations to help them: secure resources (funding and volunteers); operate safely and effectively; have a voice in shaping the future of their communities.
Employees: 3
Income: £90,000 (2015–16)

## Brainwave Centre Ltd

Marsh Lane, Huntworth Gate, Bridgwater,
Somerset TA6 6LQ
T: 01278 429089
E: joannesmith@brainwave.org.uk
www.brainwave.org.uk
Chief Executive: Phil Edge
Brainwave is a Charity that exists to help children with disabilities and additional needs to achieve greater independence. It aims to improve mobility, communication skills and learning potential, through a range of educational and physical therapies. The children we work with have a range of conditions including autism, brain injuries such as cerebral palsy and genetic conditions such as Down's Syndrome.
Employees: 96
Volunteers: 200+
Regional offices: 3

## Breaking Free – Primarily Supporting Women Survivors of Child Sexual Abuse

Marshall House, 124 Middleton Road,
Morden, Surrey SM4 6RW
T: 0845 108 0055
F: 020 8687 4134
E: info@breakingfreesupport.co.uk
Breaking Free provides a confidential, safe, supportive and understanding environment in which women can deal with issues arising from their experiences of abuse. It offers support to women survivors regardless of race, colour, creed, religious beliefs or ability/disability and increases awareness of the issue of child sexual abuse.
Employees: 3
Volunteers: 44

## Breakthrough UK Ltd

The Kevin Hyett Suite,
Abraham Moss Centre, Crescent Road,
Crumpsall, Manchester,
Greater Manchester M8 5UF
T: 0161 234 3950
E: admin@breakthrough-uk.co.uk
www.breakthrough-uk.co.uk
Chief Executive: Michelle Scattergood
Our mission is to promote the rights, responsibilities and respect of disabled people. Our mission is broken into four main aims. These are: influencing government, local, regional and national agencies about barriers to disabled people's participation; enabling disabled people to pursue and develop their careers; providing greater choice, control and independent living; working towards being financially stable, politically aware with healthy growth.
Employees: 16
Regional offices: 1

## Breast Cancer Care

5–13 Great Suffolk Street,
London SE1 0NS
T: 0845 092 0800
Helpline: 0808 800 6000
E: joanne.stewart@breastcancer.org.uk
www.breastcancercare.org.uk
Breast Cancer Care is here for anyone affected by breast cancer. We bring people together, provide information and support and campaign for improved standards of care. We use our understanding of people's experience of breast cancer and our clinical expertise in everything we do. All our services are free.
Employees: 119
Volunteers: 350
Regional offices: 4

## Breast Cancer Now

Ibex House, 42–47 Minories,
London EC3N 1DY
T: 0333 207 0300
E: community@breastcancernow.org
www.breastcancernow.org
Chief Executive: Delyth Morgan
We're Breast Cancer Now, the UK's largest
breast cancer charity – and we're dedicated
to funding research into this devastating
disease. We believe that if we all act now, by
2050, everyone who develops breast cancer
will live.
Employees: 180
Volunteers: 600
Regional offices: 2

## Breast Cancer Research Trust

PO Box 861, Bognor Regis PO21 9HW
T: 01243 583143 (also fax)
E: bcrtrust@btinternet.com
www.breastcancerresearchtrust.org.uk
Executive Administrator:
Rosemary Sutcliffe
The Trust promotes scientific research into
the origins, causes and nature of breast
cancer. It improves methods of prevention
and techniques in the treatment, cure and
control of breast cancer and develops aids
to assess the clinical needs of patients and
potential patients. It establishes clinics
for the therapeutic treatment of breast
cancer and encourages the public to take
appropriate measures.
Income: £123,914 (2014–15)

## Breastcancer Haven

Effie Road, London SW6 1TB
T: 020 7384 0000
F: 020 7384 0001
E: louise@clearsilver.co.uk
www.thehaven.org.uk
Chief Executive: Pamela Healy OBE
Being diagnosed with breast cancer and
undergoing treatment affects people
physically and emotionally. The Haven offers
a free programme of care to support patients
and their families during this time. Staffed
by a specialist team, Havens are welcoming
places providing support, information and
complementary therapies before, during and
after medical treatment. Working alongside
healthcare professionals, Havens promote
integrated breast cancer care where

conventional and complementary medicine
work together.
Employees: 45
Volunteers: 75
Regional offices: 4
Income: £3,000,000 (2013–14)

## Bridging the Gap

c/o SMCA, Cobham Court,
Haslemere Avenue, Mitcham,
Surrey CR4 3PR
T: 020 8090 1486
E: james@btguk.org
www.btguk.org
Chief Executive: Dr James Stevens-Turner
A registered charity helping prisoners and
ex-prisoners adjust to life outside prison. It
encourages local and global understanding of
problems faced by people leaving prison and
helps people leaving prison to restart their
lives, stay crime free and become useful
members of society.
Volunteers: 20
Regional offices: 1

## Britain-Nepal Medical Trust

Export House, 130 Vale Road, Tonbridge,
Kent TN9 1SP
T: 01732 360284
E: info@britainnepalmedicaltrust.org.uk
www.britainnepalmedicaltrust.org.uk
Co-Chairs: Dr G Holdsworth and
Dr S Subedi
BNMT aims to assist the people of Nepal to
improve their health through realisation of
their health rights. It does this by working in
partnership with the Ministry of Health,
international and local non-governmental
organisations, local committees and
communities.
Employees: 54
Volunteers: 11
Regional offices: 2

## British Accreditation Council for Independent Further and Higher Education

Ground Floor, 14 Devonshire Square,
London EC2M 4YT
T: 0300 330 1400
E: info@the-bac.org
www.the-bac.org
Chief Executive: Paul Fear
The British Accreditation Council has
provided a comprehensive quality assurance
scheme for independent further and higher
education in the UK since 1984. Our
accreditation is recognised the world over

by students, agents and government officials
as a clear mark of educational quality in the
private sector.
Employees: 8
Regional offices: 1

## British Acoustic Neuroma Association

Oak House B, Ransomwood Business Park,
Southwell Road West, Mansfield,
Nottinghamshire NG21 0HJ
T: 01623 632143
E: admin@bana-uk.com
www.bana-uk.com
Formed in 1992, BANA is organised and
administrated by people affected by acoustic
neuroma. It is a registered charity and exists
for mutual support, information exchange
and listening. We aim to support those
affected (both patients and family members)
by acoustic neuroma and other similar
conditions.
Employees: 2
Volunteers: 50+
Regional offices: 1

## British Acupuncture Council

63 Jeddo Road, London W12 9HQ
T: 020 8735 0400
F: 020 8735 0404
E: info@acupuncture.org.uk
www.acupuncture.org.uk
The Council works to establish the status,
maintain a register, regulate the conduct
and protect the interests of practitioners of
acupuncture, so as to promote and maintain,
in the public interest, proper standards for
the practice of acupuncture. It promotes
and encourages the study and knowledge of
acupuncture, which is a branch of medicine
founded upon the principle that health is
dependent upon a proper balance of vital
energy forces within the body.
Employees: 9
Volunteers: 15

## British Albanian Kosovar Council

21 Winchester Road, London NW3 3NR
T: 020 7586 8731
F: 020 8674 0860
E: carolineffrenchblake@gmail.com
www.bakc.org.uk/
The charity's object and its principal activity
is that of providing assistance to Albanian-
speaking young people, children and families,
as well as unaccompanied minors.
Employees: 7
Volunteers: 6

## British and International Federation of Festivals

Festivals House, 198 Park Lane,
Macclesfield, Cheshire  SK11 6UD
T: 01625 428297
F: 01625 503229
E: info@federationoffestivals.org.uk
www.federationoffestivals.org.uk
Chief Executive Officer: Terry Luddington
The Federation is the largest UK organisation for the participatory arts of music, dance and speech. Our aim is to advance, promote and encourage generally, and by means of the amateur festival movement in particular, the study and practice of the arts of music, dance, speech, literature and acting.
Employees: 4
Volunteers: 16500
Income: £250,000 (2013–14)

## British Archaeological Association

18 Stanley Road, Oxford  OX4 1QZ
E: dacruz@liv.ac.uk
www.archeologyuk.org
The Association promotes the study of archaeology. It aims to preserve our national antiquities, encourages original research and publishes new work, covering art and antiquities from the Roman to the post-medieval periods.

## British Association and College of Occupational Therapists

106–114 Borough High Street, Southwark, London  SE1 1LB
T: 020 7357 6480
F: 020 7480 2299
E: vandita.chisholm@cot.co.uk
www.cot.org.uk
The British Association and College of Occupational Therapists champions the unique and vital work of occupational therapy staff. Occupational therapy promotes health, wellbeing and independence through participation in activities or occupation. It gives people the tools and skills to do the things they need or want to do, removing obstacles to disability, injury, illness or other conditions.
Employees: 60
Volunteers: 200
Regional offices: 20

## British Association for Adoption and Fostering

Saffron House, 6–10 Kirby Street, London  EC1N 8TS
T: 020 7421 2600
F: 020 7421 2601
E: mail@baaf.org.uk
www.baaf.org.uk
Membership organisation for local authorities, voluntary adoption agencies, fostering agencies, legal advisers, childcare practitioners and the general public with an interest in adoption and fostering. The organisation aims to promote high standards in adoption and fostering, to promote public and professional understanding of the issues and to be an independent voice in the field of childcare, informing and influencing policy makers.
Employees: 140
Volunteers: 5
Regional offices: 9

## British Association for Cancer Research

c/o Leeds Institute of Cancer and Pathology, Clinical Sciences Building, St James University Hospital, Beckett Street  LS9 7TF
T: 0113 206 5611
E: bacr@leeds.ac.uk
www.bacr.org.uk
The Association aims to advance research in all aspects of cancer by encouraging the exchange of information.
Employees: 1
Volunteers: 1200

## British Association for Counselling and Psychotherapy

BACP House, 15 St John's Business Park, Lutterworth, Leicestershire  LE17 4HB
T: 01455 883300
F: 01455 550243
E: bacp@bacp.co.uk
www.bacp.co.uk
The Association promotes education and training for those involved in counselling and psychotherapy, full or part time, in either professional or voluntary contexts, with a view to raising standards. It also promotes the understanding of counselling and psychotherapy.
Employees: 75
Volunteers: 180

## British Association for Early Childhood Education

136 Cavell Street, London  E1 2JA
T: 020 7539 5400
F: 020 7539 5409
E: office@early-education.org.uk
www.early-education.org.uk
Chief Executive: Beatrice Merrick
The British Association for Early Childhood Education (Early Education), founded in 1923, is the leading national voluntary organisation for early years practitioners and parents, with members and branches across the UK. Early Education promotes the right of every child to education of the highest quality. It provides support, training, advice and information on best practice for all those concerned with the education and care of young children from birth to eight years.
Employees: 7
Volunteers: 200
Income: £425,882 (2014–15)

## British Association for Immediate Care

Turret House, 2 Turret Lane, Ipswich, Suffolk  IP4 1DL
T: 01473 218407
F: 01473 280585
E: cx@basics.org.uk
www.basics.org.uk
Chief Executive: Phill Browne
The aims of BASICS are: to foster co-operation between immediate care schemes and to encourage the formation of new schemes; to strengthen and develop cooperation between all services in coping with emergencies that may result in injury or risk to life; to encourage and assist research into all aspects of immediate care; to raise standards of care and training of practitioners; to disseminate information and encourage and assist international exchange of information and co-operation.
Employees: 3
Volunteers: 1

## British Association for Local History

PO Box 6549, Somersal Herbert, Ashbourne, Staffordshire  DE6 5WH
T: 01283 585947
E: mail@balh.co.uk
www.balh.co.uk
The Association works to advance understanding and knowledge of local history.
Employees: 4
Volunteers: 22

## British Association for the Advancement of Science

Wellcome Wolfson Building,
165 Queen's Gate  SW7 5HD
T: 020 7973 3503
F: 0870 770 7102
E: info@britishscienceassociation.org
www.britishscienceassociation.org
Chief Executive: Sir Roland Jackson
We are the UK's nationwide, open
membership organisation, which provides
opportunities for people of all ages to learn
about, discuss and challenge the sciences and
their implications.
Employees: 40
Volunteers: 5000
Regional offices: 14

## British Association of Dermatologists

4 Fitzroy Square, London  W1T 5HQ
T: 020 7383 0266
E: rachael@bad.org.uk
www.bad.org.uk
The Association publishes and promotes
information, teaching and research in
dermatology.

## British Association of Friends of Museums

141A School Road, Brislington, Bristol,
Avon BS4 4LZ
T: 0117 977 7435
E: jayneselwood@live.co.uk
www.bafm.org.uk
BAFM encourages support for museums
of all kinds. Its aims are: to publicise the
achievements of museums and their friends;
to advise those wishing to set up new groups;
to assist and encourage existing groups. It
liaises with all other bodies concerned with
museums, art galleries and heritage centres,
and voluntary support for them.
Employees: 1

## British Association of Social Workers

16 Kent Street, Birmingham  B5 6RD
T: 0121 622 3911
F: 0121 622 4860
E: info@basw.co.uk
www.basw.co.uk
Chief Executive: Dr Ruth Allen
BASW is the professional association for
social workers in the UK.
Employees: 66
Volunteers: 150
Regional offices: 3

## British Blind Sport

Pure Offices, Plato Close, Tachbrook Park,
Warwick, Warwickshire  CV34 6WE
T: 01926 424247
E: info@britishblindsport.org.uk
www.britishblindsport.org.uk
Chief Executive: Alaina MacGregor
Provides sport and recreation for blind and
visually impaired people.
Employees: 3

## British Cardiac Patients Association

15 Abbey Road, Bingham,
Nottingham NG13 8EE
T: 01949 837070
E: admin@bcpa.co.uk
www.bcpa.co.uk
Chairman: Keith Jackson
The Association provides support,
reassurance and advice to cardiac patients,
their families and carers. Whether it be heart
attack, angina, cardiac investigations,
arrhythmias, implantable cardiac devices
or surgery for bypass, valve replacement
aneurysm or transplant, we are able to offer
free advice and information.
Volunteers: 80

## British Cardiovascular Society

9 Fitzroy Square, London  W1T 5HW
T: 020 7383 3887
E: enquiries@bcs.com
www.bcs.com
The objective of the British Cardiovascular
Society is to advance the knowledge of
diseases of the heart and circulation for the
benefit of the public.
Employees: 12

## British Cave Research Association

Old Methodist Chapel, Great Hucklow,
Buxton, Derbyshire SK17 8RG
T: 01298 873810
F: 01298 873801
E: publications@british-caving.org.uk
www.bcra.org.uk
Chairman: David Checkley
Promotes cave research and exploration, and
related activities.
Employees: 1
Volunteers: 20+
Regional offices: 1

## British Centre for Science Education

12 Millbeck Approach, Morley,
West Yorkshire LS27 8WA
E: committee@bcseweb.org.uk
www.bcse.org.uk
The British Centre for Science Education is a
single-issue pressure group dedicated solely
to keeping creationism and intelligent design
out of the science classroom in publicly
funded schools in the UK.

## British Colostomy Association

Enterprise Hose, 95 London Street,
Reading, Berkshire  RG1 4QA
T: 0118 939 1537
Helpline: 0800 328 4257
E: jo.mckenzie@colostomyassociation.org.uk
www.colostomyassociation.org.uk
Chairman: Monty Taylor
The Association offers help and reassurance
to anyone who has had, or is about to have,
a colostomy operation and runs a 24-hour
helpline, provides a range of literature,
publishes a quarterly magazine and promotes
a network of support groups. Its team of
UK-wide volunteers provide one-to-one
support on the phone or in person if needed.
Employees: 4
Volunteers: 100

## British Council

10 Spring Gardens, London  SW1A 2BN
E: general.enquiries@britishcouncil.org
www.britishcouncil.org
The UK's international organisation for
educational opportunities and cultural
relations.

## British Deaf Association

18 Leather Lane, London EC1N 7SU
F: 020 7405 0090
E: bdn@bda.org.uk
www.bda.org.uk
Chairman: Terry Riley
Promoting the rights of deaf people who use
British Sign Language.
Employees: 25
Volunteers: 120
Regional offices: 4

## British Dental Health Foundation

Smile House, 2 East Union Street, Rugby,
Warwickshire CV22 6AJ
T: 01788 546365
Helpline: 0845 063 1188
F: 01788 541982
E: sharon@dentalhealth.org
www.dentalhealth.org
Chief Executive: Dr Nigel Carter
The UK's leading oral health charity, with a
40-year track record of providing public
information and influencing government
policy. It: maintains a Dental Helpline
consumer free-advice service; runs a product
accreditation scheme to provide consumer
assurance; publishes and distributes a wide
range of educational literature for the
profession and consumers; runs National
Smile Month between May and June, and
Mouth Cancer Action Month throughout
November.
Employees: 15

## British Dyslexia Association

Unit 8, Bracknell Beeches,
Old Bracknell Lane, Bracknell,
Berkshire RG12 7BW
T: 0333 405 4555
Helpline: 0333 405 4567
F: 0333 405 4570
E: helpline@bdadyslexia.org.uk
www.bdadyslexia.org.uk
Chief Executive: Dr Kate Saunders
The British Dyslexia Association is the voice
for 10% of the population that experience
dyslexia. We aim to influence government
to promote a dyslexia friendly society that
enables dyslexic people of all ages to reach
their full potential. We provide the only
national helpline supporting tens of
thousands of people each year.
Employees: 25
Volunteers: 50

## British Ecological Society

Charles Darwin House, 12 Roger Street,
London WC1N 2JU
T: 020 7685 2500
F: 020 7685 2501
E: amelia@britishecologicalsociety.org
www.britishecologicalsociety.org
The British Ecological Society aims to
promote the science of ecology through
research and to use the findings of such
research to educate the public and influence
policy decisions that involve ecological
matters.
Employees: 20

## British Endodontic Society

PO Box 707, Gerrards Cross,
Buckinghamshire SL9 0XS
T: 01494 581542 (also fax)
E: bes@athomas99.freeserve.co.uk
www.britishendodonticsociety.org.uk
The object of the charity is to promote and
advance the study of endodontology and to
ensure that the dental health of the nation is
both maintained and improved.
Employees: 1
Volunteers: 20

## British False Memory Society (BFMS)

The Old Brewery, Newtown,
Bradford-on-Avon, Wiltshire BA15 1NF
T: 01225 868682
F: 01225 862251
E: carolyn@bfms.org.uk
www.bfms.org.uk
Director: Madeline Greenhalgh
Formed in 1993 to raise awareness of dangers
of recovered memory through flawed
therapeutic trauma theories and investigative
systems. Aims to promote accurate
differentiation between true and false
allegations of child sexual abuse through
raising public, professional and policy maker
awareness, organising conferences and
seminars, information provision, newsletters
and encouraging academic research plus
working with the media. BFMS incorporates
a telephone helpline to support families and
individuals affected by false memory and false
accusations.
Employees: 3
Regional offices: 1

## British Future

Kean House, 6 Kean Street,
London WC2B 4AS
T: 020 7632 9069
E: elizabeth@britishfuture.org
www.britishfurture.org
Director: Sunder Katwala
British Future is an independent, non-
partisan thinktank seeking to involve people
in an open conversation that addresses
people's hopes and fears about identity and
integration, migration and opportunity, so
that we feel confident about Britain's future.
Employees: 5

## British Geriatrics Society

Marjory Warren House, 31 St John's Square,
London EC1M 4DN
T: 020 7608 1369
E: pr@bgs.org.uk
www.bgs.org.uk
CEO: Colin Nee
The society promotes better care in old age
and seeks to improve the quality and provision
of healthcare services for older people.
Employees: 11

## British Heart Foundation

Great London House, 180 Hampstead,
London NW1 7AW
T: 020 7554 0000
F: 020 7554 0100
E: internet@bhf.org.uk
www.bhf.org.uk
Plays a leading role in the fight against heart
disease.
Employees: 1584
Volunteers: 26000
Regional offices: 9

## British HIV Association

BHIVA Secretariat, Mediscript Ltd,
1 Mountview Court, 310 Friern Barnet Lane,
London N20 0LD
T: 020 8369 5380
F: 020 8446 9194
E: bhiva@bhiva.org
www.bhiva.org
Chair: Dr Chloe Orkin
The objectives of BHIVA are: to relieve
sickness and to protect and preserve health
through the development and promotion of
good practice in the treatment of HIV and
HIV-related illnesses; to advance public
education in the subjects of HIV and the
symptoms, causes, treatment and prevention
of HIV-related illnesses through the
promotion of research.

## British Holistic Medical Association

PO Box 371, Bridgwater,
Somerset TA7 9AA
E: contactbhma@aol.co.uk
www.bhma.org
Chair: David Peters
The BHMA is an open association of
mainstream healthcare professionals, CAM
practitioners and members of the public who
want to adopt a more holistic approach in
their own life and work. We do not endorse,
accredit or recommend individual
practitioners or organisations.
Employees: 4
Volunteers: 7
Regional offices: 1

## British Home and Hospital for Incurables

Crown Lane, London SW16 3JB
T: 020 8670 8261
E: home.stmvolunteercoord@
thebritishhome.co.uk
www.britishhome.org.uk
The British Home provides specialist nursing care and support to chronically sick and disabled people. Our residents are offered the highest standard of care and support to: maintain their independence; participate in the planning of their care; retain personal prospects; have access to their health records.

## British Homeopathic Association

Hahnemann House, 29 Park Street West,
Luton LU1 3BE
T: 0870 444 3950
F: 0870 444 3960
E: info@trusthomeopathy.org
www.britishhomeopathic.org
Chief Executive: Cristal Sumner
The charity was founded in 1902 to promote homeopathy and raise money for research and the homeopathic training of healthcare professionals including doctors, dentists, nurses, podiatrists, pharmacists and vets. It is committed to making homeopathy more widely available on the NHS and provides information for the public and lobbies and campaigns for NHS homeopathy.
Employees: 9
Volunteers: 1

## British Horse Society

Abbey Park, Stareton, Kenilworth,
Warwickshire CV8 2XZ
T: 024 7684 0500
F: 024 7684 0501
E: enquiries@bhs.org.uk
www.bhs.org.uk
The Society aims to improve standards of care for horses and ponies, improve standards of riding and driving, encourage the use of horses and ponies and promote the interests of horse and pony breeding.
Employees: 71
Volunteers: 1000
Regional offices: 9

## British Humanist Association

1 Gower Street, London WC1E 6HD
T: 020 7079 3580
F: 020 7079 3588
E: info@humanism.org.uk
www.humanism.org.uk
Chief Executive: Andrew Copson
The BHA promotes Humanism and supports and represents people who seek to live good lives without religious or superstitious beliefs. The BHA: provides educational resources for schools and students; organises public lectures and other events; campaigns against religious privilege and for equality on grounds of religion or beliefs; and provides humanist funerals, weddings, civil partnership celebrations, namings and other ceremonies.
Employees: 12
Volunteers: 6

## British Institute of Human Rights

School of Law,
Queen Mary University of London,
Mile End Road, London E1 4NS
T: 020 7882 5850
E: info@bihr.org.uk
www.bihr.org.uk
Director: Stephen Bowen
The Institute aims to further the education of the public and public authorities in the field of human rights in the UK and internationally.
Employees: 10
Volunteers: 3

## British Institute of Learning Disabilities

Campion House, Green Street,
Kidderminster DY10 1JL
T: 01562 723010
F: 01562 723029
E: enquiries@bild.org.uk
www.bild.org.uk
Chief Executive: Keith Smith
BILD aims to improve the quality of life for people with learning disabilities by involving them and their families in all aspects of our work. This includes working with government and public bodies to achieve full citizenship and human rights for people with learning disabilities, turning research and policy into practice and supporting service providers to develop and share person-centred approaches.
Employees: 28
Volunteers: 1

## British Institute of Radiology

48–50 St John Street, Farringdon,
London EC1M 4DG
E: admin@bir.org.uk
www.bir.org.uk
The Institute brings together all the professions in radiology, medical and scientific disciplines to share knowledge and educate the public, thereby improving the prevention and detection of disease and the management and treatment of patients.
Employees: 15

## British Kidney Patient Association

3 The Windmills, St Mary's Close,
Turk Street, Alton, Hampshire GU34 1EF
T: 01420 541424
F: 01420 89438
E: info@britishkidney-pa.co.uk
www.britishkidney-pa.co.uk
Chief Executive: Paddy Tabor
The British Kidney Patient Association exists to provide support for the benefit and welfare of kidney patients throughout the UK, offering information, advice, financial aid and direct patient support services as well as funding improvements in health and social care practice and campaigning on behalf of patients and their families.
Employees: 11
Volunteers: 20

## British Liver Trust

6 Dean Park Crescent, Bournemouth,
Dorset BH1 1HL
T: 01425 481320
Helpline: 0800 652 7330
E: info@britishlivertrust.org.uk
www.britishlivertrust.org.uk
Chief Executive: Andrew Langford
We aim to help everyone affected by liver disease through information, support and research.
Employees: 13

## British Lung Foundation

73–75 Goswell Road, London EC1V 7ER
T: 020 7688 5555
Helpline: 0300 003 0555
F: 020 7688 5556
E: enquiries@blf.org.uk
www.blf.org.uk
Chief Executive: Penny Woods
The British Lung Foundation is here for everyone affected by a lung condition. It understands lung disease and fights to beat it through prevention, support and research.
Employees: 75
Volunteers: 500
Regional offices: 3

## British Lymphology Society

Garth House, Rushey Lock, Tadpole Bridge,
Buckland Marsh, Oxfordshire SN7 8RF
T: 01452 790178
E: info@thebls.com
www.thebls.com
Chair: Jane Rankin
The Society's objects are: to advance education and knowledge in the field of lymphology and related subjects; to foster

interest in and co-ordinate a strategy for improving the management of chronic oedema, particularly lymphoedema; to produce and maintain a register of specialist centres in the United Kingdom and Ireland; to benefit patients by improving the knowledge, expertise and skills of health care professionals treating them.

**Employees: 2**
**Volunteers: 14**
**Regional offices: 1**

## British Medical Acupuncture Society

Royal London Hospital for
Integrated Medicine,
60 Great Ormond Street,
London WC1N 3HR
T: 020 7713 9437
F: 020 7713 6286
E: bmaslondon@aol.com
www.medical-acupuncture.co.uk
**Support Manager to Medical Director:
Allyson Brown**
A registered charity established to encourage the use and scientific understanding of acupuncture within medicine for the public benefit. BMAS seeks to enhance the education/training of suitably qualified practitioners, and to promote high standards of working practices in acupuncture.

**Employees: 5**

## British National Temperance League

18 Warwick Avenue, Carlton in Lindrick,
Worksop, Nottinghamshire S81 9BP
T: 01909 731435
E: bntl@btconnect.com
www.bntl.org
**Chief Executive: Barbara Pike**
BNTL is an organisation that responds to alcohol and other drug-related problems by seeking to promote healthy drug-free lifestyles and to inform on the effect of alcohol and drugs on individuals and communities. This is achieved through the production of teaching resources based around the national curriculum for teachers and others working with young people.

**Employees: 2**
**Volunteers: 15**

## British Naturalists' Association

BNA, BM 8129, London WC1N 3XX
T: 0844 892 1817
E: mo.norrington@bna-naturalists.org
www.bna-naturalists.org
**President: David Bellamy**
One of the UK's oldest natural history societies, BNA was founded in 1905 for the sole purpose of promoting awareness and the

study of all aspects of British natural history, an aim which it continues to pursue to the present day.

**Volunteers: 300**
**Regional offices: 10**

## British Obesity Surgery Patient Association

PO Box 805, Taunton, Somerset TA1 9DU
T: 0845 602 0446
E: zanetabospa@sky.com
www.bospa.org
BOSPA (British Obesity Surgery Patient Association) was launched in December 2003 to provide support and information to the thousands of patients in the UK for whom obesity surgery can provide an enormous benefit.

**Employees: 1**

## British Ornithologists' Union

Department of Zoology,
University of Oxford, South Parks Road,
Oxford OX1 3PS
E: bou@bou.org.uk
www.bou.org.uk
The Union promotes the study of the science of ornithology, encourages links between amateur and professional ornithologists and encourages and supports research and training.

## British ORT

Ort House, 126 Albert Street,
London NW1 7NE
T: 020 7446 8520
E: info@ortuk.org
www.ortuk.org
ORT's mission is to provide education and vocational training, helping the young and not so young to gain skills they need to become proud, independent, contributing members of their own culture and society.

## British Pain Society

3rd Floor, Churchill House,
35 Red Lion Square, London WC1R 4SG
T: 020 7269 7840
F: 020 7831 0859
E: info@britishpainsociety.org
www.britishpainsociety.org
The Society promotes the advancement of health by raising the standard of management of pain by promotion of education, research and training.

## British Polio Fellowship

Ground Floor Unit A, Eagle Office Centre,
The Runway, South Ruislip,
Middlesex HA4 6SE
T: 0800 018 0586
F: 020 8842 0555
E: info@britishpolio.org.uk
www.britishpolio.org.uk
**Chief Executive: Ted Hill**
The aims of the Fellowship are to enable polio survivors to lead full, independent and active lives and to ensure their needs are met. It ensures that post polio syndrome (late effects of polio) is recognised and managed effectively in every polio survivor and campaigns for the rights and equality of polio survivors.

## British Pregnancy Advisory Service

20 Timothys Bridge Road,
Stratford Enterprise Park,
Stratford upon Avon CV37 9BF
T: 0845 365 5050
Helpline: 0845 730 4030
F: 0845 365 5051
E: info@bpas.org
www.bpas.org
**Chief Executive: Ann Furedi**
bpas was established in 1968 to provide a safe, legal abortion service and is a charitable, non-profit-making organisation with sites nationwide. The organisation offers information and treatment in relation to unplanned pregnancy, vasectomy, abortion, contraception and online STI testing and treatment.

**Employees: 60**

## British Psychological Society

St Andrew's House, 48 Princess Road East,
Leicester LE1 7DR
T: 0116 254 9568
F: 0116 227 1314
E: enquiries@bps.org.uk
www.bps.org.uk
**Chief Executive: Professor Ann Colley**
The British Psychological Society is the representative body for psychology and psychologists in the UK. The Society and its members develop, promote and apply psychology for the public good. We enhance the efficiency and usefulness of psychologists by setting high standards of professional education and knowledge. We cover all areas of psychological research and practice.

**Employees: 100**
**Regional offices: 4**

## British Red Cross

UK Office, 44 Moorfields EC2Y 9AL
T: 0844 871 1111
E: information@redcross.org.uk
www.redcross.org.uk
The British Red Cross helps people in crisis, whoever and wherever they are. We are part of a global voluntary network, responding to conflicts, natural disasters and individual emergencies. We help vulnerable people in the UK and abroad prepare for, withstand and recover from emergencies in their own communities.
Employees: 4000
Volunteers: 22000

## British School of Osteopathy

Avon House, 275 Borough High Street,
London SE1 1JE
T: 020 7089 5307
E: n.waters@bso.ac.uk
www.bso.ac.uk
The School undertakes osteopathic research to deliver osteopathic education and healthcare for the benefit of the whole community.

## British Sjögren's Syndrome Association

PO Box 15040, Birmingham B31 3DP
T: 0121 478 0222
Helpline: 0121 478 1133
E: office@bssa.uk.net
www.bssa.uk.net
The Association provides mutual support and information to individuals affected by Sjögren's syndrome. We aim to educate people about the condition, raise awareness surrounding its existence and symptoms, and support research into its cause and treatment.
Employees: 3

## British Society For Immunology

Vintage House, 37 Albert Embankment,
London SE1 7TL
T: 020 3031 9800
E: e.thomas@immunology.org
www.immunology.org
Office Co-ordinator/PA To CEO:
Emilie Thomas
Employees: 9

## British Society for Rheumatology

Bride House, 18–20 Bride Lane,
London EC4Y 8EE
T: 020 7842 0900
F: 020 7842 0901
E: bsr@rheumatology.org.uk
www.rheumatology.org.uk

To promote excellence in the treatment of people with arthritis and musculoskeletal conditions and to support those delivering it.
Employees: 24

## British Society of Disability and Oral Health

Dental Special Needs,
Chorley and District Hospital, Preston Road,
Chorley, Lancashire PR7 1PP
E: margaret.gregory2@nhs.net
www.bsdh.org.uk
The aims of the Society are to promote the oral health of disabled people of all ages. It promotes links with organisations representing disabled people, consults with disability groups to identify their needs and demands and studies the barriers relating to the provision of oral healthcare for disabled people.

## British Society of Psychosomatic Obstetrics Gynaecology and Andrology

Porterbrook Clinic, 75 Osborne Road,
Nether Edge, Sheffield,
South Yorkshire S11 9BF
E: info@bspoga.org
www.bspoga.org
BSPOGA aims to advance the education of the general public and medical profession by encouraging the development of a better understanding and improved management of the psychological problems associated with reproductive and associated conditions in women and men.

## British Sociological Association

Bailey Suite, Palatine House,
Belmont Business Park, Belmont,
Durham DH1 1TW
T: 0191 383 0839
F: 0191 383 0782
E: judith.mudd@britsoc.org.uk
www.britsoc.co.uk
Chief Executive: Judith Mudd
The BSA advances knowledge of sociology by lectures, publications, the promotion of research and encouragement of contact between workers in all relevant fields of enquiry.
Employees: 12
Volunteers: 500
Income: £1,220,546 (2015–16)

## British Spiritualist Federation

T: 01475 700706
E: spiritualistinfo@btinternet.com
www.sagb.org.uk

## British Stammering Association

15 Old Ford Road, London E2 9PJ
T: 020 8981 8818
E: mail@stammering.org
www.stammering.org
The Association aims to help stammerers live satisfactorily with their speech and encourages research into stammering.
Employees: 9
Volunteers: 10

## British Thyroid Foundation

Suite 12, One Sceptre House,
Hornbeam Square North, Hornbeam Park,
Harrogate, North Yorkshire HG2 8PB
T: 01423 810093
E: info@btf-thyroid.org
www.btf-thyroid.org
Director and Secretary to the Trustees:
Janis Hickey
Provides reliable information and support to people with thyroid disorders.
Employees: 6
Volunteers: 40
Regional offices: 1
Income: £110,000 (2015–16)

## British Tinnitus Association

Unit 5, Acorn Business Park,
Woodseats Close, Sheffield,
South Yorkshire S8 0TB
T: 0114 250 9933
Helpline: 0800 018 0527
F: 0114 258 2279
E: info@tinnitus.org.uk
www.tinnitus.org.uk
Chief Executive: David Stockdale
The British Tinnitus Association (BTA) provides help, support and advice to people with tinnitus, their families, friends and professionals caring for them. We provide accurate, reliable and authoritative information via: our helpline; over 20 information leaflets; Quiet, our quarterly journal; our website; attending awareness-raising events. We also support clinical research and provide training.
Employees: 12
Volunteers: 80
Income: £674,331 (2013–14)

## British Trust for Ornithology

The Nunnery, Thetford, Norfolk IP24 2PU
T: 01842 750050
F: 01842 750030
E: sophie.foulger@bto.org
www.bto.org
The BTO promotes and encourages the wider understanding, appreciation and conservation of birds through scientific studies, using the combined skills and enthusiasm of its members, other birdwatchers and staff.
Employees: 95
Volunteers: 30000
Regional offices: 130

## British Voice Association

330 Gray's Inn Road, London WC1X 8EE
T: 0300 123 2773
F: 020 3456 5092
E: administrator@britishvoiceassociation.org.uk
www.britishvoiceassociation.org.uk
The BVA recognises the human voice as an essential element of our communication and wellbeing. It is devoted to people with voice problems, ranging from severe pathology and cancer to subtle difficulties of artistic performance, all of whom are entitled to the best care available.
Volunteers: 10

## British Waterways

64 Clarendon Road
T: 01442 278738
E: robin.evans@britishwaterways.co.uk
www.britishwaterways.co.uk
Chief Executive: Robin Evans

## British Wireless for the Blind Fund

10 Albion Place, Maidstone,
Kent ME14 5DZ
T: 01622 754757
F: 01622 751725
E: dave@blind.org.uk
www.blind.org.uk
The Fund provides, on a permanent free-loan basis, radios, radio-cassette recorders and CD radio-cassette recorders to UK registered blind and partially sighted persons, over the age of eight, who are in need.
Employees: 5
Volunteers: 300

## British Youth Council

49–51 East Road, London N1 6AH
T: 0845 458 1489
E: mail@byc.org.uk
www.byc.org.uk
The Council works to advance the spiritual educational and physical welfare of young people in conjunction with similar bodies working in the same field in countries overseas.

## Broken Rainbow LGBT Domestic Violence Service UK

J414, 83 Ducie Street,
Greater Manchester M1 2JQ
T: 0845 260 5560
Helpline: 0300 999 5428
E: mail@brokenrainbow.org.uk
www.broken-rainbow.org.uk
Broken Rainbow UK runs the only National LGBT Domestic Violence Helpline providing confidential support to all members of the lesbian, gay, bisexual and transgender (LGBT) communities, their family and friends, and agencies supporting them.
Employees: 6
Volunteers: 15
Regional offices: 1

## Bromley Y

E: valeriemichelet@gmail.com

## Brook

50 Featherstone Street, London EC1Y 8RT
T: 020 7284 6040
Helpline: 0808 802 1234
F: 020 7284 6050
E: admin@brook.org.uk
www.brook.org.uk
National Director: Simon Blake
The country's largest young people's sexual health charity. For 50 years, we have been providing sexual health services, support and advice to young people under 25. Brook wants a society that values all children, young people and their developing sexuality. We want all children and young people to be supported to develop the self-confidence, skills and understanding they need to enjoy and take responsibility for their sexual lives, sexual health and wellbeing.
Employees: 27
Volunteers: 21
Regional offices: 23

## Brothers of Charity Services

Lisieux Hall, Dawson Lane,
Whittle-le-Woods, Chorley PR6 7DX
T: 01257 266311
F: 01257 265671
E: info@brothersofcharity.org.uk
www.brothersofcharity.org.uk
Aims to assist people who have learning difficulties to live an ordinary life in which they are respected and valued in their local community.

## BUAV

16A Crane Grove, London N7 8NN
T: 020 7700 4888
F: 020 7700 0252
E: meg.griffiths@buav.org
www.crueltyfreeinternational.org
Chief Executive: Michelle Thew
The BUAV's vision is to create a world where nobody wants or believes we need to experiment on animals.
Employees: 18
Volunteers: 2

## Buglife – The Invertebrate Conservation Trust

Bug house, Ham Lane, Orton Waterville,
Peterborough, Cambridgeshire PE2 5UU
T: 01733 201210
F: 01733 315410
E: info@buglife.org.uk
www.buglife.org.uk
Chief Executive: Matt Shardlow
The food we eat, the birds we see, the flowers we smell and the hum of life we hear simply would not exist without bugs. Invertebrates truly underpin all life on earth. Sadly, many amazing and beautiful creatures are declining. Three species of bumblebees are now extinct in the UK and over 70% of butterfly species are in significant decline. Buglife is the only organisation in Europe devoted to the conservation of all invertebrates.
Employees: 24
Volunteers: 50
Regional offices: 4
Income: £1,175,816 (2014–15)

## Build Africa

Vale House, Clarence Road,
Tunbridge Wells, Kent TN1 1HE
T: 01892 519619
E: hello@build-africa.org.uk
www.build-africa.org.uk
Build Africa combines education and livelihoods projects to help communities in Kenya and Uganda live happier, healthier and more fulfilled lives.

## Building and Social Housing Foundation

Memorial Square, Coalville,
Leicestershire LE67 3TU
T: 01530 510444
F: 01530 510332
E: bshf@bshf.org
www.bshf.org
Director: David Ireland
BSHF is an independent housing research
organisation which identifies and promotes
good practice in housing throughout
the world.
Employees: 10

## Business and Education London South

E: michaelmanningprior@bels.org.uk

## Business in the Community

137 Shepherdess Walk, London N1 7RQ
T: 020 7566 8650
E: hq.reception@bitc.org.uk
www.bitc.org.uk
Chief Executive: Julia Cleverdon
Business in the Community is a unique
movement of over 800 member companies,
representing one in five of the UK private
sector workforce. A further 3,000 companies
are engaged through our programmes and
campaigns, which we operate through a local
network of more than 100 business-led
partnerships and we lead a global partners
network of 112 organisations operating in over
60 countries.
Employees: 343
Regional offices: 11

## Butler Trust

Howard House, 32–34 High Street,
Croydon, Surrey CR0 1YB
T: 020 8688 6062
F: 020 8688 6056
E: info@butlertrust.org.uk
www.butlertrust.org.uk
Director: Simon Shepherd
The Butler Trust is an independent charity
that recognises excellence and innovation
by people working with offenders in the UK.
Through its Annual Award Scheme and
Development Programme, the Trust helps
to: identify and promote excellence and
innovation; develop and disseminate best
practice in the care and resettlement of
offenders throughout the UK; provide
professional and personal development
opportunities for award-winning staff.
Employees: 6
Volunteers: 14

## Buttle UK

Audley House, 13 Palace Street,
London SW1E 5HX
T: 020 7828 7311
E: info@buttleuk.org
www.buttleuk.org
Chief Executive: Gerri McAndrew
Buttle UK helps children and young people
living in poverty in the UK. We make grants to
meet the critical needs of individual children
and young people whose safety, health or
development are at risk, launching them into
a brighter future. Objectives include
providing grant aid, carrying out research,
policy work and fundraising.
Employees: 20
Regional offices: 4

## BYHP

2 Chandos Close, Banbury,
Oxfordshire OX16 4TL
T: 01295 259442
E: linda.slide@byhp.org.uk
www.byhp.org.uk
Head Of Business: Tim Tarby Donald
BYHP is a registered charity that exists to
support and assist vulnerable young people
aged 13–25 in finding and maintaining a safe
home. We provide free, confidential advice,
information and support services and have
developed a range of services to support
young people in securing and maintaining
housing.
Employees: 8
Volunteers: 8
Regional offices: 1

## Cabrini Children's Society

E: himare.peterkin@cabrini.org.uk

## Caldecott Foundation

Caldecott House, Hythe Road, Smeeth,
Ashford, Kent TN25 6SP
T: 01303 815678
F: 01303 815677
E: info@caldecottfoundation.co.uk
www.caldecottfoundation.co.uk

The Caldecott Foundation provides high-
quality childcare and education within a
therapeutic setting, enabling children to
attain life skills and self-esteem. We ensure
children and young people achieve their
educational potential via personal educational
plans and delivery of the National
Curriculum.
Employees: 178

## CALIBRE Audio Library

New Road, Weston Turville, Aylesbury,
Buckinghamshire HP22 5XQ
T: 01296 432339
F: 01296 392599
E: membershipservices@calibre.org.uk
www.calibre.org.ok
Director: Mike Lewington
The CALIBRE Audio Library is a free
nationwide postal library of audio books
for people with sight problems or physical
disabilities. 7,000 fiction and non-fiction
books recorded on cassette or MP3 disks
(unabridged) and no special playback
equipment is required. 1,200 titles are
available in the Young Calibre library. A small
charge is made for print catalogues – full
catalogue available on the website. Contact
the Membership Services Team for further
details and an application form.
Employees: 52
Volunteers: 95

## Camberwell After School Project

14 Badsworth Road, Camberwell,
London SE5 0JY
T: 020 7708 2711
E: carmen.lindsay@caspuk.org
www.caspuk.org
Chief Executive Officer: Carmen Lindsay
MBE
To advance the education of children by the
provision of safe and satisfying group play and
supplementary learning. For primary school
children, this entails the provision of a safe
and happy environment before and after
school, safe travel to and from school and
full day service during school holidays. The
mission is also to enable children to develop
both socially and academically by the
provision of appropriate group play and
through structured learning.
Employees: 17
Volunteers: 5
Regional offices: 2
Income: £266,006 (2015–16)

## Cambridge House

Cambridge House, 1 Addington Square,
London SE5 0HF
T: 020 7358 7000
E: kwoodley@ch1889.org
www.ch1889.org
Chief Executive: Karin Woodley

Cambridge House is a people's social action centre that works innovatively to tackle poverty and social injustice. Occupying our own building in Southwark for more than 126 years, we deliver specialist frontline services to address the needs of people facing multiple disadvantage and complex interrelated needs. Working nationally and internationally, we remain firmly rooted in our local neighbourhood as a community asset and hub working one person, one family and one community at a time.
**Employees: 51**
**Volunteers: 43**
**Income: £1,500,000 (2014–15)**

## Camfed International

**St Giles Court, 24 Castle Street,**
**Cambridge CB3 0AJ**
**T: 01223 362648**
**E: info@camfed.org**
**www.camfed.org**
Camfed is an international non-profit organisation tackling poverty and inequality by supporting girls to go to school and succeed and empowering young women to step up as leaders of change. Since 1993, Camfed's innovative education programmes in Zimbabwe, Zambia, Ghana, Tanzania and Malawi have directly supported over 1,202,000 students to attend primary and secondary school, and over 3 million children have benefited from an improved learning environment.

## Campaign Against Drinking and Driving

**1st Floor, 16 Market Street, Brighouse,**
**West Yorkshire HD6 1AP**
**T: 01484 723649 (also fax)**
**Helpline: 0845 123 5542**
**E: info@cadd.org.uk**
**www.scard.org.uk**
**Chair: Carole Whittingham**
Campaigns against drink and/or drug driving. Supports victims who have been bereaved or injured as a result of drink/drugs or any other bereavement related to road collisions or incidents.

## Campaign for Better Transport Charitable Trust

**44–48 Wharf Road, London N1 7UX**
**T: 020 7566 6480**
**E: info@bettertransport.org.uk**
**www.bettertransport.org.uk**
We are the Campaign for Better Transport and since 1973 we have been helping to create transport policies and programmes that give people better lives. Working

nationally and locally, collectively and as individuals, through high-level lobbying and strong public campaigning, we make good transport ideas a reality and stop bad ones from happening.
**Employees: 11**
**Volunteers: 3**

## Campaign for Freedom of Information

**c/o ARTICLE 19, Free Word Centre,**
**60 Farringdon Road, London EC1R 3GA**
**T: 020 7324 2519**
**E: admin@cfoi.org.uk**
**www.cfoi.org.uk**
**Director: Maurice Frankel**
We seek to improve and defend the Freedom of Information Act. We advise the public about their rights to information under FOI and related laws, help people challenge unreasonable refusals to disclose information, encourage good practice and provide FOI training.
**Employees: 2**
**Income: £100,000 (2015–16)**

## Campaign for Learning

**24 Greencoat Place, Westminster,**
**London SW1P 1RD**
**T: 020 7798 6067**
**F: 020 7798 6001**
**E: jwright@cflearning.org.uk**
**www.campaignforlearning.org.uk**
**Chief Executive: Tricia Hartley**
The Campaign for Learning is working for a society where learning is at the heart of social inclusion. Research shows that lifelong learners are more likely to be happier, healthier, have better jobs, contribute more to society and live longer and more fulfilled lives. We work to build motivation, create opportunities and provide support for learning in families and communities, workplaces and schools that leads to positive change.
**Employees: 17**
**Volunteers: 2**
**Regional offices: 2**

## Campaign for Nuclear Disarmament (CND)

**Mordechai Vanunu House,**
**162 Holloway Road, London N7 8DQ**
**T: 020 7700 2393**
**F: 020 7700 2357**
**E: enquiries@cnduk.org**
**www.cnduk.org**
**Chair: Dave Webb**
CND campaigns non-violently to rid the world of nuclear weapons and other weapons of mass destruction and to create genuine

security for future generations. CND is funded entirely by its members and supporters.
**Employees: 11**
**Volunteers: 20**
**Regional offices: 6**

## Campaign to Protect Rural England

**5–11 Lavington Street, London SE1 0NZ**
**T: 020 7981 2800**
**F: 020 7981 2899**
**E: info@cpre.org.uk**
**www.cpre.org.uk**
**Chief Executive: Shaun Spiers**
CPRE campaigns for a sustainable future for the English countryside, a vital but undervalued environmental, economic and social asset to the nation. We highlight threats and promote positive solutions. Our in-depth research supports active campaigning, and through reasoned argument and lobbying we seek to influence public opinion and decision-makers at every level.
**Employees: 38**
**Volunteers: 1500**
**Regional offices: 43**
**Income: £4,000,000 (2013–14)**

## Camphill Village Trust Ltd

**9 Saville Street, Malton,**
**North Yorkshire YO17 7LL**
**T: 01653 228322**
**F: 0845 094 4639**
**E: trustoffice@cvt.org.uk**
**www.cvt.org.uk**
**CEO: Huw John**
To provide support for adults with special needs by establishing and maintaining intentional communities of purpose where all may continue to develop as individuals through meaningful work of a productive nature alongside a range of chosen therapeutic activities and further education, as well as a healthy cultural, social and spiritual life.
**Employees: 470**
**Regional offices: 10**

## CAN

32–36 Loman Street, Southwark,
London SE1 0EH
T: 020 7922 7700
E: r.chadha@can-online.org.uk
www.can-online.org.uk
**Chief Executive: Adele Blakebrough**
Supporting social enterprise, CAN supports
social entrepreneurs to scale up their
businesses and maximise their social impact.
We provide office space, business support
and funds. We do this through social
investment.
**Employees: 16**

## Cancer Care Society

48 Mountbatten Drive, Ferndown,
Dorset BH22 9EL
T: 01202 894896
E: peter.j.hayes@btinternet.com
The Society aims to relieve, aid and support
persons who are suffering or have suffered
from cancer. Grants are given to associated
charities and not to individuals.

## Cancer Laryngectomee Trust

PO Box 618, Halifax HX3 8WX
T: 01422 205522 (also fax)
E: info@cancerlt.org
www.cancerlt.org
**Trustee: Carole Stainton**
The Trust exists to improve the quality of life
for all neck breathers in the UK and to provide
support for all cancer of the larynx patients
after surgery.
**Volunteers: 20**
**Income: £13,111 (2013–14)**

## Cancer Research UK

Angel Building, 407 St Johns Street,
London EC1V 4AD
T: 020 7242 0200
F: 020 7269 3100
E: supporter.services@cancer.org.uk
www.cancerresearchuk.org
The aims of the Trust are to: carry out
world-class research into the biology
and causes of cancer; develop effective
treatments and improve the quality of life
for cancer patients; reduce the number
of people getting cancer and provide
authoritative information on cancer.
**Employees: 3380**
**Volunteers: 30000**
**Regional offices: 1000**

## Cancerkin

The Cancerkin Centre, Royal Free Hospital,
Pond Street, London NW3 2QG
T: 020 7830 2323
F: 020 7830 2324
E: info@cancerkin.org.uk
www.cancerkin.org.uk
Cancerkin provides information, treatment,
supportive care and rehabilitation for breast
cancer patients and support for relatives. It
also offers support for, and collaboration in,
research; education and training for health
professionals, students and volunteers; and
evolves with the changing management of
breast cancer.

## CANS Legal Information

Camelford House, London SE1 7TP
T: 020 7820 3456
F: 020 7820 7890
E: canstrust@aol.com
www.cans.org.uk
**Legal Editor: Robert Jack**
We provide legal information that is
comprehensive, accurate, affordable and
always up to date. We work to promote a
better understanding of the law by widening
access to legal information.
**Employees: 4**
**Regional offices: 1**

## Canterbury Diocesan Board of Finance

Diocesan House, Lady Wootton's Green
T: 01227 459401
E: cmccaulay@diocant.org
www.canterburydiocese.org
**Reception and Hospitality Manager:
Charlotte McCaulay**

## Canterbury Oast Trust

Highlands Farm, Woodchurch, Ashford,
Kent TN26 3RJ
T: 01233 861493
F: 01233 860433
E: enquiries@c-o-t.org.uk
www.c-o-t.org.uk
**Chief Executive: David Jackson**
The Trust provides homes, training and
supported employment for people with
a learning disability.
**Employees: 178**
**Volunteers: 130**
**Regional offices: 1**

## CapeUK

31 The Calls, Leeds LS2 7EY
T: 0845 450 3700
E: lisa.ibbetson@capeuk.org
www.capeuk.org
**Chief Executive: Pat Cochrane**

We are an independent not-for-profit
organisation committed to improving the lives
of children and young people, preparing them
to face the future with creativity and self-
belief. We work with schools, youth and
community organisations, universities, the
cultural and creative sector and other
agencies that share our aims.
**Employees: 21**
**Regional offices: 3**
**Income: £133,606 (2013–14)**

## Capital Project

Safe Haven, 32 Sudley Road, Bognor Regis,
West Sussex PO21 1EL
T: 01243 869662
E: clare.ockwell@capitalproject.org
capitalproject.org
**CEO: Clare Ockwell**
CAPITAL is a peer-run charity committed
to helping people in West Sussex who
experience mental distress to reach their
full potential through training, involvement
opportunities, a wide variety of peer led
activities and mutual support.
**Employees: 16**
**Volunteers: 31**
**Income: £20,500 (2013–14)**

## CARA (Centre for Action on Rape and Abuse)

PO Box 548, Colchester, Essex CO1 1YP
T: 01206 367881
Helpline: 01206 769795
E: info@caraessex.org.uk
www.caraessex.org.uk
**Director: Helen Parr**
CARA supports children, young people and
adult women who have experienced any form
of sexual violence, directly or indirectly,
recently or in the past. We operate across
the whole of mid, north and west Essex.
**Employees: 12**
**Volunteers: 16**
**Regional offices: 1**
**Income: £208,000 (2013–14)**

## Cara Trust

240 Lancaster Road, London W11 4AH
T: 020 7243 6147
F: 020 7243 5821
E: mail@caralife.com
www.caralife.com
**Director: Chris Woolls**
The Cara Trust works to reduce the impact of
HIV on people living with the virus through
provision of a range of social welfare and
spiritual support services. We also offer
education services to faith communities.

Our service guides can be downloaded from our website.
Employees: 4
Volunteers: 30

## Cardiomyopathy UK

Unit 10 Chiltern Court, Asheridge Road, Chesham, Buckinghamshire HP5 2PX
T: 01494 791224
Helpline: 0800 018 1024
F: 01494 797199
E: fundraising@cardiomyopathy.org
www.cardiomyopathy.org
Chief Executive: Joel Rose
Our vision is for everyone affected by cardiomyopathy to lead long and fulfilling lives. We are at an important point in our 25 year history, with ambitious plans for growth, so that we can improve diagnosis and care and increase support for everyone affected by the heart muscle disease cardiomyopathy. Although it is the most common medical cause of sudden death under 35, most of those affected can lead a long and fulfilling life if diagnosed promptly and given correct treatment.
Employees: 10
Volunteers: 200
Income: £600,000 (2013–14)

## Cards for Good Causes Ltd

1 Edison Gate, West Portway, Andover, Hampshire SP10 3SE
T: 01264 361555
F: 01264 362333
E: jill.grigg@cfgc.org.uk
www.cardsforcharity.co.uk
Cards for Good Causes assists charities through a forum where charities can exchange useful information and share ideas and solutions relating to their administration, promotion and fundraising. It encourages and promotes voluntary work for these charities by their members, supporters, local community groups and the general public.
Employees: 20
Volunteers: 6300

## Care and Repair England

The Renewal Trust Business Centre, 3 Hawksworth Street, Nottingham, Nottinghamshire NG3 2EG
T: 0115 950 6500
E: info@careandrepair-england.org.uk
www.careandrepair-england.org.uk
Chief Executive: Sue Adams
Care and Repair England innovates, develops, promotes and supports housing-related policies and practical initiatives that enable older people to live independently in their own homes for as long as they wish.
Employees: 7
Volunteers: 11
Regional offices: 3

## Care for the Wild International

72 Brighton Road, Horsham, West Sussex RH13 5BU
T: 01403 249832
E: info@careforthewild.com
www.careforthewild.org
Chief Executive Officer: Philip Mansbridge
Care for the Wild is dedicated to the protection of wildlife in the UK and around the world. Our vision is to live in a world where caring for wildlife is a global priority. Our mission is to rescue, protect and defend wildlife. Join us today www.careforthewild.org.
Employees: 10
Volunteers: 48
Regional offices: 1

## CARE International UK

9th Floor, 89 Albert Embankment, Vauxhall, London SE1 7TP
T: 020 7091 6000
F: 020 7582 0728
E: thomas@careinternational.org
www.careinternational.org.uk
Chief Executive: Geoffrey Dennis
CARE International is a leading development and humanitarian charity supporting the poorest communities in 84 countries around the world. Our aim is to bring sustainable and innovative solutions to complex poverty issues and last year we supported 1,015 poverty-fighting projects that reached more than 122 million people. Our mission is to create lasting change in poor communities and we put money where it is needed most.
Employees: 110
Volunteers: 4

## Careers Research and Advisory Centre Ltd

Sheraton House, Castle Park, Cambridge CB3 0AX
T: 01223 460277
E: hayley.evans@vitae.ac.uk
www.crac.org.uk
CRAC works to advance the education of the public in lifelong career-related learning for all, to enable employers and the world of education to work successfully together and promote best practice and the highest standards of professionalism and execution amongst those offering careers advice and development. Vitae (CRAC's biggest programme) is the UK organisation championing the personal, professional and career development of doctoral researchers and research staff in higher education institutions and research institutes.
Employees: 16
Regional offices: 1

## Carer Support Wiltshire

Independent Living Centre, St George's Road, Semington, Trowbridge, Wiltshire BA14 6JQ
T: 01380 871690
Helpline: 0800 181 4118
E: dianaf@carersinwiltshire.co.uk
carersinwiltshire.co.uk
Chief Executive: Catharine Hurford
Our aim is to ensure carers in Wiltshire are supported. We do this partly by delivering support services directly to carers, and partly by raising awareness of carers and the issues they face. As part of this work, we provide training on good practice with health and social care staff, and run a GP award scheme and employers' award scheme (Working For Carers).
Employees: 46
Volunteers: 75
Regional offices: 2
Income: £1,260,279 (2014–15)

## Carers Association Southern Staffordshire

E: michele.mcdonald@carersinformation.org.uk

## Carers Centre (Leicestershire and Rutland)

Unit 19 Matrix House, Constitution Hill, Leicester, Leicestershire LE1 1PL
T: 0116 251 0999
F: 0116 251 3514
E: enquiries@claspthecarerscentre.org.uk
www.org.uk
Centre Manager: Charles Huddleston
To promote any charitable purposes for the benefit of carers in the city and county of Leicestershire and in particular the advancement of education and furtherance of health and the relief of poverty distress and sickness.
Employees: 9
Volunteers: 25

## Carers Network

E: alison.katerji@carers-network.co.uk

## Carers Trust

32–36 Loman Street, London  SE1 0EH
T: 0844 800 4361
F: 0844 800 4362
E: info@carers.org
www.carers.org or www.babble.carers.org or www.matter.carers.org
**Chief Executive: Gail Scott-Spicer**
Carers Trust is a major new charity for, with and about carers. We work to improve support, services and recognition for anyone living with the challenges of caring, unpaid, for a family member or friend who is ill, frail, disabled or has mental health or addiction problems. To find your nearest Carers Trust Network Partner, call 0844 800 4361 or visit www.carers.org.
**Employees: 50+**
**Volunteers: 2**
**Regional offices: 6**

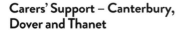

## Carers UK

20 Great Dover Street, London  SE1 4LX
T: 020 7378 4999
Helpline: 0808 808 7777
F: 020 7490 8824
E: david.titmas@carersuk.org
www.carersuk.org
**Chief Executive: Heléna Herklots**
Carers UK makes life better for the millions of people who look after older, ill or disabled family and friends.
**Employees: 65**
**Volunteers: 250**
**Regional offices: 4**

## Carers' Support – Canterbury, Dover and Thanet

80 Middle Street, Deal, Kent  CT14 6HL
T: 01304 364637
E: admin@carers-doverdistrict.org
www.carers-doverdistrict.org
**CEO: Patricia Cole**
Supporting those who care for a relative or friend.
**Employees: 11**

## Caritas Social Action Network (CSAN)

39 Eccleston Square, London  SW1V 1BX
T: 020 7901 4875
F: 020 7901 4874
E: admin@csan.org.uk
www.csan.org.uk

Promotes Catholic social action in England and Wales.
**Employees: 7**
**Regional offices: 100**

## Carplus Trust

**Round Foundry Media Centre, Foundry Street, Leeds, West Yorkshire  LS11 5QP**
T: 0113 394 4590
E: info@carplus.org.uk
www.carplus.org.uk
**Chief Executive: Chas Ball**
Carplus is the UK's pioneering transport NGO supporting the development of affordable, accessible and low-carbon car-sharing clubs and ride-sharing services. It is Carplus' mission to promote sustainable transport and, specifically, to stimulate and facilitate a rethink in the role of the private car as part of the urban mobility mix.
**Employees: 7**
**Regional offices: 2**

## CASE Kent

**Berwick House, 8 Elwick Road, Ashford, Kent  TN23 1PF**
T: 01233 610171
E: janperfect@casekent.org.uk
www.casekent.org.uk
**CEO: Jan Perfect**
CASE Kent provides specialist expertise, information and support to develop the skills local people need to run successful not-for-profit organisations and groups, primarily in the districts of Ashford, Dover, Shepway and Thanet.
**Employees: 7**
**Volunteers: 4**
**Regional offices: 3**
**Income: £137,015 (2013–14)**

## Caspari Foundation for Educational Therapy and Therapeutic Teaching

**225–229 Seven Sisters Road, London  N4 2DA**
T: 020 7527 5161
E: admin@caspari.org.uk
www.caspari.org.uk
The Foundation aims to develop the theory and practice of therapy as a mode of treatment for children and young people with emotional, behavioural and learning difficulties, to establish professional standards in its practice and to disseminate knowledge and understanding of the method.

## Cass Centre for Charity Effectiveness

**Cass Business School, 106 Bunhill Row, London  EC1Y 8TZ**
T: 020 7040 5562
E: casscce@city.ac.uk
www.cass.city.ac.uk/cce
**Director: Professor Paul Palmer**
The Centre for Charity Effectiveness at Cass (Cass CCE) is the leading nonprofit and philanthropy centre in the UK. Cass CCE focuses on driving positive change within the nonprofit sector, enabling organisations and individuals to extend their reach into wider society by increasing their operating effectiveness. The Centre achieves this through a mix of consulting assignments, professional development programmes and five specialist MScs.
**Employees: 15**
**Volunteers: 20**
**Income: £1,200,000 (2014–15)**

## Castle Point Association of Voluntary Services (CAVS)

**The Tyrells Centre, 39 Seamore Avenue, Thundersley, Essex  SS7 4EX**
T: 01268 638416
F: 01268 638415
E: office@castlepointavs.org.uk
www.castlepointavs.org.uk
**CEO: Janis Gibson**
CAVS provides support and guidance to voluntary sector organisations in the borough of Castle Point. Frontline projects include children's services, volunteer centre, befriending service, Ways to Wellness (social prescribing) and Be Safer Essex (a learning disability project).
**Employees: 30**
**Volunteers: 220**
**Regional offices: 1**
**Income: £802,598 (2014–15)**

## Catholic Agency for Overseas Development

**Romero Close, Stockwell Road, London  SW9 9TY**
T: 020 7733 7900
F: 020 7274 9630
E: cafod@cafod.org.uk
www.cafod.org.uk
CAFOD funds relief and development projects overseas and raises awareness in England and Wales of the root causes of poverty.
**Employees: 172**
**Volunteers: 80**
**Regional offices: 12**

## Catholic Association for Racial Justice

9 Henry Road, Manor House,
London N4 2LH
T: 020 8802 8080
F: 020 8211 0808
E: rosie@carj.org.uk
www.carj.org.uk
National Coordinator: Rosie Bairwal
To overcome racial discrimination in the Church and in society through policy work and programmes. Each year we produce materials for Racial Justice Sunday (on the second Sunday in September each year) with CTBI. We work with parishes, dioceses, networks and others throughout the year to promote equality for all disadvantaged groups including black minority ethnic people, Muslim communities, migrants, sanctuary seekers and refugees, gypsies, Roma and travellers, disadvantaged white communities and Dalits.
Employees: 3
Volunteers: 2

## Catholic Children's Society

E: paulw@cathchild.org.uk

## Catholic Clothing Guild

5 Dark Lane, Shrewsbury,
Shropshire SY2 5LP
T: 01743 243858
E: carmel.edwards@btinternet.com
www.catholicclothingguild.org.uk
The Guild supplies new, useful and warm clothing for those who, through unfortunate circumstances, are unable to provide for themselves and their families.

## Catholic Concern for Animals

15 Rosehip Way, Bishops Cleeve,
Cheltenham, Gloucestershire GL52 8WP
T: 01242 677423
E: deborahjark@aol.com
www.catholic-animals.org
Chairman: Mgr John Chaloner
We aim to put animals on the agenda of the Church, and to promote authentic Christian teaching on animals. The wellbeing of all animals is our priority, and cultivating non-cruelty to help make this a better, gentler and more compassionate world for all.
Employees: 1
Volunteers: 10

## Catholic Truth Society

40–46 Harleyford Road, London SE11 5AY
T: 020 7640 0042
E: f.martin@ctsbooks.org
www.ctsbooks.org

The Society: publishes and disseminates low-priced devotional and teaching works; assists all Catholics to a better knowledge of their religion; spreads information about the faith among non-Catholics and assists the circulation of Catholic books.

## Catholic Women's League

PO Box 303, Malvern WR14 9DX
T: 01684 540414 (also fax)
E: natsec@cwlhq.org.uk
www.catholicwomensleague.org
The League: aims to unite Catholic women in a bond of common fellowship; promotes religious, educational and social welfare interests on parish, diocesan, national and international levels; ensures Catholic representation of these interests on major public bodies and initiates and maintains charitable works.

## Cats Protection

National Cat Centre, Chelwood Gate,
Haywards Heath, West Sussex RH17 7TT
T: 01825 741211
F: 01825 741005
E: volunteering@cats.org.uk
www.cats.org.uk
From humble beginnings in 1927, Cats Protection has grown to become the UK's leading feline welfare charity. We now help around 235,000 cats and kittens every year through our network of over 260 volunteer-run branches, 29 adoption centres and our homing centre.
Employees: 350
Volunteers: 9000
Regional offices: 260

## Cavell Nurses' Trust

Grosvenor House, Prospect Hill, Redditch,
Worcestershire B97 4DL
T: 01527 595999
F: 01527 67245
E: vickyl@cavellnursestrust.org
www.cavellnursestrust.org
Chief Executive Officer: John Orchard
Cavell Nurses' Trust helps nurses, midwives and healthcare assistants, whether studying, working or retired, who are in need or suffering hardship or distress. Support is offered in the form of financial grants and advice as well as signposting to other agencies.
Employees: 12
Volunteers: 20
Income: £516,860 (2013–14)

## Caxton Trust (working name Catch Up)

Catch Up, Keystone Innovation Centre,
Croxton Road, Thetford, Norfolk IP24 1JD
T: 01842 752297
F: 01842 824490
E: info@catchup.org
www.catchup.org
Director: Julie Lawes
To address the problem of underachievement that has its roots in literacy and numeracy difficulties.
Employees: 12

## CCS Adoption

162 Pennywell Road, Easton, Bristol,
Avon BS5 0TX
T: 0117 935 0005
E: info@ccsadoption.org
www.ccsadoption.org
Chief Executive: Jadwiga Ball
CCS Adoption is a voluntary, independent and registered adoption agency that offers a comprehensive adoption service that includes recruiting, assessing and preparing adoptive families, supporting child and family throughout the adoption process and beyond, working with birth parents who may be considering adoption for their child in partnership with local authority social services departments and providing a counselling service to adult adoptees and their relatives.
Employees: 20
Volunteers: 2
Regional offices: 1

## CDH UK

The Denes, Lynn Road, Tilney All Saints,
King's Lynn, Norfolk PE34 4RD
T: 01553 828382
Helpline: 0800 731 6991
E: committee@cdhuk.org.uk
www.cdhuk.org.uk
Chair: Brenda Lane
The charity supports families whose children are diagnosed with congenital diaphragmatic hernia; it supports both those who survive and those who are bereaved. It also aims to educate and raise awareness, both with the general public and medical professionals, and promotes research.
Volunteers: 15
Regional offices: 2
Income: £141,124 (2014–15)

## Centre 404

Centre 404, 404 Camden Road,
London N7 0SJ
T: 020 7607 8762
F: 020 7700 0085
E: amyc@centre404.org.uk
www.centre404.org.uk
**Chief Executive: Amy Curtis**
Centre 404 is working towards a world where
people with a learning disability and their
families have the support they need to enjoy
the same rights, freedom, responsibilities,
respect, choices and quality of life as people
within the wider community. We aim to
contribute to this by providing excellent
quality services and by supporting people
with a learning disability and their carers to
get their voices and views heard.
**Employees: 173**
**Volunteers: 90**
**Regional offices: 1**

## Centre for Accessible Environments

Holyer House, 20–21 Red Lion Court,
London EC4A 3EB
T: 020 7822 8232
E: info@cae.org.uk
www.cae.org.uk
**Director: Jean Hewitt**
The Centre for Accessible Environments is
a leading authority on inclusive design and
management. We provide training, guidance
publications, research and consultancy on
access and inclusion – offering pan disability
access audits, design reviews and workplace
assessments. We produce regular
professional journals for our subscribing
members.
**Employees: 6**
**Volunteers: 1**
**Income: £250,000 (2014–15)**

## Centre for Crime and Justice Studies

2 Langley Lane, London SW8 1GB
T: 020 7840 6110
E: info@crimeandjustice.org.uk
www.crimeandjustice.org.uk
The Centre: promotes the exchange of
knowledge and experience of criminal
justice matters among all interested people,
both professional and lay; initiates and
disseminates research into the causes,
prevention and treatment of crime
and delinquency.

## Centre for Effective Dispute Resolution

International Dispute Resolution Centre,
70 Fleet Street, London EC4Y 1EU
T: 020 7536 6000
E: info@cedr.com
www.cedr.co.uk
The Centre encourages and develops
mediation and other dispute resolution and
prevention techniques in commercial and
public sectors.

## Centre for Fun and Families Limited

177/179 Narborough Road, Leicester,
Leicestershire LE3 0PE
T: 0116 223 4254
F: 0116 275 8558
E: robert@funandfamilies.org.uk
www.funandfamilies.co.uk
**Chief Executive: Jayne Ballard**
The Centre assists families where parents are
experiencing behaviour difficulties with their
children/young people; promotes good
practice by providing parent training packs
based on social learning theory; provides
services direct to families and offers skills
training to professional staff in both statutory
and voluntary agencies.
**Employees: 7**
**Volunteers: 22**

## Centre for Innovation In Voluntary Action

9–10 Mansfield Place, London NW3 1HS
T: 020 7431 1412
E: norton@civa.org.uk
www.civa.org.uk
The Centre promotes new ideas and
approaches, encourages innovation in
voluntary action in the UK and abroad,
facilitates the dissemination of ideas,
experiences and issues and promotes
exchanges.

## Centre for Policy on Ageing

28 Great Tower Street, London EC3R 5AT
T: 020 7553 6500
F: 020 7553 6501
E: cpa@cpa.org.uk
www.cpa.org.uk
The Centre encourages better services for
older people by initiating informed debate,
stimulating awareness of the needs of older
people, formulating and promoting social
policies and encouraging the spread of good
practice.
**Employees: 7**

## Centre for Studies on Inclusive Education

The Park Centre, Daventry Road, Knowle,
Bristol BS4 1DQ
T: 0117 353 3150
F: 0117 353 3151
E: admin@csie.org.uk
www.csie.org.uk
**CSIE Director: Dr Artemi Sakellariadis**
The Centre for Studies on Inclusive
Education (CSIE) is an independent centre,
set up in 1982, actively supporting inclusive
education as a basic human right of every
child. The Centre is funded by charitable
donations, with additional income from sale
of publications and small grants for research
or other projects. CSIE's work is driven by
a commitment to overcome barriers to
learning and participation for all children and
young people.
**Employees: 3**

## Centre for Sustainable Energy

3 St Peters Court, Bedminster Parade,
Bristol BS3 4AQ
T: 0117 934 1400
E: info@cse.org.uk
www.cse.org.uk
**Chief Executive: Simon Roberts OBE**
We are an independent national charity that
shares our knowledge and experience to help
people change the way they think and act
about energy.
**Employees: 50**

## Centre for the Advancement of Interprofessional Education

PO Box 680, Fareham PO14 9NH
E: admin@caipe.org.uk
www.caipe.org.uk
**Chair: Marilyn Hammick**
CAIPE promotes and develops
interprofessional education as a way of
improving collaboration between
practitioners and organisations, engaged in
both statutory and non-statutory public
services and improving the quality of care that
is delivered to the public. CAIPE's some 200
members form a network of mutual support
and interest that facilitates intellectual
engagement with interprofessionalism.
**Employees: 1**

## Centre for Volunteering and Community Leadership

University of Central Lancashire, School of Education and Social Science, Livesey House, Room 213, Preston, Lancashire PR1 2HE
T: 01772 893662
Helpline: 01772 893669
E: amelling@uclan.ac.uk
communityleadership.org.uk
Director of the Centre for Volunteering :
Alethea Melling
The University of Central Lancashire's award-winning Centre for Volunteering and Community Leadership (CVCL) is a social enterprise that has delivered significant regional, national and international high-impact outcomes in the areas of youth development and community volunteering programmes alongside academic, vocational and bespoke Continuing Professional Development (CPD) courses at UCLan. We aim to engage, empower and enable everyone who comes into contact with our work in local, national and international settings.
Employees: 7
Volunteers: 2000+
Regional offices: 2

## Centre for Youth and Community Development

94–106 Leagrave Road, Luton, Bedfordshire LU4 8HZ
T: 01582 519500
E: contact@cycd.org.uk
www.cycd.org.uk
Director: Mir Juma
Through a dedicated and professional system of youth and community development work, the Bangladesh Youth League will seek to improve the quality of life of the community, alleviate poverty and promote good health through the provision of: education and training, including social education programmes; advocacy; advice; information; outreach and centre-based activities; liaison with other similar service providers. BYL actively promotes equality of opportunity and diversity, is non-religious and non-political.

## Centrepoint

Central House, 25 Camperdown Street, London E1 8DZ
T: 0845 466 3400
E: reception@centrepoint.org
www.centrepoint.org.uk

Centrepoint aims to give young people on a downward spiral a chance to turn things around and build a more fulfilling future.
Employees: 250
Volunteers: 70
Regional offices: 2

## Centris

Crane House, 19 Apex Business Village, Annitsford, Northumberland NE23 7BF
T: 0191 250 1969
F: 0191 250 2563
E: centris@cranehouse.eu
www.centris.org.uk
The Centre exists to advance education, to promote the relief of sickness and the preservation and protection of health and to promote the relief of poverty in particular by promoting research into the role of individual self-awareness, self-development and personal responsibility in these fields and the dissemination of the useful results of that research.

## CfBT Education Trust

60 Queens Road, Reading RG1 4BS
T: 0118 902 1000
F: 0118 902 1434
E: enquiries@cfbt.com
www.cfbt.com
Chief Executive: Steve Munby
CfBT Education Trust is a top 30 UK charity providing education services in the UK and internationally. Established more than 40 years ago, CfBT has an annual turnover exceeding £100 million and employs 2,000 staff worldwide. We teach in schools, academies and the secure estate, manage national programmes in the UK and special projects overseas, provide support for school improvement as well as consultancy services to education professionals. CfBT finances a substantial research and development programme.
Employees: 2000

## Challenge Fund – The Fight Against Cancer in the Emerging World

INCTR Challenge Fund, Prama House, 267 Banbury Road, Oxford OX2 7HT
T: 01865 339510
F: 01865 339300
E: mlodge@canet.org
challengefund.org
Chair, Board of Trustees: Dr Max Parkin
65% of cases of cancer and 70% of all cancer deaths occur in the developing countries. We are the UK charity that raises money to treat children and adults with cancer in these poorer countries. We support the work of the International Network for Cancer Treatment and Research (www.inctr.org)

and help build capacity in cancer control in Africa, Asia and Latin America through professional training and carefully managed treatment programmes.
Volunteers: 2
Regional offices: 1

## Chance UK

2nd Floor, London Fashion Centre, 89–93 Fonthill Road, London N4 3JH
T: 020 7281 5858
F: 020 7281 4402
E: admin@chanceuk.com
www.chanceuk.com
Chance UK provides a year-long, one-to-one mentoring programme for primary school children with behavioural difficulties who are at risk of developing anti-social or criminal behaviour.
Employees: 25
Volunteers: 160
Regional offices: 1

## Change People

4th Floor, Calls Landing, 36–38 The Calls, Leeds, West Yorkshire LS2 7EW
T: 0113 242 6619
F: 0113 242 6142
E: info@changepeople.org
www.changepeople.org
CHANGE is a national rights organisation led by disabled people. We campaign for equal rights for all people with learning disabilities. We make information accessible and we give a strong voice to parents with a learning disability.
Employees: 21
Volunteers: 5
Regional offices: 1

## Changing Faces

The Squire Centre, 33–37 University Street, London WC1E 6JN
T: 0845 450 0275
F: 0845 450 0276
E: info@changingfaces.org.uk
www.changingfaces.org.uk
Chief Executive: James Partridge
Changing Faces supports and represents the interests of children, teenagers, adults and their families who have disfigurements from birth, accident or disease, helping them to build self-esteem, to gain access to the best health and social services and to enjoy full civil rights and equal opportunities in all aspects of life.
Employees: 24
Volunteers: 150
Regional offices: 3

## Chapter 1

2 Exton Street, London SE1 8UE
T: 020 7593 0470
F: 020 7593 0478
E: mail@chapter1.org.uk
www.ch1.org.uk
**Chief Executive: Geoff Hawkins**
Changing lives one by one. Supported
housing for vulnerable people and those
at risk. Work with single parents and their
children, women's refuge, family contact
centres, single homeless persons, private
sector leasing schemes, student
accommodation, empty homes and
social enterprise.
**Employees: 300**
**Volunteers: 20**
**Regional offices: 1**

## Charities Advisory Trust

Radius Works, Back Lane,
London NW3 1HL
T: 020 7794 9835
E: pa@charitiesadvisorytrust.org.uk
www.charitiesadvisorytrust.org.uk
The Trust works: to relieve poverty
throughout the world; to advance education;
to preserve buildings and monuments of
architectural merit; to assist charities to make
better use of their assets and resources both
generally and in relation to trading and/or
fundraising activities on their behalf.

## Charities Aid Foundation

25 Kings Hill Avenue, Kings Hill,
West Malling, Kent ME19 4TA
T: 0300 012 3000
Helpline: 01732 520000
F: 01732 520001
E: enquiries@cafonline.org
www.cafonline.org
**CEO: John Low**
The Charities Aid Foundation is a registered
charity that works to create greater value for
charities and social enterprise. We do this by
transforming the way donations are made and
the way charitable funds are managed. We
also help shape the charitable sector through
our research and events.
**Employees: 375**
**Regional offices: 3**

## Charities HR Network

43 Kingfisher Way, Marchwood,
Southampton SO40 4XS
T: 023 8086 0984
E: charhrnet@aol.com
www.chrn.org.uk
**Chair of Steering Group: Peter Reeve**
A network of senior HR representatives who
work together to advance the education in
and promote improved standards of human

resource management in national charities,
with the aim of increasing their effectiveness
and efficiency.
**Income: £11,000 (2013–14)**

## Charity Administration, Resourcing and Accountability

5 St George's Avenue, Rugby,
Warwickshire CV22 5PN
T: 01788 810146
F: 01788 522888
E: carargd@aol.com
**Executive Director: Greyham Dawes**
CARA provides free advice via its volunteer
executive director on best practice in annual
financial reporting and regulatory compliance
issues for small charities generally (on
request) and 'Special Trust' administration
services for spiritually minded charitable
projects/activities designed to awaken and
nurture the mutually respectful, caring
humanity revealed to us as the ideal we can
and must now attain to here on earth in the
New Knowledge from the Holy Grail.
**Volunteers: 6**
**Regional offices: 1**
**Income: £24,000 (2013–14)**

## Charity Bank

Fosse House, 182 High Street, Tonbridge,
Kent TN9 1BE
T: 01732 441900
F: 01732 441998
E: marketing@charitybank.org
www.charitybank.org
**Chief Executive: Patrick Crawford**
Charity Bank is an ethical bank that exists to
lend to organisations with a social purpose.
Our mission is to use loan finance to support
charities and social enterprises, so you can
be confident that we'll work with you side by
side. You can apply for loans from £50,000
to £3.25m and more in partnership with
other lenders.
**Employees: 61**
**Regional offices: 2**
**Income: £4,458,000 (2014–15)**

## Charity Finance Group

15–18 White Lion Street, London N1 9PG
T: 0845 345 3192
F: 0845 345 3193
E: info@cfg.org.uk
www.cfg.org.uk
**Chief Executive: Caron Bradshaw**
CFG (Charity Finance Group) is the charity
that champions best practice in finance
management in the voluntary sector. Our
training and development programmes
enable finance managers to give the essential

leadership on finance strategy and
management that their charities need.
With more than 2,000 members, managing
over £18 billion, we are uniquely placed to
challenge regulation that threatens the
effective use of charity funds.
**Employees: 24**

## Charity IT Leaders (CITL)

Chester House, 68 Chestergate,
Macclesfield, Cheshire SK11 6DY
T: 01625 664500
E: admin@charityitleaders.org.uk
www.charityitleaders.org.uk
**Chair: Laura Dawson**
As the premier membership group for IT
directors of major UK charities, the object is
the promotion for the public benefit of the
efficiency and effectiveness of charities and
not-for-profit organisations through the
promotion of study, sharing of knowledge
and advancement of the use of information
technology. We do this by providing
opportunities of networking, sharing and
giving advice.
**Volunteers: 15**

## Charity Retail Association

356 Holloway Road, London N7 6PA
T: 020 7697 4080
Helpline: 020 7697 4252
E: liam@charityretail.org.uk
www.charityretail.org.uk
**Chief Executive : Warren Alexander**
Aims to: monitor policy and legislative
changes affecting charity retailing and lobby
governments to achieve and maintain a
supportive regulatory environment; promote
charity retailing to public and policy makers
including its reuse/recycling/sustainability
contributions; respond to developments in
charity retailing and the needs of members
through provision of services and activities; be
a major source of expertise and information
on issues affecting the sector; promote good
practice, efficiency and self-regulation
through sharing of information; work closely
with organisations to support the sector.
**Employees: 8**

## Chartered Institute of Environmental Health

Chadwick Court, 15 Hatfields,
London SE1 8DJ
T: 020 7928 6006
E: membership@cieh.org
www.cieh.org
The Institute maintains, enhances and promotes improvements in public and environmental health.

## Chartered Institute of Housing

Octavia House, Westwood Way,
Coventry CV4 8JP
T: 024 7685 1700
E: claire.spendley@cih.org
www.cih.org
**Chief Executive: Grainia Long**
The Chartered Institute of Housing is the independent voice for housing and the home of professional standards. Our goal is simple – we want to provide everyone involved in housing with the advice, support and knowledge they need to be brilliant.

## Chartered Institute of Library and Information Professionals

7 Ridgmount Street, London WC1E 7AE
T: 020 7255 0500
F: 020 7255 0501
E: memberservices@cilip.org.uk
www.cilip.org.uk
CILIP works to enable its members to achieve and maintain the highest professional standards and encourages and supports them in delivery and promotion of high-quality library and information services responsive to the needs of users.
**Employees: 45**
**Regional offices: 2**

## Chartered Institute of Taxation

First Floor, Artillery House,
11–19 Artillery Row, London SW1P 1RT
T: 020 7340 0550
E: info@ciot.org.uk
www.tax.org.uk
**Head of Finance: Stephen Hines**
**Employees: 56**
**Volunteers: 140**

## Chartered Institution of Highways and Transportation

119 Britannia Walk, London N1 7JE
T: 020 7336 1555
E: daniel.isichei@ciht.org.uk
www.ciht.org.uk
**Chief Executive: Sue Percy**

CIHT, founded in 1930, has over 12,000 members concerned with the design, construction, maintenance and operation of transport systems and infrastructure across all transport modes in both the public and private sectors. CIHT promotes excellence in transport systems and infrastructure.
**Employees: 20**
**Volunteers: 250**
**Income: £2,000,000 (2013–14)**

## Chartered Quality Institute

2nd Floor North, Chancery Exchange,
10 Furnival Street, London EC4A 1AB
T: 020 7245 6722
E: sreeve@thecqi.org
www.thecqi.org
**Chief Executive: Simon Feary**
The Chartered Quality Institute is the chartered body for quality management professionals. Established in 1919, we gained a Royal Charter in 2006 and became the CQI shortly afterwards. The philosophy that came with the new name was simple: 'through innovation and care we create quality'. This is something that we now base all our activity on and will continue to do so.
**Employees: 50**
**Volunteers: 300**

## Chaseley Trust

South Cliff, Eastbourne,
East Sussex BN20 7JH
T: 01323 744200
F: 01323 744208
E: info@chaseleytrust.org
www.chaseley.org.uk
**Chief Executive: Sue Wyatt**
The Chaseley Trust operates two nursing care homes in Eastbourne, providing residential, respite and day care for people with spinal injury, acquired brain injury, a wide range of neurological conditions and other severe physical disabilities. It also has a multidisciplinary therapy team experienced in assessments, treatment, rehabilitation and bespoke splinting.
**Employees: 136**
**Volunteers: 45**

## Child Accident Prevention Trust (CAPT)

PO Box 3588, Barnet, London EN5 9QU
T: 020 7608 3828
E: kevin.lowe@capt.org.uk
www.capt.org.uk
**Chief Executive: Katrina Phillips**
The Child Accident Prevention Trust (CAPT) is the UK's leading charity working to reduce the number of children and young people

killed, disabled or seriously injured in accidents. CAPT provides information for professionals and parents; runs the annual community education programme Child Safety Week; trains professionals; runs projects; provides consultancy and expert advice to all organisations concerned with reducing avoidable child injuries.
**Employees: 6**

## Child Bereavement UK

Claire Charity Centre, Wycombe Road,
Saunderton, Buckinghamshire HP14 4BF
T: 01494 568900
Helpline: 0800 028 8840
F: 01494 568920
E: support@childbereavementuk.org
www.childbereavementuk.org
**Chief Executive: Ann Chalmers**
Child Bereavement UK supports families and educates professionals when a baby or child of any age dies or is dying, or when a child is facing bereavement. Every year we train over 7,000 professionals, helping them to better understand and meet the needs of grieving families.
**Employees: 38**
**Volunteers: 50+**

## Child Brain Injury Trust

Unit 1, The Great Barn,
Baynards Green Farm, Bicester,
Oxfordshire OX27 7SG
T: 01869 341075
Helpline: 0303 303 2248
E: info@cbituk.org
www.childbraininjurytrust.org.uk
**Chief Executive: Lisa Turan**
The Child Brain Injury Trust is a UK-wide charity offering support to anyone affected by childhood brain injury that has happened after birth. Acquired brain injury isn't something families prepare for. The Child Brain Injury Trust responds to the needs of these families by providing child and family support, training, information and awareness raising.
**Employees: 19**
**Volunteers: 5**
**Regional offices: 6**

## Child Death Helpline

York House, 37 Queen Square,
London WC1N 3BH
T: 0800 282986
Helpline: 0808 800 6019
F: 020 7813 8516
E: contact@childdeathhelpline.org
www.childdeathhelpline.org.uk
The Child Death Helpline aims to provide a
quality freephone service to anyone affected
by the death of a child of any age, from
pre-birth to adult, under any circumstances,
however recently or long ago. It is a listening
service that offers emotional support to all
those affected by the death of a child.
**Volunteers: 50**

## Child Growth Foundation

2 Mayfield Avenue, London W4 1PW
T: 020 8912 0720
E: ros.chaplin@childgrowthfoundation.org
www.childgrowthfoundation.org
Honorary Chairman: Tam Fry
The Foundation offers support to anybody
who is concerned about the growth of a child.
It aims to promote a wider understanding
of the importance of monitoring growth
from birth by running training sessions and
publishing booklets on growth disorders.
It also funds research into treatments for
conditions as yet untreatable. It is the
umbrella organisation for growth hormone
insufficiency, Turner syndrome, IUGR/
Russell Silver, bone dysplasia, Sotos and
premature sexual maturation patient/parent
support groups.
**Employees: 5**

## Child Migrants Trust

124 Musters Road, West Bridgford,
Nottingham, Nottinghamshire NG2 7PW
T: 0115 982 2811
F: 0115 981 7168
E: enquiries@childmigrantstrust.com
www.childmigrantstrust.com
CMT provides a professional social work,
counselling, family research and advisory
service for former child migrants and their
families. The Trust is an international agency
that enables former child migrants to reclaim
their personal identity and reunite with
members of their families.
**Employees: 9**
**Regional offices: 1**

## Child Poverty Action Group

94 White Lion Street, London N1 9PF
T: 020 7837 7979
F: 020 7837 6414
E: info@cpag.org.uk
www.cpag.org.uk
Chief Executive: Alison Garnham
Promotes action for the relief, directly or
indirectly, of poverty among children and
families with children. We get a better life for
low-income families through campaigning
and lobbying, and ensure they get good
advice with our welfare rights work,
publications and training.
**Employees: 35**
**Regional offices: 2**

## Child Soldiers International

4th Floor, 9 Marshalsea Road, Borough,
London SE1 1EP
T: 020 7367 4110
F: 020 7367 4129
E: info@child-soldiers.org
www.child-soldiers.org
Child Soldiers International is an international
human rights research and advocacy
organisation. We seek to end the military
recruitment and the use in hostilities, in any
capacity, of any person under the age of 18
by state armed forces or non-state armed
groups. We advocate for the release of
unlawfully recruited children, promote
their successful reintegration into civilian
life and call for accountability for those who
unlawfully recruit or use them.
**Employees: 8**
**Income: £675,000 (2013–14)**

## Childhood Eye Cancer Trust

The Royal London Hospital,
Whitechapel Road, London E1 1BB
T: 020 7377 5578
F: 020 7377 0740
E: info@chect.org.uk
www.chect.org.uk
Chief Executive: Patrick Tonks
The Childhood Eye Cancer Trust is a UK-
wide charity for families and individuals
affected by retinoblastoma. Our aims are: to
provide information and support to individuals
and families affected by retinoblastoma; to
raise awareness of retinoblastoma; to raise
funds for research; to influence those bodies
responsible for healthcare delivery in the UK;
to ensure retinoblastoma patients get the
best possible quality of care.
**Employees: 9**
**Volunteers: 20**

## ChildLine

45 Folgate Street, London E1 6GL
T: 020 7650 3200
F: 020 7650 3201
E: help@nspcc.org.uk
www.childline.org.uk
ChildLine is the UK's free, 24-hour helpline
for children and young people. Trained
volunteer counsellors provide comfort, advice
and protection to the children who call and
refer children in danger to appropriate helping
agencies. ChildLine also works to bring to the
attention of the public and of government
issues affecting children's welfare and rights.
**Employees: 246**
**Volunteers: 1000**
**Regional offices: 11**

## Childlink

10 Lion Yard, Tremadoc Road,
London SW4 7NQ
T: 020 7501 1700
F: 020 7498 1791
E: info@childlink.co.uk
www.childlink.org.uk
Chief Executive: Caroline Hesslegrave
Recruitment, preparation, assessment and
approval of adopters.
**Employees: 20**

## Childnet International

Studio 14, Brockley Cross Business Centre,
96 Endwell Road, London SE4 2PD
T: 020 7639 6967
F: 020 7639 7027
E: info@childnet.com
www.childnet.com
Chief Executive Officer: Will Gardner
Childnet International is a registered charity,
established in 1995, with the aim of helping to
help make the internet a great and safe place
for children, both in the UK and on a global
level. For the past 20 years, Childnet has
sought to promote the positive use of
technology, by highlighting the creative and
beneficial things that children are doing with
new technology, as well as responding to the
potential risks.
**Employees: 10**

## Children and Families Across Borders (Formerly ISS UK)

Unit 1.03 Canterbury Court,
1–3 Brixton Road, London SW9 6DE
T: 020 7735 8941
F: 020 7582 0696
E: laura.parker@cfab.org.uk
www.cfab.org.uk
CEO: Laura Parker
CFAB identifies and protects children who
have been separated from family members

due to conflict, trafficking, abduction, migration, divorce and asylum. It is the only charity specifically set up to help children, families and vulnerable people whose socio-welfare problems involve the UK and another country. We provide expert advice, guidance, skilled professional services, and emotional support and are guided by the UN Convention on the Rights of the Child.
**Employees: 16**

## Children and Young People's Empowerment Project

11 Southey Hill, Southey, Sheffield, South Yorkshire  S5 8BB
T: 0114 234 8846
E: lesley.pollard@chilypep.org.uk
www.chilypep.org.uk
**Manager: Lesley Pollard**
Chilypep works with children and young people to make the most of opportunities to influence and improve their lives and communities through empowerment and participation in a challenging, fun and action-packed way. We aim to: increase children and young people's involvement in decision-making processes; increase their skills base through training and personal development; develop, deliver and promote models that remove barriers to participation; provide training to organisations and projects that promote good youth work practice.
**Employees: 8**
**Volunteers: 50**
**Regional offices: 1**
**Income: £358,081 (2014–15)**

## Children England

Unit 30 Angel Gate, City Road, London EC1V 2PT
T: 020 7833 3319
E: nick.davies@childrenengland.org.uk
www.childrenengland.org.uk
**Chief Executive: Kathy Evans**
We are the leading membership organisation and collective voice for the CYPF voluntary sector. Our mission is to create a fairer world for children, young people and families by championing the voluntary organisations working on their behalf. We act as an independent, fearless voice for the values, contribution and expertise of the sector. We empower the sector through brokering strong relationships and active networks. We build the capacity of a thriving, sustainable sector.

## Children of Africa

1 Beechwood, Cavendish Road, Bowdon, Altrincham, Cheshire  WA14 2NH
T: 07974 161027
E: liezl.hesketh@btinternet.com
childrenofafrica.org/en
**Trustee: Liezl Hesketh**
We support orphaned children in South Africa suffering from or orphaned as a result of HIV/AIDS and advancement of education among children and young people attending schools, by the provision of financial support to meet the costs of progressing to higher education.

## Children's Burns Trust

2 Grosvenor Gardens, London  SW1W 0DH
T: 020 7881 0902
F: 020 7233 8200
E: info@cbtrust.org.uk
www.cbtrust.org.uk
The Trust offers support to specialist burns units and assistance with long-term rehabilitation of children suffering from burns. It provides education for children in burn prevention and activates public awareness of the severe problem of scalding.
**Employees: 3**
**Volunteers: 25**
**Regional offices: 1**

## Children's Country Holidays Fund

Stafford House, 91 Keymer Road, Hassocks, West Sussex  BN6 8QJ
T: 01273 847770
E: info@cchf-allaboutkids.org.uk
www.cchf-allaboutkids.org.uk
CCHF exists to provide holidays for children in need and their families from London.
**Employees: 8**
**Volunteers: 600**

## Children's Family Trust

MKA House, 4–6 St Andrews Road, Droitwich, Worcestershire WR9 8DN
T: 01905 798299
F: 01905 798230
E: shelley.candlin@thecft.org.uk
www.thecft.org.uk
**Chief Executive: Thomas Gormley**
The charity's aims are the relief of children and young people in need, in particular those in the care of, or accommodated by, a local authority.
**Employees: 19**
**Regional offices: 2**

## Children's Heart Federation (CHF)

Dragon Enterprise Centre, Cullen Mill, Braintree Road, Witham, Essex CM8 2DD
T: 01376 780044
Helpline: 0808 808 5000
E: info@chfed.org.uk
www.chfed.org.uk
**Chief Executive: Anne Keatley-Clarke**
The Children's Heart Federation (CHF) is the UK's leading children's heart charity, providing support for children and teens with heart conditions as well as their families. CHF advances public education about the challenges experienced by children with heart conditions and their families. CHF also promotes collaborative work within its own federation and among UK-based heart, health and educational organisations and international partners.
**Employees: 5**
**Volunteers: 30**

## Children's Hope Foundation

15 Palmer Place, London N7 8DH
T: 020 7700 6855
Helpline: 020 7700 6919
F: 020 7700 4432
E: tomdoran@childrenshopefoundation.org.uk
www.childrenshopefoundation.org.uk
**Chief Executive: Tom Doran**
Our aim is to improve the quality of life for children affected by illness, disability or indeed poverty, by responding to their needs in a practical way, based on the recommendation of their health and/or education professionals, to ensure they have the opportunity to fulfil their dreams and achieve their full potential.
**Employees: 5**
**Volunteers: 10**
**Regional offices: 2**

## Children's Links

Holland House, Horncastle College, Mareham Road, Horncastle, Lincolnshire LN9 6BW
T: 01507 528300
F: 01507 528301
E: info@childrenslinks.org.uk
www.childrenslinks.org.uk
Children's Links promotes the care and education of children and provides facilities for recreation and leisure time for children in the interests of social welfare.
**Employees: 61**
**Volunteers: 8**
**Regional offices: 2**

## Children's Society

c/o The Children's Society,
Edward Rudolf House, Margery Street,
London WC1X 0JL
E: venisha.douse@childrenssociety.org.uk
www.childrenssociety.org.uk
One of the UK's leading children's charities,
for more than 120 years the Church of
England Children's Society has worked with
and for children, helping them face life's
toughest challenges. Whoever they are and
whatever their issues, we believe that no child
is beyond hope, love or understanding, and
we work with those most in need to help them
face the future with confidence.
**Employees: 1050**
**Regional offices: 3**

## Children's Trust

Tadworth Court, Tadworth,
Surrey KT20 5RU
T: 01737 365000
F: 01737 365001
E: enquiries@thechildrenstrust.org.uk
www.thechildrenstrust.org.uk
**CEO: Dalton Leong**
The Children's Trust was established: for the
care, treatment, rehabilitation and education
of children with physical disabilities, learning
disabilities and complex medical needs,
including life-limiting or life-threatening
conditions and neurological damage acquired
through accident or other causes; for the
support of families and other carers involved;
and for the prevention of such disabilities
and disorders.
**Employees: 500**
**Volunteers: 500**
**Regional offices: 1**

## Chinese in Britain Forum

239 Old Street, London EC1V 9EY
T: 020 7553 7180
F: 020 7251 3130
E: firstcontact@cibf.org.uk
www.cibf.org.uk
Provides support and access to resources
and services for the Chinese communities
organisations in Britain.
**Employees: 6**
**Volunteers: 18**
**Regional offices: 1**

## Chinese Information and Advice Centre

Lower Ground Floor,
London Chinatown Market,
71–73 Charing Cross Road,
London WC2H 0ND
T: 020 7437 0112
F: 020 7734 1039
E: info@ciac.co.uk
www.ciac.co.uk
**Chair: Mr Edmond Yeo, JP**
Since being founded in 1982, the Chinese
Information and Advice Centre (CIAC) has
been a leading Chinese charity providing
immigration legal services, women's support,
refugee and asylum support, benefits advice
and information development. We aim to
help the disadvantaged Chinese individuals
and groups with compassion, care and
professionalism and have successfully
assisted a great number of service users in
getting immigration status and welfare
benefits as well as supporting women
domestic violence victims.
**Employees: 3**
**Volunteers: 20**
**Regional offices: 1**

## Chinese Mental Health Association

2/F Zenith House, 155 Curtain Road,
London EC2A 3QY
T: 020 7613 1008
F: 020 7739 6577
E: info@cmha.org.uk
www.cmha.org.uk
The charity exists to promote the
preservation and the safeguarding of mental
health and the relief of persons who are of
Chinese origin suffering from mental illness
or distress.
**Employees: 8**

## Chiropractic Patients' Association

Twingley Centre, The Portway,
Winterbourne Gunner, Salisbury,
Wiltshire SP4 6JL
T: 01980 610218
F: 01980 611947
E: info@chiropatients.org.uk
www.chiropatients.org.uk
**Chairman: Maureen Atkinson**
The Association aims to raise public
awareness and hasten acceptance of
chiropractic by the health professions
and health service. It promotes research
and chiropractic treatment for the benefit
of patients, encourages the adoption
of chiropractic as a professional career

and assists in the education of chiropractic
students.
**Volunteers: 7**

## Christian Aid

35–41 Lower Marsh, Waterloo SE1 7RL
T: 020 7523 2000
E: mraffay@christian-aid.org
www.christian-aid.org.uk
**Chief Executive : Loretta Minghella**
Christian Aid is supported and sustained by
the churches of the UK and Ireland. Our
essential purpose is to expose the scandal
of poverty, contribute to its eradication and
challenge structures and systems that keep
people poor and marginalised.

## Christian Camping International

World Vision House, Opal Drive, Fox Milne,
Milton Keynes,
Buckinghamshire MK15 0DH
T: 01908 477951
E: office@cci.org.uk
www.cci.org.uk
**Executive Director: Keith Hagon**
CCI is an association of Christian residential
providers across the UK. Members offer a
wide range of conference and meeting
facilities to meet all budgets. The automated
online venue finding service is a great place
to find your conference venue.
**Employees: 4**
**Volunteers: 20**
**Income: £90,000 (2013–14)**

## Christian Education

1020 Bristol Road, Selly Oak,
Birmingham B29 6LB
T: 0121 472 4242
E: diane.horton@christianeducation.org.uk
www.christianeducation.org.uk
Promotes human development within a
context of faith, aspiring to an education
system that offers full opportunities for
spiritual and moral development.

## Christian Family Concern

Wallis House, 42 South Park Hill Road,
South Croydon CR2 7YB
T: 020 8688 0251
F: 020 8686 7114
E: info@christianfamilyconcern.org.uk
www.christianfamilyconcern.org.uk
**Operations Manager: Mari Walters**
The charity's main purpose is the care of
children, parents and young mothers in need

of support through our nursery and bed-sit accommodation scheme.

**Employees: 35**
**Volunteers: 8**

## Chronic Granulomatous Disorder Society

199A Victoria Street, London SW1E 5NE
T: 0800 987 8988
E: hello@cgdsociety.org
www.cgdsociety.org
**Chief Executive: Caroline Harding**
The CGD Society is the leading source of support for individuals and families affected by chronic granulomatous disorder in the UK. The charity provides comprehensive information on CGD and associated issues; offers direct support to patients and affected families; funds nursing services and patient and family events; supports research to improve treatments and find a cure.
**Volunteers: 10**

## CHS Alliance

Resource Centre, 356 Holloway Road, London N7 6PA
T: 020 3137 3590
E: info@chsalliance.org
www.chsalliance.org
The Alliance supports its organisational members to advance their performance, credibility and reputation, both operationally and among the international community and donors, through strengthening quality, accountability and people management in their activities and management practices.
**Employees: 20**

## Church Action on Poverty

Dale House, 35 Dale Street, Manchester M1 2HF
T: 0161 236 9321
E: info@church-poverty.org.uk
www.church-poverty.org.uk
**Director: Niall Cooper**
CAP works to achieve lasting solutions to problems of poverty, debt and exclusion amongst communities across the UK. We: advocate for local and national policies that enable people in poverty to achieve more sustainable livelihoods; enable people with first-hand experience of poverty to speak out and campaign for lasting changes in their own communities and nationally; equip churches

to work with others to achieve real and long-term change.
**Employees: 10**
**Volunteers: 2**
**Regional offices: 1**

## Church Army

Wilson Carlile Centre, 50 Cavendish Street, Sheffield, South Yorkshire S3 7RZ
T: 0300 123 2113
E: info@churcharmy.org.uk
www.churcharmy.org.uk
**Chief Executive: Mark Russell**
Church Army is a charity affiliated with the Church of England which is committed to sharing the Christian faith through words and action with those in need across the United Kingdom and Ireland. To find out more about its work visit www.churcharmy.org.uk.

## Church Housing Trust

PO Box 50296, London, County Londonderry EC1P 1WF
T: 020 7269 1630
E: info@churchhousingtrust.org.uk
www.churchhousingtrust.org.uk
The Trust raises funds to support projects to benefit homeless people.

## Church of England: Archbishops' Council

Archbishops' Council, Church House, 27 Great Smith Street SW1P 3AZ
T: 020 7898 1000
E: william.nye@churchofengland.org
www.churchofengland.org
**Secretary-General: William Nye**
The Archbishops' Council is a body charged with the responsibility at national level to coordinate, promote, aid and further the work and mission of the Church of England.
**Employees: 252**

## Church Pastoral Aid Society

Sovereign Court One (Unit 3), Sir William Lyons Road, University of Warwick Science Park, Coventry CV4 7EZ
T: 0300 123 0780
E: info@cpas.org.uk
www.cpas.org.uk
**General Director: John Dunnett**
The Church Pastoral Aid Society exists to inspire and enable churches to reach everyone in their communities with the good news of Jesus Christ.
**Employees: 22**
**Regional offices: 1**

## Church Urban Fund

Church House, Great Smith Street, London SW1P 3NZ
T: 020 7898 1647
F: 020 7898 1601
E: admin@cuf.org.uk
www.cuf.org.uk
Promotes any charitable purpose in urban areas within the provinces of Canterbury and York that are in need of spiritual and material assistance by reason of social and economic changes with a view to reinforcing the work of the Church of England among the people of those areas.
**Employees: 16**
**Regional offices: 43**

## Churches Child Protection Advisory Service

PO Box 133, Swanley, Kent BR8 7UQ
T: 0845 120 4550
F: 0845 120 4552
E: info@ccpas.co.uk
www.ccpas.co.uk
**Chief Executive Officer: Simon Bass**
CCPAS is a professional Christian-based safeguarding charity offering resources, training, advice and support in all areas of safeguarding children and vulnerable adults to churches, faith groups and organisations, and those with no religious affiliation. CCPAS offers a 24-hour helpline and is an umbrella body for the Criminal Records Bureau.
**Employees: 24**
**Volunteers: 1**
**Regional offices: 1**

## Churches Community Work Alliance

St Chad's College, North Bailey, Durham DH1 3RH
T: 0191 334 3346
F: 0191 334 3371
E: uk@ccwa.org.uk
www.ccwa.org.uk
We initiate, support and encourage community development work in the life of the churches; we help the churches to reflect theologically on their response to social and economic change; we promote good community development work practice; we provide help and guidance for community development work projects and we support practitioners.
**Employees: 2**
**Volunteers: 20**
**Regional offices: 4**

## Churches Together in Britian and Ireland

39 Eccleston Square, London SW1V 1BX
E: info@ctbi.org.uk
www.ctbi.org.uk
General Secretary: Revd Bob Fyffe
To assist the many different Christian churches of Britain and Ireland to work together for the good of all people, deepening their fellowship with each other and, without losing their distinctive differences, to work towards a greater visible unity.
Employees: 7

## Cicely Northcote Trust

Camelford House, 15th Floor,
87–89 Albert Embankment,
London SE1 7TP
T: 020 7582 9996
E: cntrust@btconnect.com
www.cicelynorthcotetrust.org.uk
Chairman: Gary Loke
The Trust sets up projects that address gaps in the health and social services provided by statutory and voluntary organisations and, where possible, identifies ways of filling these gaps.
Employees: 1

## Cinema For All (British Federation of Film Societies)

Unit 411, The Workstation,
15 Paternoster Row, Sheffield,
South Yorkshire S1 2BX
T: 0114 221 0314
E: info@cinemaforall.org.uk
www.cinemaforall.org.uk
CEO: Deborah Parker
Cinema For All is the national support and development agency for the film society and community cinema sector. Cinema For All has supported specialised (art-house) cinema exhibition in the voluntary sector since its inception 70 years ago and today continues to provide advice, technical support and education opportunities to communities across the UK. Cinema For All is the trading name of the British Federation of Film Societies.
Employees: 7
Volunteers: 10
Regional offices: 1

## Circles Network

The Penthouse, Coventry Road, Cawston,
Rugby CV23 9JP
T: 01788 816671
F: 01788 816672
E: info@circlesnetwork.org.uk
www.circlesnetwork.org.uk
The ultimate aim of Circles Network is to build inclusive communities where everyone belongs and to demonstrate that all people can live self-determined lives, regardless of their ability or difference.
Employees: 45
Volunteers: 30
Regional offices: 9

## Circles UK

E: stephen.hanvey@circles-uk.org.uk

## Circulation Foundation

Leeds Vascular Institute,
Leeds General Infirmary,
Great George Street, Leeds LS1 3EX
T: 0113 392 3190
E: info@circulationfoundation.org.uk
www.circulationfoundation.org.uk
The Foundation encourages, promotes and assists research into the treatment of vascular disease and its related problems.

## Citizen's Income Trust

286 Ivydale Road, London SE15 3DF
T: 020 7635 7916
E: info@citizensincome.org
www.citizensincome.org
Director: Malcolm Torry
The Citizen's Income Trust promotes debate on the feasibility and desirability of a citizen's income: an automatic, unconditional and non-withdrawable income for every citizen.
Volunteers: 15
Income: £3,947 (2015–16)

## Citizens Advice

Myddelton House,
115–123 Pentonville Road, London N1 9LZ
T: 020 7833 7118
F: 020 7837 0279
E: alistair.gibbons@citizensadvice.org.uk
www.citizensadvice.org.uk
Citizens Advice helps people resolve their money, legal and other problems by providing information and advice, and by influencing policy makers.
Employees: 5000
Volunteers: 20000
Regional offices: 2000

## Citizens Online

1 Town Square, West Swindon Centre,
Tewkesbury Way, Swindon,
Wiltshire SN5 7DL
T: 01793 882800
F: 01793 882801
E: info@citizensonline.org.uk
www.citizensonline.org.uk
Citizens Online's initial remit was to explore the impact of the internet and IT on today's society. From these findings we campaign and work with other not-for-profit organisations to ensure all citizens are given the opportunity to experience the internet and IT, especially those citizens which could be judged as socially excluded.
Employees: 17
Volunteers: 5
Regional offices: 7

## Citizens UK

112 Cavell Street, London E1 2JA
T: 020 7375 1658
F: 020 7375 2034
E: colin.weatherup@cof.org.uk
www.citizensuk.org
The Citizen Organising Foundation (COF) has built a large, broad-based and diverse alliance of organisations, such as faith congregations, trade unions, schools and local community associations. Our experience, as community organisers, has demonstrated that the connectivity between individuals, family, community and society is extremely fragile and that these alliances are vital for a healthy democracy and vibrant civil society.
Employees: 7
Regional offices: 2

## Citizenship Foundation

50 Featherstone Street, London EC1Y 8RT
T: 020 7566 4141
F: 020 7566 4131
E: info@citizenshipfoundation.org.uk
www.citizenshipfoundation.org.uk
CEO: Andy Thornton
The Citizenship Foundation inspires young people to take part in society as equal members. We help them to understand the law, politics and democratic life. We promote participation, we help teachers to teach citizenship and we work with young people on issues that concern them. We want society to be fairer, more inclusive and more cohesive. We want a democracy in which everyone has the knowledge, skills, and confidence to take part and drive change as effective citizens, both as individuals and as communities.
Employees: 25
Volunteers: numerous
Regional offices: 1

## City Bridge Trust

City of London, PO Box 270, Guildhall,
London EC2P 2EJ
T: 020 7332 3710
F: 020 7332 3127
E: citybridgetrust@cityoflondon.gov.uk
www.citybridgetrust.org.uk
Chief Grants Officer: David Farnsworth
City Bridge Trust, the City of London
Corporation's charity, is the grant-making
arm of Bridge House Estates. We aim to
address disadvantage by supporting
charitable activity across Greater London
through quality grant-making and related
activities within clearly defined priorities.
Employees: 16

## City South Manchester

Turing House, Archway 5, Hulme,
Manchester, Lancashire M15 5RL
T: 0161 227 1360
E: sarah.roberts@citysouthmanchester.co.uk
www.citysouthmanchester.co.uk
Placement and Volunteer Coordinator:
Sarah Roberts
Our vision: By 2014 City South will be a
strong, viable business focused on our
customers, providing cost-effective services.
City South will grow in terms of the number
of homes we own and manage, the range of
products we offer and the areas in which we
work. We will be more than a landlord;
providing supportive services and products
to our customers that will help build and
sustain neighbourhoods, households and
our business.
Employees: 140
Volunteers: 20
Regional offices: 1

## City Year UK

58–62 White Lion Street, London N1 9PP
T: 020 7014 2680
E: info@cityyear.org.uk
www.cityyear.org.uk
Chief Executive: Sophie Livingstone
City Year UK is a leading youth and education
charity and a beacon for a volunteer service
year. Its mission is to galvanise the talent,
energy and idealism of young role models to
help vulnerable children succeed in school.
Employees: 25
Volunteers: 150
Regional offices: 2

## Civic Trust

Essex Hall, 1–6 Essex Street,
London WC2R 3HU
T: 020 7539 7900
F: 020 7539 7901
E: info@civictrust.org.uk
www.civictrust.org.uk
Managing Director: Peter Bembridge
An independent and national organisation.
It is the umbrella body for over 750 civic
societies, representing over 250,000
individuals committed to improving and
caring for places where people live and work.
It is the leading UK charity dedicated to
bringing vitality, sustainability and high-
quality design to the built environment. The
Trust works with people to promote thriving
towns and villages, developing dynamic
partnerships between communities,
government and business to deliver
regeneration and local improvement.
Employees: 35
Volunteers: 5
Regional offices: 1

## Civil Service Retirement Fellowship

Suite 2, 80a Blackheath Road SE10 8DA
T: 020 8691 7411
E: enquiries@csrf.org.uk
www.csrf.org.uk
Acting Chief Executive: David Tickner
The CSRF provides social welfare assistance
to retired civil servants, their widows/
widowers and their dependants to ensure
they do not become isolated in retirement.
We have a UK-wide network of social groups
and national befriending schemes and provide
advice, signposting and information to any
beneficiary needing help.
Employees: 5
Volunteers: 1000

## CIWEM

15 John Street, London WC1N 2EB
T: 020 7831 3110
F: 020 7405 4967
E: reception@ciwem.org
www.ciwem.org.uk
The Chartered Institution of Water and
Environmental Management (CIWEM) is
the leading professional and examining body
for scientists, engineers, other environmental
professionals, students and those committed
to the sustainable management and
development of water and the environment.
Employees: 17
Volunteers: 180
Regional offices: 17

## Claire House – Hospice For Children

Clatterbridge Road, Bebington, Wirral,
Merseyside CH63 4JD
T: 0151 343 0883
F: 0151 334 5493
E: keelan.early@claire-house.org.uk
www.claire-house.org.uk
CEO: David Pastor
The principal aim of Claire House is to provide
specialist palliative and end-of-life care for
children and young people across the North
West (Merseyside, Cheshire, North Wales
and the Isle of Man) who are living with a
life-threatening or life-limiting illness and
to provide support for their families.

## CLCGB – Church Lads' and Church Girls' Brigade

2 Barnsley Road, Wath-upon-Dearne,
Rotherham, South Yorkshire S63 6PY
T: 01709 876535
F: 01709 878089
E: audreysimm@clcgb.org.uk
www.clcgb.org.uk
Chief Executive: Audrey Simm
The Church Lads' and Church Girls' Brigade
(CLCGB) is the Anglican Churches' own
uniformed youth organisation and was
established in 1891. The CLCGB traditionally
works in inner-city areas where there is little
or no positive youth provision but more
recently within highly diverse communities,
with significant ethnic, cultural and faith
diversity. We provide a safe environment, for
youth to engage in positive, structured
activities and self-development programmes.
Employees: 9
Volunteers: 3500

## Clean Break

2 Patshull Road, London NW5 2LB
T: 020 7482 8600
F: 020 7482 8611
E: general@cleanbreak.org.uk
www.cleanbreak.org.uk
Clean Break uses theatre for personal and
political change, working with women whose
lives have been affected by the criminal
justice system.
Employees: 15
Volunteers: 4

## Climb

**Climb Building, 176 Nantwich Road, Crewe, Cheshire CW2 6BG**
T: 0845 241 2173
Helpline: 0800 652 3181
F: 0845 241 2174
E: pam@climb.org.uk
www.climb.org.uk
**Interim Executive Director: Pam Davies**
The only charity to provide information on over 700 inherited metabolic diseases. Climb is also the National Information Centre for Metabolic Disease. Supporting everyone linked with a metabolic disease.
Employees: 5
Volunteers: 40

## Clinks

**Tavis House, 1–6 Tavistock Square, London WC1H 9NA**
T: 020 7383 0966
E: info@clinks.org
www.clinks.org
**CEO: Anne Fox**
Clinks supports the voluntary and community sector working with offenders in England and Wales. Our aim is to ensure the sector, and all those with whom it works, are informed and engaged in order to transform the lives of offenders and their communities.
Employees: 20
Regional offices: 1

## Clothing Solutions for Disabled People

**Clothing Solutions For Disabled People, Unit 13, Inspire Bradford Business Park, Newlands Way, Bradford, West Yorkshire BD10 0JE**
T: 01274 292291
E: enquiries@clothingsolutions.org.uk
www.clothingsolutions.org.uk
**Manager: Sandra Hunt**
Clothing Solutions for Disabled People is a registered charity providing a unique clothing service for learning and physically disabled children, adults and elderly people. The service offers solutions to dressing and undressing difficulties by offering a made-to-measure garment alteration/adaptation and dressmaking facility. We also provide an outreach service where we visit the person for consultation, as well as an information service about specialist clothing. We make beanbags with unique breathable and waterproof lining.
Employees: 4
Volunteers: 2
Regional offices: 1
Income: £79,436 (2013–14)

## CMT United Kingdom

**PO Box 5089, Christchurch, Dorset BH23 7ZX**
T: 01202 432048
Helpline: 0800 652 6316
E: enquiries@cmt.org.uk
www.cmt.org.uk
**Chair: Lisa Welsh**
We are the national support group for people affected by Charcot-Marie-Tooth disease, the most common inherited neurological condition in the UK, affecting approximately 25,000 individuals. We provide a service of support, advice and information, with publications, a magazine and an annual conference.
Employees: 1
Volunteers: 20
Regional offices: 8

## Co-operatives UK

**Holyoake House, Hanover Street, Manchester M60 0AS**
T: 0161 246 2900
F: 0161 831 7684
E: linda.barlow@uk.coop
www.uk.coop
**Secretary General: Ed Mayo**
Represents and promotes the interests of the co-operative sector, and develops and extends the co-operative sector through provision of a range of targeted services to members.
Employees: 28
Regional offices: 1

## Coeliac UK

**Suites A–D, Octagon Court, High Wycombe, Buckinghamshire HP11 2HS**
T: 01494 437278
Helpline: 0870 444 8804
F: 01494 474349
E: generalenquiries@coeliac.org.uk
www.coeliac.org.uk
**Chief Executive: Sarah Sleet**
Coeliac UK is a national charity providing support and advice to those living with coeliac disease and dermatitis herpetiformis. The charity also campaigns for awareness of the disease and promotes the need for early diagnosis. Advice is given by a team of dietetic professionals and ranges from the gluten-free diet to symptoms of the disease and related health issues.
Employees: 20
Volunteers: 1000
Regional offices: 1

## Collage Arts

**Chocolate Factory 2, 4 Coburg Road, Wood Green, London N22 6UJ**
T: 020 8365 7500
F: 020 8365 8686
E: info@collage-arts.org
www.collage-arts.org
**Executive Director: Manoj Ambasna**
A leading arts development, training and creative regeneration organisation based in Haringey's Cultural Quarter and established in 1985. For over 20 years the organisation has created opportunities for greater access and participation in the arts and creative industries for the whole community.
Employees: 15
Volunteers: 10

## College of Sexual and Relationship Therapists (COSRT)

**PO Box 13686, London SW20 9ZH**
T: 020 8543 2707 (also fax)
E: info@cosrt.org.uk
www.cosrt.org.uk
National specialist charity for sexual and relationship therapy.
Employees: 4

## College of St Barnabas

**College of St Barnabas, Blackberry Lane, Lingfield, Surrey RH7 6NJ**
T: 01342 870260
F: 01342 871672
E: bursar@collegeofstbarnabas.com
www.st-barnabas.org.uk
**Bursar: Paul Wilkin**
A retirement home providing sheltered flats and nursing rooms for those who are clergy or who have worked with a Bishop's license for the Church of England or recognised Anglican missionary bodies overseas. The spouses, widows and widowers of the above along with those in communion with the Church of England.
Employees: 80
Volunteers: 5
Income: £1,970,640 (2013–14)

## Combat Stress

**Tyrwhitt House, Oaklawn Road, Leatherhead, Surrey KT22 0BX**
T: 01372 587100
Helpline: 0800 138 1619
F: 01372 587081
E: contactus@combatstress.org.uk
www.combatstress.org.uk
**Chief Executive: Sue Freeth**
Combat Stress is the UK's leading mental health charity for veterans of the UK Armed Forces, providing free specialist clinical

treatment and support to ex-servicemen and women across the UK with mental health conditions. We provide specialist treatment at our three treatment centres, practical and clinical support in the community and a free 24-hour helpline. For more information, visit our website combatstress.org.uk. Our free 24-hour Helpline is available on 0800 138 1619.
**Employees: 316**
**Regional offices: 4**

## Comic Relief

5th Floor, Camelford House,
87–89 Albert Embankment,
London  SE1 7TP
T: 020 7820 5555
F: 020 7820 5500
E: info@comicrelief.com
www.comicrelief.com
Comic Relief tackles poverty and social injustice by helping disadvantaged people in the UK and Africa.
**Employees: 90**
**Volunteers: 20**

## Common Ground

Gold Hill House, 21 High Street,
Shaftesbury, Dorset  SP7 8JE
T: 01747 850820
E: adrian@commonground.org.uk
commonground.org.uk
Common Ground helps people explore, celebrate and take action for their place by emphasising the value of our everyday surroundings and the positive investment people can make in their own localities. It forges links between the arts and the conservation of nature and our cultural landscapes.

## Common Purpose

Discovery House, 28–42 Banner Street,
London  EC1Y 8QE
T: 020 7608 8134
E: enquiries@commonpurpose.org.uk
www.commonpurpose.org.uk
For a democracy to be strong, it needs an active civil society in which citizens are both informed and connected. Common Purpose's vision is that we can improve the way society works by increasing the number of informed and engaged individuals who are actively involved in the future of the areas in which they live and work.

## Commonwealth Education Trust

New Zealand House, 80 Haymarket,
London  SW1Y 4TE
T: 020 7024 9822
F: 020 7024 9833
E: gyoung@cet1886.org
www.cet1886.org
**Chief Executive: Judy Curry**
The Trust invests in primary and secondary education and the training and professional development of teachers in the Commonwealth, thereby enhancing the opportunities for children in the Commonwealth to develop the skills necessary to contribute to the economic and social development of their communities. CET works in partnership with educationalists to use financial and business skills to structure sustainable, scalable and transferable projects based on applied research.

## Community Accountancy Self-Help

1 Thorpe Close, London  W10 5XL
T: 020 8969 0747
E: tom@cash-online.org.uk
www.cash-online.org.uk
**CEO: Tom Fitch**
A community accountancy service for charities and social enterprises that: provides courses on accountancy for charities and bespoke training for trustees; undertakes bookkeeping, preparation of management accounts, payroll, independent examinations, (mini audits), corporation tax returns, registration of charities and social enterprises and prepares business plans, all on a fee basis throughout London and South East England. Free grant-funded one-to-one support in Hammersmith and Fulham and Kensington and Chelsea. Free fact sheets at www.cash-online.org.uk.
**Employees: 3**
**Volunteers: 2**
**Income: £150,000 (2015–16)**

## Community Action Network

E: c.mott@can-online.org.uk
**Head of CAN Mezzanine Operations:**
**Peter Murray**

## Community Action Project

The CAP Centre, Windmill Lane,
Smethwick, West Midlands  B66 3LX
T: 0121 565 3273
F: 0121 565 0471
E: cap.smeth@talk21.com
The Project fosters and supports the needs and aspirations of the African Caribbean community primarily but not exclusively, as CAP adopts an open-door policy whereby anyone is welcome to utilise our services.
**Employees: 9**
**Volunteers: 10**

## Community Action Wyre Forest

Suite B, 3rd floor, 26 Church Street,
Kidderminster, Worcester  DY10 2AR
T: 01562 67008
Helpline: 01384 671060
E: cvs@communityactionwf.org.uk
communityactionwf.org.uk
**Chief Officer: Irene Walker**
Supporting the community and voluntary sector across Worcestershire. Delivering frontline services supporting long-term unemployed, people with mental ill health and other barriers to wellbeing. Developing micro business and social enterprise.
**Employees: 6**
**Volunteers: 12**
**Regional offices: 2**

## Community Development Finance Association (cdfa)

Hatton Square Business Centre,
16 Baldwin Gardens, London  EC1N 7RJ
T: 020 7430 0222
F: 020 7430 2112
E: info@cdfa.org.uk
responsiblefinance.org.uk
**Chief Executive: Bernie Morgan**
The Community Development Finance Association (cdfa) is the trade association for UK Community Development Finance Institutions (CDFIs). CDFIs are independent organisations that provide finance and support to people who have had trouble getting such services from the usual sources, such as banks and building societies. CDFIs typically work to benefit businesses and individuals in disadvantaged communities.
**Employees: 12**
**Regional offices: 3**

## Community Development Foundation

Unit 5, Angel Gate, 320–326 City Road,
London EC1V 2PT
T: 020 7833 1772
E: diane.williams@cdf.org.uk
www.cdf.org.uk
**Chief Executive: Alison Seabrooke**
CDF is the leading national organisation in
community development and engagement.
We are passionate about empowering
communities where local people are at the
centre of change. We have unique expertise
in working alongside local communities to
strengthen local voices, improve people's lives
and create better places to live. Our purpose
is to bring together resources, insight and
people so that communities can thrive.
**Employees: 22**

## Community First

Wyndhams, St Josephs Place, Devizes,
Wiltshire SN10 1DD
T: 01380 722475
F: 01380 728476
E: reception@communityfirst.org.uk
www.communityfirst.org.uk
**Chief Executive: Philippa Read**
Community First is Wiltshire's Rural
Community Council, a charity that works at
the forefront of community development to
help improve the quality of life and economic
wellbeing of people and local communities
throughout Wiltshire and Swindon. We have
been a dependable source of support to
communities in Wiltshire and Swindon since
1965. Our extensive networks involve parish
and town councils, village and community
hall committees, youth clubs, community
transport and community leaders across
the county.
**Employees: 65**
**Volunteers: 2**
**Regional offices: 1**

## Community Foundation for Lancashire and Merseyside

Third Floor, Stanley Building,
43 Hanover Street, Merseyside L1 3DN
T: 0151 232 2444
E: james.mcmahon@cflm.email
www.cfmerseyside.org.uk
As an independent, registered charity, we are
part of a national movement of community
foundations that undertakes strategic grant
making, facilitates philanthropy and

contributes to achieving positive social
change in our local communities.
**Employees: 10**

## Community Housing and Therapy

24/5–6 Coda Studios, 189 Munster Road,
London SW6 6AW
T: 020 7381 5888
F: 020 7610 0608
E: co@cht.org.uk
www.cht.org.uk
**Chief Executive: John Gale**
Community Housing and Therapy is a charity
that runs residential and non-residential
services for those with severe and enduring
mental ill health and ex-service personnel
who are homeless and have psychological
difficulties. The charity's objectives are to help
people experiencing mental ill-health and
emotional distress by providing residential
accommodation with psychotherapy, care
and support. Its therapeutic and rehabilitative
programme is designed to create a structure
that will lead to recovery, employment and
eventual independence.
**Employees: 43**
**Volunteers: 8**
**Regional offices: 6**

## Community Hygiene Concern

22 Darin Court, Crownhill, Milton Keynes,
Bucks MK8 0AD
T: 01908 561928
F: 01908 261501
E: bugbusters2k@yahoo.co.uk
www.chc.org
**Manager: Frances Fry**
Community Hygiene Concern offers advice
on head lice.
**Employees: 3**
**Regional offices: 1**

## Community Integrated Care

2 Old Market Court, Miners Way, Widnes,
Cheshire WA8 7SP
T: 0151 422 5326
F: 0151 424 0299
E: information@c-i-c.co.uk
www.c-i-c.co.uk
CIC was founded to assist vulnerable people
to have a life rather than an existence.
**Employees: 3500**

## Community Links

105 Barking Road, London E16 4HQ
T: 020 7473 2270
E: michelle.clark@community-links.org
community-links.org
**CEO: Athena Lamnisos**
Leading social action charity based in east
London working with the whole community
to find new solutions to old problems. We
focus on early action programmes that
prevent problems. Our focus is on helping
young people gain skills, getting adults into
work, providing spaces for families to thrive
and supporting entrepreneurs to develop.
We have a national policy and campaigning
programme which is driven by the learning
and insights from our service delivery.
**Employees: 300**
**Volunteers: 600**

## Community Links Bromley

E: alisonn@communitylinksbromley.org.uk

## Community Media Association

The Workstation, 15 Paternoster Row,
Sheffield S1 2BX
T: 0114 279 5219
Helpline: 0844 357 0442
E: info@commedia.org.uk
www.commedia.org.uk
**Chair: Dom Chambers**
The Community Media Association is the
UK representative body for the community
broadcasting sector and is committed to
promoting access to the media for people
and communities. We enable people to
establish and develop community-based
communications media promoting: social
cohesion and inclusion; cultural and
creative expression; social and economic
regeneration; empowerment through giving
communities a voice; media literacy; tackling
the digital divide; inter-cultural and inter-
generational dialogue; training and
employment opportunities; and provide
information and entertainment.
**Regional offices: 1**

## Community Network

Archway Resource Centre,
1b Waterlow Road, London N19 5NJ
T: 020 7923 5250
E: robert@community-network.org
www.communitynetworkprojects.org
**Chief Executive Officer: Robert Edmonds**
Community Network is a national charity
combating loneliness and isolation by bringing
people together in Talking Communities on
the telephone, helping them to remain active
and connected to others via peer support

groups. We provide training to other organisations in facilitating groups on the phone. NB: Our teleconferencing service is operated by The Phone Co-op. You can contact them on 020 3559 9000. Please tell them you have been referred by Community Network.
**Employees: 4**
**Volunteers: 25**
**Income: £147,904 (2015–16)**

## Community of Congolese Refugees in Great Britain (CORECOG)

Stephen Laurence House,
90 Greengate Street, Plaistow,
London E13 0AS
T: 020 8548 4073
F: 020 8552 0473
E: wgpambu@aol.co.uk
www.corecog.org.uk
The Community of Congolese Refugees in Great Britain (CORECOG) is a charity registered in England and Wales since 1993. Created as a national charity for all groups in the UK, its headquarters is based in the London Borough of Newham, which has the largest population of Congolese in England.
**Employees: 4**
**Volunteers: 3**
**Regional offices: 25**

## Community of Reconciliation and Fellowship

Prideaux House,
10 Church Crescent E9 7DL
T: 020 8986 6000
E: prideaux.house@btconnect.com
Director: Rev Gualter De Mello
The main aim of the fellowship is the improvement of conditions of life in the community, including the relief of poverty, distress and sickness, and the provision of facilities in the interest of social welfare.
**Employees: 7**
**Volunteers: 38**

## Community Resilience

16th Floor Portland House,
Bressenden Place, London SW1E 5RS
T: 0300 999 2004
F: 0300 999 2005
E: contact-us@emergencyaid.org.uk
www.communityresilience.cc
CEO: David Cloake
A not-for-profit social enterprise dedicated to helping communities respond to and recover from major emergencies.

## Community Security Trust (CST)

Shield House, Harmony Way, Hendon,
London NW4 2BZ
T: 020 8457 9999
E: enquiries@cst.org.uk
www.cst.org.uk
Chief Executive: David Delew
CST advises on and provides security for the UK Jewish community, monitors levels of antisemitism, and represents the Jewish community on antisemitism, terrorism and security to police, government and the media. The Trust promotes good race relations between the Jewish community and other members of society by working towards the elimination of racism in the form of antisemitism.
**Employees: 58**
**Volunteers: 1000**

## Community Transport

National Office, Office Suite E107,
Dean Clough, Halifax,
West Yorkshire HX3 5AX
T: 01422 364964
F: 01422 322720
E: murray.seccombe@communitytransport.org
www.communitytransport.org
Chief Executive: Murray Seccombe
We provide services in three themed areas: passenger transport for individuals with mobility needs, VCS groups and statutory agencies; furniture re-use/recycling; training, volunteering and work experience. We operate in Tyne and Wear, Greater Manchester, West Midlands and Staffordshire.
**Employees: 130**
**Volunteers: 100**
**Regional offices: 15**

## Community Transport Association

Highbank, Halton Street, Hyde,
Cheshire SK14 2NY
T: 0161 351 1475
Helpline: 0845 130 6195
F: 0161 351 7221
E: info@ctauk.org
www.ctauk.org
Chief Executive: Keith Halstead
The Community Transport Association is a not-for-profit organisation that provides advice and training for operators of community and voluntary transport. We also administer the prestigious MiDAS and Pats range of training courses for minibus drivers and passenger assistants.
**Employees: 30**
**Regional offices: 6**

## Compassion in World Farming

River Court, Mill Lane, Godalming,
Surrey GU7 1EZ
T: 01483 521950
F: 01483 861639
E: compassion@ciwf.org.uk
www.ciwf.org.uk
Chief Executive: Philip Lymbery
Compassion in World Farming is the leading charity campaigning exclusively for the welfare of farm animals throughout the world. Our vision is a world where farm animals are treated with compassion and respect and where cruel factory farming practices end. Our mission is to advance the wellbeing of farm animals worldwide. We have pioneered engagement with the food industry, rewarding good practice and highlighting welfare failures.
**Employees: 40**
**Volunteers: 6**

## Computers for Charities

Cemetery Lodge, Ersham Road, Hailsham,
East Sussex BN27 3LJ
T: 01323 840641
E: info@computersforcharities.org
www.computersforcharities.org
Chair: Simon Rooksby
Computers for Charities is a registered charity. It provides IT advice and services to UK and overseas charities and voluntary organisations including low-cost refurbished PC and Mac computer systems. CfC also undertakes social, educational, vocational and humanitarian projects.
**Employees: 1**
**Volunteers: 40**
**Regional offices: 1**

## Concern Universal

21 King Street, Hereford HR4 9BX
T: 01432 355111
F: 01432 355086
E: cu.uk@concern-universal.org
www.concern-universal.org
Chief Executive Officer: Kathryn Llewellyn
Concern Universal is an international development organisation tackling poverty from the grassroots. We create opportunities for people around the world to improve their lives and shape their own futures. By building skills and connecting people at all levels in society, we help communities deliver practical solutions with long-term impact.
**Employees: 30**
**Volunteers: 20**

## Concern Worldwide UK

13/14 Calico House, Clove Hitch Quay
T: 020 7801 1850
E: rose.caldwell@concern.net
www.concern.org.uk
Executive Director: Rose Caldwell

## Concordia International Volunteers

19 North Street, Portslade BN41 1DH
T: 01273 422218
F: 01273 421182
E: info@concordiavolunteers.org.uk
www.concordiavolunteers.org.uk
Concordia is a charity committed to
international volunteering as a means to
promoting intercultural understanding and
peace. Our International Volunteer
Programme offers the opportunity to join
international teams of volunteers working on
short-term projects in over 60 countries
worldwide. Types of international volunteer
projects include conservation, restoration,
archaeology, construction, arts, children's
play-schemes and teaching. Projects last
from two to four weeks up to one year.
Employees: 4
Volunteers: 1

## Confederation of Indian Organisations (UK)

25 Buller Road, Leicester,
Leicestershire LE4 5GB
T: 0116 266 8068
F: 0116 266 8072
E: info@conf-indian.org.uk
www.ciostrokeproject.co.uk
Project Coordinator: Vinod Kotecha
The South Asian Stroke Prevention Project
aims to set up outreach, advocacy and
support services in the East Midlands for
people from South Asian communities who
have suffered from a stroke or are at a high
risk. The project is a partnership between the
Confederation of Indian Organisations (UK)
and The Big Lottery Fund.
Employees: 4
Volunteers: 113
Regional offices: 1

## CONNECT – the Communication Disability Network

St Alphege Hall, King's Bench Street,
London SE1 0HX
T: 020 7367 0840
E: info@ukconnect.org
www.ukconnect.org
Chief Executive: Sally McVicker
Connect exists to improve the lives of people
with the communication disability 'aphasia',
caused most commonly by stroke. Aphasia
can affect a person's ability to speak, read,

write and manage numbers. We aim to
empower people with aphasia by helping
them reconnect with life. We do this through
a range of activities including drop-ins, special
interest groups and befriending schemes
around the country.
Employees: 12
Volunteers: 20

## Conquest Art – Enriching the Lives of People with Disabilities and long term health issues

Office 92, Trident Court,
One Oakcroft Road, Chessington,
Surrey KT9 1BD
T: 020 3044 2731
E: conquestart@hotmail.com
www.conquestart.org
Chairman and Trustee: John Gumbel
Conquest Art is a charity inspiring people
living with disabilities and long-term health
issues to discover their creative energy and
build self-confidence through art. Working at
their own pace in supportive groups, our
members find both relaxation and fresh
stimulus, along with the opportunity to make
new friends. Anyone over 18 whose life is
narrowed by disabling health issues is
welcome to join us. No artistic talent or
previous experience is necessary.
Employees: 1
Volunteers: 75

## Conscience: taxes for peace not war

Archway Resource Centre,
1b Waterlow Road, London N19 5NJ
T: 020 3515 9132
E: info@conscienceonline.org.uk
www.conscienceonline.org.uk
Conscience: taxes for peace not war, works
for a world where taxes are used to nurture
peace, not pay for war. We campaign for an
increase in the amount of UK tax spent on
peace-building and a decrease in the amount
spent on war and preparation for war. We
campaign for the legal right of those with a
conscientious objection to war to have the
entire military part of their taxes spent on
peace-building.
Employees: 3
Volunteers: 1

## Conservation Foundation

1 Kensington Gore, London SW7 2AR
T: 020 7591 3111
E: info@conservationfoundation.co.uk
www.conservationfoundation.co.uk
Executive Director: David Shreeve
The Conservation Foundation was launched
by David Bellamy and David Shreeve in 1982

to provide a means for people in public,
private and not-for-profit sectors to
collaborate on environmental causes.

## Consortium of Bengali Associations

100 Gatesden (Basement Offices),
Argyle Street, London WC1H 8EB
T: 020 7713 8610
F: 020 7289 8115
E: contact.cbauk@gmail.com
www.cba.dsl.pipex.com
Since being established CBA has played an
important part in the development of many
Bengali-led voluntary organisations that
serve the Bengali community. It provides a
range of services to encourage and support
voluntary action and to promote the
increasingly important role of the Bengali
voluntary and community sector in the UK.
Employees: 1

## Consortium of Lesbian, Gay, Bisexual and Transgendered Voluntary and Community Organisations

Unit 204, 34 Buckingham Palace Road,
London SW1W 0RH
T: 020 7064 6500
E: information@lgbconsortium.org.uk
www.lgbconsortium.org.uk
CEO: Paul Roberts
We are a national membership organisation
focusing on the development and support of
LGBT groups, projects and organisations, so
they can deliver direct services and campaign
for individual rights.
Employees: 5
Volunteers: 10

## Consortium of Voluntary Adoption Agencies

Caritas Care, 218 Tulketh Road,
Ashton on Ribble, Preston,
Lancashire PR2 1ES
Helpline: 07775 910009
E: info@cvaa.org.uk
cvaa.org.uk
Chief Executive Officer: Annie Crombie
The CVAA works to ensure CVAA member
agencies of voluntary adoption are enabled
to deliver services of excellence to children,
adoptive families and all those considering
adoption or who have been affected by it.
Employees: 6

## Construction Industry Trust for Youth

The Building Centre, 26 Store Street,
London WC1E 7BT
T: 020 7467 9540
E: cyt@cytrust.org.uk
www.constructionyouth.org.uk
**Executive Director: Christine Townley**
Construction Youth Trust is a registered
charity working with young people aged 14.

## Consumers' Association

2 Marylebone Road, London NW1 4DF
T: 020 7770 7810
E: which@which.co.uk
www.which.net
The Association aims to improve the
standards of goods and services available
to the public as consumers.

## Contact a Family

209–211 City Road, London EC1V 1JN
T: 020 7608 8700
F: 020 7608 8701
E: debbie.gordon@cafamily.org.uk
www.cafamily.org.uk
Contact a Family is the only UK-wide charity
providing advice, information and support to
parents of all disabled children – no matter
what their health condition.
**Employees: 65**
**Volunteers: 100**
**Regional offices: 13**

## Contact the Elderly

2 Grosvenor Gardens, London SW1W 0DH
T: 020 7240 0630
Helpline: 0800 716543
F: 020 7379 5781
E: info@contact-the-elderly.org.uk
www.contact-the-elderly.org.uk
**CEO: Mary Rance**
Contact the Elderly aims to relieve the
loneliness of frail, isolated elderly people, who
live alone with little or no support from family
or friends. Our volunteer network offers a
simple yet effective act of friendship. Every
month our volunteer drivers take otherwise-
housebound elderly guests to the home of
volunteer hosts, enjoying the warmth of
friendship for a few hours. The effect
becomes cumulative as new friendships
blossom.
**Employees: 32**
**Volunteers: 7199**

## Conway Hall Ethical Society

Conway Hall, 25 Red Lion Square,
London WC1R 4RL
T: 020 7405 1818
E: jim@ethicalsoc.org.uk
www.conwayhall.org.uk
**CEO: Dr Jim Walsh**
The landmark of London's independent
intellectual, political and cultural life.
**Employees: 11**
**Volunteers: 12**
**Regional offices: 1**
**Income: £800,000 (2014–15)**

## Coram Children's Legal Centre

University of Essex, Wivenhoe Park,
Colchester, Essex CO4 3SQ
T: 01206 877910
F: 01206 877963
E: info@coramclc.org.uk
www.childrenslegalcentre.com or
www.lawstuff.org.uk
**Managing Director: Kawaldip Sehmi**
Coram Children's Legal Centre, part of the
Coram group of charities, specialises in law
and policy affecting children and young
people. CCLC provides free legal information,
advice and representation to children, young
people, their families, carers and professionals,
as well as international consultancy on child
law and children's rights.
**Employees: 41**
**Regional offices: 2**

## Coram Family

49 Mecklenburgh Square,
London WC1N 2QA
T: 020 7520 0300
F: 020 7520 0301
E: matt@coram.org.uk
www.coram.org.uk
Coram Family works with vulnerable children
and young people to enable them to take
responsibility for their lives and achieve their
full potential.
**Employees: 144**
**Volunteers: 100**

## Coram Voice

320 City Road, London EC1V 2NZ
T: 020 7833 5792
Helpline: 0808 800 5792
F: 020 7713 1950
E: info@coramvoice.org.uk
www.coramvoice.org.uk
**Managing Director: Andrew Radford**
Coram Voice exists to enable children and
young people to actively participate in
shaping their own lives and to hold to account
the services that are responsible for their

care. We serve children and young people
who are vulnerable to harm or exclusion from
society, and who rely on the state or its
agencies for their rights and wellbeing.
**Employees: 60**
**Volunteers: 25**
**Regional offices: 3**

## Cord

1 New Street, Leamington Spa,
Warwickshire CV31 1HP
T: 01926 315301
E: info@cord.org.uk
www.cord.org.uk
**Chief Executive: Brian Wakley**
Cord is an international organisation working
to build lasting peace in partnership with
people living and working in conflict, or
post-conflict situations. We believe these
people hold the keys to peace and we
work alongside them to make lasting peace
a reality.
**Employees: 800**
**Volunteers: 20**
**Regional offices: 1**

## CORDA preventing heart disease and stroke

Chelsea Square, London SW3 6NP
T: 020 7349 8686
E: corda@rbht.nhs.uk
www.corda.org.uk
The charity raises funds to support high-
quality clinical research into the early
diagnosis and prevention of heart disease
and stroke through non-invasive methods
(magnetic resonance and ultrasound).

## CORE

3 St Andrews Place, London NW1 4LB
T: 020 7486 0341
F: 020 7224 2012
E: info@corecharity.org.uk
www.corecharity.org.uk
**Chief Executive: Warren Alexander**
CORE works for the advancement of
science and the practice of medicine and
surgery for the benefit of the public in the
field of gastroenterology. It promotes the
study of and research into medicine and
surgery with reference to the physiology
and pathology of the digestive system
and disseminates the results.
**Employees: 4**

## Cornelia de Lange Syndrome Foundation

The Tower, Guardian Ave, North Stifford,
Grays, Essex RM16 5US
T: 01375 376439
E: info@cdls.org.uk
www.cdls.org.uk
Chairman: James May
The CdLS Foundation: exists to ensure early
and accurate diagnosis of CdLS; promotes
research into the causes and manifestations
of the syndrome; helps people with a
diagnosis of CdLS to make informed
decisions throughout their lifetime.
Employees: 1
Volunteers: 16
Regional offices: 1

## Corona Worldwide

Southbank House, Black Prince Road,
London SE1 7SJ
T: 020 7793 4020
E: corona@coronaworldwide.org
www.coronaworldwide.org
Corona Worldwide helps and educates
people going to live and work overseas and
helps returners and foreigners adjust to life
in the UK.

## Council for Awards in Care, Health and Education

CACHE Head Office, Apex House,
81 Camp Road, St Albans,
Hertfordshire AL1 5HL
T: 01727 818616
F: 01727 818618
E: info@cache.org.uk
www.cache.org.uk
Chief Executive: Richard Dorrance
CACHE has been qualifying the care, health
and education workforce since 1945. Over
these 65 years, we have continually invested
in innovative, high-quality qualifications and
customer service.
Employees: 124

## Council for British Archaeology

Beatrice de Cardi House, 66 Bootham,
York YO30 7BZ
T: 01904 671417
F: 01904 671384
E: mikeheyworth@archaeologyuk.org
www.archaeologyuk.org
Director: Dr Mike Heyworth MBE
The Council aims to advance the study and
care of Britain's historic environment, and to
improve public awareness and enjoyment of
Britain's past.
Employees: 15
Volunteers: 600
Income: £1,125,000 (2014–15)

## Council for Dance Education and Training

Old Brewers Yard, 17–19 Neal Street,
Covent Garden, London WC2H 9UY
T: 020 7240 5703
F: 020 7240 2547
E: info@cdet.org.uk
www.cdet.org.uk
Director: Sean Williams
The Council aims to advance the education of
all people in the art, practice and appreciation
of the cultural significance of dance.
Employees: 3

## Council for Music in Hospitals

74 Queens Road, Walton, Surrey KT12 5LW
T: 01932 252809
E: info@music-in-hospitals.org.uk
www.music-in-hospitals.org.uk
The Council uses high-quality live music to
improve the quality of life of patients and
residents in hospitals, nursing homes,
hospices, etc.

## Council of British Pakistanis

415 Bordesley Green, Birmingham B9 5RE
T: 0845 658 1057
F: 0845 658 1067
E: info@thedoliproject.net
The prime objective of the Council is the
welfare of British Pakistanis, to promote
better understanding between the British and
Pakistani community and to promote social,
cultural and educational activities of British
Pakistanis.
Employees: 7
Volunteers: 25
Regional offices: 15

## Council of Christians and Jews

1st Floor, 89 Albert Embankment,
London SE1 7TP
T: 020 7820 0090
F: 020 7820 0504
E: cjrelations@ccj.org.uk
www.ccj.org.uk
The Council exists: to combat all forms of
religious and racial intolerance; to promote
mutual understanding and goodwill between
Christians and Jews; to foster cooperation in
educational activities and in social and
community service.

## Council of Voluntary Welfare Work

Room 118/119, Block 16, Chelsea Barracks,
Chelsea Bridge Road, London SW1H 8RF
T: 020 7259 9392
E: gensec@cvww.org.uk
The Council advances charitable work carried
out by member organisations among the
armed forces.

## Counsel and Care

6 Avonmore Road, West Kensington,
London W14 8RL
T: 020 7605 4200
Helpline: 0845 300 7585
F: 020 7605 4201
E: sara.campbell@counselandcare.org.uk
www.independentage.org
Chief Executive: Janet Morrison
Counsel and Care merged with Independent
Age in 2011. Independent Age is a unique and
growing charity, providing information, advice
and support for thousands of older people
across the UK and the Republic of Ireland.
Not only did it merge with Counsel and Care
but also with UBS and so together the whole
organisation is able to provide a broader range
of services than any of the charities could
provide separately.
Volunteers: 6

## Counselling

62 Douglas Towers, Radwell Drive, Bradford,
West Yorkshire BD5 0QR
T: 01924 377119
E: info@counselling.ltd.uk
www.counselling.ltd.uk
Aims to relieve poverty by the provision of
counselling. We do this by compiling and
displaying a web-based database of trained
and experienced counsellors and providing
free counselling to those on low incomes.

## Counselling and Support For Young People

16 London Road, Newark,
Nottinghamshire NG24 1TW
T: 01636 704620
E: n.hunter@casy.org.uk
www.casy.org.uk
CEO: Neil Hunter
We promote the preservation of good mental
and emotional health among young people
age 6–25 within Nottinghamshire and
Lincolnshire. We do this through the provision
of a confidential counselling service and by
working in the community delivering training
courses, workshops and conferences. We
focus on the individual needs of the young

person, building our service around them, to help them reach their full potential.
**Employees:** 6
**Volunteers:** 40
**Regional offices:** 1
**Income:** £260,000 (2014–15)

## Countryside Restoration Trust

Bird's Farm, Haslingfield Road, Barton, Cambridgeshire  CB23 7AG
T: 01223 262999
E: martin@countrysiderestorationtrust.com
www.countrysiderestorationtrust.com
**Director: Martin Carter**
The Countryside Restoration Trust is a farming and conservation charity that aims to protect and restore Britain's countryside through wildlife-friendly and commercially viable land management. Through education, demonstration and community involvement, the Trust is committed to promoting the importance of a living and working countryside.
**Employees:** 9
**Volunteers:** 75
**Income:** £3,128,849 (2013–14)

## Cranfield Trust

Court Room Chambers, 1 Bell Street, Romsey, Hampshire  SO51 8GY
T: 01794 830338
F: 01794 830340
E: admin@cranfieldtrust.org
www.cranfieldtrust.org.uk
The Trust helps charities improve their effectiveness through the provision of free management consultancy and online HR support.
**Employees:** 7
**Volunteers:** 850

## Cranstoun

1st Floor St Andrew's House, St Andrew's Road, Surbiton, Surrey  KT6 4DT
T: 020 8335 1830
F: 020 8399 4153
E: info@cranstoun.org.uk
www.cranstoun.org
**Chief Executive Officer: Steve Rossell**
Since 1969 Cranstoun has been making life better for those affected by alcohol and drugs. Our skilled and compassionate people work closely with services users and their families to change and save lives. We combine proven expertise in treatment and recovery with innovative approaches and actively

involve those we help in improving the design of the services we provide.
**Employees:** 156
**Volunteers:** 93
**Regional offices:** 15
**Income:** £11,103,000 (2013–14)

## CRASH

10 Barley Mow Passage, London  W4 4PH
T: 020 8742 0717
F: 020 8747 3154
E: info@crash.org.uk
www.crash.org.uk
CRASH is the construction and property industry charity for the homeless. It harnesses the skills, products, talents and goodwill of the industry to improve buildings and premises for voluntary agencies working with homeless people, throughout the UK.
**Employees:** 3

## Creative and Supportive Trust

37–39 King's Terrace, Camden Town, London  NW1 0JR
T: 020 7383 5228
F: 020 7388 7252
E: info@castwomen.org.uk
www.castwomen.org.uk
The Trust provides free education and training to women ex-offenders or those at risk of offending due to drug, alcohol or mental health issues. It aims to realise the potential of each woman for their development (personal, education, employment) and make effective changes.

## Creative Youth Network

Kingswood Estate, 20 Old School House, Britannia Road, Bristol, Avon  BS15 8DB
T: 0117 947 7948
E: info@creativeyouthnetwork.org.uk
www.creativeyouthnetwork.org.uk
**CEO: Sandy Hore Ruthven**
Inspiration through the arts: we provide creative opportunities and challenges to unlock young people's talent and personality. Our aim is for young people to excel. We help them grow and succeed through the inspiration of the arts. Our work takes place across sites in Bristol and beyond, with the aim of reaching as many young people as we can.
**Employees:** 45
**Volunteers:** 5
**Regional offices:** 2

## CRI

3rd Floor, North West Suite, Tower Point, 44 North Road, Brighton, West Sussex  BN1 1YR
T: 01273 677019
F: 01273 693183
E: queries@cri.org.uk
www.cri.org.uk
**Chief Executive: David Biddle**
CRI is a social care and health charity working with individuals, families and communities across England and Wales that are affected by drugs, alcohol, crime, homelessness, domestic abuse and antisocial behaviour. Our projects, delivered in communities and prisons, encourage and empower people to regain control of their lives and motivate them to tackle their problems.
**Employees:** 2128
**Volunteers:** 1100
**Regional offices:** 4

## Crimestoppers Trust

Apollo House, 66A London Road, Morden, Surrey  SM4 5BE
T: 020 8254 3200
F: 020 8254 3201
E: cst@crimestoppers-uk.org
www.crimestoppers-uk.org
Crimestoppers is an independent UK-wide charity working to stop crime. Crimestoppers works for you, your family and your community.
**Employees:** 30
**Volunteers:** 500

## Crisis

66 Commercial Street, London  E1 6LT
T: 0300 636 1967
F: 0300 636 2012
E: enquiries@crisis.org.uk
www.crisis.org.uk
**Chief Executive: John Sparkes**
Crisis is the national charity for single homeless people. Our purpose is to end homelessness. Crisis helps people rebuild their lives through housing, health, education and employment services. We are also determined campaigners, working to prevent people from becoming homeless and to change the way society and government think and act towards homeless people.
**Employees:** 200
**Volunteers:** 10000

## Crisis Counselling for Alleged Shoplifters

Box 147, Stanmore, Middlesex HA7 2QT
T: 020 8954 8987
E: crisiscounselling@gmail.com
Chairman: Harry Kauffer
Provides counselling and advice to people wrongfully accused of shoplifting offences and refers such cases to a solicitor, doctor or social worker where appropriate. It has a particular concern for the problems of children accused of shoplifting offences and liaises with MPs, local authorities and other organisations to discuss aspects of social or legal policy and practice. We do not condone premeditated shoplifting, which is theft. Office hours: 9:30 to 18:30 Monday to Friday.

## Crohn's and Colitis UK

45 Grosvenor Road, St Albans, Hertfordshire AL1 3AW
T: 01727 830038
Helpline: 0300 222 5700
E: david.barker@crohnsandcolitis.org.uk
www.crohnsandcolitis.org.uk
Chief Executive: David Barker
We're the UK's leading charity in the battle against Crohn's disease and ulcerative colitis. Founded as a patients' association in 1979, we now have 29,000 members across the UK. Our mission is to work with all those affected by these conditions to achieve a better quality of life, improve services and ultimately find a cure. We want to see a world in which people's lives are not limited by Crohn's and Colitis.
Employees: 45
Volunteers: 750
Income: £4,227,745 (2014–15)

## Crohn's in Childhood Research Association

Pat Shaw House, 13–19 Ventnor Road, Sutton, Surrey SM2 6AQ
T: 020 8949 6209
E: support@cicra.org
www.cicra.org
Chair, Board of Trustees: Margaret Lee
CICRA supports families of children and young adults affected by Crohn's disease and ulcerative colitis including regional meetings. CICRA also funds peer-reviewed, research fellowships, PhD studentships and research projects in major gastroenterological centres nationwide. This investment has led to new treatments and trained many of the

specialists throughout the UK who today treat children with these conditions.
Employees: 2
Volunteers: 6
Income: £277,480 (2014–15)

## Crowthorne Old Age To Teen Society (COATS)

The COATS Centre, Pinewood Avenue, Crowthorne, Berkshire RG45 6RQ
T: 01344 773464
E: secretary@coatscrowthorne.org.uk
www.coatscrowthorne.org.uk
Chairman of Trustees: John Barnes
We support the welfare of older people living in and around Crowthorne, Berkshire. At present we run a day centre, providing companionship, freshly cooked meals, activities and entertainment. We own a minibus to transport older people to the centre from their own homes.
Employees: 7
Volunteers: 100
Income: £316,571 (2015–16)

## Cruse Bereavement Care

PO Box 800, Richmond, Surrey TW9 1RG
T: 020 8939 9530
Helpline: 0808 808 1677
E: info@cruse.org.uk
www.cruse.org.uk
Chief Executive: Debbie Kerslake
Cruse Bereavement Care exists to promote the wellbeing of bereaved people and to enable anyone bereaved by death to understand their grief and cope with their loss. We offer information, advice and support with helplines, publications and face-to-face sessions through a network of branches, as well as external education and training with bespoke courses. Cruse welcomes and trains new volunteers. There's a special interactive website for bereaved young people: www.hopeagain.org.uk.
Employees: 129
Volunteers: 5500
Regional offices: 12

## CSV Cathedral Camps

CSV Social Action and Volunteering, 237 Pentonville Road, London N1 9NJ
T: 020 7278 6601
E: cathedralcamps@csv.org.uk
www.cathedralcamps.org.uk
Helps conserve, restore and maintain cathedrals, churches and historical buildings through community engagement and volunteering.

## CTBI Christians Abroad

22 Ebenezer Close, Witham, Essex CM8 2HX
Helpline: 0300 012 1201
E: support@cabroad.org.uk
www.cabroad.org.uk
Lead Consultant: Colin South
Christians Abroad provides opportunities for those who wish to work overseas for short periods within the Christian community in Africa, Asia, the Caribbean and South America. It provides travel insurance with accident and emergency and other specialist insurances for those working overseas in mission and development.
Employees: 2
Volunteers: 3
Income: £10,000 (2013–14)

## CTC – UK's National Cycling Organisation

Parklands, Railton Road, Guildford, Surrey GU2 9JX
T: 0870 873 0060
F: 0870 873 0064
E: carol.mckinley@ctc.org.uk
www.ctc.org.uk
CEO: Kevin Mayne
Promotes and encourages the use of cycles and provides services to cyclists.
Employees: 60
Volunteers: 400
Regional offices: 200

## Cued Speech Association UK

9 Jawbone Hill, Dartmouth, Devon TQ6 9RW
Helpline: 01803 832784
E: info@cuedspeech.co.uk
www.cuedspeech.co.uk
Executive Director: Anne Worsfold
We provide information about and training in Cued Speech throughout the UK with the aim of improving the communication and literacy skills of deaf and hearing-impaired children and adults by giving them full access to spoken language through vision.

## Cult Information Centre

BCM Cults, London WC1N 3XX
T: 01689 833800
E: info@cultinformation.org.uk
www.cultinformation.org.uk
The centre researches and supplies information on cults. It offers advice and an international network of contacts for further information and counselling.

## Cumberland Lodge

Cumberland Lodge, The Great Park,
Windsor, Berkshire SL4 2HP
T: 01784 432316
Helpline: 01784 497780
F: 01784 497799
E: martinnewlan@cumberlandlodge.ac.uk
www.cumberlandlodge.ac.uk
Principal: Canon Dr Edmund Newell
Cumberland Lodge is an educational charity
in a 17th-century royal house, established
in 1947 to provide a place where university
students could consider wider moral, ethical
and social issues than their courses permit.
The objective remains the same, but
Cumberland Lodge is now a comfortable
and inspiring residential conference centre
in the stunning and peaceful surroundings
of Windsor Great Park, only 40 minutes
from London Waterloo and 20 minutes
from Heathrow.
Employees: 70
Volunteers: 18
Income: £2,800,000 (2015–16)

## Cumbria CVS

6 Hobson Court, Gillan Way, Penrith,
Cumbria CA10 2NH
T: 01768 800350
E: info@cumbriacvs.org.uk
www.cumbriacvs.org.uk
Chief Officer: Karen Bowen
Cumbria CVS is a membership organisation,
a registered charity and a company limited by
guarantee. It is the only provider of generalist
infrastructure support to third sector
organisations in Cumbria. The third sector
comprises community and voluntary groups
and organisations, as well as faith groups,
sports groups and social enterprises.
Employees: 25
Volunteers: 3

## CXK

The Old Court, Tufton Street, Ashford,
Kent TN23 1QN
T: 01233 224244
E: info@cxk.org
www.cxk.org
CEO: Matthew Roberts
CXK is a charity that delivers inspirational
advice, guidance, support, counselling and
training for those in need. Our services, which
cover early help, youth services, career
management and training programmes, are
delivered across Kent, Medway, East and
West Sussex, Essex and into South East
London. On average we impact on the lives
of approximately 34–40,000 individuals,
regardless of their age, circumstance or
background, each year. In 2015 we became

the lead organisation throughout the South
East for the delivery of the National Careers
Service and the National Citizen Service
programme.
Employees: 183
Volunteers: 14
Regional offices: 3
Income: £14,620,000 (2014–15)

## Cyclical Vomiting Syndrome Association UK

77 Wilbury Hills Road,
Letchworth Garden City,
Hertfordshire SG6 4LD
Helpline: 0151 342 1660
E: info@cvsa.org.uk
www.cvsa.org.uk
Chair: Dr Robin Dover
The Association offers relief to people
suffering from cyclical vomiting syndrome
by providing and assisting in the provision
of treatment, advice, information and
counselling for sufferers and their families.
Volunteers: 10

## Cystic Fibrosis Trust

11 London Road, Bromley, Kent BR1 1BY
T: 020 8464 7211
Helpline: 0845 859 1000
E: enquiries@cftrust.org.uk
www.cftrust.org.uk
Chief Executive: Ed Owen
The Trust funds medical research and
provides advice, information and support
to all those affected by Cystic Fibrosis.
Employees: 90
Volunteers: 200
Income: £10,000,000 (2013–14)

## Daisy Network

PO Box 183, Rossendale BB4 6WZ
E: daisy@daisynetwork.org.uk
www.daisynetwork.org.uk
The Daisy Network Premature Menopause
Support Group is a registered charity

for women who have experienced a
premature menopause.
Volunteers: 20

## Dance UK

Unit A402A, The Biscuit Factory,
100 Clements Road,
Bermondsey SE16 4DG
T: 020 7713 0730
F: 020 7223 0074
E: info@danceuk.org
www.danceuk.org
Dance UK works to create a diverse,
dynamic and healthy future for dance and
to build a stronger sense of a UK-wide
dance community.
Employees: 7
Volunteers: 25

## Dark Horse Theatre

The Lawrence Batley Theatre, Queen Street,
Huddersfield, West Yorkshire HD1 2SP
T: 01484 484441
F: 01484 484443
E: info@darkhorsetheatre.co.uk
www.darkhorsetheatre.co.uk
Executive Director: Lynda Hornsby
Dark Horse is a theatre company that
trains learning-disabled actors at the
highest vocational level. Dark Horse tours
professional productions with learning-
and non-learning-disabled casts regionally
and nationally.
Employees: 4
Volunteers: 1
Regional offices: 1

## Dartington Social Research Unit

Lower Hood Barn, Totnes, Dartington,
Devon TQ9 6AB
T: 01803 762400
E: jaddy@dartington.org.uk
www.dartington.org.uk
The Dartington Social Research Unit
(DSRU) is an independent charity that brings
science and evidence to bear on policy and
practice in children's services to improve the
health and development of children and
young people.
Employees: 25

## darts (Doncaster Community Arts)

The Point, 16 South Parade, Doncaster,
South Yorkshire DN1 2DR
T: 01302 341662
F: 01302 341668
E: sophy@thepoint.org.uk
www.thepoint.org.uk
Co-Directors: Elaine Hirst/Duncan
Robertshaw

darts is a participatory arts organisation,
firmly rooted in and focused on Doncaster
communities. At the heart of our work is
a passionate belief that the arts can fuel
change for individuals and communities
and that creativity enhances the abilities
and opportunities of every person who
participates in it. Our mission is to engage
those who are described as hard to reach and/
or who have little or no access to the arts.
Employees: 39
Volunteers: 50
Regional offices: 1
Income: £1,408,143 (2015–16)

## David Lewis

Mill Lane, Warford, Near Alderley Edge,
Cheshire SK9 7UD
T: 01565 640000
F: 01565 640100
E: enquire@davidlewis.org.uk
www.davidlewis.org.uk
CEO: Anthony Waters

David Lewis is the UK's largest provider of
care, education, assessment, treatment
and life skill development for people aged
16 upwards with complex epilepsy, physical
and learning disabilities and other neurological
conditions.
Employees: 1000

## Deaf Education through Listening and Talking (DELTA)

DELTA, 83 Sherwin Road, Nottingham,
Nottinghamshire NG7 2FB
T: 0300 365 7200
E: enquiries@deafeducation.org.uk
www.deafeducation.org.uk
Chair: Andy Stubbs

DELTA is a national charity that supports
deaf children, their families and practitioners
following the Natural Aural Approach. This
approach helps the deaf child learn to listen
and talk using their residual hearing and
natural spoken language, even those with a
severe or profound loss. DELTA provides a
range of information, advice and practical
help at summer schools, weekend and
information days for parents, teachers and
other professionals.
Employees: 1
Volunteers: 250
Regional offices: 1

## Deaf Ex-Mainstreamers Group

Unit 9, Milner Way, Ossett, Wakefield,
West Yorkshire WF5 9JN
F: 01226 700326
E: info@dex.org.uk
www.dex.org.uk
Chair: Brian Daltrey

The Deaf Ex-Mainstreamers' Group (DEX) is
a deaf-led organisation concerned about the
limited lack of access deaf children have to
the National Curriculum and to the school
environment. DEX has conducted a Best
Value Review of deaf children in the UK,
Sweden, Norway and Canada, a literature
review, and a study of the needs of parents of
deaf children and deaf young people. DEX
now markets its services to local government
and health.
Employees: 1

## Deaf PLUS

1st Floor, Trinity Centre, Key Close,
Whitechapel, London E1 4HG
T: 020 7790 6147
E: clare.kennedy@deafplus.org
www.deafplus.org
Chief Executive: Clare Kennedy

Deaf and hearing people working together to
achieve equality.
Employees: 26
Volunteers: 15
Regional offices: 6

## Deafax

Clare Charity Centre, Wycombe Road,
Saunderton, Buckinghamshire HP14 4BF
T: 01494 568885
E: info@deafax.org
www.deafax.org
Chief Executive: Helen Lansdown

Deafax works with deaf people providing
innovative and high-quality deaf-friendly
resources and training courses (online and
face to face) which cover areas such as life
skills, personal health, drug and alcohol
awareness, sexual health, identity issues, etc.

## Deafblind UK

National Centre For Deafblindness,
John and Lucille Van Geest Place,
Cygnet Road, Hampton, Peterborough,
Cambridgeshire PE7 8FD
T: 01733 358100
Helpline: 0800 132320
F: 01733 358356
E: info@deafblind.org.uk
www.deafblind.org.uk
Chief Executive: Jeff Skipp

Deafblind UK is a national charity offering
specialist services and human support to
deafblind people and those who have
progressive sight and hearing loss acquired
throughout their lives. Our aim is to enable
people living with this unique disability to
maintain their independence and quality
of life and to reduce the isolation that
Deafblindness creates. Further information
about Deafblind UK is available on our
website.
Employees: 200
Volunteers: 200
Regional offices: 1

## Deafconnect

Spencer Dallington Community Centre,
Tintern Avenue, Northampton NN5 7BZ
T: 01604 589011
F: 01604 754529
E: joanna.steer@deafconnect.org.uk
deafconnect.org.uk
CEO: Joanna Steer

Deafconnect supports and empowers
deaf and hearing impaired people to be
independent. We offer support, advice,
information and advocacy to deaf and hearing
impaired people of all ages, their families,
carers and professionals working with them.
We provide an interpreting service for hearing
impaired communication to support our aims.
We work closely with other organisations to
improve access to other services and
information.
We also offer competitively priced sign
language courses and deaf awareness
training.
Employees: 13
Volunteers: 22
Regional offices: 1
Income: £220,000 (2014–15)

## Deafness Support Network

144 London Road, Northwich,
Cheshire CW9 5HH
T: 0808 208 2440
F: 01606 49456
E: dsn@dsnonline.co.uk
www.dsnonline.co.uk
Chief Executive Officer: Bob Birchall

Providing support services to Deaf, deafened
and Hard of Hearing people of all ages, across
Cheshire.
Employees: 70
Volunteers: 150
Regional offices: 3

## Deafway

Deafway, Brockholes Brow, Preston,
Lancashire PR2 5AL
T: 01772 796461
F: 01772 693416
E: info@deafway.org.uk
www.deafway.org.uk
Deafway works towards providing equality
of opportunity and access in all areas of
life for deaf, sign language users in the UK
and abroad.
Employees: 64
Volunteers: 2
Regional offices: 1

## DEBRA

Unit 13, Wellington Business Park,
Dukes Ride, Crowthorne,
Berkshire RG45 6LS
T: 01344 771961
E: debra@debra.org.uk
www.debra.org.uk
DEBRA is the national charity that supports
individuals and families affected by
Epidermolysis Bullosa (EB) – a genetic
condition which causes the skin to blister and
shear at the slightest touch. DEBRA provides
an enhanced specialist EB Nursing Service, in
partnership with the NHS and community
support staff to work directly with families.
The charity also commissions world-leading
research into the condition with the aim of
finding effective treatments and, ultimately,
a cure for EB.

## Democratic Progress Institute

E: info@democraticprogress.org

## DEVELOP Enhancing Community Support

3–4 New Road, Chippenham,
Wiltshire SN15 1EJ
T: 0845 034 5250
F: 01249 655696
E: hello@wearedevelop.org.uk
www.wearedevelop.org.uk
Chief Executive Officer: Janice Fortune
DEVELOP Enhancing Community Support
is an independent organisation which
operates across Wiltshire and the surrounding
areas. We are a registered charity set up,
owned and run by local groups to support,
develop and enhance local voluntary and
community action.
Employees: 17
Volunteers: 5
Regional offices: 1

## Diabetes Foundation

1 Constable's Gate, Winchester SO23 8GE
T: 01962 842070
E: judith.rich@btinternet.com
www.diabetesfoundation.org.uk
Chair: Judith Rich
The Foundation supports and advances
research in the field of diabetes, particularly
juvenile (insulin dependent) diabetes in the
UK and throughout the world.
Volunteers: 10

## Diabetes UK

Macleod House, 10 Parkway,
London NW1 7AA
T: 020 7424 1106
F: 020 7424 1080
E: info@diabetes.org.uk
www.diabetes.org.uk
Chief Executive: Chris Askew
Our aim is to improve the lives of people with
diabetes, to work towards a future without
diabetes and to set people free from the
restrictions of diabetes. We work towards the
highest quality care and information for all, an
end to discrimination and ignorance, universal
understanding of diabetes and Diabetes UK
and a world without diabetes.
Employees: 180
Volunteers: 10000
Regional offices: 10

## Diagrama Foundation

E: julie.firth@diagrama.org

## DIAL Basildon and South Essex

75 Southernhay, Basildon, Essex SS14 1EU
T: 01268 285676
E: jan@dialbasildon.co.uk
www.dialbasildon.co.uk
Manager: Jan Stevens
DIAL provides a free, confidential
information and advice service on all issues
affecting disabled people's everyday lives, to
enable and empower individuals to improve
their quality of life. We currently offer advice,
support, advocacy and guidance services to
local disabled people, assisting them with a
number of topics related to disability. Our
own unique experience of living with disability
allows us to assist others with understanding
and expertise.
Employees: 5
Volunteers: 12
Regional offices: 1
Income: £180,000 (2014–15)

## DIAL UK

6 Market Road, London N7 9PW
F: 020 7619 7100
E: dialnetwork@scope.org.uk
www.dialuk.org.uk
Dial UK is the national organisation for the
DIAL network – 140 disability advice centres
run by and for people with disabilities.
Employees: 8
Volunteers: 8

## DIAL West Cheshire

DIAL House, Hamilton Place, Chester,
Cheshire CH1 2BH
T: 01244 345655
E: k.roper@dialwestcheshire.org.uk
www.dialhousechester.org.uk
Chief Officer: Keith Roper
DIAL West Cheshire (DIAL House) aims
to enable disabled people and older people
to live sustained, independent lives. We
provide a range of disability-related services
including: advice and information; community
cafe; shopmobility; volunteering and training.
Employees: 12
Volunteers: 80+
Income: £320,000 (2014–15)

## Different Strokes

9 Canon Harnett Court, Wolverton Mill,
Milton Keynes,
Buckinghamshire MK12 5NF
T: 01908 317618
Helpline: 0845 130 7172
F: 01908 313501
E: info@differentstrokes.co.uk
www.differentstrokes.co.uk
Chief Executive: Debbie Wilson
Different Strokes provides a free service to
younger stroke survivors throughout the UK.
Run by stroke survivors for stroke survivors,
for active self-help and mutual support. We
help stroke survivors of working age to
optimise their recovery and regain as much
independence as possible by offering
rehabilitative services, information and
advice. Our services include the Strokeline,
access to exercise sessions, practical
information packs, an interactive website,
regular newsletters and assistance finding
counselling services.
Employees: 6
Volunteers: 150
Regional offices: 50

## Dignity in Dying

181 Oxford Street, London  W1D 2JT
T: 020 7479 7730
E: info@dignityindying.org.uk
www.dignityindying.org.uk
Dignity in Dying is the leading campaigning organisation promoting patient choice at the end of life. We are also a major information source on end-of-life issues. Dignity in Dying is independent of any political, religious or other organisation. We are supported entirely by voluntary contributions from members of the public.
Employees: 21

## Dimbleby Cancer Care

4th Floor Management Offices,
Bermondsey Wing, Guy's Hospital,
Great Maze Pond, London  SE1 9RT
T: 020 7188 7889
Helpline: 020 7188 5918
E: admin@dimblebycancercare.org
www.dimblebycancercare.org
Chairman of Trustees: Jonathan Dimbleby
Provides psychological and social support, complementary therapies and benefits advice to patients with cancer at Guy's and St Thomas' Hospitals, London. Provides research funding for national projects looking into the psycho-social and practical support needs of people with cancer and their families.
Employees: 3
Income: £450,573 (2014–15)

## DIPEx Charity

23–28 Hythe Bridge Street, Oxford,
Oxfordshire  OX2 7LX
T: 01865 201330
E: info@healthtalkonline.org
www.healthtalkonline.org
In partnership with Oxford University we provide information about people's experiences of illnesses and health conditions via video interviews, shared on our websites Healthtalkonline and Youthhealthtalk. The award-winning websites are aimed at patients, their carers, family and friends, and health professionals. We aim to help them understand the impact of issues such as cancer, being a carer, bereavement, infertility and chronic pain on people's everyday lives.
Employees: 5
Volunteers: 20

## Direct Help and Advice (DHA)

Phoenix Street, Derby,
Derbyshire  DE1 2ER
T: 01332 287850
Helpline: 0845 345 4345
F: 01332 287863
E: annette.barrett@dhadvice.org
www.dhadvice.org
Interim Chief Executive: Ian Grostate
DHA provides direct help via specialist advice, advocacy and representation for families and individuals facing crisis, to prevent and alleviate homelessness, debt and housing difficulty. Our free, independent and confidential services offer support to the most vulnerable people in our communities, often requiring immediate intervention, support and advice. We also offer accessible training and skills development to a wide range of people to help reduce unemployment and promote social and financial inclusion.
Employees: 36
Volunteers: 5
Regional offices: 2

## Directory of Social Change – London

24 Stephenson Way, London  NW1 2DP
T: 0845 077 7707
F: 020 7391 4804
E: dsc@dsc.org.uk
www.dsc.org.uk
The Directory of Social Change, set up in 1975, aims to be an internationally recognised independent source of information and support to voluntary and community sectors worldwide. We enable the community and voluntary sectors to achieve their aims through being an independent voice, providing training and information.
Employees: 45
Regional offices: 1

## Disabilities Trust

32 Market Place, Burgess Hill,
West Sussex  RH15 9NP
T: 01444 239123
F: 01444 244978
E: info@thedtgroup.org
www.disabilities-trust.org.uk
The Trust: provides purpose-built accommodation and a full range of support facilities for people with physical disabilities, acquired brain injuries and autism; provides the most modern facilities in a homely, caring atmosphere; offers residents a stage between institutionalised care and total independence, and encourages them to lead as independent a lifestyle as possible while receiving individual attention and the security offered by residential staff.
Employees: 1160

## Disability Awareness in Action

46 The Parklands, Hullavington,
Wiltshire  SN14 6DL
T: 01666 837671
E: info@daa.org.uk
www.daa.org.uk
The Alliance provides information to disabled people, their organisations and allies worldwide, supports their self-help activities and ensures their equality of opportunity. It raises awareness that disability is a human rights issue.

## Disability Foundation

RNOH, Brockley Hill, Stanmore,
Middlesex  HA7 4LP
T: 020 8954 7373
F: 020 8954 7414
E: info@tdf.org.uk
www.tdf.org.uk
TDF welcomes any person with a disability by offering help, support and guidance to them, their families and care/support associates, creating hope and inspiration for the future. TDF has a holistic approach offering complementary therapies at heavily reduced rates and provides information, promoting best practice at all times.
Employees: 6
Volunteers: 10
Regional offices: 1

## Disability Law Service

39–45 Cavell Street, London  E1 2BP
T: 020 7791 9800
F: 020 7791 9802
E: advice@dls.org.uk
www.dls.org.uk
Director: Aydin Djemal
For over 30 years the Disability Law Service (DLS) has continued to provide high-quality information and advice to disabled and deaf people. As a national registered charity DLS is independent, run by and for disabled people.
Employees: 8
Volunteers: 20–30

## Disability Partnership and MOVE

Wooden Spoon House, 5 Dugard Way,
London  SE11 4TH
T: 020 7414 1495
E: office@disabilitypartnership.co.uk
www.disabilitypartnership.co.uk
The Disability Partnership is a small but influential charity that exists primarily as a launch-pad for initiatives that ultimately change the daily lives of many disabled people for the better. We change lives through

working to overcome the attitudinal and physical barriers that most affect disabled people in the UK and worldwide.

## Disability Pregnancy and Parenthood

N10 1HU
E: info@dppi.org.uk
www.disabledparent.org.uk
Disability, Pregnancy and Parenthood (DPPI) is the national information charity on disability and parenthood. We promote better awareness and support for disabled people considering, during and after pregnancy and as parents.

## Disability Rights UK

CAN Mezzanine, 49–51 East Road, London N1 6AH
T: 020 7250 8181
E: enquiries@disabilityrightsuk.org
www.disabilityrightsuk.org
Chief Executive: Liz Sayce
Disability Rights UK campaigns to create a society where everyone can participate equally. We publish the Disability Rights Handbook, sell the RADAR accessible toilet key, produce free benefits factsheets and operate the Disabled Student Helpline and the Personal Budgets Helpline.
Employees: 20
Volunteers: 5

## Disability Snowsport UK (Bromley)

20 Foxearth Close, Biggin Hill, Kent TN16 3HQ
T: 01959 574108
E: m.martineau@btinternet.com
www.disabilitysnowsport.org.uk or www.uphill-skiing.org.uk
Chair of Bromley Group: Barbara Crow
Skiers and snowboarders with a disability should be able to ski alongside the able bodied as equals at all ski facilities and resorts. A disabled person chooses both freedom and independence when they snap into bindings or transfer from a wheelchair to sit ski. They also make a choice to actively access adventure, a choice that may be made in spite of chronic health problems or a physical or learning disability. Snowsport provides people with a method to conquer the barriers that confront them in daily life and add to their potential.
Volunteers: 40
Income: £1,000 (2013–14)

## Disabled Living Foundation

380–384 Harrow Road, London W9 2HU
T: 020 7289 6111
Helpline: 0845 130 9177
F: 020 7266 2922
E: info@dlf.org.uk
www.dlf.org.uk
Chief Executive: Nicole Penn-Symons
The Disabled Living Foundation (DLF) is a national charity that provides free, impartial advice and information about all types of equipment for daily living for older and disabled people. Every year we respond to up to 25,000 requests for information via our helpline service. We provide an equipment demonstration centre, free factsheets, an online self-assessment tool, AskSARA, and our personal care search and comparison website.
Employees: 30
Volunteers: 4

## Disabled Living Foundation

84 St Gothard Road, West Norwood, London SE27 9QP
T: 07904 694089
E: peter.acton@dls.org.uk
www.livingmadeeasy.org.uk
Co-Founder: Jean Leigh
Our main aims are to research into the needs and requirements of disabled people, especially young adults with learning difficulties and to work with other organisations to have these 'needs' met whilst raising disability awareness as an everyday issue.
Volunteers: 10
Income: £602 (2013–14)

## Disabled Motoring UK

National Office, Ashwellthorpe, Norwich NR16 1EX
T: 01508 489449
E: info@disabledmotoring.org
www.disabledmotoring.org
CEO: Graham Footer
Disabled Motoring UK is the campaigning charity for Blue Badge holders, disabled motorists and wheelchair and scooter users. We run the Baywatch campaign against parking abuse and represent disabled people's needs at a national level. Membership includes a monthly magazine, one-to-one advice and member benefits and concessions. Membership is £24 a year (£36 for joint members).
Employees: 10
Volunteers: 1

## Disabled Motorists' Federation

145 Knoulberry Road, Washington, Tyne and Wear NE37 1JN
T: 0191 416 3172
E: jkillick2214@yahoo.co.uk
www.dmfed.org.uk
Chairman: Noel Muncey
The Federation helps disabled people overcome their handicaps and become as independent as possible so that they may lead fuller and more active lives. It gives free advice on motoring, travel, etc to all disabled people and their carers.
Volunteers: 8

## Disabled Parents Network

Poynters House, Poynters Road, Dunstable, Bedfordshire LU5 4TP
T: 0300 330 0639
E: information@disabledparentsnetwork.org.uk
www.disabledparentsnetwork.org.uk
Chair: Terri Balon
Disabled Parents Network (DPN) is a national user-led organisation providing information, advice and support to parents and parents to be, who are disabled or have a long-term health condition, their families, etc. Helping disabled parent families access appropriate support, grow in knowledge and self-confidence.
Volunteers: 20

## Disabled Photographers' Society

43 Burge Court, Cirencester, Gloucestershire GL7 1JY
T: 01285 654984
E: enquiries@disabledphotographers.co.uk
www.dps-uk.org.uk
The Society encourages disabled people to undertake photography as a therapeutic and creative activity.

## Disaster Action

PO Box 849, Woking, Surrey GU21 8WB
T: 01483 799066
E: admin@disasteraction.org.uk
www.disasteraction.org.uk
Disaster Action provides support and guidance to individuals and groups affected by disasters.

## Disasters Emergency Committee

1st Floor, 43 Chalton Street,
London NW1 1DU
T: 020 7387 0200
F: 020 7387 2050
E: info@dec.org.uk
www.dec.org.uk
At times of overseas emergency, the DEC brings together a unique alliance of the UK's aid, corporate, public and broadcasting sectors to rally the nation's compassion, and ensure that funds raised go to DEC agencies best placed to deliver effective and timely relief to people most in need.
Employees: 9
Volunteers: 1

## Disaway Trust

11 Larchwood Close, Banstead,
Surrey SM7 1HE
T: 01737 214805
E: lynnesimpkins@hotmail.com
www.disaway.co.uk
Treasurer: Lynne Simpkins
We organise group holidays with physically disabled people. Each disabled person has their own helper, either a friend or family member or a helper supplied by the Trust. The helper pays approximately 50% of the cost.
Volunteers: varies

## Diversity Hub

The Learning Exchange, Wygston's House,
Applegate, Leicester,
Leicestershire LE1 5LD
T: 0116 222 9977
F: 0116 222 9970
E: info@diversityhub.org.uk
www.diversityhub.org.uk
Director: Val Carpenter
Diversity Hub is a leadership-training organisation dedicated to ending prejudice and discrimination, whether because of nationality, race, gender, religion, class, sexual orientation, age, physical ability, occupation or life circumstance.
Employees: 4
Volunteers: 30
Regional offices: 1

## Diversity Role Models

St Anne's Church, 55 Dean Street,
London W1D 6AF
T: 020 3795 9201
E: info@diversityrolemodels.org
www.diversityrolemodels.org
Chief Executive: Suran Dickson
Our vision is a world where all children and young people can live, learn, grow and play safely, regardless of issues relating to gender and sexuality. Our mission is to eliminate homophobic, biphobic and transphobic bullying. We achieve this by providing high-quality, pioneering educational workshops and teacher training involving role models who share their personal experiences of being LGBT. We value diversity and equality, creativity and innovation, communication and role modelling, and inter-generational learning.
Employees: 7
Volunteers: 250
Regional offices: 1
Income: £508,409 (2014–15)

## Diving Diseases Research Centre

8 Research Way, Plymouth Science Park,
Derriford, Plymouth, Devon PL6 8BU
T: 01752 209999
F: 01752 209115
E: info@ddrc.org
www.ddrc.org
Chief Executive Officer: Gary Smerdon
A medical research, training and service charity working with hyperbaric oxygen, its uses and effects in humans. Providing services to the NHS and private sector for difficult to heal wounds, soft tissue infections and carbon monoxide poisoning in particular as well as treatment for divers with decompression illness (the bends).
Employees: 28
Regional offices: 2

## DoBe.org

NW1 1EU
E: info@alberyfoundation.org
www.alberyfoundation.org

## Dog AID (Assistance In Disability)

CVS Building, Arthur Street, Chadsmoor,
Cannock, Staffordshire WS11 5HD
T: 01543 899463
E: general_admin@dogaid.org.uk
www.dogaid.org.uk
Chairperson: Sandra Fraser
Dog AID provides access to dog training for people with physical disabilities, enabling them to train their own dog in basic control and specialised tasks, which will assist them manage their disability in everyday life.

## Dogs for Good

The Frances Hay Centre, Blacklocks Hill,
Banbury, Oxfordshire OX17 2BS
T: 01295 252600
F: 01295 252668
E: info@dogsforgood.org
www.dogsforgood.org
Chief Executive: Peter Gorbing
Dogs for the Disabled provides specially trained assistance dogs for adults and children with physical disabilities, and families with a child with autism, to help them lead fuller and more independent lives.
Employees: 50
Volunteers: 140

## Dogs Trust

17–26 26 Wakley Street,
London EC1V 7RQ
T: 020 7837 0006
F: 020 7833 2701
E: info@dogstrust.org.uk
www.dogstrust.org.uk
Dogs Trust is working towards the day when all dogs can enjoy a happy life, free from the threat of unnecessary destruction. We care for stray and abandoned dogs through our network of 15 rehoming centres nationwide. No healthy dog is ever destroyed. Our subsidised neutering campaigns aim to prevent the birth of unwanted litters. Additionally, our schools education programme promotes responsible dog ownership to young people.
Employees: 400
Volunteers: 200
Regional offices: 15

## Donkey Sanctuary

Slade Farm House, Sidmouth,
Devon EX10 0NU
T: 01395 578222
F: 01395 579266
E: amanda.gordon@thedonkeysanctuary.com
www.thedonkeysanctuary.org.uk
Chief Executive: David Cook
The Donkey Sanctuary has taken over 13,000 donkeys into its care since 1969. Some of these donkeys may have been neglected, mistreated, retired from working on beaches or their owners could no longer care for them. The Donkey Sanctuary also brings urgent veterinary assistance to working donkeys in Egypt, Ethiopia, India, Kenya and Mexico. Further projects exist in Europe where more donkeys are in need of help. Admission is free at its headquarters in Sidmouth.
Employees: 526

## Dorset and Somerset Air Ambulance

Landacre House, Castle Road,
Chelston Business Park, Wellington,
Somerset TA21 9JQ
T: 01823 669604
E: bill.sivewright@dsairambulance.org.uk
www.dsairambulance.org.uk
Chief Executive Officer: Bill Sivewright
To save and enhance lives through the funding and provision of a helicopter emergency medical service.
Employees: 17
Volunteers: 80
Regional offices: 2

## Dorset Youth Association

**County Headquarters, Lubbecke Way, Dorchester, Dorset DT1 1QL**
T: 01305 262440
E: info@dorsetyouth.com
www.dorsetyouth.com
**Director: Dave Thompson**
Improves the quality of life for children and young people in Dorset by: delivering positive activities and support to affiliated clubs and groups; providing information, advice and guidance for young people; helping young people gain the skills and confidence to 'move on'; supporting programmes which enable young people to make a positive contribution to their communities; providing targeted support for young people who are disadvantaged; administering and providing support to VCS 0–19 Forum and Sector.
**Employees: 12**
**Volunteers: 300**
**Income: £307,995 (2015–16)**

## Douglas Haig Memorial Homes (Haig Homes)

**Alban Dobson House, Green Lane, Morden, Surrey SM4 5NS**
T: 020 8685 5777
E: haig@haighomes.org.uk
www.haighomes.org.uk
Provides housing for the ex-service community.

## Down's Heart Group

**PO Box 4260, Dunstable, Bedfordshire LU6 2ZT**
T: 0300 102 1644
F: 0300 102 1645
E: info@dhg.org.uk
www.dhg.org.uk
**Director: Penny Green**
Provides support and information relating to heart problems associated with Down's syndrome.
**Employees: 2**
**Volunteers: 10**
**Income: £15,000 (2014–15)**

## Down's Syndrome Association

**2a Langdon Park, Langdon Centre, Teddington TW11 9PS**
F: 0333 121 2300
E: info@downs-syndrome.org.uk
www.downs-syndrome.org.uk
We are the only organisation in this country focusing solely on all aspects of living successfully with Down's syndrome. We are a national charity with over 20,000 members, a national office in Teddington Middlesex, regional offices in Northern Ireland and

Wales and over 130 affiliated local groups. We provide support, training, information and advice for people with Down's syndrome, their families and professionals.
**Employees: 36**
**Regional offices: 130**

## Down's Syndrome Educational Trust

**The Sarah Duffen Centre, Belmont Street, Southsea, Hampshire PO5 1NA**
T: 023 9289 3889
F: 023 9289 3895
E: info@dseinternational.org
www.downsed.org
Promotes the development and education of individuals with Down's syndrome.
**Employees: 20**
**Volunteers: 10**
**Regional offices: 3**

## Dr Hadwen Trust

**Suite 8, Portmill House, Portmill Lane, Hitchin, Hertfordshire, Portmill Lane SG5 1DJ**
T: 01462 436819 (also fax)
E: b.lloyd@drhadwentrust.org
www.drhadwentrust.org
**Development Director: Kay Miller**
The Dr Hadwen Trust (DHT) is the UK's leading non-animal medical research charity that funds and promotes the development of techniques and procedures to replace the use of animals in biomedical research and testing.
**Employees: 10**
**Volunteers: 10**
**Regional offices: 1**
**Income: £700,000 (2012–13)**

## Drake Music

**60–61 Old Nichol Street, London E2 7HP**
T: 020 7739 5444
E: info@drakemusic.org
www.drakemusic.org
**CEO: Carien Meijer**
Drake Music is the leading national charity working in music, disability and technology. We specialise in the use of assistive technology to break down both physical and societal barriers to music-making. We offer a wide range of high-quality, life-long learning opportunities for people of all ages, working in partnership with schools, music hubs, universities, healthcare professionals, artists, technologists and more to improve access to music. Our team has an excellent track record in delivering outreach, training and education initiatives, as well as developing new technologies and commissioning

disabled practitioners to produce new artistic works.
**Employees: 8**
**Regional offices: 3**

## Dreamflight

**7C Hill Avenue, Amersham, Buckinghamshire HP6 5BD**
T: 01494 722733
F: 01494 722977
E: office@dreamflight.org
www.dreamflight.org
Dreamflight is a UK charity that takes seriously ill and disabled children on their 'holiday of a lifetime' to the theme parks of Central Florida. Other charities do some wonderful things like funding research or purchasing medical equipment, but Dreamflight believes that fun and joy are just as important, especially for children who perhaps can't wait long enough for the breakthrough they need or whose illnesses and treatments have brought pain, distress and disruption.
**Employees: 2**

## Dreams Come True Charity

**Exchange House, 33 Station Road, Liphook, Hampshire GU30 7DW**
T: 01428 726330
F: 01428 724953
E: info@dctc.org.uk
www.dctc.org.uk
The charity aims to try and fulfil the dreams of young people aged 2-21 who suffer from serious, degenerative or terminal illnesses.
**Employees: 12**
**Volunteers: 3**
**Regional offices: 1**

## Drug and Alcohol Action Programme

**KAS House, Unit K, Middlesex Business Centre, Bridge Road, Southall, Middlesex UB2 4AB**
T: 020 8843 0945
F: 020 8843 1068
E: info@daap.org.uk
www.daap.org.uk
The Programme advances the education of the public about all aspects of substance misuse and related issues particularly: by working towards eradicating addiction by and through education; by developing and managing appropriate programmes and treatment services; by conducting research on addictive behaviour.
**Employees: 4**

## Duchenne Family Support Group

78 York Street, London W1H 1DP
T: 0870 241 1857
Helpline: 0800 121 4518
E: info@dfsg.org.uk
www.dfsg.org.uk
**Development Officer: Phillippa Farrant**
We provide support to families affected by Duchenne muscular dystrophy by a national helpline, our website and a quarterly newsletter. We organise subsidised holidays and social events so that parents and siblings can share experiences. We also organise conferences and workshops on topics of interest to our families. We work with other related charities on a variety of topics including research and improving services.
**Employees: 1**
**Volunteers: 55**
**Regional offices: 1**

## Dudley Caribbean and Friends Association

3rd Floor, Trident House,
14 Wolverhampton Street, Dudley,
West Midlands DY1 1DB
T: 01384 868085
E: levene.bruce@btconnect.com
**Manager: Levene Bruce**
The charity's objects are to impact the educational and socio-economic needs of ethnic communities, in particular the African Caribbean community within the metropolitan borough of Dudley and other likeminded community associations in the wider West Midlands. To achieve this the charity has established several projects to address the educational, training, employment and social welfare needs of the community.
**Employees: 9**
**Volunteers: 6**
**Income: £134,931 (2013–14)**

## Durrell Wildlife Conservation Trust

Les Augres Manor, La Profonde Rue, Trinity,
Jersey JE3 5BP
T: 01534 860000
F: 01534 860001
E: info@durrell.org
www.durrell.org
Durrell Wildlife is a charity with a mission to save species from extinction.
**Employees: 88**
**Volunteers: 200**

## Dyslexia Action

Dyslexia Action House, 10 High Street,
Egham, 10 High Street, Surrey TW20 9EA
T: 0300 303 8357
F: 01784 770484
E: info@dyslexiaaction.org.uk
www.dyslexiaaction.org.uk
**Chief Executive: Stephen Hall**
Dyslexia Action is a national charity and the UK's leading provider of services and support for people with dyslexia, literacy and numeracy difficulties. We specialise in offering free advice, assessments, teaching, training and consultancy. We also develop and distribute teaching materials and undertake research. Our services are available through our centres and teaching locations around the UK. Over half a million people benefit from our work each year.
**Employees: 300**
**Regional offices: 26**

## Dyspraxia Foundation

8 West Alley, Hitchin,
Hertfordshire SG5 1EG
T: 01462 455016
F: 01462 455052
E: admin@dyspraxiafoundation.org.uk
www.dyspraxiafoundation.org.uk
**General Manager/Company Secretary: Eleanor Howes**
The Foundation puts parents and children in contact with other sufferers, locally and nationally. It provides a regular newsletter, promotes better diagnostic and treatment facilities for dyspraxic children and encourages a wider understanding of dyspraxia from childhood into adulthood by health and education professionals and by the general public.
**Employees: 5**
**Volunteers: 100**
**Regional offices: 1**

## Dystonia Society

2nd Floor, 89 Albert Embankment,
London SE1 7TP
T: 020 7793 3651
Helpline: 020 7793 3650
E: info@dystonia.org.uk
www.dystonia.org.uk
**Chief Executive: Guy Parckar**
The Dystonia Society is a UK-wide charity providing practical and emotional support for the 70,000 people with dystonia and their families. Dystonia is a neurological movement disorder characterised by involuntary and sustained muscle spasms, which can be very painful and debilitating.
**Employees: 15**
**Volunteers: 200**
**Income: £707,114 (2014–15)**

## Ealing Centre for Independent Living

1 Bayham Road, West Ealing,
London W13 0TQ
T: 020 8840 8717
E: ellen.collins@ecil.org
www.ecil.org
**Chief Executive: Alan Murray**
To provide advice, information, advocacy, peer support, counselling, respite and social events for disabled people and their unpaid carers in the London Borough of Ealing, enabling them to live a full and independent life.
**Employees: 13**
**Volunteers: 25**
**Regional offices: 1**
**Income: £350,000 (2015–16)**

## Ealing Community Transport

Greenford Depot, Greenford Road,
Greenford, Middlesex UB6 9AP
T: 020 8813 3210
F: 020 8813 3211
E: ealing@ectcharity.co.uk
www.ectcharity.co.uk
**Chief Executive: Anna Whitty**
ECT is a national charity with a local focus on the specialist provision of high-quality, safe, accessible and affordable transport for the many communities we serve. We are committed to charity, partnership and social business excellence. Under the banner ;ECT Charity', we operate in Ealing, Cheshire, Dorset, Bournemouth and Cornwall.
**Employees: 180**
**Volunteers: 300**
**Regional offices: 3**

## Earl Mountbatten Hospice

Halberry Lane, Newport,
Isle of Wight PO30 2ER
T: 01983 529511
E: richard.dent@iwhospice.org
www.iwhospice.org
Chief Executive: Nigel Hartley
Earl Mountbatten Hospice is an independent charity providing comprehensive end-of-life healthcare for the Isle of Wight community. We support and care for people living with and dying from a life-limiting illness.
Employees: 150
Volunteers: 550

## Earthwatch (Europe)

267 Banbury Road, Summertown,
Oxford, Oxfordshire OX13 5ET
T: 01865 318838
F: 01865 311383
E: info@earthwatch.org.uk
www.earthwatch.org/europe
Executive Director: Nigel Winser
Aims to advance the education and awareness of the public in the sciences and humanities and in all matters relating to the existence and development of life, human and non-human.
Employees: 55
Volunteers: 650

## East Anglian Air Ambulance

Hangar E, Gambling Close,
Norwich Airport, Norwich,
Norfolk NR6 6EG
T: 01603 269320
E: info@eaaa.org.uk
www.eaaa.org.uk
Chief Executive: Tim Page
The East Anglian Air Ambulance is a 365-day helicopter emergency medical service covering Bedfordshire, Cambridgeshire, Norfolk and Suffolk. We fly with a doctor and critical care paramedic, bringing A&E to the patient. We are 100% charity and receive no government or lottery funding.
Employees: 48
Volunteers: 250
Regional offices: 6

## East London Advanced Technology Training

E: orla@elatt.org.uk

## Eaves Housing for Women Limited

Lincoln House, 1–3 Brixton Road,
London SW9 6DE
T: 020 7735 2062
F: 020 7820 8907
E: post@eaveshousing.co.uk
www.eavesforwomen.org.uk
Provides housing for homeless women in need of supported housing; provides information about the causes of women's homelessness; campaigns for increased housing provision for single homeless women; encourages appropriate housing provision for single women.

## ECPAT UK

4 A Chillingworth Road, Holloway,
London N7 8QJ
T: 020 7607 2136
E: info@ecpat.org.uk
www.ecpat.org.uk
Chief Executive Officer: Bharti Patel
ECPAT UK (End Child Prostitution, Pornography and Trafficking) is a leading children's rights organisation campaigning to protect children from commercial sexual exploitation in the UK. In particular, we focus on the protection of trafficked children and children exploited in tourism.
Employees: 7
Volunteers: 1

## Ecumenical Council for Corporate Responsibility

c/o The United Society (Us), Harling House,
47–51 Great Suffolk Street,
London SE1 0BS
T: 07880 437131
E: info@eccr.org.uk
www.eccr.org.uk
Chair: Christopher Stockwell
ECCR works for economic justice, human rights and environmental sustainability. It acts as a forum where issues of corporate and investor responsibility are researched and studied, information and ideas are exchanged and strategies are planned and implemented.
Employees: 4

## EDP Drug and Alcohol Service

Suite 2:11, 2nd Floor, Renslade House,
Bonhay Road, Exeter, Devon EX4 3AY
T: 01392 666710
E: info@edp.org.uk
www.edp.org.uk
Chief Executive: Lucie Hartley
When people have problems with drugs and alcohol they may feel they have less control over their lives, and they may struggle to engage with their families and communities.

We provide accessible services in Devon and Dorset, which support people to move towards a place of wellbeing where they feel empowered and reconnected to their family and/or community.
Employees: 200
Regional offices: 17

## Education and Services for People with Autism Ltd

2A Hylton Park Road, Wessington Way,
Sunderland, Sunderland,
Tyne and Wear SR5 3HD
T: 0191 516 5080
F: 0191 549 8620
E: lesley.lane@espa.org.uk
www.espa.org.uk
Chief Executive: Lesley Lane
Provides specialist further education, residential, day and domiciliary services for people with an autism spectrum disorder.
Employees: 425
Regional offices: 1

## Education for Choice

The Resource Centre, 356 Holloway Road,
London N7 6PA
T: 020 7700 8190 (also fax)
E: efc@efc.org.uk
www.efc.org.uk
Director: Lisa Hallgarten
Education for Choice is the only UK organisation dedicated to enabling young people to make and act on informed choices about pregnancy and abortion. EFC works with young people, delivers training and consultancy for professionals and produces a range of information resources.
Employees: 4
Volunteers: 2

## Educational Centres Association

21 Ebbisham Drive, Norwich NR4 6HQ
T: 0870 161 0302
E: info@e-c-a.ac.uk
www.e-c-a.ac.uk
The Educational Centres Association is a practice-based organisation concerned with adult education and lifelong learning. Its work in the arts and cultural sectors complements the role of its constituent institutions and organisations. These extend across the range of adult community learning, FE colleges and HE. In England, much of this work is funded by the Learning and Skills Council, LSC, with which we have effective relationships at national and local levels.

## Edward's Trust

43A Calthorpe Road, Edgbaston,
Birmingham, West Midlands B15 1TS
T: 0121 456 4838
E: christine.bodkin@edwardstrust.org.uk
www.edwardtrust.org.uk
The aims of Edward's Trust are: to provide
support to children with a serious illness and
requiring hospital treatment, and their
families; to provide support to families
suffering a bereavement; to provide training
to those involved in bereavement services
following the death of a child; to raise
awareness of complementary approaches to
childhood concerns; to promote and support
research into complementary approaches to
childhood illnesses.
Employees: 22

## Ehlers-Danlos Support Group

PO Box 337, Aldershot GU12 6WZ
T: 01252 690940
E: director@ehlers-danlos.org
www.ehlers-danlos.org
Trustee: Frances Gawthrop
The aims of the Group are to support those
with Ehlers-Danlos syndrome and provide
education, information and research for
medical and caring professionals. It produces
books, information sheets and a newsletter.
A national conference is held biennially. The
group endeavours to heighten awareness of
EDS among the medical professionals and
support EDS research.
Volunteers: 24
Regional offices: 1

## EIRIS Foundation

80–84 Bondway, London SW8 1SF
T: 020 7840 5707
E: ethics@eiris.org
www.eiris.org
The Foundation provides information on a
wide range of issues to help concerned
investors apply positive or negative ethical
and social criteria. It identifies forms of
investment that meet certain non-financial
requirements on the part of the investor and
promotes wider understanding of, and debate
on, corporate responsibility.

## Elderly Accommodation Counsel

3rd Floor, 89 Albert Embankment,
London SE1 7TP
T: 020 7820 3755
Helpline: 020 7820 1343
F: 020 7820 3970
E: ros.lucas@eac.org.uk
www.housingcare.org
EAC provides information, advice and
support to older people and their families on

their housing and care options. It does this via
its Advice Line service and its website.
Employees: 12
Volunteers: 10

## Elfrida Society

34 Islington Park Street, London N1 1PX
T: 020 7359 7443
F: 020 7704 1358
E: elfrida@elfrida.com
www.elfrida.com
The Elfrida Society promotes and advances
the welfare, education, training and
advancement in life of people with learning
difficulties.
Employees: 60
Volunteers: 7

## Elimination of Leukaemia Fund

Burnhill House, 50 Burnhill Rd,
Beckenham BR3 3LA
T: 020 8249 6038
E: admin@elf-fund.org.uk
www.elf-fund.org.uk
Executive Director: Angela Smith-Morgan
ELF is a major funder of leukaemia research
at King's College Hospital, London, and is
also funding work at a number of other major
centres including the Institute of Child
Health, Great Ormond Street Hospital and
Belfast City Hospital. ELF favours patient-
centred work so that there is an immediate or
near future benefit to sufferers of leukaemia
and the related blood disorders.
Income: £260,000 (2015–16)

## Elizabeth Finn Care

1 Derry Street, London W8 5HY
T: 020 7396 6700
F: 020 7396 6739
E: info@elizabethfinn.org.uk
www.elizabethfinncare.org.uk
Chief Executive: Jonathan Welfare
Elizabeth Finn Care helps individual
British and Irish people who come from
a professional or similar background who
have fallen below the poverty line, and their
immediate families, by offering grants,
information and advice.
Employees: 750
Volunteers: 700
Regional offices: 8

## Elizabeth Foundation

Southwick Hill Road, Cosham,
Portsmouth PO6 3LL
T: 023 9237 2735
F: 023 9232 6155
E: sally.moger@elizabeth-foundation.org
www.elizabeth-foundation.org
Chief Executive: Sue Campbell

The Elizabeth Foundation facilitates early
diagnosis for babies and preschool children
with hearing loss, and provides
comprehensive educational and support
services to them and their families. By doing
so we enable these children to develop their
listening skills and natural speech and give
parents the confidence and knowledge
to make informed decisions on behalf of
their child.
Employees: 20
Volunteers: 8
Regional offices: 1
Income: £857,938 (2013–14)

## ella Forums CIC

17 Peters Lodge, 2 Stonegrove,
Edgware, Middlesex HA8 7TY
T: 020 7164 6206
E: brian@ella-forums.org
www.ella-forums.org
ella Forums is a leadership development
programme specifically designed to inspire
and develop the leaders of charities and social
enterprises to grow their organisations.
Employees: 5
Volunteers: 25
Regional offices: 1
Income: £140,000 (2014–15)

## Elmham Charitable Trust

224 Hills Road, Cambridge,
Cambridgeshire CB2 2QE
T: 01223 247661
E: elmham@gn.apc.org
Very small family charity with no capital. It
channels the income that trustees donate to
charities the trustees agree upon. They do not
spend any money on running the charity and
do not accept any applications for funding.

## Embrace

Selby Centre, Selby Road, London N17 8JL
T: 020 8801 9224
F: 020 8801 0244
E: post@embraceuk.org
www.embraceuk.org
Executive Director: Alem Gebrehiwot
Provides information, advice and guidance
for migrants, refugees and asylum seekers
(particularly but not exclusively of Ethiopian
origin) on education and training, welfare
benefits, housing, immigration, money and
debt, health-related issues with a particular
focus on HIV/AIDS and mental health, and
also conducts research as necessary.
Employees: 12
Volunteers: 45

## emerge poverty free

5 Skylines Village, Limeharbour,
London E14 9TS
T: 020 7839 3854
E: info@emergepovertyfree.org
emergepovertyfree.org
emerge poverty free is a small but highly
efficient international development agency.
We believe in a world where every person has
the opportunity to reach their full potential
poverty free.
Employees: 8
Volunteers: 2

## Emmaus UK

48 Kingston Street, Cambridge,
Cambridgeshire CB1 2NU
T: 01223 576103
F: 01223 576203
E: contact@emmaus.org.uk
www.emmaus.org.uk
Director: Tim Page
Emmaus Communities enable people to
move on from homelessness by providing
home and work in a supportive, family
environment. Residents work together,
collecting donated furniture and selling it in
community shops to support themselves and
reduce waste going to landfill. Any surplus
made by the Communities is used to benefit
other people in need. Emmaus UK is the
central support office for the Federation of
Emmaus Communities in the UK.
Employees: 26
Volunteers: 5
Regional offices: 26

## Empowering West Berkshire

Broadway House, 4–8 The Broadway,
Northbrook Street, Newbury,
Berkshire RG14 1BA
T: 01635 760501
E: info@empoweringwb.org.uk
www.empoweringwb.org.uk
Manager: Shelly Hambrecht
Providing support, information and training
for the voluntary community sector of West
Berkshire. Working in partnership with West
Berkshire's, statutory and community sector
to ensure quality service provision for West
Berkshire's communities.
Employees: 2
Regional offices: 1
Income: £70,000 (2014–15)

## Empty Homes Agency

Downstream Building, 1 London Bridge,
London SE1 9BG
T: 020 7828 6288
F: 020 7681 3214
E: info@emptyhomes.com
www.emptyhomes.com
Chief Executive: David Ireland
The Agency is an independent campaigning
charity that aims to raise awareness of the
potential of empty homes in England to meet
housing need and to devise and promote, with
others, sustainable solutions that will bring
empty homes back into use.
Employees: 6
Volunteers: 5

## End Child Poverty

94 White Lion Street, London N1 9PF
T: 020 7843 1913
F: 020 7843 1918
E: info@ecpc.org.uk
www.ecpc.org.uk
Employees: 5

## Endeavour Training Ltd

5–6 Sheepbridge Centre, Sheepbridge Lane,
Chesterfield, Derbyshire S41 9RX
T: 0870 770 3250
F: 0870 770 3254
E: info@endeavour.org.uk
www.endeavour.org.uk
Employees: 26
Volunteers: 250
Regional offices: 3

## Endometriosis SHE Trust (UK)

Unit 14, Moorland Way, Lincoln LN6 7JW
T: 01522 682300 (also fax)
E: shetrust@shetrust.org.uk
www.shetrust.org.uk
Chair: Diane Carlton
Aims include: the relief of persons suffering
from endometriosis by the provision of
advice and guidance including that of holistic
methods of treatment; the advancement
of the education of the public, including
the medical professions, by raising awareness
in all matters relating to endometriosis and
its treatment.
Volunteers: 12

## Endometriosis UK

Suites 1 and 2, 46 Manchester Street,
London W1U 7LS
T: 020 7222 2781
Helpline: 0808 808 2227
F: 020 7222 2786
E: admin@endometriosis-uk.org
www.endometriosis-uk.org
Chief Executive Officer: Helen North
1.5 million UK women live with endometriosis,
a chronic gynaecological condition that has a

huge impact on quality of life. Despite being
so common, awareness and understanding
is staggeringly low. Endometriosis UK
is the lead charity offering vital support
and information for those living with
endometriosis, working hard to reduce
the inherent isolation of this condition.
Employees: 5
Volunteers: 50
Regional offices: 30 (local support groups)

## Enfield Carers Centre

Britannia House, 137–143 Baker Street,
Enfield, Middx EN1 3JL
T: 020 8366 3677
E: info@enfieldcarers.org
enfieldcarers.org
Chief Executive: Pamela Burke
Enfield Carers Centre is a local charity
offering support and advice for all unpaid
carers living in Enfield. A carer is someone
of any age who provides unpaid support to a
partner, relative or friend with a short- or
long-term illness, a disability, a substance-
misuse problem, a life-limiting illness or
terminal diagnosis. We support the following
carers: older carers; working carers; former
carers; parent carers; bereaved carers; young
adult carers (16–25 years); BME carers.
Employees: 14
Volunteers: 10
Income: £641,406 (2014–15)

## Enfield Voluntary Action (EVA)

Community House, 311 Fore Street,
London N9 0PZ
T: 020 8373 6268
F: 020 8373 6267
E: evanews@enfieldva.org.uk
www.enfieldva.org.uk
Chief Executive: Paula Jeffery
EVA provides services to local voluntary
and community organisations in the London
Borough of Enfield, including community
accountancy, development and funding
advice, news and information services and
volunteer centre Enfield.
Employees: 8
Volunteers: 4

## Engineers Against Poverty

2nd Floor, Weston House,
246 High Holborn, London  WC1V 7EX
T: 020 3206 0488
F: 020 3206 0401
E: p.matthews@engineersagainstpoverty.org
www.engineersagainstpoverty.org
**Executive Director: Petter Matthews**
Engineers Against Poverty works with
industry, government and civil society to fight
poverty and promote sustainable development.
**Employees: 4**
**Volunteers: 2**

## English Federation of Disability Sport

SportPark, Loughborough University,
3 Oakwood Drive, Loughborough,
Leicestershire LE11 3QF
T: 01509 227750
F: 01509 227777
E: federation@efds.co.uk
www.efds.co.uk
**Chief Executive: Barry Horne**
The English Federation of Disability Sport
(EFDS) was established in September 1998
as the national body and charity dedicated to
disabled people in sport throughout England.
We work closely with a number of key
partners to improve and increase the
opportunities offered, ensuring disabled
people have a memorable experience of sport
and physical activity. Our partners include
the National Disability Sports Organisations
(NDSOs) recognised by Sport England,
who form part of our membership.
**Employees: 19**
**Volunteers: 200**
**Regional offices: 1**

## Enham Trust

Enham Place, Enham Alamein, Andover,
Hampshire SP11 6JS
T: 01264 345850
E: info@enham.org.uk
www.enhamtrust.org.uk
**Chief Executive: Peta Wilkinson**
Enham delivers a wide range of essential
services, from housing and employment to
personal development and care, that provide
choices and empower people to make their
own decisions about their lives. Enham also
operates a number of commercial enterprises
that provide direct employment opportunities
for disabled people, improve access to
essential products and services and generate

income to support Enham's charitable
objectives.
**Employees: 280**
**Volunteers: 90**
**Regional offices: 8**

## Enterprising Futures

Kingsley, The Brampton,
Newcastle under Lyme ST5 0QW
T: 01782 854803
E: wnixon@enterprisingfutures.org.uk
www.pmtraining.org.uk
**CEO: Will Nixon**
**Employees: 7**

## Enviromental Vision

47–49 Pitfield Street, London N1 6DA
T: 020 7096 1714
E: vision@envision.org.uk
www.envsion.org.uk
**CEO: Jennie Butterworth**
Envision's programme supports 16–19 year
olds from over 130 schools and colleges in
Birmingham, Bristol and London. Envision
programmes help young people to design
their own local community projects tackling
issues of their own choice. We seek to provide
individuals with a powerful and rewarding
experience of making a positive difference so
they will be both willing and able to continue
acting as effective role models for their
communities building powerful legacies
of their own.
**Employees: 25**
**Volunteers: 20**
**Regional offices: 3**
**Income: £650,000 (2014–15)**

## Environment Africa Trust

110 Colleys Lane, Nantwich,
Cheshire CW5 6NT
T: 01270 662692 (also fax)
E: mike.chandler@environmentafricatrust.
org.uk
www.environmentafricatrust.org.uk
**Executive Director: Mike Chandler**
Environment Africa Trust supports
organisations and projects within Sub-
Saharan Africa that encourage sound
environmental management and biodiversity
conservation through a strong community
development focus to achieve sustainable
livelihoods. Our partner Mpingo Conservation
and Development Initiative in Tanzania is
developing a fair trade in African Blackwood
that is being promoted by Sound and Fair.
EAT welcomes approaches from projects
that have the above vision and focus in

Sub-Saharan Africa that are seeking a
UK partner.
**Volunteers: 6**

## Environmental Investigation Agency Trust

62–63 Upper Street, London N1 0NY
T: 020 7354 7960
E: ukinfo@eia-international.org
www.eia-international.org
**Executive Director: Mary Rice**
The Environmental Investigation Agency
(EIA) is an independent campaigning
organisation committed to bringing about
change that protects the natural world from
environmental crime and abuse. Our vision is
a future where humanity respects, protects
and celebrates the natural world for the
benefit of all.
**Employees: 26**
**Volunteers: 5**

## Environmental Law Foundation

Suite 309, 16–16a Baldwins Gardens,
London EC1N 7RJ
T: 020 7404 1030
E: info@elflaw.org
www.elflaw.org
ELF helps community groups and individuals
gain access to the law in order to protect
their environment.

## Environmental Protection

44 Grand Parade, Brighton BN2 9QA
T: 01273 878777
E: secretariat@environmental-protection.
org.uk
www.environmental-protection.org.uk
Aims to secure environmental improvement
by promoting clean air through the reduction
of air pollution, noise and other contaminants,
while having regard for other aspects of
the environment.

## Epic Arts

Bradbury Studios, 138 Kingsland Road,
London E2 8DY
T: 020 7613 6440 (also fax)
E: info@epicarts.org.uk
www.epicarts.org.uk
**CEO: Rachel Duncombe-Anderson**
The aim is to create arts opportunities for
people who previously lacked access,
especially those who are disadvantaged
because of disability, poverty or age.
**Employees: 6**
**Volunteers: 4**
**Regional offices: 1**

## Epilepsy Action

New Anstey House, Gate Way Drive,
Yeadon, Leeds  LS19 7XY
T: 0113 210 8800
Helpline: 0808 800 5050
F: 0113 391 0300
E: epilepsy@epilepsy.org.uk
www.epilepsy.org.uk
Chief Executive: Philip Lee
Aims: to increase public awareness and
understanding of epilepsy; to provide
information and advice; to promote research
into the condition; to raise funds for epilepsy;
to campaign for change.

## Epilepsy Research UK

PO Box 3004, London  W4 4XT
T: 020 8747 5024
E: info@eruk.org.uk
www.epilepsyresearch.org.uk
Chairman: Dr Graeme Sills
Epilepsy Research UK funds research into
the causes, treatment and prevention of
epilepsy, with the aim of identifying new
means to control the condition and improve
the quality of life of those with epilepsy.
Epilepsy Research UK is the only national
charity exclusively dedicated to funding
epilepsy research.
Employees: 6

## Epilepsy Society

Chalfont Centre, Chalfont St Peter,
Gerrards Cross, Buckinghamshire  SL9 0RJ
T: 01494 601300
Helpline: 01494 601400
E: judy.consden@epilepsysociety.org.uk
www.epilepsysociety.org.uk
Chief Executive: Angela Geer
Epilepsy Society's mission is to enhance the
quality of life of people affected by epilepsy
by promoting research, education and public
awareness and by delivering specialist medical
care and support services.

## Equality and Diversity Forum

Tavis House, 1–6 Tavistock Square,
London WC1H 9NA
T: 020 3033 1454
E: info@edf.org.uk
www.edf.org.uk
CEO: Ali Harris
The Equality and Diversity Forum (EDF) is
the network of national NGOs working on
equality and human rights. Our vision is of a
society: in which everyone can fulfill their
potential and make a distinctive contribution;
where diversity is celebrated, people can
express their identities free from the threat of
violence and everyone is treated with dignity
and respect; where your chance to flourish is
not limited by who you are or where you
come from. EDF uses its strength as a
network of committed and influential
organisations to work for a society in which
everyone can fulfill their potential, everyone
is treated with respect regardless of
background or circumstances and diversity
is celebrated.
Employees: 5
Volunteers: 1
Income: £279,285 (2014–15)

## Equity Trust Fund

222 Africa House, 64 Kingsway,
London  WC2B 6BD
T: 020 7404 6041
E: kaethe@equitycharitabletrust.org.uk
www.equitytrustfund.org.uk
Aims to assist professional performers in
need, in particular past and present members
of British Actors Equity.

## ERIC (Education and Resources for Improving Childhood Continence)

36 Old School House, Britannia Road,
Kingswood, Bristol BS15 8DB
T: 0117 960 3060
Helpline: 0845 370 8008
F: 0117 960 0401
E: info@eric.org.uk
www.eric.org.uk
Interim CEO: David Derbyshire
ERIC provides information and support on
bedwetting, daytime wetting, soiling and
constipation, and potty training. Our
telephone helpline is available Mondays and
Wednesdays from 9:30 to 4:30. Leaflets
and further information to download and a
moderated message board are available on
the ERIC website. Useful and practical
resources are available to purchase from
www.ericshop.org.uk.
Employees: 12
Volunteers: 2
Regional offices: 1
Income: £650,000 (2013–14)

## Eritrean Relief Association (UK)

Robin House, 2a Iverson Road,
London  NW6 2HE
T: 020 7328 7888
Helpline: 07957 113307
E: seble@era-uk.org
www.era-uk.org
Chairman: Seble Ephrem
The Eritrean Relief Association (UK) is
set up to provide relief, rehabilitation and
development support and assistance to
humans and their livestock affected by
drought, war and displacement in Eritrea.
ERA-UK also provides capacity-building
advice, information and guidance to people
from Eritrea living in the UK.
Volunteers: 10
Regional offices: 1

## Ernest Foundation

45 Cardiff House, Peckham Park Road,
London  SE15 6TT
T: 020 7635 9607
E: theernestfoundation@hotmail.com
www.theernestfoundation.org
Coordinator: Ernest Nkrumah
Carries out activities and projects that will
bring support and relief to people living
with HIV/AIDS and related diseases among
the Ghanaian and other West African
communities in England and Wales.
Working with children and young people.

## Esmee Fairbairn Foundation

Kings Place, 90 York Way, London  N1 9AG
T: 020 7812 3700
F: 020 7812 3701
E: info@esmeefairbairn.org.uk
www.esmeefairbairn.org.uk
Chief Executive: Caroline Mason
The Esmee Fairbairn Foundation aims to
improve the quality of life throughout the
UK by funding the charitable activities of
organisations that have the ideas and ability to
achieve change for the better. We take pride
in supporting work that might otherwise be
considered difficult to fund. Our primary
interests are in the arts, children and young
people, environment, social change and food.
Employees: 28

## Ethical Property Foundation

Development House, London  EC2A 4LT
T: 020 7065 0760
F: 020 7065 0768
E: mail@ethicalproperty.org.uk
www.ethicalproperty.org.uk
The Ethical Property Foundation is a charity
committed to empowering charities and
community groups to make the most of their
property. The Foundation is also committed
to improving the environmental and social
performance of the commercial property
sector.
Employees: 5
Regional offices: 1

## Ethical Trading Initiative

8 Coldbath Square, London EC1R 5HL
Helpline: 020 7841 5180
F: 020 7831 7852
E: eti@eti.org.uk
www.ethicaltrade.org
Director: Dan Rees
We are an alliance of global brands and retailers, trade unions, campaigning organisations and charities that work together to improve the lives of workers in global supply chains. We provide practical tools and guidance for companies to help them implement codes of labour practice in their supply chains, and are widely recognised as a global leader in this area.
Employees: 15

## Ethiopian Community In Britian

2a Lithos Road, London NW3 6EF
T: 020 7794 4265
F: 020 7794 4116
E: postmaster@ethiopiancommunity.co.uk
www.ethiopiancommunity.co.uk
Co-Coordinator: Eyoel F Mengesha
Provides information, advice, advocacy and referral services and training for Ethiopians and members of other communities, as well as outreach, sports and leisure activities. It also runs ESOL and IT training courses for unemployed refugees and asylum seekers, irrespective of their country of origin.
Volunteers: 1

## Europe Trust

PO Box MAR005, Markfield,
Leicestershire LE67 9RY
T: 01530 245919
E: info@europetrust.eu.com
europetrust.eu.com
Provides support to community-based organisations.
Employees: 3

## European Atlantic Movement

Start Farm, Harlow Road, Ongar,
Essex CM5 0DT
T: 01277 890282
E: info@european-atlantic.org.uk
www.european-atlantic.org.uk
President: Lord Watson of Richmond
TEAM is an independent educational foundation that aims to promote understanding and discussion of European and world affairs.
Volunteers: 40

## European League of Stuttering Associations

31 Grosvenor Road, Jesmond,
Newcastle upon Tyne NE2 2RL
T: 0191 281 8003
E: elsa.europe@ymail.com
www.elsa.info
Chair: Edwin Farr
Coordinates, links together and furthers the cooperation of Europe's national stuttering associations.
Volunteers: 10
Regional offices: 2

## Eva Women's Aid

E: julie@eva.org.uk

## Evangelical Alliance

176 Copenhagen Street, London N1 0ST
T: 020 7520 3830
E: info@eauk.org
www.eauk.org
General Director: Steve Clifford
A Christian charity founded in 1846 to promote unity and truth, and represent evangelical concerns to the wider world of the church, state and society.

## Evelyn 190 Centre

Evelyn 190 Centre, 190 Evelyn Street,
Deptford, London SE8 5DB
T: 020 8691 7180
F: 020 8692 9305
E: admin@evelyn190centre.org.uk
Centre Manager : Elona Elliott
To provide advice services (housing, welfare rights, employment and debt) to the residents of the Borough of Lewisham.
Employees: 6
Volunteers: 2
Income: £230,000 (2013–14)

## EveryChild

4 Bath Place, Rivington Street,
London EC2A 3DR
T: 020 7749 2468
F: 020 7729 8339
E: gen@everychild.org.uk
www.everychild.org.uk
EveryChild works with some of the world's most vulnerable and marginalised children to enable them to grow up free from disease, poverty and exploitation. We work with children, communities and governments across 18 countries to ensure that every child

has the right to an education, to healthcare and to grow up in a loving family environment.
Employees: 50
Volunteers: 15
Regional offices: 1

## Evidence For Development

E: celiapetty@gmail.com

## Examination Officers' Association (EOA)

Eilean Donan, Russell Road, Tokers Green,
Near Reading, Oxfordshire RG4 9EJ
Helpline: 0118 946 2588
E: andrew.harland@examofficers.org.uk
www.examofficers.org.uk
CEO: Andrew Harland
The EOA is an independent, not-for-profit professional body and registered charity whose key role is to support the professional development of all exam office personnel working in centres throughout the UK and abroad, so they can support an exam system that will benefit all learners.
Employees: 2
Volunteers: 15
Regional offices: 2
Income: £150,000 (2015–16)

## Explore

The EWR Centre, Cloudesley Street,
London N1 0HU
T: 020 7278 0699
F: 020 7278 0589
E: info@theexploreexperience.co.uk
www.theexploreexperience.co.uk
Explore is a registered educational charity that enables young people in schools, colleges and prisons to explore the experience of couples and, through this study, to appreciate lasting relationship skills, emotional literacy, family life and marriage.

## EXTEND Exercise Training Ltd

2 Place Farm, Wheathampstead,
Hertfordshire AL4 8SB
T: 01582 832760 (also fax)
E: admin@extend.org.uk
www.extend.org.uk
CEO: Cynthia Robinson
EXTEND Exercise delivers accredited training courses and CPD to fitness teachers and provides Exercise to Music and Chair Based Exercise classes to 25,000 older adults and disabled people nationwide. EXTEND classes are delivered by qualified, insured and experienced instructors, working in the community or in care facilities. EXTEND Exercise ensures that all classes are tailored to meet the needs of every participant, delivering increased mobility,

improved strength, coordination and balance and countering loneliness and isolation.

**Employees: 6**
**Volunteers: 5**

## Eye on the Wild

Unit 10, The Glasshouse,
49a Goldhawk Road, London W12 8QP
T: 020 8204 8466
E: charity@foxtrot.org.uk
www.eyeonthewild.org
Chair: Lord Brian Hamilton

A small environmental charity that focuses on damage or influences caused by tourism. It identifies causes and concerns in flora, fauna, environment and communities globally directly or indirectly influenced by tourism and travel. Extensive operations and projects globally.

**Volunteers: 4**

## Fable Charity

Lower Ground Floor, 305 Glossop Road, Sheffield, South Yorkshire S10 2HL
T: 0114 275 5335
Helpline: 0800 521629
F: 0114 275 6444
E: sarah-fable@btconnect.com
www.fable.org.uk
Founder: Sandra Howard

For A Better Life with Epilepsy or FABLE is a national charity that helps people with epilepsy, or issues or associated with epilepsy, to increase their quality of life. It operates a free phone advice line and drop-in advice and information centre in Sheffield, along with a national patient support network.

**Employees: 7**
**Volunteers: 10**
**Regional offices: 1**

## Fair Play for Children Association/ Charitable Trust

32 Longford Road, Bognor Regis, West Sussex PO21 1AG
T: 0845 330 7635
E: fairplay@arunet.co.uk
www.fairplayforchildren.org
National Secretary: Jan Cosgrove

Campaigns for children's right to play, including more, better and safer facilities and services for all children. Provision of information, news and services such as CRB Enhanced Disclosures.

**Employees: 3**
**Volunteers: 12**

## Fair Trials International

Temple Chambers, 3/7 Temple Avenue, London EC4Y 0HP
T: 020 7822 2370
F: 020 7822 2371
E: office@fairtrials.net
www.fairtrials.net
Chief Executive Officer: Jago Russell

Works for fair trials according to international standards of justice and defends the rights of those facing charges in a country other than their own.

**Employees: 9**
**Volunteers: 5**

## Fairtrade Foundation

3rd Floor, Ibex House, 42–47 Minories, London EC3N 1DY
T: 020 7405 5942
F: 020 7977 0101
E: mail@fairtrade.org.uk
www.fairtrade.org.uk
Chief Executive: Mike Gidney

Fairtrade is about better prices, decent working conditions and fair terms of trade for farmers and workers. We support over 1.65 million farmers and workers in 1,226 producer organisations across the Fairtrade system. But there are many more still urgently in need of a fair deal. As a certification scheme, our Fairtrade Standards provide one of our primary and also most visible tools for empowering small farmer and worker organisations. But beyond the standards and certification, the Fairtrade system also provides direct and indirect support to producers and their organisations to deepen social and environmental sustainability.

**Employees: 125**
**Volunteers: 20**
**Income: £11,437,000 (2015–16)**

## Faith Based Regeneration Network UK

12–20 Baron Street, London N1 9LL
T: 020 7713 8193
E: doreenf@fbrn.org.uk
www.fbrn.org.uk
Executive Director: Doreen Finneron

FbRN UK is the leading national multi-faith network for community development, regeneration and social action. It encourages the active engagement of faith groups in civil society by linking practitioners across the different faith traditions for mutual learning, and provides an interface between policy makers and communities. It is managed by a trustee body drawn from nine faith traditions: Baha'i, Buddhist, Christian, Hindu, Jain, Jewish, Muslim, Sikh and Zoroastrian.

**Employees: 5**

## Faith in Families

7 Colwick Road, West Bridgford, Nottingham NG2 5AF
T: 0115 955 8811
F: 0115 955 8822
E: enquiries@faithinfamilies.org
www.faithinfamilies.org
Chief Executive Officer: Sumerjit Ram

Faith in Families is a registered charity and voluntary adoption agency. The charity is based in Nottingham and works throughout the East Midlands. Faith in Families' vision is to provide nurturing, innovative, high-quality services for children and families. We believe that the services we provide will enable all children to develop into confident, secure, caring individuals, with the capacity to reach their full potential in life.

**Employees: 35**
**Volunteers: 100**
**Regional offices: 1**

## Families for Children

Southgate Court, Buckfast, Devon TQ11 0EE
T: 01364 645480
F: 01364 645499
E: marketing@familiesforchildren.org.uk
www.familiesforchildren.org.uk
CEO: Caroline Davis OBE

Families for Children is a vibrant adoption agency based in the south west. We place vulnerable children from all over country with adoptive families in Devon, Dorset and Cornwall. We are a specialist adoption agency providing advice and support for those who are considering adoption and also offer our 'forever' policy of support. This means that we can offer adoption support to the child and new family for as long as they need us.

**Employees: 40**
**Regional offices: 2**

## Families Need Fathers

134 Curtain Road, London EC2A 3AR
T: 0300 030 0110
Helpline: 0300 030 0363
F: 020 7739 3410
E: admin@fnf.org.uk
www.fnf.org.uk
Chairman of Trustees: Jerry Karlin
FNF is a charity chiefly concerned with the problems of maintaining a child's relationship with both parents and extended family during and after family breakdown. FNF provides emotional and practical support via their helpline, 50 UK branches, comprehensive website and other resources for members that will help them to have a meaningful relationship with their children. Helpline available: 9am–10pm Monday–Friday and 10am–3pm at weekends: 0300 0300 363.
Employees: 4
Volunteers: 60–100

## Family Action

501–505 Kingsland Road, London E8 4AU
T: 020 7254 6251
F: 020 7249 5443
E: info@family-action.org.uk
www.family-action.org.uk
Chief Executive: Helen Dent
Assists families and individuals to overcome the effects of poverty and disadvantage in tangible ways, by providing services offering practical, emotional and financial support.
Employees: 750
Volunteers: 500
Regional offices: 8

## Family and Childcare Trust

2nd Floor, The Bridge,
81 Southwark Bridge Road,
London SE1 0NQ
T: 020 7940 7510
E: info@familyandchildcaretrust.org
www.familyandchildcaretrust.org
Chief Executive: Julia Margo
The Family and Childcare Trust works to make the UK a better place for families. Our vision is of a society where government, business and communities do all they can to support every family to thrive. Through our research, campaigning and practical support we are creating a more family friendly UK.
Employees: 25

## Family Education Trust (Family and Youth Concern)

The Atrium, 31 Church Road, Ashford,
Middlesex TW15 2UD
T: 01784 242340
F: 01784 252343
E: info@familyeducationtrust.org.uk
www.familyeducationtrust.org.uk
Director: Norman Wells
An independent educational charity conducting and promoting research into the causes and consequences of family breakdown. Through its publications, media profile and responses to government consultations and inquiries, the Trust seeks to promote the welfare of children and families in line with the research evidence.

## Family Holiday Association

16 Mortimer Street, London W1T 3JL
T: 020 7436 3304
E: info@fhaonline.org.uk
www.fhaonline.org.uk
Director: John McDonald
Aims to increase access to holidays for families on a low income.
Employees: 10
Volunteers: 100

## Family Links

Units 2 and 3 Fenchurch Court,
Bobby Fryer Close, Cowley, Oxford,
Oxfordshire OX4 6ZN
T: 01865 401800
F: 01865 401820
E: info@familylinks.org.uk
www.familylinks.org.uk
Chief Executive: Nick Haisman-Smith
Family Links is a national charity dedicated to empowering children, parents, families and schools to be emotionally healthy. Our vision is a world where adults and children live flourishing lives, fulfil their potential and make a positive contribution to their community. We deliver innovative, high-quality training in the Nurturing Programme to health and social care services, third-sector organisations, schools and universities.
Employees: 28
Volunteers: 9
Regional offices: 1

## Family Lives

15–17 The Broadway, Hatfield,
Hertfordshire AL9 5HZ
Helpline: 0808 800 2222
E: rachelt@familylives.org.uk
www.familylives.org.uk
Chief Executive: Jeremy Todd

Family Lives is a national charity that has over 40 years' experience of supporting families. We provide advice and support to thousands of families every year through our online advice, helpline and community services.
Employees: 134
Volunteers: 260
Regional offices: 6
Income: £3,465,000 (2015–16)

## Family Matters Institute

Moggerhanger Park, Park Road,
Moggerhanger, Bedfordshire MK44 3RW
T: 01767 641002 (also fax)
E: family@familymatters.org.uk
www.familymatters.org.uk
Family Matters Institute is an educational charity motivated by the Christian faith to provide affordable training in order to mobilise church and community groups to support the family in marriage and couple relationships, parenting and money issues. We also carry out research in these areas.
Employees: 10
Volunteers: 4
Regional offices: 1

## Family Rights Group

The Print House, 18 Ashwin Street,
London E8 3DL
T: 020 7923 2628
F: 020 7923 2683
E: office@frg.org.uk
www.frg.org.uk
Supports and advises families involved with social services; promotes the involvement of children, parents and families in the decision-making process, so that the best decisions are made; develops and promotes policies and practices that help secure the best possible futures for children and families.
Employees: 16

## Farm Africa

9th Floor, Bastion House, 140 London Wall,
London EC2Y 5DN
T: 020 7430 0440
F: 020 7430 0460
E: farmafrica@farmafrica.org.uk
www.farmafrica.org
Chief Executive: Nigel Harris
Farm Africa reduces poverty permanently by unleashing African farmers' abilities to grow their incomes and manage their natural resources sustainably. We work with different types of farmers (pastoralists, agro-pastoralists, smallholders and forest dwellers) in a range of regions in eastern Africa. Their specific situations vary but most are

facing increasing economic, health and environmental vulnerability.

**Employees: 265**
**Volunteers: 2**
**Regional offices: 24**

## Farm Animal Welfare Network

Farm Animal Welfare Trust,
Northfield Farmhouse, Wytham,
Oxford OX2 8QJ
T: 01865 244315
E: fawcsecretariat@defra.gsi.gov.uk
www.farmanimalwelfaretrust.org.uk
Campaigns for the worldwide abolition of the battery cage system for laying hens, and opposes other intensive and cruel systems for all farmed animals.

## Farms for City Children

Exeter Community Centre,
17 St David's Hill, Exeter, Devon EX4 3RG
T: 01392 276381
E: admin@farmsforcitychildren.org
www.farmsforcitychildren.org
Chief Executive: Dr Tessa Stone
Aims to enrich the lives and develop the potential of children from disadvantaged urban areas by providing a residential week on a working farm, where groups of school children participate purposefully in the life of the farm.

**Employees: 65**
**Regional offices: 4**

## FAS Aware UK

c/o 4 Wakefield Crescent, Standish, Wigan,
Lancashire WN6 0AU
T: 01257 432423
E: fasawareuk@blueyonder.co.uk
www.fasaware.co.uk
Full-time Volunteer Coordinator:
Gloria Armistead MBE
To provide information, training and accredited courses. Support to improve the health and social wellbeing of all those affected by foetal alcohol spectrum disorders. To develop and support autonomous support groups.

**Volunteers: 20**

## FATIMA Women's Network

Innovation Centre, Oxford Street, Leicester,
Leicestershire LE1 5XY
T: 0845 331 2373
F: 0870 005 2608
E: parvin@fatima-network.com
www.fatima-network.com
Chief Executive: Parvin Ali
FATIMA (Forum for Advocacy, Training and Information in a Multicultural Arena) Women's Network is a BME-led socially responsible enterprise supporting the social and economic empowerment of women and

their families, particularly those from diverse and disadvantaged communities, through personal development, advocacy, research, training, business support and cross-community networking. As a national infrastructure organisation we seek to build the resilience and connectivity of women's groups.

**Employees: 6**
**Volunteers: 15**

## Fawcett Society

The Print Rooms, Unit 204,
168–180 Union Street, London SE1 0LH
T: 020 3598 6154
E: info@fawcettsociety.org.uk
www.fawcettsociety.org.uk
Chief Executive: Sam Smethers
Fawcett is the UK's leading campaigning organisation for women's equality and rights – at home, at work and in public life. We are the UK's largest independent membership organisation with a dedicated focus on advancing women's equality and rights in modern Britain. We effect change by combining direct lobbying within the political system with campaigns that increase and demonstrate public support for action.

**Employees: 9**
**Volunteers: 3**

## Federal Trust for Education and Research

84 Moorgate, London EC2M 6SQ
T: 020 7320 1677
E: info@fedtrust.co.uk
www.fedtrust.co.uk
Director: Brendan Donnelly
Promotes research and education about federal solutions to national, European and global problems.

**Employees: 2**

## Federation for Community Development Learning

3rd Floor, The Circle, 33 Rockinghan Lane,
Sheffield, South Yorkshire S1 4FW
T: 0114 253 6770
F: 0114 253 6771
E: info@fcdl.org.uk
www.fcdl.org.uk
Head of Agency: Janice Marks
FCDL welcomes the membership of everyone who is interested in or who practises community development, whether community activists or voluntary or paid workers. This includes generic CD practitioners or practitioners from other occupations (eg health, housing, environment) who are interested in using

a CD approach to engage with and work effectively with communities. We support a network of individuals, groups and organisations who share information and good training practice and provide opportunities for CD learning.

**Employees: 8**

## Federation of British Artists

17 Carlton House Terrace,
London SW1Y 5BD
T: 020 7930 6844
E: info@mallgalleries.com
www.mallgalleries.org.uk
Director: Lewis McNaught
Mall Galleries is one of central London's largest, friendliest and most accessible exhibition spaces. Our aim is to promote, inspire and educate audiences about the contemporary visual arts. Many of our exhibitions focus on contemporary representational art, each of them offering paintings, sculpture, prints or drawings for sale at affordable prices.

**Employees: 15**
**Volunteers: 600**

## Federation of City Farms and Community Gardens

The Greenhouse, Hereford Street,
Bedminster, Bristol, Avon BS3 4NA
T: 0117 923 1800
E: admin@farmgarden.org.uk
www.farmgarden.org.uk
Director: Charlie Powell
Supports, represents and promotes community-managed farms and gardens in the UK.

**Employees: 26**
**Volunteers: 20**
**Regional offices: 6**
**Income: £900,000 (2015–16)**

## Federation of English Karate Organisations (international)

234 West Park Drive West, Roundhay,
Leeds, West Yorkshire LS8 2BD
T: 0113 269 0383
E: jimreece@tradka.org.uk
www.feko.co.uk
Chair: Noel Mantock
FEKO is a Federation of Karate Associations offering its members support, guidance and a range of services to enable them to manage their own organisations.

## Federation of Merchant Mariners

16 Glebe Road, Brampton, Huntingdon,
Cambridgeshire PE28 4PH
T: 01480 412958
E: info@merchant-mariners.co.uk
www.merchant-mariners.co.uk
FMM brings together many associations/
organisations connected to the Merchant
Navy, filling a gap that had existed in the
maritime scene for over 60 years. Its aim is to
gain recognition for the role that merchant
seafarers have played in the defence and
development of our nation.

## Federation of Private Residents Associations Ltd

PO Box 10271, Epping, Essex CM16 9DB
T: 0871 200 3324
E: info@fpra.org.uk
www.fpra.org.uk
Chairman: Bob Smytherman
FPRA is a not-for-profit advice, support and
lobbying organisation for private residential
leaseholders and residents.
Volunteers: 20

## Fellowship of Depressives Anonymous

Self Help Nottingham, Ormiston House,
32–36 Pelham Street,
Nottingham NG1 2EG
T: 0870 774 4319
E: fdainfo@hotmail.com
www.depressionanon.co.uk
Supports and encourages people suffering
from, or who have suffered from, depression
and those who care about them, on a self-
help/mutual support basis.

## Fellowship of Postgraduate Medicine

12 Chandos Street, Cavendish Square,
London W1G 9DR
T: 020 7636 6334
F: 020 7436 2535
E: admin@fpm-uk.org
www.fpm-uk.org
President: Donald Singer
The Fellowship achieves its objectives of
development of postgraduate educational
programmes in all branches of medicine
through the publication of its international
journal, the Postgraduate Medical Journal,
and by hosting a range of seminars
and conferences.
Employees: 1

## Fellowship of Reconciliation

E: emma@for.org.uk

## Fellowship of the School of Economic Science

11 Mandeville Place, London W1U 3AJ
T: 020 7034 4000
F: 020 7034 4001
E: secretary@fses.org
www.schooleconomicscience.org
Promotes the study of natural laws governing
the relations between men in society and the
study of the laws, customs and practices by
which communities are governed.
Employees: 15

## Female Prisoners Welfare Project and Hibiscus

18 Borough High Street, London SE1 9QG
T: 020 7357 6543
E: fpwphibiscus@aol.com
Provides welfare advice and support for
women in prison, especially those
disadvantaged by the criminal justice system
such as foreign nationals and those from
ethnic minorities.

## FIA Foundation for the Automobile and Society

60 Trafalgar Square, London WC2N 5DS
T: 020 7930 3882
F: 020 7930 3883
E: j.pearce@fiafoundation.org
www.fiafoundation.org
Director General: David Ward
The Foundation was established in the
UK by the Federation Internationale de
l'Automobile (FIA), the non-profit federation
of motoring organisations and the governing
body of world motor sport. The foundation
manages and supports an international
programme of activities promoting road
safety, environmental protection and
sustainable mobility, as well as funding
specialist motor sport safety research.
Employees: 13

## Field Lane Foundation

16 Vine Hill, London EC1R 5EA
T: 020 7837 0412
E: info@fieldlane.org.uk
www.fieldlane.org.uk
Field Lane is a Christian charity that is
committed to providing innovative
accommodation and day-centre support
services for families who are homeless,
older people and people with disabilities.

## Fieldfare Trust Ltd

Volunteer House, 69 Crossgate,
Cupar KY15 5AS
T: 01334 657708
F: 0844 443 1139
E: info@fieldfare.org.uk
www.fieldfare.org.uk
Chief Executive: Ian Newman
The Fieldfare Trust works with, not for,
people with disabilities to promote disabled
access and provide environmental education
opportunities for all.
Employees: 5
Regional offices: 3

## Fields In Trust

2nd Floor, 15 Crinan Street,
London N1 9SQ
T: 020 7427 2110
E: helen.griffiths@fieldsintrust.org
www.fieldsintrust.org
Chief Executive: Helen Griffiths
Fields in Trust (FIT) is the only independent
UK-wide organisation dedicated to
protecting and improving outdoor sports and
play spaces and facilities. We want to make
sure that everyone – young and old alike, and
wherever they live – has somewhere nearby
to go for healthy outdoor activities. Through
our work we improve the wellbeing of millions
of people nationwide.
Employees: 18
Regional offices: 3

## Filipino International Emergency Services Training

12 Montgomery Crescent, Bolbeck Park,
Milton Keynes MK15 8PR
T: 01908 233120
E: dalejohno@aol.com
www.fiestauk.homestead.com/homepage.
html
Chair: John Dale
Provides support for the emergency services
of the Philippines in the form of equipment,
training and other assistance. The website also
lists all the countries of the world and their
emergency telephone numbers.

## Find a Future

157–197 Buckingham Palace Rd,
London SW1W 9SZ
T: 0800 612 0742
F: 020 7543 7489
E: enquiries@worldskillsuk.org
www.findafuture.org.uk
UK Skills is a charity that promotes
excellence in vocational skills and training
through competitions and major awards. UK
Skills recognises that investing in high-quality
training and vocational education leads to a

well-equipped workforce that is the key to the success of the UK economy.
Employees: 10

## Finn-Guild

1a Mornington Court, Mornington Crescent, London NW1 7RD
T: 020 7387 3508
F: 020 7529 8750
E: mail@finn-guild.org
www.finn-guild.org
Works for the advancement of Finnish culture and language in the UK, educating about Finland, supporting the work of the Finnish Church in London. Supports the wellbeing and relief of poverty among the Finnish-British community.
Employees: 8
Volunteers: 150

## Fire Fighters Charity

Level 6, Belvedere, Basing View, Basingstoke RG21 4HG
T: 01256 366568
F: 01256 366599
E: vfox@firefighterscharity.org.uk
www.firefighterscharity.org.uk
Employees: 136

## First Step Trust

32–34 Hare Street, Woolwich, London SE18 6LZ
T: 020 8855 7386 (also fax)
E: comms@firststeptrust.org.uk
www.fst.org.uk
FST offers people with enduring mental health problems, learning disabilities and other disadvantages the chance to work, experiencing the challenges of working in a small business, trading with the local community. This enables them to overcome their problems and become less dependent on health and social care services. Many go on to make the transition to paid employment.

## fit4funding

Lightwaves, Lower York Street, Wakefield, West Yorkshire WF1 3LJ
T: 01924 239063
E: info@fit4funding.org.uk
www.fit4funding.org.uk
fit4funding is nationally recognised as a quality provider of training (face to face and online) on all aspects of fundraising and commissioning for voluntary and community organisations, funders and funding advisers. Much of our training is OCN accredited. We can offer bespoke training for groups, infrastructure organisations or consortia. We provide extensive information through our website and the fit4funding e-newsletter

and offer consultancy support on strategic planning and fundraising.
Employees: 5
Regional offices: 1
Income: £172,309 (2013–14)

## FitzRoy

FitzRoy House, 8 Hylton Road, Petersfield, Hampshire GU32 3JY
T: 01730 711111
Helpline: 0808 168 4662
F: 01730 710566
E: info@fitzroy.org
www.fitzroy.org
Chief Executive: Anna Galliford
FitzRoy transforms the lives of people with disabilities and autism, helping them live more independently at home and in the community. We are a national charity that provides a mix of residential and community services and support including supported volunteering.
Employees: 800
Volunteers: 200
Regional offices: 3

## FLACK Cambridge

City Life House, Sturton Street, Cambridge CB1 2QF
T: 01223 366532
E: info@flackcambridge.org.uk
flackcambridge.org.uk
Chairman of the Board of Trustees: Quentin Millington
FLACK supports adults in the Cambridge area who, through homelessness, have experienced social and economic exclusion. We assist individuals to explore their personal development needs, learn relevant skills and undertake meaningful activities. In a nurturing environment, we encourage creativity, foster a sense of belonging and help people to regain confidence and self-esteem. In providing this bridge back into the wider community, we also challenge unhelpful perceptions about individuals who have experienced exclusion.
Employees: 7
Volunteers: 5
Regional offices: 1

## Fledglings Family Services

Wenden Court, Station Approach, Wendens Ambo, Saffron Walden, Essex CB11 4LB
T: 0845 458 1124
F: 0845 280 1539
E: enquiries@fledglings.org.uk
www.fledglings.org.uk
Founder, Trustee and Director: Ruth Lingard
Fledglings helps parents and carers of disabled children and those with additional

needs to find solutions to the practical problems of everyday living. We do this by searching for, testing and supplying a range of helpful products (at affordable prices) to address specific needs. We also share information via our monthly e-News, our product brochure and an informative website.
Employees: 9
Volunteers: 12
Income: £211,884 (2014–15)

## FOCUS

73 Church Gate, Leicester LE1 3AN
T: 0116 251 0369
F: 0116 262 0187
E: admin@focus-charity.co.uk
www.focus-charity.co.uk
Director: Matt Lilley
FOCUS is a charity that aims to inspire and empower young people to become more actively involved in their local community and in so doing raise their aspirations, develop their skills and self-confidence and improve their life chances.
Employees: 5
Volunteers: 50
Regional offices: 1
Income: £126,000 (2013–14)

## Food Chain (UK) Ltd

Acorn House, 314–320 Gray's Inn Road, London WC1X 8DP
T: 020 7843 1800
F: 020 7843 1818
E: katie.smith@foodchain.org.uk
www.foodchain.org.uk
Chief Executive: Siobhán Lanigan
The Food Chain provides nutrition services including home-delivered meals, essential groceries and nutrition advice to men, women and children who are chronically sick as a result of HIV-related illness. We aim to ensure that no one living with the virus has their ability to get well and stay well adversely affected by lack of access to appropriate food.
Employees: 11
Volunteers: 600
Income: £800,000 (2013–14)

## Foresight the Association for the Promotion of Preconceptual Care

3 Lower Queens Road, Clevedon,
Somerset BS21 6LX
T: 01275 878953
E: info@foresight-preconception.org.uk
www.foresight-preconception.org.uk
Promotes natural approaches to optimal
health in both parents prior to the conception
of a child, with a view to minimising the risks of
miscarriage, foetal damage or compromised
health in the infant. Promotes research on
environmental hazards to foetal life.
Employees: 4
Regional offices: 2

## Forever Hounds Trust

PO Box 4243, Radstock BA3 3ZL
Helpline: 0300 011 1100
E: enquiries@foreverhoundstrust.org
www.foreverhoundstrust.org
Chief Executive: Rachel Grocott
Our vision is that one day every greyhound
will be free from risk or need. In the
meanwhile we rescue, rehabilitate and find
loving homes for abused and abandoned
greyhounds and lurchers. The charity receives
no financial help from the greyhound racing
industry and is completely reliant on
donations, legacies and public support.
We operate nationally and home around
500 of these special dogs every year.
Employees: 5
Volunteers: 200
Income: £679,823 (2013–14)

## Foundation for Community Dance

LCB Depot, 31 Rutland Street, Leicester,
Leicestershire LE1 1RE
T: 0116 253 3453
F: 0116 261 6801
E: emma@communitydance.org.uk
www.communitydance.org.uk
Executive Director: Chris Stenton
The Foundation for Community Dance is
the UK development agency for access,
participation and progression in dance for all.
Employees: 14

## Foundation for Conductive Education

Cannon Hill House, Russell Road, Moseley,
Birmingham B13 8LD
T: 0121 449 1569
E: foundation@conductive-education.org.uk
www.conductive-education.org.uk
Aims to develop and advance the science
and skill of conductive education and
especially its teaching.

## Foundation for Public Service Interpreting

12 Tudor Rose Court, Fann Street,
London EC2Y 8DY
T: 020 7623 9191
E: director@fpsi.org
www.fpsi.org
Chief Executive: Mark Kiddle
The Foundation aims to promote a national
minimum standard in public service
interpreting, together with an affordable
telephone interpreting service.
Employees: 3
Volunteers: 5

## Foundation for Women's Health Research and Development

Unit 4, 765–767 Harrow Road,
London NW10 5NY
T: 020 8960 4000
F: 020 8960 4014
E: yasmin@forwarduk.org.uk
www.forwarduk.org.uk
The Foundation aims to improve women's
and children's health, with special emphasis
on the eradication of female genital
mutilation.
Employees: 3

## Foundation of Nursing Studies (FoNS)

11–13 Cavendish Square, London W1G 0AN
T: 020 7307 2857
E: theresa.shaw@fons.org
www.fons.org
Chief Executive: Dr Theresa Shaw
Our vision: To inspire and enable a culture
across health and social care that values
people, where patients experience care that
is the best it can be and staff feel appreciated
and supported. Our mission: To work in
partnership with health and social care
organisations to foster a commitment to
person-centredness by valuing staff and
enabling them to develop the knowledge,
skills and expertise to deliver care that is safe,
effective and compassionate.
Employees: 4
Income: £365,941 (2013–14)

## Foundation66

7 Holyrood Street, London SE1 2EL
T: 020 7234 9940
F: 020 7357 6712
E: info@foundation66.org.uk
www.foundation66.org.uk
CEO: Sally Scriminger
Foundation is a London-based charity and
a registered social landlord. We exist to
reduce the harm caused by problem alcohol
and drug use. We provide client-focused
community and accommodation-based
services, supporting people to achieve
positive change and freedom from the
harmful effects of alcohol and other drugs.
Employees: 150
Volunteers: 6

## Foundations UK

2 Augustine Road, London W14 0HZ
T: 020 7602 0862 (also fax)
E: info@foundationsuk.org
www.foundationsuk.org
Aims to relieve those suffering with eating
disorders or disordered eating and those
affected by such suffering.
Employees: 1
Volunteers: 4

## Foyer Federation

3rd Floor, 5–9 Hatton Wall,
London EC1N 8HX
T: 020 7430 2212
F: 020 7430 2213
E: joel@foyer.net
www.foyer.net
The Foyer Federation works with young
people through a network of 140 accredited
Foyers across the UK. Foyers are integrated
learning and accommodation centres
providing safe and secure housing, support
and training for young people aged 16.
Employees: 17

## FPA

45 Park Mount, Harpenden,
Hertfordshire AL5 3AS
T: 020 7923 5211
E: johng@fpa.org.uk
www.fpa.org.uk
The FPA promotes sexual health and the
reproductive rights and choice of all people
throughout the UK.

## Fragile X Society

Rood End House, 6 Stortford Road,
Great Dunmow, Essex CM6 1DA
T: 01371 875100
E: info@fragilex.org.uk
www.fragilex.org.uk
Managing Director: Tim Potter
The Society provides mutual support and
information to families, encourages research
and increases public and professional
awareness of fragile X syndrome.
Employees: 6
Volunteers: 27

## Fraud Advisory Panel

Chartered Accountants' Hall,
Moorgate Place, London  EC2R 6EA
T: 020 7920 8637
E: info@fraudadvisorypanel.org
www.fraudadvisorypanel.org
Manager: Mia Campbell

The Fraud Advisory Panel is an independent voice of the anti-fraud community. It champions anti-fraud best practice and works to improve fraud awareness, understanding and resilience. Free resources include practical self-help guides on anti-fraud measures and UK legislation, together with dedicated prevention advice for charities.
Employees: 2
Volunteers: 500
Income: £157,250 (2014–15)

## Free Word

60 Farringdon Road, London  EC1R 3GA
T: 020 7324 2571
E: eleanor@freewordonline.com
Executive Director: Eleanor Lang

## Freedom From Torture

111 Isledon Road, Finsbury Park,
London  N7 7JW
T: 020 7697 7777
F: 020 7697 7799
E: northeast@freedomfromtorture.org
www.freedomfromtorture.org
Chief Executive: Simon Carruth

Provides adult and child survivors of torture and organised violence living in the UK with medical, psychotherapeutic and social care and practical assistance; documents evidence of torture; provides training for health and social care professionals and others who work with torture survivors; educates the public and decision-makers about torture and its consequences; campaigns to improve the law and practice in the UK regarding the treatment of survivors in the asylum system.
Employees: 171
Volunteers: 250
Regional offices: 4

## Freeplay Foundation

56–58 Conduit Street, London  W1S 2YZ
T: 020 7851 2616
E: jfairbairn@freeplayfoundation.org
www.freeplayfoundation.org
Chief Executive: Kristine Pearson

The Freeplay Foundation is unlike any other non-profit humanitarian organisation in the world. Our mission is to enable access to information and education for the most vulnerable populations through appropriate and sustainable technologies, particularly self-powered radios. The Freeplay Foundation collaborates with in-country non-governmental organisations (NGOs), government ministries, international organisations and broadcasters to ensure radio information and education reaches the widest possible rural populations.
Employees: 10

## Freshwinds

Prospect Hall, 12 College Walk, Selly Oak,
Birmingham, West Midlands  B29 6LE
T: 0121 415 6670
F: 0121 415 6699
E: office@freshwinds.org.uk
www.freshwinds.org.uk

Freshwinds offers care and support, without charge, to adults and children living with life-limiting illnesses, as well as to individuals from socially excluded backgrounds. The charity manages a wide range of projects, including the provision of integrated complementary therapy, debt counselling and community-based initiatives. Please check the charity's website for up-to-date information regarding current projects.
Employees: 37
Volunteers: 200
Regional offices: 1

## Friends of Cathedral Music

21 Bradford Road, Trowbridge,
Wiltshire  BA14 9AL
T: 01225 768607
E: info@fcm.org.uk
www.fcm.org.uk

The Friends publicise cathedral music, assist cathedrals in maintaining their musical activities and encourage as many people as possible to discover and enjoy cathedral music.

## Friends of Friendless Churches

St Ann's Vestry Hall, 2 Church Entry,
London  EC4V 5HB
T: 020 7236 3934
E: office@friendsoffriendlesschurches.org.uk
www.friendsoffriendlesschurches.org.uk
Director: Matthew Saunders

Founded in 1957 to save redundant churches from demolition, decay and unsympathetic conversion. We now own 47 such buildings, half in England and half in Wales (where our work is almost wholly funded by CADW and the Church in Wales). Joint membership with the Ancient Monuments Society.
Employees: 3
Volunteers: 100

## Friends of the Earth

26–28 Underwood Street, London  N1 7JQ
T: 020 7490 1555
F: 020 7490 0881
E: info@foe.co.uk
www.foe.co.uk
Executive Director: Andy Atkins

We campaign on issues of environmental and social justice, making life better for people by inspiring solutions to environmental problems.
Employees: 170
Volunteers: 30
Regional offices: 12

## Friends of the Elderly

40–42 Ebury Street, London  SW1W 0LZ
T: 020 7730 8263
E: enquiries@fote.org.uk
www.fote.org.uk

Supports older people, often frail, confused or with dementia, to maintain a level of independence and choice by providing a complete range of services for them in any one locality.

## Friends of the Western Buddhist Order

51 Roman Road, Bethnal Green,
London  E2 0HU
T: 0845 458 4716
E: info@lbc.org.uk
www.lbc.org.uk

Aims: to advance the Buddhist religion by encouraging members and others to live in accordance with the Buddha's teachings; to support ordained members of the Western Buddhist Order wherever possible; to maintain close contact with other groups with similar objectives.

## Friendship Works

Studio 442, Highgate Studios,
London  NW5 1TL
T: 020 7485 0900
E: info@family-action.org.uk
www.friendshipworks.org.uk
Employees: 12
Volunteers: 150

## Fulham Football Club Foundation

Fulham FC Training Ground, Motspur Park
T: 020 8336 7432
E: enquiries@fulhamfc.com
Operations Manager: Jamie Morgan

## Fund for the Replacement of Animals in Medical Experiments

96–98 North Sherwood Street,
Nottingham NG1 4EE
T: 0115 958 4740
E: frame@frame.org.uk
www.frame.org.uk
**Director: Robert Combes**
FRAME was founded in 1969 to promote the concept of alternatives to the use of live animals in medical research and toxicity testing. FRAME believes in reducing the number of animals used, refining procedures so that the suffering of animals necessarily used is minimised and ultimately eliminating the need for live animal experiments altogether.
**Employees: 8**

## Furniture Re-use Network

48–54 West Street, St Philips, Bristol,
Avon BS2 0BL
T: 0117 954 3578
Helpline: 0845 602 8003
E: info@frn.org.uk
www.frn.org.uk
**Chief Executive: Craig Anderson**
The FRN promotes and supports the re-use of household and office items such as furniture, domestic appliances, TVs and computers to support low-income households and community-based organisations. We are a representative body with over 300 members working across the UK.
**Employees: 10**
**Volunteers: 1**
**Regional offices: 1**

## Furzedown Family Centre

Graveny School Site, Welham Road,
London SW17 8DN
T: 020 8672 6924
E: info@furzedownfamilycentre.org.uk
www.furzedownfamilycentre.org.uk
**Centre Manager: Barbara Vine**
We are a charitable organisation dedicated to providing a safe and nurturing environment for pre-school children to thrive and learn through play. The FFC is committed to providing parents/carents in the community with a warm and welcoming place to bring their children to learn by engaging with stimulating activities. It is a place for both parents/carers and children to build friendships and provides an invaluable sense of belonging in the community.
**Employees: 7**
**Volunteers: 2–4**

## Fylde Coast YMCA

St Annes YMCA, St Albans Road,
Lytham St Annes, Lancashire FY8 1XD
T: 01253 893928
E: enquiries@fyldecoastymca.org
fyldecoastymca.org
**Chief Executive : John Cronin**
Fylde Coast YMCA strives to transform people's lives by providing an inspirational journey which supports and develops individuals, with a focus on young people. We believe that by fulfilling this vision we can change and enhance lives.
**Employees: 559**
**Volunteers: 50**
**Regional offices: 18**
**Income: £8,835,842 (2014–15)**

# G

## Gaia House

West Ogwell, Newton Abbot,
Devon TQ12 6EN
T: 01626 335256
F: 01626 352650
E: info@gaiahouse.co.uk
www.gaiahouse.co.uk
Preserves, protects and enhances physical, mental, emotional and spiritual health by the provision of a centre for the instruction and practice of meditation.
**Employees: 6**
**Volunteers: 10**

## Galapagos Conservation Trust

28 Portland Place, London W1B 1LY
T: 020 7399 7440
E: gct@gct.org
www.galapagosconservation.org
**Chief Executive: Sharon Johnson**
The Galapagos Conservation Trust (GCT) was founded in 1995 with two aims: to raise awareness of the issues facing the Galapagos Islands; to raise much-needed funds to support the expanding conservation work.
**Employees: 7**
**Volunteers: 15**
**Regional offices: 1**

## GamCare

2nd Floor, 7–11 St John's Hill,
Clapham Junction, London SW11 1TR
T: 020 7801 7000
F: 020 7378 5233
E: info@gamcare.org.uk
www.gamcare.org.uk
Works in a gambling-neutral manner with all sections of society and delivers services that address the social impact of gambling; improves the understanding of gambling issues; promotes the concept of responsible gambling; addresses the needs of those adversely affected by a gambling dependency.
**Employees: 15**
**Volunteers: 15**

## Game & Wildlife Conservation Trust

Burgate Manor, Fordingbridge,
Hampshire SP6 1EF
T: 01425 652381
F: 01425 655848
E: london@gwct.org.uk
www.gwct.org.uk
Promotes for the public benefit the conservation and study of game species, their habitats and the other species associated with those habitats.
**Employees: 120**
**Volunteers: 10**
**Regional offices: 6**

## Garden History Society, The

70–77 Cowcross Street, London EC1M 6EJ
T: 020 7608 2409
E: enquiries@gardenhistorysociety.org
www.gardenhistorysociety.org
Aims: to promote the study of history of gardening, landscape gardening and horticulture; to promote protection and conservation of historic designed landscapes; to encourage creation of new parks and designed landscapes. GHS is a statutory consultee on all planning applications relating to or affecting sites entered on the English Heritage Register of Parks and Gardens of Historic Interest.

## Garden Organic

Ryton Organic Gardens,
Coventry CV8 3LG
T: 024 7630 3517
F: 024 7663 9229
E: enquiry@gardenorganic.org.uk
www.hdra.org.uk
Garden Organic is the working name of the Henry Doubleday Research Association (HDRA). We are a registered charity, and

Europe's largest organic membership organisation. We are dedicated to researching and promoting organic gardening, farming and food.

**Employees:** 120
**Volunteers:** 50
**Regional offices:** 3

## Gardening for Disabled Trust

Appleton Oast, Frittenden, Kent TN17 2EG
T: 01580 852372
F: 01580 852218
E: sally@thetukes.com
gardeningfordisabledtrust.org.uk

Provides assistance, both practical and financial, to help disabled people wishing to take an active part in gardening. Grants may be made to help with the design of special gardens, both to individuals and to institutions, schools, hospitals, etc.

## Gateway Community Action

c/o Lee Omar, Refugee Action,
64 Mount Pleasant, Liverpool,
Merseyside L3 5SD
T: 07817 152444
E: festog@yahoo.com
www.gcscap.org

## Gauchers Association Ltd

3 Bull Pitch, Dursley,
Gloucestershire GL11 4NG
T: 01753 646737
E: ga@gaucher.org.uk
www.gaucher.org.uk

## General Assembly of Unitarian and Free Christian Churches

Essex Hall, 1–6 Essex Street,
London WC2R 3HY
T: 020 7240 2384
F: 020 7240 3089
E: amason@unitarian.org.uk
www.unitarian.org.uk
**Chief Executive: Rev Steve Dick**

Promotes a free and inquiring religion through the worship of God, the celebration of life, the service of humanity and respect for all creation and the upholding of the liberal Christian tradition.

**Employees:** 9
**Volunteers:** 100
**Regional offices:** 177

## General Council and Register of Naturopaths

PO Box 122, Midhurst,
West Sussex GU29 1BN
T: 01458 840072
E: admin@gcrn.org.uk
www.gcrn.org.uk
**President: Clare Badrick**

The Council is the largest naturopathic register in the UK. For the benefit and protection of the public, it sets and monitors educational standards in naturopathic training, sets and enforces a code of ethics and publishes annually a listing of suitably qualified naturopathic practitioners. The GCRN operates, in association with the British Naturopathic Association, a HealthLine service for the public.

**Employees:** 2
**Volunteers:** 12

## Generation for Change and Development

PO Box 2108, Ilford, Essex IG1 9LE
T: 020 8911 8767
E: abdirashid@gencad.org
www.gencad.org

GENCAD's vision is to be an exemplary organisation that contributes to the socio-economic development of pastoralist communities in the Horn of Africa. Pastoralist communities experience extreme poverty, lack of education, political and economic marginalisation in the Horn of Africa. GENCAD's mission is to increase their access to educational opportunities and health services, and to empower these communities to actively participate in and take ownership of their socio-economic development.

## Genetic Alliance UK

Unit 4D, Leroy House, 436 Essex Road,
London N1 3QP
T: 020 7704 3141
E: contactus@geneticalliance.org.uk
www.geneticalliance.org.uk
**Director: Alastair Kent**

Genetic Alliance UK is the national alliance of patient organisations with a membership of over 150 charities supporting all those affected by genetic disorders. Our aim is to improve the lives of people affected by genetic conditions by ensuring that high-quality services and information are available to all who need them.

**Employees:** 15

## Genetic Disorders UK

199A Victoria Street, London SW1E 5NE
T: 020 7199 3300
Helpline: 0800 987 8987
E: hello@geneticdisordersuk.org
www.geneticdisordersuk.org
**Chief Executive: Caroline Harding**

The mission of Genetic Disorders UK is to improve the lives of children and adults who are affected by genetic disorders. The charity aims to offer support and information to affected individuals and families as well as providing resources and grants for disorder-specific UK-based support groups and charities. Genetic Disorders UK organises the annual Jeans for Genes Day event in schools and workplaces to raise funds and awareness for its cause.

**Employees:** 9
**Volunteers:** 5

## Get Connected Helpline

PO Box 7777, London W1A 5PD
T: 020 7009 2500
Helpline: 0808 808 4994
E: admin@getconnected.org.uk
www.getconnected.org.uk
**Chief Executive: Fiona Clark**

Get Connected is the UK's free, confidential helpline for young people under 25 who need help and don't know where to turn. Our service is available 365 days a year and young people can contact us by phone, webchat, email, text message or use our online directory, WebHelp 24/7. Our mission is to be the home of help and support for young people, enabling them to find free confidential help, whenever they need it, however they want it, no matter what the issue.

**Employees:** 15
**Volunteers:** 100

## Get Hooked on Fishing

Old Billingham Business Centre,
Chapel Road, Billingham, Stockton-on-Tees,
Durham TE23 1EN
E: hello@ghof.org.uk
www.ghof.org.uk
**Chief Executive Officer: Sarah Collins**

We work with children and young people at risk of social exclusion across the UK. We use the vehicle of angling to help them access the personal, social, educational, community, health and well-being benefits.

**Employees:** 9
**Volunteers:** 100
**Regional offices:** 16

## Get Well UK

9 Delancey Street, Camden Town NW1 7NL
T: 0870 438 9355
F: 0870 438 9356
E: boo@getwelluk.com
www.getwelluk.com
**Managing Director: Boo Armstrong**
Get Well UK makes it possible for GPs
to confidently refer their patients to
complementary therapists, by providing
information, support and a team of highly
skilled and qualified practitioners. With NHS
funding, this service is free to patients. We
believe that complementary medicine can
play an important role in improving health and
wellbeing and want to ensure that many more
people have access to effective healthcare,
not just people who can afford to pay for
it privately.
Employees: 3

## GFS Platform for Young Women

Unit 2, Angel Gate, 326 City Road,
London EC1V 2PT
T: 020 7837 9669
F: 020 7837 4107
E: info@gfsplatform.org.uk
www.gfsplatform.org.uk
**Director: Joy Lauezzari**
The Girls Friendly Society is a movement
for young women that aims to widen horizons
and celebrate individuality and talents,
with love and understanding. Our vision
is to inspire young women and challenge
them to break down barriers, building on
their achievements to become independent
women.
Employees: 30
Volunteers: 175
Income: £748,881 (2013–14)

## Gharweg Advice Training and Careers Centre

5 Westminster Bridge Road,
London SE1 7XW
T: 020 7620 1430
F: 020 7620 1431
E: gharweg@aol.com
Provision of welfare advice on benefits,
immigration, health, housing, employment
training and career guidance and counselling
for black and minority communities.

## Gideons International in the British Isles

24 George Street, Lutterworth,
Leicestershire LE17 4EE
T: 01455 554241
E: hq@gideons.org.uk
www.gideons.org.uk
**Executive Director: Iain Mair**

An interdenominational association of
Christian business and professional men and
their wives, which freely provides copies of
the Bible or New Testament and psalms to
public institutions such as hotels, hospitals,
schools, homes for the elderly and prisons.
Employees: 13
Volunteers: 3600
Regional offices: 1

## Gingerbread

530 Highgate Studios,
53–79 Highgate Road, London NW5 1TL
T: 020 7428 5400
Helpline: 0808 802 0925
F: 020 7482 4851
E: info@gingerbread.org.uk
www.gingerbread.org.uk
**Chief Executive: Fiona Weir**
We provide expert advice and practical
support and campaign for single parents.
Employees: 76
Regional offices: 2

## Girlguiding UK

17–19 Buckingham Palace Road,
London SW1W 0PT
T: 020 7834 6242
F: 020 7828 8317
E: executive.assistant@girlguiding.org.uk
www.girlguiding.org.uk
Girlguiding UK, as part of a worldwide
movement, enables girls and young women
to fulfil their potential and to take an active
and responsible role in society through a
distinctive, stimulating and enjoyable
programme of activities delivered by trained
volunteer leaders. Our vision is to be
recognised as the leading organisation for
girls and young women and to widen and
increase our membership.
Employees: 150
Volunteers: 80000
Regional offices: 9

## Girls' Brigade England and Wales

Cliff College, Calver, Hope Valley,
Derbyshire S32 3XG
T: 01246 582322
E: gbco@girlsbrigadeew.org.uk
www.girlsb.org
**National Director: Ruth Gilson**
A membership organisation that specialises
in working with churches to provide fun
and inspiring local groups where girls and
young women can belong, achieve and
discover Jesus. GB companies are primarily
for girls and young women, aged four to 18,
and meet most weeks of the year in safe and
friendly environments.

## Girls' Venture Corps Air Cadets

1 Bawtry Gate, Sheffield S9 1UD
T: 0114 244 8405
E: gvcac@toucansurf.com
www.gvcac.org.uk
**Corps Director: Brenda Layne**
An organisation for girls aged between 11 and
20 years of age who are interested in aviation,
Duke of Edinburgh award, leadership training,
camps and courses, outdoor activities and
community service.
Employees: 1
Volunteers: 300
Regional offices: 6

## Glebe House

Glebe House, Church Road, Shudy Camps,
Cambridge, Cambridgeshire CB21 4QH
T: 01799 584359
F: 01799 584098
E: jeanette.hurworth@glebehouse.org.uk
www.glebehouse.org.uk
**Director: Peter Clarke**
Glebe House (The Friends Therapeutic
Community Trust) is a Quaker charity that
provides holistic support for young men with
challenging behaviour.
Employees: 55

## Global Action Plan

9 Kean Street, London WC2B 4AY
T: 020 7420 4444
F: 020 7836 7345
E: all@globalactionplan.org.uk
www.globalactionplan.org.uk
**CEO: Trewin Restorick**
Global Action Plan is the UK's leading
environmental behaviour change charity and,
since 1993, has helped businesses, schools
and communities reduce their impact on the
environment. We achieve environmental and
financial savings in the UK by empowering
people to take action on energy, waste, water
and travel. We are the only UK charity whose
programmes are endorsed by the United
Nations Environment Programme.
Employees: 27
Volunteers: 500
Regional offices: 1

## Global Care

2 Dugdale Road, Coventry CV6 1PB
T: 024 7660 1800
F: 024 7660 1444
E: info@globalcare.org.uk
www.globalcare.org.uk
Employees: 21
Volunteers: 50

## Global Connections

Caswell Road, Leamington Spa,
Warwickshire CV31 1QD
T: 01926 487755
E: info@globalconnections.org.uk
www.globalconnections.org.uk
**Executive Director: Martin Lee**
Promotes and encourages the spread of the
Christian Gospel by putting mission at the
heart of the church and the church at the
heart of mission.
**Employees: 10**
**Income: £500,000 (2014–15)**

## Global Justice Now

66 Offley Road, London SW9 0LS
T: 020 7820 4900
F: 020 7820 4949
E: offleyroad@globaljustice.org.uk
www.globaljustice.org.uk
**Director: Nick Dearden**
Global Justice Now tackles the underlying
causes of poverty. We lobby decision-makers
to change the policies that keep people
poor. We research and promote positive
alternatives. We work alongside people
in the developing world who are standing
up to injustice.
**Employees: 30**
**Volunteers: 5**
**Regional offices: 1**

## Global Witness Limited

PO Box 6042, London N19 5WP
T: 020 7561 6375
E: mail@globalwitness.org
www.globalwitness.org
Focuses on areas where environmental
exploitation causes human rights abuses
and funds conflict.

## Golden Buddha Centre

The Grove, Totnes, Devon TQ9 5EP
T: 01803 897550
E: guidestar@goldenbuddha.org
www.goldenbuddha.org
The twin objectives of the Golden Buddha
Centre project are to have an active Buddhist
centre together with related residential
accommodation for retired Buddhists.
**Volunteers: 20**

## Good Gardeners' Association

Pinetum Lodge, Churcham,
Gloucester GL2 8AD
T: 07901 815647
E: david@igeek.co.uk
www.goodgardeners.org.uk
The purpose of the Good Gardeners'
Association is the improvement and
encouragement of horticulture along
compost or organic lines, and the daily
study of organic methods of gardening.
**Volunteers: 8**

## Gordon Moody Association

47 Maughan Street, Dudley,
West Midlands DY1 2BA
T: 01384 241292
F: 01384 217649
E: elaine.smethurst@gordonmoody.org.uk
www.gordonmoody.org.uk
**Managing Director: Elaine Smethurst**
We provide advice, education and high-
quality and innovative therapeutic support
to problem gamblers and those affected by
problem gambling, through residential, online
and outreach services. Gordon Moody
Association offers a unique and intensive
residential treatment programme in the UK
for those gamblers most severely addicted as
well as online support and advice to problem
gamblers overseas through our Gambling
Therapy website.
**Employees: 18**
**Volunteers: 12**
**Regional offices: 2**
**Income: £909,308 (2014–15)**

## Gorlin Syndrome Group

11 Blackberry Way, Penwortham, Preston,
Lancashire PR1 9LQ
Helpline: 01772 496849
E: info@gorlingroup.org
www.gorlingroup.porg
The Gorlin Syndrome Group was formed in
the UK in 1992. It supports: those affected
by Gorlin syndrome and their families and
carers; the advancement of the education
of the medical profession and the general
public regarding Gorlin syndrome and
its implications; the promotion and
dissemination of research into the causes,
effects, treatment and management of
Gorlin syndrome.
**Volunteers: 6**

## Gosport Voluntary Action

Martin Snape House, 96 Pavilion Way,
St George's Barracks, Gosport,
Hampshire PO12 1FG
T: 023 9258 3836
E: gosportvb@gva.org.uk
www.gosport-voluntary-action.org.uk
**Chief Officer: Nicky Stavely**
We are at the heart of the Gosport
community providing support to voluntary
sector organisations and running in-house
projects to benefit under-represented
groups, as well as offering a volunteer
centre service.
**Employees: 20**
**Volunteers: 30**
**Regional offices: 1**

## Grail

125 Waxwell Lane, Pinner,
Middlesex HA5 3ER
T: 020 8866 0505
E: m.grasar@grailsociety.org.uk
www.grailsociety.org.uk
A Roman Catholic organisation involved in
the education and formation of adults and
young people, which encourages young
people and adults to work out their Christian
commitment in modern society and take
their full share in meeting the needs of
the community.
**Employees: 8**

## Grandparents Plus

18 Victoria Park Square, Bethnal Green,
London E2 9PF
T: 020 8981 8001
Helpline: 0300 123 7015
E: info@grandparentsplus.org.uk
www.grandparentsplus.org.uk
**Chief Executive: Lucy Peake**
Grandparents Plus incorporating The
Grandparents' Association, is the national
charity which champions the vital role of
grandparents and the wider family in
children's lives – especially when they
take on the caring role in difficult family
circumstances and when they have lost
contact with children. We do this because
we want to make children's lives better.
Grandparents Plus provides: policy solutions
and campaigns, a free support network, an
advice and information service and training
and guidance.
**Employees: 20**
**Volunteers: 57**
**Regional offices: 1**

## GrantScape

Office E, Whitsundoles, Broughton Road,
Salford, Milton Keynes MK17 8BU
T: 01908 247630
E: steven.hargreaves@grantscape.org.uk
www.grantscape.org.uk
Chief Executive: Steven Hargreaves
The charity's aim is to improve the life of
communities and the environment by
managing and administering grant
programmes for deserving and quality
projects.
Employees: 7
Volunteers: 35

## Great Ormond Street Hospital Children's Charity

Great Ormond Street Hospital,
Great Ormond Street, London WC1N 3JH
T: 020 7405 9200
E: karen.atkinson@gosh.org
www.gosh.org

## Greater London Volunteering

27 Old Gloucester Street,
London WC1N 3AX
T: 020 7125 0151
E: info@glv.org.uk
www.glv.org.uk
Chief Executive Officer: James Banks
Greater London Volunteering is an umbrella
body representing, consulting and co-
ordinating volunteer centres and volunteer
development agencies across Greater
London. Activities include consultation, event
organisation, training, marketing and
promotion.
Employees: 2
Regional offices: 1
Income: £168,440 (2013–14)

## Greater Manchester Centre for Voluntary Organisation

St Thomas Centre, Ardwick Green North,
Manchester, Greater Manchester M12 6FZ
T: 0161 277 1000
F: 0161 273 8296
E: gmcvo@gmcvo.org.uk
www.gmcvo.org.uk
Chief Executive: Alex Whinnom
GMCVO supports local voluntary action by
local people by providing specialist support,
knowledge, voice, infrastructure and
innovation, working in partnership with other
support organisations and with the public and
private sectors. We aspire to be a channel for
information for and about our sector, and to
provide co-ordination and leadership. A large
element of our work involves representing the
views and needs of people involved in local
voluntary groups, sharing ideas and brokering
relationships.
Employees: 28

## Greater World Christian Spiritualist Association

The Greater World Spiritual Centre,
3–5 Conway Street, Fitzrovia,
London W1T 6BJ
T: 020 7436 7555
E: greaterworld@btconnect.com
greaterworld.co.uk
National President: Megan Long
To spread in all directions the truth of
survival after death, of spirit communion,
of healing by the power of Holy Spirit and
to disseminate the teachings of Jesus the
Christ and additional teachings received
from highly evolved spirit messengers.
Employees: 3
Volunteers: many
Regional offices: 51
Income: £77,606 (2013–14)

## Green Alliance

36 Buckingham Palace Road,
London SW1W 0RE
T: 020 7630 4518
F: 020 7233 9033
E: ga@green-alliance.org.uk
www.green-alliance.org.uk
Green Alliance's mission is to promote
sustainable development by ensuring
that the environment is at the heart of
decision-making.
Employees: 11
Volunteers: 3

## Green Life UK

39 Marlborough Road, Forest Gate,
39 Marlborough Road, London E7 8HA
T: 07415 345761 (also fax)
E: jamaluddin@outlook.com
www.greenlifecharity.org
Chairman: Jamal Uddin
Green Life UK is a non-governmental,
non-profit-making, non-partisan charity
striving to meet the basic human needs of
the underprivileged and people of limited
resources. The organisation was founded by
a native Bangladeshi philanthropist, Jamal
Uddin who is based in the UK.
Volunteers: 4
Regional offices: 1

## GreenNet Educational Trust

Development House, 56–
64 Leonard Street, London EC2A 4LT
T: 0845 055 4011
E: info@greenneteducationaltrust.org.uk
www.greenneteducationaltrust.org.uk
Promotes the strategic use of electronic
networking for the benefit of social
movements internationally and at home
in the UK.

## Greenpeace UK

Canonbury Villas, Islington,
London N1 2PN
T: 020 7865 8100
Helpline: 0800 269065
E: info.uk@greenpeace.org
www.greenpeace.org.uk
Executive Director: John Sauven
Aims to protect the environment through
peaceful direct action, scientific research and
finding solutions to environmental problems.
Employees: 100
Volunteers: 40

## Greenwich & Bexley Community Hospice

Greenwich and Bexley Community Hospice,
185 Bostall Hill, Abbey Wood,
London SE2 0GB
T: 020 8312 2244
E: info@gbch.org.uk
www.communityhospice.org.uk
Chief Executive: Kate Heaps
To provide specialist palliative care and
support, free of charge, to patients and
their families living within the boroughs of
Greenwich and Bexley in our inpatient unit,
day hospice, community or outpatient clinic.
Psychological care, bereavement support
and advice are also offered.
Employees: 160
Volunteers: 600
Regional offices: 1
Income: £7,500,000 (2015–16)

## Groundwork North East

Grosvenor House, 29 Market Place,
Bishop Auckland, Co Durham DL14 7NP
T: 0191 567 2550 ext 32
E: stephen.armstrong@groundwork.org.uk
www.groundwork.org.uk/sites/northeast

## Groundwork UK

Lockside, 5 Scotland Street,
Birmingham B1 2RR
T: 0121 236 8565
F: 0121 236 7356
E: info@groundwork.org.uk
www.groundwork.org.uk
**Chief Executive: Graham Duxbury**
Groundwork supports communities in need,
working with partners to help improve the
quality of people's lives, their prospects and
potential and the places where they live,
work and play. Our vision is of a society of
sustainable communities that are vibrant,
healthy and safe, that respect the local and
global environment and where individuals
and enterprise prosper.
**Employees: 31**
**Regional offices: 1**
**Income: £19,402,466 (2013–14)**

## Group B Strep Support

PO Box 203, Haywards Heath,
West Sussex RH16 1GF
T: 01444 416176
F: 0870 803 0024
E: info@gbss.org.uk
www.gbss.org.uk
**Chief Executive: Jane Plumb MBE**
Group B Strep Support (GBSS) is the only
UK charity dedicated to preventing group B
Strep (GBS) infections in newborn babies
and supporting affected families. GBS is the
most common cause of life-threatening
infection in newborn babies, infections which
are usually preventable. GBSS regularly sends
information materials to maternity units and
GPs nationwide. We receive no government
funding – families affected by GBS raise
most of the charity's funds.
**Employees: 4**
**Income: £176,575 (2013–14)**

## Grubb Institute

Cloudesley Street, London N1 0HU
E: enquiries@grubbinstitute.org.uk
www.grubbinstitute.org.uk
**Executive Director: Bruce Irvine**
The Institute is an applied research
foundation working globally to mobilise
values, faiths and beliefs as a resource for
the transformation, healing and repair of
organisations, people and society. The
Institute's work is informed by a Christian
theology that recognises the heritage, culture
and traditions of the many diverse faiths and
spiritualities present in our society.

## Guernsey Arts Commission

Guernsey Arts Commission,
Guernsey Information Centre,
North Esplanade, St Peter Port,
Guernsey GY1 2LQ
T: 01481 709748
E: joanna.littlejohns@cultureleisure.gov.gg
www.arts.gg
**Head of Arts Development:**
**Joanna Littlejohns**
The Guernsey Arts Commission's aim is to
help the arts in Guernsey to grow and develop
and to involve more people in the arts; for the
arts to be recognised and valued as a vital part
of island life.
**Employees: 4**
**Volunteers: 35**

## Guideposts Trust Ltd

Willow Tree House, Two Rivers,
Station Lane, Witney,
Oxfordshire OX28 4BH
T: 01993 893560
E: gpt@guidepoststrust.org.uk
www.guidepoststrust.org.uk
Guideposts aims to provide services to help all
individuals lead independent lives, fulfil their
aspirations and maximise their potential. We
work with people who have mental health
issues, dementia, learning disabilities, physical
impairments, and their carers and families, to
help them make the best possible choices for
quality care. We seek to achieve excellence in
our work and lead the way in researching,
delivering and disseminating good practice.
**Employees: 100**
**Volunteers: 100**
**Regional offices: 7**

## Guild of Aid

10 St Christopher's Place,
London W1U 1HZ
T: 020 7935 0641
E: admin@professionalsaid.org.uk
www.guild-of-aid.org.uk
**Chief Executive Officer: Finola McNicholl**
Aims to help UK citizens aged over 18 who
are of good education in need of financial
assistance. We offer weekly grants and
contributions towards essential household
goods. To apply, you must have claimed state
benefits and have approached other funds
for help.
**Employees: 4**
**Volunteers: 19**

## Guild of Health Ltd

9 St Georges Road, Folkestone,
Kent CT19 4BE
T: 01303 277399
E: director@gohealth.org.uk
www.gohealth.org.uk
Helps people to experience within the
fellowship of God's family the freedom of
life promised by Jesus Christ.

## Guild of Pastoral Psychology

82 Boston Gardens, Brentford,
Middlesex TW8 9LP
T: 020 8568 2195
E: administration@
guildofpastoralpsychology.org.uk
www.guildofpastoralpsychology.org.uk
Acts as a meeting ground for all those
interested in the relationship between
religion and depth psychology, particularly
the work of CG Jung and his followers and
communicates the results of recent practice
and research to everyone interested
professionally or personally.

## Guild of St Raphael

St John's Church, 2 Green Lane,
Stoneycroft, Liverpool L13 7EA
T: 0151 228 2023
E: guildofstraphael@gmail.com
www.guild-of-st-raphael.org.uk
Teaches and practises the ministry of Christ's
healing in the Church of England through the
sacraments and prayer in full co-operation
with the medical profession.

## GuildHE Limited

Woburn House, 20 Tavistock Square,
London WC1H 9HB
T: 020 3393 6132
E: info@guildhe.ac.uk
www.guildhe.ac.uk
**CEO: Andrew Westwood**
GuildHE is one of the two recognised
representative bodies for Higher Education
in the UK.
**Employees: 7**

## Guillain Barre & Associated Inflammatory Neuropathies

Woodholme House,
Heckington Business Park, Station Road,
Heckington, Sleaford,
Lincolnshire NG34 9JH
T: 01529 469910
Helpline: 0800 374803
F: 01529 469915
E: director@gaincharity.org.uk
www.gaincharity.org.uk
Director: Caroline Morrice
To provide support, information and other assistance to sufferers and their families; to promote research into causes, prevention and treatments; and to advance the education of the public and of the medical professionals.
Employees: 3
Volunteers: 150
Income: £244,105 (2015–16)

## Habitat for Humanity Great Britain

10 The Grove, Slough, Berkshire SL1 1QP
T: 01295 264240
F: 01295 264230
E: supporterservices@habitatforhumanity.org.uk
www.habitatforhumanity.org.uk
Chief Executive: Rebecca Martin
Habitat for Humanity Great Britain is an international development charity. Our vision is for a world where everyone has a safe and decent place to live through the elimination of housing poverty and homelessness.
Employees: 18
Volunteers: 250
Regional offices: 2

## Haemochromatosis Society

PO Box 6356, Rugby,
Warwickshire CV21 9PA
T: 0303 040 1101
Helpline: 0303 040 1102
E: office@haemochromatosis.org.uk
www.haemochromatosis.org.uk
Chief Executive: David Head
Advice and support for people affected by genetic haemochromatosis (GH) and

their families. A patient representative organisation.

## Haemophilia Society

Petersham House, 57a Hatton Garden,
London EC1N 8JG
T: 020 7380 0600
Helpline: 0800 018 6068
F: 020 7387 8220
E: sue@haemophilia.org.uk
www.haemophilia.org.uk
The Haemophilia Society works to secure the best possible care, treatment and support for people with haemophilia and related or associated bleeding disorders, and their families.
Employees: 9
Volunteers: 350
Regional offices: 18

## Hambleton and Richmondshire Carers Centre

32 High Street, Northallerton,
Northallerton, North Yorkshire DL7 8EE
T: 01609 780872
F: 01609 788489
E: info@hrcarers.org.uk
www.hrcarers.org.uk
Chief Executive: Andrea Hobbs
Our principal aim is to support carers of all ages in a way that is centred on individual needs and supports their general health and well-being. We: provide advice and information to carers and their families; provide emotional support; work in partnership to raise awareness of issues; provide social groups and activities to reduce isolation; signpost and refer to other support agencies; undertake carers assessments; work in partnership and collaborate where appropriate to strengthen local and sub-regional services for carers.
Employees: 8
Volunteers: 10
Income: £200,000 (2013–14)

## Hambleton Community Action

Community House, 10 South Parade,
Northallerton, North Yorkshire DL7 8SE
T: 01609 780458
E: admin@hambletoncommunityaction.org
www.hambletoncommunityaction.org
Manager: Hazel Kirby
Hambleton Community Action is a registered charity providing advice, information, training and support to volunteers and voluntary and community

groups in the local area. We also provide some services for local people.
Employees: 12
Volunteers: 100+

## Hamlet Trust

c/o Mental Health Foundation, 9th Floor,
Sea Containers House, 20 Upper Ground,
London SE1 9QB
T: 020 7803 1160
E: office@hamlet-trust.org.uk
www.hamlet-trust.org.uk
Pursues development, education and research initiatives in mental health in central and Eastern Europe, with special emphasis on the social integration of people with long-term mental health problems in the community.

## Hammersmith Management College

E: s.khan@hmclondon.com

## Handicap International UK

CAN Mezzanine, 32–36 Loman Street,
London SE1 0EH
T: 0870 774 3737
F: 0870 774 3738
E: hi-uk@hi-uk.org
www.handicap-international.org.uk
We support people in situations of vulnerability who, due to a physical, mental or psychological condition, have difficulty in playing their role in society, thus finding themselves in a situation of disability.
Employees: 6
Volunteers: 155

## Hannahs

Woodland Road, Ivybridge,
Devon PL21 9HQ
T: 01752 898100
F: 01752 898116
E: charlotte.simonds@discoverhannahs.org
www.discoverhannahs.org
Chief Executive Officer: Bronwen Hewitt
Hannahs offers education, care and life opportunities for children and adults with a range of disabilities. The Trust offers a school, respite centre, children's home, adult transition project and an innovative service for adults. We have two centres – Hannahs at Ivybridge and Hannahs at Seale-Hayne.
Employees: 300
Volunteers: 150
Regional offices: 2

## Hansard Society

40–43 Chancery Lane, London  WC2A 1JA
T: 020 7438 1222
F: 020 7438 1229
E: pressoffice@lse.ac.uk
www.hansardsociety.org.uk
Chief Executive: Fiona Booth
The Hansard Society is the UK's leading non-partisan political research and education charity, which exists to strengthen parliamentary democracy and encourage greater public involvement in politics.
Employees: 22
Volunteers: 2

## Happy Days Children's Charity

Clody House, 90–100 Collingdon Street, Luton, Bedfordshire LU1 1RX
T: 01582 755999
F: 01582 755900
E: happydayscharity@yahoo.co.uk
www.happydayscharity.org
Chief Executive: Ryan Sinclair
We fund and organise holidays, days out and theatre trips throughout the UK for disadvantaged young people with special needs. We help young people in special needs schools, in hospitals and in hospices, and we help individual families.
Employees: 10
Volunteers: 1

## Harvest Fields Commissioning International

PO Box 740, Hemel Hempstead, Hertfordshire HP1 3RH
T: 07941 502613
E: info@hfci.net
www.hfci.net
Offers leadership training and materials as well as TV, film and media production and media training in over 50 countries worldwide. We also provide humanitarian assistance in developing countries.

## Havering Mind

Harrow Lodge House, Hornchurch Road, Hornchurch RM11 1JU
T: 01708 457040
F: 01708 457141
E: reach.us@haveringmind.org.uk
www.haveringmind.org.uk
CEO: Vanessa Bennett
We are a local mental health charity based in Hornchurch Havering. We provide advice and support to people who are experiencing mental health problems and also their carers. We campaign to improve local mental health services, raise awareness and promote understanding. We provide a range of services to support older people, younger adults and adolescents, children and those most at risk of social isolation.
Employees: 26
Volunteers: 73
Income: £385,940 (2013–14)

## HCPT (Hosanna House and Children's Pilgrimage Trust)

Oakfield Park, 32 Bilton Road, Rugby, Warwickshire CV22 7HQ
T: 01788 564646
E: hq@hcpt.org.uk
www.hcpt.org.uk
Chief Executive: Phil Sparke
Disabled and disadvantaged children and adults enjoy life-changing pilgrimage holidays to Lourdes in the south of France, supported by volunteers, thanks to HCPT.
Employees: 15
Volunteers: 5000
Income: £4,400,000 (2010–11)

## Headliners (formerly known as Children's Express)

Rich Mix, 35–47 Bethnal Green Road, London  E1 6LA
T: 020 7749 9360
E: fiona.wyton@headliners.org
www.headliners.org
Director: Fiona Wyton
Aims to inspire children and young people to investigate and challenge the world around them, enhance their personal development and promote their right to be heard as equals. We provide learning through journalism, participation and volunteering.
Employees: 25
Volunteers: 8
Regional offices: 4

## Headlines, the Craniofacial Support Group

8 Footes Lane, Frampton Cotterell, Bristol BS36 2JQ
T: 01454 850557
E: info@headlines.org.uk
www.headlines.org.uk
Group Administrator: Gil Ruff
Provides help, advice and contact to anyone (including their families) having or dealing with craniosynostosis or craniostenosis and all of the associated conditions and syndromes. Merged with Apert Syndrome Support Group.
Employees: 1
Volunteers: 10

## Headway – the Brain Injury Association

190 Bagnall Road, Old Basford, Nottingham  NG6 8SF
T: 0115 924 0800
F: 0115 958 4446
E: enquiries@headway.org.uk
www.headway.org.uk
Our aim is to promote understanding of all aspects of brain injuries and to provide information, support and services to people with brain injuries, their families and carers.
Employees: 35
Volunteers: 7
Regional offices: 112

## Headway Devon

The XCentre, Commercial Road, Exeter, Devon EX2 4AD
T: 01392 211822
E: info@headwaydevon.org.uk
www.headwaydevon.org.uk
Chief Executive: Anne Mattock
Headway Devon is an independent registered charity working to provide care, support and information for people with brain injuries and their families including: centre-based social rehabilitation and respite care; community support programme providing one-to-one care and enabling in the community; carer support; information and advice including signposting and advocacy; training – internal and external; campaigning and awareness raising – raising public awareness of brain injury ('the hidden disability').
Employees: 50
Regional offices: 1
Income: £914,000 (2014–15)

## Healing Foundation

The Royal College of Surgeons, 35–45 Lincoln's Inn Fields, London WC2A 3PE
T: 020 7869 6920
F: 020 7869 6929
E: info@thehealingfoundation.org
www.thehealingfoundation.org
Chief Executive: Brendan Eley
Employees: 5
Volunteers: 30

## Health Foundation

90 Long Acre, London WC2E 9RA
T: 020 7257 8000
F: 020 7257 8001
E: jacquelyn.bell@health.org.uk
www.health.org.uk
Chief Executive: Stephen Thornton
The Health Foundation is an independent
charitable foundation working to improve
the quality of healthcare across the UK
and beyond.
Employees: 25

## Health Poverty Action

Ground Floor, 31–33 Bondway,
London SW8 1SJ
T: 020 7840 3777
F: 020 7840 3770
E: general@healthpovertyaction.org
www.healthpovertyaction.org
Director: Martin Drewry
Health Poverty Action works to strengthen
poor and marginalised people in their struggle
for health through development initiatives in
13 countries and campaigning for change.
Employees: 500
Volunteers: 10
Regional offices: 14

## HealthProm

Star House, 104–108 Grafton Road,
London NW5 4BA
T: 020 7284 1620
F: 020 7284 1881
E: general@healthprom.org
www.healthprom.org
Working in partnership to promote health and
social care for women and children in Eastern
Europe and Asia.
Employees: 4
Volunteers: 9

## Hearing Dogs for Deaf People

The Grange, Wycombe Road, Saunderton,
Princes Risborough,
Buckinghamshire HP27 9NS
T: 01844 348100
F: 01844 348101
E: info@hearingdogs.org.uk
www.hearingdogs.org.uk
Supplies trained dogs to assist the profoundly
deaf by alerting them to specific household
sounds by touch and provide companionship
and independence.
Employees: 99
Volunteers: 500
Regional offices: 60

## Hearing Link

27–28 The Waterfront, Eastbourne,
East Sussex BN23 5UZ
T: 0300 111 1113
E: helpdesk@hearinglink.org
www.hearinglink.org
Chief Executive: Dr Lorraine Gailey
Hearing Link is a UK charity active in England,
Scotland, Wales and Northern Ireland for
people living with hearing loss, their family
and friends. We offer a helpdesk, support
programmes, useful website and membership
scheme. Find out more at www.hearinglink.org.
Employees: 18
Volunteers: 130
Regional offices: 3

## Heart UK, the Cholesterol Charity

7 North Road, Maidenhead,
Berkshire SL6 1PE
T: 01628 777046
Helpline: 0345 450 5988
E: jp@heartuk.org.uk
www.heartuk.org.uk
Chief Executive: Jules Payne
Over half of the adults in the UK have raised
cholesterol. One in 500 people are born with
an inherited high cholesterol condition,
meaning they have a high risk of a heart
attack, stroke or sudden death in their 20s,
30s and 40s. We provide expert support,
guidance and education to people who have
high cholesterol, their families and health care
professionals.
Employees: 10
Volunteers: 6

## Helen & Douglas House

E: lcrowley@helenanddouglas.org.uk

## Helen Arkell Dyslexia Centre

Frensham, Farnham, Surrey GU10 3BW
T: 01252 792400
E: enquiries@arkellcentre.org.uk
www.arkellcentre.org.uk
The Centre: helps people of all ages with
dyslexia and other specific learning difficulties
to fulfil their potential by optimising their
educational opportunities and quality of life;
trains teachers in the special skills needed;
helps schools manage dyslexics in the
classroom; raises public awareness of how
dyslexia can be helped.

## Help A Poor Child

Devonshire House, Manor Way,
Borehamwood, Hertfordshire WD6 1QQ
T: 020 8236 2953
F: 020 8731 4322
E: info@hapc.co.uk
hapc.co.uk
A non-profit, voluntary organisation, founded
in 1980, to provide assistance to children and
families struggling in terrible poverty.

## Help Age International

PO Box 32832, London N1 9ZN
T: 020 7278 7778
E: info@helpage.org
www.helpage.org
Operates a global network of not-for-profit
organisations with a mission to work with and
for disadvantaged older people worldwide to
achieve a lasting improvement in the quality
of their lives.

## Helplines Partnership

Business Design Centre, 52 Upper Street,
London N1 0HQ
T: 0300 330 7777
E: mirelle.frost@helplines.org
www.helplines.org
Chief Executive: Theodore Spyrou
Helplines Partnership is the membership
body for organisations that provide helpline
services in the UK and internationally. We
facilitate high-quality service delivery to
callers by providing a range of services,
including training (accredited qualifications),
innovative contact solutions, quality
standards, individually tailored support and
information resources through web portals.
We raise the profile of the sector through
representation of our members' interests and
influencing the social policy agenda, giving
providers of helpline services a voice to build
sustainability and promote excellence, choice
and accessibility for everyone.
Employees: 25
Volunteers: 10
Regional offices: 3

## HemiHelp

6 Market Road, London N7 9PW
T: 0345 120 3713
Helpline: 0345 123 2372
E: info@hemihelp.org.uk
www.hemihelp.org.uk
Provides information and support for children and young people with hemiplegia and increases public awareness of the condition. Facilitates research into hemiplegia and its associated conditions.
Employees: 12
Volunteers: 15
Income: £330,621 (2015–16)

## Henry George Foundation of Great Britain Ltd

212 Piccadilly, London W1J 9HG
T: 020 7377 8885
F: 020 8393 3526
E: office@henrygeorgefoundation.org
www.henrygeorgefoundation.org
Raises awareness of social injustice stemming from unjust property ownership and capitalisation of land rent and other resource rents.

## Henry Smith Charity

65 Leadenhall Street, London EC3A 2AD
T: 020 7264 4970
E: dc@henrysmithcharity.org.uk
www.henrysmithcharity.org.uk
Director: Nick Acland

## Heritage Care

Connaught House, 112–120 High Road, Loughton, Essex IG10 4HJ
T: 020 8502 3933
F: 020 8502 3543
E: dave.chopra@heritagecare.co.uk
www.heritagecare.co.uk
Chief Executive: Kim Foo
Heritage Care is a registered charity that provides a range of flexible individualised services that support independence and choice for people with learning disabilities, mental health support needs and older people. Our care and support services include supported living, domiciliary services, packages for self-directed support, extra-care schemes, registered care homes, day services and respite/short-break services. We support 1,000 service users each day and employ over 1,800 staff employed across 130 locations.
Employees: 1850
Volunteers: 50
Regional offices: 7

## Herpes Viruses Association (also called HVA or SPHERE)

41 North Road, London N7 9DP
T: 020 7607 9661
Helpline: 0845 123 2305
E: info@herpes.org.uk
www.herpes.org.uk
Director: Marian Nicholson
Helps and advises people with herpes simplex (cold sores and genital herpes) and herpes zoster. The HVA: answers phone calls, emails and letters; supports an informative and calming website; offers one-to-one counselling; promotes public awareness of the virus and reduces anxiety; disseminates information to the public and the medical profession; acts as a pressure group for research; undertakes research wherever possible; encourages and promotes s elf-help groups. Certified by the Information Standard.
Employees: 2
Volunteers: 15
Income: £110,000 (2015–16)

## HFT the Home Farm Trust

Peter Needham, Merchants House North, Wapping Road, Bristol BS1 4RW
T: 0117 930 2600
E: info@hft.org.uk
www.hft.org.uk
Provides, for people with learning disabilities, residential and other services that develop their potential and sustain their rights.

## Hi8us Projects Ltd

Ground Floor, Toepath House, Limehouse Court, London E14 7EQ
T: 020 7538 8070
F: 020 7987 4522
E: jerry@hi8us.co.uk
www.hi8us.co.uk
Hi8us Projects Limited was established in 1994 to produce innovative media with young people in their communities.
Employees: 5
Regional offices: 1

## High/Scope UK

Anerley Business Centre, Anerley Road, Anerley, London SE20 8BD
T: 0870 777 7680
F: 0870 777 7682
E: susan.noble@southtyneside.gov.uk
www.high-scope.org.uk
Aims to improve the life chances of children through high-quality care and education using the high/scope approach. Disseminates information on the effectiveness of using the high/scope approach to care and education for young children. Aims to increase the use

of the approach within social service, education, voluntary and independent settings.
Employees: 7

## Highbury Vale Blackstock Trust

Elizabeth House, 2 Hurlock Street, London N5 1ED
T: 020 7690 1300
E: director@elizabeth-house.org.uk
www.elizabeth-house.org.uk
Centre Director: Centre Director
A community centre serving the local community by offering play services (after-school clubs and playscheme), youth work programmes and health and wellbeing activities, as well as facilities to local groups and individuals willing to serve the local community.
Employees: 13
Volunteers: 2
Income: £227,088 (2014–15)

## Hillingdon Autistic Care and Support

E: louise@hacs.org.uk

## Historical Association

59a Kennington Park Road, London SE11 4JH
T: 0300 100 0223
F: 020 7582 4989
E: enquiries@history.org.uk
www.history.org.uk
The Historical Association is the national charity for history. It exists to bring together people of all communities who have an interest in the past. It promotes and supports the study and teaching of history at all levels: teacher, student, amateur and professional.
Employees: 9
Volunteers: 229
Regional offices: 50

## Hollybank Trust

Roe Head, Far Common Road, Mirfield,
West Yorkshire WF14 0DQ
T: 01924 490833
F: 01924 483902
E: s.hughes@hollybanktrust.com
www.hollybanktrust.com
**Chief Executive and Principal:**
**Steven Hughes**
A charity trust working with children, young
people and adults who have profound physical
disabilities. We have a commitment for life
for those in our care. We have a specialist
school with an attached children's home,
independence homes and homes for life in
the neighbouring communities. We are open
52 weeks a year. Our multidisciplinary staff
number 450. Internationally renowned for
our work in IT, access technology and social
care.
Employees: 450
Volunteers: 45
Regional offices: 1

## Home from Hospital Care after Treatment

Prospect Hall, College Walk, Selly Oak,
Birmingham, West Midlands B29 6LE
T: 0121 472 4499
E: enquiries@home-from-hospital-care.
org.uk
www.home-from-hospital-care.org.uk
**Director: Geraldine Amos**
Volunteers from our Welcome Home Service
offer practical, common-sense support for
up to six weeks after discharge from hospital.
We will shop, call in for a friendly chat, go to
the bank, help with completing benefit forms,
etc. Our volunteers call in at least once a
week. We can also supply lists of cleaners,
gardeners, hairdressers, chiropodists etc.
Employees: 7
Volunteers: 60
Regional offices: 1

## Home-Start Canterbury and Coastal

E: sari@homestartcanterbury.org

## Home-Start Haringey

100 Tower Gardens Road, Tottenham,
London N17 7QA
T: 020 8352 4151
Helpline: 020 8352 4152
E: fatmata@home-start-haringey.org
www.home-start-haringey.org
**Scheme Manager: Fatmata Bah**
We: recruit and train local parents as family
support volunteers; provide one-to-one
practical and emotional peer support for
vulnerable and socially excluded families; help

reduce family crisis and breakdown; increase
parenting confidence and knowledge; provide
personal development and accreditation
opportunities for volunteers; deliver
managing money, parenting education,
HENRY and domestic abuse training for
local Haringey parents.
Employees: 4
Volunteers: 69
Income: £112,000 (2015–16)

## Home-Start South Hams, Plymouth and Tavistock

Age Concern Building, Ilbert Road,
Kingsbridge, Ilbert Road, Kingsbridge,
Devon TQ7 1DZ
T: 01548 854513
E: andreachandler.homestart@gmail.com
homestart-southhams.org.uk
**Scheme Manager: Andrea Chandler**
We believe every child deserves the best start
in life and parents are best placed to provide it
but that sometimes, for some families this
can be difficult. We offer one-to-one
befriending and mentoring support to families
with a child under five, who are experiencing
difficulties. We also offer gentle group
support to parents at risk of exclusion.
Employees: 5
Volunteers: 100
Regional offices: 1

## Home-Start UK

2 Salisbury Road, Leicester LE1 7QR
T: 0116 233 9955
Helpline: 0800 068 6368
F: 0116 233 0232
E: info@home-start.org.uk
www.home-start.org.uk
**Chief Executive: Kay Bews**
Home-Start offers support, friendship and
practical help to parents with young children,
in local communities throughout the UK and
with British Forces in Germany and Cyprus.
337 independent schemes managed by and
offering support from 20,226 volunteers,
supported 34,952 families and 69,672
children during 2007/8.
Employees: 117
Volunteers: 20226
Regional offices: 12

## Home-Start Worthing and Adur

E: lisa.green@wahomestart.org.uk

## Homeless Action in Barnet

36B Woodhouse Road, London N12 0RG
T: 020 8446 8400
F: 020 8446 8480
E: joe@habcentre.org
www.habcentre.org
**Chief Executive: Joe Lee**
Our mission is to work with vulnerable people
so that they gain access to housing, health
and other services in order: to achieve dignity;
to make their own effective choices; to
express themselves as fully independent
members of society. HAB should be a 'Place
of Change' – enabling and facilitating
practical change for individuals and
promoting the needs of homeless people
within our society.
Employees: 16
Volunteers: 30
Income: £340,589 (2014–15)

## Homeless International

Queen's House, 16 Queens Road, Coventry,
West Midlands CV1 3EG
T: 024 7663 2802
F: 024 7663 2911
E: info@homeless-international.org
www.homeless-international.org
**Chief Executive: Larry English**
Aims to relieve poverty, in particular that
caused by homelessness, internationally.
We work through lasting relationships with
local partners in Asia and Africa, within which
there is confidence to create solutions to
the challenge of urban poverty. Typically
we provide resources, technical assistance
and financial services for community-led
processes.
Employees: 16

## Homeless Link

1st Floor, 10–13 Rushworth Street,
London SE1 0RB
T: 020 7960 3010
F: 020 7960 3011
E: irmani.darlington@homelesslink.org.uk
www.homeless.org.uk
The Citizenship Foundation is an independent
charity that aims to empower individuals to
engage in the wider community through
education about the law, democracy and
society.
Employees: 30
Volunteers: 15

## Homeopathy Action Trust

PO Box 9022, Melton Mowbray,
Leicestershire LE13 9BZ
T: 0844 800 2840 (also fax)
E: info@homeopathyactiontrust.org
www.homeopathyactiontrust.org
Executive Director: Simon Wilkinson-Blake
The principal activity of the company is the
promotion of homeopathy through funding
of education and research and the raising of
funds to support homeopathic activities.
Employees: 2
Volunteers: 8

## HOPE

17 Queen Street, Worksop S80 2AN
T: 01909 531294
Helpline: 01909 489990
E: director@hopeservices.org.uk
www.hopeservices.org.uk
CEO: Alan Diggles
Aims to help those in crisis or without
somewhere to live, through the provision
of help, advice and practical support.
Employees: 25
Volunteers: 35
Income: £900,000 (2013–14)

## Hope and Homes for Children

East Clyffe, Salisbury, Wiltshire SP3 4LZ
T: 01722 790111
F: 01722 790024
E: sue.rooke@hopeandhomes.org
www.hopeandhomes.org
Chief Executive: Rick Foulsham
Provides family-based care for orphaned and
vulnerable children in Central and Eastern
Europe and Africa.
Employees: 45
Volunteers: 7

## Hope for Children

Hope House, 14a Queensway,
Hemel Hempstead, Hertfordshire HP1 1LR
T: 0870 751 9861
E: hope@hope4c.org
www.hope4c.org
Aims to assist children, in particular those
living in developing countries and the UK,
who suffer through being handicapped,
orphaned, poor and exploited.

## Hope UK

25(F) Copperfield Street, London SE1 0EN
T: 020 7928 0848
F: 020 7401 3477
E: m.watson@hopeuk.org
www.hopeuk.org
Chief Executive Officer: Sarah Brighton
Hope UK enables children and young people
to make drug-free choices. A network of 116
volunteer drug educators, trained to Open
College Network accreditation standards,
provide interactive drug awareness sessions
for children and young people and any group
with an interest in them. Hope UK also
provides accredited two-day courses for
family and youth workers.
Employees: 12
Volunteers: 116
Regional offices: 3
Income: £645,943 (2014–15)

## HOPE worldwide

360 City Road, London EC1V 2PY
T: 020 7713 7655
F: 020 7812 1236
E: wil.horwood@hopeworldwide.org.uk
www.hopeworldwide.org.uk
Chief Executive: Wil Horwood
Bringing hope to, and changing the lives of,
disadvantaged and vulnerable people. In the
UK we work in the areas of homelessness and
addiction recovery. Overseas, we support a
wide range of poverty reduction initiatives
through grants and management support.
We have a strong volunteerism ethos and
develop initiatives that connect volunteers
with poverty issues.
Employees: 10
Volunteers: 890
Regional offices: 2

## Horder Centre for Arthritis

St John's Road, Crowborough,
East Sussex TN6 1XP
T: 01892 665577
E: info@hordercentre.co.uk
www.hordercentre.co.uk
Provides professional help by all available
methods for people suffering the pain and
disabling effects of all forms of arthritis in
order to restore maximum independence and
alleviate pain wherever possible.

## Horse Rangers Association (Hampton Court) Ltd

E: director@horserangers.com

## Horsham and Mid Sussex Voluntary Action

4th Floor Martlet Heights, 49 The Martlets,
Burgess Hill, West Sussex RH15 9NN
T: 01444 258102
E: adminfinance@hamsva.org.uk
www.hamsva.org.uk
Chief Officer: Christine Hardisty
Practical support services for voluntary and
community groups who work with people
of all ages, faiths and abilities including
community development, volunteer services,
training opportunities, voluntary and
statutory sector networking events, co-
ordination and facilitation of open meetings,
seminars and forums together with
representation and liaison with local voluntary
organisations and community groups
encouraging them to put forward their views
on local and national policies and events.
Employees: 8
Regional offices: 3

## Hospice Information Service

51–59 Lawrie Park Road, Sydenham,
London SE26 6DZ
T: 020 8768 4500
E: info@stchristophers.org.uk
www.stchristophers.org.uk
An information exchange and
communication network for the hospice
movement; phone and written enquiries
welcomed from healthcare professionals
and members of the public.

## Hospice UK

Hospice House, 34–44 Britannia Street,
London WC1X 9JG
T: 020 7520 8200
F: 020 7278 1021
E: info@hospiceuk.org
www.hospiceuk.org
Chief Executive: David Praill
Hospice UK is the national membership
organisation for hospice care. It champions
and supports the work of more than 200
services providing hospice care across the
UK, so that they can deliver the highest
quality care for people with terminal or
life-limiting conditions and support their
families.
Employees: 60
Volunteers: 5

## Hospitality Action

62 Britton Street, London EC1M 5UY
T: 020 3004 5500
F: 020 7253 2094
E: help@hospitalityaction.org.uk
www.hospitalityaction.org.uk
Chief Executive: Penny Moore
Hospitality Action helps those who work/have worked within the UK hospitality industry. We check all applicants are receiving their full state entitlement when unable to work and can assist where the state is unable to. In addition to signposting and support we offer one-off grants for essential needs, short-term ongoing support for periods of crisis and a befriending scheme for socially isolated individuals. We also provide educational seminars on drug and alcohol misuse.
Employees: 12
Volunteers: 40

## HOST UK

Unit K106, Tower Bridge Business Complex, 100 Clements Road, London SE16 4DG
T: 020 7739 6292
E: info@hostuk.org
www.hostuk.org
Chief Executive: Susie Alemayehu
HOST's mission is to offer international students the chance to visit a British home and thereby promote international understanding and friendship.
Employees: 5
Volunteers: 1700

## House of Saint Barnabas in Soho

1 Greek Street, Soho Square, Soho, London W1V 6NQ
T: 020 7434 1894
F: 020 7434 1746
E: finance@hosb.org.uk
hosb.org.uk
Provides temporary housing and care to homeless women (18–55 years of age).

## Housing Associations' Charitable Trust (HACT)

Octavia House, 50 Banner Street, London EC1Y 8ST
T: 020 7247 7800
F: 020 7247 2212
E: hact@hact.org.uk
www.hact.org.uk
Director: Heather Petch
HACT pioneers housing solutions for people on the margins. We identify emerging need, and then develop, test and promote practical solutions for social inclusion. We work through partnerships and networks, acting as a bridge between housing associations and the wider third sector.
Employees: 9
Volunteers: 1

## Housing Justice

256 Bermondsey Street, London SE1 3UJ
T: 020 3544 8094
E: info@housingjustice.org.uk
www.housingjustice.org.uk
Chief Executive: Alison Gelder
The national voice for churches and Christians on housing and homelessness. We help churches help homeless people through practical support, training, resources, consultancy and events. We raise awareness about housing and homelessness and campaign for positive change, particularly through the annual Homeless Sunday campaign.
Employees: 10
Volunteers: 25
Regional offices: 2

## Howard League for Penal Reform

1 Ardleigh Road, London N1 4HS
T: 020 7249 7373
F: 020 7249 7788
E: info@howardleague.org
www.howardleague.org
The Howard League for Penal Reform works for a safe society where fewer people are victims of crime. The Howard League for Penal Reform believes that offenders must make amends for what they have done and change their lives. The Howard League for Penal Reform believes that community sentences make a person take responsibility and live a law-abiding life in the community.
Employees: 13
Volunteers: 300

## Hull Churches Home from Hospital Service

E: administrator@hchfh.org.uk

## Human Givens Foundation

Chalvington, East Sussex BN27 3TD
T: 01323 811662
E: info@hgfoundation.com
www.hgfoundation.com
Aims to promote research and public education into the 'givens' of human nature and their application in the treatment and care of those suffering from mental illness.
Employees: 1

## Human Relief Foundation

PO Box 194, Bradford, Yorkshire BD7 1YW
T: 01274 392727
E: mohammed@hrf.co.uk
www.hrf.org.uk

## Human Scale Education

Unit 8, Fairseat Farm, Chew Stoke, Bristol BS40 8XF
T: 01275 332516
E: info@hse.org.uk
www.hse.org.uk
The charity aims to promote education in small groups, in which effective learning can be encouraged and undertaken with mutual respect. The charity also supports and campaigns for state funding for small alternative schools and it supports the restructuring of state secondary schools.

## Humane Research Trust

Brook House, 29 Bramhall Lane South, Bramhall, Stockport, Cheshire SK7 2DN
T: 0161 439 8041
E: info@humaneresearch.org.uk
www.humaneresearch.org.uk
The Humane Research Trust encourages and supports new medical research that does not include the use of animals, with the objectives of advancing the diagnosis and treatment of disease in humans. The Trust encourages scientists to develop innovative alternatives to the use of animals and so eliminate the suffering of animals that occurs in medical research and testing. The Trust fulfils an important role in educating the next generation of researchers.
Employees: 3
Volunteers: 50
Regional offices: 1

## Humane Slaughter Association

The Old School, Brewhouse Hill, Wheathampstead, St Albans, Hertfordshire AL4 8AN
T: 01582 831919
E: info@hsa.org.uk
www.hsa.org.uk
Promotes humane methods of slaughter.

## Humanity at Heart

22–24 Keymer Road, Hassocks, West Sussex BN6 8AN
T: 01273 846135
E: humanity@humanityatheart.org.uk
www.humanityatheart.org.uk
Aims to relieve the suffering and poverty of children in Romania and elsewhere and to effect this by giving aid, support and training where appropriate, either directly or through the agency of other charities.

## Huntington's Disease Association

Suite 24, Liverpool Science Park,
Innovation Centre 1, 131 Mount Pleasant,
Liverpool L3 5TF
T: 0151 331 5444
F: 0151 331 5441
E: info@hda.org.uk
www.hda.org.uk
**Chief Executive: Cath Stanley**
Provides care, advice, support and education
to both families and professionals affected by
Huntington's disease.
Employees: 30
Volunteers: 200+
Regional offices: 20

## Hyperactive Children's Support Group

71 Whyke Lane, Chichester,
West Sussex PO19 7PD
T: 01243 539966
E: hyperactive@hacsg.org.uk
www.hacsg.org.uk
**Founder/Director: Sally Bunday MBE**
Provides support, ideas and information to
parents, carers and professionals concerned
for ADHD/hyperactive children. Non-
medication therapies are a priority.
Employees: 2
Volunteers: 8

## Hypothalamic Hamartoma Uncontrolled Gelastic Seizures UK

ABS House, 35 Chiltern Avenue,
Amersham, Buckinghamshire HP6 5AE
T: 0800 999 4847
E: hhugsuk@hotmail.com
www.hhugs-uk.com
**Trustee: Vivianne Gattoc**
To provide support to individuals and families
who are affected with Hypothalamic
Hamartoma.
Income: £500 (2013–14)

## Hysterectomy Association

Bakehouse Cottage, Clifton Hill,
Clifton Maybank, Bakehouse Cottage,
Clifton Maybank, Dorset BA22 9UZ
T: 0843 289 2142 (also fax)
E: info@hysterectomy-association.org.uk
www.hysterectomy-association.org.uk
**CEO: Linda Parkinson-Hardman**
The Hysterectomy Association provides
impartial, timely and appropriate information,
products, books and support to women facing
a hysterectomy.
Volunteers: 2
Income: £20,000 (2012–13)

## I CAN

31 Angel Gate, Goswell Road,
London EC1V 2PT
T: 020 7843 2510
Helpline: 020 7843 2544
F: 0845 225 4072
E: info@ican.org.uk
www.ican.org.uk
**Chief Executive: Bob Reitemeier**
I CAN supports children from 0–19 through
our Talk programmes and specialist schools.
We provide resources and information for
parents, families and people who work with
children and young people through our
Enquiry Service. We work in nurseries and
schools across the UK with our evidence-
based programmes and run two special
schools for children with the most severe and
complex needs.
Employees: 235

## IA (The Ileostomy and Internal Pouch Support Group)

Danehurst Court, 35–37 West Street,
Rochford, Essex SS4 1BE
T: 0800 018 4724
Helpline: 01702 849859
F: 01702 597990
E: info@iasupport.org
www.iasupport.org
**National Secretary: Jackie King**
IA is a national support charity specialising
in supporting people with an ileostomy or
internal pouch, their families and their carers.
The core objectives are to help those facing
these operations to return to a normal, active
lifestyle as soon as possible after surgery. IA is
totally funded by donations and subscriptions
and most of the members have either an
ileostomy or an internal pouch.
Volunteers: 800
Regional offices: 49 UK groups

## ICA:UK

41 Old Birley Street, Unit 14,
Manchester M15 5RF
T: 0161 232 8444
E: martin@ica-uk.org.uk
www.ica-uk.org.uk
**Chief Executive: Martin Gilbraith**
Employees: 5
Volunteers: 30
Regional offices: 1

## iDE UK

8a Accommodation Road,
London NW11 8ED
T: 020 8905 5597
E: info@ide-uk.org
www.ide-uk.org
**Chief Executive: Lewis Temple**
International Development Enterprises UK
(iDE UK) helps poor farming families in
Africa and Asia to escape from poverty by
doubling their income. IDE's mission is to
create income and livelihood opportunities
for the rural poor.
Employees: 3
Volunteers: 15

## IGD

Grange Lane, Letchmore Heath,
Watford WD25 8GD
T: 01923 851950
F: 01923 852531
E: itmanager@igd.com
www.igd.com
IGD is a charity that actively helps people to
grow by bringing together intelligence,
opinion and experience from the food and
grocery chain. IGD's principal objectives are:
to promote education and training,
particularly industrial and technical education
and training required for persons working in
the food industry.
Employees: 78
Volunteers: 11

## Imkaan

**Tindlemanor, 52–54 Featherstone Street,
London EC1Y 8RT**
T: 020 7250 3933
E: policy@imkaan.org.uk
www.imkaan.org.uk
**Chair: Amrit Wilson**

Our mission is to act as a collective voice for
the South Asian women's and other refuges,
by promoting their needs and views to
relevant policy makers and agencies and by
providing targeted organisational support.

## Immigrant Counselling and Psychotherapy

**96 Moray Road, Finsbury Park,
London N4 3LA**
T: 020 7272 7906
F: 020 7272 6920
E: info@icap.org.uk
www.icap.org.uk

The charity's objective and its principal
activity is to provide culturally sensitive
counselling for people of Irish origin.
**Employees: 4**
**Volunteers: 15**

## Immigration Advisory Service

**County House, 190 Great Dover Street,
London SE1 4YB**
T: 020 7967 1221
E: info@iasservices.org.uk
www.iasuk.org

Provides the best possible free legal advice
and representation to immigrants and asylum
seekers, without prejudice or discrimination,
in which the interests and welfare of the client
are paramount.

## Impact Foundation

**151 Western Road, Haywards Heath,
West Sussex RH16 3LH**
T: 01444 457080
F: 01444 457877
E: impact@impact.org.uk
www.impact.org.uk

Promotes activities for the prevention of
disablement, and for the cure, mitigation
and relief of disabling conditions.
**Employees: 6**
**Volunteers: 8**

## Impetus – The Private Equity Foundation (Impetus-PEF)

**183 Eversholt Street, London NW1 1BU**
T: 020 3474 1000
E: lisa.dorstek@impetus-pef.org.uk
www.impetus-pef.org.uk
**Chief Executive Office:
Daniela Barone Soares**

Impetus-PEF is committed to transforming
the lives of 11–24 year olds from

disadvantaged backgrounds by ensuring they
get the support they need to succeed in
education, find and keep jobs and achieve
their potential. It finds the most promising
charities and social enterprises working with
these children and young people. It helps
them become highly effective organisations
that transform lives, and then helps them
expand significantly to dramatically increase
the number of young people they serve.
**Employees: 35**

## In Kind Direct

**62 Cornhill, London EC3V 3NH**
T: 020 7398 5510
F: 020 7398 5544
E: robin@inkinddirect.org
www.inkinddirect.org
**Chief Executive: Robin Boles**

In Kind Direct, one of The Prince's Charities
redistributes new goods donated by 930 of
Britain's best-known manufacturers and
retailers to UK voluntary and community
organisations. Since 1997, we've distributed
£130 million in value of goods to 6,700
organisations assisting millions of people in
need. We created In Kind Direct International
to spread product philanthropy to other
countries. Start-up charity Innatura in
Germany and Dons Solidaires in France
are now members of the IKDI network.
**Employees: 18**

## Inclusion London

**336 Brixton Road, London SW9 7AA**
T: 020 7237 3181
E: info@inclusionlondon.org.uk
www.inclusionlondon.org.uk
**CEO: Tracey Lazard**

Inclusion London is a pan-London disability
equality organisation. We provide policy,
campaigning and capacity-building support
for deaf and disabled people's organisations
(DDPOs) in London. Inclusion London's
mission is to promote deaf and disabled
people's equality and inclusion by supporting
deaf and disabled people's organisations
(DDPOs) and campaigning for rights for
deaf and disabled people across the UK. Our
work is rooted in the social model of disability
and the cultural model of deafness.
**Employees: 9**
**Income: £353,053 (2014–15)**

## Independence Initiative

**64–68 Balliol Road, Bootle,
Liverpool L20 7EJ**
T: 0151 284 1100
F: 0151 286 0015
E: joewelsh@independenceinitiative.co.uk
www.independenceinitiative.co.uk

The Independence Initiative works with
individuals, agencies and the community to
facilitate the long-term rehabilitation of
people with a history of drug misuse and also
provides support for their families. It provides
a personal programme, addressing individual
needs, overcoming barriers to social inclusion
and assisting integration into the community.

## Independent Custody Visiting Association

**PO Box 1053, Colne, Lancashire BB9 4BL**
T: 01282 870325
F: 020 7278 9027
E: info@icva.org.uk

## InDependent Diabetes Trust (IDDT)

**PO Box 294, Northampton NN1 4XS**
T: 01604 622837
F: 01604 622838
E: enquiries@iddtinternational.org
www.iddtinternational.org

Offers care and support to people with
diabetes and their families and ensures that
people with diabetes have an informed-
choice treatment; informs and disseminates
information to the general public and
health professionals to create a better
understanding of life with diabetes.
**Employees: 5**
**Volunteers: 50**

## Independent Home Solutions CIC

**The Old Crumpet Factory,
16 Brockham Lane, Brockham,
Surrey RH3 7EL**
T: 01737 845630
F: 01737 841650
E: info@ihscic.org.uk
www.independenthomesolutions.org.uk
**Managing Director: Alison Goodall**

Our experienced team specialises in
providing quality and bespoke home
adaptations for our disabled or elder clients.
Popular alterations are: level access shower
rooms, ground floor extensions, garage
conversions, ramps, improved access,
through floor or stair lifts. We help our clients
to retain their independence, safety and
dignity. The IHS team oversees every project
from conception to completion so that we

ensure a successful outcome and peace of mind for our clients.
**Employees: 14**
**Volunteers: 2**
**Regional offices: 1**

## Independent Living Alternatives

Trafalgar House, Grenville Place, Mill Hill,
London NW7 3SA
T: 020 8906 9265
F: 020 8959 1910
E: paservices@ilanet.co.uk
www.ilanet.co.uk
**Director: Tracey Jannaway**
Independent Living Alternatives is a user-controlled disability organisation established in 1989 promoting the right of disabled people to live independently. ILA provides innovative and flexible alternatives to institutional and domiciliary care and has a comprehensive range of personal assistance services.
**Employees: 4**
**Volunteers: 15**
**Regional offices: 1**

## Independent Theatre Council

The Albany, Douglas Way,
London SE8 4AG
T: 020 7403 1727
E: admin@itc-arts.org
www.itc-arts.org
**Chief Executive: Charlotte Jones**
The Independent Theatre Council represents, supports and develops the professional performing arts in the UK. We are a community of over 400 companies and producers, united in the knowledge that we are stronger together. ITC's commitment to representing your interests includes advice on management, financial and legal matters, peer learning, training opportunities and a professional network. ITC is a strong voice.
**Employees: 5**

## India Welfare Society

177 Kensal Road, London W10 5BJ
T: 020 8960 2637 (also fax)
E: iwslondon@hotmail.com
facebook/indiawelfaresociety
**President: SK Gupta**
Attends to the welfare of people in the UK, particularly members of the Indian community who are in need, hardship or distress.
**Volunteers: 30**
**Income: £9,000 (2015–16)**

## Industry and Parliament Trust

Suite 101, 3 Whitehall Court,
London SW1A 2EL
T: 020 7839 9400
F: 020 7839 9401
E: angelahodder@ipt.org.uk
www.ipt.org.uk
**Chief Executive: Sally Muggeridge**
Established in 1977, the Trust is dedicated to fostering mutual understanding between business and parliament for the public benefit. The IPT is independent, non-partisan and non-lobbying. IPT facilitates educational exchange Fellowships for MPs, MEPs, peers and officers of both Houses with a range of companies from different sectors of commerce and industry.
**Employees: 10**

## Infertility Network UK

Charter House, 43 St Leonards Road,
Bexhill on Sea, East Sussex TN40 1JA
T: 0800 008 7464
F: 01424 731858
E: clarelewisjones@infertilitynetworkuk.com
www.infertilitynetworkuk.com
**Chief Executive: Clare Lewis-Jones**
At I N UK we aim to ease the feelings of isolation on both an emotional and practical level. Members of I N UK tell us frequently that by accessing our services, they are helped in the management of their illness.
**Employees: 12**
**Volunteers: 80**
**Regional offices: 3**

## Information Point for Centronuclear and Myotubular Myopathy

12 Bluebell Close, Huntington, Chester,
Cheshire CH3 6RR
T: 01244 316531
E: centronuclear.org@btinternet.com
www.centronuclear.org.uk
**Founder: Toni Abram**
The Information Point is a website for anyone affected by centronuclear/myotubular myopathy, the aim of which is to reach out to more families globally, to give them information about managing the condition. It is currently the only organisation in Europe/UK that provides comprehensive information and resources for the condition.
**Volunteers: 1**

## Inland Waterways Association

Island House, Moor Road, Chesham,
Buckinghamshire HP5 1WA
T: 01494 783453
E: iwa@waterways.org.uk
www.waterways.org.uk
**Chief Executive: Neil Edwards**

The goals of the Association are the preservation, conservation, restoration and development of the inland waterways of Great Britain.
**Employees: 14**
**Volunteers: 17000**

## Innovative Vision Organisation (IVO)

Innovative Vision Organisation,
123 High Cross Road, Tottenham,
London N17 9NR
T: 020 8365 0349
Helpline: 07943 317905
F: 020 8365 1477
E: info@ivo.org.uk
**Executive Director: Daisy Byaruhanga**
IVO provides care and support, and advice to African people living with HIV/AIDS.
**Employees: 2**
**Volunteers: 25**
**Regional offices: 1**

## INQUEST

89–93 Fonthill Road, London N4 3JH
T: 020 7263 1111
F: 020 7561 0799
E: inquest@inquest.org.uk
www.inquest.org.uk
**Co-Directors: Deborah Coles and Helen Shaw**
INQUEST is the only registered charity in England and Wales that provides a free advice service to bereaved people and their advisors on contentious deaths and their investigation, with a particular focus on deaths in custody. INQUEST gives advice and a free handbook to any bereaved family about inquest procedure. Informed by casework, INQUEST undertakes research and develops policy proposals to campaign for changes to the inquest and investigation process.
**Employees: 9**
**Volunteers: 3**

## Inspire!

E: david.blagbrough@inspire-ebp.org.uk

## Institute for Community and Development Studies

Day Lewis House, 324 Bensham Lane, Thornton Heath, London CR7 7EQ
T: 020 8664 2600
F: 020 8664 2656
E: icdsabcd@aol.com
www.partnershipventure.com
The charity exists primarily to advance education in accordance with Christian beliefs, values and identity, and biblical teachings in particular, by training students wishing to become community development leaders and facilitators working in inner-city areas.
**Employees: 15**
**Volunteers: 80**

## Institute for Complementary Medicine

Unit 25, Tavern Quay Business Centre, Sweden Gate, London SE16 7TX
T: 020 7231 5855
F: 020 7237 5175
E: info@icnm.org.uk
icnm.org.uk
**Director: Frances Fewell**
The ICM believes in promoting the standard of best practice and safe practice for all practitioners and therapists who work within complementary medicine. ICM facilitates the British Register of Complementary Practitioners and can supply names of highly qualified practitioners of various kinds of complementary medicine. It also has contact with other support groups.
**Employees: 5**
**Volunteers: 1**
**Regional offices: 1**

## Institute for Conservation

3rd Floor, Downstream Building, 1 London Bridge, London SE1 9BG
T: 020 7785 3805
F: 020 7785 3806
E: admin@icon.org.uk
www.ukic.org.uk
Acts as a professional body for conservators of objects, for example, works of art, stonework, metalwork, etc. The Institute educates its members and the public about conservation techniques and developments in the profession.
**Employees: 4**
**Volunteers: 80**

## Institute for European Environmental Policy London

28 Queen Annes Gate, London SW1H 9AB
T: 020 7799 2244
E: jlindblad@ieep.eu
www.ieep.org.uk
Aims to analyse environmental policies in Europe, to increase the awareness of the European dimension of environmental policy and advance European environmental policy making.

## Institute for Jewish Policy Research

4th Floor, 7–8 Market Place, London W1W 8AG
T: 020 7436 1553
E: jpr@jpr.org.uk
www.jpr.org.uk
**Executive Director: Dr Jonathan Boyd**
The Institute for Jewish Policy Research is an independent think-tank that informs and influences policy, opinion and decision-making on social, political and cultural issues affecting Jewish life.
**Employees: 6**

## Institute for Outdoor Learning

Plumpton Old Hall, Plumpton, Penrith, Cumbria CA11 9NP
T: 01768 885800
E: institute@outdoor-learning.org
www.outdoor-learning.org
The aim of the Institute is to advance the education of the public in and through outdoor education.
**Employees: 3**

## Institute for War and Peace Reporting

48 Gray's Inn Road, London WC1X 8LT
T: 020 7831 1030
F: 020 7831 1050
E: gerryb@iwpr.net
www.iwpr.net
Aims to advance education and training in public-interest journalism and in the causes, conduct, effects and resolution of international, ethnic and group conflict and civil war for the public benefit. IWPR: links local writers for story development, research, writing and training; organises public seminars and workshops; provides communications, networking, collaboration and financial support for local media; undertakes consultancy and research.
**Employees: 19**
**Volunteers: 5**

## Institute of Alcohol Studies

Elmgren House, 1 The Quay, St Ives, Cambridgeshire PE27 5AR
T: 01480 466766
E: info@ias.org.uk
www.ias.org.uk
**Chairman: Derek Rutherford**
Aims to increase knowledge of alcohol and of the social health consequences of its use and abuse and to encourage and support the adoption of effective measures for the management and prevention of alcohol-related problems.

## Institute of Business Ethics

24 Greencoat Place, London SW1P 1BE
T: 020 7798 6040
F: 020 7798 6044
E: info@ibe.org.uk
www.ibe.org.uk
**Director: Philippa Foster Back**
The Institute aims to advance public education and good practice in business ethics.
**Employees: 9**

## Institute of Cancer Research

123 Old Brompton Road, London SW7 3RP
T: 020 7352 8133
F: 020 7370 5261
E: stewart.northcott@icr.ac.uk
www.icr.ac.uk
**Chief Executive: Peter Rigby**
The Institute is one of the world's leading cancer research organisations and is internationally renowned for the quality of its science. Together with the Royal Marsden NHS Foundation Trust it also forms the leading and largest comprehensive cancer centre in Europe. Our integrated work in genetics, molecular biology and drug development is unrivalled in the world and provides the opportunity for Institute scientists to transform the prospects for cancer patients.
**Employees: 943**

## Institute of Fundraising

Park Place, 12 Lawn Lane, London SW8 1UD
T: 020 7840 1000
F: 020 7840 1001
E: info@institute-of-fundraising.org.uk
www.institute-of-fundraising.org.uk
**Chief Executive: Lindsay Boswell**
The professional body for UK fundraising. We support fundraisers, through leadership, representation, setting standards and training, and we champion fundraising as a career choice.
**Employees: 42**
**Volunteers: 300**
**Regional offices: 13**

## Institute of Group Analysis

1 Daleham Gardens, London NW3 5BY
T: 020 7431 2693
E: iga@groupanalysis-uk.co.uk
www.groupanalysis.org
Executive Director: Sharon Kalsy

The Institute of Group Analysis (IGA) is the leading provider of group analytic and group work training in the UK. We offer professional and academic qualifications in Group Analysis and Group Work Practice across the country, providing education, short courses and continuing professional development for over 1,100 individuals each year. Alongside our core training programme we also offer bespoke training/consultancy and a national clinical referral service for members of the public seeking therapy.
Employees: 10–15
Volunteers: 35
Income: £600,000 (2015–16)

## Institute of Money Advisers

1st Floor, 4 Park Court, Park Cross Street, Leeds, West Yorkshire LS1 2QH
T: 0113 242 0048 (also fax)
E: robert.halstead@i-m-a.org.uk
www.i-m-a.org.uk
Institute of Money Advisers:
Robert Wilson

The IMA's mission statement is assuring quality in the money advice profession. Our objective is to systematically drive up the standards of advice, by championing professionalism and good practice and regulating compliance with our Professional Code of Conduct. The Institute aims to: develop professional standards; provide support services to its members; promote free money advice; influence policy and practice relating to personal finance.

## Institute of Psychoanalysis

Byron House, 112a Shirland Road, London W9 2BT
T: 020 7563 5000
F: 020 7563 5001
E: nick.childs@iopa.org.uk
www.psychoanalysis.org.uk
CEO: Dr J Levett

Founded in 1924, the Institute of Psychoanalysis has trained psychoanalysts, many of whom have become leaders in the mental health field. The Institute welcomes applicants from all types of professional and academic backgrounds, from all over the world. Many students are psychiatrists or medically qualified, some are child or adult psychotherapists, psychologists, social workers or academics, and some come from other backgrounds altogether. The Institute

training leads to the title 'psychoanalyst', as recognised by the IPA.
Employees: 18
Regional offices: 1

## Institute of Transactional Analysis

Broadway House, 149–151 St Neots Road, Hardwick, Cambridge CB23 7QJ
T: 0845 009 9101
E: admin@ita.org.uk
www.uktransactionalanalysis.co.uk
Promotes the study and application of transactional analysis in the UK; maintains a register of approved practitioners and monitors standards of application; provides information and support for any individual or organisation that wishes to know more about transactional analysis.

## Inter Faith Network for the United Kingdom

Ground Floor, 2 Grosvenor Gardens, London SW1W 0DH
T: 020 7730 0410
F: 020 7730 0414
E: ifnet@interfaith.org.uk
www.interfaith.org.uk
Executive Director: Harriet Crabtree

The Inter Faith Network for the UK works, with its member bodies to advance public knowledge and mutual understanding of the teachings, traditions and practices of the different faith communities in Britain and to promote good relations between people of different faiths in this country. It links in membership national faith community representative bodies, national, regional and local inter-faith organisations and educational and academic bodies.

## Inter-Action Associated Charitable Trusts and Companies

HMS President (1918),
Near Blackfriars Bridge,
Victoria Embankment, London EC4Y 0HJ
T: 020 7583 2652
F: 020 7515 4450
E: edbiaction@aol.com
Inter-Action applies entrepreneurial skills to obtain social and community benefits. It sets up model projects, especially in the areas of digital media, social enterprise training and education, which incorporate these aims, and offers training and consultancy to other groups locally and internationally, helping them to adapt model projects to their own communities' needs.
Employees: 3
Volunteers: 5

## Interact Worldwide

325 Highgate Studios,
53–79 Highgate Road, London NW5 1TL
T: 020 7241 8500
F: 020 7267 6788
E: programmes@interactworldwide.org
www.interactworldwide.org
Interact Worldwide is an international charity with over 30 years' experience and relies on donations to fund its overseas projects and programmes. Interact Worldwide works on issues of sexual and reproductive health and HIV/AIDS in solidarity with indigenous partner organisations in Africa, Asia and Latin America. We take a rights-based approach, which is a framework that allows poor and marginalised people to demand as a 'right' the basic conditions that allow them to live in dignity.
Employees: 26
Volunteers: 5
Regional offices: 2

## Intercontinental Church Society

Unit 11 Ensign Business Centre, Westwood Way, Westwood Business Park, Coventry, West Midlands CV4 8JA
T: 024 7646 3940
F: 024 7767 5868
E: enquiries@ics-uk.org
www.ics-uk.org
Mission Director: Rev Richard Bromley
Aims to advance the Christian gospel by evangelical mission and ministry to English-speaking people throughout the world.
Employees: 5
Regional offices: 1

## Intercountry Adoption Centre

22 Union Street, Barnet, Hertfordshire EN5 4HZ
T: 020 8449 2562
Helpline: 020 8447 4753
E: pa@icacentre.org.uk
www.icacentre.org.uk
Chief Executive: Gill Haworth
Intercountry Adoption Centre (IAC) is a registered Voluntary Adoption Agency which specialises in intercountry adoptions but also offers a domestic service, including for adopters who have previously adopted overseas through IAC and who wish subsequently to adopt children from the UK. We provide intercountry adoption assessments and subscription services nationally to local authorities and other voluntary adoption agencies. IAC is unique in being internationally accredited by some states of origin as their partner agency.
Regional offices: 1

## InterHealth Worldwide

Partnership House, 157 Waterloo Road,
London SE1 8US
T: 020 7902 9000
F: 020 7928 0927
E: info@interhealth.org.uk
www.interhealth.org.uk
InterHealth provides whole-person
healthcare to individuals and organisations
involved in service throughout the world.
InterHealth is motivated by Christian beliefs
and values and by humanitarian ideals to
provide compassionate and professional
care without discrimination.
Employees: 22
Volunteers: 4

## Interights

Lancaster House, 33 Islington High Street,
London N1 9LH
T: 020 7278 3230
E: ir2@interights.org
www.interights.org
Interights works to ensure that human rights
are defended effectively in domestic courts
and before regional and international bodies.
We contribute to the development of a
cumulative and progressive interpretation of
universal human rights and to their effective
use in both international and regional arenas
as well as national courts.
Employees: 25

## Interlink Foundation

Fourth Floor Offices, 97 Stamford Hill,
London N16 5DN
T: 020 8802 2469
F: 020 8800 5153
E: admin@interlink-foundation.org.uk
www.interlink-foundation.org.uk
Chief Executive: Chaya Spitz
The Interlink Foundation strengthens and
improves community services by supporting
the work of Orthodox Jewish charities and
community organisations. We provide
specialist advice to community groups,
advocate on their behalf and build bridges
between the Orthodox Jewish community
and public bodies.
Employees: 10
Regional offices: 2

## International Action Network on Small Arms

56–64 Leonard Street, London EC2V 4JX
T: 020 7065 0870
F: 020 7065 0871
E: contact@iansa.org
www.iansa.org

The International Action Network on Small
Arms (IANSA) is the global movement
against gun violence.
Employees: 4
Volunteers: 4

## International Alert

346 Clapham Road, London SW9 9AP
T: 020 7627 6800
F: 020 7627 6900
E: info@international-alert.org
www.international-alert.org
CEO: Harriet Lamb
International Alert has been working for
30 years with people directly affected
by conflict to find peaceful solutions. We
believe in a world where people resolve their
differences without violence and can build a
more peaceful future for their families and
communities. We build a more peaceful world
by collaborating with people from across
divides to resolve the root causes of conflict,
because everyone can play a part in building
peace, every day.
Employees: 200
Regional offices: 17
Income: £15,118,000 (2014–15)

## International Cat Care

Taeselbury, High Street, Tilsbury,
Wiltshire SP3 6LD
T: 01747 871872
E: info@icatcare.org
icatcare.org
Promotes: the wellbeing of cats in sickness
and health; the increased understanding of
feline diseases; the improvement of standards
of boarding; humane behaviour towards, and
increased understanding of, the cat.

## International Children's Trust

67A Lincoln Road, Peterborough,
Cambridgeshire PE1 2SD
T: 01733 319777
E: admin@theict.org
www.theict.org
Executive Director: Dave Christie
The International Children's Trust funds,
develops and supports partners who are
working with severely disadvantaged and
'at risk' children, their families and their
communities in low- and middle-income
countries. It develops an effective network
between its partners whose similarities and
differences combine to form a collective
experience in the field of international child

development for the purpose of learning and
giving strength through mutual support.
Employees: 3
Volunteers: 2
Income: £500,000 (2014–15)

## International Community Assist

Churchview, 13 Woodland Road, Patney,
Devizes, Wiltshire SN10 3RD
T: 01380 840990
E: icauk@btopenworld.com
www.ica-uk.co.uk
Aims to alleviate poverty through provision
of general assistance in the developing world.

## International Development Partnerships

5 Cleveland Mansions, Widley Road,
London W9 2LA
T: 020 7286 9756
E: office@idp-uk.org
www.idp-uk.org
Director: Andrew Chadwick
We provide broad-based humanitarian
assistance to rural communities in Ethiopia,
particularly: improving access to healthcare;
providing clean water and sanitation facilities;
rehabilitating schools; improving agricultural
production; protecting the environment and
preserving Ethiopia's heritage.
Volunteers: 8
Income: £90,000 (2014–15)

## International Fund for Animal Welfare

8th Floor, Camelford House,
87–89 Albert Embankment,
London SE1 7UD
T: 020 7587 6700
F: 020 7587 6720
E: info@ifaw.org
www.ifaw.org
Promotes the compassionate treatment of
animals as sentient beings; to protect them
from cruelty; to preserve their natural
habitat; to preserve them from extinction.

## International Glaucoma Association

Woodcote House,
15 Highpoint Business Village, Henwood,
Ashford, Kent TN24 8DN
T: 01233 648164
Helpline: 01233 648170
F: 01233 648179
E: info@iga.org.uk
glaucoma-association.com
Chief Executive: David Wright
Provides a fellowship for those suffering from
the eye disease glaucoma and those
concerned in its diagnosis and treatment;
presses for increased resources for what is

frequently a neglected condition so that there is an improved awareness and better long-term monitoring of the disease. This is necessary because the loss of sight from glaucoma is largely preventable yet it accounts for 13% of the registered blind.
Employees: 14

## International Guide Dog Federation

Hillfields, Burghfield Common,
Reading RG7 3YG
T: 0118 983 8356
E: enquiries@igdf.org.uk
www.igdf.org.uk
First and foremost, membership of the IGDF enables guide dog organisations around the world to join a community where all organisations have meet to the internationally recognised IGDF standards. That community wants to show it meets internationally recognised standards and wants to share its knowledge and the IGDF facilitates that.
Employees: 1

## International Institute for Environment and Development

3 Endsleigh Street, London WC1H 0DD
T: 020 7388 2117
F: 020 7388 2826
E: morris.kagkwo@iied.org
www.iied.org
Director: Camilla Toulmin
IIED seeks to make the world a fairer and more sustainable place, in alliance with like-minded partners. Acting as a catalyst, broker and facilitator, we seek to add voice to poorer and more vulnerable groups to ensure their interests are heard in decision-making and can bring about progressive change.
Employees: 70

## International Institute of Communications

The Glasshouse, 177–187 Arthur Road,
Wimbledon, London SW19 8AE
T: 020 8947 3535
F: 020 8944 6083
E: info@iicom.org
www.iicom.org
The Institute's principal activity is the organisation of overseas meetings and conferences, carrying out research and publishing material in the field of worldwide communications.
Employees: 5
Volunteers: 20

## International League for the Protection of Horses

Anne Colvin House, Snetterton,
Norfolk NR16 2LR
T: 0870 870 1927
F: 0870 904 1927
E: nagtrader08@gmail.com
www.ilph.org
Our aim is a world where horses are used but never abused. Our mission is to protect horses from abuse and alleviate their suffering by rehabilitation, campaigning and educating worldwide.
Employees: 131
Volunteers: 8
Regional offices: 5

## International Longevity Centre-UK

22–26 Albert Embankment, Vauxhall,
London SE1 7TJ
T: 020 7735 7565
E: louisetasker@ilcuk.org.uk
www.ilcuk.org.uk
Chief Executive: Baroness Sally Greengross
The International Longevity Centre-UK is an independent, non-partisan think-tank dedicated to addressing issues of longevity, ageing and population change. We develop ideas, undertake research and create a forum for debate.
Employees: 8
Regional offices: 1

## International Network for the Availability of Scientific Publications

60 St Aldates, Oxford OX1 1ST
T: 01865 249909
F: 01865 251060
E: inasp@inasp.info
www.inasp.info/en
The charity exists for the benefit of people in resource-poor countries, to promote education, knowledge and learning by enhancing local capabilities to manage and use information and knowledge.
Employees: 16

## International Seafarers Welfare & Assistance Network

3rd Floor, Suffolk House, George Street,
Croydon, Surrey CR0 1PE
T: 0300 012 4279
Helpline: 020 7323 2737
F: 0300 012 4280
E: iswan@iswan.org.uk
www.seafarerswelfare.org
Executive Director: Roger Harris
The objectives of ISWAN are to promote the relief of need, hardship or distress

amongst seafarers of all nationalities, races, colours and creeds.
Employees: 16

## International Seafarers' Assistance Network

8th Floor, Cygnet House,
12–14 Sydenham Road, Croydon,
Surrey CR0 2EE
T: 020 8680 2232
F: 020 3251 0221
E: info@seafarerhelp.org
www.seafarerhelp.org
Provides support, information and advice to seafarers around the world, through a network of maritime agencies.
Employees: 3

## International Service

2nd Floor, Rougier House, 5 Rougier Street,
York YO1 6HZ
T: 01904 647799
F: 01904 652353
E: contact@internationalservice.org.uk
www.internationalservice.org.uk
Chief Executive: Jo Baker
An international development agency that has been changing lives for more than 60 years by empowering some of the world's poorest and most marginalised people. International Service works in Latin America, West Africa and the Middle East, supporting in-country partners to develop and deliver sustainable solutions to inequality and poverty. Partners range from a local, grassroots level to government departments. Promoting social and economic inclusion is at the core of our work.
Employees: 18
Volunteers: 250
Regional offices: 6

## International Stress Management Association UK

PO Box 108, PO Box 108, Caldicot,
Avon NP26 9AP
T: 0117 969 7284
E: stress@isma.org.uk
www.isma.org.uk
Chair: Jenny Edwards
ISMA is a registered charity with a multidisciplinary professional membership. It exists to promote sound knowledge and best practice in the prevention and reduction of human stress. It sets professional standards for the benefit of individuals and organisations using the services of its members.
Employees: 1

## International Students House

229 Great Portland Street,
London W1W 5PN
T: 020 7631 8300
F: 020 7631 8307
E: marketing@ish.org.uk
www.ish.org.uk
Helps students achieve the academic and personal aims that have brought them to the UK; provides the best opportunities for international students to experience the many facets of life in the UK and give them a deeper understanding of British society; gives British students the opportunity for friendship with people from widely differing backgrounds and cultures and by these means makes an effective contribution to better international relations.
Employees: 130

## International Tree Foundation

Mayfield House, 256 Banbury Road,
Oxford, Oxfordshire OX2 7DE
T: 01865 318838
E: misty@internationaltreefoundation.org
www.internationaltreefoundation.org
Chief Executive: Andy Egan
Since 1924 ITF has worked with communities in UK and internationally to protect the environment through safeguarding forests, re-forestation and improving livelihoods through agroforestry. Our programmes: Tree Power schools programme combining global and outdoor learning to encourage environmental awareness; Africa Drylands programme tackles desertification in the Sahel region; Sustainable Community Forestry Programme supports community-led forestry, bio-diversity and livelihoods projects across sub-Saharan Africa; UK Community Tree Planting provides grants for community and schools forestry projects.
Employees: 5
Volunteers: 2
Income: £267,490 (2013–14)

## International Voluntary Service

Thorn House, 5 Rose Street, Edinburgh,
Lothian EH2 2PR
T: 0131 243 2745
F: 0131 243 2747
E: info@ivsgb.org
www.ivsgb.org
Development Director:
Helen Wass O'Donnell
IVS GB is a peace organisation that promotes intercultural cooperation and intercultural understanding through voluntary work. Volunteer projects work for sustainable development of local and global communities throughout the world. IVS is open to everyone from 18 to 70 years. We offer short-term projects of two to four weeks and long-term opportunities and we are a sending organisation for EVS (European Voluntary Service).
Employees: 4
Volunteers: 3
Regional offices: 1

## International Youth Hostel Federation

2nd Floor, Gate House, Fretherne Road,
Welwyn Garden City,
Hertfordshire AL8 6RD
T: 01707 324170
F: 01707 323980
E: jpowell@hihostels.com
www.hihostels.com
Chief Executive: Mikael Hansson
Promotes the education of all young people by encouraging in them a greater knowledge, love and care of the countryside, towns and cities in all parts of the world; provides hostel accommodation with no distinction of race, nationality, colour, religion, sex, class or political opinions; develops a better understanding of other people, both at home and abroad.
Employees: 20

## Internet Watch Foundation

Suite 7310, First Floor Building 7300,
Cambridge Research Park,
Waterbeach CB25 9TN
T: 01223 203030
E: bill@iwf.org.uk
www.iwf.org.uk
Chief Executive: Susie Hargreaves
The IWF is the UK reporting hotline for images of child sexual abuse online, extreme adult pornography and non-photographic images of child sexual abuse. Our vision is to eliminate online child sexual abuse.
Employees: 20
Regional offices: 1

## INTRAC

PO Box 563, Oxford OX2 6RZ
T: 01865 201851
F: 01865 201852
E: info@intrac.org
www.intrac.org
Provides specially designed management training, consultancy and research services to organisations involved in international relief and development; improves the organisational effectiveness and programme performance of northern NGOs and southern partners.
Employees: 28
Volunteers: 3
Regional offices: 3

## involve Community Services

The Court House, Town Square, Bracknell,
Berkshire RG12 1AE
T: 01344 304404
E: reception@involve.community
involve.community
General Manager: Phillip Cook
involve is an independent organisation whose role is to enhance the quality of life of the people of Bracknell Forest and Wokingham Borough by promoting and supporting the work of voluntary, community and faith organisations. We are a central support for voluntary and community action and a local development agency and provide back office support for our members.
Employees: 16
Volunteers: 120
Regional offices: 1
Income: £350,000 (2015–16)

## Involvement and Participation Association (IPA)

42 Colebrook Row, London N1 8AF
T: 0171 354 8040
F: 020 7354 8041
E: involve@ipa-involve.com
www.ipa-involve.com
Promotes employee information and consultation processes and partnership in the workplace.
Employees: 6

## Iranian Association

Palingswick House, 241 King Street,
London W6 9LP
T: 020 8748 6682
F: 020 8563 7549
E: info@iranianassociation.org.uk
www.iranianassociation.org.uk
Aims to assist the development of the Iranian ethnic community in Britain in terms of settlement, social welfare, training and education.
Employees: 13
Volunteers: 35

## Irish in Britain

356 Holloway Road, London N7 6PA
T: 020 7697 4081
F: 020 7697 4271
E: info@irishinbritain.org
www.irishinbritain.org
CEO: Jennie McShannon

Irish in Britain is the national representative body for the Irish in Britain. Working together with over 100 Irish cultural and community members we endeavour to raise the profile and contribution of the Irish community in Britain through research, policy and parliamentary work, campaigns and community development support. Our mission is to achieve a confident, healthy and empowered Irish community participating fully in Britain.
**Employees: 11**
**Volunteers: 10**
**Regional offices: 3**

## Isbourne Foundation

Wolseley House, Oriel Road,
Cheltenham GL50 1TH
T: 01242 254321
E: info@isbourne.org
www.isbourne.org
The Foundation helps individuals to develop their self-awareness in harmony with natural and spiritual laws.
**Employees: 3**
**Volunteers: 10**

## Islamic Relief

19 Rea Street South, Digbeth, Birmingham,
West Midlands B5 6LB
T: 0121 605 5555
F: 0121 622 5003
E: saleh.saeed@irworldwide.org
www.islamic-relief.com
**Chief Executive Officer: Saleh Saeed**
Dedicated to the service of the world's poorest people through emergency intervention at the time of disasters and through long-term development in the fields of education, health, income generation and water and sanitation.
**Employees: 240**
**Volunteers: 100**
**Regional offices: 25**

## IVAR

26 Russell Square, Bloomsbury,
London WC1B 5DQ
T: 020 7631 6608
F: 020 7631 6688
E: kulwinder@ivar.org.uk
www.ivar.org.uk
**Director: Ben Cairns**
IVAR's mission is to support the development and sustainability of charities and other voluntary, community and not-for-profit organisations through research, education and training.
**Employees: 3**

## Iyengar Yoga Institute

223A Randolph Avenue, London W9 1NL
T: 020 7624 3080
F: 020 7372 2726
E: office@iyi.org.uk
www.iyi.org.uk
Aims to advance public education in the classical teachings of the science of yoga; promotes and advances the study and practice of yoga; supports research into the therapeutic effects of yoga as a means of improving the mental and physical health of the community and publishes the results of such research.

## JAT

Berkeley House, 1st Floor,
18–24 High Street, Edgware HA8 7RP
T: 020 8952 5253
F: 020 8952 8893
E: admin@jat-uk.org
www.jat-uk.org
**Director: Janine Clements**
JAT provides sexual health and HIV education for Jewish youth in schools, youth groups and summer camps. We also run a programme for parents on how to talk to their children about sex. We offer financial, practical and emotional support for Jewish people with HIV.
**Employees: 4**
**Volunteers: 20**

## Jewish Association for the Mentally Ill

Olympia House, Armitage Road,
London NW11 8RQ
T: 020 8458 2223
F: 020 8731 7395
E: info@jamiuk.org
www.jamiuk.org
Provides services and support to people with severe and enduring mental health problems.
**Employees: 8**
**Volunteers: 37**

## Jewish Bereavement Counselling Service

Bet Meir, 44A Albert Road, Hendon,
London NW4 2SJ
T: 020 8385 1874
E: enquiries@jbcs.org.uk
jvisit.org.uk
Offers emotional help and support to members of the Jewish community who have been bereaved, and serves as a resource and information centre to both the Jewish and the non-Jewish community within London and around the UK.

## Jewish Council for Racial Equality (JCORE)

PO Box 47864, London NW11 1AB
T: 020 8455 0896
E: admin@jcore.org.uk
www.jcore.org.uk
**Executive Director: Dr Edie Friedman**
Since 1976, The Jewish Council for Racial Equality (JCORE) has been working to promote race equality in the UK through education, campaigning and dialogue. We have a particular interest in achieving justice for refugees and asylum seekers, safeguarding their human rights and giving them practical support. We also work closely with other ethnic minority groups in order to understand our common experiences and develop a collective voice on race and asylum issues.
**Employees: 3**
**Volunteers: 30**

## Jewish Lads and Girls Brigade including Outreach/Kiruv and Hand-in-Hand Young Volunteers

3 Beechcroft Road, South Woodford,
London E18 1LA
T: 020 8989 8990
F: 020 8530 3327
E: getinvolved@jlgb.org
www.jlgb.org
Aims to train its members in loyalty, honour, discipline and self-respect so that they may become a credit to their country and their community. We are committed to enhancing the lives of Jewish young people through a diverse range of experiences and activities within a friendly and safe environment, encouraging development within the Jewish and wider community.
**Employees: 10**
**Volunteers: 250**
**Regional offices: 1**

## Jewish Marriage Council

23 Ravenshurst Avenue, Hendon,
London NW4 4EE
T: 020 8572 2691
E: info@jmc-uk.org
www.jmc-uk.org
Chair: Martyn Zeidman
Provides confidential support for all Jewish people.
Employees: 2
Volunteers: 20
Regional offices: 1

## Jewish Women's Aid

PO Box 65550, London N3 9EG
T: 020 8445 8060
Helpline: 0808 801 0500
E: info@jwa.org.uk
www.jwa.org.uk
Executive Director: Naomi Dickson
Aims to raise awareness of the issues of domestic abuse against women within the Jewish community and to campaign on their behalf; provides a refuge for Jewish women and their children fleeing domestic abuse; fosters links with organisations in both the Jewish and the wider community; provides professional advice services; researches, develops and produces resources and publicity material.
Employees: 15
Volunteers: 160
Regional offices: 1

## Jigsaw4U Ltd

40 Mill Green Road, Mitcham,
Surrey CR4 4HY
T: 020 8687 1384
F: 020 8687 9730
E: info@jigsaw4u.org.uk
www.jigsaw4u.org.uk
Director of Operations: Pam Byfield
Jigsaw4U is a child-centred charity supporting children and young people through grief, loss and trauma whilst also empowering them to have a voice in decision-making about their own lives. The organisation delivers a wide range of projects including those that work with sexual exploitation, home school links, domestic abuse, participation for disabled young people, pre and post bereavement, advocacy and going missing.
Employees: 21
Volunteers: 60
Income: £655,021 (2013–14)

## John Ellerman Foundation

Aria House, 23 Craven Street,
London WC2N 5NS
T: 020 7930 8566
E: enquiries@ellerman.org.uk
www.ellerman.org.uk
Director: Nicola Pollock
The Foundation is a generalist grant-making trust, which mainly funds charities working in the arts, environment and welfare in the UK.
Employees: 5
Income: £3,692,000 (2014–15)

## John Huntingdon's Charity

John Huntingdon Centre, 189 High Street,
Sawston, Cambridge CB22 3HJ
T: 01223 830599
E: jill@johnhuntingdon.org.uk
johnhuntingdon.org.uk
Charity Manager: Jill Hayden
To bring relief either generally or to individual persons who are in conditions of need, hardship or distress in particular, but not exclusively, for the benefit of those who live, work and study in the Parish of Sawston and elsewhere locally. We achieve these objectives by supporting individuals and families with free advice through the JHC Support Service, giving grants to individuals and organisations and housing those most in need in our almshouses.
Employees: 5
Volunteers: 14
Income: £350,000 (2014–15)

## Joint Committee of the Order of St John and British Red Cross Society

5th Floor, 22–26 Albert Embankment,
London SE1 7TJ
E: balwinder@jointcommittee.freeserve.co.uk
Provides financial assistance in the form of grants to ex-service men and women disabled in the First and Second World Wars. Help is also available for widows of war disability pensioners, for sick and elderly ex-members of the nursing services of HM Forces and to officers and members of the Voluntary Aid Detachment of the Red Cross and St John Ambulance who gave service to the wounded in the Second World War or earlier.

## Joint Council for the Welfare of Immigrants

115 Old Street, London EC1V 9RT
T: 020 7251 8708
F: 020 7251 8707
E: info@jcwi.org.uk
www.jcwi.org.uk
Chief Executive: Habib Rahman
JCWI was established in 1967 to provide immediate and direct support to immigrants and to respond to the injustice and unfairness of UK immigration control. JCWI exists to campaign for justice in immigration, nationality and refugee laws and policy.
Employees: 10
Volunteers: 2

## Joint Epilepsy Council

PO Box 186, Leeds,
West Yorkshire LS20 8WY
T: 01943 87182
E: sharon.jec@btconnect.com
www.jointepilepsycouncil.org.uk
Chief Executive: Sharon Wood
The Joint Epilepsy Council of the UK and Ireland (JEC) is an umbrella charity providing the representative voice working for the benefit of people affected by epilepsy.
Employees: 1
Volunteers: varies

## Joseph Levy Foundation

1 Bell Street, London NW1 5JY
T: 020 7616 1200
F: 020 7616 1206
E: info@jlf.org.uk
www.jlf.org.uk
Director: Sue Nyfield
The Foundation supports general charitable purposes, giving grants to registered charities. The trustees believe in an inclusive society and recognise the needs of all its citizens. The Foundation works with charities that enable people to build a better future in their communities and to improve their quality of life. The Foundation is currently closed to unsolicited applications.
Employees: 2

## Joseph Rowntree Foundation

The Homestead, 40 Water End, York,
North Yorkshire YO30 6WP
T: 01904 629241
F: 01904 620072
E: sarah.carrette@jrf.org.uk
www.rowntreesociety.org.uk
Chief Executive: Julia Unwin
The Joseph Rowntree Foundation's aim is to search, demonstrate and influence, providing research, evidence, solutions and ideas that will

help to overcome the causes of poverty and inequality. Our three main research themes are Poverty, Place and An Ageing Society.
**Employees: 700**

## Josephine Butler Educational Trust

**4 The Hedges, Penenden Heath, Maidstone, Kent ME14 2JW**
**T: 01622 679630**
**E: jbt@liverpool.anglican.org**
**www.josephinebutler.org.uk**
The Trust disseminates knowledge and educates the public about the law as it affects prostitution of women and children, international sexual slavery and all forms of exploitation of prostitution by third parties.

## Journalists Charity

**Dickens House, 35 Wathen Road, Dorking, Surrey RH4 1JY**
**T: 01306 887511**
**F: 01306 888212**
**E: enquiries@pressfund.org.uk**
**www.journalistscharity.org.uk**
**Director: David Ilott**
Helps journalists and their dependants in times of need. Also provides sheltered housing and a nursing home.
**Employees: 20**
**Volunteers: 30**

## Jubilee Sailing Trust

**Merlin Quay, Hazel Road, Southampton, Hampshire SO19 7GB**
**T: 023 8044 9108**
**F: 023 8044 9145**
**E: rebecca.withers@jst.org.uk**
**www.jst.org.uk**
**Chief Executive: Amanda Butcher**
The JST was founded in 1977 to give disabled people the opportunity to discover the thrill and adventure of offshore tall ship sailing as a member of a mixed-ability crew. The JST operates two beautiful purpose designed and built tall ships, Lord Nelson and Tenacious, and is the only organisation in the world that can integrate mixed-ability crews on year-round voyages to northern Europe, the Canaries and the Caribbean.
**Employees: 58**
**Volunteers: 500**

## Judith Trust

**5 Carriage House, 90 Randolph Avenue, London W9 1BG**
**T: 020 7266 1073**
**F: 020 7289 5804**
**E: judith.trust@lineone.net**
**www.judithtrust.org.uk**
**Chair: Annette Lawson**
The Judith Trust's vision is a world without struggle: a better life for people with both learning disabilities and mental illness needs and their carers. The Trust funds commissioned research and, on the basis of outcomes, advocates for policy change and implementation.
**Employees: 1**

## Julia Margaret Cameron Trust

**Dimbola Museum and Galleries, Terrace Lane, Freshwater Bay, Isle of Wight PO40 9QE**
**T: 01983 756814**
**E: elissa.blizzard@dimbola.co.uk**
**www.dimbola.co.uk**
**Chairman: Brian Hinton**
Former home and work place of pioneering Victorian photographer Julia Margaret Cameron, now a museum and gallery. The charity aims to educate the public about the work of Cameron, the history of photography and the Freshwater Circle and to encourage an appreciation of modern photography as an art.
**Employees: 3FTE**
**Volunteers: 26**
**Income: £99,698 (2012–13)**

## Just a Drop

**Gateway House, 28 The Quadrant, Richmond, Surrey TW9 1DN**
**T: 020 8910 7981**
**F: 020 8334 0555**
**E: nikki.davis@reedexpo.co.uk**
**www.justadrop.org**
Polluted water is the world's biggest killer of children under five. Just a Drop raises money to build wells, install hand pumps and carry out health and sanitation programmes to give them and their families clean, accessible water.
**Employees: 1**
**Volunteers: 10**

## JustGiving

**1st Floor, 30 Eastbourne Terrace, London W2 6LA**
**E: press@justgiving.com**
**www.justgiving.com**
**CEO: Zarine Kharas**
JustGiving has been helping charities and their supporters raise money online since 2001. Whether it's online fundraising, regular giving, text donations, automatic Gift Aid reclaim or detailed reporting, we make sure you have the tools you need all in one place.

## JUSTICE

**59 Carter Lane, London EC4V 5AQ**
**T: 020 7329 5100**
**F: 020 7329 5055**
**E: admin@justice.org.uk**
**www.justice.org.uk**
**Director: Roger Smith**
JUSTICE is an independent law reform and human rights organisation. Since its formation in 1957, JUSTICE has been at the cutting edge of the debate on legal reform. It is widely respected for the breadth, depth and quality of its analysis. Today, more than ever, JUSTICE is involved in the issues that will shape the future legal landscape.
**Employees: 8**
**Volunteers: 6**

## Kairos Community Trust

**110 Brixton Road, London SW9 6BE**
**F: 020 7582 4211**
**E: kairosoffice@kairoscommunity.org.uk**
**www.kairoscommunity.org.uk**
Helps homeless people to recover from situations causing their marginalisation, providing detox and treatment for substance misuse and suitable accommodation. It fosters their recovery in a community residential setting and alleviates poverty.
**Employees: 21**
**Volunteers: 20**

## Karuna Trust

**72 Holloway Road, London N7 8JG**
**T: 020 7700 3434**
**F: 020 7700 3535**
**E: info@karuna.org**
**www.karuna.org**
Works for the relief of poverty, the advancement of education, cultural conservation and advancement of the Buddhist religion. Continues to expand the funding work begun by Aid for India, both in India and elsewhere and promotes, amongst the poorest people of the world, dignity, initiative and self-reliance.
**Employees: 9**
**Volunteers: 5**

## Keep Britain Tidy

Elizabeth House, The Pier, Wigan,
Greater Manchester WN3 4EX
T: 01942 612621
F: 01942 824778
E: press@keepbritaintidy.org
www.keepbritaintidy.org
**Chief Executive: Phil Barton**
Keep Britain Tidy is a campaigning
environmental charity that encourages
everyone to be litter free, to waste less and
to live more. It runs a variety of programmes
including WasteWatch, Eco-Schools in
England, the Blue Flag Award for beaches
and the Keep Britain Tidy Network for local
authorities and land managers as well as a
number of volunteering programmes.
**Employees: 100**
**Volunteers: 75000**

## Keep Fit Association

Suite 105, Astra House, Arklow Road,
London SE14 6EB
T: 01403 266000
F: 020 8692 8383
E: office@emdp.org
www.keepfit.org.uk
Provides the opportunity for people of all
ages and aptitudes to develop their individual
potential through the medium of movement,
dance and exercise by making full use of
their physical and intellectual capabilities
and social involvement.
**Employees: 2**
**Volunteers: 20**
**Regional offices: 82**

## Kent Volunteers

E: caroline.reade@kent.gov.uk

## Kenward Trust

Kenward Road, Yalding ME18 6AH
T: 01622 814187
F: 01622 815805
E: audrey.pie@kenwardtrust.org.uk
www.kenwardtrust.org.uk
**Chief Executive: Angela Painter**
The Kenward Trust is a registered social and
healthcare Christian charity that provides
drug and alcohol recovery, reintegration and
resettlement services in Kent and East Sussex.
**Employees: 52**
**Volunteers: 29**

## Keratec

Keratec Eyebank, Department of Anatomy,
St Georges, University of London,
Cranmer Terrace, London SW17 0RE
T: 020 8672 2325
F: 020 8682 3026
E: rostron@sgul.ac.uk
www.kerateceyebank.co.uk
**Medical Director: Chad Rostron**
The charity is committed to developing
the treatment of corneal disease. Corneal
opacity is a major cause of blindness
worldwide, and we are researching new
methods of treatment to restore sight in
those suffering from conditions such as
keratoconus, trachoma and corneal scarring.
**Employees: 1**
**Volunteers: 1**

## Keratoconus Self-Help and Support Association

PO Box 26251, London W3 9WQ
Helpline: 020 8993 4759
E: anneklepacz@aol.com
www.keratoconus-group.org.uk
The association provides information and
support to those with this eye condition.
It organises conferences and members
meetings and produces a regular newsletter
and other information.
**Volunteers: 12**
**Income: £10,802 (2012–13)**

## Keychange Charity

5 St Georges Mews,
43 Westminster Bridge Road,
London SE1 7JB
T: 020 7633 0533
E: info@keychange.org.uk
www.keychange.org.uk
**CEO: Graham Waters**
Provides residential care for older people
(care homes) and for homeless young
people (hostels).
**Employees: 400+**
**Regional offices: 15**

## KeyRing

65 Dalston Lane E8 2NG
T: 020 3119 0960
E: enquiries@keyring.org
www.keyring.org
**Chief Executive: Karyn Kirkpatrick**
KeyRing supports vulnerable adults to
live independently at the heart of their
community. KeyRing has been supporting
people for over 20 years and over 1,000

people across England and Wales are
unlocking their potential through KeyRing.
**Employees: 200**
**Volunteers: 100**
**Regional offices: 3**

## KIDS

49 Mecklenburgh Square,
London WC1N 2NY
T: 020 7520 0420
F: 020 7520 0406
E: kevin.williams@kids.org.uk
www.kids.org.uk
**Chief Executive: Kevin Williams**
Provides services to disabled children
and young people and their families.
**Employees: 600**
**Volunteers: 200**
**Regional offices: 5**

## Kids Can Achieve

E: pat.lee@kidscanachieve.co.uk

## Kidsaid

4 St Giles Terrace, Northampton NN1 2BN
T: 01604 630332
E: info@kidsaid.org.uk
www.kidsaid.org.uk
**Chair of Trustees: Patrick Conrad**
A Northamptonshire based charity that
provides therapy and support to children who
have suffered bereavement, abuse, domestic
violence, family breakdown, bullying or any
form of trauma.
**Employees: 3**
**Volunteers: 10**
**Regional offices: 1**
**Income: £120,000 (2014–15)**

## Kidscape Campaign for Children's Safety

2 Grosvenor Gardens, London SW1W 0DH
T: 020 7730 3300
F: 020 7730 7081
E: contact@kidscape.org.uk
www.kidscape.org.uk
**CEO: Claude Knights**
Kidscape is committed to keeping children
safe. Launched in 1985, it is the only
nationwide charity dedicated exclusively
to preventing child sexual abuse and bullying
before it happens.
**Employees: 22**
**Volunteers: 1**
**Regional offices: 1**

## Kidsout UK

14 Church Square, Leighton Buzzard,
Bedfordshire LU7 1AE
T: 01525 385252
F: 01525 385533
E: kidsout@kidsout.org.uk
www.kidsout.org.uk
CEO: Gordon Moulds CBE

Our mission is to help transform the lives of disadvantaged children and young people in the UK by providing fun opportunities and positive experiences to significantly enhance their wellbeing and outlook for a happier future. Our projects currently support children who have experienced domestic violence, children with disabilities, children with English as an additional language, children struggling academically and those not in education, employment or training.
Employees: 7
Volunteers: 50

## King's Medical Research Trust

Weston Education Centre,
10 Cutcombe Road, London SE5 9RJ
T: 020 7848 5866
E: peter@wiard.ws

The Trust aims to relieve suffering and cure illness and disease by continuous research into causes, prevention, diagnosis and treatment, and by publishing the results for public good.

## Kingham Hill Trust

Oak Hill College, Chase Side, Southgate
T: 020 8449 0467
E: tonys@oakhill.ac.uk
www.oakhill.ac.uk
Bursar: Tony Sims

## Kingston Centre for Independent Living

River Reach, 31–35 High Street, Kingston,
Surrey KT1 1LF
T: 020 8546 9603
E: robert.reilly@kcil.org.uk
www.kcil.org.uk
CEO: Lisa Ehlers

We: enable disabled people in and around the Royal Borough of Kingston (RBK) to lead independent and empowering lives; lobby for full equality of status, opportunity and inclusion for all; promote the recognition and acceptance of the social model of disability; represent the interests of disabled people in and around RBK using appropriate forms of user consultation and engagement.
Employees: 10
Volunteers: 10
Income: £345,000 (2015–16)

## Kingsway International Christian Centre

KICC Prayer City, Buckmore Park,
Maidstone Road, Chatham,
Kent ME5 9QG
T: 020 8525 0000
E: ade_d'almeida@kicc.org.uk
www.kicc.org.uk
CEO: Oladipo Oluyomi

KICC is an independent, interdenominational and international church. KICC actively supports the community via a range of counselling services, skills training and a supplementary school for GCSE pupils. KICC also works in partnership with statutory and voluntary organisations to improve social conditions.
Employees: 51
Volunteers: 1200

## Kingwood Trust

2 Chalfont Court, Chalfont Close,
Lower Earley, Reading RG6 5SY
T: 0118 931 0143
F: 0118 931 1937
E: info@kingwood.org.uk
www.kingwood.org.uk
Chief Executive: Sue Osborn
Employees: 130

## Kith and Kids

c/o Haringey Irish Centre, Pretoria Road,
London N17 8DX
T: 020 8801 7432
F: 020 8885 3035
E: projects@kithandkids.org.uk
www.kithandkids.org.uk

Aims to achieve empowerment and social inclusion with families living with disability.

## Koestler Trust

168A Du Cane Road, London W12 0TX
T: 020 8740 0333
E: bcrosland@koestlertrust.org.uk
www.koestlertrust.org.uk

The charity promotes the creative enterprise of inmates and former inmates of prisons, young offender institutions and secure units.
Employees: 6

## Krishnamurti Foundation Trust

Brockwood Park, Bramdean,
Hampshire SO24 0CQ
T: 01962 771525
F: 01962 771159
E: kft@brockwood.org.uk
www.kfoundation.org

The Trust works to advance the education of the public in philosophy, sociology, psychology and comparative religion and, in particular, to promote the study of the teachings in those fields of Jiddu Krishnamurti.
Employees: 48
Volunteers: 20

## Kurdish Cultural Centre

14–16 Stannary Street, London SE11 4AA
T: 020 7735 0918
E: admin@kcclondon.org.uk
www.kcclondon.org.uk/english

Aims to: assist and advise the Kurdish community in matters relating to education, health, immigration, integration, legal issues, housing, social activities and welfare; support cultural events, meetings and seminars; encourage a positive relationship and wider co-operation between the Kurdish community and other communities.

## L'Arche

10 Briggate, Silsden, Keighley,
West Yorkshire BD20 9JT
T: 01535 656186
F: 01535 656426
E: info@larche.org.uk
www.larche.org.uk
National Leader: John Sargent

We are people with and without learning disabilities sharing life in communities, belonging to an international federation. Our mission is to: nurture communities of faith in which mutually transforming relationships can flourish; promote the gifts of people with learning disabilities enabling them to take a full part in L'Arche and society; be open and outward looking and actively engaged with those around us responding to changing needs and circumstances.
Employees: 400
Volunteers: 178
Regional offices: 11

## La Leche League Great Britain

PO Box 29, West Bridgford, Nottingham,
Nottinghamshire NG2 7NP
Helpline: 0845 120 2918
E: admin@laleche.org.uk
www.laleche.org.uk
Chair of Council of Directors:
Eden Anderson
Provides information and support for
breastfeeding mothers through a national
telephone helpline, email help and a network
of local groups, all run by trained volunteers.
Publishes books and leaflets on breastfeeding.
Promotes the benefits of breastfeeding and
works with health professionals nationally and
locally; trains mothers with the help of health
professionals through the national peer
counsellor programme.
Employees: 1
Volunteers: 260
Regional offices: 72

## Landlife

National Wildflower Centre,
Court Hey Park, Liverpool L16 3NA
T: 0151 737 1819
E: info@landlife.org.uk
www.wildflower.co.uk
Aims to protect and promote wildlife, working
with people for nature – working with nature
for people and creating new habitats for
people to enjoy.

## Landmine Action

1st Floor, 89 Albert Embankment,
London SE1 7TP
T: 020 7820 0222
F: 020 7820 0057
E: info@landmineaction.org
www.aoav.org.uk
Landmine Action is a not-for-profit
organisation committed to good governance
and the development of civil society through
the promotion of international humanitarian
law, the relief of poverty and the
empowerment of communities marginalised
by conflict.
Employees: 7
Volunteers: 2

## Landscape Institute

33 Great Portland Street,
London W1W 8QG
T: 020 7299 4508
E: mail@landscapeinstitute.org
www.landscapeinstitute.org
The Landscape Institute is the Royal
Chartered body for landscape architects and
professionals who inspire people to expect
the best from natural and built environments.
Employees: 20

## Langley House Trust

PO Box 181, Witney,
Oxfordshire OX28 6WD
T: 01993 774075
F: 01993 772425
E: info@langleyhousetrust.org
www.langleyhousetrust.org
The Langley House Trust is a national
Christian charity that provides resettlement
support for ex-offenders (and those at risk
of offending) working towards crime-free
independence and reintegration into society.
The Trust's residential projects along with
move-on accommodation provide a range of
supported accommodation. The Trust works
with those who are hard to place and accepts
both men and women of any or no faith.
Employees: 205
Volunteers: 20
Regional offices: 3

## Lasa

1st Floor, Kinnaird House, 1 Pall Mall East,
London SW1Y 5BP
T: 020 7377 2748
E: cashcroft@lasa.org.uk
www.lasa.org.uk
Chief Executive: Terry Stokes
Lasa is a social welfare law and technology
charity. Established in 1984, we're dedicated
to supporting organisations in their use of
technology and the delivery of social welfare
law advice to the disadvantaged communities
they serve.
Employees: 8
Income: £581,865 (2015–16)

## Lattitude Global Volunteering

Lattitude, 44 Queens Road,
Reading RG1 4BB
T: 0118 959 4914
F: 0118 957 6634
E: nadie@lattitude.org.uk
www.lattitude.org.uk
Chief Executive: Belinda Coote
Lattitude Global Volunteering has 35 years'
experience of working with young people.
Every year we place 2,000 UK and overseas
volunteers in 23 different countries. Our
aims: to provide placements that allow young
people to develop their skills and broaden
their education; to promote access to
volunteering opportunities for all young
people, regardless of background; to help
overseas communities by providing volunteer
support whilst empowering our young people
to make a real difference.
Employees: 28
Volunteers: 150

## Law Centres Network

Floor 1 Tavis House, 1–6 Tavistock Square,
Tavis House, London WC1H 9NA
T: 020 3637 1330
F: 020 3637 1342
E: info@lawcentres.org.uk
www.lawcentres.org.uk
Director: Julie Bishop
Established in 1978, the Law Centres
Network (a business name of the Law
Centres Federation) is a charity and a
company limited by guarantee. LCN
supports and promotes Law Centres in
England, Wales and Northern Ireland. Law
Centres provide free legal advice on social
welfare law to disadvantaged people in their
communities, helping them alleviate their
poverty and disadvantage.
Employees: 10
Regional offices: 44

## LawWorks

10–13 Lovat Lane, London EC3R 8DN
T: 020 7929 5601
F: 020 7929 5722
E: rg@lawworks.org.uk
www.lawworks.org.uk
Chief Executive: Robert Gill
Brokers and develops pro bono legal services
linking those who need free legal help with
lawyers willing to provide it.
Employees: 14
Volunteers: 2000
Regional offices: 1

## LDN Research Trust

PO Box 1083, Buxton, Norwich,
Norfolk NR10 5WY
T: 01603 279014
E: contact@ldnresearchtrust.org
www.ldnresearchtrust.org
Trustee: Linda Elsegood
We aim to raise awareness of LDN for
autoimmune conditions, cancers and
addictions, while helping initiate clinical
trials for conditions where LDN could be
of benefit.
Volunteers: 30
Income: £65,852 (2013–14)

## Leadership Trust Foundation

Weston under Penyard, Ross on Wye,
Herefordshire HR9 7YH
T: 01989 767667
F: 01989 768133
E: enquiries@leadership.co.uk
www.leadership.org.uk

Aims to enhance and develop leadership in all aspects of society.
**Employees: 80**
**Volunteers: 200**

## League Against Cruel Sports

**New Sparling House, Holloway Hill, Godalming, Surrey GU7 1QZ**
**F: 020 7378 7745**
**E: info@league.uk.com**
**www.league.org.uk**
Campaigns for the abolition of cruel sports where animals are hurt, at risk of trauma, injury or death for sport. Seeks change where abolition is not politically achievable and provides protection for animals endangered by cruel sports.
**Employees: 25**
**Volunteers: 50**
**Regional offices: 30**

## League of British Muslims

**Ilford Muslim Community Centre, Eton Road, Ilford, Essex IG1 2UE**
**T: 020 8514 0706**
**F: 020 8599 7052**
**E: leagueofbm@btconnect.com**
**www.leagueofbritishmuslims.co.uk**
The principal objectives of the charity are to advance the religion of Islam and to advance Islamic education amongst Muslims resident in England and Wales.
**Employees: 1**
**Volunteers: 12**

## League of Jewish Women

**6 Bloomsbury Square, London WC1A 2LP**
**T: 020 7242 8300**
**E: office@theljw.org**
**www.theljw.org**
**President: Marilyn Brummer**
The League of Jewish Women (LJW) is one of the leading voluntary Jewish women's service organisations in the UK. Affiliated to more than 30 other national and international organisations, membership is open to all Jewish men and women. LJW is the UK affiliate of the International Council of Jewish Women. LJW is a voluntary service organisation that provides help wherever it is needed, within both the Jewish and the wider community.
**Employees: 2**
**Volunteers: 2500**
**Regional offices: 1**

## League of Mercy

**PO Box 68, Lingfield, Surrey RH7 6QQ**
**T: 020 8660 4496 (also fax)**
**E: admin@leagueofmercy.co.uk**
**www.leagueofmercy.co.uk**
Works for: the advancement of the Christian faith; the relief of persons who are in need, hardship or distress; the advancement of education on the basis of Christian principles.

## League of Remembrance

**55 Great Ormond Street, London WC1N 3HZ**
**T: 020 7829 7818 (also fax)**
**E: info@leagueofremembrance.com**
**leagueofremembrance.org.uk**
Provides companionship, financial assistance and support to dependants and retired members of the armed forces and retired nurses.
**Employees: 1**
**Volunteers: 38**

## Learning and Work Institute

**21 De Montfort Street, Leicester, Leicestershire LE1 7GE**
**T: 0116 204 4200**
**F: 0116 285 4514**
**E: juliana.hancock@learningandwork.org.uk**
**www.learningandwork.org.uk**
**Chief Executive Officer: David Hughes**
Learning and work is an independent policy and research organisation dedicated to lifelong learning, full employment and inclusion. We bring together over 90 years of combined history and heritage from NIACE and CESI. We want everyone to have an opportunity to realise their ambitions and potential in learning, work and throughout life. We believe a better skilled workforce, in better paid jobs, is good for business, the economy and for society.
**Employees: 71**
**Regional offices: 3**
**Income: £6,195,000 (2014–15)**

## Learning for Life

**2 Rickett Street, London SW6 1RU**
**T: 020 7385 8765**
**F: 020 7385 9154**
**E: info@learningforlifeuk.org**
**www.learningforlifeuk.org**
**Director: Ujwala Samant**
Learning for Life assists and relieves needy persons and their dependants who are employed or have been employed in the motor, agricultural engineering and cycle and allied trades and industries.
**Employees: 3**
**Volunteers: 30**

## Learning from Experience Trust

**Goldsmiths College, Deptford Town Hall, New Cross Road, London SE14 6AF**
**T: 020 7919 7739**
**F: 020 7919 7762**
**E: su@gold.ac.uk**
**www.learningexperience.org.uk**
Aims to advance education by promoting research into, and developing the concept of, experiential learning and its assessment, and encouraging its recognition and use in education, training, industry, commerce and the public service.
**Employees: 5**

## Learning Plus UK

**1st Floor, Kings Lodge, 194 Kings Road, Reading, Berkshire RG1 4NH**
**T: 0118 956 8408**
**E: donna.roberts@learningplusuk.org**
**www.learningplusuk.org**
**Office Manager: Donna Roberts**
**Employees: 6**

## Learning Through Landscapes

**Ground Floor, F Block, Clarendon House, Monarch Way, Winchester, Hampshire SO22 5PW**
**T: 01962 846258**
**E: enquiries@ltl.org.uk**
**www.ltl.org.uk**
**Executive Director: Juno Hollyhock**
Learning through Landscapes is the UK charity dedicated to enhancing outdoor learning and play for children. Our vision is that every child benefits from stimulating outdoor learning and play in their education. We aim to enable children to connect with nature, be more active, be more engaged with their learning, develop their social skills and have fun!
**Employees: 20**
**Volunteers: 5**
**Regional offices: 2**
**Income: £750,000 (2015–16)**

## Leeds Church Institute

**E: haydn@leedschurchinstitute.org**

## Legal Action Group

3rd Floor, Universal House,
88–94 Wentworth Street, London E1 7SA
T: 020 7833 2931
F: 020 7837 6094
E: lag@lag.org.uk
www.lag.org.uk
**Director: Steve Hynes**
LAG is a national, independent charity that
aims to promote equal access to justice
for all members of society who are socially,
economically or otherwise disadvantaged. To
this end, it seeks to improve law and practice,
the administration of justice and legal services
through campaigning as well as publishing
legal books, its magazine Legal Action and
providing training for solicitors, barristers
and legal advisers.
**Employees: 9**
**Volunteers: 2**

## Legislation Monitoring Service for Charities, Voluntary Organisations and their Advisers

Church House, Great Smith Street,
London SW1P 3AZ
T: 020 7222 1265
E: info@lmsconline.org
www.charitylaw.info
LMSC's principal objective is monitoring and
disseminating information about legislative
and policy developments in the UK and
Europe likely to have an impact on charities.

## Leicestershire Centre for Integrated Living

West End Centre, Andrewes Street,
Leicester, Leicestershire LE3 5PA
T: 0116 222 5005
E: admin@lcil.org.uk
www.lcil.org.uk
**CEO: Stephen Cooper**
LCiL is an organisation of disabled people,
supporting disabled people. Based upon our
own experiences and skills we work closely
with Leicester City, the voluntary sector and
areas of the private sector to deliver support
advice and guidance to anyone directly or
indirectly affected by matters arising because
of a disability. Working to the social model of
disability, we offer support whatever the age
or condition.
**Employees: 12**
**Volunteers: 4**
**Income: £373,000,000 (2013–14)**

## Leo Baeck College

The Sternberg Centre for Judaism,
80 East End Road, London N3 2SY
T: 020 8349 5600
E: info@lbc.ac.uk
www.lbc.ac.uk
**Principal: Rabbi Dr Deborah Kahn-Harris**
Established in 1956, Leo Baeck College:
trains rabbis for Progressive Jewish
congregations in the UK, Europe and
worldwide with over 250 graduates;
promotes the study of Judaism in a spirit of
reverence for Jewish tradition; instills the love
of learning in the Jewish community by raising
the level of knowledge. Resources include
Judaica and research library.
**Employees: 13**
**Volunteers: 2**

## Leo Trust

Boldshaves Oast, Woodchurch, Ashford,
Kent TN26 3RA
T: 01233 860039
F: 01233 860060
E: leotrust@btconnect.com
www.leotrust.com
**Chief Executive: Joe Graham**
The Leo Trust is a residential care home for
adults with learning difficulties, which seeks to
promote the relief, welfare and preservation
of health of the residents and to provide
opportunities to develop them into
productive members of the community.
**Employees: 32**
**Volunteers: 1**

## Leonard Cheshire Disability

66 South Lambeth Road SW8 1RL
T: 020 3242 0200
F: 020 7802 8250
E: info@leonardcheshire.org
www.leonardcheshire.org
**Chief Executive: Clare Pelham**
We are the UK's leading charity supporting
disabled people. We work for a society in
which every person is equally valued. We
believe that disabled people should have
the freedom to live their lives the way they
choose – to live independently, contribute
economically and participate fully in society.
**Employees: 7100**
**Volunteers: 4000**
**Regional offices: 10**
**Income: £162,200,000 (2014–15)**

## Lepra

28 Middleborough, Colchester CO1 1TG
T: 01206 216700
E: lepra@lepra.org.uk
www.lepra.org.uk
**Chief Executive: Sarah Nancollas**
We are a UK-registered international charity
fighting disease, poverty and prejudice. We
work on the ground in Bangladesh, India
and Mozambique with people affected by
neglected diseases such as leprosy and
lymphatic filariasis and also malaria and TB.
**Employees: 50**
**Volunteers: 3**
**Regional offices: 1**
**Income: £4,970,000 (2014–15)**

## Lesbian and Gay Christian Movement

Oxford House, Derbyshire Street,
London E2 6HG
T: 020 7739 1249 (also fax)
E: info@lgcm.org.uk
www.lgcm.org.uk
**Chief Executive: Rev Sharon Ferguson**
We aim to encourage fellowship, friendship
and support among individual lesbian and gay
Christians and to help the whole church
re-examine its understanding of human
sexuality and to challenge homophobia.
**Employees: 2**
**Volunteers: 10**

## Let's Face It Support Network for the Facially Disfigured

72 Victoria Avenue, Westgate-on-Sea,
Kent CT8 8BH
T: 01843 833724
E: chrisletsfaceit@aol.com
www.lets-face-it.org.uk
**Founder/Chief Executive: Christine Piff**
Aims to provide counselling, advice and
support to patients with facial disfigurement,
however caused, and their families, by
meetings, letter writing, telephone contact
and hospital visits. This includes head and
neck cancer patients.
**Employees: 1**
**Volunteers: 40**
**Regional offices: 8**

## Leukaemia Care

1 Birch Court, Blackpole East,
Worcestershire WR3 8SG
T: 01905 755977
F: 01905 755166
E: care@leukaemia.org.uk
www.leukaemiacare.org.uk

Provides support, information and assistance to people affected by leukaemia or allied blood disorders.
Employees: 8
Volunteers: 125

## Lewy Body Society

Hudson House, 8 Albany Street,
Edinburgh EH1 3QB
T: 0131 473 2385
E: info@lewybody.org
www.lewybody.org
CEO: Jacqueline Cannon
Founded in 2006 and run entirely by volunteers, the LBS is the only charity in Europe dedicated exclusively to Lewy body disease. The Society's mission is to support research into and raise awareness of this terrible neurogenerative disease. The Society is committed to not having paid employees nor ever soliciting donations.
Volunteers: 10

## Liberal Judaism

The Montagu Centre, 21 Maple Street
E: shelley@liberaljudaism.org
Operations Director:
Shelley Shocolinsky-Dwyer

## Liberty

21 Tabard Street, London SE1 4LA
T: 020 7403 3888
Helpline: 0845 123 2307
E: webmaster@liberty-human-rights.org.uk
www.liberty-human-rights.org.uk
Liberty is also known as the National Council for Civil Liberties. Founded in 1934, we are a cross-party, non-party membership organisation at the heart of the movement for fundamental rights and freedoms in England and Wales. We promote the values of individual human dignity, equal treatment and fairness as the foundations of a democratic society.

## Library Campaign

13 Shrublands Close, Chelmsford CM2 6LR
T: 01273 887321
E: www.librarycampaign.com
Supports friends and user groups of publicly funded libraries to advocate and lobby for library provision support.

## Life

Life House, 1 Mill Street, Leamington Spa,
Warwickshire CV31 1ES
T: 01926 312272
F: 01926 336497
E: vickyobrien@lifecharity.org.uk
www.lifecharity.org.uk
Chief Executive: Stephen Sharpe

LIFE is a charity that offers an innovative approach to supporting women and families throughout pregnancy and beyond, including the provision of supported housing for pregnant women and mothers of young children.
Employees: 100
Volunteers: 380
Regional offices: 60

## Life Education Centres

County House, 14 Hatton Garden,
London EC1N 8AT
T: 020 7831 9311
F: 020 7831 9939
E: jeani@lifeeducation.org.uk
www.lifeeducation.org.uk
National Director: Stephen Burgess
Helping children make healthy choices. Life Education's main work is with primary schools and with parents, delivered through local trusts, to ensure that children develop the vital knowledge, skills and attitudes needed to make informed choices about health that will enhance and enrich their lives.
Employees: 7
Volunteers: 400
Regional offices: 40

## Life For The World

Micklefield Christian Centre,
Buckingham Drive, High Wycombe,
Buckinghamshire HP13 7YB
T: 01494 462008
Helpline: 0845 241 0973
E: wycombe@lftw.org
www.living-recovery.org
Chief Executive: John Lowton
Provides training, education, advice and consultancy for service providers (drug and alcohol misuse).
Employees: 5
Volunteers: 10
Regional offices: 2

## Life Opportunities Trust

Hempstead House, 1 Hempstead Road,
Kings Langley, Hertfordshire WD4 8BJ
T: 01923 299770
F: 01923 299771
E: atierney@lot-uk.org.uk
www.lot-uk.org.uk
Chief Executive: Ralph Verlander
Provides domiciliary and residential services for adults with learning disabilities.
Employees: 165
Volunteers: 14

## Lifeline Community Projects

LifeLine House, Neville Road, Dagenham,
Essex RM8 3QS
T: 020 8597 2900
F: 020 8597 1990
E: andriasoteriou@lifelineprojects.co.uk
www.lifelineprojects.co.uk
PA to Chief Executive: Andria Soteriou
LifeLine is a social enterprise which impacts individuals and influences systems. Characterised by renewed hope, developed confidence and improved skills, our programmes release people to be agents of change in their communities.
Employees: 81
Volunteers: 5
Regional offices: 2

## Lifeline International

25 Jellicoe Road N17 7BL
T: 020 8365 9815
F: 020 8805 9411
E: dupsy25@hotmail.com
www.lli.org.uk
Chair: Grace Labaran
Works to relieve the poverty and hardship of teenage mothers and their babies in Africa, whether through deprivation of family, skills, education, or otherwise, so that they may participate in a learning environment and/or life skills programme, enabling them to integrate into their communities and gain employment.
Employees: 10
Volunteers: 3
Regional offices: 5

## Lifeline Project Ltd

39–41 Thomas Street, Manchester M4 1NA
E: fazackerley2@btinternet.com
www.lifeline.org.uk
The charity aims to relieve poverty, sickness and distress among those persons affected by addiction to drugs of any kind, and to educate the public on matters relating to drug misuse.
Employees: 460

## Lifeworks

Blacklers, Park Road,
Dartington Hall Estate, Totnes,
Devon TQ9 6EQ
T: 01803 840744
E: laurabambrey@lifeworks-uk.org
lifeworks-uk.org
CEO: Richard Hanlon
A charity that supports learning disabled children and young adults. Our services include respite care (short breaks), residential care, a specialist FE college, youth clubs, life skills training and sports and leisure events.

## Lightforce International

Christian Centre, Strudwick Drive,
Oldbrook, Milton Keynes,
Buckinghamshire MK6 2TG
T: 01908 553070
F: 01908 553077
E: grr@lightforce.org.uk
www.lightforce.org.uk
**International Director: George Ridley**
Aims to advance the Christian religion and
to relieve people in any part of the world
who are in condition of need, hardship and
distress, in particular by deploying human
and material resources.
**Employees: 235**
**Volunteers: 15**
**Regional offices: 4**

## Lin Berwick Trust

Eastgate House, Upper East Street,
Sudbury, Suffolk CO10 1UB
T: 01787 372343
E: info@thelinberwicktrust.org.uk
www.thelinberwicktrust.org.uk
Provides relief for physically disabled people,
their families and carers, through the
provision of holiday accommodation.
**Employees: 3**
**Volunteers: 15**

## Linkage Community Trust

Scremby Grange, Spilsby PE23 5RW
T: 01754 890339
F: 01754 890538
E: info@linkage.org.uk
www.linkage.org.uk
Works to advance the general education and
social development of people with disabilities,
to develop such skills as are necessary to
enable such people to qualify for useful
occupation and, where this is not possible,
to provide long-term care facilities.

## LionHeart

Surveyor Court, Westwood Way, Coventry,
West Midlands CV4 8BF
T: 0845 603 9057
F: 024 7647 4701
E: mcarter@lionheart.org.uk
www.lionheart.org.uk
**Chief Executive: Mike Carter**
LionHeart provides advice, information,
counselling, befriending, financial help by
grant or loan and help in kind to members
of the Royal Institution of Chartered
Surveyors (RICS) and their dependants who
experience difficulties in their lives, including
bereavement, unemployment, ill-health,
accident or disability, separation of families
or difficulties in retirement.
**Employees: 11**
**Volunteers: 225**

## Lions Clubs International and British Isles and Ireland

257 Alcester Road South, Kings Heath,
Birmingham B14 6DT
T: 0121 441 4544
F: 0121 441 4510
E: secretary@lions.org.uk
www.lionsmd105.org
**Council Chairman: Martin Morgan**
Lions Clubs International is the world's largest
service club organisation. It has 1.4 million
members in 206 countries who work
together through selfless, effective
community service to answer the needs that
challenge communities around the world.
**Employees: 4**
**Volunteers: 17000**
**Regional offices: 13**

## Listening Books

12 Lant Street, London SE1 1QH
T: 020 7407 9417
E: info@listening-books.org.uk
www.listening-books.org.uk
**Director: Bill Dee**
Listening Books supplies an online and postal
audiobook library service to anyone across
the UK who struggles to read due to an
illness, disability or learning difficulty.
Members can choose from thousands of
titles across a range of formats (MP3 CDs,
internet streaming or downloads).
**Employees: 9**
**Volunteers: 10+**
**Regional offices: 1**

## Little Hearts Matter

11 Greenfield Crescent, Edgbaston,
Birmingham B15 3AU
T: 0121 455 8982
F: 0121 455 8983
E: info@lhm.org.uk
www.lhm.org.uk
The charity promotes the relief and welfare of
persons affected by single ventricle cardiac
disease and advances the education of the
medical profession and the general public on
the subject of single ventricle cardiac disease
and its implications for the family.
**Employees: 3**
**Volunteers: 12**

## Little Sisters of the Poor

St Peter's Residence, 2A Meadow Road,
South Lambeth, London SW8 1QH
T: 020 7735 0788
E: lsplondonstpeter@aol.com
www.littlesistersofthepoor.co.uk
Cares for elderly people of modest means
of all denominations or those of none.

## Livability

50 Scrutton Street, London EC2A 4XQ
T: 020 7452 2000
F: 020 7452 2001
E: info@livability.org.uk
www.livability.org.uk
**Chief Executive: Dave Webber**
Livability offers a wide range of innovative
services that support and enable disabled
people throughout their lives and provides
community organisations with the resources,
advice and confidence to bring life to local
neighbourhoods. Livability was formed in
2007 by the merger of John Grooms and
the Shaftesbury Society.
**Employees: 2000**

## Live Music Now!

Mill House, Newsham Bridge, Malton,
North Yorkshire YO17 6TZ
T: 01653 668551
E: keisha@macfarlane.org.uk
www.livemusicnow.org.uk
Provides performance opportunities for
talented young professional musicians under
the age of 27 years and brings the experience
of live music back into everyday life.

## Living Paintings

Unit 8, Kingsclere Park, Kingsclere,
Newbury, Berkshire RG20 4SW
T: 01635 299771 (also fax)
E: camilla@livingpaintings.org
www.livingpaintings.org
**Charity Director: Camilla Oldland**
Living Paintings helps blind and partially
sighted people feel visual images. We make
special versions of pictures with raised
surfaces that come to life when fingers feel
them. Sound recordings direct the fingers,
telling the stories of the pictures and
describing their features. For children and
adults the senses of touch and hearing
combine to make up for the missing sense
of sight.
**Employees: 7**
**Volunteers: 120**

## Living Streets

31–33 Bondway, London SW8 1SJ
T: 020 7820 1010
F: 020 7820 8208
E: info@livingstreets.org.uk
www.livingstreets.org.uk
Aims to improve conditions for walking journeys and for safe, convenient and environment friendly ways for people on foot. Represents the interests of walkers (particularly in urban areas) to central and local government and the media.
Employees: 12
Volunteers: 150
Regional offices: 76

## Local Investment Fund

Seventh Floor, Ibex House, 42–47 Minories, London EC3N 1DY
T: 020 7680 1028
E: information@lif.org.uk
www.lif.org.uk
LIF is dedicated to providing loan finance to economically viable, community-based voluntary organisations that are run as not-for-profit enterprises. It bridges the gap between grant dependency and mainstream banking finance.

## Local Trust

Unit 5, Angel Gate, 320–326 City Road, London EC1V 2PT
T: 020 3588 0571
E: info@localtrust.org.uk
www.localtrust.org.uk
Funding Administrator: Michael Williams
Employees: 11

## Localgiving

Localgiving, 6th Floor, 233 High Holborn, London WC1V 7DN
T: 0300 111 2340
E: help@localgiving.com
www.localgiving.com
Founder and CEO: Marcelle Speller
Localgiving is dedicated to providing funding opportunities and advocacy for local charities and community groups in the UK. Our mission is to safeguard the sustainability of the local voluntary sector by empowering charitable organisations to connect with supporters, fundraise online and take control of their future.
Employees: 14
Regional offices: 1

## Locality

33 Corsham Street, London N1 6DR
T: 0345 458 8336
E: info@locality.org.uk
www.locality.org.uk
CEO: Tony Armstrong
Locality is the national network of ambitious and enterprising community-led organisations. Our vision is a fair and diverse society where every neighbourhood thrives and where local people determine their future together. We represent community businesses across England, helping them to work in enterprising ways to improve their communities. With our members, we influence decision makers, both locally and nationally, to help create a fair, diverse society which puts local people in control.

## Locality

33 Corsham Street, London N1 6DL
T: 0845 458 8336
E: info@locality.org.uk
www.locality.org.uk
Locality is the leading nationwide network of settlements, development trusts, social action centres and community enterprises.

## London Funders

314–320 Grays Inn Road, London WC1X 8DP
T: 020 7255 4488
E: info@londonfunders.org.uk
www.londonfunders.org.uk
Director: David Warner
London Funders fulfils its mission by providing a unique space where funders can discuss issues affecting London and the work that they do, learn from each other, share experience and knowledge, be briefed on changes in public policy and the implications for London, and – increasingly – look at how they can work better together to improve the lives of Londoners.
Employees: 3

## London Gypsy and Traveller Unit

6 Westgate Street, London E8 3RN
T: 020 8533 2002
F: 020 8533 7110
E: srowles@lgtu.org.uk
www.lgtu.org.uk
Joint Chief Executive: Debby Kennett and Lorraine Sweeney
We support Travellers and Gypsies living in London to: influence decisions affecting their lives; improve their quality of life and the opportunities available to them; challenge

the discrimination they routinely experience. We do this by providing the following services: community development; youth work programme for young Irish Travellers in North and East London; advocacy and advice service on accommodation, benefits and access to services; learning support in literacy, IT and life skills; strategic and policy work.
Employees: 12
Volunteers: 7
Income: £316,919 (2014–15)

## Long-Term Conditions Alliance

202 Hatton Square, 16 Baldwins Gardens, London EC1N 7RJ
T: 020 7813 3637
F: 020 7813 3640
E: thelongtrail@ltca.org.uk
www.ltca.org.uk
Chief Executive: David Pink
Umbrella body of over 100 patient groups and professional organisations working to improve the lives of people with long-term conditions.
Employees: 5

## Look National Office

Queen Alexandra College,
49 Court Oak Road, Harborne,
Birmingham B17 9TG
T: 0121 428 5038
E: information@look-uk.org
www.look-uk.org
CEO: Aliona Laker
Provides practical help, support and information to families with visually impaired children. Promotes improved services nationally.
Employees: 4
Volunteers: 2

## Lubavitch Youth

107–115 Stamford Hill, London N16 5RP
T: 020 8800 0022
F: 020 8809 7324
E: info@lubavitchuk.com
www.lubavitchuk.com
Works to further the needs of the Jewish ethnic minority, in the widest possible context.
Volunteers: 200
Regional offices: 18

## LUpus Patients Understanding and Support (LUPUS)

8 Shakespeare Drive, Borehamwood,
Hertfordshire WD6 2FD
E: roz@lupus-support.org.uk
www.lupus-support.org.uk or
www.lupus-support.org
**Director: Rosalind M Share**
A non-profit organisation providing free
information and free online psychological
support for individuals affected by SLE, lupus
variant conditions and the antiphospholipid
antibody (Hughes) syndrome. The Lupus
Counselling Service is maintained by qualified
psychotherapists/counsellors. We offer
online psychological support services and
research into the unmet needs of individuals
affected by lupus. We also offer information
and support to carers and families as well as
doctors, nurses and other health
professionals.
**Volunteers: 3**

## LUPUS UK

St James House, Eastern Road, Romford,
Essex RM1 3NH
T: 01708 731251
E: headoffice@lupusuk.org.uk
www.lupusuk.org.uk
**Director: Chris Maker**
Provides communication between patients;
educates patients, the general public and the
medical profession about the symptoms and
problems of systemic lupus erythematosus;
raises funds and provides practical help and
lupus research.
**Employees: 7**
**Volunteers: 250**

## Lutheran Council of Great Britain

30 Thanet Street, London WC1H 9QH
T: 020 7388 4044
E: enquiries@lutheran.org.uk
www.lutheran.org.uk
**General Secretary: James Laing**
Established in 1948, the Lutheran Council is
a communion of churches that have come
together to express their shared Lutheran
heritage and identity through common work
in Britain, enriched by their cultural and
linguistic diversity.
**Employees: 20**
**Income: £868,000 (2014–15)**

## Lyme Disease Action

Sand, Sidbury, Sidmouth,
Devon EX10 0QN
E: lda@lymediseaseaction.org.uk
www.lymediseaseaction.org.uk
**Chairman: Stella Huyshe-Shires**
Lyme Disease Action was established for the
relief of persons suffering from Lyme disease,
other borrelioses and associated diseases by
raising awareness of the public at large and
scientific and medical education and research
in topics related to Lyme disease, other
borrelioses and associated diseases.
**Volunteers: 8**

## Lyme Trust

39 London Road, Newcastle,
Staffordshire ST5 1LN
T: 01782 634725
F: 01782 634510
E: heather.perry@thelymetrust.co.uk
www.thelymetrust.co.uk
The charity provides accommodation for
people with mild to moderate mental health
difficulties and assists them into a successful
return to life in the community.
**Employees: 18**
**Volunteers: 1**

## Lymphoedema Support Network

St Luke's Crypt, Sydney Street,
London SW3 6NH
T: 020 7351 0990
Helpline: 020 7351 4480
F: 020 7349 9809
E: adminlsn@lymphoedema.freeserve.co.uk
www.lymphoedema.org/lsn
**Chair: Anita Wallace**
Provides information and support to people
with lymphoedema and promotes better
awareness of lymphoedema as a major
health condition to local health authorities,
healthcare professionals and politicians.
**Employees: 2**
**Volunteers: 15**

## Lymphoma Association

PO Box 386, Aylesbury,
Buckinghamshire HP20 2GA
T: 01296 619400
Helpline: 0808 808 5555
F: 01296 619415
E: j.coldwell@lymphomas.org.uk
www.lymphomas.org.uk
**Chief Executive: Sally Penrose**
The Lymphoma Association is the only
specialist UK charity that provides accurate
medical information and support to lymphatic
cancer patients, their families, friends and
carers. Support services include a freephone
helpline, a buddy scheme that puts people in
touch with others who have been through a
similar experience of lymphoma, a network
of support groups throughout the UK, free
literature and an interactive website with a
chatroom and forum.
**Employees: 23**

## Macfarlane Trust

Alliance House, 12 Caxton Street,
London SW1 0QS
T: 020 7233 0057
F: 020 7233 0839
E: june@macfarlane.org.uk
www.macfarlane.org.uk
Works to meet the needs of those people
with haemophilia who became infected with
HIV through treatment with contaminated
blood products in the UK, and their
dependants, and dependants of those who
have died.
**Employees: 5**
**Volunteers: 10**

## MacIntyre Care

602 South Seventh Street,
Milton Keynes MK9 2JA
T: 01908 230100
F: 01908 694452
E: customer.solutions@macintyrecharity.org
www.macintyrecharity.org
MacIntyre is a national charity that provides
learning, support and care for more than 700
children and adults with learning disabilities,
at more than 120 MacIntyre services across
the UK.
**Employees: 1320**
**Volunteers: 50**

## Macmillan Cancer Support

89 Albert Embankment, London SE1 7UQ
T: 020 7840 4648
F: 020 7840 7841
E: contactus@macmillan.org.uk
www.macmillan.org.uk
**Volunteers: 70000**

## Macular Society

PO Box 1870, Andover,
Hampshire SP10 9AD
T: 01264 350551
Helpline: 0845 241 2041
F: 01264 350558
E: info@macularsociety.org
www.macularsociety.org
Chief Executive: Helen Jackman
Macular disease is the UK's most common cause of sight loss. The Macular Disease Society is the only UK charity supporting people with macular disease and seeking a cure. We provide information and support to anyone affected by macular disease and professionals working with people with the condition. We have over 15,000 members and support many more through our national network of local support groups and our telephone helpline, counselling, advocacy and low vision services.
Employees: 23
Volunteers: 1000

## Magdi Yacoub Institute

Heart Science Centre, Harefield,
Middlesex UB9 6JH
T: 01895 828952
F: 01895 828954
E: preay@myi.ac
The Institute aims to improve the understanding of important clinical cardiac problems by combining a broad basis of research at both clinical and fundamental levels.
Employees: 3

## Magistrates' Association

28 Fitzroy Square, London W1T 6DD
T: 020 7383 2672
F: 020 7383 4020
E: sandra.whitear@magistrates-association.org.uk
www.magistrates-association.org.uk
CEO: Chris Brace
We are a membership organisation that provides our members with information and training by publishing our magazine, email news bulletin and training materials. We promote public awareness of the magistracy and support our 60 local branches to work locally and regionally to promote the voice of the magistracy. We represent the magistracy at the highest levels of government and provide robust evidence for our policy positions using our own in-house research.
Employees: 13
Volunteers: 15000

## Maharishi Foundation

The Golden Dome, Woodley Park Road,
Skelmersdale, Lancashire WN8 6UQ
T: 01695 557403
E: info@t-m.org.uk
www.maharishifoundation.org.uk
Promotes the full development of the individual, using scientifically verified programmes that have been shown to unfold the full potential of the mind, create better health, improve social behaviour and relationships and establish a more peaceful world.

## Maidstone Community Support Centre

E: matt@mcsc.org.uk

## Make-A-Wish Foundation UK

329–331 London Road, Camberley,
Surrey GU15 3HQ
T: 01276 24127
F: 01276 683727
E: info@make-a-wish.org.uk
www.make-a-wish.org.uk
Works to grant the wishes of children living with life-threatening illnesses.
Employees: 48
Volunteers: 750
Regional offices: 16

## Making Space

46 Allen Street, Warrington,
Cheshire WA2 7JB
T: 01925 571680
E: business.support@makingspace.co.uk
www.makingspace.co.uk
Senior Administrator: Sarah Thomas
Employees: 512
Volunteers: 116

## Mammal Society

18 St Johns Church Lane, London E9 6EJ
T: 023 8001 0981
E: finance@themammalsociety.org
www.mammal.org.uk
Chair: Fiona Matthews
Established in 1954, The Mammal Society is a charity advocating science-led mammal conservation, leading efforts to collect and share information on mammals, encourage research to learn more about their ecology and distribution, and contribute meaningfully to efforts to conserve them.
Employees: 4
Volunteers: 20
Regional offices: 1

## Management Strategies for Africa

5 Westminster Gardens, Barkingside, Ilford,
Essex IG6 1PL
T: 020 8550 7607
E: info@msforafrica.org
www.msforafrica.org
Chairman/Chief Executive Officer:
Marc A Okunnu, Sr.
Management Strategies for Africa (MSA) is a charitable private company limited by guarantee, with country offices in Ghana and Nigeria. MSA advocates and supports organisational capacity development to strengthen the institutional effectiveness of public and civil society organisations engaged in social and health development. MSA is concerned with organisational effectiveness and performance improvement in relation to social development, especially meeting sexual and reproductive health (SRH) goals, within the context of health systems strengthening.
Employees: 1
Volunteers: 3
Income: £6,315 (2014–15)

## Mankind

PO Box 124, Newhaven,
East Sussex BN9 9TQ
T: 01273 510447
E: admin@mankindcounselling.org.uk
www.mankindcounselling.org.uk
CEO: Martyn Sullivan
Mankind offers counselling services to men over the age of 18 who are suffering the continuing effects of childhood sexual abuse and/or adult sexual assault at any time in their lives. Counselling services are also offered to partners, family and those affected by sexual violence towards males.
Employees: 5
Volunteers: 15
Regional offices: 1

## Marfan Association UK

Rochester House, 5 Aldershot Road, Fleet,
Hampshire GU51 3NG
T: 01252 810472
F: 01252 810473
E: contactus@marfan-association.org.uk
www.marfan-association.org.uk
Chairman/Support Coordinator: Diane Rust
Provides updated Marfan information to patients, their families and the medical profession; provides means for patients and relatives to share their experience, to support one another, and to improve medical care; supports and fosters research.
Employees: 2
Volunteers: 3
Regional offices: 1

## Marie Stopes International

153–157 Cleveland Street,
London W1T 6QW
T: 020 7574 7400
E: services@mariestopes.org.uk
www.mariestopes.org.uk
Provides reproductive healthcare/family
planning services and information, to enable
individuals all over the world to have children
by choice, not chance. MSI's goal is the
prevention of unwanted births.

## Marine Conservation Society

Unit 3, Wolf Business Park, Alton Road,
Ross-on-Wye, Herefordshire HR9 5NB
T: 01989 566017
E: info@mcsuk.org
www.mcsuk.org
Chief Executive: Sam Fanshawe
UK charity is dedicated to the protection
of the marine environment and its wildlife.
Employees: 50
Regional offices: 1

## Marine Stewardship Council

3rd Floor, Mountbarrow House,
6–20 Elizabeth Street, London SW1W 9RB
T: 020 7811 3300
F: 020 7811 3301
E: info@msc.org
www.msc.org
Conserves marine fish populations and the
ocean environment on which they depend
and promotes to the public the benefit of
effective management of marine fisheries.
Employees: 12
Volunteers: 1

## Mark Hall and Netteswell Community Association

Moot House, The Stow, Harlow,
Essex CM20 3AG
T: 01279 424074
F: 01279 453200
E: moothouseca@moothouse.plus.com
www.moothouse.org.uk
President: Derek Fenny
We have an open-door policy to offer social
and educational activities. We are a venue for
civil partnerships and civil weddings. We want
social interaction for all ages.
Employees: 6
Regional offices: 1

## Maroa Christian Counselling International

37 Clothworkers Road, Plumstead,
London SE18 2PD
T: 020 8316 7074 (also fax)
Helpline: 07719 229897
E: maroacounselint@aol.com
www.maroa.org.uk
Director: Rebecca Adeosun
Our aim is to enable those we serve to live
their lives to the fullest through counselling.
Volunteers: 2
Regional offices: 1

## Marriage Care

Bishops Park House,
25–29 Fulham High Street,
London SW6 3JH
T: 0800 389 3801
Helpline: 0845 660 6000
E: volunteer@marriagecare.org.uk
www.marriagecare.org.uk
Chief Executive: Mark Molden
Marriage Care is the largest faith-based
provider of relationship support services in
England and Wales. Our marriage preparation
and support service enables couples to
nurture marriages that last, as we draw on
Catholic Christian tradition and contemporary
research to help couples focus on the quality
of their relationship with each other. Through
our relationship counselling service we
accompany, with compassion and practical
wisdom, couples who find themselves in need
of support on their journey.
Employees: 21
Volunteers: 750

## Mary Frances Trust

E: patrickwolter@maryfrancestrust.org.uk

## Mary Ward Centre

42 Queen Square, London WC1N 3AQ
T: 020 7269 6061
E: mwenquiries@marywardcentre.ac.uk
www.marywardcentre.ac.uk
Aims to work for the advancement of public
education and the promotion of social service
for the benefit of the community.

## Maternity Action

52–54 Featherstone Street,
London EC1Y 8RT
T: 020 7253 2288
Helpline: 0845 600 8533
E: info@maternityaction.org.uk
www.maternityaction.org.uk
Director: Ros Bragg
To improve the health and wellbeing of
pregnant women, new parents and their
babies. Maternity Action offers free advice
on maternity and parental rights and benefits.
Employees: 5
Volunteers: 5

## Mathematics in Education and Industry

Monckton House, Epsom Centre,
White Horse Business Park, Trowbridge,
Wiltshire SN12 6EL
T: 01225 776776
F: 01225 775755
E: office@mei.org.uk
www.mei.org.uk
Chief Executive: Charlie Stripp
MEI is an independent charity committed to
improving mathematics education, and also
an independent UK curriculum development
body. Income generated through our work is
used to support the teaching and learning of
mathematics. MEI provides professional
development for teachers and specialist
tuition for students. We work with industry to
enhance mathematical skills in the workplace.
We also develop innovative teaching and
learning resources, including extensive online
materials. MEI manages the government-
funded Further Mathematics Support
Programme.
Employees: 50

## Matthew Trust

PO Box 604, London SW6 3AG
T: 020 7736 5976
E: amt@matthewtrust.org
www.matthewtrust.org
The Matthew Trust is a small registered
charity providing last-stop support and care
for people aged eight years old and upwards,
living in all communities of our society
throughout the UK, who have a mental health
problem of any kind.

## ME Association

7 Apollo Office Court, Radclive Road,
Gawcott, Buckinghamshire MK18 4DF
T: 01280 818968
Helpline: 0844 576 5326
E: meconnect@meassociation.org.uk
www.meassociation.org.uk
Chairman: Neil Riley
We are a campaigning national charity that
provides information and support to an
estimated 250,000 people in the UK who
have ME/chronic fatigue syndrome, their
families and carers. This is provided through
a quarterly magazine, literature, education
and training. We also run ME Connect,
the UK's premier helpline for people with
ME/CFS, and fund biomedical research.
Employees: 5
Volunteers: 30

## Medact

The Grayston Centre, 28 Charles Square,
London N1 6HT
T: 020 7324 4739
E: office@medact.org
www.medact.org
Director: David McCoy
Medact educates, analyses and campaigns
for global health on issues related to conflict,
poverty and the environment.
Employees: 2
Volunteers: 10
Income: £130,000 (2013–14)

## Media Trust

4th Floor, Block A, Centre House,
Wood Lane, London W12 7SB
T: 020 7871 5600
F: 020 7871 5601
E: info@mediatrust.org
www.mediatrust.org
CEO: Caroline Diehl
Media Trust works in partnership with the
media industry to build effective voluntary
and community sector communications. Its
vision is of a society in which: the voluntary
and community sector is widely visible and
celebrated for what it achieves; the public can
easily access the voluntary and community
sector; voluntary organisations can access
the resources, skills and contacts they need
to communicate effectively with target
audiences via a wide range of media and
communication.
Employees: 70
Volunteers: 20
Regional offices: 1

## Mediation Works Milton Keynes

Acorn House, 379 Midsummer Boulevard,
Central Milton Keynes,
Buckinghamshire MK9 3HP
T: 01908 200828
F: 01908 200842
E: mkcms@mkcommediation.org.uk
mediationworksmk.org.uk
We operate in and around Milton Keynes.
Our main aim is to resolve conflict amicably
and to open communication between all
disputants. Our second aim is to recruit
and train volunteers to CROCNAC and
Community Legal Service QM standards in
Community Mediation and provide support
and ongoing training to our mediators.
Employees: 6
Volunteers: 35
Regional offices: 1

## MediaWise Trust

University of the West of England,
Canon Kitson, Oldbury Court Road, Bristol,
Avon BS16 2JP
T: 0117 939 9333
F: 0117 902 9916
E: info@mediawise.org.uk
www.mediawise.org.uk
Director: Mike Jempson
Provides information, advice, research and
training on media ethics issues.
Employees: 2

## Medical Council on Alcohol

5 St Andrews Place, London NW1 4LB
T: 020 7487 4445
F: 020 7935 4479
E: info@m-c-a.org.uk
www.m-c-a.org.uk
Aims to improve medical understanding of
alcohol-related problems.
Employees: 5
Volunteers: 55
Regional offices: 33

## Medical Engineering Resource Unit

Unit 2 Eclipse Estate, 30 West Hill,
Epsom, Surrey KT19 8JD
T: 01372 725203
F: 01372 743159
E: info@meru.org.uk
www.meru.org.uk
Chief Executive: Jonathan Powell
Provides individual aids and services for
disabled children and young adults that are
not available commercially. Carries out
research and development of devices and
equipment that may have a more widespread
use for the same disabled group.
Employees: 11
Volunteers: 20

## Medical Women's Federation

Entrance B, Tavistock House North,
Tavistock Square, London WC1H 9HX
T: 020 7387 7765
E: admin.mwf@btconnect.com
www.medicalwomensfederation.co.uk
The MWF promotes the personal and
professional development of women in
medicine and women's health issues.

## Medway Youth Trust

Connexions, 205–217 New Road,
Chatham, Kent ME4 4QA
T: 01634 334343
F: 01634 335555
E: graham.clewes@themtrust.org
www.medwayyouthtrust.org
Chief Executive: Graham Clewes
We deliver the Connexions service in
Medway to provide information and guidance
to young people. Whilst our focus is careers
we look to provide a much wider service to
include delivery of the Prince's Trust
programme, National Citizenship Service
amongst others.
Employees: 49
Volunteers: 9
Regional offices: 1

## Men's Health Forum

32–36 Loman Street, London SE1 0EH
T: 020 7922 7908
E: office@menshealthforum.org.uk
www.menshealthforum.org.uk
Chief Executive: Martin Tod
The Men's Health Forum works to improve
the health of men and men's health services.
Employees: 8

## Mencap

123 Golden Lane, London EC1Y 0RT
T: 020 7454 0454
Helpline: 0808 808 1111
F: 020 7696 5548
E: help@mencap.org.uk
www.mencap.org.uk
Mencap is the leading charity working with
people with a learning disability in England,
Wales and Northern Ireland. We campaign to
ensure that people with a learning disability
have the best possible opportunities to live
as full citizens and aim to influence new
legislation. We can support people with a
learning disability to get a job, take a college
course or find a place of their own to live in.
Employees: 5500
Volunteers: 20000
Regional offices: 15

## Meniere's Society

The Rookery, Surrey Hills Business Park,
Wotton, Dorking, Surrey RH5 6QT
T: 01306 876883
Helpline: 0845 120 2975
E: info@menieres.org.uk
www.menieres.org.uk
**Director: Natasha Harrington-Benton**
The Meniere's Society is the only registered
charity in the UK dedicated solely to
supporting people with vestibular (inner ear)
disorders causing dizziness and imbalance.
The Meniere's Society is a national
organisation offering information and support
to those affected by vestibular conditions
and those who care for them, as well as
health professionals and the general public.
Research is also funded.
**Employees: 2**
**Volunteers: 15**

## Meningitis Now

Fern House, Bath Road, Stroud,
Gloucestershire GL5 3TJ
T: 01453 768000
Helpline: 0808 801 0388
F: 01453 768001
E: info@meningitisnow.org
www.meningitisnow.org
**Chief Executive: Sue Davie**
Meningitis Now is a charity with almost
30 years' experience. It was formed in 2013
by bringing together Meningitis UK and
Meningitis Trust, founders of the meningitis
movement in the UK. We exist to save lives
and rebuild futures by funding research,
raising awareness and providing support.
Our vision is a future where no one in the UK
loses their life to meningitis and everyone
affected gets the support they need to
rebuild their lives.
**Employees: 66**
**Volunteers: 750**

## Meningitis Research Foundation

Newminster House, Baldwin Street,
Bristol BS1 1LT
T: 0333 405 6262
Helpline: 0808 800 3344
E: miket@meningitis.org
www.meningitis.org
**Chief Executive: Vincent Smith**
Meningitis Research Foundation's vision is a
world free from meningitis and septicaemia.
The charity works in the UK, Ireland and
overseas to fund research to prevent
meningitis and septicaemia, and to improve
survival rates and outcomes. It promotes

education and awareness to reduce death and
disability, and gives support to people affected.
**Employees: 45**
**Volunteers: 30**
**Regional offices: 4**
**Income: £2,334,715 (2015–16)**

## Meningitis UK

25 Cleeve Wood Road, Downend,
Bristol BS16 2SF
T: 0117 373 7373
F: 0117 373 7374
E: information@meningitisuk.org
www.meningitisuk.org
**Chief Executive: Steve Dayman**
Meningitis UK's sole focus is to eradicate
meningitis. Meningitis is a terrifying disease,
which can kill in less than four hours and
tragically is most prevalent in children. We
feel that focusing on prevention, as opposed
to treatment, is the only way to successfully
eradicate the disease and prevent its
devastating consequences. We are confident
that with enough support we will be able to
put a stop to the heartache and devastation
it causes.
**Employees: 12**
**Volunteers: 5**

## Mental Health Foundation

1st Floor, Colechurch House,
1 London Bridge Walk, London SE1 2SX
T: 020 7803 1100
F: 020 7803 1111
E: info@mhf.org.uk
www.mentalhealth.org.uk
**CEO: Jenny Edwards CBE**
The Foundation provides information, carries
out research, campaigns and works to
improve services for anyone affected by
mental health problems. We aim to help
people survive, recover from and prevent
mental health problems by: learning what
makes and keeps people mentally well;
communicating our findings widely; turning
our research into practical solutions that
make a difference to people's lives.
**Employees: 50**
**Volunteers: 10**
**Regional offices: 4**

## Mental Health Matters

Avalon House, St Catherine's Court,
Sunderland Enterprise Park, Sunderland,
Tyne and Wear SR5 3XJ
T: 0191 510 3399
F: 0191 487 7945
E: ghiscox@mentalhealthmatters.co.uk
www.mentalhealthmatters.com
The principal aim of the charity is to act
as a national organisation for all matters
concerning mental health and mental illness

and to assist sufferers and carers of sufferers
of mental health problems.
**Employees: 200**

## Mental Health Providers Forum

c/o Mental Health Foundation, 9th Floor,
Sea Containers House, 20 Upper Ground,
London SE1 9QB
T: 020 7803 1107
F: 020 7803 1111
E: i.petit@mhpf.org.uk
www.mhpf.org.uk
**Chief Executive: Judy Weleminsky**
The Mental Health Providers Forum is a
not-for-profit umbrella organisation that
brings together voluntary sector service
providers to improve services for people with
mental health needs. We work to: influence
national and regional mental health strategies;
improve the quality and accessibility of
services in the community; increase
opportunities for voluntary and community
sector providers to delivery quality services.
**Employees: 6**

## Mentor Foundation (International)

Unit 1, Elms Lodge Farm, Melton Road,
Barrow upon Soar, Loughborough,
Leicestershire LE12 8HX
T: 01509 221622
F: 01509 808111
E: mandy@mentorfoundation.org
www.mentorfoundation.org
**Executive Director: Jeff Lee**
The Mentor Foundation is an international
non-government not-for-profit organisation
with a focus on the prevention of drug misuse
and the promotion of health and wellbeing
of young people. Mentor seeks to identify,
support and share information on effective
practice that will protect young people from
the harm that drugs can cause.
**Employees: 5**
**Volunteers: 1**
**Regional offices: 1**

## Mentoring and Befriending Foundation

T: 0161 272 6042
E: infomandbf@ncvo.org.uk
www.mandbf.org
The Mentoring and Befriending Foundation
(MBF) aims to increase the effectiveness and
quality of mentoring and befriending as
methods of enabling individuals to transform
their lives and/or reach their full potential.
MBF does this by providing training and
resources, quality assurance, network
membership, consultancy services and
contract/project management for

organisations and people interested in mentoring and befriending. Part of NCVO.

## Merchant Navy Welfare Board

30 Palmerston Road, Southampton,
Hampshire SO14 1LL
T: 023 8033 7799
F: 023 8063 4444
E: enquiries@mnwb.org.uk
www.mnwb.org
Chief Executive: David Parsons
The Board is the umbrella for those charities involved in the welfare of merchant seafarers, fishermen and their dependants visiting, or residing in, UK and Gibraltar. It manages 17 Port Welfare Committees and provides grants, training and support services for its constituent charities. It also advises and acts as a clearing house for seafarers and their families seeking assistance.
Employees: 6

## Merlin

12th Floor, 207 Old Street,
London EC1V 9NR
T: 020 7014 1600
F: 020 7014 1601
E: carolyn.miller@merlin.org.uk
www.merlin.org.uk
Chief Executive: Carolyn Miller
Merlin is the UK's leading international health charity. Undaunted and determined, Merlin saves lives. We deliver medical expertise to the toughest places and stay to help build lasting healthcare. Our mission is to end the needless loss of life in the poorest countries caused by a lack of effective healthcare. We help communities set up medical services for the long term including hospitals, clinics, surgeries and training nurses and other health workers.
Employees: 96 UK 168 internatio
Regional offices: 16 international

## Merseyside Jewish Community Care

Shifrin House, 433 Smithdown Road,
Liverpool, Merseyside L15 3JL
T: 0151 733 2292
F: 0151 734 0212
E: info@mjccshifrin.co.uk
merseysidejewishcommunitycare.co.uk
Chief Executive: Lisa Dolan
MJCC offers caring welfare services to Jewish people facing a crisis or needing longer term support. We provide practical assistance to Jewish parents and children, older people, disabled people, the visually impaired, people coping with mental health problems, families on low income and people who have become

isolated from the community. We offer daytime activities, kosher meals services, small crisis grants and links and referrals to other caring agencies.
Employees: 11
Volunteers: 263

## Metamorphic Association

26 York Street, London W1U 6PZ
T: 0845 154 7222
E: office@metamorphicassociation.net
www.metamorphicassociation.org
Promotes good health and wellbeing through awareness, understanding and use of the metamorphic technique in the UK and internationally and to uphold standards in practising and teaching the technique.

## Metanoia Institute

13 North Common Road, Ealing,
London W5 2QB
T: 020 8579 2505
F: 020 8832 3070
E: kate.fromant@metanoia.ac.uk
www.metanoia.ac.uk
Chief Executive: Sheila Owen-Jones
Metanoia Institute is a higher education institute and professional training establishment, specialising in the training of counsellors, psychotherapists, counselling psychologists, supervisors, coaches and organisational development consultants. We also have a clinic, staffed by students in fully supervised supervision, offering lower cost counselling and psychotherapy services to the general public.
Employees: 100
Volunteers: 100
Income: £3,000,000 (2013–14)

## MHA Care Group

Epworth House, 3 Stuart Street,
Derby DE1 2EQ
T: 01332 296200
E: enquiries@mha.org.uk
www.mha.org.uk
Provides a range of accommodation and care services, based on Christian principles, which are open to all older people in need, whatever their beliefs.

## Middlesbrough Voluntary Development Agency

St Mary's Centre, 82–90 Corporation Road,
Middlesbrough TS1 2RW
T: 01642 249300
F: 01642 249600
E: general@mvdauk.org.uk
www.mvda.info
CEO: Dinah Lane
MVDA exists to support an effective and enterprising voluntary and community sector (VCS) that makes a difference to the lives of Middlesbrough people. It supports, promotes and develops local voluntary and community action by: providing information, training and one-to-one support for VCOs; promoting and developing volunteering, through a brokerage service and support for good practice in volunteer management; representing the interests of the VCS and organising meetings and events to enable networking and collaboration.
Employees: 13
Volunteers: 3

## Migraine Action

Floor 4, 27 East Street, Leicester,
Leicestershire LE1 6NB
T: 0845 601 1033
E: info@migraine.org.uk
www.migraine.org.uk
Chief Executive: Simon Evans
We are a national charity supporting all those affected by migraine and their families. We work to raise awareness of this disabling condition and challenge the stigmas and misconceptions associated with it. We strive to ensure that no one is misdiagnosed, misunderstood or missing out.
Employees: 6
Volunteers: 3
Regional offices: 1
Income: £250,000 (2011–12)

## Migrant Helpline

The Rendezvous Building,
Freight Service Approach Road,
Eastern Docks, Dover, Kent CT16 1JA
T: 01304 203977
F: 01304 203995
E: oli.gennbash@migranthelpuk.org
www.migranthelpuk.org
Provides relief for asylum seekers, refugees and migrants who are in distress.
Employees: 205
Volunteers: 28
Regional offices: 8

## Migrants Resource Centre

24 Churton Street, London SW1V 2LP
T: 020 7834 2505
F: 020 7931 8187
E: info@migrants.org.uk
www.migrantsresourcecentre.org.uk
The Migrants Resource Centre works with
migrants and refugees and in partnership with
other agencies to effect social justice and
change, enabling migrants and refugees to
fully participate in this society.
**Employees: 14**
**Volunteers: 12**

## Mind

Granta House, 15–19 Broadway,
London E15 4BQ
T: 020 8519 2122
F: 020 8522 1725
E: contact@mind.org.uk
www.mind.org.uk
Aims to raise awareness of mental health
and to campaign for the rights of everyone
experiencing mental distress.
**Employees: 116**
**Volunteers: 20**

## Mind in Camden

Barnes House, 9–15 Camden Road,
London NW1 9LQ
T: 020 7911 0822
F: 020 7485 0842
E: rdean@mindincamden.org.uk
www.mindincamden.org.uk
**Chief Executive: Brian Dawn**
Mind in Camden provides services for people
whose mental health and difficult life
experiences are proving challenging including:
hearing voices, extremes of mood, anxiety,
unusual beliefs and post-traumatic reactions.
We have: a wellbeing and recovery service; a
service to support people who are dependent
on benzodiazepines; projects for young voice
hearers; for voice hearers in London prisons;
a London-wide Paranoia project.
**Employees: 14**
**Volunteers: 60**

## Mind in Tower Hamlets and Newham

Open House, 13 Whitethorn Street
T: 020 7510 1081
E: cecilia.morkeh-yamson@mithn.org.uk
www.mithn.org.uk
**Finance Manager: Cecilia Morkeh-Yamson
Pelligrin**

## Mind the Gap

Silk Warehouse, Patent Street, Bradford,
West Yorkshire BD9 4SA
T: 01274 487390
F: 01274 493973
E: arts@mind-the-gap.org.uk
www.mind-the-gap.org.uk
Mind the Gap believes in quality, equality and
inclusion. Our mission is to dismantle the
barriers to artistic excellence so that learning
disabled and non-disabled artists can perform
alongside each other as equals.

## Minority Rights Group International

54 Commercial Street, London E1 6LT
T: 020 7422 4200
E: minority.rights@mrgmail.org
www.minorityrights.org
MRG works to secure the rights of ethnic,
religious and linguistic minorities, and
indigenous peoples, and acts as an advocate
of the rights of minorities. MRG works across
groups to build units and raise awareness of
minority rights within a clear framework of
international standards in a non-partisan way.

## Miscarriage Association

17 Wentworth Terrace, Wakefield,
West Yorkshire WF1 3QW
T: 01924 200795
Helpline: 01924 200799
F: 01924 298834
E: info@miscarriageassociation.org.uk
www.miscarriageassociation.org.uk
**National Director: Ruth Bender Atik**
Miscarriage can be a very unhappy,
frightening and lonely experience. The
Miscarriage Association strives to make a
positive difference to those it affects. We
offer support, provide information, promote
good practice amongst health professionals
and work to raise public awareness about
the facts and feelings of pregnancy loss.
**Employees: 5**
**Volunteers: 100**

## Missing People

Roebuck House,
284 Upper Richmond Road West,
London SW14 7JE
T: 020 8392 4590
Helpline: 116000
F: 020 8878 7752
E: info@missingpeople.org.uk
www.missingpeople.org.uk
**Executive Director: Jo Youle**
We are a lifeline when someone disappears.
We are caring and highly trained staff and
volunteers working in collaboration with
partners across the UK. For those left behind,
we provide specialised support to end the

heartache and confusion and search for their
missing loved one.
**Employees: 67**
**Volunteers: 400**
**Regional offices: 1**

## Mission Aviation Fellowship UK

Castle House, Castle Hill Avenue,
Folkestone, Kent CT20 2TQ
T: 01303 850950
F: 01302 852800
E: alex.finlow@maf-uk.org
www.maf-uk.org
**Chief Executive: Ruth Whitaker**
Mission Aviation Fellowship is a Christian
organisation with the mission to fly light
aircraft in developing countries so that
people in remote areas can receive the help
they need.
**Employees: 79**
**Volunteers: 700**
**Regional offices: 2**
**Income: £13,600,000 (2014–15)**

## Mission Care

Graham House, 2 Pembroke Road, Bromley,
Kent BR1 2RU
T: 020 8289 7925
E: admin@missioncare.org.uk
www.missioncare.org.uk
Works for the relief of sickness and poverty,
the relief of the aged, handicapped or infirm
and the advancement of the Christian religion.

## Mobility Information Service

20 Burton Close, Dawley, Telford,
Shropshire TF4 2BX
T: 01743 340269
E: info@starthere.org
www.mis.org
Provides an information service by letter,
email and phone, with a 24-hour answering
service. Leaflets are available covering various
aspects of disability.
**Volunteers: 10**

## Mobility Trust

17B Reading Road, Pangbourne, Reading,
Berkshire RG8 7LR
T: 0845 450 0359
F: 0118 984 2544
E: mobility@mobilitytrust.org.uk
www.mobilitytrust.org.uk
Provides powered wheelchairs and scooters
for severely disabled children and adults who
cannot obtain them through statutory
sources or purchase such equipment
themselves. We do not give grants.
**Employees: 4**

## MOC Foundation

341 Lauderdale Tower, Barbican,
London EC2Y 8NA
T: 020 7256 6066
E: info@mocfoundation.org
www.mocfoundation.org
Chair: Jose Carlos Martines
Provides humanitarian aid for the relief of
poverty in less developed regions of the world.
Volunteers: 9
Income: £35,000 (2014–15)

## Money Advice Trust

21 Garlick Hill, London EC4V 2AU
T: 020 7489 7796
Helpline: 0808 808 4000
F: 020 7489 7704
E: info@moneyadvicetrust.org
www.moneyadvicetrust.org
Chief Executive: Joanna Elson
The Money Advice Trust (MAT) is a charity
formed in 1991 to increase the quality and
availability of free, independent money advice
in the UK. MAT's vision: to help people across
the UK to tackle their debts and manage their
money wisely. MAT does this through direct
service provision (National Debtline, Business
Debtline and My Money Steps) as well as
supporting the advice sector through training
(wiseradviser).
Employees: 173

## More Music

13–17 Devonshire Road, Morecambe,
Lancashire LA3 1QT
T: 01524 831997
E: sandra.wood@moremusic.org.uk
www.moremusic.org.uk
Artistic Director: Peter Moser
More Music is a community music and
education charity based in the West End of
Morecambe, working throughout Lancashire,
the North West and internationally. We
provide a year-round programme that covers
a breadth of music making activity involving
people of all ages and all backgrounds. We are
one of the longest running and most highly
regarded community music and education
organisations in the UK.

## MOSAIC Black and Mixed Parentage Family Group

Community Base, 113 Queens Road,
Brighton BN1 3XG
T: 01273 234017
F: 01273 234018
E: info@mosaicbrighton.org.uk
mosaicequalities.org.uk
Director: Naima Nouidjem

MOSAIC exists to empower black, Asian and
mixed-parentage families to combat racism
and to support the development of positive
cultural and racial identity.
Employees: 4
Volunteers: 30
Regional offices: 1

## Mosaic Clubhouse

65 Effra Road, Brixton, London SW2 1BZ
T: 020 7924 9657
E: m.ness@mosaic-clubhouse.org
www.mosaic-clubhouse.org
Chief Executive: Maresa Ness
The aim of Mosaic Clubhouse is to provide
opportunities for individuals, who have been
socially and vocationally disadvantaged by
mental ill health, to regain the confidence and
skills necessary to lead productive and
satisfying lives. The services we deliver assist
our members with: increased social networks;
better mental health; improved skills;
increased take up of education and
employment opportunities; the self-
confidence to make informed choices
about their future.
Employees: 16
Volunteers: 4
Regional offices: 1
Income: £900,174 (2014–15)

## Mothers Apart from their Children

BM Box 6334, London WC1N 3XX
E: enquiries@matchmothers.org
www.matchmothers.org
MATCH offers non-judgemental emotional
support to mothers apart because of their
own short- or long-term mental or physical
ill-health when children are fostered or
adopted, to mothers whose children have
been abducted abroad by their fathers, to
mothers apart as a result of alienation
following high-conflict family breakdown
when children profess not to want to see their
mothers and to mothers of adult children
apart as a result of family rows.
Volunteers: 10
Income: £5,000 (2013–14)

## Mothers Union

Mary Sumner House, 24 Tufton Street,
London SW1P 3RB
T: 020 7222 5533
F: 020 7222 1591
E: mu@themothersunion.org
www.themothersunion.org

The Mothers' Union is an Anglican
organisation that promotes the wellbeing
of families worldwide.
Employees: 47
Volunteers: 36,000,000
Regional offices: 70

## Motivation

Brockley Academy, Brockley Lane,
Backwell, Bristol BS48 4AQ
T: 01275 464012
F: 01275 464019
E: info@motivation.org.uk
www.motivation.org.uk
President : David Constantine
Motivation is an international charity
transforming the lives of disabled people.
Our wheelchairs and training give people
independence, confidence and hope for
the future.
Employees: 38
Volunteers: 4
Regional offices: 1

## MS Trust

Spirella Building, Bridge Road, Letchworth,
Hertfordshire SG6 4ET
T: 01462 476700
Helpline: 0800 032 3839
E: info@mstrust.org.uk
www.mstrust.org.uk
Chief Executive: Pam Macfarlane
The MS Trust is dedicated to supporting
people living with MS now. We provide the
information you trust and support the health
professionals you need.
Employees: 30
Volunteers: 2
Regional offices: 1

## Multiple Births Foundation

Hammersmith House, Level 4,
Queen Charlotte's Hospital, Du Cane Road,
London W12 0HS
T: 020 3313 3519
E: mbf@imperial.nhs.uk
www.multiplebirths.org.uk
Director: Jane Denton
The Multiple Births Foundation offers
professional advice, education and support to
parents and carers of twins, triplets and more,
and to the health professionals who care for
them.

## Multiple Sclerosis International Federation

3rd Floor, Skyline House, 200 Union Street, London SE1 0LX
T: 020 7620 1911
E: info@msif.org
www.msif.org
Works in worldwide partnership with member MS societies and the international research community to eliminate multiple sclerosis and its consequences, and speaks out globally on behalf of those affected by multiple sclerosis.

## Multiple Sclerosis National Therapy Centres

Bradbury House, 155 Barkers Lane, Bedford MK41 9RX
T: 01234 325781
E: info@msntc.org.uk
www.ms-selfhelp.org
Supports multiple sclerosis therapy centres with training, education, information, etc.

## Multiple Sclerosis Society of Great Britain and Northern Ireland

MS National Centre, 372 Edgware Road, London NW2 6ND
T: 020 8438 0700
Helpline: 0808 800 8000
F: 020 8438 0701
E: volunteering@mssociety.org.uk
www.mssociety.org.uk
Chief Executive: Michelle Mitchell
Over 100,000 of us in the UK have multiple sclerosis (MS). It can cause problems with how we walk, move, see, think and feel. It can make it hard for us to work and do the things we enjoy. We're the MS Society community of people living with MS, scientists, campaigners, volunteers and fundraisers. We understand what life's like with MS, we support each other, we drive research into more and better treatments.
Employees: 250
Volunteers: 5500

## Muntham House School Ltd

Muntham Drive, Barns Green, Near Horsham, West Sussex RH20 2QZ
T: 01403 730302
F: 01403 730510
E: triciajeffs@muntham.org.uk
www.muntham.org.uk
Principal: Tricia Jeffs
Boarding and day school for boys (8–18) with a range of social and emotional difficulties including ADHD, Asperger's Syndrome and conduct disorders. Muntham has a local, regional, national and international reputation for innovative practice, successful outcomes for young people and trains professionals in managing challenging behaviour.
Employees: 84

## Murdered Abroad (formerly known as Support After Murder and Manslaughter Abroad)

SISEC Ltd, 21 Holborn Viaduct, London EC1A 2DY
T: 0845 123 2384
E: eve@murdered-abroad.org.uk
www.murdered-abroad.org.uk
Director/Trustee: Eve Henderson
Murdered Abroad (formerly Support After Murder and Manslaughter Abroad) started in 2001. We provide peer support, emotional support, information and practical support. We also work to improve the support families receive in the UK after a murder abroad. We seek to provide feedback to the many government agencies involved after a murder abroad, so that they may improve the services they offer and reduce the distress they cause to bereaved families.
Volunteers: 6
Income: £10,000 (2014–15)

## Muscular Dystrophy Campaign

61A Great Suffolk Street, London SE1 0BU
T: 020 7803 4800
Helpline: 0800 652 6352
F: 020 7401 3495
E: info@muscular-dystrophy.org
www.muscular-dystrophy.org
Chief Executive: Robert Meadowcroft
The Muscular Dystrophy Campaign is the leading UK charity fighting muscle-wasting conditions. We are dedicated to beating muscular dystrophy and related neuromuscular conditions by finding treatments and cures and to improving the lives of everyone affected by them.
Employees: 60
Volunteers: 30000
Regional offices: 11

## Museums Association

24 Calvin Street, London E1 6NW
T: 020 7426 6910
F: 020 7426 6961
E: info@museumsassociation.org
www.museumsassociation.org
Director: Mark Taylor
Represents museums and art galleries and their staff; protects and develops professional standards in museums.
Employees: 26

## Music Education Council

54 Elm Road, Hale, Altrincham, Cheshire WA15 9QP
T: 0161 928 3065
E: ahassan@easynet.co.uk
www.mec.org.uk
Promotes and advances music education and training in the UK.

## Muslim Aid

PO Box 3, London E1 1WP
T: 020 7377 4200
F: 020 7377 4201
E: hr@muslimaid.org
www.muslimaid.org
Muslim Aid was established to provide humanitarian relief aid to the poorest, more deprived and most vulnerable in society worldwide. Emergency relief for victims of disasters like floods, earthquakes, famines as well as war is an important part of the aid we provide.
Employees: 10
Volunteers: 10
Regional offices: 5

## Myaware

The College Business Centre, Uttoxeter New Road, Derby, Derbyshire DE22 3WZ
T: 01332 290219
Helpline: 0800 919912
E: mg@myaware.org
www.myaware.org
CEO: Ruth Bury
Funds research into the cause of myasthenia gravis in order to find a cure; provides a support network for myasthenics and their families; increases public and medical awareness of the problems of myasthenia gravis (rebranded from Myasthenia Gravis Association).
Employees: 15
Volunteers: 100+
Regional offices: 57

## Myositis Support Group

146 Newtown Road, Woolston, Southampton SO19 9HR
T: 023 8044 9708
E: irene@myositis.org.uk
www.myositis.org.uk
Promotes the relief of persons suffering from dermatomyositis, polymyositis and inclusion body myositis; promotes research for a cure

and better treatment. We also help to relieve the isolation felt when diagnosed with a rare condition and give support and up-to-date information to sufferers and their families.
**Employees: 1**
**Volunteers: 8**

## Myotonic Dystrophy Support Group

19/21 Main Road, Gedling, Nottingham, Nottinghamshire NG4 3HQ
T: 0115 987 5869
Helpline: 0115 987 0080
E: mdsg@tesco.net
www.myotonicdystrophysupportgroup.org
National Coordinator: Margaret Bowler
We support families who have myotonic dystrophy, both congenital and adults. We supply information to the medical practitioners. There is a website and helpline, annual conference and area informal meetings.
**Employees: 2**
**Volunteers: 25**
**Regional offices: 1**

## Nacro

First Floor, 46 Loman Street, London SE1 0EH
T: 0300 123 1889
E: contactus@nacro.org.uk
www.nacro.org.uk
CEO: Jacob Tas
As an established charity with 50 years of experience, Nacro has been repositioning itself as a champion of social justice which continues to put crime prevention and reduction at its core. Throughout England and Wales we deliver interventions which are consistently high quality, evidence based and outcome focused so that we can maximise our impact in communities.
**Employees: 830**
**Volunteers: 150**

## NAGALRO

PO Box 264, Esher, Surrey KT10 0WA
T: 01372 818504
E: nagalro@globalnet.co.uk
www.nagalro.com
NAGALRO is the professional association for children's guardians, children and family reporters and independent social workers. NAGALRO: promotes good practice; provides support and advice to individual members; contributes to developments in the Guardian and Family Court service; supports communication between individual guardians and Cafcass; encourages quality standards in independent social work with children and families; makes links with childcare solicitors and other professionals; provides professional insurance cover; produces a quarterly journal; organises interdisciplinary conferences and training.
**Volunteers: 15**

## Nakuru Environmental and Conservation Trust

5 Kingsend Court, Kingsend, Ruislip HA4 7DB
T: 01895 633650
E: nectecology@yahoo.co.uk
www.nectuk.org
Chair: Nim Njuguna
Promoting global citizenship and sustainable development through undertaking environmental service projects with communities in Kenya's Rift Valley Province. Encouraging young people from Kenya and the UK Diaspora to work and learn from each other by discovering, celebrating and exploring similarities and differences between their cultures through 'Kenya's Story in a 100 Objects' programme.
**Volunteers: 6**

## NAPAC

Herald House, 15 Lamb's Passage, Bunhill Row, London EC1Y 8TQ
T: 020 7614 1801
Helpline: 0808 801 0331
E: tim.barclay@napac.org.uk
www.napac.org.uk
Chief Executive Officer: Gabrielle Shaw
NAPAC provides relief and support to people who have experienced abuse in childhood, and to those affected by abuse. NAPAC also advances the education of the

public and relevant professional bodies with regard to child abuse.
**Employees: 10**
**Volunteers: 30**
**Regional offices: 1**
**Income: £419,783 (2014–15)**

## Narcolepsy Association UK (UKAN)

PO Box 13842, Penicuik EH26 8WX
T: 0845 450 0394
E: nicola.rule@narcolepsyuk.co.uk
www.narcolepsy.org.uk
An association of people with narcolepsy, their relatives and others interested in improving their lot. Objectives are: the benefit, relief and aid of persons suffering from narcolepsy; to promote awareness and provide authoritative information to narcoleptics, to the medical profession and to the public; to encourage research into the causes and treatment of narcolepsy.
**Employees: 1**
**Volunteers: 12**

## National AIDS Trust

New City Cloisters, 196 Old Street, London EC1V 9FR
T: 020 7814 6767
F: 020 7216 0111
E: info@nat.org.uk
www.nat.org.uk
Chief Executive: Deborah Gold
The National AIDS Trust is the UK's leading independent policy and campaigning charity on HIV. We develop policies and campaign to halt the spread of HIV and improve the quality of life of people affected by HIV, both in the UK and internationally.
**Employees: 16**
**Volunteers: 15**

## National Alliance of Women's Organisations

Suite 405, Davina House, 137, London EC1V 7ET
T: 020 7490 4100
E: info@nawo.org.uk
www.nawo.org.uk
Aims to bring together all women's organisations in the country working to eliminate all forms of discrimination against women.

## National Animal Welfare Trust

Tyler's Way, Watford, Watford,
Hertfordshire WD25 8WT
T: 020 8950 0177
F: 020 8420 4454
E: d.warner@nawt.org.uk
www.nawt.org.uk
Chief Executive: David Warner
The National Animal Welfare Trust's primary
purpose is to rescue and re-home domestic
animals and provide a place of sanctuary or
retirement for animals of all types.
Employees: 110
Volunteers: 350

## National Ankylosing Spondylitis Society (NASS)

4 Albion Court, Galena Road,
Hammersmith, London W6 0QT
T: 020 8741 1515
E: admin@nass.co.uk
www.nass.co.uk
Director: Debbie Cook
NASS provides advice, support and
information for patients with AS. We support
research in this field, have over 100 branches
in the UK and also campaign for access
to treatments and better services for all
AS patients.
Employees: 7
Volunteers: 200
Income: £350,000 (2013–14)

## National Association for Able Children in Education

PO Box 242, Arnold's Way,
Oxford OX2 9FR
T: 01865 861879
F: 01865 861880
E: info@nace.co.uk
www.nace.co.uk
NACE is a network of educators passionate
about enabling able pupils to fulfil their
potential within inclusive school communities.
We: develop and exchange strategies for
effective practice and further the professional
development of our members; provide
responses on issues affecting the education
of able children and advice to government
agencies; undertake development projects;
provide professional expertise, advice, training
and consultancy services, conferences,
events, publications and resources.

## National Association for Children of Alcoholics

PO Box 64, Bristol, Avon BS16 2UH
T: 0117 924 8005
Helpline: 0800 358 3456
E: admin@nacoa.org.uk
www.nacoa.org.uk
CEO: Hilary Henriques MBE
Nacoa provides information, advice and
support for children, young people and adults
struggling with parental alcohol problems and
people concerned with their welfare through
our free, confidential telephone and email
helpline and website. We raise awareness of
the problems they face and services available
to them. We also initiate and take part in
research studies into the scope and scale of
the problem and the prevention of alcoholism
developing in this vulnerable group.
Employees: 3
Volunteers: 341
Regional offices: 1
Income: £86,000 (2013–14)

## National Association for Environmental Education (UK)

University of Wolverhampton,
Walsall Campus, Gorway, Walsall,
West Midlands WS1 3BD
T: 07479 287183
E: info@naee.org.uk
www.naee.org.uk
NAEE is a membership organisation with
an aim of supporting all those who deliver
environmental education to young people.
Particular emphasis is given to linking
teaching with the national curriculum.
NAEE has an active website and shares
good practice here and also through our
journal 'Environmental Education'. Please
do visit our website and become part of our
voluntary charity.
Employees: 1
Volunteers: 10

## National Association for Pastoral Care in Education

University of Warwick, Gibbet Hill Road,
Coventry CV4 7AL
T: 024 7652 3810
E: base@napce.org.uk
www.napce.org.uk
NAPCE establishes links between all those
who have an interest in pastoral care and
personal-social education. It has a
membership of 600 individuals and
organisations. NAPCE: supports all who
have a professional concern for pastoral care;
promotes the theoretical study of pastoral
care; disseminates good practice; promotes

the education, training and development of
those engaged in pastoral care; liaises with
other organisations with similar aims.

## National Association for Patient Participation

10 Rosegarth Avenue, Aston,
Sheffield S26 2DD
T: 0870 774 3666 (also fax)
E: admin@napp.org.uk
www.napp.org.uk
NAPP is the umbrella group for patient
participation groups (PPGs) in primary care.
NAPP offers guidance on starting and
maintaining PPGs and advice to primary care
organisations on PPGs as well as identifying
and disseminating good practice.
Volunteers: 15

## National Association for Premenstrual Syndrome

41 Old Road, East Peckham, Tonbridge,
Kent TN12 5AP
T: 0870 777 2178
E: contact@pms.org.uk
www.pms.org.uk
Provides clinically authoritative, independent
advice, information and support to all those
experiencing, and treating, PMS and
menstrual ill health.

## National Association for Special Educational Needs

NASEN House,
4–5 Amber Business Village, Amber Close,
Amington, Tamworth,
Staffordshire B77 4RP
T: 01827 311500
F: 01827 313005
E: welcome@nasen.org.uk
www.nasen.org.uk
NASEN is the leading organisation in the
UK that aims to promote the education,
training, advancement and development
of all those with special and additional support
needs. NASEN reaches a huge readership
through its journals: British Journal of Special
Education, Support for Learning, the
new online publication Journal of Research
in Special Educational Needs and the
magazine Special.
Employees: 14

## National Association for the Teaching of English

50 Broadfield Road, Sheffield,
South Yorkshire S8 0XJ
T: 0114 255 5419
F: 0114 255 5296
E: info@nate.org.uk
www.nate.org.uk

NATE currently has over 3,000 members, affiliated to a network of regional branches. The association has a range of committees and working parties that address current concerns, disseminate knowledge and ideas, promote the work of the association and seek to represent the views of the association to national bodies, local authorities, the DfES, OFSTED, QCA, examination boards, etc.
**Employees: 8**
**Volunteers: 70**

## National Association for Voluntary and Community Associations

The Tower, 2 Furnival Square,
Sheffield S1 4QL
T: 0114 278 6636
F: 0114 278 7004
E: navca@navca.org.uk
www.navca.org.uk
**Chief Executive: Kevin Curley**
NAVCA is the national voice of local voluntary and community sector infrastructure in England. Our 360 members work with 170,000 local community groups and voluntary organisations, which provide services, regenerate neighbourhoods, increase volunteering and tackle discrimination, in partnership with local public bodies.
**Employees: 40**
**Volunteers: 8**
**Regional offices: 398**

## National Association of Child Contact Centres

Minerva House, Spaniel Row,
Nottingham NG1 6EP
T: 0845 450 0280
E: contact@naccc.org.uk
www.naccc.org.uk
**Chief Executive: Yvonne Kee**
Promotes safe child contact within a national framework of around 350 child contact centres. These are safe, neutral places where children of separated families can spend time with one or both parents and sometimes other family members. NACCC offers a range of support services to its membership and also provides a voice for child contact centres, promoting their role with national and regional decision-makers.
**Employees: 7**
**Volunteers: 12**

## National Association of Deafened People

Dalton House, 60 Windsor Avenue,
London SW19 2RR
T: 0845 055 9663
E: enquiries@nadp.org.uk
www.nadp.org.uk
**Chair: Lidia Best**
NADP supports all those who have suffered hearing loss during their lifetime. We provide our newsletter Network and monthly EBulletins to provide information and updates on any developments affecting our members. We campaign and also provide information and advice on employment, telecommunications, equipment and other subjects. NADP has some local groups and other contacts in various parts of the country, which arrange social events and provide support at grassroots level.
**Volunteers: 12**
**Income: £10,270 (2013–14)**

## National Association of Decorative and Fine Arts Societies

NADFAS House, 8 Guilford Street,
London WC1N 1DA
T: 020 7430 0730
F: 020 7242 0686
E: enquiries@nadfas.org.uk
www.nadfas.org.uk
Aims to increase the enjoyment, knowledge and care of the arts, and to stimulate interest in the preservation of our cultural heritage.
**Employees: 14**
**Volunteers: 10000**

## National Association of Independent Schools and Non Maintained Special Schools

PO Box 705, York YO30 6WW
T: 01904 621243 (also fax)
E: cdorer@nasschools.org.uk
www.nasschools.org.uk
**Chief Executive: Claire Dorer**
The umbrella organisation for non-maintained special schools and independent schools catering for pupils with special educational needs. Works as the voice of the sector to ensure high-quality education and care for children with special educational needs.
**Employees: 2**

## National Association of Laryngectomee Clubs

Lower Ground Floor,
152 Buckingham Palace Road,
London SW1W 9TR
T: 020 7381 9993
E: website@nalc.gov.uk
www.laryngectomy.org.uk
Promotes the welfare and rehabilitation, in any way possible, of laryngectomy patients and their families within the British Isles.

## National Association of Local Councils

109 Great Russell Street,
London WC1B 3LD
T: 020 7637 1865
F: 020 7436 7451
E: nalc@nalc.gov.uk
www.nalc.gov.uk
NALC represents the interests of around 8,500 town and parish councils in England. These councils serve electorates ranging from small rural communities to major cities, and are independently elected. Working with our member councils, NALC lobbies national government to advance and protect the interests of these councils and their communities. NALC provides support and advice to our members through a network of county associations and is committed to developing the role of town and parish councils.

## National Association of Round Tables of Great Britain and Ireland

Marchesi House, 4 Embassy Drive,
Edgbaston, Birmingham B15 1TP
T: 0121 456 4402
F: 0121 456 4185
E: hq@roundtable.org.uk
www.roundtable.org.uk
**General Secretary: John Handley**
A young men's fellowship organisation.
**Employees: 6**
**Regional offices: 670**

## National Association of Small Schools

Quarrenden, Upper Red Cross Road,
Goring, Oxfordshire RG8 9BD
T: 01491 873548
E: quarrenden.tay@btinternet.com
www.smallschools.org.uk
**Chairman: Neil Short**
Provides a voice and a link for those who believe that small schools, in rural and urban areas, have educational and social roles too precious to lose.

## National Association of Swimming Clubs for the Handicapped

The Willows, Mayles Lane, Wickham,
Fareham, Hampshire PO17 5ND
T: 01329 833689
E: r.a.oleary@btinternet.com
www.nasch.org.uk
**Chairman: Tracey Kitching**
Encourages, promotes and develops
swimming among handicapped people,
in recognition of the immense value
of swimming for both physical and
psychological rehabilitation.

## National Association of Women's Clubs

5 Vernon Rise, London WC1X 9EP
T: 020 7837 1434
E: nawc@btconnect.com
www.nawc.org.uk
**National Chairman: Maureen Harwood**
Provides facilities for social life and
opportunities for informal education within
the means of all women.
**Employees: 3**
**Regional offices: 120**

## National Association of Youth Theatres

c/o York Theatre Royal, St Leonard's Place,
York YO24 3LD
T: 07515 651481
E: info@nayt.org.uk
www.nayt.org.uk
**Chief Executive: Jill Adamson**
NAYT works with over 1,000 groups and
individuals to support the development of
youth theatre activity through information
and support services, advocacy, training,
participation and partnerships.
**Employees: 1**

## National Benevolent Fund for the Aged

32 Buckingham Palace Road,
London SW1W 0RE
T: 020 7828 0200
F: 020 7828 0400
E: trusteesnbfa@gmail.com
www.nbfa.org.uk
**Interim Executive Director: Andrew Ross**
NBFA was founded to improve the quality of
life for older people who live on a low income.
NBFA does this by providing direct, practical
assistance through the provision of

emergency alarms, TENS pain relief
machines and free break-aways.
**Employees: 4**
**Volunteers: 10**

## National Benevolent Institution

Peter Herve House, Eccles Court, Tetbury,
Gloucestershire GL8 8EH
T: 01666 505500
Helpline: 01666 505200
F: 01666 503111
E: welfare@nbi.org.uk
www.thenbc.org.uk
The NBI was founded in 1812 by Peter Herve
to provide a regular payment and one-off
grants to people who have reached pension
age or are over 50 years of age with a
disability.
**Employees: 5**
**Regional offices: 1**

## National Campaign for the Arts

1 Kingly Street, London W1B 5PA
T: 020 7287 3777
E: hello@forthearts.org.uk
forthearts.org.uk
Aims to inform the public, brief the media
and alert politicians to the need for greater
public funding of the arts and campaigns for
improvements in arts funding, arts education
and access to the arts.

## National Centre for Social Research

35 Northampton Square,
London EC1V 0AX
T: 020 7250 1866
E: info@natcen.ac.uk
www.natcen.ac.uk
**Chief Executive: Norman Glass**
Our aim is a society better informed through
high-quality social research.

## National Childbirth Trust

Alexandra House, Oldham Terrace,
London W3 6NH
T: 0870 770 3236
Helpline: 0870 444 8707
F: 0870 770 3237
E: enquiries@national-childbirth-trust.co.uk
www.nct.org.uk
**Chief Executive: Belinda Phipps**
The NCT wants all parents to have an
experience of pregnancy, birth and early
parenthood that enriches their lives and
gives them confidence in being a parent.
It provides local support and puts parents
in touch for social networking. The NCT
also runs antenatal classes and provides
information on maternity issues,
breastfeeding and postnatal support,
including specialist groups for caesareans

and miscarriage. It has approximately 300
branches throughout the UK.
**Employees: 80**
**Volunteers: 7000**
**Regional offices: 300**

## National Children's Bureau

8 Wakley Street, London EC1V 7QE
T: 020 7843 6000
E: pbell@ncb.org.uk
www.ncb.org.uk
**Chief Executive: Anna Feuchtwang**
The National Children's Bureau is a leading
charity that for 50 years has been improving
the lives of children and young people,
especially the most vulnerable. We work
with children and for children, to influence
government policy, be a strong voice for
young people and practitioners and provide
creative solutions on a range of social issues.

## National Children's Centre

Brian Jackson House, New North Parade,
Huddersfield, West Yorkshire HD1 5JP
T: 01484 519988
F: 01484 435150
E: info@nccuk.org.uk
yorkshirechildrenscentre.org.uk
Aims to advance public awareness in subjects
connected with the care and upbringing of
children in order to promote a better quality
of life for the child.
**Employees: 30**
**Volunteers: 10**

## National Coastwatch Institution (NCI)

1 Walk Terrace, West Street,
Polruan by Fowey, Cornwall PL23 1PN
T: 01726 870659 (also fax)
Helpline: 0300 111 1202
E: public.relations@nci.org.uk
www.nci.org.uk
**Chairman: Alan Richards**
NCI was set up in 1994 to restore a visual
watch along the coast after many coastguard
stations were closed. Today 50 stations are
operational and manned by over 2,000
volunteers at no cost to the public purse. Our
mission is to assist in saving lives at sea and
along the UK coastline. NCI is part of the
national Search and Rescue organisation
and is dependent on public support to cover
running costs.
**Volunteers: 2000**

## National Communities Resource Centre

Trafford Hall, Ince Lane,
Wimbolds Trafford, Chester CH2 4JP
T: 01244 300246
E: s.wyatt@traffordhall.com
www.traffordhall.com
Offering training and support to all those living and working in low-income communities around the UK. The centre develops skills, confidence and capacity to tackle problems and reverse poor conditions.

## National Community Safety Network

1 Hunters Walk, Canal Street,
Chester, Cheshire CH1 4EB
T: 01244 322314
E: enquiries@community-safety.net
communitysafetyinstitute.net
NCSN is the leading practitioner-led organisation supporting those involved in promoting community safety/crime reduction throughout the UK. It has just under 400 organisational members and individual members in the public, private and voluntary sectors, all with a common interest in promoting safer communities. NCSN: gives a national voice to practitioners; influences national policy and practice; supports the professional development of practitioners; promotes joint working in the UK and Europe.
Employees: 3
Volunteers: 1

## National Confederation of Parent Teacher Associations

39 Shipbourne Road, Tonbridge,
Kent TN10 3DS
T: 01732 375460
F: 01732 375461
E: dwb@ncpta.org.uk
www.pta.org.uk
NCPTA is the only membership organisation for PTAs and other home/school groups in England, Wales and Northern Ireland. Members enjoy high levels of support and advice on a variety of subjects such as fundraising ideas, running a PTA, registering as a charity and holding successful events.
Employees: 20
Volunteers: 130000
Regional offices: 11

## National Confidential Enquiry Into Patient Outcome and Death

Ground Floor, Abbey House,
74–76 St John Street, London EC1M 4DZ
T: 020 7251 9060
F: 020 7250 0020
E: info@ncepod.org.uk
www.ncepod.org.uk
NCEPOD aims to review medical clinical practice and to make recommendations to improve the quality of the delivery of care. We do this by undertaking confidential surveys covering many different aspects of medical care and making recommendations for clinicians and management to implement.
Employees: 12

## National Consumer Federation

24 Hurst House, Penton Rise, London,
Surrey WC1X 9ED
T: 020 7837 8545
E: secretary@ncf.info
www.ncf.info
Chair: Arnold Pindar
Aims to educate and inform consumers, with reference to the key guiding principles of choice, information, representation, access to goods and services, quality, fairness, safety and redress.
Employees: 1
Volunteers: 25

## National Council for Palliative Care

The Fitzpatrick Building,
188–194 York Way, London N7 9AS
T: 020 7697 1520
F: 020 7697 1530
E: enquiries@ncpc.org.uk
www.ncpc.org.uk
Chief Executive: Eve Richardson
NCPC is the umbrella organisation for all those providing, commissioning and using palliative care and hospice services in England, Wales and Northern Ireland. NCPC promotes the extension and improvement of palliative care services for all people with life-threatening and life-limiting conditions. NCPC promotes palliative care in health and social care settings across all sectors to government, national and local policy makers.
Employees: 17

## National Council for Voluntary Organisations

Society Building, 8 All Saints Street,
London N1 9RL
T: 020 7713 6161
F: 020 7713 6300
E: caroline.grais@ncvo.org.uk
www.ncvo.org.uk
Chief Executive: Sir Stuart Etherington
NCVO's vision is of a society in which people are inspired to make a positive difference to their communities. NCVO believes that a vibrant voluntary and community sector deserves a strong voice and the best support. NCVO aims to be that support and voice.
Employees: 130
Regional offices: 1
Income: £9,588,000 (2013–14)

## National Council of Women of Great Britain

72 Victoria Road, Darlington DL1 5JG
T: 01325 367375
E: info@ncwgb.org
www.ncwgb.org
President: Gwenda Nicholas
Works for the removal of discrimination against women; encourages the effective participation of women in public life and acts as a coordinating body to which societies with similar aims may associate.
Employees: 1

## National Day Nurseries Association

National Early Years Enterprise Centre,
Longbow Close, Huddersfield,
West Yorkshire HD2 1GQ
T: 0870 774 4244
F: 0870 774 4243
E: info@ndna.org.uk
www.ndna.org.uk
NDNA is a national charity dedicated to the support and promotion of high-quality care and education for all children in the early years. It provides a code of practice for provider members and encourages all providers to follow the accreditation scheme, Quality Counts.
Employees: 50
Volunteers: 250
Regional offices: 5

## National Deaf Children's Society (NDCS)

Ground Floor South, Castle House,
37–45 Paul Street, London EC2A 4LS
T: 020 7490 8656
Helpline: 0808 800 8880
F: 020 7251 5020
E: helpline@ndcs.org.uk
www.ndcs.org.uk
Chief Executive: Susan Daniels
In all our work we aim to: empower deaf children, young people and their families to determine what happens in their lives and shape the services they receive; increase awareness of the support deaf children and young people need to achieve and challenge social attitudes which prevent them achieving; influence and challenge key decision-makers to make deaf children and young people a political priority.
Employees: 140
Volunteers: 240
Regional offices: 5
Income: £18,000,000 (2011–12)

## National Development Team for Inclusion

First Floor, 30–32 Westgate Buildings,
Bath BA1 1EF
T: 01225 789135
F: 01225 338017
E: mark.collings@ndti.org.uk
www.ndti.org.uk
Chief Executive: Rob Greig
The National Development Team for Inclusion is a not-for-profit organisation concerned with promoting inclusion and equality for people who risk exclusion and who need support to lead a full life. We have a particular interest in issues around age, disability, mental health and children and young people.
Employees: 20
Volunteers: 10

## National Eczema Society

Hill House, Highgate Hill,
London N19 5NA
T: 020 7281 3553
Helpline: 0800 089 1122
E: fundraising@eczema.org
www.eczema.org
Chief Executive: M Cox
Provides information and support to people with eczema and their carers, including health professionals.
Employees: 8
Volunteers: 20

## National Energy Action (NEA)

West One, Level 6 (Elswick), Forth Banks,
Newcastle upon Tyne NE1 3PA
T: 0191 261 5677
F: 0191 261 6496
E: info@nea.org.uk
www.nea.org.uk
Chief Executive: Jenny Saunders OBE
The national energy efficiency charity which campaigns to end fuel poverty by influencing decision-makers and working with stakeholders to develop policies and practices to tackle the heating and insulation problems of low-income households through improvements in energy efficiency.
Employees: 68
Volunteers: 2
Regional offices: 9

## National Energy Foundation

Davy Avenue, Knowlhill,
Milton Keynes MK5 8NG
T: 01908 665555
F: 01908 665577
E: enquiries@nef.org.uk
www.nef.org.uk
CEO: Kerry Mashford
NEF aims to give people, organisations and government the knowledge, support and inspiration they need to understand and improve the use of energy in buildings.
Employees: 25
Volunteers: 3

## National Extension College

23 Castalia Square, Docklands,
London E14 3NG
T: 0870 385 1213
Helpline: 0870 385 1218
F: 0870 385 1217
E: info@nec.ac.uk
www.nec.ac.uk/
The European Extension College is a non-profit educational association established in London. The mission of the College is to provide opportunities for learning throughout life by enabling access to individualised and flexible quality education and training, and to support the advancement and improvement of education at all levels for the benefit of the public.
Volunteers: 10
Regional offices: 2

## National Extension College Trust Ltd

Joydon, 33 Adelaide Close, Stanmore,
Middlesex HA7 3EN
T: 020 8420 6055
E: info@nec.ac.uk
www.nec.ac.uk
Provides the learning resources and opportunities to enable individuals to meet their vocational and personal goals.

## National Eye Research Centre

Bristol Eye Hospital, Lower Maudlin Street,
Bristol BS1 2LX
E: nerc-charity@bris.ac.uk
www.nerc.co.uk
The NERC funds and publishes research into the causes and treatment of eye diseases and disabilities and the prevention of blindness. The major part of the research it supports is carried out by the Unit of Ophthalmology at the University of Bristol, but research is also supported in Yorkshire, where it has a branch known as Yorkshire Eye Research, and in other eye research establishments throughout the UK.

## National Family Mediation

4 Barnfield Hill, Exeter, Devon EX1 1SR
T: 0300 400 0636
F: 01392 271945
E: general@nfm.org.uk
www.nfm.org.uk
CEO: Jane Robey
NFM is a network of local not-for-profit family mediation services in England and Wales, which offers help to couples, married or unmarried, who are in the process of separation and divorce. We provide high-quality mediation to everyone who needs it in all communities, helping clients to reach joint decisions about the issues associated with their separation
Employees: 12
Volunteers: 1
Regional offices: 47

## National Federation of Shopmobility

2–4 Meadow Close,
Ise Valley Industrial Estate, Wellingborough,
Northamptonshire NN8 4BH
T: 01933 229644 (also fax)
E: shopmobility@bhta.com
www.nfsuk.org
Provides advice, guidance and support to organisations and individuals considering developing Shopmobility in their locality. Influences policy on mobility and access

issues and supports the organisations and individuals campaigning for improvements.
Employees: 1

## National Federation of the Blind of the UK

Sir John Wilson House, 215 Kirkgate, Wakefield, West Yorkshire WF1 1JG
T: 020 8452 8336
Helpline: 01924 291313
F: 01924 200244
E: admin@nfbuk.org
www.nfbuk.org
President: Norma Town
The Federation, through its blind and partially sighted membership, seeks to promote a better quality of life for all visually impaired people through local activities at branch level and nationally through campaigning.
Employees: 2
Volunteers: 1
Regional offices: 19

## National Federation of Women's Institutes

104 New Kings Road, London SW6 4LY
T: 020 7371 9300
F: 020 7736 4333
E: pr@nfwi.org.uk
www.thewi.org.uk
General Secretary: Jana Osborne
The largest women's voluntary organisation in the UK, with over 212,000 members in over 6,600 WIs in England, Wales and the Islands. We offer women the best opportunity: to make an impact in their communities; to influence local, national and world issues affecting the social, economic and environmental life of families and communities; to learn new and traditional skills.
Regional offices: 70

## National Federation of Young Farmers' Clubs

YFC Centre, 10th Street, Stoneleigh Park, Kenilworth, Warwickshire CV8 2LG
T: 024 7685 7200
F: 024 7685 7229
E: james.eckley@nfyfc.org.uk
www.nfyfc.org.uk
Chief Executive: James Eckley
The National Federation of Young Farmers
Employees: 70
Volunteers: 5000
Regional offices: 49

## National Flood Forum

Old Snuff Mill Warehouse, Park Lane, Bewdley, Worcestershire DY12 2EL
T: 01299 403055
E: amanda.davies@floodforum.org.uk
www.nationalfloodforum.org.uk
Chief Executive: Paul Cobbing
The National Flood Forum is a charity dedicated to supporting and representing flood risk communities. It helps people to recognise, understand and reduce their flood risks and also helps people to recover if they have been flooded. The National Flood Forum also works to ensure that the needs of communities are fully recognised by government, Environment Agency, local government and the insurance industry.
Employees: 14
Regional offices: 10
Income: £426,777 (2013–14)

## National Gardens Scheme

Hatchlands, East Clandon, Guildford, Surrey GU4 7RT
T: 01483 211535
E: ngs@ngs.org.uk
www.ngs.org.uk
Opens gardens of quality, character and interest to the public for charity.

## National Group on Homeworking

Office 26, 30–38 Dock Street, Leeds, Yorkshire LS10 1JF
T: 0113 245 4273
F: 0113 246 5616
E: admin@ngh.org.uk
www.ngh.org.uk
Aims: to educate the public and policy makers on issues concerning homeworking; to alleviate poverty among homeworkers by working, campaigning and lobbying to improve their working terms and conditions.
Employees: 8
Volunteers: 9

## National Gulf Veterans and Families Association

Building E Office 8, Chamberlain Business Centre, Chamberlain Road, Hull, Humberside HU8 8HL
T: 0845 257 4853
F: 01482 808731
E: info@ngvfa.org.uk
www.ngvfa.org.uk
Chair: Nigel Graveston
The relief of persons who served as members of the armed forces or as civilians in the conflict in the Gulf and their families and dependants who are in condition of need, hardship, sickness or distress. The relief of

persons who served as members of the armed forces or as civilians in any future desert conflict and their families and dependants who are in condition of need, hardship, sickness or distress.
Employees: 5
Volunteers: 30
Income: £179,083 (2015–16)

## National Housing Federation

Lion Court, 25 Procter Street WC1V 6NY
T: 020 7067 1010
F: 020 7067 1011
E: info@housing.org.uk
www.housing.org.uk
Chief Executive: David Orr
The National Housing Federation is the voice of affordable housing in England. We believe that everyone should have the home they need at a price they can afford. That's why we represent the work of housing associations and campaign for better housing. Our members provide two and a half million homes for more than five million people. Each year they invest in a diverse range of projects that help create strong, vibrant communities.
Employees: 135
Regional offices: 3

## National Institute of Medical Herbalists

Clover House, James Court, South Street, Exeter, Devon EX1 1EE
T: 01392 426022
F: 01392 498963
E: info@nimh.org.uk
www.nimh.org.uk
President: Desiree Shelley
Promotes the importance of herbal medicine; makes people more aware of herbal medicine and its benefits; assists with training to those who wish to pursue as a career.
Employees: 2

## National Justice and Peace Network

NJPN, 39 Eccleston Square,
London SW1V 1BX
T: 020 7901 4864
E: admin@justice-and-peace.org.uk
www.justice-and-peace.org.uk
Chair: Anne Peacey
We are a grassroots body working with groups
and individuals of all faiths and none who
share our aims and values based in the
Christian Gospels and Catholic Social
Teaching. We engage with all who seek to
challenge unjust structures which perpetuate
poverty, violence and environmental
degradation, including individuals, diocesan
and local groups, national agencies and
religious communities, offering opportunities
for action, information sharing, friendship and
mutual support.
Employees: 1
Volunteers: 9
Income: £70,000 (2014–15)

## National Kidney Federation

The Point, Coach Road, Shireoaks,
Worksop, Nottinghamshire S81 8BW
T: 01909 544999
Helpline: 0845 601 0209
F: 01909 481723
E: nkf@kidney.org.uk
www.kidney.org.uk
Chief Executive Officer: Timothy Statham
The National Kidney Federation (NKF) is the
patient's voice and is fighting to achieve
high-quality renal treatment across the UK.
It is the only national kidney charity run by
patients, for patients. It is funded entirely by
donations and sponsorships. The Federation
is able to monitor and compare renal services
across the country because of its unique
structure. It is run by representatives of the
78 separate Kidney Patient Associations
geographically spread across the UK.
Employees: 18

## National Literacy Trust

68 South Lambeth Road, London SW8 1RL
T: 020 7587 1842
F: 020 7587 1411
E: contact@literacytrust.org.uk
www.literacytrust.org.uk
Director: Jonathan Douglas
The National Literacy Trust is a national
charity dedicated to raising literacy levels in
the UK. Our research and analysis make us
the leading authority on literacy. We run
projects in the poorest communities,
campaign to make literacy a priority for
politicians and parents and support schools.
Employees: 55
Volunteers: 5
Income: £3,144,000 (2014–15)

## National Music for the Blind

2 High Park Road, Southport,
Merseyside PR9 7QL
T: 01704 228010
E: music4blind@gmail.com
www.music4blind.webs.com
Director: Chris Mills
Provides a free fortnightly USB service to all
visually handicapped persons in the UK. The
USB memory stick contains nostalgic music
programmes, plays, documentaries, comedy
shows, old radio and much more from the
vast library of the charity. Fourteen days to
listen then return using freepost wallets.
Volunteers: 2

## National Operatic and Dramatic Association

Peterborough PE1 2RZ
T: 0870 770 2480
F: 0870 770 2490
E: info@noda.org.uk
www.noda.org.uk
Promotes and improves the art of amateur
theatre to cultivate the improvement of
public taste in the art.
Employees: 8
Volunteers: 180
Regional offices: 11

## National Organisation for the Treatment of Abusers

PO Box 356, Hull HU12 8WR
T: 01482 896990 (also fax)
E: notaoffice@nota.co.uk
www.nota.co.uk
NOTA has a growing multidisciplinary
membership comprising practitioners,
managers and policy makers from the public,
private and voluntary sectors. NOTA brings a
wide variety of perspectives to interventions
with sexual aggressors. It is the only
professional multidisciplinary organisation in
the UK and Ireland dedicated to work with
sexual abusers. It is consequently in a unique
position to promote and develop work in this
area of public protection.
Regional offices: 13

## National Osteoporosis Society

Camerton, Bath BA2 0PJ
T: 01761 471771
F: 01761 471104
E: h.kingman@nos.org.uk
www.nos.org.uk
The National Osteoporosis Society (NOS)
campaigns to ensure that all people with or
at risk of osteoporosis receive appropriate
advice and treatment to enable them to avoid
fractures and to enjoy a better quality of life.
The NOS provides information and support
for people with osteoporosis and their carers
by promoting education for the public and
health professionals, by lobbying government
and health organisations and by encouraging
fundraising for support services.
Employees: 60
Volunteers: 500

## National Patients Support Trust

First Floor, 162 Shepherds Bush Road,
Hammersmith, London W6 7PB
T: 020 7603 9770
E: npstcharity@btconnect.com
www.npst.co.uk
Trustee: Cornelius Oconnor
Provides relief and assistance for patients
and former patients of NHS hospital trusts
suffering from disease and from other
physical and or mental disability or disabilities.
Employees: 6

## National Pensioners Convention

Walkden House, 10 Melton Street,
London NW1 2EJ
T: 020 7383 0388
E: info@npcuk.org
www.npcuk.org
The NPC is Britain's biggest campaigning
organisation for older people, representing
over 1,000 local, regional and national
pensioner groups with a total of 1.5 million
members. The NPC promotes the welfare
and interests of all pensioners. It lobbies MPs
and government on policies affecting older
people and stages an annual three-day
Pensioners- Parliament in Blackpool, where
over 1,000 representatives discuss issues
of concern.
Employees: 4
Regional offices: 18

## National Playbus Association

Brunswick Court, Brunswick Square,
Bristol BS2 8PE
T: 01458 850804
E: playbus@playbus.org.uk
www.workingonwheels.org
Promotes the use of playbuses and converted
vehicles as mobile community resources
and acts as an umbrella organisation
that promotes good practice in mobile
community work.

## National Portage Association

Kings Court, 17 School Road, Hall Green,
Birmingham, West Midlands B28 8JG
T: 0121 244 1807
F: 0121 244 1801
E: info@portage.org.uk
www.portage.org.uk
Portage is a home-visiting educational service
for pre-school children with additional
support needs and their families.
**Employees: 5**

## National Rheumatoid Arthritis Society

Unit B4, Westacott Business Centre,
Westacott Way, Littlewick Green,
Maidenhead, Berkshire SL6 3RT
T: 0845 458 3969
Helpline: 0800 298 7650
F: 0845 458 3971
E: enquiries@nras.org.uk
www.nras.org.uk
Chief Executive: Ailsa Bosworth
NRAS provides support, information and
advocacy for people with rheumatoid arthritis
and juvenile idiopathic arthritis, their families,
friends and carers. We are also a resource for
health professionals with an interest in
rheumatology and work closely with
rheumatology teams across the UK.
**Employees: 20**

## National Society of Allotments and Leisure Gardeners

O'Dell House, 8 Hunters Road, Corby,
Northamptonshire NN17 5JE
T: 01536 266576
E: natsoc@nsalg.org.uk
www.nsalg.org.uk
Operations and Legal Manager: Liz Bunting
National representative body for the
allotment movement.
**Employees: 5**

## National Trust

Heelis, Kemble Drive, Swindon,
Wiltshire SN2 2NA
T: 01793 817400
F: 01793 817401
E: enquiries@thenationaltrust.org.uk
www.nationaltrust.org.uk
We protect and open to the public over 300
historic houses and gardens and 49 industrial
monuments and mills. We also look after
forests, woods, fens, beaches, farmland,
downs, moorland, islands, archaeological
remains, castles, nature reserves and villages.
**Employees: 4000**
**Volunteers: 40000**
**Regional offices: 11**

## National Voices

1st Floor, Bride House, 18–20 Bride Lane,
London EC4Y 8EE
T: 020 3176 0738
E: info@nationalvoices.org.uk
www.nationalvoices.org.uk
Chief Executive: Jeremy Taylor
National Voices is the coalition of health and
social care charities working to strengthen
the voice of patients, service users and those
who represent them.
**Employees: 9**
**Income: £506,474 (2013–14)**

## National Women's Register

23 Vulcan House, Vulcan Road North,
Norwich, Norfolk NR6 6AQ
T: 01603 406767
F: 01603 407003
E: office@nwr.org.uk
www.nwr.org.uk
Chair of Trustees: Pamela McKee
NWR is an international organisation of
women's discussion groups. Each group aims
to provide its members with the opportunity
to take part in stimulating discussions on a
wide range of topics.
**Employees: 5**
**Volunteers: 24**

## National Youth Agency

Eastgate House, 19–23 Humberstone Road,
Leicester, Leicestershire LE5 3GJ
T: 0116 242 7350
F: 0116 285 3777
E: nya@nya.org.uk
www.nya.org.uk
Chief Executive: Fiona Blacke
We are the national charity for youth work
in England. Founded in 1964, we believe
investing in young people's personal and
social development helps them overcome
challenges and reach their potential. We want

to ensure young people get access to the
youth workers they need, so we seek to
secure youth work through policy and
advocacy supporting youth workers to do
their jobs better and securing new resources.
**Employees: 48**
**Regional offices: 1**

## National Youth Orchestra of Great Britain

32 Old School House, Britannia Road,
Kingswood, Bristol BS15 8DB
T: 0117 960 0477
E: info@nyo.org.uk
www.nyo.org.uk
Works: to discover and foster exceptional
musical talent in young people and to help
provide them with tuition and experience in
orchestral musical skills; to give concerts of
the highest standard; to inspire young people
to take an interest in music.

## National Youthbike

PO Box 27, Horncastle,
Lincolnshire LN9 6XB
T: 01507 524432
E: nationalyouthbike@yahoo.co.uk
www.youthbike.com
Chair: Tony Nightingale
Promotes the education and social
development of young people in the UK in life
skills, engineering, design and information
technology by assisting them in their
preparation for and participation in the annual
National Youthbike weekend event.
**Volunteers: 17**

## Natural Death Centre

In The Hill House, Watley Lane, Twyford,
Winchester SO21 1QX
T: 01962 712690
E: contact@naturaldeath.org.uk
www.naturaldeath.org.uk
Manager: Rosie Inman-Cook
Aims to improve the quality of dying and
funerals. Gives information for families caring
for the dying at home, and on how to get your
affairs in order. Empowers people organising
inexpensive and or environmentally friendly
funerals, sometimes without funeral
directors. Gives advice on rights and laws
concerning burials on private land or at
natural burial grounds. List suppliers, who
deal direct with the public. Advice on keeping
costs down. Telephone helpline on all
related topics.
**Volunteers: 5**

## Nautilus International

1–2 The Shrubberies, George Lane,
South Woodford, London E18 1BD
T: 020 8989 6677
F: 020 8530 1015
E: rcunningham@nautilusinc.org
www.nautilusint.org
General Secretary: Mark Dickinson
The Nautilus Welfare Fund, a charity
administered by Nautilus International,
provides support and assistance for retired
seafarers and their dependants.
Employees: 65
Regional offices: 2

## Naz Foundation International

2nd Floor, 5 Harbour Exchange,
London E14 9GE
T: 020 7570 6092
F: 020 7691 7062
E: kim@nfi.net
www.nfi.net
Chief Executive: Shivananda Khan
With a primary focus on males who have sex
with males (MSM), NFI's mission is to
empower socially excluded and disadvantaged
males to secure for themselves social justice,
equity, health and wellbeing through
technical, institutional and financial support.
Regional offices: 1

## NCVO Charities Evaluation Services (CES)

Society Building, 8 All Saints Street,
London N1 9RL
T: 020 7713 6161
F: 020 7713 6300
E: consultancy@ncvo.org.uk
www.ncvo.org.uk
Employees: 21
Volunteers: 12

## Nell Bank

Denton Road, Ilkley,
West Yorkshire LS29 0DE
T: 01943 602032
F: 01943 601690
E: dan.goodey@bradford.gov.uk
www.nellbank.com
Centre Manager: Bruce Fowler
Educates young people in the principles of
responsible citizenship by providing them
with training and recreation and community
service opportunities. Provides affordable day
and residential outdoor education experience
in stunning and contrasting environments to
20,000 children and young people each
year. Enables hard-to-reach groups to

access outdoor experience via nationally
significant activities, adapted accommodation
and equipment.
Employees: 9
Volunteers: 100

## Network 81

1–7 Woodfield Terrace, Stansted,
Essex CM24 8AJ
T: 0845 077 4056
Helpline: 0845 077 4055
F: 0845 077 4057
E: network81@btconnect.com
www.network81.org
Chair: Eirwen Grenfell-Essam
Network 81 offers help and support to
parents throughout all stages of assessment
and statementing as outlined in the
Education Act 1996 and Code of Practice
2001. Our national helpline offers an
individual service linked to a national network
of local contacts. Network 81 produces a
range of literature aimed at familiarising
parents with the assessment and
statementing procedures. We also run
extensive training programmes for parents
and those working with parents.
Employees: 4
Volunteers: 80

## Network for Peace

5 Caledonian Road, London N1 9DY
T: 07794 036602
E: mail@networkforpeace.org.uk
www.networkforpeace.org.uk
Coordinator: Claire Poyner
After the demise of the National Peace
Council, one of the oldest peace
organisations in the UK, Network for Peace
was set up with the aim of continuing with the
networking role of the NPC. NfP provides a
regularly updated website, which includes
links to websites of members, news and an
extensive diary of events. This information is
also available as a bi-monthly newsletter.
Employees: 1
Income: £2,500 (2014–15)

## Neuroblastoma UK

54 Forest Road, Richmond TW9 3BZ
T: 020 8940 4353
E: secretary@neuroblastoma.org.uk
www.neuroblastoma.org.uk
Chair: Susan Hay
Funding vital research to find new treatments
and improve existing treatments for

neuroblastoma, an aggressive childhood
cancer.
Volunteers: 10
Income: £300,000 (2015–16)

## Neurological Alliance

Neurological Alliance, c/o Parkinsons UK,
215 Vauxhall Bridge Road,
London SW1V 1EJ
T: 020 7963 3994
E: sarah.vibert@neural.org.uk
www.neural.org.uk
Chief Executive: Sarah Vibert
The Neurological Alliance is the only
collective voice for 80 organisations working
together to make life better for millions of
people in England with a neurological
condition. We work with our member
organisations to campaign nationally and
locally to ensure better services and outcomes
for all those with a neurological condition.
Employees: 2
Regional offices: 13

## New Bridge Foundation

1a Elm Park, London SW2 2TX
T: 020 8671 3856
E: info@newbridgefoundation.org.uk
www.newbridgefoundation.org.uk
New Bridge was founded in 1956 to create
links between the offender and the community.
The keynote service remains the friendship
and support given by volunteers to longer-
term prisoners, especially those no longer
in contact with family and friends.
Employees: 3
Volunteers: 200

## New Choices for Youth

E: marcias@ncytrust.org

## New Economics Foundation

3 Jonathan Street, Vauxhall,
London SE11 5NH
T: 020 7820 6300
F: 020 7820 6301
E: info@neweconomics.org
www.neweconomics.org
Executive Director: Stewart Wallis
Aims to put people and the environment a
t the centre of economic thinking. We aim
to improve quality of life by promoting
innovative solutions that challenge
mainstream thinking on economic,
environment and social issues. We work
in partnership and put people and the
planet first.
Employees: 45
Volunteers: 2
Regional offices: 1

## New Horizon Youth Centre

68 Chalton Street, London NW1 1JR
T: 020 7388 5560
F: 020 7388 5848
E: info@nhyouthcentre.org.uk
www.nhyouthcentre.org.uk
Director: Shelagh O'Connor
New Horizon Youth Centre is a day centre working with young people age 16 to 21 who are vulnerable, homeless or at risk. New Horizon Youth Centre aims to enable young people to gain skills and knowledge to improve their life chances and to help them move from adolescence into adulthood.
Employees: 28
Volunteers: 45
Regional offices: 1

## New Kadampa Tradition – International Kadampa Buddhist Union

Conishead Priory, Ulverston
T: 01229 588533
E: info@kadampa.org
www.kadampa.org
General Secretary: Stephen Cowing

## New Philanthropy Capital

3rd Floor, 185 Park Street, 185 Park Street, London, County Londonderry SE1 9BL
T: 020 7620 8450
Helpline: 020 7620 4869
F: 020 7620 8451
E: info@thinknpc.org
www.thinknpc.org
Chief Executive: Dan Corry
NPC advises donors on how to make their giving to charities more effective. Our aim is to increase the quantity and quality of resources available to the charitable sector. We do this through a combination of independent research and tailored advice. Our research identifies charities that are achieving excellent results and where funds and resources can be targeted most effectively. Our advice for donors guides them on how to ensure their money has high impact.
Employees: 45

## Newcastle Action for Parent and Toddler Groups Initiative

Heaton Community Centre, Trewhitt Road, Heaton, Newcastle upon Tyne,
Tyne and Wear NE6 5DY
T: 0191 265 6158 (also fax)
E: karen@napi.org.uk
www.napi.org.uk
Project Manager: Karen Williams
To promote the education and development of under school aged children in the City of Newcastle upon Tyne by the provision of advice, information and support services for parent and toddler groups and like groups.
Employees: 12

## Newcastle Council for Voluntary Service

Higham House, Higham Place, Newcastle upon Tyne NE1 8AF
T: 0191 232 7445
F: 0191 230 5640
E: sally.young@cvsnewcastle.org.uk
cvsnewcastle.org.uk
Chief Executive: Sally Young
Newcastle CVS works to support, develop, promote, connect and represent voluntary and community organisations in Newcastle. Our work helps to make Newcastle a better place by helping to develop a thriving voluntary and community sector. We do this through our three service areas: supporting and developing local organisations to thrive; networking and involving local organisations to engage; representing and influencing on behalf of the voluntary and community sector. Newcastle CVS also runs Ellison Services, a community accountancy organisation providing payroll.
Employees: 32
Volunteers: 70
Regional offices: 1

## Newcastle Tenants and Residents Federation

Fawdon Community Centre, Fawdon Park Road, Fawdon, Newcastle upon Tyne,
Tyne and Wear NE3 2PL
T: 0191 285 2724
E: enquiries@newcastletenantsfed.org.uk
www.newcastletenantsfed.org.uk
Newcastle Tenants and Residents Federation is a registered charity representing tenants and residents associations (TARAs) throughout Newcastle upon Tyne. We are also one of the oldest federation's in the country, having been formed in 1977. Our focus is on working with tenants and residents to relieve deprivation and improve housing conditions and living environments across the city.
Employees: 4
Volunteers: 2

## Newlife

Newlife Centre, Hemlock Way, Cannock, Staffordshire WS11 7GF
T: 01543 462777
E: info@newlifecharity.co.uk
www.newlifecharity.co.uk
Medical research, awareness and service, relevant to all birth defects.

## NHS Confederation

29 Bressenden Place, London SW1E 5DD
T: 020 7074 3282
F: 020 7959 7273
E: info@nhsconfed.org
www.nhsconfed.org
We help our members provide better health and healthcare by: influencing the development and implementation of policy and the wider public debate on the full range of health and health services issues, speaking out independently on behalf of our members; supporting health leaders through information sharing and networking; promoting excellence in employment to improve the working lives of staff and, through them, to provide better care for patients; providing tailored services and products to enable boards to develop their objectives.
Employees: 40

## Niemann-Pick Disease Group UK

Suite 2, Vermont House, Concord, Washington, Tyne and Wear NE37 2SQ
T: 0191 415 0693
E: niemann-pick@zetnet.co.uk
www.niemannpick.org.uk
Executive Director: Toni Mathieson
The group aims to make a positive difference to the lives of those affected by Niemann-Pick diseases and their families, through the provision of effective support in the three main areas of care, information and research.
Employees: 4
Volunteers: 12

## No Panic

Jubilee House, 74 High Street, Madeley, Telford, Shropshire TF5 4AH
T: 01952 680460
Helpline: 0844 967 4848
E: admin@nopanic.org.uk
www.nopanic.org.uk
Chairperson: Keith Stenning
Works for the relief and rehabilitation of people suffering from panic attacks, phobias and obsessive/compulsive disorders.
Employees: 3
Volunteers: 51
Regional offices: 1

## Noise Abatement Society

44 Grand Parade, Brighton  BN2 9QA
T: 01273 682223
E: nas@noiseabatementsociety.fsnet.co.uk
www.noiseabatementsociety.com
The Noise Abatement Society is a registered
charity. Its aims are to eliminate excessive
noise in all its forms by campaigning to raise
awareness, by lobbying parliament and
through education to improve the quality
of life for all. It is an active and effective
problem-solving organisation with strong
contacts in government. The society runs the
only telephone noise helpline in the UK.

## Nordoff-Robbins Music Therapy

2 Lissenden Gardens, London  NW5 1PQ
T: 020 7267 4496
F: 020 7267 4369
E: admin@nordoff-robbins.org.uk
www.nordoff-robbins.org.uk
Provides music therapy treatment for people
with special needs and training for music
therapists.
Employees: 50
Volunteers: 50

## Norfolk Community Law Service Ltd

St Clements House, 2–16 Colegate,
Norwich, Norfolk  NR3 1BQ
T: 01603 496623
F: 01603 618320
E: admin@ncls.co.uk
www.ncls.co.uk
Chief Executive Officer: Ros Brown
We are a registered charity dedicated to
providing access to justice and equality in
Norfolk. All our services are free,
independent and confidential.
Employees: 15
Volunteers: 110
Regional offices: 1

## Norm UK

PO Box 71, Stone, Staffordshire  ST15 0SF
T: 01785 814044 (also fax)
E: info@norm-uk.org
www.15square.org.uk
Aims to advance the education of the public
in all matters relating to circumcision and
other forms of surgical alteration of the
genitals, including alternative treatments
and offering information and advice on
such matters.
Employees: 1
Volunteers: 14

## North Taunton Partnership

Priorswood Community Centre,
13–14 Priorswood Place, Eastwick Road,
Taunton, Somerset  TA2 7JW
T: 01823 353643
E: lesley.priorswoodcc@yahoo.co.uk
www.priorswoodcommunitycentre.co.uk
Manager: Lesley Thomas
The Charity's objects are to promote
charitable purposes for the benefit of the
community of North Taunton and in
particular the advancement of education,
the promotion of health and the relief of
poverty, sickness and distress. These aims are
achieved by offering advice surgeries, social
groups, exercise classes and activities for
young people during the school holidays
through our Pride in Priorswood program.
Employees: 4
Volunteers: 32
Regional offices: 1
Income: £81,087 (2014–15)

## Northern Ireland Council for Voluntary Action

61 Duncairn Gardens, Belfast  BT15 2GB
T: 028 9087 7777
F: 028 9087 7799
E: info@nicva.org
www.nicva.org
Chief Executive: Seamus McAleavey
NICVA is an umbrella organisation, seeking
to represent the interests of voluntary and
community organisations throughout
Northern Ireland. In its role as a voluntary
sector development agency, NICVA acts
as a catalyst to promote innovation and new
approaches to the challenge of social need.
Employees: 45

## Norwich Door To Door

Norwich Community Hospital,
Bowthorpe Rd, Norwich, Norfolk  NR2 3TU
T: 01603 776735
E: n-norwich@btconnect.com
www.norwichdoortodoor.org.uk
CEO: Door to Door
Norwich Door to Door is a caring welfare
charity that provides a minibus transport
service in Norwich for people with disabilities
and mobility issues who are unable to access
general public transport. Our aim is to enable
social inclusion and enhance the quality of
life of local people on low incomes. We do
this by providing a mobility service at an
affordable cost. This allows passengers to
gain independence and equality, safely and
securely, building their confidence and

empowering them to make a contribution
to their community.
Employees: 20
Volunteers: 50
Regional offices: 1

## Norwood

Broadway House, 80–82 The Broadway,
Stanmore, Middlesex  HA7 4HB
T: 020 8954 4555
F: 020 8420 6800
E: suzanne.nehard@norwood.org.uk
www.norwood.org.uk
Chief Executive: Norma Brier
Norwood is Anglo-Jewry's largest children
and family services organisation, supporting
children and their families, and adults, in
coping with learning disabilities and social
disadvantage. Every year we help thousands
of children and their families by providing
vital, specialised care to the most vulnerable
members of our community.
Employees: 1100
Volunteers: 700
Regional offices: 4

## Notts Housing Advice

E: admin@nottshousingadvice.org.uk

## Nova Wakefield District Limited

11 Upper York Street, Wakefield, Wakefield,
West Yorkshire  WF1 3FQ
T: 01924 367418
E: fiona.cooper@nova-wd.org.uk
www.nova-wd.org.uk
CEO: Alison Haskins
Nova Wakefield District is the support
agency for the community and voluntary
sector. We work with organisations big and
small throughout the district, helping with
development, volunteering, funding,
contracts, governance and influencing issues
pertinent to the sector.
Employees: 13
Volunteers: 13

## NSPCC

Weston House, 42 Curtain Road,
London EC2A 3NH
T: 020 7825 2500
Helpline: 0808 800 5000
F: 020 7825 2525
E: info@nspcc.org.uk
www.nspcc.org.uk
**Chief Executive: Andrew Flanagan**
The NSPCC's purpose is to end cruelty to
children. Our vision is of a society where all
children are loved, valued and able to fulfil
their potential.
Employees: 2600
Volunteers: 27500
Regional offices: 60

## Nubian Life Resource Centre Ltd

50 Commonwealth Avenue,
London W12 7QR
T: 020 8749 8017
E: info@nubianlife.org.uk
www.nubianlife.org.uk
Provides for the relief of elderly African
Caribbean people living in the UK.
Employees: 14

## Nuffield Trust

59 New Cavendish Street,
London W1G 7LP
T: 020 7631 8450
F: 020 7631 8451
E: info@nuffieldtrust.org.uk
www.nuffieldtrust.org.uk
**Chief Operating Officer: Kim Beazor**
The Trust's mission is to promote independent
analysis and informed debate on UK
healthcare policy, with a particular focus on
long-term, strategic direction. The core
objectives are: to improve the health of the
people of the UK, to improve the quality of
healthcare and to improve the quality of
health policy; to communicate evidence and
encourage an exchange around developed or
developing knowledge in order to illuminate
recognised and emerging issues.
Employees: 5

## Number One Community Trust (TW) Ltd

1 Rowan Tree Road, Tunbridge Wells,
Kent TN2 5PX
T: 01892 514544
E: onecommunity@btconnect.com
numberonecommunitytrust.org.uk
**Chair of Trustees: Adrian Cory**
Runs a community centre in a deprived area
offering a wide range of services including
pre-school, café and a variety of clubs/groups
for people of all ages. Aims to: promote the
physical, mental and spiritual health and
wellbeing of local residents; improve the social
and economic wellbeing of local residents;
support the advancement of education and
training;assist those who are seeking
employment; and encourage environmental
improvements in the neighbourhood.
Employees: 9
Volunteers: 47
Regional offices: 1

## Nurture Group Network

18a Victoria Park Square, Bethnal Green,
London E2 9PF
T: 020 3475 8980
E: info@nurturegroups.org
www.nurturegroups.org
**Chief Executive: Kevin Kibble**
The Nurture Group Network exists to
promote the development of nurture
groups and to ensure the continuing quality
of their delivery through accredited training
programmes, research on effective practice,
relevant publications and information
exchange. Its aim is to make the nurture
group approach available to all pupils
who need it and also to ensure that the
connections between learning and
early development are understood
throughout education.
Employees: 15
Regional offices: 2
Income: £911,081 (2014–15)

## NYAS (National Youth Advocacy Service)

Egerton House, 2 Tower Road, Birkenhead,
Wirral, Merseyside CH41 1FF
T: 0151 649 8700
Helpline: 0300 330 3131
F: 0151 649 8701
E: main@nyas.net
www.nyas.net
**Chief Executive: Rita Waters**
NYAS offers an unusual range of preventive
interdisciplinary welfare and legal services,
information, consultation, support and
representation to children, young people and
vulnerable adults in England and Wales. It has
a team of in-house lawyers and a sessional
workforce of more than 350 children's
advocates and caseworkers, who include
some of the most experienced welfare
professionals in the country.
Employees: 135
Volunteers: 65
Regional offices: 8

## Nystagmus Network

PO Box 70580, London SE12 2BL
T: 0345 634 2630
E: info@nystagmusnet.org
www.nystagmusnetwork.org
**Chair: Richard Wilson**
The Nystagmus Network provides support
and information to everyone affected by
congenital or acquired nystagmus, including
parents, adults and the professionals
supporting those with nystagmus in
education or employment. We raise
awareness of nystagmus all year round but
especially on Wobbly Wednesday, the first
Wednesday in November. We also raise
funding for and foster scientific, medical
and social research into nystagmus.
Employees: 2
Volunteers: 12
Income: £120,000 (2015–16)

## Oakleaf Enterprise

Oakleaf Enterprise, 101 Walnut Tree Close,
Guildford, Surrey GU1 4UQ
T: 01483 303649
F: 01483 537069
E: deeptiparmar@oakleaf-enterprise.org
www.oakleaf-enterprise.org
**Chief Executive: Clive Stone**
Oakleaf is the only mental health charity in
Surrey working as a social enterprise to
provide vocational training for those suffering
from mental health issues. We offer training
in horticulture, upholstery and IT, enabling
people to acquire new skills and ultimately
return to work. Alongside these we offer a
range of social inclusion activities that cater
to building confidence, physical health and
wellbeing. Through their placement at
Oakleaf, clients are able to gain up-to-date
qualifications and practical experience and
increase their confidence levels.
Employees: 20
Volunteers: 40

## Oasis Charitable Trust

Oasis Trust, 1 Kennington Road,
London SE1 7QP
T: 020 7921 4200
E: enquiries@oasisuk.org
www.oasistrust.org
Group CEO: Joy Madeiros
Oasis is a community, housing, education and
social-transformation charity committed to
building communities where everyone can
belong, overcome life's obstacles and reach
their God-given potential. Working in 36
communities we pioneer integrated services
such as academies, food banks, youth work,
housing provision and community churches.
Inspired by the teachings of Jesus Christ,
Oasis is a fully inclusive movement working to
make life in all its fullness a greater reality for
every person and community.

## OCD Action

Suite 506–507, Davina House,
137–149 Goswell Road, London EC1V 7ET
T: 020 7253 5272
Helpline: 0845 390 6232
E: info@ocdaction.org.uk
www.ocdaction.org.uk
Director: Joel Rose
OCD Action is the largest national charity
focusing on Obsessive Compulsive Disorder.
The charity provides support and information
to anybody affected by OCD, works to raise
awareness of the disorder amongst the public
and healthcare workers and strives to secure a
better deal for people with OCD. Formed by
a group of leading professionals and volunteers
in 1994, the charity is recognised as a strong
voice for people with OCD and a vital source
of help.
Employees: 7
Volunteers: 30
Regional offices: 2

## Ockenden International

Constitution Hill, Woking,
Surrey GU22 7UU
T: 01483 772012
E: enquiries@ockendenprizes.org
www.ockenden.org.uk
Ockenden works to promote independence
and self-reliance amongst refugees, displaced
people, returnees and their host communities
throughout the world.

## Odyssey Trust (UK)

Omnibus Business Centre,
39–41 North Road, London N7 9DP
T: 020 7700 6177
F: 020 7700 6232
E: info@theodyssey.co.uk
www.theodyssey.co.uk
The Trust provides high-quality treatment
and support services that respond to the
changing needs of people affected by
substance misuse.

## Off Centre Hackney

E: martin.williams@offcentre.org.uk

## Officers' Association

1st Floor, Mountbarrow House,
6–20 Elizabeth Street, London SW1W 9RB
T: 020 7808 4160
F: 020 7808 4161
E: info@officersassociation.org.uk
www.officersassociation.org.uk
The Officers' Association (OA), founded
over 90 years ago, is the only charity
dedicated exclusively to supporting officers
and ex-officers and their dependants from
all three services. It achieves this in two ways:
providing employment services for service
leavers and ex-serving officers; providing
benevolence services in the form of financial
and welfare support. The OA offers a
resource based on a thorough understanding
of the background and needs of
commissioned officers and their families.
Employees: 24
Volunteers: 600

## Olmec

London SE11 5JA
T: 0845 880 0110
E: iwebunor.aniya@olmec-ec.org.uk
www.olmec-ec.org.uk
We are a dynamic community investment
foundation and work alongside disadvantaged
communities to deliver programmes that lead
to positive impact. We are driven by principles
of self-help, empowerment and social justice
and our work ranges from addressing issues
of under-representation of minority
communities, to breaking down the barriers
to employment faced by refugees. We also
engage in research and use it as a tool to
influence policy and provision.
Employees: 8

## One Plus One Marriage and Partnership Research

1 Benjamin Street, London EC1M 5QG
T: 020 7553 9530
E: kb@oneplusone.org.uk
www.oneplusone.org.uk
Director: Penny Mansfield
OnePlusOne puts research into practice,
investigating what makes relationships work
– or fall apart. We support individuals and
couples to manage relationship issues earlier
and more effectively, and champion the
adoption and implementation of policies and
services that value relationships, espouse
early relationship support and encourage a
culture of relationship support. We run
self-help websites www.thecoupleconnection.
net for individuals and couples and www.
theparentconnection.org.uk for separated
parents or those considering separation.
Employees: 23
Volunteers: 8
Income: £2,387,000 (2014–15)

## One World Trust

3 Whitehall Court, London SW1A 2EL
T: 020 7766 3470
F: 020 7839 7718
E: info@oneworldtrust.org
www.oneworldtrust.org
The One World Trust promotes education
and research into the changes required within
global organisations in order to achieve the
eradication of poverty, injustice and war. It
conducts research on practical ways to make
global organisations more responsive to the
people they affect and on how the rule of law
can be applied equally to all. It educates
political leaders and opinion-formers about
the findings of its research.
Employees: 8
Volunteers: 12

## Online Centres Foundation

The Workstation, 15 Paternoster Row,
Sheffield, Unknown S1 2BX
T: 0114 227 0035
E: alison.broadley@ukonlinecentres.com
www.ukonlinecentres.com

## Onside

E: martine.vantomme@onside-advocacy.
org.uk

## Open College Network YHR

OCNYHR, OCN House,
Lower Warrengate, Wakefield,
West Yorkshire  WF1 1SA
T: 01924 434600
F: 01924 364213
E: enquiries@ocnyhr.org.uk
www.ocnyhr.org.uk
**Chief Executive: John Lawton**
OCNYHR is a national awarding organisation committed to providing a high-quality and responsive accreditation service. Regulated by Ofqual, OCNYHR offers a wide range of qualifications within the Qualifications and Credit Framework (QCF). At OCNYHR, we also provide our Recognised Centres with bespoke accreditation through our Customised Accreditation Service. OCNYHR is also an Access Validating Agency, licensed by the Quality Assurance Agency (QAA), to develop, approve and certificate Access to Higher Education Diplomas.
**Employees: 30**

## Open Doors International Language School

E: croberts@odils.com

## Open Spaces Society

25a Bell Street, Henley-on-Thames,
Oxfordshire  RG9 2BA
T: 01491 573535
E: hq@oss.org.uk
www.oss.org.uk
**General Secretary: Kate Ashbrook**
We campaign to create and conserve common land, village greens, open spaces and rights of public access, in town and country, in England and Wales.
**Employees: 5**
**Volunteers: 40**

## Operation Black Vote

18A Victoria Park Square, London  E2 9PB
T: 020 8983 5474
F: 020 7684 3889
E: info@obv.org.uk
www.obv.org.uk
Operation Black Vote began in July 1996 as a collaboration between two organisations: Charter88 (which campaigns for democratic reform) and the 1990 Trust, the only national black generic policy research and networking organisation, which uses information technology as a primary means of communication.
**Employees: 8**
**Volunteers: 4**

## Operation Florian

6 Worcester Close, Bracebridge Heath,
Lincoln, Lincolnshire  LN4 2TY
T: 01522 569728 (also fax)
E: opflorian@aol.com
www.operationflorian.com
Operation Florian was established as a charity in 1995. It is a UK Fire Service Humanitarian Charity working to promote the protection of life amongst communities in need, worldwide, by the provision of equipment and training to improve fire fighting and rescue capabilities.
**Employees: 1**

## Opportunity Links

Trust Court, Vision Park, Histon,
Cambridge  CB24 9PW
T: 01223 566522
F: 01223 500281
E: info@openobjects.com
www.opportunity-links.org.uk
**Managing Director: Paul Bogen**
Opportunity Links works with the public sector to develop and manage quality information that supports families in making important life choices.
**Employees: 62**
**Volunteers: 4**
**Regional offices: 2**

## Optua

Optua House, Hill View Business Park,
Claydon, Ipswich, Suffolk  IP6 0AJ
T: 01473 836777
F: 01473 836778
E: enquiries@optua.org.uk
www.optua.org.uk
**Chief Executive: Colin Poole**
We are a Suffolk-based disability charity providing a range of services and opportunities for disabled people including leisure and sport activities, community transport, advice and advocacy, community brain injury services and homecare.
**Employees: 230**
**Volunteers: 300**
**Regional offices: 2**

## OPUS

26 Fernhurst Road, London  SW6 7JW
T: 020 7736 3844
E: director@opus.org.uk
www.opus.org.uk
**Chair: Steve Oram**
OPUS is an organisation of people who believe that it is important that we and others develop a deeper understanding of organisational and societal processes and the way in which we relate to them, and that we use such understanding to act with authority and responsibility in our various roles. OPUS

exists therefore to promote the development of the reflective citizen.
**Volunteers: 350**
**Regional offices: 24**
**Income: £89,330 (2014–15)**

## Orbis Charitable Trust

4th Floor, Fergusson House,
124–128 City Road, London  EC1V 2NJ
T: 020 7608 7260
F: 020 7278 5231
E: info@orbis.org.uk
www.orbis.org.uk
Orbis is a nonprofit humanitarian organisation dedicated to blindness prevention and treatment in developing countries.
**Employees: 28**
**Volunteers: 1**

## Orione Care

13 Lower Teddington Road, Hampton Wick,
Kingston upon Thames  KT1 4EU
T: 020 8977 5130
E: info@orionecare.org
www.orionecare.org
Orione Care is a working name of The Sons of Divine Providence, a charity that provides housing and care services for older people and people with learning disabilities. The charity has a Roman Catholic ethos but people of all faiths and none are welcome to use its services.
**Employees: 112**

## Ormiston Families

Central Office, 333 Felixstowe Road,
Ipswich, Suffolk  IP3 9BU
T: 01473 705038
F: 01473 705025
E: income.generation@ormiston.org
www.ormiston.org
**Chief Executive: Mark Heasman**
Ormiston Families supports children, young people and their families to manage the challenges they face and improve their life chances. We run four core programmes across the East of England supporting young children, prisoners' families, school students and local communities. Our vision is that 'every child and young person is loved, nurtured and valued'.
**Employees: 240**
**Volunteers: 200**
**Regional offices: 1**

## Orphans In Need

22a Atlas Way, Sheffield S4 7QQ
T: 0800 999 0852
E: info@orphansinneed.org
www.orphansinneed.org
Orphans in Need helps some of the world's
most vulnerable and needy people. It is
committed to the alleviation of all forms of
poverty and deprivation, in all parts of the
globe. However, the organisation's primary
focus is on orphans and widows, often the
weakest members of any society, and the
most affected by the scourge of poverty.
Employees: 4
Volunteers: 30
Regional offices: 2

## Orphans Relief Fund and Charitable Trust

163–165 Dukes Road, Park Royal,
London W3 0SL
T: 020 8205 8272
F: 020 8205 8922
E: orfact@hotmail.com
www.orfact.co.uk
Works for the relief of poverty and
advancement of education for orphans,
widows, refugees, the impoverished and the
vulnerable around the world. This is carried
out through education and support services,
vocational training and development projects
and emergency aid and relief.
Employees: 6
Volunteers: 6

## Outreach International

The Cambodia Trust, 4C Station Yard,
Thame, Oxfordshire OX9 3UH
T: 01844 214844
E: www.outreachinternational.co.uk
www.cambodiatrust.com
Outreach International is committed to
cross-cultural exchange and education. We
combine the desire of young people to travel
and work overseas with the needs of local
communities. We give volunteers a deep
understanding of traditional life in Ecuador,
Cambodia and the Pacific coast of Mexico,
whilst providing benefits to the host
communities and children from humble
backgrounds.

## Outsiders

4S Leroy House, 436 Essex Road,
London N1 3QP
T: 01997 421019
F: 020 7460 2247
E: trust@outsiders.org.uk
www.outsiders.org.uk/outsidersclub
Provides help for people with physical and
social disabilities, especially those who live in
emotional isolation.

## Ovacome

B5 City Cloisters, 196 Old Street,
London EC1V 9FR
T: 020 7299 6654
Helpline: 020 7299 6650
E: ovacome@ovacome.org.uk
www.ovacome.org.uk
Ovacome is a support organisation for all
those affected by ovarian cancer. It links
sufferers, provides information and runs a
support line and awareness-raising activities.
Employees: 6

## Ovarian Cancer Action

8–12 Camden High Street,
London NW1 0JH
T: 0300 456 4700
F: 0300 456 4708
E: info@ovarian.org.uk
www.ovarian.org.uk
Chief Executive: Gilda Witte
Ovarian Cancer Action (OCA) is the UK's
leading ovarian cancer charity, dedicated to
improving survival rates for women with
ovarian cancer. It: funds innovative research
into the disease at the Ovarian Cancer Action
Research Centre (OCARC); raises awareness
of the symptoms with national awareness
campaigns aimed at women and healthcare
workers; gives a voice to those affected by it,
acting as an advocate with policy makers,
healthcare professionals and scientists.
Employees: 10
Volunteers: 50
Regional offices: 1

## Overeaters Anonymous

PO Box 19, Stretford,
Manchester M32 9EB
T: 07000 784985
E: general@oagb.org.uk
www.oagb.org.uk
Welcomes those with the desire to stop
eating compulsively, offering identification
and acceptance; relieves our compulsion to
overeat/undereat, or an obsession with food/
dieting by living by spiritual principles based
on the 12 steps of Alcoholics Anonymous.

## Overseas Development Institute

203 Blackfriars Road, London SE1 8NJ
T: 020 7922 0300
F: 020 7922 0399
E: p.gee@odi.org.uk
www.odi.org.uk
Director: Alison Evans
Our mission is to inspire and inform policy
and practice that lead to the reduction of
poverty, the alleviation of suffering and the
achievement of sustainable livelihoods in

developing countries. We do this by locking
together high-quality applied research,
practical policy advice and policy-focused
dissemination and debate. We work with
partners in the public and private sectors, in
both developing and developed countries.
Employees: 184
Volunteers: 20

## Oxfam GB

John Smith Drive, Cowley, Oxford,
Oxfordshire OX4 2JY
T: 0300 200 1300
F: 01865 472600
E: givetime@oxfam.org.uk
www.oxfam.org.uk
CEO: Mark Goldring
Oxfam is a development, relief, and
campaigning organisation that works with
others to achieve a just world without poverty.
Employees: 4951
Volunteers: 27000
Regional offices: 8

## PAC-UK Ltd

5 Torriano Mews, Torriano Avenue,
Kentish Town, London NW5 2RZ
Helpline: 020 7284 5879
E: advice@pac-uk.org
www.pac-uk.org
CEO: Peter Sandiford
PAC provides confidential advice,
information and support for anyone affected
by adoption or any other form of permanent
care, including adoptive parents, adopted
adults, birth parents and other birth family
members, foster carers where permanence is
the plan, special guardians and prospective
adopters. Services include: advice line;
individual counselling; individual, couple and
family consultations; family therapeutic work;
support with contact arrangements between
adoptive and birth families; support for birth
relatives, including fortnightly birth mothers'
drop-in.
Employees: 50
Volunteers: 4
Regional offices: 2

## PACE

34 Hartham Road, London N7 9JL
T: 020 7715 0385
Helpline: 020 7700 1323
E: info@pacehealth.org.uk
www.pacehealth.org.uk
**Chief Executive Officer: Margaret Unwin**
PACE is London's leading charity promoting the mental health and emotional well-being of the lesbian, gay, bisexual and transgender community. PACE also provides online services that can be accessed nationally. We are committed to responding to the changing needs of LGBT people, and offering appropriate, sensitive, LGBT-delivered support services to help people move through their difficult times.
**Employees: 23**
**Volunteers: 22**

## PACT (Parents and Children together)

7 Southern Court, South Street, Reading, Berkshire RG1 4QS
T: 0300 456 4800
E: info@pactcharity.org
www.pactcharity.org
**Chief Executive: Jan Fishwick**
PACT helps hundreds of families every year through adoption services and community projects. PACT is one of the UK's leading Voluntary Adoption Agencies (VAA) placing children with secure and loving families and supporting them with specialist therapeutic support.
**Employees: 70**
**Volunteers: 50**
**Regional offices: 3**
**Income: £4,851,000 (2014–15)**

## Paget's Association (AKA National Association for the Relief of Paget's Disease)

Suite 5, Moorfield House, Moorside Road, Swinton, Manchester M27 0EW
T: 0161 799 4646
E: diana.wilkinson@paget.org.uk
www.paget.org.uk
**Chair: Prof Roger Francis**
Our aims are: to raise awareness of Paget's disease of bone among the public and the medical profession; to offer information and support to those with the condition; to support and sponsor research into the causes and treatment of the disease.
**Employees: 2**
**Volunteers: 6**
**Regional offices: 1**

## Pain Relief Foundation

Clinical Sciences Centre,
University Hospital Aintree, Lower Lane,
Liverpool L9 7AL
T: 0151 529 5820
F: 0151 529 5821
E: secretary@painrelieffoundation.org.uk
www.painrelieffoundation.org.uk
**Administrator: D Emsley**
Aims to research human chronic pain to find the causes and mechanisms of why chronic pain persists and to find new and improved methods of treating all such conditions to ease the suffering of patients. Our ultimate aim is to find cures for all pain. Additionally, we provide ongoing education for health professionals at all levels and disciplines who are dealing with human chronic pain at the point of treatment.
**Employees: 6**
**Regional offices: 1**

## Painswick Rococo Garden Trust

E: rococogarden@hotmail.co.uk

## Paintings in Hospitals

Floor One, Menier Chocolate Factory,
51 Southwark Street, London SE1 1RU
T: 020 7407 3222
F: 020 7403 7721
E: mail@paintingsinhospitals.org.uk
www.paintingsinhospitals.org.uk
**Director: Stuart Davie**
Aims to relieve sick, infirm and convalescent persons by providing pictures and works of art on loan in order to improve the environment of hospitals and other healthcare establishments.
**Employees: 5**
**Volunteers: 50**
**Regional offices: 7**

## Papworth Trust

Bernard Sunley Centre, Papworth Everard,
Cambridge, Cambridgeshire CB23 3RG
T: 01480 357200
Helpline: 0800 952 5000
F: 01480 357201
E: info@papworth.org.uk
www.papworth.org.uk
**Chief Executive: Adrian Bagg**
Papworth Trust is a leading disability charity. We support over 20,000 people each year through a wide range of services, including accessible homes, personal care, leisure and learning opportunities, and support for people to find and keep jobs.
**Employees: 500**
**Regional offices: 24**

## Parents for Inclusion

London
E: info@parentsforinclusion.org
www.parentsforinclusion.org
Parents for Inclusion is a network of parents of disabled children and children with special needs. In our families and as an organisation we have worked together with disabled people to build inclusive communities in ordinary life, where all people are truly welcome. We work closely with disabled adults, to bring their understanding and experience to parents, so that parents can become real allies to their disabled children.
**Employees: 2**
**Volunteers: 5**

## Parents in Partnership

Carers Support Centre,
24–26 George Street, Croydon CR0 1PB
T: 020 8663 5626
E: office@pipcroydon.com
pipcroydon.com
**Chairman: Liam Mallon**
**Employees: 6**
**Volunteers: 4**
**Regional offices: 1**

## PARITY

Constables, Windsor Road, Ascot,
Berkshire SL5 7LF
T: 01344 621167 (also fax)
E: postmaster@parity-uk.org
www.parity-uk.org
**Chair: John Mays**
Fosters and promotes equal treatment of the sexes under the law and by public authority, for example in state pensions, other social security provisions, bus concessions, etc.
**Volunteers: 10**
**Regional offices: 1**

## Parkinson's Disease Society of the UK

215 Vauxhall Bridge Road,
London SW1V 1EJ
T: 020 7931 8080
F: 020 7233 9908
E: enquiries@parkinsons.org.uk
www.parkinsons.org.uk
Helps and supports people with Parkinson's and their relatives; collects and shares information on Parkinson's; encourages and provides funds for research into the disease.
**Employees: 150**
**Volunteers: 3500**
**Regional offices: 14**

## Parliamentary Advisory Council for Transport Safety

3rd Floor, Clutha House, 10 Storey's Gate,
London SW1P 3AY
T: 020 7222 7732
F: 020 7222 7106
E: admin@pacts.org.uk
www.pacts.org.uk
**Executive Director: Robert Gifford**
To protect human life through the promotion of transport safety for the public benefit; to exercise scrutiny of legislative and policy proposals.
**Employees: 3**
**Volunteers: 5**

## Partially Sighted Society

1 Bennetthorpe, Doncaster,
South Yorkshire DN2 6AA
T: 0844 477 4966
F: 0844 477 4969
E: info@partsight.org.uk
partsight.org.uk
**Executive Director: Anita Plant**
Provides help, advice and training in enabling people with a visual impairment to make the best use of their remaining vision; directly assists partially sighted people in their daily lives; promotes research and development in order to better understand the problems of being partially sighted. In-house design and print facility to produce heavily lined stationery.
**Employees: 4**
**Regional offices: 1**

## Partners of Prisoners and Families Support Group

Valentine House, 1079 Rochdale Road,
Blackley, Manchester M9 8AJ
T: 0161 702 1000
Helpline: 0808 808 2003
F: 0161 850 1988
E: mail@partnersofprisoners.co.uk
www.partnersofprisoners.co.uk
**CEO: Diane Curry OBE**
Provides information, advice and support to the partners, families and friends of those in prison.

## Patients Association

PO Box 935, Harrow HA1 3YJ
T: 020 8423 9111
Helpline: 020 8423 8999
F: 020 8423 9119
E: mailbox@patients-association.com
www.patients-association.org.uk
**Chief Executive Officer: Katherine Murphy**

The Patients Association is a healthcare charity that for more than 40 years has advocated for greater and equitable access to high-quality, accurate and independent information for patients, for greater and equitable access to high-quality care and for involvement in decision-making as a right.
**Employees: 10**
**Volunteers: 11**

## Patients Forum

Riverbank House,
1 Putney Bridge Approach,
London SW6 3JD
T: 020 7736 7903
F: 020 7736 7932
E: support@datadial.net
www.thepatientsforum.org.uk
The Patients Forum is a network of national and regional organisations concerned with the healthcare interests of patients and their families and carers. Full membership is open to national and umbrella organisations representing the interests of users of health services and their families and carers. Associate (non-voting) membership can be obtained for healthcare service providers, as well as all regulatory bodies.
**Employees: 1**
**Regional offices: 1**

## Pax Christi

Christian Peace Education Centre,
St Joseph's, Watford Way,
London NW4 2LH
T: 020 8203 4884
F: 020 8203 5234
E: info@paxchristi.org.uk
www.paxchristi.org.uk
Founded in the Catholic Church, but open to all faiths, Pax Christi is a gospel-based lay-inspired peacemaking movement. It strives to help both the Church and the wider community proclaim peace through the witnesses and actions of its members. The three major objectives of Pax Christi are: reconciliation; the promotion of a culture of peace and non-violence; providing the means to bring about peace (for example through training and education resources).
**Employees: 1**
**Volunteers: 9**

## Pay and Employment Rights Service (Yorkshire) Ltd

E: fawzia@pers.org.uk

## PayPal Giving Fund

Surrey TW9 1EH
T: 020 8439 2381
E: info@paypalgivingfund.org
www.paypalgivingfund.org.uk
**CEO: Nick Aldridge**

PayPal Giving Fund UK is a registered charity and enables eBay and PayPal users to give to good causes quickly and easily. PayPal Giving Fund certifies charities to participate in the eBay for Charity programme, and collects donations from eBay and PayPal users. It also distributes those donations and Gift Aid to donors' chosen charities, which receive 100% of the funds raised.

## PDSA for Pets in Need of Vets

Head Office, Whitechapel Way, Priorslee,
Telford TF2 9PQ
T: 01952 290999
F: 01952 291035
E: rydstrom.marilyn@pdsa.org.uk
www.pdsa.org.uk
**Director General: Marilyn Rydstrom**
PDSA cares for the pets of people in need by providing free veterinary services to their sick and injured animals and promoting responsible pet ownership.
**Employees: 1780**
**Volunteers: 4850**
**Regional offices: 6**

## Peace Brigades International UK Section (PBI UK)

1B Waterlow Road, London N19 5NJ
T: 020 7281 5370
E: admin@peacebrigades.org.uk
www.peacebrigades.org.uk
**Director: Susi Bascon**
Peace Brigades International provides protective accompaniment to human rights defenders (HRDs) at risk in Colombia, Guatemala, Honduras, Kenya, Mexico and Nepal. The presence of PBI volunteers represents the international community's concerns and deters against threats being carried out. This is backed up by international political and diplomatic support and dialogue with authorities at all levels. PBI UK also lobbies the UK government, EU and UN bodies for better mechanisms and policies to protect HRDs worldwide.
**Employees: 3**
**Volunteers: 30**
**Regional offices: 1**

## Peace Direct

Development House,
56–64 Leonard Street, London EC2A 4JX
T: 0845 456 9714
F: 020 7794 2489
E: robert@peacedirect.org
www.peacedirect.org
Peace Direct's focus is grassroots peace-building in areas of conflict across the world. This is achieved through funding projects, including: collaborative projects and one-off grants; persuasion and promotion of the value

of non-violent approaches; learning through peace activities around the world.
Employees: 7

## Peace Pledge Union

1 Peace Passage, Brecknock Road,
London N7 0BT
T: 020 7424 9444
F: 020 7482 6390
E: mail@ppu.org.uk
www.ppu.org.uk
Co-ordinator: Symon Hill
The Peace Pledge Union (PPU) is a UK-based network of people who have pledged not to participate in war. Our work includes challenging militarism, advocating disarmament, promoting active nonviolence and producing educational resources on peace and nonviolent conflict resolution. Founded in 1934, we are the oldest secular pacifist organisation in Britain.
Employees: 4
Volunteers: 10
Income: £155,813 (2014–15)

## Peacemakers

41 Bull St, Birmingham,
West Midlands B4 6AF
T: 0121 236 4796
E: info@peacemakers.org.uk
www.peacemakers.org.uk
Director: Sara Hagel
Peacemakers exists to help create a more peaceful world, with more caring and resilient communities. We want a world where people are equipped to deal non-violently and creatively with the inevitable conflicts that arise. Our contribution to promoting a more harmonious society in the West Midlands is the development of peace-making behaviour of children and adults in schools.
Employees: 5
Volunteers: 1
Income: £153,000 (2014–15)

## Peel Institute

Peel Centre, Percy Circus,
London WC1X 9EY
T: 020 7837 6082
F: 020 7278 3855
E: admin@peelinstitute.org.uk
www.peelinstitute.org.uk
Chief Executive: Rob Hamilton
A community hub in the heart of King's Cross, providing a wide range of services for all ages and sections of the local community. Activities include crèche, child care, youth services, adult education, advice and advocacy to sports and older people's

projects, all provided in a fully accessible purpose built community centre.
Employees: 33
Volunteers: 50
Income: £750,000 (2013–14)

## Pelvic Pain Support Network

PO Box 6559, Poole, Dorset BH12 9DP
T: 01202 603447
E: info@pelvicpain.org.uk
www.pelvicpain.org.uk
The Network's volunteers are patients and carers who have been supporting those with pelvic pain, their carers and families since the year 2000. We attend local, national and international events and represent pelvic pain patients at many meetings, seminars and conferences.
Volunteers: 5

## Pensions Advisory Service

11 Belgrave Road, London SW1V 1RB
T: 020 7630 2272
F: 020 7592 7000
E: jonathan.kalemera@pensionsadvisoryservice.org.uk
www.pensionsadvisoryservice.org.uk
Chief Executive: Malcolm McLean
The Pensions Advisory Service is an independent non-profit organisation that provides free information, advice and guidance on the whole spectrum of pensions covering state, company, personal and stakeholder schemes.
Employees: 35
Volunteers: 450

## Penwith Community Development Trust

E: enquiries@pcdt.org.uk
www.pcdt.org

## People & Planet

16–17 Turl Street, Oxford,
Oxfordshire OX1 3DH
T: 01865 264180
E: people@peopleandplanet.org
www.peopleandplanet.org
People and Planet is the largest student network in Britain campaigning to end world poverty, defend human rights and protect the environment. We're a student-led movement that empowers young people with the skills, confidence and knowledge they need to make change happen, at home and globally.

## People of God Trust

1 Carysfort House, 14 West Halkin Street,
London SW1X 8JS
T: 020 7235 2841
E: pogtrust@gmail.com
ccc4vat2.org.uk
Honorary Secretary: Simon Bryden-Brook
A lay initiative, promoting the Catholic religion in accordance with the Second Vatican Council, largely by making grants to appropriate organisations.
Volunteers: 2
Regional offices: 1
Income: £5,500 (2014–15)

## People Potential Possibilities (P3)

P3 Eagle House, Cotmanhey Road, Ilkeston,
Derbyshire DE7 8HU
T: 0115 850 8190
E: comms@p3charity.org
www.p3charity.org
Chief Executive Officer: Mark Simms
Promotes social inclusion to socially excluded and vulnerable adults, families and young people from a range of backgrounds and with a range of needs.
Employees: 600
Volunteers: 60
Regional offices: 40
Income: £18,000,000 (2015–16)

## People's Trust for Endangered Species

15 Cloisters House, 8 Battersea Park Road,
London SW8 4BG
T: 020 7498 4533
F: 020 7498 4459
E: jill@ptes.org
www.ptes.org
Chief Executive: Jill Nelson
PTES protects endangered species worldwide and advances public awareness of which species are endangered, rare or threatened. It gives grants and runs selected conservation programmes. The prime aims of PTES activities are: to protect endangered species through conservation strategies that are informed by scientific research; to educate the public and promote open debate between the public, policy makers and conservation scientists about issues surrounding endangered species and their conservation.
Employees: 13
Volunteers: 1000

## Permaculture Association (Britain)

BCM Permaculture Association,
London WC1N 3XX
T: 0845 458 1805
E: office@permaculture.org.uk
www.permaculture.org.uk
CEO: Andy Goldring
The Permaculture Association is the
national charity that supports and promotes
permaculture design throughout the UK
and worldwide through education, research
and networking.
Employees: 13
Volunteers: 150

## Perthes Association

PO Box 773, Guildford, Surrey GU1 1XN
T: 01483 306637
E: info@perthes.org.uk
www.perthes.org.uk
Perthes disease is a form of osteochondritis.
A potentially crippling disease of the hip,
Perthes disease is a childhood disorder, which
affects the head of the femur. The association
supports children with Perthes disease and
associated conditions through the purchase
of wheelchairs, buggies and more specialist
equipment loaned free to members (parents
and carers) allowing the children to play with
their siblings and friends and enjoy a better
quality of life.
Employees: 4
Volunteers: 20

## Pestalozzi International Village Trust

Ladybird Lane, Sedlescombe, Battle,
East Sussex TN33 0UF
T: 01424 870444
F: 01424 870655
E: debbie.martin@pestalozzi.org.uk
www.pestalozzi.org.uk
Chief Executive: Paul Evans
Employees: 20
Volunteers: 6
Regional offices: 1

## Pesticide Action Network UK

56–64 Leonard Street, London EC2A 4LT
T: 020 7065 0905
F: 020 7065 0907
E: admin@pan-uk.org
www.pan-uk.org
Director: Linda Craig
PAN UK works to eliminate the dangers of
toxic pesticides, our exposure to them and
their presence in the environment where
we live and work. Nationally and globally, we
promote safer alternatives, the production
of healthy food and sustainable farming.
Employees: 15
Volunteers: 3

## Peter le Marchant Trust

Canalside Moorings Beeches Road,
Loughborough, Leicestershire LE11 2NS
T: 01509 265590
E: lynnsmith@peterlemarchanttrust.co.uk
www.peterlemarchanttrust.co.uk
The Trust provides trips and holidays
on special boats for adults and children
with disabilities.

## Peter Rigby Trust

The London Centre for Children with
Cerebral Palsy, 54 Muswell Hill,
London N10 3ST
T: 020 8444 7242
F: 020 8444 7241
E: kath@cplondon.org.uk
www.cplondon.org.uk
CEO: Marc Crank
We provide educational services for children
with cerebral palsy. We have an independent
approved school for children aged 3 to 11
years. We specialise in an approach known as
Conductive Education. We also have an early
intervention service and outreach support
service within mainstream schools.
Employees: 26
Volunteers: 11
Regional offices: 1

## PEYTU

2nd Floor, Scrapstore House,
21 Sevier Street, St Werburgh's, Bristol,
Avon BS2 9LB
T: 0117 908 0601
F: 0117 908 0622
E: admin@peytu.co.uk
www.peytu.co.uk
Chief Executive Officer: Sandra Meadows
Independent, not-for-profit and approved
by local authorities. As a registered charity,
our aim is to improve outcomes for children
and young people by providing training,
information, consultancy and support for
those working with and/or caring for them.
Our work broadly encompasses workforce
development and enhancing opportunities
for employment, further education and the
promotion of social welfare and recreation
for all families.
Employees: 6
Regional offices: 1

## PFEG (Personal Finance Education Group)

Fifth Floor, 14 Bonhill Street,
London EC2A 4BX
T: 020 7330 9470
Helpline: 0300 666 0127
F: 020 7374 6147
E: info@pfeg.org
www.pfeg.org
Chief Executive: Wendy van den Hende
PFEG is an educational charity and its
mission is to make sure that all young people
leaving school have the confidence, skills and
knowledge in financial matters to take part
fully in society. It offers a range of advice and
resources and supports UK teachers working
with children and young people aged 4 to 19
from all backgrounds.
Employees: 17
Volunteers: 100

## PHAB

Summit House, Wandle Road,
Croydon CR0 1DF
T: 020 8667 9443
F: 020 8681 1399
E: anne.joyce@phab.org.uk
www.phab.org.uk
Via a network of clubs, projects, publications
and activities, PHAB promotes and
encourages people with and without physical
disabilities to come together on equal terms
to achieve complete integration within the
wider community.
Employees: 30
Volunteers: 15000
Regional offices: 4

## Pharmacist Support

5th Floor, 196 Deansgate, Manchester,
Greater Manchester M3 3WF
T: 0808 168 2233
F: 0161 441 0319
E: info@pharmacistsupport.org
www.pharmacistsupport.org
Charity Manager: Diane Leicester-Hallam
Pharmacist Support is an independent charity
providing a range of free and confidential
services to pharmacists and their families,
former pharmacists, pre-registration trainees
and pharmacy students. Support includes
financial assistance, an information and
enquiry service, a stress helpline, debt,
benefits and employment advice and
addiction support.
Employees: 9
Volunteers: 30

## Philadelphia Association

4 Marty's Yard, 17 Hampstead High Street,
London NW3 1QW
T: 020 7794 2652 (also fax)
E: office@philadelphia-association.co.uk
www.philadelphia-association.org.uk
The Association helps: to relieve mental
illness of all descriptions; to maintain
therapeutic community households; to offer
a forum for research, study and training in
community therapy and psychotherapy
according to the Association's own
philosophy; to publish relevant texts.
**Employees: 1**

## Phoenix Domestic Abuse & Support Services Ltd

E: andrew.luisis@cvsc.org.uk

## Phoenix Futures

3rd Floor, Asra House, 1 Long Lane,
London SE1 4PG
T: 020 7234 9740
F: 020 7234 9770
E: info@phoenix-futures.org.uk
www.phoenix-futures.org.uk
**Chief Executive: Karen Biggs**
Phoenix Futures is the leading provider of
care and rehabilitation services for people
with drug and alcohol problems in the UK.
**Employees: 550**
**Volunteers: 50**
**Regional offices: 4**

## Pilgrim Hearts Trust

24 Yorkshire Place, Warfield,
24 Yorkshire Place, Bracknell RG42 3XE
T: 01344 307030 (also fax)
E: pilgrim.hearts@gmail.com
www.pilgrimhearts.org.uk
**Director: Elaine Chalmers-Brown**
Pilgrim Hearts is there to assist those who are
homeless and on the edge and those who for
whatever reason are not able to benefit from
all of life's opportunities. It is a Christian
organisation devoted to helping marginalised
people, and those with disabilities, from all
walks of life and backgrounds. We provide
assistance to other organisations and
community groups both in the voluntary
and public sector.
**Employees: 5**

## Pilgrim Trust

Cowley House, 9 Little College Street,
London SW1P 3HS
T: 020 7222 4723
E: georgina@thepilgrimtrust.org.uk
www.thepilgrimtrust.org.uk

## Pilotlight

15–17 Lincoln's Inn Fields, Holborn,
London WC2A 3ED
T: 020 7396 7414
F: 020 7396 7467
E: info@pilotlight.org.uk
www.pilotlight.org.uk
Pilotlight helps small charities to build their
capacity in order to plan for sustainability,
growth and, where appropriate, replication.
The membership of senior business people
donate their time to supporting the charities
through a combination of coaching and
consultancy. The Pilotlight process is
designed to enable members to make a
difference to small charities in just a few
hours a month and educates this influential
group about the charitable sector through
practical experience.
**Employees: 3**

## Pituitary Foundation

The Pituitary Foundation,
86 Colston Street, Bristol BS1 5BB
T: 0117 370 1333
Helpline: 0117 370 1320
E: helpline@pituitary.org.uk
www.pituitary.org.uk
The Pituitary Foundation is a national support
and information organisation for pituitary
patients, their families, friends and carers.
The Pituitary Foundation's objectives are to:
promote the relief and treatment of persons
suffering from pituitary disorders and related
conditions and diseases, and their families,
friends and carers, and to provide information
and support; to promote and support
research and to disseminate for the public
benefit the results of any such research.
**Employees: 12**
**Volunteers: 110**
**Regional offices: 31**

## Place2Be

13–14 Angel Gate, 326 City Road,
London EC1V 2PT
T: 020 7923 5527
F: 020 7481 1894
E: enquiries@theplace2be.org.uk
www.theplace2be.org.uk
The Place2Be was established in 1994 in
response to increasing concern about
the extent and depth of emotional and
behavioural difficulties displayed in
classrooms and playgrounds.
**Volunteers: 350**

## Plan International

5–6 Underhill Street, London NW1 7HS
T: 020 7482 9777
F: 020 7482 9778
E: hrod@plan-international.org
plan-international.org/
Plan is a child-centred development agency
with no political or religious affiliations,
enabling families and communities in the
poorest countries to make lasting
improvements to the lives of their children.
**Employees: 64**
**Volunteers: 34**

## Plant Heritage

12 Home Farm, Loseley Park, Guildford,
Surrey GU3 1HS
T: 01483 447540
F: 01483 458933
E: info@plantheritage.org.uk
www.plantheritage.com
**Chief Executive Officer: Chief Executive Officer**
Plant Heritage (or National Council for the
Conservation of Plants and Gardens to give
its full name) is the only charity working to
conserve cultivated plants through the
National Plant Collections scheme and the
Threatened Plants Project.
**Employees: 8**
**Volunteers: 500**

## Plunkett Foundation

2–3 The Quadrangle, Banbury Road,
Woodstock, Oxfordshire OX20 1LH
T: 01993 810730
F: 01993 810849
E: info@plunkett.co.uk
www.plunkett.co.uk
The Plunkett Foundation is an educational
charity, based near Oxford in the UK, which
supports the development of rural group
enterprise worldwide. The Foundation draws
on 80 years' practical experience of working
with partners from the private sector to
promote and implement economic self-help
solutions to rural problems.
**Employees: 16**

## Police Foundation

Room 1.13, The Foundry, 17 Oval Way,
Kennington, London SE11 5RR
T: 020 3752 5630
E: sue.roberts@police-foundation.org.uk
www.police-foundation.org.uk
**Director: Dr Rick Muir**
The Police Foundation is the country's only
independent charity focused on responding
to public concerns about policing, informing
their understanding of policing issues and
challenging the police service and the
government to improve policing for the
benefit of all citizens. It does so by promoting
debate on policing and police reform,
providing commentary, knowledge and
insight on important issues and contemporary
developments and turning new ideas into
policy and practice.
**Employees: 8**
**Volunteers: 1**
**Regional offices: 1**
**Income: £580,790 (2015–16)**

## Policy Studies Institute

50 Hanson Street, London W1W 6UP
T: 020 7911 7500
F: 020 7911 7501
E: psi-admin@psi.org.uk
www.psi.org.uk
One of Britain's leading independent
research institutes, conducting research to
promote economic wellbeing and improve
quality of life. PSI undertakes and publishes
research studies relevant to social, economic,
industrial and environmental policy. In 1998 it
merged to become an independent subsidiary
of the University of Westminster. PSI takes a
politically neutral stance on issues of public
policy and its income is derived from funds for
individual research projects: funding sources
include government, professional agencies,
charitable trusts and private companies.
**Volunteers: 46**

## Polycystic Kidney Disease Charity

91 Royal College Street, London NW1 0SE
T: 020 7387 0543
Helpline: 0300 111 1234
E: tess.harris@pkdcharity.org.uk
www.pkdcharity.org.uk
**Chief Executive: Tess Harris**
We provide information, advice and support
to those affected by polycystic kidney
disease (PKD). We aim to fund research into
determining the causes of PKD, discovering
treatments and a cure, and raise awareness
of PKD, providing information about PKD to
patients, the public, the medical community
and the media.
**Employees: 2**
**Volunteers: 100**
**Income: £200,000 (2011–12)**

## Pontifical Mission Societies

23 Eccleston Square, London SW1V 1NU
T: 020 7821 9755
E: director@missio.org.uk
www.missio.org.uk

## Portchester Community Association

The Portchester Hub, 2 New Parade,
38 West Street, Portchester, Fareham,
Hampshire PO16 9UY
T: 023 9221 0048
E: admin@portchesterca.org.uk
portchesterca.org.uk
**Manager: Sarah Moss**
Provide social, educational and leisure
activities, facilities and services to local people
(all ages) and groups through the Portchester
Hub, outreach and partnerships. Also run
community learning, pre-school/ancillary
services; sections (sports, arts, interest
groups); community projects, specific
activities for older people and volunteering.
**Employees: 10**
**Volunteers: 80**
**Regional offices: 1**

## Portman Group Trust

7–10 Chandos Street, London W1G 9DQ
T: 020 7907 3700
F: 020 7907 3710
E: advice@portmangroup.org.uk
www.portmangroup.org.uk
Supported by the UK's leading drinks
producers, the Trust is concerned solely
with social responsibility issues surrounding
alcohol. It endorses the preservation,
protection and promotion of public health
through the provision of education and
research on alcohol-related matters.

## Positive Body Image

PO Box 23266, London SE14 5FQ
E: info@positivebodyimage.co.uk
Positive Body Image aims to use a holistic
approach to health and fitness to help
individuals improve their physical, mental
and spiritual wellbeing and, in so doing, help
them to improve their self-image and achieve
their potential. Positive Body Image was
established to help address the health
inequalities experienced by ethnic minority
women, but its programmes and services
are open to all women.

## Positively UK

345 City Road, London, London EC1V 1LR
T: 020 7713 0444
E: info@positivelyuk.org
www.positivelyuk.org
Positively UK is the only national charity
working to improve the quality of life of
people affected by HIV, enabling them to
make informed choices and challenging
stigma and discrimination. All direct support
is carried out by people who are themselves
HIV positive and therefore have personal
experience of the social and health
implications of living with the virus.

## Potential Plus UK

Suite 1.2, Challenge House, Sherwood Drive,
Bletchley, Milton Keynes MK3 6DP
T: 01908 646433
E: amazingchildren@nagcbritain.org.uk
www.potentialplusuk.org
**Chief Executive: Denise Yates**
Supports gifted children, their parents,
families and teachers and disseminates
information concerning gifted children.
**Employees: 9**
**Volunteers: 120**

## Powerhouse

St Luke's Community Centre,
85 Tarling Road, Canning Town,
London E16 1HN
T: 020 7366 6336
F: 020 7366 6337
E: info@thepowerhouse.org.uk
www.thepowerhouse.org.uk
Powerhouse is an organisation of women with
learning difficulties. It is committed to
promoting women's rights through advocacy,
campaigning, one-to-one support, training
and awareness-raising.

## Practical Action

The Schumacher Centre,
Bourton on Dunsmore, Rugby,
Warwickshire CV23 9QZ
T: 01926 634400
E: practicalaction@practicalaction.org.uk
www.practicalaction.org
**Chief Executive: Paul Smith Lomas**
We believe technology can transform lives
and should be available to the many not the
few. Through technology we enable poor
communities to build on their skills and
knowledge to produce sustainable solutions,
finding out what people are doing and helping
them do it better. Founded in 1966 by EF

Schumacher, for 50 years we've been delivering life-changing projects alongside local communities, building access to knowledge and influencing change for poor men and women.

**Employees: 250**
**Regional offices: 8**
**Income: £26,000,000 (2015–16)**

## Prader-Willi Syndrome Association UK

125A London Road, Derby,
Derbyshire DE1 2QQ
T: 01332 365676
F: 01332 360401
E: admin@pwsa.co.uk
www.pwsa.co.uk
**Chief Executive Officer: Susan Passmore**
Prader-Willi syndrome is a complex genetic disorder, present from birth. The Association exists: to contact and support families concerned with the disorder; to inform health professionals, families and the public in general about the disorder; to raise funds and foster research into its causes and alleviation.

**Employees: 9**
**Volunteers: 70**
**Regional offices: 1**

## Pre-school Learning Alliance

50 Featherstone Street, London EC1Y 8RT
T: 020 7697 2595
F: 020 7700 0319
E: info@pre-school.org.uk
www.pre-school.org.uk
**Chief Executive: Neil Leitch**
The Pre-school Learning Alliance is the largest and most representative early years membership organisation in England. A registered educational charity, the Alliance represents 14,000 member settings and supports them to deliver care and learning to over 800,000 families every year. We offer information and advice, produce specialist publications, run acclaimed training and accreditation schemes and campaign to influence early years policy and practice.

**Employees: 2000**
**Volunteers: 763**
**Regional offices: 30**
**Income: £36,110,000 (2013–14)**

## Primary Ciliary Dyskinesia Family Support Group

15 Shuttleworth Grove, Wavendon Gate,
Milton Keynes MK7 7RX
T: 01908 281635
Helpline: 0300 111 0122
E: chair@pcdsupport.org.uk
www.pcdsupport.org.uk
**Chairman: Fiona Copeland**
The Group provides support to patients with PCD (also known as Kartagener's syndrome and immotile cilia syndrome) and parents of children known to have the syndrome. It brings the disease to the attention of the medical profession and the public and raises funds for research.

**Volunteers: 8**

## Primary Sclerosing Cholangitis Trust

Hollibury House, 12 Limont Road,
Southport, Merseyside PR8 3NJ
T: 01704 808740
E: info@psctrust.com
www.psctrust.com
The Primary Sclerosing Cholangitis (PSC) Trust is dedicated to discovering the cause and cure of PSC, a chronic progressive liver disease, and related conditions.

**Volunteers: 12**

## PRIMHE

c/o Tipton Care Org,
Glebefields Health Centre, St Marks Road,
Tipton, West Midlands DY4 0SN
T: 0121 530 8021 (also fax)
E: admin@primhe.org.uk
www.primhe.org.uk
**Chair of Trustees: Dr Ian Walton**
Helping primary healthcare professionals and staff achieve and deliver the best standards of mental healthcare. PRIMHE provides mental health support, services, resources, education and training.

**Volunteers: 5**
**Regional offices: 1**

## Prince's Trust

Clarence House, London SW1A 1BA
T: 020 7543 1234
E: customer.services@princes-trust.org.uk
www.princes-trust.org.uk
**Employees: 800**
**Volunteers: 10000**
**Regional offices: 9**

## Prison Advice and Care Trust

Park Place, 12 Lawn Lane,
London SW8 1UD
T: 020 7735 9535
E: info@prisonadvice.org.uk
www.prisonadvice.org.uk
**Director: Andy Keen-Downs**
The Trust's mission is to support prisoners and their families to make a fresh start and to minimise the harm that can be caused by imprisonment on offenders, families and communities.

**Employees: 83**
**Volunteers: 300**
**Regional offices: 1**

## Prison Chat UK

PO Box 49449, Penge, London SE20 8YG
T: 020 8778 7741
E: prisonchatuk@aol.com
www.prisonchatuk.com
An online community giving support to those who have a loved one inside the British prison system. All members are connected to the prison system in some way and can offer advice and share their experiences, so creating a community for people to go and get support and answers when a loved one has been taken into custody.

## Prison Fellowship England and Wales

PO Box 68226, London SW1P 9WR
T: 020 7799 2500
E: info@prisonfellowship.org.uk
www.prisonfellowship.org.uk
**Chief Executive: Natalie Cronin**
Prison Fellowship aims to show Christ's love to prisoners by coming alongside them, praying and supporting them to change. We offer our services to all who request them, regardless of their beliefs. We do this through our network of volunteer members and have over 1,500 volunteers throughout England and Wales.

**Employees: 18**
**Volunteers: 1600**

## Prison Reform Trust

The Old Trading House,
15 Northburgh Street, London EC1V 0JR
T: 020 7251 5070
F: 020 7251 5076
E: geoff.dobson@prisonreformtrust.org.uk
www.prisonreformtrust.org.uk
Promotes public understanding of the need for improvements in our prison system and encourages public interest in penal policy and practice.

**Employees: 13**
**Volunteers: 3**

## Prisoners Abroad

89–93 Fonthill Road, London N4 3JH
T: 020 7561 6820
Helpline: 0808 172 0098
F: 020 7561 6821
E: info@prisonersabroad.org.uk
www.prisonersabroad.org.uk
Chief Executive: Pauline Crowe
Provides practical and emotional support
to British citizens in prison overseas, their
families and friends, and to ex-prisoners
returning to the UK.
Employees: 25

## Prisoners Advice Service

PO Box 46199, London EC1M 4XA
T: 020 7253 3323
Helpline: 0845 430 8923
F: 020 7253 8067
E: advice@prisonersadvice.org.uk
www.prisonersadvice.org.uk
PAS provides free, expert legal advice and
information to prisoners in England and
Wales regarding their rights and conditions
of imprisonment; it takes up prisoners'
complaints about their treatment inside
prison by providing free advice and assistance
on an individual and confidential basis. The
service also produces a quarterly bulletin
on new prison case law and policy, entitled
Prisoners' Legal Rights Bulletin.
Employees: 7
Volunteers: 20
Income: £350,000 (2015–16)

## Prisoners Education Trust

Wandle House, Riverside Drive, Mitcham,
Surrey CR4 4BU
T: 020 8648 7760
F: 020 8648 7762
E: info@prisonerseducation.org.uk
www.prisonerseducation.org.uk
Interim Director: Rachel Youngman
The Trust aims to offer prisoners a chance to
change through education and promotes the
importance of education in the successful
resettlement of offenders. It makes grants to
enable prisoners to study through distance
learning and other courses that will enhance
their chances of employment after release.
It also runs projects developing support and
advice for prisoner learners and enables
prisoner learners to have a voice about
education and learning.
Employees: 12
Volunteers: 12

## Prisoners' Families and Friends Service

20 Trinity Street, London SE1 1DB
T: 020 7403 4091
F: 020 7403 9359
E: info@prisonersfamiliesandfriends.org.uk
www.prisonersfamiliesandfriends.org.uk
The main aims of the Service are: to provide
the families and friends of anyone sentenced
to imprisonment or remanded in custody
with advice and information; support and
assistance at court; support and friendship.
Employees: 4
Volunteers: 58

## Professional Association for Childcare and Early Years (PACEY)

Royal Court, 81 Tweedy Road, Bromley,
Kent BR1 1TG
T: 0300 003 0005
E: info@pacey.org.uk
www.pacey.org.uk
Chief Executive: Liz Bayram
PACEY is the Professional Association for
Childcare and Early Years. A standard-setting
organisation, we promote best practice and
support childcare professionals to deliver high
standards of care and learning. Since 1977
we have provided high-quality support to our
members and have worked with government,
local authorities and others to raise standards.
Together with our members – childminders,
nannies and nursery workers – we are
working to become the professional
association for everyone in childcare and
early years and ensure our members are
recognised for the vital role they play in
helping children get the best start in life.
Employees: 160
Regional offices: 7

## Progress Educational Trust

140 Gray's Inn Road, London WC1X 8AX
T: 020 7278 7870
E: admin@progress.org.uk
www.progress.org.uk
Aims: to enhance the public understanding
of reproduction and genetics; to encourage
discussion of their social, legal and ethical
implication and to promote the need for
further research in these areas of science
and medicine.

## Progress Employment Support

The Enterprise Centre,
291–305 Lytham Road, Blackpool,
Lancashire FY4 1EW
T: 01253 477287
F: 01253 477276
E: deborah.parker@progressemployment.org
www.progressemployment.org
CEO: Deborah Parker
A values-driven supported employment
agency achieving inclusive employment and
business success, by supporting disabled
people and their employers to benefit from
working together.
Employees: 5
Regional offices: 1

## Progressio

Units 9–12, The Stable Yard,
Broomgrove Road, London SW9 9TL
T: 020 7733 1195
F: 020 7326 2059
E: enquiries@progressio.org.uk
www.progressio.org.uk
Executive Director: Mark Lister
Progressio is a UK-based charity working
internationally to enable people in developing
countries to change the situations that keep
them poor. We work in 11 countries and have
a history of working in fragile, post-conflict
states, developing long-term partnerships
with local organisations and community
groups in Africa, Latin America, the
Caribbean, the Middle East and Asia,
providing practical support through around
100 development workers, mostly from the
south, who share skills, know-how and training.
Employees: 80
Volunteers: 104

## Promise Dreams

Promise House, Edwin House,
Boundary Industrial Estate, Stafford Road,
Wolverhampton, West Midlands WV10 7EL
T: 01902 212451
F: 01902 783625
E: info@promisedreams.co.uk
www.promisedreams.co.uk
Charity Manager: Beverley Bird
Promise Dreams is a national registered
charity, dedicated to helping seriously ill and
terminally ill children and their families turn
a very special wish into reality.
Employees: 5
Regional offices: 1

## Prospect Hospice

E: andrewthompson@prospect-hospice.net

## Prospects for People with Learning Disabilities

69 Honey End Lane, Reading,
Berkshire RG30 4EL
T: 0118 950 8781
E: paula@prospects.org.uk
www.prospects.org.uk
CEO: Paul Ashton
Prospects is a Christian organisation supporting people with learning disabilities so that they live their lives to the full through: residential homes and supported living; overseas partnerships; church-based ministry; involvement in Christian conferences.
Employees: 700
Volunteers: 1300
Regional offices: 7

## Prostate Cancer UK

Fourth Floor, The Counting House,
53 Tooley Street, London SE1 2QN
T: 020 3310 7000
Helpline: 0800 074 8383
F: 020 3310 7107
E: info@prostatecanceruk.org
www.prostatecanceruk.org
Chief Executive: Owen Sharp
Prostate Cancer UK fight to help more men survive prostate cancer and enjoy a better quality of life. We support men through: our helpline staffed by specialist nurses, our work in the community and by providing vital information on all aspects of prostate disease. We find answers by funding research into causes, tests and treatments. And we lead change, raising the profile of the disease and improving care. We believe that men deserve better.
Employees: 185
Volunteers: 1263
Regional offices: 6

## Psoriasis and Psoriatic Arthritis Alliance

PO Box 111, St Albans AL2 3JQ
T: 0870 770 3212
F: 0870 770 3213
E: info@papaa.org
www.papaa.org
Aims to preserve, protect and relieve persons suffering from psoriatic arthropathy and associated conditions.

## Psoriasis Association

Dick Coles House, 2 Queensbridge,
Northampton,
Northamptonshire NN4 7BF
T: 01604 251620
Helpline: 0845 676 0076
F: 01604 251621
E: mail@psoriasis-association.org.uk
www.psoriasis-association.org.uk
Chief Executive: Helen McAteer
The Association supports people with psoriasis, raises awareness of the condition and funds research into the causes, treatment and care.
Employees: 6
Volunteers: 2

## Psychiatric Rehabilitation Association

Bayford Mews, Bayford Street,
London E8 3SF
T: 020 8985 3570
E: ppra528898@aol.com
www.centreforbetterhealth.org.uk
Promotes the rehabilitation of the mentally sick on their return home, to employment and society by preparatory work and after-care in the community; promotes practical measures in research for the prevention and combating of mental stress within the community.

## Psychosynthesis and Education Trust

92–94 Tooley Street, London SE1 2TH
T: 020 7403 2100
F: 020 7403 5562
E: enquiries@petrust.org.uk
www.psychosynthesis.edu
The Trust's main purpose is to gain recognition for the central role of soul and self in psychology and to renew the soul in the everyday life of individuals, the family, groups, organisations and society. Other activities include promoting the practice of transpersonal counselling and psychotherapy by providing a training centre of excellence, and providing psychosynthesis educational techniques suitable for schools and adult education.
Employees: 29
Regional offices: 1

## Public Concern at Work

Suite 301, 16 Baldwins Gardens,
London EC1N 7RJ
T: 020 7404 6609
E: whistle@pcaw.co.uk
www.pcaw.org.uk
Acting as a leading, independent authority on public interest whistleblowing, PCaW aims to improve standards in the public, private and voluntary sectors and to assert the accountability of people in the workplace.

## Public Fundraising Regulatory Association

Unit 11, Europoint Centre,
5–11 Lavington Street, London SE1 0NZ
T: 020 7401 8452
E: info@pfra.org.uk
www.pfra.org.uk
Chief Executive: Sally de la Bedoyere
The PFRA regulates the use of face-to-face fundraising by charities and professional fundraising organisations, principally on the street and doorstep. We work with local authorities to agree equitable access to fundraising sites and monitor their use to ensure fundraisers abide by the Institute of Fundraising's codes of practice.
Employees: 9
Regional offices: 1

## Public Law Project

150 Caledonian Road, London N1 9RD
T: 020 7843 1260
F: 020 7837 7048
E: office@publiclawproject.org.uk
www.publiclawproject.org.uk
Aims to improve access to public law remedies, such as judicial review, for people whose access is limited because of poverty, discrimination or other disadvantages.
Employees: 8
Volunteers: 3
Regional offices: 1

## PublicMedia CIC

82A Highfield Road, Dartford,
Kent DA1 2JJ
T: 01322 405540
E: vb@publicmedia.co.uk
www.publicmedia.co.uk
Enterprise Director: Vince Braithwaite
PublicMedia is a social enterprise, community interest company which has been set up to support the introduction of new media services. These services aim to support the social and economic regeneration of local communities and empower people to engage more effectively in civic society. They would also create a space for the creative industries sector to produce content which is both entertaining and engaging.

## QED – UK

Quest House, 243 Manningham Lane,
Bradford BD8 7ER
T: 01274 483267
F: 01274 305689
E: admin@qed-uk.org
www.qed-uk.org
Aims to improve the economic, social and
education development of minority ethnic
groups. Mainly focusing on disadvantaged
South Asian communities.
Employees: 15
Volunteers: 20

## Quaker Social Action

QSA, 17 Old Ford Road, Bethnal Green,
London E2 9PJ
T: 020 8983 5030
E: info@qsa.org.uk
www.quakersocialaction.org.uk
Director: Judith Moran
We enable people on low incomes in East
London and beyond to seek solutions to the
issues affecting their lives. To do this we listen
and respond to the needs of the community
by running practical, sustainable and
collaborative projects. We share our work
with others when it is clear that it has the
potential to bring benefits to communities
outside of our own.
Employees: 25
Volunteers: 115
Regional offices: 1
Income: £994,218 (2014–15)

## Queen Alexandra College

Court Oak Road, Harborne,
Birmingham B17 9TG
T: 0121 428 5050
F: 0121 428 5048
E: enquiries@qac.ac.uk
www.qac.ac.uk
Queen Alexandra College aims to challenge
discrimination and exclusion by providing
opportunities for people with visual impairment
and other disabilities to learn, live and work
independently.
Employees: 115
Volunteers: 10

## Queen Elizabeth's Foundation for Disabled People

Leatherhead Court, Woodlands Road,
Leatherhead, Surrey KT22 0BN
T: 01372 841100
F: 01372 844072
E: sue.moller@qef.org.uk
www.qef.org.uk
Chief Executive: Jonathan Powell
QEF works with people living with physical
and learning disabilities or acquired brain
injuries to gain new skills and increase
independence. Whether it's learning
everyday skills, rebuilding a life affected by
brain injury, acquiring the skills to drive a
specially adapted car or training for future
employment, QEF supports disabled people
to achieve goals for life.
Employees: 300
Volunteers: 300

## Queen Victoria Seamen's Rest

121–131 East India Dock Road, Poplar,
London E14 6DF
T: 020 7987 5466
E: enquiries@qvsr.org.uk
www.qvsr.org.uk
Provides secure and comfortable
accommodation; fosters a spirit of
community internally and externally;
supports, empowers and enables individuals
to enhance their quality of life; provides active
rehabilitation opportunities; integrates our
services into the lives of the local community.

## Race on the Agenda

c/o Resource for London,
356 Holloway Road, London N7 6PA
T: 020 7697 4093
E: rota@rota.org.uk
www.rota.org.uk
Chief Executive: Andy Gregg
To be a BAME-led social policy think-tank
that focuses on race equality and issues
affecting Britain's BAME communities, and
create an environment for the equalities third
sector to flourish. To strengthen the voice of
BAME communities through increased civic
engagement and participation in society and
provide representation of issues affecting

BAME communities and the sector that was
set up to serve them.
Employees: 7
Volunteers: 3
Regional offices: 1

## Raglan Housing Association

Wright House, 12–14 Castle Street, Poole,
Dorset BH15 1BQ
T: 01202 678731
Helpline: 0845 070 7772
F: 01202 665091
E: info@raglan.org
www.raglan.org
Chief Executive: Alan Seabright
Raglan's purpose is to meet a variety of
housing needs by providing quality, affordable
homes, high-standard services and by
promoting and encouraging sustainable
communities. Our resident involvement
policy offers a wide range of opportunities
for volunteers to monitor performance
and contribute to our drive for continuing
improvement in the homes and services
we deliver.
Employees: 400
Volunteers: 150
Regional offices: 6

## Railway Children

1st Floor, 1 The Commons, Sandbach,
Cheshire CW11 1EG
T: 01270 251571 (also fax)
E: enquiries@railwaychildren.org.uk
www.railwaychildren.org.uk
Railway Children exists to help street
children. No child should have to live alone
and at risk on the streets, and this belief is
reflected in the charity's vision, which is to
create a world of safety and opportunity
for children who are at risk on the streets.
Employees: 6
Volunteers: 5

## Rainbow Centre for Children affected by Life-Threatening Illnesses or Bereavement

27 Lilymead Avenue, Knowle,
Bristol BS4 2BY
T: 0117 985 3343
E: contact@rainbowcentre.org.uk
www.rainbowcentre.org.uk
Centre Director: Angela Emms
The Rainbow Centre supports children and
their families experiencing cancer and other
life-threatening illnesses or bereavement, using
counselling and complementary therapies.
Regional offices: 1

## Rainbow Trust Children's Charity

6 Cleeve Court, Cleeve Road, Leatherhead,
Surrey KT22 7UD
T: 01372 363438
F: 01372 363101
E: louise.whitby@rainbowtrust.org.uk
www.rainbowtrust.org.uk
**Chief Executive: Heather Wood**
Rainbow Trust provides emotional and
practical support for families who have a child
with a life-threatening or terminal illness. We
offer the whole family individually tailored,
high-quality support for as long as they need it.
**Employees: 80**
**Volunteers: 50**
**Regional offices: 8**

## Rainforest Foundation UK

233A Kentish Town Road,
London NW5 2JT
T: 020 7485 0193
F: 020 7485 0315
E: info@rainforestuk.org
www.rainforestfoundationuk.org
**Executive Director: Simon Counsell**
The Rainforest Foundation UK supports
indigenous peoples of the world's rainforests
in their efforts to protect the environment
and fulfill their rights to life, land and livelihoods.
**Employees: 20**
**Volunteers: 2**

## Rainy Day Trust

Federation House, 10 Vyse Street,
Birmingham B18 6LT
T: 0121 237 1132
Helpline: 020 3192 0486
E: diane@rainydaytrust.org.uk
www.rainydaytrust.org.uk
**General Secretary: Diane Stevens**
The Rainy Day Trust is a charity that exists
solely to help people who have worked in
the UK's home improvement and home
enhancement industry including DIY/
hardware stores, garden centres, pottery and
glass, housewares and all the manufacturers,
distributors and wholesalers who supply them.
We can assist in variety of ways, however all
applicants should have worked for one or
more of the above industries for at least
three years.
**Employees: 2**
**Volunteers: 5**
**Income: £193,933 (2014–15)**

## Raleigh International Trust

3rd Floor, Dean Bradley House,
52 Horseferry Road, London SW1P 2AF
T: 020 7183 1270
F: 020 7504 8094
E: s.adams@raleighinternational.org
www.raleighinternational.org
**Chief Executive: Stacey Adams**
Raleigh International supports people and
communities to overcome the challenges
they face, and help them to find the best
solutions. By bringing together teams of
young volunteers with communities in rural
areas, and through a hands-on learning
approach, we inspire and empower them
to create lasting change. Our programmes
focus on improving access to safe water and
sanitation, building community resilience
and empowering communities to sustainably
manage their natural resources.
**Employees: 102**
**Volunteers: 2125**
**Regional offices: 5**
**Income: £6,867,000 (2013–14)**

## Ramblers' Association

2nd Floor, Camelford House, 87–
89 Albert Embankment, London SE1 7TW
T: 020 7339 8571
F: 020 7339 8501
E: ramblers@london.ramblers.org.uk
www.ramblers.org.uk
Promotes walking, protects rights of way,
campaigns for access to open country and
defends the beauty of the countryside.
**Employees: 60**
**Volunteers: 5000**
**Regional offices: 3**

## Rape and Sexual Abuse Support Centre – Rape Crisis South London

PO Box 383, Croydon, Surrey CR9 2AW
T: 020 8683 3311
Helpline: 0808 802 9999
F: 020 8683 3366
E: info@rasasc.org.uk
www.rasasc.org.uk
**Chief Executive Officer: Yvonne Traynor**
A professional and passionate team working
in a centre of excellence dedicated to the
healing and empowerment of survivors of
sexual violence by providing counselling,
helpline support, advocacy through the
criminal justice system, outreach to women
involved in prostitution, ex-offenders and
homeless women, training and information
for other agencies including schools, colleges
and teacher training. Services are provided in

Croydon, Kingston, Southwark, Bexley and
Crawley.
**Employees: 48**
**Volunteers: 40**
**Regional offices: 4**
**Income: £750,000 (2015–16)**

## Rapid Effective Assistance for Children with Potentially Terminal Illness

St Luke's House, 270 Sandycombe Road,
Richmond Upon Thames, Surrey TW9 3NP
T: 020 8940 2575
F: 020 8940 2050
E: react@reactcharity.org
www.reactcharity.org
Identifies and responds to the needs of
children and young people diagnosed as
suffering from potentially terminal illnesses.
**Employees: 4**
**Volunteers: 30**
**Regional offices: 1**

## Rare Breeds Survival Trust

Stoneleigh Park, Kenilworth,
Warwickshire CV8 2LG
T: 024 7669 6551
F: 024 7669 6706
E: enquiries@rbst.org.uk
www.rbst.org.uk
**CEO: Tom Beeston**
The Rare Breeds Survival Trust is the leading
national charity working to conserve and
protect the UK's rare native breeds of farm
animals from extinction. We believe in the
value of the UK's rich and varied livestock
heritage and that this needs to be conserved
as a vital genetic resource for future
generations and the benefit of agriculture.
**Employees: 9**
**Volunteers: 250**
**Regional offices: 20**
**Income: £700,000 (2010–11)**

## Rare Disease UK

Unit 4D, Leroy House, 436 Essex Road,
London N1 3QP
T: 020 7704 3141
E: info@raredisease.org.uk
www.raredisease.org.uk
**Chair: Alastair Kent**
The national alliance for people with rare
diseases and all who support them.

## Rathbone

4th Floor, Churchgate House,
56 Oxford Street, Manchester M1 6EU
T: 0161 236 5358
F: 0161 238 6356
E: julie.lewis@rathboneuk.org
www.rathboneuk.org
**Chief Executive: Richard Williams**
Rathbone is a charity that provides education
and training opportunities to over 14,000
young people annually. Rathbone is dedicated
to working with young people who have
not had their needs met by mainstream
education. Many such young people require
support to access opportunities that are
tailored to their learning and social needs.
Rathbone has four core areas: alternative
school curriculum for young people aged
14–16, apprenticeships, pre-vocational
activities and youth engagement.
**Employees: 750**
**Volunteers: 40**
**Regional offices: 89**

## Raw Material Music and Media Education

2 Robsart Street SW9 0DJ
T: 020 7737 6103
F: 020 7733 7533
E: tim@raw-material.org
www.raw-material.org
Promotes education and training in the
creative and expressive arts and media.

## Raynaud's & Scleroderma Association (RSA)

112 Crewe Road, Alsager, Cheshire ST7 2JA
T: 01270 872776
E: info@raynauds.org.uk
www.raynauds.org.uk
**Chief Executive Officer: Elizabeth Bevins**
Raynaud's is a common condition in which
blood is prevented from reaching the
extremities of the body, mainly the fingers
and toes, on exposure to the cold or any slight
change in temperature. Scleroderma is an
uncommon disease of the blood vessels, the
immune system and the connective tissue.
The Association's aims are to promote a
better communication between doctors and
patients, to disseminate information and to
raise funds for research and welfare projects.
**Employees: 6**

## RCJ Advice Bureau

Royal Courts of Justice, Strand,
London WC2A 2LL
T: 020 7947 7119
F: 020 7947 7167
E: admin@rcjadvice.org.uk
www.rcjadvice.org.uk
**Chief Executive: James Banks**
Works to provide access to justice to
unrepresented litigants in the Royal Courts
of Justice and the Principal Registry of the
Family Division, through the provision of legal
and other advice services.
**Employees: 21**
**Volunteers: 35**

## Re-Solv

30A High Street, Stone,
Staffordshire ST15 8AW
T: 01785 817885
F: 01785 813205
E: information@re-solv.org
www.re-solv.org
**Director: Stephen Ream**
Re-Solv works to contribute to happier,
healthier, safer social environments by
preventing the death, suffering and crime,
which may result as a consequence of solvent
and volatile substance abuse (VSA).
**Employees: 5**
**Volunteers: 14**
**Regional offices: 1**

## Re-Start

56 Davids Way, Hainault, Ilford,
Essex IG6 3BQ
T: 020 8501 1096
Helpline: 020 3087 5699
E: restartoffice@gmail.com
www.restartoffice.blogspot.com
**CE: Moinul Khalique**
Re-Start is a social-work-led voluntary
organisation, working in partnership with Job
Centre Plus. We currently run a number of
programmes, mainly of a solution-focused
therapeutic nature, targeting specific groups,
such as claimants of incapacity benefits in
some of the most deprived parts of east and
north east London. Many of the clients
referred to us sometimes lack the motivation
and determination to change their
circumstances.
**Employees: 1**
**Volunteers: 5**

## REACH

Camelford House,
87–89 Albert Embankment,
London SE1 7TP
T: 020 7582 6543
F: 020 7582 2423
E: mail@reachskills.org.uk
www.reachskills.org.uk
REACH's aims are to recruit and support
people with managerial, professional, business
and technical experience and match them
with part-time voluntary roles throughout
the UK, and to help voluntary organisations
gain access to these potential volunteers and
benefit fully from their expertise.
**Employees: 7**
**Volunteers: 60**
**Regional offices: 1**

## Reach – Association for Children with Upper Limb Deficiency

Pearl Assurance House, Brook Street,
Tavistock, Devon PL19 0BN
T: 0845 130 6225
E: reach@reach.org.uk
www.reach.org.uk
**National Coordinator: Jo Dixon**
Reach was formed in 1978 by parents of
children who were missing part of their arm
or a hand, in order to lobby for the provision
of a new artificial arm under the NHS.
Since then Reach has grown to become a
national organisation providing support and
information for children with hand or arm
deficiencies, and their parents.
**Employees: 2**
**Volunteers: 25**
**Regional offices: 14**

## Reading Matters

Western House, Western Way,
Halifax Road, Bradford,
West Yorkshire BD6 2SZ
T: 01274 692219
E: rachel@readingmatters.org.uk
readingmatters.org.uk
**Chief Executive: Rachel Kelly**
Reading Matters improves reading skills. We
specialise in one-to-one support to motivate
children and young people to reach their
potential by becoming confident and
enthusiastic readers. As an effective literacy
support charity, we support a network of
trained volunteer reading mentors across
West and South Yorkshire and train adults,

young people and children across the UK and beyond to offer reading support.

**Employees: 6**
**Volunteers: 100**
**Regional offices: 1**
**Income: £183,390 (2014–15)**

## Reading Mencap

21 Alexandra Road, Reading,
Berkshire RG1 5PE
T: 0118 966 2518
E: businessrelations@readingmencap.org.uk
www.readingmencap.org.uk
CEO: Mandi Smith

We provide services from birth and throughout life for carers and children and adults with Learning Disability and Difficulties (LDD) and aim to reduce inequality in statutory services, combat isolation and discrimination, and bring to local people an experience of having people with LDD as part of their community.

**Employees: 22**
**Volunteers: 30**

## Real Life Options

A1 Business Park, Knottingley Road,
Knottingley, West Yorkshire WF11 0BL
T: 01977 781800
F: 01977 795361
E: dave.rawnsley@reallifeoptions.org
www.reallifeoptions.org
Chief Executive: Brian Hutchinson

We all strive to enjoy our lives, experience excitement, make our own decisions and aim for the stars. Some of us may need support to help us achieve our goals and aspirations; this includes people with learning disabilities, autism or intellectual impairments. That's where Real Life Options excels. Across the UK we support people to make their own choices, to have the same experiences we take for granted and, above all, to enjoy their lives.

**Employees: 2000**
**Volunteers: 2**
**Regional offices: 15**

## Realife Trust

3 The Courtyard, Windhill,
Bishop's Stortford,
Hertfordshire CM23 2ND
T: 01279 504735
F: 01279 757658
E: info@realife.org.uk
www.realife.org.uk
**Employees: 12**
**Volunteers: 20**

## Redbridge Council for Voluntary Service

3rd Floor, Forest House,
16–20 Clements Road, Ilford IG1 1BA
T: 020 8553 1004
F: 020 8911 9128
E: ross@redbridgecvs.net
redbridgecvs.net
Chief Officer: Ross Diamond

Redbridge CVS is the umbrella body for the voluntary sector in the north east London Borough of Redbridge. We provide the functions of a CVS and a volunteer centre and provide a range of support services to local groups. We exist to support a strong, effective and independent voluntary and community sector in Redbridge.

**Employees: 31**
**Volunteers: 20**
**Regional offices: 1**
**Income: £1,672,910 (2014–15)**

## RedR UK

250A Kennington Lane, London SE11 5RD
T: 020 7840 6000
F: 020 7582 8669
E: jo.barrett@redr.org.uk
www.redr.org.uk
CEO: Martin McCann

RedR is a leading international disaster relief charity that trains aid workers and provides skilled professionals to humanitarian programmes worldwide.

**Employees: 120**
**Volunteers: 8**
**Regional offices: 6**

## Reedham Children's Trust

The Lodge, 23 Old Lodge Lane, Purley,
Surrey CR8 4DJ
T: 020 8660 1461
F: 020 8763 1293
E: info@reedham-trust.org.uk
www.reedham-trust.org.uk
CEO: Sarah Smart

We help some of the most vulnerable children in our society who though death, illness, disability or substance abuse of a parent are left with a home environment that does not provide them with care and stability. We assist them to attend boarding schools thereby giving them space and security to thrive and receive a great education whilst also keeping the families together.

**Employees: 4**

## Refuge

4th Floor, International House,
1 St Katharine's Way, London E1W 1UN
T: 020 7395 7700
Helpline: 0808 200 0247
F: 020 7395 7721
E: info@refuge.org.uk
www.refuge.org.uk

Refuge is the national charity that provides a wide range of specialist domestic violence services to women and children experiencing domestic violence. On any given day our services support 3,000 women and children.

**Employees: 175**
**Volunteers: 12**

## Refuge Action

11 Belgrave Road, London SW1V 1RB
T: 020 7952 1511
E: lyna@refugee-action.org.uk
www.refugee-action.org
Chief Executive: Dave Garratt

Across England, Refugee Action works to: provide high-quality reception, advice and information to refugees and asylum seekers; promote the development of refugee communities; improve access to employment and mainstream services, and enhance opportunities for refugees and asylum-seekers; raise awareness, influence policy, and campaign for refugee rights; advise and assist asylum seekers and irregular migrants who are considering voluntary return.

**Employees: 205**
**Volunteers: 200**
**Regional offices: 9**

## Refugee Council

240–250 Ferndale Road,
London SW9 8BB
T: 020 7346 6700
F: 020 7582 9929
E: supporter@refugeecouncil.org.uk
www.refugeecouncil.org.uk

The Refugee Council gives practical advice and promotes refugees' rights in the UK and abroad

**Employees: 350**
**Volunteers: 200**
**Regional offices: 8**

## Refugee Legal Centre

Nelson House, 153–157 Commercial Road,
London E1 2DA
T: 020 7780 3320
E: rlc@refugee-legal-centre.org.uk
www.refugee-legal-centre.org.uk

Provides legal advice and representation (free of charge) to asylum seekers and refugees.

## Refugee Therapy Centre

40 St John's Way, London  N19 3RR
T: 020 7272 2565
E: info@refugeetherapy.org.uk
www.refugeetherapy.org.uk
Provides counselling, psychotherapy and
associated treatment to children, adolescents
and young refugees and asylum seekers and
their families.

## Regard

BM Regard, London  WC1N 3XX
E: secretary@regard.org.uk
www.regard.org.uk
A national organisation of lesbians, gay men,
bisexuals and transgender people (LGBT)
who self-identify as disabled. We follow the
Social Model of Disability. This is a way of
thinking about disability that says it is society
that needs to change by removing the
barriers that deny us inclusion and equal
rights. We offer information, support and
campaign. Regard is run by its members for
its members and has no paid staff.

## Regional Studies Association

PO Box 2058, Seaford  BN25 4QU
T: 01323 899698 (also fax)
E: support@rsc-london.ac.uk
www.regionalstudies.org
Provides, as an interdisciplinary group, a
forum in which to discuss regional issues and
to publish the results of related research.
Employees: 3
Volunteers: 12

## Registry Trust Limited

E: mhurlston@hurlstons.com

## Relate Brighton, Hove, Worthing and Districts

E: jo.carden@brightonrelate.org.uk

## Relate Central Office

Herbert Gray College, Little Church Street,
Rugby, Warwickshire  CV21 3AP
T: 01788 563824
F: 01788 563825
E: enquiries@relate.org.uk
www.relate.org.uk
Aims to educate the public concerning the
benefits of secure couple relationships,
marriage and family life in order to improve
the emotional, sexual and spiritual wellbeing
of individuals that is derived from committed
relationships.

## Relate Lincolnshire

138 High Street, Lincoln,
Lincolnshire  LN5 7PJ
T: 01522 524922
F: 01522 569238
E: enquiries@relate-lincs.org.uk
relate-lincs.org.uk
Centre Manager: Marilyn Merry
To enhance the health of adults and children
by increasing public awareness of the benefit
of committed relationships, marriage, and
family life and working to prevent poverty,
hardship and distress caused by the
breakdown of such relationships. Providing
counselling, advice, education, guidance and
relief to adults and/or children in relation to
any aspect of contemporary life or work.
Employees: 40
Volunteers: 20
Regional offices: 11
Income: £560,000 (2013–14)

## Relatives and Residents Association

24 The Ivories, 6–18 Northampton Street,
London  N1 2HY
T: 020 7359 8148
Helpline: 020 7359 8136
F: 020 7226 6603
E: gillian.dalley@relres.org
www.relres.org
Chief Executive: Gillian Dalley
The Association exists for older people
needing, or living in, residential care and the
families and friends. As well as a listening ear,
relatives need to know how to understand the
complex regulations about paying for care, or
to complain about the quality of care their
loved ones are receiving. It offers support and
information via its helpline; specific project
work; influencing policy and practice; and
working with local relatives and residents
groups in care homes.
Employees: 5
Volunteers: 6
Regional offices: 20

## Release

124–128 City Road, London  EC1V 2NJ
T: 020 7324 2979
Helpline: 020 7324 2989
F: 020 7324 2977
E: ask@release.org.uk
www.release.org.uk
Executive Director: Niamh Eastwood
Release is the national centre of expertise on
drugs, law and human rights. We provide legal
advice to those affected by the UK drugs
laws. We also provide a specialist drugs

helpline. Advice can be sought via telephone
or email.
Employees: 13
Volunteers: 50
Income: £600,000 (2014–15)

## REMA

The Unity Centre,
St Leonards Road  S65 1PD
T: 01709 720744
E: team@rema-online.org.uk
www.rema-online.org.uk
Chief Executive: Azizzum Akhtar
REMA is the infrastructure support
organisation for the black and minority
ethnic voluntary and community sector of
Rotherham. Our mission is to support the
development of voluntary and community
action that is effective, sustainable and brings
about positive social change for the BME
voluntary, community and faith sector
(VCFS) and communities. We provide
small group support, capacity building and
recruitment advice. We also support voice
and influence activity by hosting networks
for the BME communities.
Employees: 5
Volunteers: 5

## Remap

D9 Chaucer Business Park, Watery Lane,
Kemsing, Kent  TN15 6YU
T: 01732 760209
F: 01732 760204
E: data@remap.org.uk
www.remap.org.uk
Remap is an established national charity
which provides one-off pieces of equipment
for people with disabilities. Each year Remap
helps about 4,000 people in this way,
helping them to lead more fulfilling and
independent lives.
Employees: 5
Volunteers: 1500

## Renaisi Limited

21 Garden Walk, London  EC2A 3EQ
T: 020 7033 2600
F: 020 7033 2631
E: info@renaisi.com
www.renaisi.com
Chief Executive: Clive Tritton
Renaisi is an award-winning social enterprise
that helps people and places to thrive. We do
this by: developing strategies to maximise
economic, social and cultural assets to create
successful places; equipping and empowering
individuals to find sustainable and secure

employment; enabling resilient, confident, cohesive and flourishing communities.
**Employees: 60**
**Income: £2,500,000 (2014–15)**

## Rescare

Steven Jackson House, 31 Buxton Road, Heaviley, Stockport SK2 6LS
T: 0161 474 3723
Helpline: 0800 032 7330
E: office@rescare.org.uk
www.rescare.org.uk
Works for the relief and welfare of people with a learning disability in all types of residential accommodation. Gives help, support and advice to the families of such disabled people.

## Rescue: the British Archaeological Trust

15A Bull Plain, Hertford SG14 1DX
T: 01992 553377
E: rescue@rescue-archaeology.freeserve.co.uk
rescue-archaeology.org.uk
Aims to preserve and record the archaeological and historic environment. Acts as a fundraising body and publications outlet, and works to increase public awareness of the destruction of our heritage.

## Research Society of Process Oriented Psychology UK

c/o Interchange Studios,
Hampstead Town Hall Centre,
213 Haverstock Hill, London NW3 4QP
T: 0870 429 5296
E: contact@processworkuk.org
www.rspopuk.com
RS POP UK is the national forum and organising body for process work in the UK. It organises a full and exciting annual programme of workshops, classes, supervision, training and private therapy with teachers and therapists from the British and international process work community.

## Resources for Autism

858 Finchley Road, Temple Fortune,
London NW11 6AB
T: 020 8458 3259
F: 020 8458 3222
E: liza.dresner@resourcesforautism.org.uk
www.resourcesforautism.org.uk
Director: Liza Dresner
Provides practical services including play and youth clubs, respite schemes, outreach home support, music and art therapy and advice

and information for individuals with an autistic spectrum condition and their families.
**Employees: 220**
**Volunteers: 200**
**Regional offices: 1**
**Income: £1,500,000 (2015–16)**

## Respect

4th Floor, Development House,
56–64 Leonard Street, London EC2A 4LT
T: 020 7549 0578
Helpline: 0808 802 4040
E: info@respect.uk.net
www.respect.uk.net
Respect is the UK membership association for domestic violence perpetrator programmes and associated support services. Its key focus is on increasing the safety of those experiencing domestic violence through promoting effective interventions with perpetrators. An information and advice phone line is central to Respect's activities: this is used both by those carrying out abuse and those who have suffered it, as well as professionals who come into contact with domestic violence situations.
**Employees: 12**
**Regional offices: 1**

## Respond

Respond, 3rd Floor,
24–32 Stephenson Way,
London NW1 2HD
T: 020 7383 0700
E: admin@respond.org.uk
www.respond.org.uk
Chief Executive: Noelle Blackman
Respond exists to: lessen the effect of trauma and abuse on people with learning disabilities their families and supporters. We do this through providing psychotherapy for people with learning disabilities; advice and support for staff and families; training for professionals; education for people with learning disabilities; influencing generic services to make their services accessible; influencing learning disability services to consider the psychological impact of living with learning disabilities; undertaking research and disseminating our findings.
**Regional offices: 1**

## Response International (HMD)

Office 11, Interlink House,
73a Maygrove Road, London NW6 2EG
T: 020 7372 6972
E: ri@responseinternational.org.uk
www.responseinternational.org.uk
Chief Executive: Philip Garvin

Emergency and rehabilitation services for victims of conflict: primary health, landmine action, rehabilitation of torture victims and amputees, reconstruction of health infrastructure, provision of prosthetics, training of health professionals.
**Employees: 50**
**Volunteers: 15**
**Regional offices: 4**

## Restorative Justice Council

Beacon House, 113 Kingsway, Holborn,
London WC2B 6PP
T: 020 7831 5700
E: enquiries@restorativejustice.org.uk
www.restorativejustice.org.uk
Chief Executive Officer: Jon Collins
The Restorative Justice Council (RJC) is the independent third sector membership body for the field of restorative practice. It provides quality assurance and a national voice advocating the widespread use of all forms of restorative practice, including restorative justice. The RJC's vision is of a restorative society where everyone has access to safe, high-quality restorative practice wherever and whenever it is needed.
**Employees: 19**

## Restricted Growth Association

PO Box 99, Lydney,
Gloucestershire GL15 9AW
T: 0300 111 1970
F: 0300 111 2454
E: office@restrictedgrowth.co.uk
www.restrictedgrowth.co.uk
The RGA is a self-help charity dealing with the medical and social consequences of restricted growth/dwarfism. It provides a telephone helpline, dedicated medical and benefits advisers and regular opportunities to meet others in a supportive social setting. The RGA also produces a variety of information publications about the different forms of dwarfism and provides members with regular e-newsletters.

## Retirement Trust

Silton Cottage, Chantlers Hill,
Paddock Wood, Tonbridge, Kent TN12 6LX
T: 01892 838474
E: info@theretirementtrust.org.uk
www.theretirementtrust.org.uk
Chair: Roger Parkes
The Trust aims to bring pre-retirement advice, support and education to a wide range of employees.
**Volunteers: 5**

## Rett UK

Langham House West, Mill Street,
Luton LU1 2NA
T: 01582 798910
Helpline: 01582 798911
E: info@rettuk.org
www.rettuk.org
Offers support, friendship and practical help
to those families and carers who have a child
or adult with Rett syndrome. Rett UK helps
inform and train professionals in the fields of
research, education, treatment, diagnosis,
care and understanding of the condition.
Employees: 5
Volunteers: 120
Income: £301,000 (2015–16)

## Returned Volunteer Action

5 Balls Pond Road, London N1 4AX
T: 020 7247 6406
E: retvolact@lineone.net
Returned Volunteer Action is a membership
organisation open to both people who have
been development volunteers or workers
and those interested in the field. It provides
information and training materials for
those interested in becoming volunteers.
A resource list is available on request.
Volunteers: 20
Income: £3,500 (2014–15)

## Revolving Doors Agency

Units 28, The Turnmill,
63 Clerkenwell Road, London EC1M 5NP
T: 020 7253 4038
F: 020 7553 6079
E: admin@revolving-doors.org.uk
www.revolving-doors.co.uk
Revolving Doors Agency is the UK's leading
independent charity dedicated to working
with people with mental health problems in
touch with the criminal justice system.
Employees: 30
Volunteers: 1

## Rica (Research Institute for Consumer Affairs)

Unit G03, The Wenlock,
50–52 Wharf Road, London N1 7EU
T: 020 7427 2460
E: mail@rica.org.uk
www.rica.org.uk
Director: Caroline Jacobs
Rica is an independent research charity
working with older and disabled consumers.
It has specialist expertise in product testing,
user trials, focus groups and mystery
shopping. Rica provides unbiased information
for older/disabled consumers, eg motoring
guides including on car adaptations, an online

car search and other relevant information.
Rica aims to increase awareness among
manufacturers, service providers and policy
makers to improve products and services to
meet the needs of disabled and older
consumers.
Employees: 8

## Richmond Fellowship

80 Holloway Road, London N7 8JG
T: 020 7697 3300
F: 020 7697 3301
E: communications@richmondfellowship.
org.uk
www.richmondfellowship.org.uk
Provides residential care, counselling and
support, as well as rehabilitation and work
skills, to men and women who are recovering
from emotional disturbance, addiction and
mental health problems. The Fellowship
encourages greater public awareness and
understanding of mental health problems.
Employees: 686
Regional offices: 4

## Riding for the Disabled Association

Norfolk House, 1A Tournament Court,
Edgehill Drive, Warwick,
Warwickshire CV34 6LG
T: 0845 658 1082
F: 0845 658 1083
E: info@rda.org.uk
www.rda.org.uk
Chief Executive: Ed Bracher
RDA is a national charity dedicated to
improving the lives of people with disabilities,
through the provision of opportunities for
riding and/or carriage driving. Through 500
member groups we enable people to improve
their health and wellbeing, delivering a real
and lasting therapy that not only benefits
mobility and co-ordination, but also
encourages confidence and self-worth whilst
having fun. Currently 28,000 people with a
wide range of disabilities and of all ages ride
with RDA.
Employees: 17
Volunteers: 18000
Regional offices: 500

## Right From the Start

84/86 Lewis Street, Aberbargoed, Bargoed,
Caerphilly, Mid Glamorgan CF81 9EA
T: 01443 879426
F: 01443 879621
E: info@rfts.org.uk
www.rightfromthestart.co.uk
Project coordinator: Sian Williams
Supports families with children within the
Caerphilly Borough. Delivering parenting

groups within the local communities and
offering housing-related support to families
within their own home, covering a range of
issues such as debt management, budgeting,
managing accommodation and healthy living
amongst other tenancy-related support to
ensure families are able to live independently
within their own communities
Employees: 12
Volunteers: 5
Regional offices: 1

## Rights of Women

52–54 Featherstone Street,
London EC1Y 8RT
E: info@row.org.uk
www.rightsofwomen.org.uk
Director: Estelle du Boulay
Rights of Women is a women's voluntary
organisation committed to informing,
educating and empowering women
concerning their legal rights. Our advice lines
provide free, confidential legal advice to
women on family law and domestic violence,
sexual violence and criminal law, and
immigration and asylum law. Details are on
our website: www.rightsofwomen.org.uk.
Income: £398,485 (2015–16)

## RNIB National Library Service

Far Cromwell Road, Bredbury,
Stockport SK6 2SG
Helpline: 0845 762 6843
F: 0161 355 2098
E: reader.advice@rnib.org.uk
www.rnib.org.uk/reading
Head of RNIB National Library Service:
Helen Brazier
Provides books and information for blind
and partially sighted children and adults in a
range of accessible formats including audio
(unabridged Daisy CDs), braille, Moon, large
print (16pt type) and giant print (24pt type).
We also provide free access to online
reference information, braille sheet music,
themed book lists and a quarterly reader
magazine.
Employees: 35
Volunteers: 950
Regional offices: 2

## RoadPeace

**Shakespeare Business Centre,**
**245a Coldharbour Lane, London SW9 8RR**
**T: 020 7733 1603**
**Helpline: 0845 450 0355**
**E: info@roadpeace.org**
**www.roadpeace.org**
**CEO: Beccie D'Cunha**
RoadPeace is Britain's national charity
for road traffic victims, set up in 1992.
RoadPeace provides support for people
bereaved and injured in road crashes through
a national helpline and gives specialist advice
and support. RoadPeace supports road
danger reduction and the promotion of
transport policies which give greater
consideration to vulnerable road users
and the environment.
**Employees: 5**
**Volunteers: 100**

## Roald Dahl's Marvellous Children's Charity

**81a High Street, Great Missenden,**
**Buckinghamshire HP16 0AL**
**T: 01494 890465**
**E: richardp@roalddahlcharity.org**
**www.roalddahlcharity.org**
**Chief Executive: Richard Piper**
Making life better for children with severe,
rare and under-supported health conditions.
We create new Roald Dahl Nurse posts, give
grants directly to families, and run a range
of proactive programmes in partnership
with others.
**Employees: 11**
**Volunteers: 6**
**Income: £869,730 (2013–14)**

## Roots HR CIC

**The Coach House, 30a Church Street,**
**Kidderminster, Worcestershire DY10 2AX**
**T: 01562 840060**
**E: admin@rootshr.org.uk**
**www.rootshr.org.uk**
**Chief Executive : Jan Golding**
Roots HR CIC is the UK's specialist
consultancy for human resources and health
and safety services for the social sector. We
enable organisations to continually improve
performance and sustainability through
better people management, whilst ensuring
an understanding of and compliance with
employment legislation. Founded in 2009,
we operate as a social enterprise, providing

high-quality and affordable services to social
sector organisations.
**Employees: 7**
**Regional offices: 1**
**Income: £230,000 (2015–16)**

## RoSA

**RoSA, PO Box 151, Rugby,**
**Warwickshire CV21 3WR**
**T: 01788 551150**
**Helpline: 01788 551151**
**E: lindalewis.rosa@btconnect.com**
**www.rosasupport.org**
**Agency Director: Linda Lewis**
We are an independent charity working with
survivors of rape, sexual assault and childhood
sexual abuse and their families. We offer a
completely confidential service and support
women, men, young people and children
from the age of five. All counsellors and
support workers at RoSA have received
comprehensive specialist training and work
to BACP guidelines. We are the founder
members of The Survivors Trust, a national
umbrella agency.
**Employees: 8**
**Volunteers: 50**
**Regional offices: 1**

## Rotary International in Great Britain and Ireland

**Kinwarton Road, Alcester,**
**Warwickshire B49 6BP**
**T: 01789 765411**
**F: 01789 765570**
**E: secretary@ribi.org**
**www.ribi.org**
There are some 58,000 Rotarians in Great
Britain and Ireland in 1,845 clubs, helping
those in need and working towards world
understanding and peace.
**Employees: 18**
**Volunteers: 60000**

## Rounders England

**Unit 15, Venture 1 Business Park,**
**Long Acre Close, Holbrook Industrial Estate,**
**Sheffield, South Yorkshire S20 3FR**
**T: 0114 248 0357**
**E: oliver.wilson@roundersengland.co.uk**
**www.roundersengland.co.uk**
**Operations Director: Alison Steel**
Rounders England is the sport's governing
body in England. Based in Sheffield it
provides a structure for the sport from the
Board, county associations and clubs right

the way through to individual members
and volunteers.
**Employees: 13**
**Volunteers: 1000+**
**Regional offices: 1**

## Rowntree Society

**Tanners Yard, Huntington Road,**
**Huntington, York,**
**North Yorkshire YO31 1ET**
**T: 01904 425499**
**E: info@rowntreesociety.org.uk**
**www.rowntreewalks.org**
**Volunteers: 12**

## Roy Castle Lung Cancer Foundation

**200 London Road, Liverpool L3 9TA**
**T: 0871 220 5426**
**F: 0871 220 5427**
**E: foundation@roycastle.co.uk**
**www.roycastle.org**
The Foundation: secures the development of
the Roy Castle International Centre for Lung
Cancer research and health promotion;
promotes and funds clinical laboratory and
epidemiological research into the causes,
prevention and treatment of lung cancer;
provides amenities intended to improve the
quality of life of the patients and relieve and
alleviate the distress of relatives of the patients.
**Employees: 60**
**Volunteers: 100**
**Regional offices: 2**

## Royal Academy of Dance

**36 Battersea Square, London SW11 3RA**
**T: 020 7326 8000**
**F: 020 7924 3129**
**E: info@rad.org.uk**
**www.rad.org.uk**
**Chief Executive: Luke Rittner**
The Royal Academy of Dance is a global
organisation with over 13,000 members.
With offices in 79 countries and headquarters
in London, it is the largest ballet examination
and teacher training institution in the world.
Its mission is to promote knowledge,
understanding and practice of dance
internationally. It seeks to accomplish its
mission through examining students of ballet,
educating and training teachers of dance
and promoting the study and performance
of dance.
**Employees: 180**

## Royal Agricultural Benevolent Institution

Shaw House, 27 West Way, Botley, Oxford, Oxfordshire OX2 0QH
T: 01865 724931
Helpline: 01865 727888
F: 01865 202025
E: info@rabi.org.uk
www.rabi.org.uk
Chief Executive: Paul Burrows
The national farming charity for England and Wales. Helping those in need in the farming community during times of hardship.
Employees: 114

## Royal Air Force Benevolent Fund

67 Portland Place, London W1B 1AR
T: 020 7580 8343
Helpline: 0800 169 2942
F: 020 7636 7005
E: enquiries@rafbf.org.uk
www.rafbf.org
Controller: Robert Wright
The Royal Air Force Benevolent Fund provides assistance to members and former members of the Royal Air Force, and their dependants, who need support as a consequence of poverty, sickness, disability, accident, infirmity or other adversity.
Employees: 120
Volunteers: 30
Regional offices: 2

## Royal Air Force Music Charitable Trust

24 Bayford Drive, Newark, Nottinghamshire NG24 2GS
T: 01636 707857
Helpline: 07748 945160
E: office@rafmct.org.uk
www.rafmct.org.uk
Founding Director and Honorary Administrator: Malcolm Goodman MBE
Promoting welfare funding through the performance of live music by Royal Air Force musicians.
Volunteers: 10
Regional offices: 1
Income: £15,000 (2013–14)

## Royal Air Forces Association

117.5 Loughborough Road, Leicester LE4 5ND
T: 0116 266 5224
Helpline: 0800 018 2361
F: 0116 266 5012
E: enquiries@rafa.org.uk
www.rafa.org.uk
Secretary General: Jane Easton
The RAF Association is a membership and charitable organisation offering support to all serving and former members of the RAF and their dependants during times of need. Its network of welfare officers provides advice, financial guidance, friendship and, where appropriate, can signpost to other agencies for assistance.
Employees: 179
Volunteers: 400
Regional offices: 9

## Royal Alfred Seafarers Society

Head Office, Weston Acres, Woodmasterne Lane, Banstead, Surrey SM7 3HA
T: 01737 353763
F: 020 8401 2592
E: royalalfred@btopenworld.com
www.royalalfredseafarers.com
Provides long-term care for retired or disabled seafarers and their dependants.
Employees: 86
Volunteers: 2

## Royal Association for Deaf people

18 Westside Centre, London Road, Stanway, Colchester, Essex CO3 8PH
T: 0845 688 2525
F: 0845 688 2526
E: info@royaldeaf.org.uk
www.royaldeaf.org.uk
RAD promote the welfare and interests of deaf people. We believe deaf people should receive the same access and opportunities as hearing people. We mainly support deaf people whose first or preferred language is British Sign Language (BSL) but also work with people with all forms of deafness including those who are hard of hearing, deafened or deafblind.
Employees: 100
Volunteers: 50
Regional offices: 3

## Royal Blind Society for the UK

RBS House, 59/61 Sea Lane, Rustington, West Sussex BN16 2RQ
T: 01903 857023
F: 01903 859166
E: royalblindsoc@aol.com
www.royalblindsociety.org
Director: Graham Booth
Aims to assist blind and partially sighted people to cope with the additional costs of blindness and to experience opportunities that they could not otherwise have.
Employees: 48
Volunteers: 25
Regional offices: 1

## Royal British Legion

Haig House, 199 Borough High Street, London SE1 1AA
T: 020 7973 7200
F: 020 7973 7399
E: info@britishlegion.org.uk
www.britishlegion.org.uk
The Royal British Legion provides financial, social and emotional support to millions who have served and are currently serving in the Armed Forces, and their dependants. Currently, nearly 10.5 million people are eligible for our support and we receive thousands of calls for help every year.
Employees: 880
Volunteers: 600000
Regional offices: 65

## Royal British Legion Industries Ltd

Hall Road, Aylesford, Kent ME20 7NL
T: 01622 795923
F: 01622 718744
E: phillip.defrain@rbli.co.uk
www.rbli.co.uk
RBLI provides employment, training and support for people, including those with disabilities, plus care and support for ex-servicemen, women and families.

## Royal British Legion Women's Section

199 Borough High Stree, London SE1 1AA
T: 020 7973 7378
E: women@britishlegion.org.uk
www.rblws.org.uk
Promotes the welfare of ex-service women, the wives, widows, children and dependants of those who have served in any of HM Forces who find themselves in difficulties; to augment the activities of the Royal British Legion and to assist them in raising funds.

## Royal College of General Practitioners

30 Euston Square, Stephenson Way, London NW1 2FB
T: 020 3188 7400
E: info@rcgp.org.uk
www.rcgp.org.uk
Encouraging, fostering and maintaining the highest possible standards in general medical practice.
Employees: 170
Regional offices: 31

## Royal College of Midwives

15 Mansfield Street, London W1G 9NH
T: 020 7312 3535
F: 020 7313 3536
E: info@rcm.org.uk
www.rcm.org.uk

Aims to advance the art and science of midwifery and to maintain high professional standards.
Employees: 70
Volunteers: 2000
Regional offices: 4

## Royal College of Obstetricians and Gynaecologists

27 Sussex Place, Regent's Park,
London NW1 4RG
T: 020 7772 6200
E: iwylie@rcog.org.uk
www.rcog.org.uk
Chief Executive: Ian Wylie
The professional membership organisation for obstetricians and gynaecologists. We educate and examine doctors in the speciality both in the UK and throughout the world and we support their continuing development. We set standards for women's health and assist developing countries with maternal health education.
Employees: 140

## Royal College of Paediatrics and Child Health

15 Nicholas Gardens, Woking,
Surrey GU22 8SD
T: 01932 346843
E: enquiries@rcpch.ac.uk
www.rcpch.ac.uk
Promotes research into the cause, treatment, cure and prevention of Reye's syndrome and Reye-like illnesses; provides support for parents whose children have suffered from these diseases and creates awareness and professional knowledge.

## Royal College of Paediatrics and Child Health

50 Hallam Street, London W1W 6DE
T: 020 7307 5616
E: enquiries@rcpch.ac.uk
www.rcpch.ac.uk
Promotes and publishes paediatric research; organises scientific meetings; advises government and other professional bodies on problems of child health; oversees the training of doctors specialising in paediatrics and child health; issues guidance on related issues.

## Royal Commonwealth Society

Award House, 7–11 St Matthew Street,
London SW1P 2JT
T: 020 3727 4300
E: info@thercs.org
www.thercs.org
Director: Michael Lake CBE

The Royal Commonwealth Society is a network of individuals and organisations committed to improving the lives and prospects of Commonwealth citizens worldwide. Promoting an understanding of the values and working of the Commonwealth, the Society engages with its educational, civil society, business and governmental networks to address issues that matter to the citizens of the Commonwealth and the world.
Employees: 9
Volunteers: 1

## Royal Corps of Signals Benevolent Fund

Regimental Headquarters, Griffin House,
Blandford Camp, Blandford Forum,
Dorset DT11 8RH
T: 01258 482081
E: soinc-rhq-regtsec@mod.uk
Regimental Secretary: Colonel Terry Canham
Employees: 5

## Royal Geographical Society

1 Kensington Gore, London SW7 2AR
T: 020 7591 3088
E: enquiries@rgs.org
www.rgs.org
A world-leading society for geographers and geographical learning dedicated to the promotion and development of knowledge together with its application to the challenges facing society and the environment.

## Royal Humane Society

50/51 Temple Chambers,
3–7 Temple Avenue, London EC4Y 0HP
T: 020 7936 2942
E: secretary@royalhumanesociety.org.uk
www.royalhumanesociety.org.uk
Secretary: Dick Wilkinson
The Royal Humane Society is a charity that assesses acts of bravery in the saving of human life and makes awards. These range from certificates and testimonials to bronze, silver and gold medals.
Employees: 2
Volunteers: 19
Income: £56,000 (2014–15)

## Royal Institute of British Architects

66 Portland Place, London W1B 1AD
T: 020 7580 5533
E: info@inst.riba.org
www.architecture.com
RIBA is the UK body for architecture and the architectural profession. Providing support for 40,500 members worldwide in the form of training, technical services, publications and events, and sets standards for the education of architects, both in the UK and overseas.

## Royal Life Saving Society UK

River House, High Street, Broom,
Warwickshire B50 4HN
T: 01789 773994
F: 01789 773995
E: lifesavers@rlss.org.uk
www.lifesavers.org.uk
Employees: 29
Volunteers: 13500
Regional offices: 50

## Royal Literary Fund

3 Johnson's Court, Off Fleet Street,
London EC4A 3EA
T: 020 7353 7159
F: 020 7353 1350
E: eileen.gunn@rlf.org.uk
www.rlf.org.uk
Chief Executive: Eileen Gunn
Provides assistance to established published authors of several books who are in financial difficulties due to personal or professional setbacks.
Employees: 4

## Royal London Society

16 Manor Road, Bexhill-on-Sea,
East Sussex TN40 1SP
T: 01424 218097
E: office@royallondonsociety.org.uk
www.royallondonsociety.org.uk

## Royal London Society for the Blind

Dorton House, Wilderness Avenue, Seal,
Sevenoaks, Kent TN15 0EB
T: 01732 592665
Helpline: 01732 592500
F: 01732 592668
E: enquiries@rlsb.org.uk
www.rlsb.org.uk
Chief Executive: Brian Cooney
The RLSB exists to provide education, training, transition and employment services that enable people who are blind or partially sighted to overcome the discrimination they face and the social exclusion and poverty that many experience.
Employees: 300
Volunteers: 25
Regional offices: 3

## Royal Masonic Benevolent Institution

20 Great Queen Street,
London WC2B 5BG
T: 020 7596 2400
E: enquiries@rmbi.org.uk
www.rmbi.org.uk
Provides support to freemasons and their dependants, by providing residential or nursing accommodation through our homes situated throughout the country.

## Royal Medical Benevolent Fund

24 King's Road, Wimbledon,
London SW19 8QN
T: 020 8540 9194
F: 020 8542 0494
E: cbogle@rmbf.org
www.rmbf.org
**Chief Executive Officer: Steve Crone**
The objectives of the charity are to prevent or relieve poverty and to relieve need arising from youth, age, ill health, disability and bereavement among people who are doctors or who have worked as doctors, and medical students and the dependants of such individuals.
Employees: 13
Volunteers: 300

## Royal National Institute of the Blind

105 Judd Street, London WC1H 9NE
T: 020 7388 1266
F: 020 7388 2034
E: helpline@rnib.org.uk
www.rnib.org.uk
RNIB are the UK's leading charity offering information, support and advice to over two million people with sight problems. We fight for equal rights for people with sight problems. We fund pioneering research into preventing and treating eye disease and promote eye health by running public health awareness campaigns.
Employees: 2923
Volunteers: 5000
Regional offices: 5

## Royal National Lifeboat Institution

West Quay Road, Poole, Dorset BH15 1HZ
T: 01202 663000
F: 01202 663167
E: info@rnli.org.uk
www.rnli.org.uk
The RNLI aims to save lives by changing attitudes and behaviour among people who use the sea regularly. Its lifeguards patrol more than 70 beaches and assisted more than 10,000 people last year. Its boats rescued more than 8,000 people
Employees: 1000
Volunteers: 4600
Regional offices: 10

## Royal National Mission to Deep Sea Fishermen

Mather House, 4400 Parkway,
Solent Business Park, Hampshire PO15 7FJ
T: 020 7487 5101
E: enquiries@rnmdsf.org.uk
www.fishermensmission.org.uk
Supports fishermen and their families throughout the UK and in the Falkland Islands.

## Royal Naval Benevolent Society for Officers

70 Porchester Terrace, Bayswater,
London W2 3TP
T: 020 7402 5231
E: rnoc@arno.org.uk
www.arno.org.uk
**CEO: Cdr Mike Goldthorpe**
The Society, working title RNOC, provides financial assistance when in need to officers of the Royal Navy and Royal Marines and their respective reserves, both active service and retired, and to their widows, ex-wives and dependants.
Employees: 3
Income: £450,000 (2014–15)

## Royal Naval Benevolent Trust

Castaway House, 311 Twyford Avenue,
Portsmouth PO2 8RN
T: 023 9269 0112
F: 023 9266 0852
E: rnbt@rnbt.org.uk
www.rnbt.org.uk
The RNBT exists to give help, in cases of need, to those who are serving or have served as ratings in the Royal Navy or as other ranks in the Royal Marines, and their dependants. The RNBT also manages its own care home in Gillingham, Kent, which offers first-class nursing and personal care in excellent

accommodation for former sailors, Royal Marines, their wives and widows.
Employees: 100
Volunteers: 30

## Royal Navy and Royal Marine Children's Fund

311 Twyford Avenue, Stamshaw,
Portsmouth, Hampshire PO2 8RN
T: 023 9263 9534
F: 023 9267 7574
E: rnchildren@btconnect.com
www.rnrmchildrensfund.org.uk
Assists children, under the age of 25, of serving and ex-serving members of RN and RM who are in need, hardship or distress. Assistance may be given in the form of grants to individuals or by paying for goods or services or facilities for those in need.
Employees: 4
Volunteers: 12
Regional offices: 1

## Royal Society

6 Carlton House Terrace,
London SW1Y 5AG
T: 020 7451 2500
E: info@royalsoc.ac.uk
royalsociety.org
Promotes the natural sciences, including mathematics and all applied sciences such as engineering and medicine. The Society encourages both national and international scientific activities (in a similar way to national academies overseas), adhering to many international, non-governmental scientific organisations and promoting co-operative research and exchanges through agreements with overseas academies.

## Royal Society for Public Health

John Snow House, 59 Mansell Street,
London E1 8AN
T: 020 7265 7300
E: info@rsph.org.uk
www.rsph.org.uk
**Chief Executive: Shirley Cramer**
RSPH is an independent, multi-disciplinary charity dedicated to the improvement of the public's health and wellbeing. Formed in October 2008 with the merger of the Royal Society of Health and the Royal Institute of Public Health, we help inform policy and practice, working to educate, empower and support communities and individuals to live healthily.
Employees: 45

## Royal Society for the Prevention of Cruelty to Animals

Wilberforce Way, Southwater, Horsham, West Sussex RH13 9RS
T: 0300 123 0100
Helpline: 0300 123 4555
F: 0303 123 0100
E: supportercare@rspca.org.uk
www.rspca.org.uk
Chief Executive: Mark Watts
The RSPCA will, by all lawful means, promote kindness to, prevent cruelty to, and alleviate suffering of animals.
Employees: 1668
Volunteers: 7000
Regional offices: 5

## Royal Society for the Protection of Birds

The Lodge, Potton Road, Sandy, Bedfordshire SG19 2DL
T: 01767 680551
F: 01767 691178
E: alan.sharpe@rspb.org.uk
www.rspb.org.uk
Chief Executive: Mike Clarke
The RSPB speaks out for birds and wildlife, tackling the problems that threaten our environment. Our work helps all nature, every buzzing, crawling, slithering, fluttering part of it, and we look after wild places for you to enjoy too. We have a million members who are inspired by nature and give it a voice. Nature is amazing! Help us keep it that way.
Employees: 2151
Volunteers: 15765
Regional offices: 14

## Royal Society of Medicine

1 Wimpole Street, London W1G 0AE
T: 020 7290 2900
F: 020 7290 2989
E: marketing@rsm.ac.uk
www.rsm.ac.uk
Chief Executive: Ian Balmer
The RSM is an independent, apolitical organisation and one of the largest providers of continuing medical education in the UK. We provide accredited courses, which are vital in allowing healthcare professionals their continuing freedom to practice. Our aims are: to provide a broad range of educational activities for medical and healthcare professionals including students of these disciplines; to promote an exchange of information and ideas on the science, practice and organisation of medicine.
Employees: 192
Volunteers: 500

## Royal Television Society

3 Dorset Rise, London EC4Y 8EN
T: 020 7822 2810
F: 020 7822 2811
E: info@rts.org.uk
www.rts.org.uk
Chief Executive: Theresa Wise
The Society's objective and principal activity is the advancement of public education in the science, practice, technology and art of television.
Employees: 12
Volunteers: 600

## Royal Theatrical Fund

11 Garrick Street, Covent Garden, London WC2E 9AR
T: 020 7836 3322
F: 020 7379 8273
E: admin@trtf.com
www.trtf.com
Chair: Paul Gane
The Fund helps those in the entertainment media who cannot work through illness, adversity or infirmity.
Employees: 2

## Royal UK Beneficent Association (Rukba)

18 Avonmore Road, London W14 8RR
T: 020 7605 4200
F: 020 7605 4201
E: charity@independentage.org
www.rukba.org.uk
Grants annuities and provides friendship for older people who are impoverished or infirm.
Employees: 218
Volunteers: 1100
Regional offices: 15

## RP Fighting Blindness

PO Box 350, Buckingham MK18 1GZ
T: 01280 821334
Helpline: 0845 123 2354
E: info@rpfightingblindness.org.uk
www.rpfightingblindness.org.uk
Chief Executive: Tina Houlihan
RP Fighting Blindness aims to raise funds for scientific research to provide treatments for retinitis pigmentosa (RP). RP Fighting Blindness provides information and support services to people with RP and their families.
Employees: 14
Volunteers: 110

## Rugby Football Foundation

Rugby House, 200 Whitton Road
T: 020 8831 7985
E: foundation@therfu.com
www.rfu.com/rff
RFF Administrator: Fran Thornber

## Runnymede Trust

7 Plough Yard, Shoreditch, London EC2A 3LP
T: 020 7377 9222
F: 020 7377 6622
E: info@runnymedetrust.org
www.runnymedetrust.org
Director: Dr Robert Berkeley
The Runnymede Trust is an independent policy research organisation focusing on equality and justice through the promotion of a successful multi-ethnic society. Founded as a charitable educational trust, Runnymede has a long track record in policy research, working in close collaboration with eminent thinkers and policy makers in the public, private and voluntary sectors.
Employees: 12
Volunteers: 2

## Rural Action Yorkshire

E: leah.swain@ruralyorkshire.org.uk

## Rural Community Action Nottinghamshire

Newstead Centre, Tilford Road, Newstead, Nottinghamshire NG15 0BS
T: 01623 727600
E: rcrowder@rcan.org.uk
www.rcan.org.uk
Chief Executive: Robert Crowder
Rural Community Action Nottinghamshire (RCAN) is an independent voluntary organisation and registered charity, which exists to promote the social and economic well-being of rural communities. Examples of our work include tackling health issues, solving transport access problems, improving community facilities and addressing social exclusion by developing initiatives which allows everyone to play a full part in the life of their community.
Employees: 17
Volunteers: 30
Income: £765,000 (2014–15)

## Rural Housing Trust

Unit 8, Graphite Square, London SE11 5EE
T: 020 7793 8114
E: info@ruralhousing.org.uk
www.ruralhousing.org.uk
Provides affordable housing for local people
in villages throughout England.

## Rural Media Company

Sullivan House, 72–80 Widemarsh Street,
Hereford, Herefordshire HR4 9HG
T: 01432 344039
F: 01432 270539
E: helenj@ruralmedia.co.uk
www.ruralmedia.co.uk
Chief Executive: Nic Millington
The Rural Media Company brings
community and informal education, training
and advocacy together with professional
filmmaking and media industry skills. Working
throughout the UK with local, regional and
national partners in public, voluntary and
independent organisations, to develop short
and long term projects, as well as undertaking
commissions for video/DVD.
Employees: 17
Volunteers: 10
Regional offices: 1

## RYA Sailability

RYA House, Ensign Way, Hamble,
Southampton, Hampshire SO31 4YA
T: 0845 345 0403
F: 023 8060 4286
E: info@ryasailability.org
www.rya.org.uk/sailability
The RYA programme for disability sailing.
Committed to development of sailing clubs
and organisations throughout the UK to
promote, encourage and find people with
disabilities to take up sailing in all its forms.
Employees: 3

## SABRE Research UK

PO Box 18653, Hampstead,
London NW3 4UJ
T: 020 7722 9394
E: office@sabre.org.uk
www.sabre.org.uk
Founder/Trustee: Susan Green
An independent charity that represents the
interests of patients and research volunteers
by raising awareness of the need to apply
rigorous research methodology to the way
animal research is conducted and evaluated.
A more evidence-based approach is essential
if the value of animal experiments is to be
determined and the safety and efficacy of
medical research to be improved. The charity
has no links to political parties, animal lobby
groups or the pharmaceutical industry.
Volunteers: 4

## SAD Association

PO Box 989, Steyning BN44 3HG
E: info@sada.org.uk
www.sada.org.uk
Informs the public and health professions
about SAD (seasonal affective disorder) and
supports and advises sufferers of the illness.
Volunteers: 7

## Safe Partnership Limited

3 East Street, Wareham,
Dorset BH20 4NN
T: 01929 55100
F: 01929 553300
E: malcolm@safepartnership.org
www.safepartnership.org
Chief Executive: Malcolm Macleod
Safe Partnership is the national charity
that provides home security and advice to
vulnerable victims of crimes such as domestic
violence, burglary, robbery, distraction
burglary, identity theft and hate crime and
to those in fear of such crimes. We also
undertake proactive, preventative work with
young people, to help them recognise the
early signs of relationship abuse to prevent
them becoming victims or perpetrators of
violence and crime when they grow up.
Employees: 11
Volunteers: 5

## SafeHands for Mothers

23 Fitzjohns Avenue, London NW3 5JY
T: 020 7433 0792
E: ndm@safehands.org
www.safehands.org
Founder Director: Nancy Durrell McKenna
Our vision is a world where no woman dies in
pregnancy and childbirth. We work to achieve
this through the production of films –
documentaries that raise awareness of
important issues such as FGM, obstetric
fistula, child marriage, HIV/AIDS, family
planning and films which educate and inspire
frontline health workers, women and their
communities.
Employees: 3
Volunteers: 2
Income: £146,146 (2014–15)

## SafeLives

Suite 2a, Whitefriars, Lewins Mead,
Bristol BS1 2NT
T: 0117 403 3220
E: info@safelives.org.uk
safelives.org.uk
SafeLives is a national charity dedicated to
ending domestic abuse. Previously called
Co-ordinated Action Against Domestic
Abuse (Caada), we chose our new name
because we're here for one reason: to make
sure all families are safe. Our experts find out
what works to stop domestic abuse. Then we
do everything we can to ensure families
everywhere benefit. It works: after getting
the right help, more than 60% of victims tell
us that the abuse stops.
Employees: 50

## Safer Places

PO Box 2489, Essex CM18 6NS
T: 0845 074 3216
Helpline: 0330 102 5811
E: allison.gardner@saferplaces.co.uk
www.saferplaces.co.uk
Director of Business Services: Allison Gardner
Safer Places is an independent domestic
abuse charity dedicated to supporting adults
and children affected by domestic abuse. We
provide a wide range of services to support
clients and respond to their individual needs
and circumstances, whether it is in our safe
accommodation or in the community. We
work in a holistic and empowering way to help
enable clients to live independent lives free
from domestic abuse. Services are available in
East Hertfordshire, Essex and Southend.
Employees: 77
Volunteers: 28
Income: £3,400,000 (2015–16)

## Saferworld

The Grayston Centre,
28 Charles Square N1 6HT
T: 020 7324 4646
F: 020 7324 4647
E: communications@saferworld.org.uk
www.saferworld.org.uk
**Executive Director: Paul Murphy**
Saferworld is an independent international
organisation working to prevent violent
conflict and build safer lives. We work with
local people affected by conflict to improve
their safety and sense of security and
conduct wider research and analysis. We use
this evidence and learning to improve local,
national and international policies and
practices that can help build lasting peace.
**Employees: 149**
**Regional offices: 12**

## SAGGA

5 Portway Drive, Tutbury, Burton-on-Trent,
Staffordshire DE13 9HU
T: 01283 520685
E: treasurer@sagga.org.uk
www.sagga.org.uk
Provides a pool of professional people with
experience of the Scout and Guide
movement who are ready to assist with
projects connected with the movement;
takes an independent look at progress and
developments within the movement;
supports and encourages Scout and Guide
clubs in institutions of higher education.

## Sahara Communities Abroad (SACOMA)

108 Cranbrook Road, Ilford, Essex IG1 4LZ
T: 020 8554 9444 (also fax)
E: perez@sacoma.org.uk
www.sacomauk.com
**Chief Executive: Perez Ochieng**
Supports African migrant communities to
develop skills for enterprise and work. We
provide information, advice and guidance on
matters such as housing, welfare, pensions,
business start up, training and education.
We provide accredited training and business
support for SMEs.
**Employees: 24**
**Volunteers: 40**

## Sailors' Children's Society

Francis Reckitt House, Cottingham Road,
Hull HU6 7RJ
T: 01482 342331
E: info@sailorschildren.org.uk
www.sailorschildren.org.uk
**Chief Officer: Deanne Thomas**
A maritime charity caring for the children of
deceased and disabled seafarers and those
in severe financial hardship. The aim of the
Society is to provide not only the basic
necessities of life such as clothing but to allow
the children to partake in everyday activities.
Financial support includes single parent
families and families where one of the parents
is too ill, or disabled, to work and the other
acts as carer.
**Employees: 6**

## Sailors' Society

74 St Annes Road, Southampton,
Hampshire SO19 9FF
T: 023 8051 5950
F: 023 8051 5951
E: admin@sailors-society.org
www.sailors-society.org
**Chief Executive: Stuart Rivers**
The objectives for which the Society is
established are the advancement of the
Christian religion, the advancement of
education and the relief of poverty and
distress among the world's seafarers and their
families.
**Employees: 76**

## Salmon Youth Centre

E: sam.adofo@salmonyouthcentre.org

## Salvation Army

Territorial HQ, 101 Newington Causeway,
London SE1 6BN
T: 020 7367 4864
F: 020 7367 4728
E: thq@salvationarmy.org.uk
www.salvationarmy.org.uk
Expresses practical Christianity through
social action regardless of class, creed or sex.
Programmes include homeless and drug
rehabilitation centres, and nearly 16,000
church and community centres. Also
supports the work of the emergency services
by providing refreshments, shelter and
counselling at major incidents.
**Employees: 4000**
**Volunteers: 40000**
**Regional offices: 18**

## Samaritans

The Upper Mill, Kingston Road, Ewell,
Surrey KT17 2AF
T: 020 8394 8300
Helpline: 0845 790 9090
F: 020 8394 8301
E: supportercare@samaritans.org
www.samaritans.org
**Chief Executive: Dominic Rudd**
Available 24 hours a day to provide
confidential emotional support for people
who are experiencing feelings of distress
and despair, including those that may lead
to suicide.
**Employees: 75**
**Volunteers: 15400**
**Regional offices: 203**

## SANE

1st Floor, Cityside House, 40 Adler Street,
London E1 1EE
T: 020 7375 1002
Helpline: 0845 767 8000
F: 020 7375 2162
E: info@sane.org.uk
www.sane.org.uk
**Chief Executive: Marjorie Wallace**
SANE is a national mental health charity that
works to: raise awareness; combat stigma and
increase understanding of mental illness;
initiate research into causes, treatments
and experiences of mental illness; provide
emotional support and information to anyone
affected by mental illness, including families,
friends and carers. One-to-one support:
helpline, Textcare and email. Peer support:
Support Forum. For more information,
visit the SANE website.
**Employees: 30**
**Volunteers: 120**
**Regional offices: 1**

## Sangat Advice Centre

Sancroft Road, Harrow HA3 7NS
T: 020 8427 0659
F: 020 8863 2196
E: info@sangat.org.uk
www.sangat.org.uk
**Manager: Kanti Nagda**
Sangat Advice Centre provides legal advice
on welfare benefits, housing, immigration,
debt, etc. We represent clients at the
immigration and welfare benefits tribunals.
We also provide IT learning facilities and assist
BME carers.
**Employees: 4**
**Volunteers: 6**
**Income: £90,000 (2010–11)**

## Savana

Wood House, Etruria Road, Hanley,
Stoke on Trent, Staffordshire ST1 5NQ
T: 01782 433205
Helpline: 01782 433204
E: info@savana.org.uk
www.savana.org.uk
**Chief Operations Officer: Kay Glover**
Savana is a company limited by guarantee
with charitable status providing support
services for those who have experienced or
who are affected by (including relatives and
supporters) any form of sexual violence or
abuse including within domestic abuse,
whether recently or in the past.
**Employees: 14**
**Volunteers: 30**
**Regional offices: 1**

## SAVE Britain's Heritage

70 Cowcross Street, London EC1M 6EJ
T: 020 7253 3500
E: save@btinternet.com
www.savebritainsheritage.org
Campaigns for the retention and
rehabilitation of historic buildings and areas.

## Save the Children UK

1 St John's Lane, London EC1M 4AR
T: 020 7012 6400
F: 020 7012 6963
E: supporter.care@savethechildren.org.uk
www.savethechildren.org.uk
Aims to relieve the distress and hardship, and
to promote the welfare of children in any
country or countries, place or places with
particular emphasis on disaster relief,
emergency response, campaigns and
programmes.
**Employees: 3673**
**Volunteers: 11000**
**Regional offices: 567**

## SBA The Solicitors' Charity

1 Jaggard Way, London SW12 8SG
T: 020 8675 6440
E: sec@sba.org.uk
www.sba.org.uk
Aims to financially assist solicitors and their
dependants in need, who are or have been on
the roll for England and Wales.

## SCA Group

Amplevine House, Dukes Road,
Southampton, Hampshire SO14 0ST
T: 023 8036 6663
F: 023 8036 6666
E: rosalind.lucas@scagroup.co.uk
www.scagroup.co.uk
**CEO: Maria Mills**
The Social Care in Action (SCA) Group is
one of the leading social enterprises in the
UK. Established over 20 years ago, SCA
provides an outstanding range of health and
social care services including care, NHS
dentistry, transport, a health and wellbeing
centre, an award-winning training centre and
consultancy services. Everything SCA does is
focussed on supporting its customers to lead
better lives.
**Employees: 596**
**Volunteers: 100**
**Regional offices: 4**

## School for Social Entrepreneurs

18 Victoria Park Square, London E2 9PF
T: 020 8981 0300
F: 020 8983 4655
E: office@sse.org.uk
www.sse.org.uk
The School for Social Entrepreneurs exists
to provide training and opportunities to
enable people to use their creative and
entrepreneurial abilities more fully for social
benefit. We also want to recruit more
innovative and capable people into voluntary
and other organisations.
**Employees: 14**

## School Governors' One-Stop Shop

Unit 11, Shepperton House, 83,
London N1 3DF
T: 020 7354 9805
F: 020 7288 9549
E: info@sgoss.org.uk
www.sgoss.org.uk
**Chief Executive: Steve Acklam**
SGOSS is dedicated to recruiting volunteers
to fill some of the 40,000 school governor
vacancies that exist across England.
Governors do not have to know about
education or be a parent, they simply need to
be over 18 and want to make a difference. All
of SGOSS's services are free to volunteers,
employers, schools and local authorities.
**Employees: 17**
**Volunteers: 11500**
**Regional offices: 1**

## School Library Association

1 Pine Court, Kembrey Park, Swindon,
Wiltshire SN2 8AD
T: 01793 530166
F: 01793 481182
E: info@sla.org.uk
www.sla.org.uk
**Director: Tricia Adams**
Promotes the development of school libraries
as central to the curriculum at primary and
secondary level and acts as a national voice
for school libraries.
**Employees: 6**
**Volunteers: 20**

## School-Home Support (SHS)

Cityside House, 40 Adler Street,
Whitechapel, London E1 1EE
T: 020 7426 5000
F: 020 7426 5001
E: enquiries@schoolhomesupport.org.uk
www.schoolhomesupport.org.uk
**Chief Executive: Jan Tallis**
Through the use of highly trained,
independent practitioners based in schools,
SHS works with disadvantaged children and
their families to overcome the barriers that
get in the way of learning. Currently working
in 90 schools in London, as well as offering
training in family support work in London,
Yorkshire and the North East.
**Employees: 100**
**Regional offices: 1**

## SciDevNet

97–99 Dean Street, London W1D 3TE
T: 020 7291 3690
F: 020 7843 4596
E: info@scidev.net
www.scidev.net
SciDev.Net aims to: promote for the public's
benefit the advancement of education in
science, technology and other matters
connected with the development of society
and in particular to disseminate useful
research findings and provide for a critical
discussion; undertake any other charitable
purpose.
**Employees: 5**

## Scoliosis Association (UK)

4 Ivebury Court, 323–327 Latimer Road,
London W10 6RA
T: 020 8964 5343
Helpline: 020 8964 1166
E: info@sauk.org.uk
www.sauk.org.uk
Chair of Trustees: Dr Stephanie Clark
SAUK is the only national support
organisation for people with scoliosis and
their families. SAUK aims to: provide advice,
support and information to people affected
by scoliosis, and their families; raise
awareness among health professionals and
the general public.
Employees: 5
Volunteers: 4

## Scope

PO Box 833, Milton Keynes MK12 5NY
Helpline: 0808 800 3333
F: 01908 321051
E: response@scope.org.uk
www.scope.org.uk
Chief Executive: Mark Atkinson
We're all about changing society for the
better, so that disabled people and their
families can have the same opportunities as
everyone else. We work with disabled people
and their families at every stage of their lives.
We offer practical support from information
services to education and everyday care. We
challenge assumptions about disability, we
influence decision-makers and we show what
can be possible. Visit the Scope website.
Employees: 3375
Regional offices: 4

## Scottish Council for Voluntary Organisations

Mansfield Traquair Centre,
15 Mansfield Place, Edinburgh EH3 6BB
T: 0131 474 8000
Helpline: 0800 169 0022
F: 0131 556 0279
E: enquiries@scvo.org.uk
www.scvo.org.uk
Chief Executive: Martin Sime
The Scottish Council for Voluntary
Organisations (SCVO) is the membership
organisation for Scotland's charities,
voluntary organisations and social enterprises.
SCVO works in partnership with the voluntary
sector to advance our shared values and
interests. We have over 1,600 members
who range from individuals and grassroots
groups to Scotland-wide organisations and
intermediary bodies. Through lobbying and
campaigning SCVO works to advance the

interests of our members and the people
and communities that they support.
Employees: 100
Volunteers: varies
Regional offices: 3
Income: £13,906,265 (2014–15)

## Scripture Union

207–209 Queensway, Bletchley,
Milton Keynes, Buckinghamshire MK2 2EB
T: 01908 856000
F: 01908 856111
E: info@scriptureunion.org.uk
www.scriptureunion.org.uk
National Director: Tim Hastie-Smith
Scripture Union is a Christian mission
movement working with churches to make
disciples of Jesus Christ among children,
young people and families. Activities include
running holidays, church-based events and
school Christian groups, producing a wide
range of publications and supporting those
who use its resources through training
programmes.
Employees: 76
Volunteers: 3900
Regional offices: 7

## Sea Watch Foundation

Ewyn y Don, Bull Bay, Amlwch,
Anglesey LL68 9SD
T: 01545 561227
E: info@seawatchfoundation.org.uk
www.seawatchfoundation.org.uk
Scientific Director: Dr Peter Evans
The principal objective of the charity is the
study, preservation and protection of
cetaceans and promoting awareness for the
benefit of the public.
Employees: 4
Volunteers: 15
Regional offices: 1
Income: £190,000 (2014–15)

## Seafarers UK

King George's Fund for Sailors,
8 Hatherley Street, London SW1P 2QT
T: 020 7932 0000
F: 020 7932 0095
E: seafarers@seafarers-uk.org
www.seafarers-uk.org
Director General: Commodore Barry Bryant
Seafarers UK (King George's Fund for
Sailors) is the UK's leading maritime welfare
charity that supports and promotes the many
organisations that look after seafarers in
need, plus their families and dependants,

across the Merchant Navy, Fishing Fleets,
Royal Navy and Royal Marines.
Employees: 22
Volunteers: 100+
Regional offices: 2

## Seafarers' Advice and Information Line

30 King William Walk,
Greenwich SE10 9HU
T: 0800 160 1842
E: advice@sailine.org.uk
www.sailine.org.uk
Manager: Miles Cowley
Seafarer's Advice and Information Line
(SAIL) is a Citizens Advice service dedicated
to working and retired seafarers and their
families across the UK. All advice is free and
confidential. See www.sailine.org.uk.
Employees: 10
Volunteers: 1

## SEAP

E: aoife.murphy@seap.org.uk

## SeeAbility

Newplan House, 41 East Street, Epsom,
Surrey KT17 1BL
T: 01372 755000
F: 01372 755001
E: d.scott-ralphs@seeability.org
www.seeability.org
Chief Executive: David Scott-Ralphs
SeeAbility works to enrich the lives of people
with sight loss and multiple disabilities across
the UK. We provide housing and personal
support, day activities, specialist therapeutic
support and a range of advisory services.
Employees: 500
Volunteers: 250
Regional offices: 2
Income: £15,122,538 (2013–14)

## Selby Trust Ltd

The Selby Centre, Selby Road,
White Hart Lane, Tottenham,
London E17 8JL
T: 020 8885 5499
F: 020 8493 8517
E: selbytrust@aol.com
www.selbytrust.co.uk
Chief Executive: Sona Mahtani
The Selby Trust promotes education
and leisure activities to local residents,
communities and young people facing
multiple disadvantages through lack of
education, poor health, living on low incomes
or in unemployment or needing new skills.
The vision of the Selby Trust to provide
affordable workspace in an environmentally
friendly manner with the strong participation
of diverse local communities of all cultures
is delivered through its motto of 'Many
Cultures One Community'.
Employees: 20
Volunteers: 10
Income: £927,570 (2013–14)

## Self Help Africa

Second Floor Suite, Westgate House,
Dickens Court, Off Hills Lane, Shrewsbury,
Shropshire SY1 1QU
T: 01743 277170
F: 01952 247158
E: infouk@selfhelpafrica.net
www.selfhelpafrica.org
Self Help Africa works with rural communities
in eight African countries to help them
improve their farms and their livelihoods. Self
Help Africa helps people in rural Africa grow
enough food to feed themselves, earn a living
and access basic services. Self Help Africa
equips people with the skills they need to
move out of poverty by training farmers in
new techniques and teaching basic business
skills.
Employees: 14
Volunteers: 50
Regional offices: 11

## Self injury Support

PO Box 3240, Bristol BS2 2EF
T: 0117 927 9600
Helpline: 0808 800 8088
E: info@selfinjurysupport.org.uk
www.selfinjurysupport.org.uk
Director: Hilary Lindsay
To provide support to women and girls
affected by self-injury/self harm. To raise
awareness of the issue by providing
information (for professionals, individuals
and family, friends and carers) and training
for workers in contact with people who

self-injure. Helpline 0808 800 8088.
Text Support 0780 047 2908.
Employees: 5
Volunteers: 45
Income: £105,000 (2013–14)

## Self management uk

32–36 Loman Street, Southwark,
London SE1 0EH
T: 0333 344 5840
E: marketing@selfmanagementuk.org
www.selfmanagementuk.org
Chief Executive: Renata Drinkwater
self management uk is a leading charity
which supports people with long-term
health conditions. We have over 10 years'
experience of delivering self-management
training, support and education to well over
120,000 patients. Our aims are: to provide
self-management support and training for
people living with long-term conditions,
increasing their wellbeing and confidence;
to promote the value of self-management;
to develop innovative and cost-effective ways
to deliver self-management education.
Employees: 40
Volunteers: 100
Regional offices: 2

## Sense

11–13 Clifton Terrace, London N4 3SR
T: 020 7272 7774
F: 020 7272 6012
E: jacqui.penalver@sense.org.uk
www.sense.org.uk
Sense is a national voluntary organisation
that works with and campaigns for the needs
of children and adults who are deafblind,
providing advice, support, information and
services for them, their families, carers and
the professionals who work with them.
Employees: 1600
Volunteers: 500
Regional offices: 13

## Sesame Institute (UK)

27 Blackfriars Road, London SE1 8NY
T: 020 7633 9690
E: info@sesame-institute.org
www.sesame-institute.org
Makes possible a fuller life, through applied
drama and movement, for those with mental
health difficulties, people working with a
physical challenge and others.

## Shaftesbury Young People

The Chapel,
Royal Victoria Patriotic Building,
John Archer Way, London SW18 3SX
T: 020 8875 1555
F: 020 8875 1954
E: info@shaftesbury.org.uk
www.shaftesbury.org.uk
Cares for, educates and encourages looked
after children and young people and children
in need.

## Shannon Trust

38 Ebury Street, London SW1W 0LU
T: 020 7730 4917
E: sue@shannontrust.org.uk
www.shannontrust.org.uk
CEO: David Ahern
Shannon Trust runs the Toe by Toe Reading
Plan, an award-winning peer mentoring
programme that encourages and supports
prisoners who can read to give one-to-one
tuition to prisoners who struggle to read.
Employees: 4
Volunteers: 160

## Shape London

Deane House Studios, 27 Greenwood Place,
London NW5 1LB
T: 0845 521 3457
F: 0845 521 3458
E: info@shapearts.org.uk
www.shapearts.org.uk
CEO: Tony Heaton
Our strategy reflects the artistic and
political 'journey' of the disability and deaf
communities and seeks to offer them a new
platform to profile their work. Our strategy
invests in disabled and deaf people as equals
and seeks to ensure that they can play an
active role in the cultural life of London and
the UK. In order to achieve these aims, Shape
will work in partnership with other arts
organisations to build their capacity and their
understanding of the creative potential of
disabled and deaf people.
Employees: 18
Volunteers: 350
Regional offices: 4

## Shaping Our Lives – National User Network

BM Box 4845, London WC1N 3XX
T: 0845 241 0383
E: information@shapingourlives.org.uk
www.shapingourlives.org.uk
Chair: Peter Beresford
Shaping Our Lives is a national user
controlled independent organisation started
in 1996. We work with a wide variety of
service users including people with physical
and/or sensory impairments, older people,
users/survivors of mental health services,

young people with experience of being 'looked after', people with learning difficulties and others. Through networking, research and development we support the development of user involvement that aims to deliver better outcomes for service users.
**Employees: 2**

## ShareAction

Ground Floor, 16 Crucifix Lane,
London SE1 3JW
T: 020 7403 7800
E: info@shareaction.org
www.shareaction.org
**Chief Executive: Catherine Howarth**
ShareAction is a groundbreaking charity that promotes responsible investment. We exist to catalyse an investment system that truly serves savers, benefits communities and protects our environment for the long term.
**Employees: 27**
**Volunteers: 60**
**Income: £1,031,043 (2015–16)**

## Shared Care Network

63–66 Easton Business Centre, Felix Road,
Easton, Bristol BS5 0HE
T: 0117 941 5361
F: 0117 941 5362
E: shared-care@bristol.ac.uk
www.shortbreaksnetwork.org.uk
We are the national organisation representing family-based short break schemes for disabled children.
**Employees: 15**
**Regional offices: 9**

## Shared Lives Plus

G04 The Cotton Exchange, Old Hall Street,
Liverpool, Merseyside L3 9JR
T: 0151 227 3499
F: 0151 236 3590
E: deborah@sharedlivesplus.org.uk
www.sharedlivesplus.org.uk
**Chief Executive: Alex Fox**
Shared Lives Plus is a UK charity established to represent the interests of all those involved in delivering very small, individualised, community-based services such as Shared Lives (formerly known as Adult Placement). Shared Lives Plus: promotes Shared Lives, Homeshare and other small community micro services as an important resource to those seeking individualised services; promotes a legislative environment that

ensures safety and quality but allows small community services to flourish.
**Employees: 14**
**Volunteers: 50**
**Regional offices: 3**

## Shaw Trust Ltd

Fox Talbot House, Greenways Business Park,
Bellinger Close, Malmesbury Road,
Chippenham, Wiltshire SN15 1BN
T: 01225 716300
Helpline: 01225 779471
F: 01225 716301
E: support@shaw-trust.org.uk
www.shaw-trust.org.uk
**Director General: Tim Pape**
Runs work programmes to help people with disabilities find employment and to remain in their jobs.
**Employees: 1200**
**Volunteers: 200**
**Regional offices: 5**

## Shelter

88 Old Street, London EC1V 9HU
T: 020 7505 2000
F: 020 7505 2169
E: info@shelter.org.uk
www.shelter.org.uk
**Employees: 800**
**Volunteers: 800**

## ShelterBox Trust

1A Water Ma Trout Industrial Estate,
Helston, Cornwall TR13 0LW
T: 01326 569782
E: ageocur@aol.com
www.shelterbox.org
**Chief Executive: Alison Wallace**
ShelterBox is an international disaster relief charity that provides emergency shelter and life-saving supplies to families around the world who are affected by disasters. Each big, green ShelterBox is tailored to every disaster but typically contains a disaster relief tent for an extended family, blankets, water purification and storage equipment, cooking utensils, a stove, a basic tool kit, a children's activity pack and other vital items.
**Employees: 60**
**Volunteers: 500**
**Regional offices: 2**

## SHINE

42 Park Road, Peterborough PE1 2UQ
T: 01733 555988
E: info@shinecharity.org.uk
www.shinecharity.org.uk
Provides services to people with spina bifida and/or hydrocephalus, and their carers, and promotes their interests in order to help

them develop their abilities, receive the best possible services and make the most of life.

## Shipwrecked Fishermen and Mariners' Royal Benevolent Society

Shipwrecked Mariners' Society,
1 North Pallant, Chichester,
West Sussex PO19 1TL
T: 01243 789329
Helpline: 01243 787761
F: 01243 530853
E: general@shipwreckedmariners.org.uk
www.shipwreckedmariners.org.uk
**Chief Executive: Malcolm Williams**
The Shipwrecked Mariners' Society exists to provide financial help to merchant seafarers, fishermen and their dependants who are in need. We pay an immediate grant to the widow of a serving seafarer who dies, whether at sea or ashore. Regular grants are paid to elderly seafarers and widows whose circumstances justify ongoing support. Special grants are made to meet particular needs in crisis situations.
**Employees: 7**
**Volunteers: 200**

## Shpresa Programme (Albanian for Hope)

Mansfield House, 30 Avenons Road,
Plaistow E13 3HT
T: 020 7511 1586
E: shpresaprogramme@yahoo.co.uk
www.shpresaprogramme.com
**Project Director: Luljeta Nuzi**
Aims to enable the Albanian-speaking community in the UK to settle and fully participate in society and realise their full potential. We want to promote a positive identity and recognition of our community's cultural and linguistic heritage, both among Albanian speakers and wider society, so that we can contribute to community cohesion in the UK.
**Employees: 5**
**Volunteers: 31**

## Sightsavers International

Grosvenor Hall, Bolnore Road,
Haywards Health, West Sussex RH16 4BX
T: 01444 446600
F: 01444 446688
E: charper@sightsavers.org
www.sightsavers.org
**Chief Executive: Caroline Harper**
Sightsavers is an international charity that
is dedicated to combating blindness in
developing countries. We work with partners
in over 33 countries, in poor and least-served
communities, to support activities that
prevent and cure blindness, restore sight
and provide education and training for the
blind and visually impaired.
**Employees: 325**
**Regional offices: 6**

## Signalong Group

Stratford House, Waterside Court,
Neptune Way, Rochester, Kent ME2 4NZ
T: 0845 450 8422
F: 0845 450 8428
E: mkennard@signalong.org.uk
www.signalong.org.uk
**Operations Manager: Tracy Goode**
Charity specialising in communication
resources and training in learning disabilities
and autism. Its aims are to improve
communication skills, leading to greater
independence, fulfilment of potential,
reduction in disturbed and challenging
behaviour, improved self-esteem and
improved relationships.
**Employees: 4**
**Volunteers: 24**

## Signature

Mersey House, Mandale Business Park,
Belmont, Durham DH1 1TH
T: 0191 383 1155
F: 0191 383 7914
E: joanne.lavender@signature.org.uk
www.signature.org.uk
Works towards the improvement of
communication with deaf, deafened, hard of
hearing and deafblind people in particular by
the education, training and examination of
students and tutors in the different modes of
communication used by such persons.
**Employees: 33**
**Regional offices: 2**

## SignHealth

5 Baring Road, Beaconsfield,
Buckinghamshire HP9 2NB
T: 01494 687600
E: info@signhealth.org.uk
www.signhealth.org.uk
**Chief Executive: Steve Powell**
SignHealth is a charity that aims for a world
where the risk of deaf people developing
preventable health problems is removed, and
where equality, respect and fulfillment are
enjoyed by deaf people experiencing mental
health problems. SignHealth is committed to
bringing better healthcare and equality of
service provision to deaf people in the UK.
**Employees: 120**
**Volunteers: 20**
**Regional offices: 6**

## Single Parent Action Network

Millpond, Baptist Street, Bristol BS5 0YW
T: 0117 951 4231
F: 0117 935 5208
E: info@spanuk.org.uk
www.singleparents.org.uk
**Director: Sue Cohen**
SPAN is a uniquely diverse organisation
supporting single parents to empower
themselves throughout the UK. SPAN aims
to give a voice to one-parent families living
in poverty and isolation, and support the
setting up and development of self-help
groups. SPAN develops partnerships with
organisations and agencies to improve
policies for one-parent families.
**Employees: 17**
**Volunteers: 5**

## Sir Halley Stewart Trust

22 Earith Road, Willingham, Cambridge,
Cambridgeshire CB24 5LS
T: 01954 260707 (also fax)
E: email@sirhalleystewart.org.uk
www.sirhalleystewart.org.uk
**Trust Administrator: Sue West**
The Trust aims to promote and assist
innovative research activities or pioneering
developments in medical, social and religious
fields. It emphasises prevention rather than
alleviation of human suffering. Certain
priorities apply, please refer to the Trust
website for current details.
**Employees: 1**
**Income: £106,300 (2013–14)**

## SITRA (Services)

3rd Floor, 55 Bondway, London SW8 1SJ
T: 020 7793 4710
F: 020 7793 4715
E: post@sitra.org
www.sitra.org
**Chief Executive: Vic Rayner**
Provides policy, information, training, events
and consultancy services to the housing with
care and support sector. Sitra has some 600
member organisations including supported
housing providers, housing associations and
local authorities. We publish a popular
monthly bulletin.
**Employees: 30**
**Regional offices: 4**

## Skill Force

Edwinstowe House, High Street,
Edwinstowe, Mansfield,
Nottinghamshire NG21 9PR
T: 01623 827619
E: enquiries@skillforce.org
www.skillforce.org
The mission of Skill Force is to develop young
people in order to raise standards in wider key
skills, self-esteem and employability.
**Employees: 250**

## Skills for Care Ltd

Albion Court, 5 Albion Place, Leeds,
West Yorkshire LS1 6JL
T: 0113 245 1716
F: 0113 243 6417
E: sharon.allen@skillsforcare.org.uk
www.skillsforcare.org.uk
**Chief Executive: Andrea Rowe**
Skills for Care is the not-for-profit
organisation that aims to improve adult
social care services across the whole of
England by supporting employers' workforce
development activity. Our vision is: to put
employers in the driving seat on social care
workforce issues; to create a trained and
qualified workforce providing high-quality
care; to provide an expert voice on the social
care workforce.
**Employees: 200**
**Volunteers: 24**
**Regional offices: 9**

## Skills for Communities

271 Anlaby Road, Hull,
Humberside HU3 2SE
T: 01482 214675
E: info@skills4communities.co.uk
www.skills4communities.co.uk
**CEO: Andre Ntenda**
Skills 4 Communities is a social enterprise set
up in 2003 to create opportunities, advance
education, empower people, improve living
standards and promote independence of the

socially excluded communities, particularly but not exclusively people from the BME community, migrants, refugees and asylum seekers. It aims to unlock potential of the disadvantaged for employment and social prospects through breaking down personal barriers and developing employability skills, basic self-reliance and transferable skills.

**Employees: 11**
**Volunteers: 2**
**Regional offices: 2**

## Skillset Sector Skills Council

Focus Point, 21 Caledonian Road N1 9GB
T: 020 7713 9800
E: michellec@skillset.org
www.skillset.org
**HR and Office Manager: Michelle Care**

## Skillshare International

Imperial House, St Nicholas Circle,
Imperial House, Leicester,
Leicestershire LE1 4LF
T: 0116 254 1862
E: info@skillshare.org
www.skillshare.org
**CEO: Dr Cliff Allum**
Skillshare International works for sustainable development in partnership with people and communities in Africa and Asia. We do this by sharing and developing skills through projects and volunteer placements. Our programmes focus on sustainable livelihoods, sport for development, HIV and AIDS, gender justice and conflict management.

**Employees: 38**
**Volunteers: 260**
**Regional offices: 7**
**Income: £1,400,000 (2014–15)**

## Small Charities Coalition

Unit 9/10, 83 Crampton Street,
London SE17 3BQ
T: 020 7358 6490
E: info@smallcharities.org.uk
www.smallcharities.org.uk
**Acting CEO: John Barrett**
Small Charities Coalition is a national umbrella and capacity-building organisation with over 7,000 members UK-wide. We exist to help trustees, staff and volunteers of small charities access the skills, tools and information they need to get going and do what they do best. We do this through a free skills matching service, free online resources and information, low cost training, free online and phone helpline and championing the voice of small charities.

**Employees: 3**
**Volunteers: 10**

## Smile International

PO Box 3, Orpington, Kent BR5 1WZ
T: 01689 870932
E: ruth.doubleday@smileinternational.org
www.smileinternational.org
**CEO: Clive Doubleday**
Smile International is passionate about helping to relieve suffering and poverty around the world through its feeding, educating, empowering and developing programmes in Africa, Asia and Europe.
**Employees: 4**
**Volunteers: 40**
**Income: £1,207,147 (2014–15)**

## Smile Support & Care

Eastleigh Community Enterprise Centre,
Unit 3, Barton Park, Eastleigh,
Hampshire SO50 6RR
T: 023 8061 6215
E: stuart.baldwin@smilesupport.org.uk
www.smilesupport.org.uk
**Chief Executive: Stuart Baldwin**
Smile Support and Care supports children and young adults with disabilities both in their own home, in the community and at our new residential respite centre in Waterlooville, Hampshire. Working in southern England, we ensure the people we support can exercise choice over the way they take short breaks or engage in any other activity. We are Care Quality Commission registered, Investors in People and ISO 9001 quality assured. For more information, see our website.

**Employees: 110**
**Volunteers: 30**
**Regional offices: 2**
**Income: £1,500,000 (2015–16)**

## Social Care Institute for Excellence

1st Floor, Goldings House, Hayes Lane,
London SE1 2HB
T: 020 7089 6871
F: 020 7089 6841
E: stephen.goulder@scie.org.uk
www.scie.org.uk
**Chief Executive: Julie Jones**
The Social Care Institute for Excellence (SCIE) was established by government in 2001 to improve social care services for adults and children in the UK. We achieve this by identifying good practice and helping to embed it in everyday social care provision.
**Employees: 65**

## Social Emotional and Behavioural Difficulties Association

C/O Goldwyn School, Godinton Lane,
Great Chart, Ashford, Great Chart,
Kent TN23 3BT
T: 01233 662958
E: admin@sebda.org
www.sebda.org
**Chair: Nicki Jennings**
SEBDA is a long-established charity that provides accredited specialist training, information and support to professionals working with children with social, emotional and behavioural difficulties. Members receive free copies of the Association's research journal, discounts on courses and conferences and detailed updates on policy and practice in its popular newsletter.
**Employees: 1**
**Volunteers: 50**

## Social Enterprise Coalition

South Bank House, Black Prince Road,
London SE1 7SJ
T: 020 7793 2323
F: 020 7968 4922
E: info@socialenterprise.org.uk
www.socialenterprise.org.uk
The Social Enterprise Coalition (SEC) is the UK trade body that brings together all types of social enterprise to promote the sector and share knowledge.
**Employees: 7**

## Social Market Foundation

11 Tufton Street, London SW1P 3QB
T: 020 7227 4400
E: enquiries@smf.co.uk
www.smf.co.uk
The Social Market Foundation is a leading UK think-tank, developing innovative ideas across a broad range of economic and social policy. It champions policy ideas that marry markets with social justice and takes a pro-market rather than free-market approach. Its work is characterised by the belief that governments have an important role to play in correcting market failures and setting the framework within which markets can operate in a way that benefits individuals and society.
**Employees: 12**

## Social Partnership

44 Castle Street, Liverpool L2 7LA
T: 0151 258 1331
F: 0151 709 7779
E: generalenquiries@tsp.org.uk
The Social Partnership (TSP) aims to reintegrate socially excluded people into the community both socially and economically through the provision of education, training and employment opportunities.
Employees: 45
Volunteers: 3

## Social Perspectives Network

c/o SCIE, Goldings House, 2 Hay's Lane, London SE1 2HB
T: 020 7089 6840
F: 020 7089 6841
E: media@scie.org.uk
www.spn.org.uk
We are a broad-based coalition of service users/survivors, carers, policy makers, academics, students and practitioners working to ensure that social perspectives are put at the heart of the evolving mental health policy, practice, research and legislative agendas. Social perspectives are holistic and look at the social issues that affect people's mental health such as experiences of stigma and discrimination, relationships, employment, access to housing and quality health and social care services.
Employees: 1
Volunteers: 25

## Social Research Association

24–32 Stephenson Way, London NW1 6QB
T: 020 7388 2391
E: admin@the-sra.org.uk
www.the-sra.org.uk
Chair of the Board of Trustees: Patten Smith
We are the professional membership body for social researchers. Promoting high-quality standards of social research, we seek to represent, support, connect and inform our members and the wider social research community.
Employees: 2
Volunteers: 10
Regional offices: 3

## Social Venture Network UK

Chandos House, 128 Cotham Brow, Bristol, Avon BS6 6AE
E: info@svnuk.org
www.svneurope.com
A network of socially and environmentally engaged entrepreneurs dedicated to changing the way the world does business. The network creates opportunities for learning, partnerships and launching new ventures and is associated with SVN United States and SVN Asia.
Volunteers: 3
Regional offices: 1

## Society for Co-operative Studies

c/o Patricia Juby, Co-operative UK, Holyoake House, Hanover Street, Manchester M60 0AS
T: 01452 308406
E: pajuby@gmail.com
www.co-opstudies.org
The Society welcomes into membership, co-operative members, employees, managers, specialist practitioners, academics and others who share an interest in the UK and world Co-operative Movement. It seeks to advance the education of members and the public on all aspects of the Co-operative Movement, co-operative forms of structure and, in particular, to commission, identify and publish research on the Co-operative Movement and the exchange of information and experience on co-operative study and research.

## Society for Endocrinology

22 Apex Court, Woodlands, Bradley Stoke, Bristol, Avon BS32 4JT
T: 01454 642200
F: 01454 642205
E: sally.spencer@endocrinology.org
www.endocrinology.org
Chief Executive: Ian Russell
The Society for Endocrinology is the major British society representing scientists, clinicians and nurses who work with hormones. It advances education and research in endocrinology, as well as acting as the discipline's voice with an aim of raising its profile.
Employees: 80

## Society for General Microbiology

Marlborough House, Basingstoke Road, Spencers Wood, Reading, Berkshire RG7 1AG
T: 0118 988 1800
E: info@sgm.ac.uk
www.sgm.ac.uk
CEO: Dr Simon Festing
Society for General Microbiology (SGM) is a membership organisation for scientists who work in all areas of microbiology. SGM publishes key academic journals in microbiology and virology, organises international scientific conferences and provides an international forum for communication among microbiologists and supports their professional development. SGM promotes the understanding of microbiology to a diverse range of stakeholders, including policy makers, students, teachers, journalists and the wider public through a framework of communication activities and resources.
Employees: 36
Volunteers: 80

## Society for Mucopolysaccharide Diseases

MPS House, Repton Place, White Lion Road, Amersham, Buckinghamshire HP7 9LP
T: 0345 389 9901
F: 0845 389 9902
E: mps@mpssociety.org.uk
www.mpssociety.org.uk
Group Chief Executive: Christine Lavery
Provides support and individual advocacy to those affected by Mucopolysaccharide, Fabry and other lysosomal diseases throughout the UK. Publishes a wide range of information booklets and a quarterly newsletter. Organises conferences, training and funds research into MPS diseases.
Employees: 16
Volunteers: 200
Regional offices: 1

## Society for Promoting Christian Knowledge

36 Causton Street, London SW1P 4ST
T: 020 7592 3900
F: 020 7592 3939
E: pphillips@spck.org.uk
www.spck.org.uk
Chief Executive: Sam Richardson
Promotes Christian knowledge by: communicating the faith in its rich diversity; helping people to understand it and to develop their personal faith; equipping Christians for mission and ministry.
Employees: 40
Income: £5,000,000 (2015–16)

## Society for the Assistance of Ladies in Reduced Circumstances

Lancaster House, 25 Hornyold Road, Malvern, Worcestershire WR14 1QQ
T: 0300 365 1886
E: john.sands@salrc.org.uk
www.salrc.org.uk
General Secretary: John Sands
The Society makes grants to working-age women resident in the UK who are living alone in their own home (either owned or

rented) and in genuine financial need, irrespective of social status.
**Employees: 4**
**Income: £886,012 (2013–14)**

## Society for the Protection of Ancient Buildings

37 Spital Square, London  E1 6DY
T: 020 7377 1644
Helpline: 020 7456 0916
F: 020 7247 5296
E: info@spab.org.uk
www.spab.org.uk
**Secretary: Philip Venning**
Aims to educate public opinion in the conservative repair of historic buildings and to prevent ill-considered and conjectural restoration. Offers advice and courses for homeowners and building professionals. SPAB is a membership organisation. Its respected magazine, Cornerstone, is sent to all members on a quarterly basis. We advise, we educate, we campaign.

## Society for the Protection of Animals Abroad

14 John Street, London  WC1N 2EB
T: 020 7831 3999
F: 020 7831 5999
E: john@spana.org
www.spana.org
**Chief Executive: Jeremy Hulme**
With 19 veterinary centres and 21 mobile clinics, SPANA treated over 300,000 animals last year throughout North and West Africa and the Middle East. Our efforts are concentrated on those areas where the need is greatest: wherever animals are mistreated, neglected or struggling to survive without proper care.
**Employees: 17**
**Volunteers: 20**

## Society for the Protection of Unborn Children

5–6 St Matthew Street, London  SW1P 2JT
T: 020 7222 5845
F: 020 7222 0630
E: information@spuc.org.uk
www.spuc.org.uk
Affirms, defends and promotes the existence and value of human life from the moment of conception; reasserts the principle laid down in UN Declaration of the Rights of the Child that the child needs special safeguards and care, including appropriate legal protection, before as well as after birth; defends and promotes welfare of mothers during pregnancy and of their children; examines existing or proposed laws, legislation or regulations relating to abortion, supporting or opposing as appropriate.
**Employees: 34**
**Volunteers: 100**
**Regional offices: 6**

## Society of Analytical Psychology

1 Daleham Gardens, Hampstead, London  NW3 5BY
T: 020 7435 7696
F: 020 7431 1495
E: chair@thesap.org.uk
www.thesap.org.uk
**Chair: Penny Pickles**
The Society's main functions are the development of analytical psychology; training of adult analysts and psychotherapists; provision of Jungian analysis to members of the public through the society's clinic, plus a consultation and referral service; education through public events and the Journal of Analytical Psychology; professional association for Jungian analysts and psychotherapists.
**Employees: 17**
**Volunteers: 100**

## Society of Antiquaries of London

Burlington House, Piccadilly, London  W1J 0BE
T: 020 7479 7080
F: 020 7287 6967
E: admin@sal.org.uk
www.sal.org.uk
**General Secretary: John Lewis**
The Society of Antiquaries of London's goals are the encouragement, advancement and furtherance of the study and knowledge of the antiquities and history of this and other countries.
**Employees: 20**
**Regional offices: 1**

## Society of Authors

84 Drayton Gardens, London  SW10 9SB
T: 020 7373 6642
F: 020 7373 5768
E: info@societyofauthors.org
www.societyofauthors.org
**General Secretary: Mark Le Fanu**
The Society is a trade union with 8,500 members. It lobbies for the profession and gives individual advice and help to members on business issues (eg. contracts, copyright, publishers, agents, etc). Members receive a quarterly journal, The Author.
**Employees: 14**

## Society of Biology

Charles Darwin House, 12 Roger Street, London  WC1N 2JU
T: 020 7685 2550
E: info@societyofbiology.org
www.societyofbiology.org
**Chief Executive: Dr Mark Downs**
Aims to advance the science and practice of biology and education in biology and to coordinate and encourage the study of biology and its application.
**Employees: 30**
**Volunteers: 200**

## Society of Homeopaths

11 Brookfield, Duncan Close, Moulton Park, Northampton, Northamptonshire NN1 6WL
T: 01604 621400
F: 01604 622622
E: julie_rowland@homeopathy-soh.org
www.homeopathy-soh.org
Established in 1978, it is the largest organisation representing professional homeopaths in Europe, with over 1,500 members on its register. Members practice in accordance with the Society's Code of Ethics and Practice and carry full public liability and indemnity insurance.
**Employees: 20**
**Volunteers: 20**
**Regional offices: 1**

## Soil Association

Bristol House, 40–56 Victoria Street, Bristol  BS1 6BY
T: 0117 914 2454
F: 0117 925 2504
E: development@soilassociation.org
www.soilassociation.org
Aims to educate the general public about organic agriculture, gardening and food, and their benefits for both human health and the environment; promotes the production and consumption of organically grown food; lobbies the authorities for an agricultural policy that is based on ecological and sustainable principles.
**Employees: 150**
**Volunteers: 10**
**Regional offices: 2**

## Solihull Carers Centre

E: sueshahmiri@solihullcarers.org

## SOLVE IT

Satra Innovation Park, Rockingham Road,
Kettering, Northamptonshire NN16 9JH
T: 01536 414690
E: manager.solveit@gmail.com
www.solveitonline.co.uk
Business Manager: Deborah Clarke
SOLVE IT provides a free service to young
people, parents, carers and those adults
affected by volatile substance abuse (VSA),
promoting a general awareness to the
dangers of these substances, working towards
the prevention of related deaths, illness,
accidents and social exclusion. It provides
education, early intervention, a confidential
support and counselling service for those
affected by such abuse, including families,
training and support for professionals.
Employees: 5
Volunteers: 8
Regional offices: 1

## SOS Children's Villages UK

St Andrew's House, 59 St Andrew's Street,
Cambridge, Cambridgeshire CB2 3BZ
T: 01223 365589
F: 01223 322613
E: info@sos-uk.org.uk
www.soschildrensvillages.org.uk
Provides loving care and a secure future for
homeless, orphaned and abandoned children
throughout the world.
Employees: 9
Volunteers: 2

## Sound and Music

3rd Floor, Somerset House,
London WC2R 1LA
T: 020 7759 1800
E: info@soundandmusic.org
www.soundandmusic.org
Chief Executive: Susanna Eastburn
Sound and Music's vision is to create a world
where new music and sound prospers,
transforming lives, challenging expectations
and celebrating the work of its creators.
Employees: 10
Regional offices: 1

## Sound Seekers

c/o UCL Ear Institute,
332–336 Gray's Inn Road,
London WC1X 8EE
T: 020 7833 0035
E: help@sound-seekers.org.uk
www.sound-seekers.org.uk
Sound Seekers is dedicated to helping deaf
people, particularly children, in the poorest
communities of the developing world. We
work in partnership with local organisations
to deliver sustainable and cost-effective
projects that advance understanding of deaf
people's needs and improve their access to
health services, education and social support,
together with initiatives that enable people to
avoid, or overcome, the effects of deafness.
Employees: 4
Volunteers: 30
Regional offices: 1
Income: £770,566 (2014–15)

## South Lancashire Learning Disability Training Consortium

E: ceo@slldtc.co.uk

## Southampton and Winchester Visitors Group

SWVG, PO Box 1615, Southampton,
Hampshire SO17 3WF
T: 07503 176350
E: info@swvg-refugees.org.uk
www.swvg-refugees.org.uk
Chair: Anne Leeming
SWVG is a group of volunteers who befriend
and support asylum seekers and refugees in
the Southampton area. We offer financial
assistance to those who are homeless and
destitute. Through our legal justice project
we have access to advice from a leading
immigration solicitor. We try to give asylum
seekers a voice by reaching out to churches,
schools and community groups and we
campaign for a fairer asylum system.
Employees: 2
Volunteers: 60
Income: £82,098 (2014–15)

## Southbank Mosaics CIC

St John's Crypt, 73 Waterloo Road,
London SE1 8UD
T: 020 7620 6070
F: 020 7928 6724
E: david@southbankmosaics.com
www.southbankmosaics.com
Director: David Tootill
To make the neighbourhood more attractive
through the highest quality public realm
installations: sculptures, fountains, seating,
murals, etc. We train students in artisan craft
and will open a small independent institute to
teach mosaic. We work with special needs
children and take referrals from health and social
services. We aim to provide an alternative to
custody for local youth in trouble with the law.
We support ex-offenders coming out of prison.
Employees: 4
Volunteers: 300
Income: £100,000 (2015–16)

## Southend Association of Voluntary Services

E: asemmence@savs-southend.co.uk

## Sova

Head Office, Unit 201, Lincoln House,
1–3 Brixton road, London SW9 6DE
T: 020 7793 0404
F: 020 7793 5858
E: mail@sova.org.uk
www.sova.org.uk
Chief Operating Officer: Sophie Wilson
Sova works in England and Wales with the
National Offender Management Service, the
Prison Service, probation areas, JobCentre
Plus, Social Services and other organisations
to strengthen communities by involving local
volunteers in promoting social inclusion and
reducing crime. Paid staff and volunteers
utilise skills to encourage the positive
development of a wide client group including
offenders, prisoners, young people on youth
offending orders, those at risk of offending
and asylum seekers.
Employees: 150
Volunteers: 1000

## Spadework Ltd

Teston Road, Offham, West Malling,
Kent ME19 5NA
T: 01732 870002
F: 01732 842827
E: spadework1@btconnect.com
www.spadework.net
Provides training opportunities for adults with
learning and/or physical disabilities to prepare
them for an independent life within the
community.
Employees: 13
Volunteers: 20
Regional offices: 2

## Spare Tyre Theatre Company

E: lucy@sparetyre.org

## Speakability (Action for Dysphasic Adults)

240 City Road, London EC1V 2PR
T: 020 7261 9572
Helpline: 0808 808 9572
E: melanie@speakability.org.uk
www.speakability.org.uk
Chief Executive: Melanie Derbyshire
Speakability is a national charity supporting
and empowering people with Aphasia
(whatever the cause) and their carers, by
offering a free helpline and information
service, training resources for carers and a
UK-wide network of Aphasia Self-Help
Groups. As the voice of people with Aphasia,
Speakability also campaigns for greater

understanding of this communication disability and better service provision.
**Employees: 5**
**Volunteers: 100+**

## Special Kids In the UK

PO Box 617, Addlestone  KT15 9AP
T: 01932 356416
E: information@specialkidsintheuk.org
www.specialkidsintheuk.org
Special Kids in the UK is a charity for families who have a child of any age with additional needs. The charity aims to bring families together, offering friendship and support.

## Spinal Injuries Association

SIA House, 2 Trueman Place, Oldbrook, Milton Keynes  MK6 2HH
T: 01908 604191
Helpline: 0800 980 0501
E: sia@spinal.co.uk
www.spinal.co.uk
Chief Executive Officer: Sue Browning
SIA is a national, user-led organisation for people with spinal cord injuries and their families. Our purpose is to promote the integration and full participation in society of our members, by encouraging them to become fulfilled and in control of their lives.
**Employees: 50**
**Volunteers: 100**

## Spinal Muscular Atrophy Support UK

40 Cygnet Court, Timothy's Bridge Road, Stratford upon Avon, Warwickshire CV37 9NW
T: 01789 267520
F: 01789 268371
E: office@smasupportuk.org.uk
www.smasupportuk.org.uk
Managing Director: Doug Henderson
We inform, support and empower families and individuals affected by all forms of SMA and raise awareness of the condition. We also fund and support the research community addressing the causes, treatment and management of SMA.
**Employees: 9**
**Volunteers: 70**
**Income: £596,485 (2015–16)**

## Spitalfields City Farm

Buxton Street, London  E1 5AR
T: 020 7247 8762
F: 020 7247 5452
E: mhairi@spitalfieldscityfarm.org
spitalfieldscityfarm.org
Director: Mhairi Weir
Spitalfields City Farm is a community space that inspires and that everyone can enjoy. We challenge people to respect themselves, each other, their environment and animals. We strive to be sustainable and lead by example. We aim to give people the opportunity to become active members of their community and encourage their participation in the development of the farm and to explore and promote the benefits of healthy and sustainable lifestyles.
**Employees: 16**
**Volunteers: 350**
**Income: £350,000 (2012–13)**

## Sport and Recreation Alliance

4th Floor, Burwood House, 14–16 Caxton House, London  SW1H 0QT
T: 020 7976 3900
F: 020 7976 3901
E: info@sportandrecreation.org.uk
www.sportandrecreation.org.uk
Chief Executive: Tim Lamb
Sport and Recreation Alliance is the trade association for governing and representative bodies of sport and recreation. It exists to protect, promote and provide for its members
**Employees: 20**

## Sports Leaders UK

Clyde House, 10 Milburn Avenue, Oldbrook, Milton Keynes  MK6 2WA
T: 01908 689194
F: 01908 393744
E: info@sportsleaders.org
www.sportsleaders.org
The new name for the British Sports Trust, Sports Leaders UK believes in inspiring people and communities through leadership qualifications in sport. Sports Leaders UK believes that everyone has the potential to make a meaningful contribution to their local community, but not everyone has the opportunity or the motivation. Our Sports Leader Awards help people learn essential skills such as working with and organising others, as well as motivational, communication and teamwork skills.
**Employees: 32**
**Volunteers: 1**

## Spurgeon's Child Care

74 Wellingborough Road, Rushden, Northamptonshire NN10 9TY
T: 01933 417405
E: info@spurgeons.org
www.spurgeons.org

## ssafa

Queen Elizabeth House, 4 St Dunstans Hill, London  EC3R 8AD
T: 020 7403 8783
F: 020 7403 8815
E: terry.c@ssafa.org.uk
www.ssafa.org.uk
We provide support for the serving men and women in today's Armed Forces and for those who have served – even if it was only for a single day. We also care for the needs of their families and dependants. Last year alone, our professional staff and trained volunteers gave assistance to more than 50,000 people. We helped to make a real difference to many lives.
**Employees: 680**
**Volunteers: 7000**
**Regional offices: 100**

## St Albans Mencap

E: enquiries@stalbansmencap.org.uk

## St Andrew's Healthcare

St Andrew's Hospital, Billing Road, Northampton, Northamptonshire NN1 5DG
T: 01604 616000
E: treading@standrew.co.uk
www.stah.org
Chief Executive and Medical Director: Philip Sugarman
St Andrew's Healthcare, a not-for-profit charity, aims to be the UK's leading independent provider of specialist mental healthcare, complementing and working in partnership with the NHS.
**Employees: 2500**
**Volunteers: 110**

## St Francis Leprosy Guild

73 St Charles Square, London W10 6EJ
T: 020 8969 1345
E: enquiries@stfrancisleprosy.org
www.stfrancisleprosy.org
President: Mr Michael Forbes Smith
St Francis Leprosy Guild supports those
caring for leprosy patients in Asia, Africa and
South America. Although leprosy can now be
cured by multi-drug therapy, many new cases
are still being discovered and thousands of
cured patients have disabilities and need care
and support. Each year the Guild sends
grants to 80 hospitals, clinics and centres in
25 countries. Its 'elective' programme helps
medical students in the UK to work with
leprosy patients abroad.
Employees: 1
Volunteers: 10
Income: £201,500 (2013–14)

## St John Ambulance

27 St John's Lane, London EC1M 4BU
T: 020 7324 4000
F: 020 7324 4001
E: chief-executive@nhq.sja.org.uk
www.sja.org.uk
Everyone who needs it should receive first
aid from those around them. No one should
suffer for the lack of trained first aiders.
Our mission is: to provide an effective and
efficient charitable first aid service to local
communities; to provide training and
products to satisfy first aid and related
health and safety needs for all of society;
to encourage personal development for
people of all ages, through training and by
membership of our organisation.
Volunteers: 44000
Regional offices: 45

## St John of God Care Services

Saint Bede's House, Morton Park Way,
Darlington, County Durham DL1 4XZ
T: 01325 373701
F: 01325 373707
E: enquiries@sjog.org.uk
Employees: 700
Volunteers: 40
Regional offices: 6

## St Joseph's Hospice Association

Jospice, Ince Road, Thornton,
Liverpool L23 4UE
T: 0151 924 3812
E: enquiries@jospice.org.uk
www.jospice.org.uk
Maintains hospices to care for the incurably
sick and destitute, both in Britain and the
third world (Central and South America, India
and Pakistan).

## St Loye's Foundation

Beaufort House, 51 New North Road,
Exeter EX4 4EP
T: 01392 255428
F: 01392 420889
E: info@stloyes.ac.uk
www.stloyes.org.uk
CEO: Eilis Rainsford
St Loye's Foundation is a national charity and
service provider, based in Exeter, Devon for
over 75 years. We also have satellite offices in
Warrington, Cardiff and North Devon. We
specialise in helping people with health,
disability and social issues by providing a range
of services, including employment training,
care and support and learning and skills.
Across all these services individuals are given
the support and practical knowledge they
need to access employment.
Employees: 120
Volunteers: 6
Regional offices: 6

## St Peters House Project

1–3 The Pavement, Grovehill Road, Redhill,
Surrey RH1 6TW
T: 01737 773917
Helpline: 01737 763000
E: stephanie@stpetershouse.org.uk
www.stpetershouse.org.uk
Project Director: Stephanie Phillips
To support people living with or affected
by HIV, to offer opportunities of choice
regarding their healthcare, continued
wellbeing and independent living. We also
work with other organisations to develop
quality and responsive services that meet,
reflect and support the diverse needs of
individuals within local communities.
Employees: 6
Volunteers: 3
Income: £124,000 (2015–16)

## St Vincent de Paul Society (England and Wales)

5th Floor, 291–299 Borough High Street,
London SE1 1JG
T: 020 7407 4644
F: 020 7407 4634
E: info@svp.org.uk
www.svp.org.uk
Chief Executive: Elizabeth Palmer
The St Vincent de Paul Society is an
international Christian voluntary organisation
dedicated to tackling poverty and
disadvantage by providing direct practical
assistance to anyone in need. Active in
England and Wales since 1844, today it

continues to address social and material
need in all its many forms.
Employees: 130
Volunteers: 10000
Regional offices: 1100

## Staffordshire Council of Voluntary Youth Services

42a Eastgate Street, Stafford,
Staffordshire ST16 2LY
T: 01785 240378
E: phil@staffscvys.org.uk
staffscvys.org.uk
Staffordshire Council of Voluntary Youth
Services is the lead body of a delivery
partnership recognised as the VCSE
Strategic Partner for Staffordshire County
Council. We will work together across four
main themes to capacity build the sector,
reduce demand on public services, develop
new expressions of social action, getting
'people to help people' and improve
outcomes for all. We aim to increase
investment into the county and help
maximise existing internal resource and
local philanthropy.
Employees: 9
Volunteers: 8300
Income: £400,000 (2015–16)

## STAGETEXT

1st Floor, 54 Commercial Street,
London E1 6LT
T: 020 7377 0540
F: 020 7247 5622
E: enquiries@stagetext.org
www.stagetext.org
Chief Executive: Tabitha Allum
STAGETEXT provides and promotes the
use of captioning and live speech-to-text
transcription (subtitling) in cultural and
entertainment venues to enable deaf,
deafened and hard of hearing people to
access the arts.
Employees: 7

## STAR (Student Action for Refugees)

356 Holloway Road N7 6PA
T: 020 7697 4130
E: staradmin@star-network.org.uk
www.star-network.org.uk
Chief Executive: Emma Williams
STAR is the national charity of students
welcoming refugees to the UK. Our 12,000
student activists run groups at over 30
universities. They volunteer at local refugee
projects, educate fellow students about

asylum in the UK, campaign for refugee protection and fundraise for STAR.
**Employees: 7**
**Volunteers: 45**

## STARS – Syncope Trust And Reflex anoxic Seizures

PO Box 175, Stratford upon Avon,
Warwickshire CV37 8YD
T: 01789 450564
F: 01789 450682
E: info@stars.org.uk
www.stars.org.uk
STARS aims to ensure that anyone presenting with unexplained loss of consciousness receives the correct diagnosis, the appropriate treatment, informed support and signposting to the appropriate medical professional. STARS offers information and advice to help manage symptoms and regain quality of life. This is achieved through our 24-hour helpline, DoH approved resources and patients' day offering advice and support to patients, carers and medical professionals.
**Employees: 1**
**Volunteers: 3**
**Regional offices: 1**

## Staying First

Mulliner House, Flanders Road W4 1NN
T: 020 8996 8893
E: lorna.revell@sbhg.co.uk
Director: Graham Raine
To provide advice, practical assistance and help to people living in West London to enable them to live in comfort and security in their own homes. Housing advice (private tenants and owner occupiers only), small repairs and home improvement agency for residents in Kensington and Chelsea. Small repairs for residents in Westminster. Furniture recycling and reuse in West London. Debt and welfare benefits advice provided to a number of registered social housing providers.
**Employees: 42**
**Volunteers: 15**
**Regional offices: 1**

## Step Together Volunteering

5 Russell Town Avenue, Bristol BS5 9LT
T: 0117 955 9042
E: admin@step-together.org.uk
www.step-together.org.uk
Director: Mike Silvey
Step Together helps those people most in need of support to transform their lives through community volunteering. Working through a team of outreach workers we provide tailored one-to-one support to help individuals into volunteering placements that

match their needs and interests, and help them develop the personal and practical skills required to build a more positive future.
**Employees: 18**

## Stephen Lawrence Charitable Trust

2nd Floor, Downstream Building,
1 London Bridge, London SE1 9BG
T: 020 8100 2800
E: information@stephenlawrence.org.uk
www.stephenlawrence.org.uk
As an educational charity, our mission is to promote diversity in architecture and associated professions, improve the educational achievements of black and ethnic-minority students, and help young people find pathways out of poverty into sustainable, rewarding careers in architecture, building construction and other fields associated with urban design and regeneration.
**Employees: 4**
**Volunteers: 20**

## Steps Charity Worldwide

Wright House, Crouchley Lane, Lymm,
Cheshire WA13 0AS
T: 01925 750271
F: 01925 750270
E: info@steps-charity.org.uk
www.steps-charity.org.uk
**Acting Chief Executive Officer:**
**Loredana Guteg Wyatt**
We provide quality support, information and a voice for families and people with lower limb conditions (hip dysplasia/clubfoot/lower limb deficiency). In order to do this we are committed to furthering research, innovation, services and best practice through a partnership approach.
**Employees: 4**
**Volunteers: 3**

## Stickler Syndrome Support Group

PO Box 3351, Littlehampton BN16 9GB
T: 01903 785771
E: info@stickler.org.uk
www.stickler.org.uk
**Founder and Honorary President: Wendy**
**Hughes**
The Stickler Syndrome Support Group provides support for sufferers and their families, plus medical and other professionals with an interest in the syndrome. This support is provided through publications, telephone, website, conferences and family days.
**Volunteers: 8**

## Stillbirth and Neonatal Death Society

28 Portland Place, London W1B 1LY
T: 020 7436 7940
F: 020 7436 3715
E: support@uk-sands.org
www.uk-sands.org
**Director: Neal Long**
SANDS provides support for anyone who has been affected by the death of a baby via: our helpline; an online support forum; a network of support groups located throughout the UK; an array of publications and support literature as well as an informative website.
**Employees: 19**
**Regional offices: 95 groups**

## Stonewall

The Tower Building, 11 York Road,
London SE1 7NX
T: 020 7593 1850
Helpline: 0800 050 2020
F: 020 7593 1877
E: info@stonewall.org.uk
www.stonewall.org.uk
**Chief Executive Officer: Ben Summerskill**
Campaigns to achieve legal and social justice for lesbians, gay men and bisexuals; challenges discrimination and prejudice; promotes new research and has an information service offering information about LGB rights.
**Employees: 70**
**Volunteers: 200**
**Regional offices: 3**

## Stonewall Housing

Unit 2A, Leroy House, 436 Essex Road,
London N1 3QP
T: 020 7359 6242
Helpline: 020 7359 5767
F: 020 7359 9419
E: bob@stonewallhousing.org
www.stonewallhousing.org
**Chief Executive: Bob Green**
Stonewall Housing provides housing, advice, care and support to lesbian, gay, bisexual and transgender people so they feel safe and secure and are able to achieve their full potential.
**Employees: 16**
**Volunteers: 2**

## Stonham

Malt House, 281 Field End Road, Eastcote,
Middlesex HA4 9XQ
T: 020 8868 9000
F: 020 8868 9292
E: robert.weatherall@homegroup.org.uk
www.stonham.org.uk
**Executive Director: Paul Rydquist**
Stonham is England's largest provider of
housing and support for socially excluded
and vulnerable adults. We run 545 projects
across the country and work with over
15,000 people each year, in a mix of
residential services and in floating support
services (where we support people living
in their own homes).
**Employees: 2500**
**Regional offices: 3**

## Stop Abuse for Everyone

1 Queens Road, Exeter EX2 9ER
T: 01392 269545
E: chris.collier@btinternet.com
www.safe-services.org.uk
**Manager: Janet Collier**
Stop Abuse For Everyone (SAFE) works
with all those affected by and experiencing
all forms of domestic violence and abuse
(DVA) in Exeter, East and Mid Devon. It
provides: a refuge for women, children and
young people; independent domestic
violence advisors who offer support through
MARAC, court and other processes; support
in the community for children, young people
and young men; awareness-raising work in
schools and colleges; pattern changing
courses for women wishing to move on in
their lives and learn how to do so in a specialist
and supportive environment.
**Employees: 7**
**Volunteers: 9**
**Regional offices: 1**
**Income: £566,263 (2013–14)**

## Strategic Planning Society

Buxton House, 7 Highbury Hill,
London N5 1SU
T: 0845 056 3663
E: membership@sps.org.uk
www.sps.org.uk
Campaigns to develop an understanding of
the need for long-range planning in both the
private and public sectors of the economy.
Aims to enhance the skills of long-range
planners and to exchange and extend the
information available to long-range planners.

## Street Child Africa

Brabant House, Portsmouth Road,
Thames Ditton, Surrey KT7 0EY
T: 020 8972 9820
F: 020 8972 9821
E: info@streetchildafrica.org.uk
www.streetchildafrica.org.uk
**Director: Anthony Morton-King**
Street Child Africa's mission is to champion
the rights of African street children and other
children at risk. We work in Senegal, Ghana,
Uganda, the DRC, Zambia and Mozambique,
directly with African partners. Through our
partners we support children with education,
skills training and a chance to return to their
families and communities.
**Employees: 10**
**Volunteers: 7**
**Regional offices: 1**

## Streetscene

StreetScene Addiction Recovery,
(Registered office), 55 Cobham Road,
Ferndown, Dorset BH21 7RB
T: 01202 540337
Helpline: 01202 551254
F: 01202 765946
E: tessa@streetscene.org.uk
www.streetscene.org.uk
**CEO: Tessa Corner**
Provider of care for people with problems
of addiction to drugs/alcohol including;
residential treatment, supported after care,
day care, re-integration, simple detox. There
are 54 beds of rehab in three different
locations; 54 beds of support in six different
locations. Based in Dorset and Hampshire.
Abstinence-based philosophy.
**Employees: 52**
**Volunteers: 15**

## Stroke Association

Stroke Association House, 240 City Road,
London EC1V 2PR
T: 020 7566 0300
Helpline: 0303 303 3100
F: 020 7490 2686
E: jane.cryer@stroke.org.uk
www.stroke.org.uk
**Chief Executive: Juliet Bouverie**
We are the UK's leading charity dedicated to
conquering stroke. We believe in life after
stroke. That's why we support stroke survivors
to make the best recovery they can. It's why
we campaign for better stroke care. And it's
why we fund research to develop new

treatments and ways of preventing stroke.
Together we can conquer stroke.
**Employees: 783**
**Volunteers: 4000**
**Regional offices: 16**
**Income: £37,500,000 (2014–15)**

## Student Christian Movement

Grays Court, 3 Nursery Road, Edgbaston,
Birmingham, West Midlands B15 3JX
T: 0121 426 4918
E: scm@movement.org.uk
www.movement.org.uk
**National Coordinator: Hilary Topp**
We're a student-led movement inspired by
Jesus to act for justice and show God's love in
the world. As a community we come together
to pray, worship and explore faith in an open
and non-judgemental environment. The
movement is made up of a network of groups
and individual members across Britain, as well
as link churches and affiliated chaplaincies.
**Employees: 7**
**Volunteers: 10**
**Regional offices: 1**
**Income: £177,913 (2014–15)**

## Student Hubs

Student Hubs, 16–17 Turl Street, Oxford,
Oxfordshire OX1 3DH
T: 01865 264156
E: info@studenthubs.org
www.studenthubs.org
**Executive Director: Sara Fernandez**
**Employees: 22**
**Volunteers: 2200**
**Regional offices: 7**
**Income: £650,000 (2015–16)**

## Sturge Weber Foundation (UK)

348 Pinhoe Road, Exeter EX4 8AF
T: 01392 464675
E: support@sturgeweber.org.uk
www.sturgeweber.org.uk
**Chair: Jenny Denham**
Sturge Weber syndrome is a rare neurological
disorder, the symptoms of which usually
occur in the child's first year of life. The
Foundation aims to help and support parents;
to raise public and professional awareness and
to raise funds in order to do so.
**Volunteers: 6**

## Sue Ryder

First Floor, 16 Upper Woburn Place,
London WC1H 0AF
T: 0845 050 1953
F: 020 7400 0441
E: info@sueryder.org
www.sueryder.org
Sue Ryder Care's mission is care that
liberates lives. We inspire, support and care
for people with long-term neurological
conditions and palliative care needs in our
care centres, hospices, their own homes
and in the community.
Employees: 2500

## Support After Murder and Manslaughter

L&D Tally Ho!, Pershore Road, Edgbaston,
Birmingham B5 7RN
T: 0121 471 1200
Helpline: 0845 872 3440
F: 0121 471 1201
E: samm.national@gmail.com
www.samm.org.uk
National Coordinator: Heather Meyer
Offers understanding and support to families
and friends bereaved through murder and
manslaughter; raises public awareness about
the effects of murder and manslaughter;
takes up issues of concern arising from the
affects of murder and manslaughter;
promotes and supports research into the
effects of murder and manslaughter on
society. All volunteers, trustees etc have
themselves been bereaved by murder.
Employees: 4
Volunteers: 55

## Supporters Direct

3rd Floor, Victoria House,
Bloomsbury Square, London WC1B 4SE
T: 020 7273 1596
F: 020 7273 1605
E: info@supporters-direct.coop
www.supporters-direct.org
Chief Executive: David Lampitt
Supporters Direct helps form and support
supporters' trusts, which are not-for-profit,
volunteer-run groups of supporters of
particular sports clubs who wish to take a
stake in the ownership and management of
their clubs and reorientate those clubs
towards their communities using social
enterprise business models.
Employees: 11
Volunteers: 11
Regional offices: 2

## SupportLine

PO Box 2860, Romford, Essex RM7 1JA
T: 01708 765222
Helpline: 01708 765200
E: info@supportline.org.uk
www.supportline.org.uk
Chair: Peter Barrell
Provides emotional support and information
by telephone helpline, email and post. A
service for children, young people and adults
primarily aimed at those who are vulnerable,
at risk, isolated and victims of any form of
abuse. We help people develop healthy
positive coping strategies, increase their
confidence and self-esteem and develop
an inner feeling of strength. The service
specialises in providing support for adult
survivors of childhood abuse.
Employees: 1
Volunteers: 6
Income: £45,057 (2014–15)

## Surf Life Saving Great Britain

19 Southernhay West, Exeter,
Devon EX1 1PJ
T: 01392 218007
F: 01392 217808
E: mail@slsgb.org.uk
www.surflifesaving.org.uk
CEO: Esther Pearson
Aims to provide a safe and enjoyable
environment on British beaches, promoting
and controlling the work of lifesaving,
resuscitation and first aid.
Employees: 8
Volunteers: 100
Regional offices: 1

## Surrey Nurturing Links

E: jharris@surreynurturinglinks.org.uk

## Survival International

6 Charterhouse Buildings, Goswell Road,
London EC1M 7ET
T: 020 7687 8700
E: info@survivalinternational.org
www.survivalinternational.org
Survival International is the global movement
for tribal peoples' rights. They help tribal
peoples to defend their lands, protect their
lives and determine their own futures.

## Survivors of Bereavement by Suicide

The Flamsteed Centre, Albert Street,
Ilkeston, Derbyshire DE7 5GU
T: 0115 944 1117
Helpline: 0300 111 5065
E: sobs.admin@care4free.net
www.uk-sobs.org.uk
Chair of the Trustees: Ann Culley

We exist to meet the needs and break the
isolation of those bereaved by the suicide of a
close relative or friend. Many of those helping
have, themselves, been bereaved by suicide.
Our aim is to provide a safe, confidential,
environment, in which bereaved people can
share their experiences and feelings, thus
giving and gaining support from each other.
Employees: 3
Volunteers: 180
Regional offices: 55

## Survivors Trust

Unit 2, Eastlands Court Business Centre,
St Peters Road, Rugby,
Warwickshire CV21 3RP
T: 01788 550554
F: 01788 551150
E: info@thesurvivorstrust.org
www.thesurvivorstrust.org
The Survivors Trust is a national umbrella
agency for 126 specialist voluntary sector
agencies providing a range of counselling,
therapeutic and support services working with
women, men and children who are victims/
survivors of rape, sexual violence and
childhood sexual abuse.
Employees: 2

## Sustain: the Alliance for Better Food and Farming

94 White Lion Street, London N1 9PF
T: 020 7837 1228
E: sustain@sustainweb.org
www.sustainweb.org
Advocates food and agriculture policies and
practices that enhance the health and welfare
of people and animals, improves the working
and living environment, and promotes equity
and enriches society and culture.

## Sustrans

Head Office, Sustrans, 2 Cathedral Square,
College Green, Bristol BS1 5DD
T: 0117 926 8893
F: 0117 929 4173
E: info@sustrans.org.uk
www.sustrans.org.uk
MD: Malcolm Shepherd
Sustrans works with communities, policy-
makers and partner organisations so that
people can choose healthier, cleaner and
cheaper journeys and enjoy better, safer
spaces where they live. All over the UK, we
make a positive difference to people's lives.
Employees: 300
Volunteers: 1200
Regional offices: 10

## Sutton Trust

9th Floor, Millbank Tower,
21–24 Millbank, London SW1P 4QP
T: 020 7802 1660
F: 020 7802 1661
E: info@suttontrust.com
www.suttontrust.com
The main objective of the Trust is to support innovative projects that provide educational opportunities for young people from non-privileged backgrounds. Projects range from early years (0–3 year olds), through primary and secondary schooling, to further and higher education, including research projects, with an emphasis on innovative start-up projects that have the scope to benefit large numbers in the future. The Trust does not fund individuals or capital projects.
Employees: 6

## Suzy Lamplugh Trust

218 Strand, London WC2R 1AT
T: 020 7091 0014
F: 020 7091 0015
E: info@suzylamplugh.org
www.suzylamplugh.org
As the leading authority on personal safety, the Trust works to reduce violence and aggression in society.
Employees: 18
Volunteers: 3

## Swan Advice Network

Leigh House, 1 Wells Hill, Radstock,
Bath BA3 3RN
Helpline: 01761 432445
E: swan.management@btconnect.com
swan.btck.co.uk
Manager: Sarah Williams
Swan exists to relieve need and hardship amongst people in Bath and North East Somerset and surrounding areas by providing a range of advice, information and access services. Current services include transport provision for the elderly or disabled on low incomes and a housing and benefits advice service for Curo tenants.
Employees: 7
Volunteers: 24
Regional offices: 1
Income: £132,377 (2015–16)

## SWAN UK (Syndromes Without A Name)

Genetic Alliance UK, Unit 4D Leroy House,
436 Essex Rd, London N1 3QP
T: 020 7704 3141
E: info@undiagnosed.org.uk
www.undiagnosed.org.uk
Director of Genetic Alliance UK:
Alastair Kent

SWAN UK supports families of children with undiagnosed genetic conditions. SWAN UK is the only dedicated support network available for families of children and young adults with undiagnosed genetic conditions in the UK. It is run by the charity Genetic Alliance UK.

## TAEN – The Age and Employment Network

Headland House, 308–312 Gray's Inn Road,
London WC1X 8DP
T: 020 7837 4762
E: info@taen.org.uk
www.taen.org.uk
Chief Executive: Chris Ball
TAEN – The Age and Employment Network works to remove age barriers to employment opportunities and for an effective job market that works better for people in mid and later life, employers and the economy. TAEN is not an employment agency but can direct individuals looking for work, who want to change direction, develop their careers or undertake training, to relevant organisations and a number of useful resources.

## Take a Break Warwickshire

Canterbury House, Exhall Grange Campus,
Easter Way, Ash Green, Coventry,
Warwickshire CV7 9HP
T: 024 7664 4909
F: 024 7664 4959
E: kim@tabw.org.uk
www.tabw.org.uk
Director: Kim Fathers
Take a Break Warwickshire provides community-based short breaks for children and young people who have a disability or life-threatening illness and adults with a learning disability.
Employees: 220
Volunteers: 20
Regional offices: 1
Income: £1,704,000 (2015–16)

## Talking Newspaper Association of the UK

10 Browning Road, Heathfield,
East Sussex TN21 8DB
T: 01435 866102
E: helpline@rnib.org.uk
www.tnauk.org.uk
Chief Executive: John Kerby
National Talking Newspapers and Magazines provides magazines and newspapers in audio and full (electronic) text for people unable to read normal print, mainly due to visual impairment, with the aim of giving them the same choice of magazines and newspapers as sighted people. Part of RNIB Group.
Employees: 30
Volunteers: 200

## Tall Ships Youth Trust

2A The Hard, Portsmouth PO1 3PT
T: 023 9283 2055
F: 023 9281 5769
E: info@tallships.org
www.tallships.org
The personal development of young people aged 16–25 through the crewing of Tall Ships
Employees: 10
Volunteers: 1500
Regional offices: 50

## Tapestry Care UK

hello@tapestry-uk.org

## Target Tuberculosis

82 Queens Road, Brighton,
East Sussex BN1 3XE
T: 01273 827070
F: 01273 821059
E: info@targettb.org.uk
www.targettuberculosis.org.uk
Tackles tuberculosis as a disease as well as the social and economic issues around it. Forms partnerships with local organisations mainly in the Indian subcontinent and sub-Saharan Africa. Aims to bring TB treatment close to the patient and improve the quality of life for patients and families.
Employees: 3
Volunteers: 6

## TASHA Foundation

Alexandra House, 241 High Street,
Brentford, Middlesex TW8 0NE
T: 020 8560 4583 (also fax)
E: enquiries@tasha-foundation.org.uk
www.tasha-foundation.org.uk
Provides one-to-one counselling for those experiencing problems with drug use, suffering from anxiety and stress.

Supports individuals experiencing mental health problems.
**Employees: 14**
**Volunteers: 15**
**Regional offices: 4**

## TaxAid UK

**Room 304, Linton House,**
**164–180 Union Street, Southwark,**
**London  SE1 0LH**
**T: 020 7803 4950**
**Helpline: 0345 120 3779**
**F: 020 7803 4955**
**E: admin@taxaid.org.uk**
**www.taxaid.org.uk**
**Director: Rosina Pullman**
TaxAid runs a free, confidential helpline, helping people on low incomes with their tax affairs. It offers face-to-face appointments in London, Birmingham, Manchester, Newcastle, Plymouth and Shropshire. It also runs training programmes for the voluntary sector.
**Employees: 11**
**Volunteers: 40**

## TBPI Group

**1 Malvern Rise, Hadfield, Glossop,**
**Derbyshire SK13 1QW**
**E: kcam26@uwclub.net**
**www.tbpi-group.org**
Supplies information and support to adults coping with a trauma brachial plexus injury and helps them achieve a better understanding of the impact these injuries may have on the individual, and their family.

## Teacher Support Network

**40A Drayton Park, London N5 1EW**
**T: 020 7697 2750**
**Helpline: 0800 056 2561**
**F: 020 7554 5239**
**E: enquiries@teachersupport.info**
**www.teachersupport.info**
**Chief Executive: Julian Stanley**
We believe that all teachers should have access to the practical and emotional support they need to improve their personal wellbeing and effectiveness. If, as a society, we are to achieve the best possible education for our young people, then supporting teachers is a must. Teacher Support Network is the largest provider of support services to UK schoolteachers. We provide counselling, coaching and advice free of charge.
**Employees: 25**
**Volunteers: 327**
**Regional offices: 3**

## Tearfund

**100 Church Road, Teddington,**
**Middlesex TW11 8QE**
**T: 0845 355 8355**
**F: 020 8943 3594**
**E: enquiries@tearfund.org**
**www.tearfund.org**
Aims to relieve poverty, suffering and distress, prevent disease and ill health among the people of the world and to promote Christian education and evangelism.
**Employees: 300**
**Volunteers: 3300**
**Regional offices: 13**

## Teenage Cancer Trust

**3rd Floor, 93 Newman Street,**
**London W1T 3EZ**
**T: 020 7612 0370**
**F: 020 7612 0371**
**E: hello@teenagecancertrust.org**
**www.teenagecancertrust.org**
**Chief Executive: Siobhan Dunn**
Teenage Cancer Trust is the only UK charity dedicated to improving the quality of life and chances of survival for young people with cancer aged 13 to 24. The charity funds and builds specialist units in NHS hospitals and provides dedicated staff, bringing young people together so they can be treated by teenage cancer experts in the best place for them. Teenage Cancer Trust relies on donations to fund its work.
**Employees: 105**

## Telephones for the Blind Fund

**7 Huntersfield Close, Reigate,**
**Surrey RH2 0DX**
**T: 01737 248032**
**E: info@tftb.org.uk**
**www.tftb.org.uk**
Provides financial support for installation and rental for a BT line for the benefit of the blind. Applicants must be registered blind or partially sighted, living alone and on low income. Applications must be made through registered support workers. Free mobile phones may also be given on application and with the same criteria.
**Volunteers: 5**

## Television Trust for the Environment

**46 Bloomsbury Street, London  WC1B 3QJ**
**T: 020 7147 7420**
**E: tve@tve.org.uk**
**www.tve.org**
Promotes global public awareness of sustainable development through television and the other audio-visual media. TVE aims to provide videos on the environment and development of NGOs in low and middle income countries free of charge, and to raise funding for film-makers in the developing world to make these programmes.

## Template Foundation

**The Centre, 1 Bath Place, Barnet,**
**Hertfordshire EN5 5XE**
**T: 020 8441 2567**
**E: info@thecentrelondon.org**
The Foundation's objectives are to advance the education of the public through the promotion and further study of human behavioural sciences, philosophy, history, the art of human expression and living derived from the Template and Emin archives, including arts such as theatre, dance and music.
**Employees: 5**
**Volunteers: 200**

## Terrence Higgins Trust

**314–320 Gray's Inn Road,**
**London WC1X 8DP**
**T: 020 7812 1600**
**Helpline: 0845 122 1200**
**F: 020 7812 1696**
**E: info@tht.org.uk**
**www.tht.org.uk**
**Chief Executive: Sir Nick Partridge**
HIV and sexual health charity.
**Employees: 350**
**Volunteers: 1000**
**Regional offices: 17**

## Textile Institute International

**1st Floor, St James's Buildings,**
**Oxford Street, Manchester  M1 6FQ**
**T: 0161 237 1188**
**E: devans@textileinst.org.uk**
**www.textileinstitute.org**
Promotes professionalism in all areas associated with the textile industries worldwide.

## Thames Reach

**E: street_rescue@thamesreach.org.uk**

## The Adolescent and Children's Trust (TACT)

303 Hither Green Lane, Hither Green,
London  SE13 6TJ
T: 020 8695 8142
F: 020 8695 8141
E: enquiries@tactcare.org.uk
www.tactcare.org.uk
**Chief Executive: Kevin Williams**
TACT is the UK's largest charity provider of
fostering and adoption services. Our core
work involves providing high-quality and
well-supported fostering or adoptive families
for children and young people in the care
of local authorities. We are dedicated to
providing creative, effective and outcome-
focused services. We also campaign and
fundraise on behalf of children and young
people in care, carers and adoptive families.
**Employees: 152**
**Volunteers: 2**
**Regional offices: 9**

## The Anscombe Bioethics Centre

38 Circus Road, London  NW8 9SE
T: 020 7806 4088
E: admin@bioethics.org.uk
www.bioethics.org.uk
Promotes understanding of the Catholic
viewpoint on bioethical issues. The Centre's
perspective is informed by Catholic moral
teaching, but in defending such teaching
it seeks also to appeal to non-religious,
philosophical reasoning to enable dialogue
with those of no religious faith.

## The Arthrogryposis Group (TAG)

45 Milton Road, Hanwell, London  W7 1LQ
Helpline: 0800 028 4447
E: admin@taguk.org.uk
www.taguk.org.uk
The Arthrogryposis Group (TAG) is the only
organisation in the UK providing contact,
information and support to people with
Arthrogryposis and their families. TAG
provides members with information about
Arthrogryposis and can put them in touch
with other families. TAG also provides an
information service for professionals involved
in the management of the condition.
TAG encourages public awareness of
Arthrogryposis and also supports research.
**Volunteers: 30**

## The Association for Post-Natal Illness

145 Dawes Road, Fulham,
London SW6 7EB
T: 020 7386 0868
E: info@apni.org
www.apni.org

Service for women with post-natal illness
and their families, friends and professionals.
Offers advice and information. Telephone
helpline staffed Monday–Friday 10:00–
14:00, answerphone at other times. Can put
people in touch with volunteers who have had
post-natal illness and are now fully recovered.
Produces information leaflets.
**Employees: 7**
**Volunteers: 300+**
**Regional offices: 1**

## The Brendoncare Foundation

The Old Malthouse, Victoria Road,
Winchester, Hampshire  SO23 7DU
T: 01962 852133
E: jlamont@brendoncare.org.uk
www.brendoncare.org.uk
**Chief Executive: Carole Sawyers**
The Brendoncare Foundation is a registered
charity dedicated to improving the quality of
life for older people through our care homes,
close-care facilities and social clubs across
the South of England. We have 10 care
homes, each with a distinctive character.
Brendoncare Clubs provide a range of styles
of clubs, giving older people a choice on
where to meet new friends in a welcoming
and supportive environment.
**Employees: 750**
**Volunteers: 600**
**Regional offices: 1**

## The British Evacuees Association

The Mill Business Centre, Mill Hill,
Gringley-on-the-Hill,
Nottinghamshire  DN10 4RA
T: 01777 816166
E: era@evacuees.org.uk
www.evacuees.org.uk
**Chief Executive: James Roffey**
The Association has 1,300 members
worldwide and mails out a 1- page bi-monthly
magazine 'The Evacuee'. We organise
events to raise the profile of the story of the
evacuation which affected 3.5 children within
the UK and abroad. We provide information
for students and give talks to numerous
groups. We are currently raising funds for a
memorial. Annual membership is £20.
**Employees: 2**
**Volunteers: 75**

## The Brooke

The Brooke, 5th Floor Friars Bridge Court,
41–45 Blackfriars Road  SE1 8NZ
T: 020 3012 3456
F: 020 3012 0156
E: info@thebrooke.org
www.thebrooke.org

The Brooke is an international animal welfare
organisation dedicated to improving the
lives of working horses, donkeys and mules
in the poorest parts of the world. We provide
veterinary treatment and community
programmes across Africa, Asia and Latin
America. The Brooke's goal is to increase the
number of working animals we help to two
million a year by 2016.
**Employees: 100**
**Volunteers: 30**

## The Cambridge Centre

E: paula.myers@cambridgecentre.org

## The Churches Conservation Trust

Society Building, 8 All Saints Street,
London N1 9RL
T: 0845 303 2760
F: 020 7841 0434
E: central@thecct.org.uk
www.visitchurches.org.uk
**Chief Executive: Crispin Truman**
CCT is the national charity protecting historic
churches at risk. We've saved over 340
beautiful buildings which attract almost two
million visitors a year. We aim to: inspire
people to enjoy, understand and support
England's historic churches; protect history
through the conservation, regeneration and
presentation of our unique collection; create
value, ensuring that its social, environmental
and economic value is realised.
**Employees: 68**
**Volunteers: 1700**
**Regional offices: 3**
**Income: £12,900,000 (2014–15)**

## The Clinic for Boundaries Studies

49–51 East Road, London  N1 6AH
T: 020 3468 4194
E: jcoe@professionalboundaries.org.uk
www.professionalboundaries.org.uk
**Managing Director: Jonathan Coe**
The clinic provides specialist support services
for the public alongside training and
professional development services for
practitioners. It is also involved in research
and development around professional
boundaries and conduct.
**Employees: 12**

## The Compassionate Friends

SE8 3HS
Helpline: 0345 123 2304
E: helpline@tcf.org.uk
www.tcf.org.uk

We are an organisation of bereaved parents offering support and befriending to others after the loss of a child, of any age, from any cause. We have a National Helpline (helpline@tcf.org.uk), with calls taken only by bereaved parents, which is available for support and information 365 days a year. We also have a website which includes a Members Forum which enables those who join up to speak electronically to others similarly bereaved.

## The Cry-sis Helpline

BM Cry-sis, London WC1N 3XX
Helpline: 0845 122 8669
E: info@cry-sis.org.uk
www.cry-sis.org.uk
From its modest beginnings, Cry-sis has developed to become a well-respected and national charity. It offers support to families with excessively crying, sleepless and demanding babies. To achieve this, Cry-sis runs a national telephone helpline that is available to callers every day of the year between 9.00am and 10.00pm. Calls cost a maximum of 2p per minute plus your telephone provider's access charge.
Employees: 1
Volunteers: 30

## The Drinkaware Trust

Samuel House, 6 St Albans Street,
London SW1Y 4SQ
T: 020 7766 9900
F: 020 7504 8217
E: llam@drinkaware.co.uk
www.drinkaware.co.uk
Chief Executive: Elaine Hindal
Drinkaware aims to change the UK's drinking habits for the better. We promote responsible drinking and find innovative ways to challenge the national drinking culture to help reduce alcohol misuse and minimise alcohol-related harm.
Regional offices: 1

## The Duke of Edinburgh's Award

Gulliver House, Madeira Walk, Windsor,
Berkshire SL4 1EU
T: 01753 727400
F: 01753 810666
E: info@dofe.org
www.dofe.org
Chief Executive: Peter Westgarth
Our mission is to inspire, guide and support young people in their self-development and recognise their achievements.
Employees: 112
Volunteers: 50000
Regional offices: 11

## The Ear Foundation

Marjorie Sherman House, 83 Sherwin Road,
Lenton, Nottingham,
Nottinghamshire NG7 2FB
T: 0115 942 1985
F: 0115 924 9054
E: info@earfoundation.org.uk
www.earfoundation.org.uk
Chief Executive: Sue Archbold
Our vision is that all deaf children, young people and adults have the opportunity to hear, communicate and develop spoken language using the latest technological interventions.
Employees: 16
Volunteers: 80
Regional offices: 1

## The Eikon Charity

The Eikon Charity, On Fullbrook School site,
Selsdon Road, New Haw, Addlestone,
Surrey KT15 3HP
T: 01932 347434
E: info@eikon.org.uk
www.eikon.org.uk
CEO: Chris Hickford
The Eikon Charity aims to help socially and economically disadvantaged young people achieve their full potential and has been working in local Surrey communities for almost two decades, delivering a variety of support programmes for vulnerable young people who are at risk of falling into crisis: developing an addiction, becoming homeless, being excluded from school, etc. We strongly believe in early intervention – helping young people overcome issues before they become significant problems.
Employees: 30
Volunteers: 50
Income: £900 (2015–16)

## The Electrical Safety Council

Unit 331–
3 Great Guildford Business Square,
30 Great Guildford Street,
London SE1 0HS
T: 020 3463 5100
E: enquiries@esc.org.uk
www.esc.org.uk
Director General: Philip Buckle
The Electrical Safety Council (ESC) is a UK charity committed to reducing deaths and injuries caused by electrical accidents in the home. We work closely with industry, government, media and consumer

organisations to raise awareness of the dangers of electricity.
Employees: 20
Regional offices: 1

## The Emily Jordan Foundation

Unit 9 Finepoint, Finepoint Way,
Kidderminster, Worcestershire DY11 7FB
T: 01562 861154
E: chris.jordan@theemilyjordanfoundation.org.uk
theemilyjordanfoundation.org.uk
Chair of Trustees: Chris Jordan
Our aim is to help individuals with learning and physical disabilities to lead fulfilled lives. This is done via developing and supplying good-quality day opportunities alongside work development projects for those who may be able to enter the workplace.
Employees: 11
Volunteers: 15
Income: £200,000 (2015–16)

## The Encephalitis Society

32 Castlegate, Malton,
North Yorkshire YO17 7DT
T: 01653 692583
Helpline: 01653 699599
E: mail@encephalitis.info
www.encephalitis.info
Chief Executive Officer: Ava Easton
Aims to improve the quality of life of all people affected, directly and indirectly, by Encephalitis. We support people affected, provide information on the condition and its consequences in different formats, raise awareness of the condition, and conduct research. The Society is the only resource of its kind in the world.
Employees: 9
Volunteers: 30
Income: £501,441 (2014–15)

## The Fairlight Trust

Fairlight, The Avenue, North Ascot,
Berkshire SL5 7LY
T: 01344 874681
E: lindsay@fairlightolc.co.uk
Chair: Josephine Collier
The charity's main aims are: to support vulnerable women, especially those in prostitution and with related issues, and their children; to provide aftercare for women and children who have previously accessed its services.
Employees: 20
Volunteers: 21

## The Farming Community Network

FCN Manor Farm, Guilsborough Road,
West Haddon, Northampton,
Northamptonshire NN6 7AQ
T: 01788 510866
Helpline: 0300 011 1999
E: mail@fcn.org.uk
www.fcn.org.uk
**Chief Executive Officer: Charles W Smith**
The Farming Community Network is a UK
network of volunteers from the farming
community and rural churches, providing a
national helpline and visiting service to
farming people and families facing difficulties.
The network provides pastoral and practical
support for as long as it is needed, helping
people to find a positive way forward through
their problems.
**Employees: 12**
**Volunteers: 401**

## The Federation

505 Barking Road, Plaistow,
London E13 8PS
T: 020 8692 2525
F: 020 8469 4103
E: info@thefederation.org.uk
www.thefederation.org.uk
The Federation is a national membership
organisation and registered charity,
representing the needs of diverse
communities and professionals from the
drug, alcohol, criminal justice, mental health
and related sectors. We offer a particular
expertise in issues pertaining to black and
minority ethnic (BME) communities and
professionals.
**Employees: 4**

## The Forum for Health and Wellbeing

Office 2/3, St Mark's Community Centre,
218 Tollgate Road, Beckton,
London E6 5YA
T: 020 7474 3176
E: manjit.notta@fhwb.co.uk
fhwb.co.uk
**Director: Sahdia Warraich**
The Forum aims to develop and improve
services that effectively meet the health and
social care needs of black and ethnic minority
communities. It develops a strong, collective
and informed voice for black and ethnic
minority groups, service users and carers.
The Forum aims to build the infrastructure
of the black and ethnic minority voluntary,
community and faith sector to deliver their
own health and social care services through
providing tailored capacity building and
development support, and access to funding.
**Employees: 11**

## The Fostering Network

87 Blackfriars Road, London SE1 8HA
T: 020 7620 6410
F: 020 7620 6401
E: info@fostering.net
www.thefosteringnetwork.org.uk
**Chef Executive: Kevin Williams**
The Fostering Network is the UK's leading
fostering charity. We are passionate about
the difference foster care makes to children
and young people. Transforming children's
lives is at the heart of everything we do.
**Employees: 62**
**Volunteers: 2**
**Regional offices: 3**

## The Giving Machine

E: joanne@me2club.org.uk

## The Grace Eyre Foundation

36 Montefiore Road, Hove,
East Sussex BN3 6EP
T: 01273 201900
E: mburgess@grace-eyre.org
www.grace-eyre.org
**CEO: Eva Eriksson**
We support people with learning disabilities
and/or mental health needs across Sussex
and the South East to develop their
independence, obtain housing, find
employment and learn new skills.
**Employees: 238**
**Volunteers: 91**
**Regional offices: 1**
**Income: £5,912,970 (2015–16)**

## The Grandparents' Association

Moot House, The Stow, Harlow,
Essex CM20 3AG
T: 01279 428040 (also fax)
Helpline: 0845 434 9585
E: info@grandparents-association.org.uk
www.grandparents-association.org.uk
**Chief Executive: Lynn Chesterman**
The Grandparents' Association is the only
national membership organisation dealing
with all grandparent issues, such as bringing
up your grandchildren full-time (kinship
care), denied contact and childcare, in public
and private law. We provide information
and support by way of our helpline, welfare
benefits advice service, support groups
and various publications and leaflets.
**Employees: 11**
**Volunteers: 80**
**Regional offices: 2**
**Income: £303,051 (2014–15)**

## The Grange

E: karen.pinchbeck@grangecentre.org.uk

## The Harland Trust

66 High Street, Weston Favell,
Northampton,
Northamptonshire NN3 3JX
T: 07752 647208
E: alan.harland@ntlworld.com
This trust supports individuals in need and
charitable causes known to the Trustees at
home and overseas. It applies charitable
resources at the point of need in an
accountable manner. This trust aims to grow
in the future. Anyone wishing to donate to
The Harland Trust or leave a legacy should
contact the trust directly using the contact
details provided here.

## The Haven

E: poppyk@havenrefuge.org.uk

## The Heritage Alliance

Clutha House, 10 Storeys Gate,
Westminster, London SW1P 3AY
T: 020 7233 0500
E: kate.pugh@theheritagealliance.org.uk
www.theheritagealliance.org.uk
**Chief Executive: Kate Pugh**
The Heritage Alliance is the largest coalition
of heritage interests in England. Established
in 2002 by key voluntary sector bodies, it
brings together nearly 90 major national and
regional non-government organisations
concerned with heritage. Between them,
Alliance members represent nearly five
million people across Britain. The Alliance
provides a forum for members to formulate
and promote policy on core issues, make
their voices heard collectively and share
information and networks.
**Volunteers: 6**

## The Hextol Foundation

14c Gilesgate, Hexham,
Northumberland NE46 3NJ
T: 01434 605253
E: contact@hextol.org.uk
www.hextol.org.uk
**Chief Executive: Chris Milner**
We offer people with a learning disability or
with poor mental health work experience,
training and a real sense of purpose. Our
aim is to help them to develop greater
self-esteem, more confidence and better
mental health and to have real opportunities

to contribute positively and regularly to society and to be seen doing so.
**Employees: 18**
**Volunteers: 8**
**Regional offices: 1**
**Income: £355,648 (2015–16)**

## The IARS International Institute

14 Dock Offices, Surrey Quays Road,
London SE16 7PQ
T: 020 7064 4380
E: t.gavrielides@iars.org.uk
www.iars.org.uk
**Director: Dr Theo Gavrielides**
The IARS International Institute is a user-led and user-focused charity with a mission to give everyone a chance to forge a safer, fairer and more inclusive society. Over the last 10 years, the Institute has been providing world-class and cutting-edge educational, research, policy and networking services of local, national and international significance. We are focused on empowering the most marginalised communities through direct service delivery, while enabling organisations to achieve, measure and improve their social impact.
**Employees: 10**
**Volunteers: 15**
**Regional offices: 1**
**Income: £450,000 (2014–15)**

## The INSPIRE Foundation

Spinal Treatment Centre,
Salisbury District Hospital,
Salisbury SP2 8BJ
T: 01722 336262
E: office@inspire-foundation.org.uk
www.inspire-foundation.org.uk
**Director: Rory Steevenson**
INSPIRE promotes research into the development of practical systems for people with damage to the spinal cord by the use of the latest advances in electronic, mechanical and medical technology. Our preferred method is to offer PhD scholarships for students to research aspects of spinal cord injury in the leading teaching hospitals, spinal injuries units or universities throughout the UK.
**Employees: 4**
**Volunteers: 100**

## The King's Fund

11–13 Cavendish Square, London W1G 0AN
T: 020 7307 2400
E: library@kingsfund.org.uk
www.kingsfund.org.uk
**Chief Executive: Chris Ham**
The King's Fund is an independent charity working to improve health and care in England. We help to: shape policy and practice through research and analysis; develop individuals, teams and organisations; promote understanding of the health and social care system; bring people together to learn, share knowledge and debate. Our vision is that the best possible care is available to all.
**Employees: 120**

## The Leprosy Mission

Goldhay Way, Orton Goldhay,
Peterborough, Cambridgeshire PE2 5GZ
T: 01733 370505
F: 01733 404880
E: post@tlmew.org.uk
www.leprosymission.org.uk
**National Director: Peter Walker**
Our vision is a world without leprosy. Our goal is to eradicate the causes and consequences of the disease. This means more than just detecting and curing the leprosy bacillus. It means addressing the underlying cause as well as working to prevent disability and restore dignity and wholeness to people's lives.
**Employees: 40**

## The Lesbian and Gay Foundation

Number 5, Richmond Street,
Manchester M1 3HF
T: 0845 330 3030
F: 0161 235 8036
E: info@lgf.org.uk
www.lgf.org.uk
**Chief Executive: Paul Martin**
The Lesbian and Gay Foundation is a community-based charity, working to end homophobia and empower people across the north west of England and beyond. In 2013/14 we provided advice, information, support and services to over 40,000 people. The Lesbian and Gay Foundation provides direct services and resources for more LGB people than any other charity of its kind in the UK.
**Employees: 49**
**Volunteers: 200**
**Regional offices: 1**

## The Lindsay Leg Club Foundation

The Lindsay Leg Club Foundation,
PO Box 689, Ipswich IP1 9BN
T: 01473 749565
E: lynn.bullock@legclubfoundation.com
www.legclub.org
**President: Ellie Lindsay**
The aims of the Lindsay Leg Cub Foundation are twofold: to support the network of Leg Clubs operating around the UK, Europe, Australia and Tasmania, and to communicate the benefits of the Leg Club model to stakeholders. The model features the treatment of patients suffering from or at risk of leg ulceration within a social model of care. Stakeholders include patients, healthcare providers, clinicians and healthcare media
**Income: £100,000 (2011–12)**

## The Lodge Trust

The Lodge, Main Street, Market Overton,
Oakham, Rutland LE15 7PL
T: 01572 767234
F: 01572 767503
E: admin@lodgetrust.org.uk
www.lodgetrust.org.uk
**CEO: David Whitmarsh**
Provides individual support for adults with learning disabilities in Christian homes and working environments.
**Employees: 75**
**Volunteers: 25**
**Regional offices: 1**

## The Log Cabin

259 Northfield Avenue, Ealing,
London W5 4UA
T: 020 8840 3400
F: 020 8840 6780
E: vivien.dymock@logcabin.org.uk
www.logcabin.org.uk
**Director: Sharon Flynn**
The Log Cabin makes a positive difference to the lives of 250 children and young people with additional needs and disabilities or who are in need by providing exciting and stimulating play opportunities in a safe, caring, inclusive and fun environment. Founded in 1978, we are open six days a week. Services include an after-school club, all-day holiday playschemes, Saturday sessions, sessions for young families and projects for older young people.
**Employees: 17**
**Volunteers: 10**
**Income: £604,370 (2014–15)**

## The Lullaby Trust

E: fundraising@lullabytrust.org.uk

## The Makaton Charity

Westmead House, Farnborough,
Hampshire GU14 7LP
T: 01276 606760
Helpline: 01276 606777
F: 01276 36725
E: info@makaton.org
www.makaton.org
**Chief Executive Officer: Lysa Schwartz**
Makaton uses signs, symbols and speech to help people communicate. Today over 100,000 children and adults use Makaton symbols and signs, either as their main method of communication or as a way to support speech. The Makaton Charity is responsible for developing and sharing Makaton so that everyone who needs to use Makaton can. We support families and professionals, provide training, resources, information and work with others to influence change for people with communication difficulties.
Employees: 14
Income: £1,096,057 (2013–14)

## The Mare and Foal Sanctuary

Honeysuckle Farm,
Haccombe with Coombe, Newton Abbot,
Devon TQ12 4SA
T: 01626 355969
E: office@mareandfoal.org
www.mareandfoal.org
Rescues, provides care for and prevents cruelty and suffering among horses and ponies that are in need of attention because of sickness, maltreatment, ill usage or other causes and provides temporary or permanent homes for such horses and ponies.
Employees: 31
Volunteers: 25

## The Marine Society and Sea Cadets

202 Lambeth Road, London SE1 7JW
T: 020 7654 7000
F: 020 7928 8914
E: info@ms-sc.org
www.ms-sc.org
**Chief Executive: Martin Coles**
To be the leading maritime charity for youth development and lifelong learning. Our vision for Sea Cadets is to give young people the best possible head start in life through nautical adventure and fun and for the Marine Society to be the first in learning and personal development for seafarers.
Employees: 180
Volunteers: 9000
Regional offices: 6

## The Matthew Project

Nedeham House, 22 St Stephens Road,
Norwich, Norfolk NR1 3QU
T: 01603 626123
F: 01603 630411
E: frankie.keith@matthewproject.org
www.matthewproject.org
**Chief Executive Officer: Paul Martin**
The Matthew Project works across Norfolk and Suffolk with young people and adults: supporting people with drug and alcohol related issues; providing innovative education about the risks of drugs and alcohol; empowering people to make more informed choices.
Employees: 135
Volunteers: 29
Regional offices: 1
Income: £3,434,000 (2013–14)

## The MedicAlert Foundation

MedicAlert House, 327–329 Witan Court,
Upper Fourth Street,
Milton Keynes MK9 1EH
Helpline: 01908 951045
F: 01908 951071
E: info@medicalert.org.uk
www.medicalert.org.uk
**CEO: Mark Rawden**
MedicAlert provides vital details in an emergency, because every moment matters. We support members with a wide range of medical conditions and allergies, which we help to describe on custom made medical ID jewellery. MedicAlert keeps secure, detailed medical records for our members. This information can be accessed in an emergency, 24/7 from anywhere in the world, using our emergency telephone number and we are able to converse in over 100 languages.
Employees: 42
Volunteers: 460

## The Migraine Trust

52–53 Russell Square, London WC1B 4HP
T: 020 7631 6970
Helpline: 020 7631 6975
F: 020 7436 2886
E: info@migrainetrust.org
www.migrainetrust.org
**Chief Executive: Wendy Thomas**
The Migraine Trust is the health and medical research charity for migraine in the UK. We seek to educate health professionals, raise awareness of migraine as a serious public health issue and empower, inform and support those affected by migraine by providing them with evidence-based information. The Migraine Trust funds and promotes research into migraine in order to

better understand it, improve diagnosis and treatment and ultimately to find a cure.

## The National Autistic Society

393–395 City Road, London EC1V 1NG
T: 020 7833 2299
Helpline: 0808 800 4104
F: 020 7833 9666
E: nas@nas.org.uk
www.autism.org.uk
**Chief Executive: Mark Lever**
The National Autistic Society (NAS) is the UK's leading charity for people affected by autism. The NAS provides: information, advice, training and support for individuals and their families; information and training for health, education and other professionals working with people with autism and their families; residential, supported living, outreach and day services for adults; specialist schools and education, outreach services for children and young people; employment training and support and social programmes for adults with autism.
Employees: 2782
Volunteers: 1000
Regional offices: 12

## The National Churchs Trust

31 Newbury Street, London EC1A 7HU
T: 020 7600 6090
F: 020 7796 2442
E: info@nationalchurchtrust.org
www.nationalchurchestrust.org
Provides for the preservation, repair, maintenance, improvement, upkeep, beautification and reconstruction of churches in the UK and of monuments, fittings, fixtures, stained glass, furniture, ornaments, etc.
Employees: 5
Volunteers: 3

## The National Society for Phenylketonuria (UK) Ltd

PO Box 3143, Purley CR8 9DD
T: 0303 040 1090
E: info@nspku.org
www.nspku.org
**Chair: Eric Lange**
The NSPKU exists to help and support people with PKU, their families and carers. The NSPKU actively promotes the care and treatment of people with PKU and works closely with medical professionals in the UK. It organises conferences and study days throughout the UK and produces a wide range of publications (including food lists) for parents, adults with PKU and medical

professionals. The NSPKU also sponsors medical research into the condition.

**Employees: 3**
**Volunteers: 15**

## The Nationwide Foundation

Nationwide House, Pipers Way, Swindon, Wiltshire SN38 2SN
Helpline: 01793 655113
E: enquiries@nationwidefoundation.org.uk
www.nationwidefoundation.org.uk
interim Chief Executive: Leigh Pearce
The Nationwide Foundation makes grants and social investments to charitable causes in the UK. It aims to create decent affordable homes for people in need. The three areas the Nationwide Foundation focuses on are: bringing empty properties into use as homes for people in need; improving the living conditions of vulnerable private rented sector tenants; supporting alternative scalable housing models.

**Employees: 3**

## The Neuro Foundation

Quayside House, 38 High Street, Kingston upon Thames, Surrey KT1 1HL
T: 020 8439 1234
F: 020 8439 1200
E: info@nfauk.org
www.nfauk.org
Charity Manager: Mike Mills
The Neuro Foundation works to: raise awareness of neurofibromatosis; provide help, support and advice to those affected, their families and the professionals working with them; provide relevant, up-to-date information and facilitate research.

**Employees: 6**
**Regional offices: 1**

## The NFSH Charitable Trust Ltd

21 York Road, Northampton, Northamptonshire NN1 5QG
T: 01604 603247
F: 01604 603534
E: office@thehealingtrust.org.uk
www.thehealingtrust.org.uk
Chair: Alan Knott
**Employees: 5**
**Volunteers: 4000**
**Regional offices: 65**

## The Not Forgotten Association

4th Floor, 2 Grosvenor Gardens, London SW1W 0DH
T: 020 7730 2400
F: 020 7730 0020
E: admin@nfassociation.org
www.nfassociation.org
Chief Executive: Piers Storie-Pugh
A tri-service charity which provides entertainment and recreation for the serving wounded, injured or sick and for ex-service men and women with disabilities. This is achieved through a unique programme of concerts, outings, holidays, events and the provision of televisions and/or TV licences. Our aim is to provide comradeship, challenge, hope and something to which ex-service men and women can look forward.

**Employees: 7**
**Volunteers: 25**
**Income: £1,082,000 (2014–15)**

## The Orpheus Centre

E: enquiries@orpheus.org.uk

## The Otherwise Club

Mailing Address Only, 1 Croxley Road, London W9 3HH
T: 020 8969 0893
E: lesliebarson@yahoo.com
www.theotherwiseclub.org.uk
Aims to advance the education of children whose families have chosen to educate them out-of-school without distinction of race, sex, political, religious or other opinions, through the provision of facilities, activities, trips and workshops.

## The Philanthropy Workshop

2 Temple Place, London WC2R 3BD
T: 020 7240 0262
F: 020 7240 8022
E: info@tpw.org
www.tpw.org
The Institute for Philanthropy works to increase effective philanthropy in the UK and internationally. We do this by: providing donor education and building donor networks; serving as a forum for new ideas; developing promising models for promoting philanthropy.

**Employees: 15**

## The Prebend Day Centre

The Prebend Day Centre, 12 Prebend Street, Bedford, Bedfordshire MK40 1QW
T: 01234 365955
Helpline: 01234 376835
F: 01234 352717
E: admin@prebendcentre.org.uk
www.prebendcentre.org.uk
Chief Executive: Ryan Flecknell
Bedford Concern for the Homeless and Rootless provides a Day Centre where our clients can get cheap hot food, clothing and washing facilities and somewhere to relax in comfort. We provide counselling services to help our clients get access to jobs, housing and generally re-enter normal society.

**Employees: 10**
**Volunteers: 30**
**Regional offices: 1**

## The Printing Charity

First Floor, Underwood House, 235 Three Bridges Road, Crawley, West Sussex RH10 1LS
T: 01293 542820
F: 01293 542826
E: info@theprintingcharity.org.uk
www.theprintingcharity.org.uk
Chief Executive : Stephen Gilbert
The Printing Charity: helps individuals and their families; helps people of all ages; wants to help more people. Whatever a person's job is or was for three years in an organisation that produces a printed output – printing, publishing, operating presses, driving, cleaning, advertising, photography, graphic arts, making ink, recycling paper – the charity is there to help through regular financial assistance, one-off grants and its two sheltered homes for retired printers.

## The Queen's Nursing Institute

1A Henrietta Place, London W1G 0LZ
T: 020 7549 1400
E: matthew.bradby@qni.org.uk
www.qni.org.uk
Chief Executive: Dr Crystal Oldman
The Queen's Nursing Institute is the charity dedicated to patient care in the home and in the community. We work with nurses and decision-makers to make sure that high-quality nursing is available for everyone, where and when they need it.

**Employees: 14**
**Income: £750,000 (2013–14)**

## The Radio Amateurs' Emergency Network

Far Cockcroft, Rishworth, Sowerby Bridge,
West Yorkshire HX6 4SB
T: 0303 040 1080
E: cosec@raynet-uk.net
www.raynet-uk.net
Chairman: C Clark
The Radio Amateurs' Emergency Network,
known as RAYNET, provides communications
to government, emergency and voluntary
organisations in times of emergency or
community support.
Volunteers: 1600
Regional offices: 14

## The Respite Association

4 Lowgate Lane, Bicker, Boston,
Lincolnshire PE20 3DG
T: 01775 820176
E: help@respiteassociation.org
www.respiteassociation.org
CEO: Preston Keeling
Aims to relieve the stress on unpaid carers by
offering assistance with funding alternative
care enabling a short respite break. As of
2013 we have also added a smaller service to
the above, now offering some carers free
holiday accommodation in Skegness or
Blackpool for a break without the person they
normally care for to enable a proper break.
Details of both schemes are on our website,
as are application forms.
Employees: 2
Volunteers: 12
Regional offices: 1
Income: £107,000 (2013–14)

## The Rivers Trust

Rain-Charm House, Kyl Cober Parc,
Stoke Climsland, Callington,
Cornwall PL17 8PH
T: 01579 372142
E: alan@theriverstrust.org
www.theriverstrust.org
Chief Executive: Arlin Rickard
The Rivers Trust is an umbrella environmental
charity representing the rivers trust
movement in England, Wales and Northern
Ireland. It works by promoting practical and
sustainable solutions at a river catchment
scale to environmental issues across the UK
and Europe.
Employees: 10
Income: £1,070,549 (2013–14)

## The Royal National College for the Blind

Gardner Hall, Venns Lane, Hereford,
Herefordshire HR1 1DT
T: 01432 265725
F: 01432 842979
E: peter.okeefe@rnc.ac.uk
www.rnc.ac.uk
Principal: Mr Mark Fisher
Vision: People with visual impairment
have true equality. Mission: Education,
employment and empowerment for people
with a visual impairment.
Employees: 174
Volunteers: 21
Income: £6,845,000 (2014–15)

## The Royal Society for the Prevention of Accidents (RoSPA)

RoSPA House, 28 Calthorpe Road,
Edgbaston, Birmingham,
West Midlands B15 1RP
T: 0121 248 2000
F: 0121 248 2001
E: sbrookes@rospa.com
www.rospa.com
Chief Executive: Tom Mullarkey
More than 14,000 people die as a result of
accidents across the UK each year, while
thousands more are maimed and millions
injured. Through our varied activities –
campaigning, carrying out research,
influencing legislation, informing and
educating, auditing and providing expert
consultancy to businesses – we're committed
to putting an end to unnecessary suffering
at work, on the road, in the home and at
leisure to achieve our mission: to save lives
and reduce injuries.
Employees: 130
Regional offices: 2

## The Royal Star and Garter Homes

15 Castle Mews, Hampton,
Middlesex TW12 2NP
T: 020 8481 7676
F: 020 8481 7677
E: general.enquiries@starandgarter.org
www.starandgarter.org
Chief Executive: Mike Barter
The Royal Star and Garter Homes is a charity
founded in 1916 to care for the severely
injured young men returning from the
battlegrounds of the First World War. Today
we provide specialist care to the whole
military family in our friendly, modern and
comfortable homes in Solihull and Surbiton.
Regional offices: 1

## The Scout Association

Gilwell Park, Chingford, London E4 7QW
T: 020 8433 7100
F: 020 8433 7108
E: info.centre@scout.org.uk
www.scouts.org.uk
Chief Executive: Matt Hyde
Scouting exists to actively engage and
support young people in their personal
development, empowering them to make
a positive contribution to society.
Employees: 240
Volunteers: 89013

## The Seeing Dogs Alliance

116 Potters Lane, Send, Woking,
Surrey GU23 7AL
T: 01483 765556
F: 01483 750846
E: info@seeingdogs.org.uk
www.seeingdogs.org.uk
Furthers the mobility of blind persons
through the use of trained training guide
dogs, known as Seeing Dogs.
Employees: 1
Volunteers: 20

## The Sequal Trust

3 Ploughmans Corner, Wharf Road,
Ellesmere, Shropshire SY12 0EJ
T: 01691 624222 (also fax)
E: info@thesequaltrust.org.uk
www.thesequaltrust.org.uk
Chair: Dorcas Munday
The Sequal Trust is a national charity that
fundraises to provide communication aids for
disabled people with speech, movement and/
or severe learning difficulties.
Employees: 4
Volunteers: 7

## The Sick Children's Trust

80 Ashfield Street, London E1 2BJ
T: 020 7791 2266
F: 020 7709 8358
E: claudette@sickchildrenstrust.org
www.sickchildrenstrust.org
Chief Executive: Claudette Watson
Provides high-quality 'home from home'
accommodation for families whose children
are receiving hospital treatment for serious
illnesses. We exist to support and promote
the child's recovery and further to support the
fabric and wellbeing of the family as a whole.
Employees: 26
Volunteers: 10
Regional offices: 7

## The Sickle Cell Society

54 Station Road, London NW10 4UA
T: 020 8961 7795
F: 020 8961 8346
E: info@sicklecellsociety.org
www.sicklecellsociety.org
Our aim is to enable and assist individuals with a sickle cell disorder to realise their full economic and social potential. Objectives are to provide relief for persons with sickle cell disorders, the relief of poverty, provision of recreational activities and improvement of public information, assisting in research into the causes, treatment of the condition and dissemination of such information.
Employees: 6
Volunteers: 20
Regional offices: 2

## The SMA Trust

1C Atherstone Barns, Atherstone on Stour,
Stratford upon Avon,
Warwickshire CV37 8NE
T: 01789 801155
E: mandy@smatrust.org
www.smatrust.org
Chief Executive: Joanna Mitchell
We are the only UK charity solely dedicated to funding medical research into Spinal Muscular atrophy (SMA). Our objective is to be active and progressive in the search for a cure and treatments for SMA.
Employees: 4
Volunteers: 6–10
Regional offices: 1
Income: £350,000 (2013–14)

## The Somerville Foundation

Saracens House, 25 St Margarets Green,
Ipswich, Suffolk IP4 2BN
T: 01473 252007
Helpline: 0800 854759
F: 01473 281823
E: admin@thesf.org.uk
www.thesf.org.uk
National Director: John Richardson
Supports young people and adults born with a heart condition in the UK. Offers support, information and advice to help them stay in control, empowering patients to enable them to take control of their lives and manage their own heart condition. We listen to the patients and respond to their needs, providing them with the support they need and want.
Employees: 5
Volunteers: 10
Regional offices: 1
Income: £107,700 (2013–14)

## The Tavistock Centre for Couple Relationships

The Tavistock Centre, 70 Warren Street,
London W1T 5PB
T: 020 7380 1975
F: 020 7388 6162
E: enquiries@tavistockrelationships.org
www.tccr.org.uk
CEO: Susanna Abse
TCCR is the leading provider of highly specialised and affordable couple counselling and psychotherapy. We offer a range of relationship, psychosexual and parenting support services throughout London. Our services include: relationship counselling; couple psychotherapy; wellbeing service – brief counselling; parenting together; psychosexual therapy; divorce and separation unit.
Employees: 42

## The Therapy Database

23 Holybourne Avenue, London SW15 4JJ
T: 020 8788 5370
E: info@thetherapydatabase.org
www.therapydatabase.info
Trustee Director: Gerard Bonham-Carter
We enable doctors to fulfil their duty to gain their patients' fully informed consent to treatment. We enable patients to fully understand their treatment options. Patients benefit from the powerful placebo effect when they undergo treatments that they believe in. We achieve both goals by enabling patients to access comprehensive and balanced information on Western mainstream treatments and on the alternatives. This fulfils a DOH requirement for valid consent.
Employees: 1
Volunteers: 9

## The Traveller Movement

The Resource Centre, 356 Holloway Road,
London N7 6PA
T: 020 7607 2002
F: 020 7607 2005
E: info@travellermovement.org.uk
travellermovement.org.uk
ITM aims to develop the capacity and skills of members of the socially and economically disadvantaged community of Irish travellers in such a way that they are better able to identify, and help meet, their needs and to participate more fully in society; and to promote equality and diversity and racial harmony for the benefit of the public by encouraging others to understand the culture and needs of Irish travellers.
Employees: 1
Volunteers: 11

## The Vince Hines Foundation

The Acton Centre, Acton Old Town Hall,
High Street, London W3 6NE
Helpline: 0303 040 2690
F: 0870 974 8524
E: cmass@ubol.com
www.ubol.com
The charity was formed in 1975 and has operated continuously since. Its focus is on self-help and grassroots support. It provides general support to members of the community on matters dealing with community, education and training. This includes information, advice and guidance, with a focus on the harder to reach and those not in education, training and employment. It provides support to volunteers and the formation of new groups, including those involved in the performing arts.

## The Who Cares? Trust

15–18 White Lion Street, London N1 9PG
T: 020 7251 3117
Helpline: 020 7017 8901
E: mailbox@thewhocarestrust.org.uk
www.thewhocarestrust.org.uk
Chief Executive: Natasha Finlayson
We provide help, support and advice to young people in care and young care leavers so that they can unleash their potential and take control of their lives. We help make the care system work better by ensuring that young people's voices and perspectives shape policy and service provision.
Employees: 18
Income: £901,679 (2015–16)

## The Wildlife Trusts

The Kiln, Waterside, Mather Road, Newark,
Nottinghamshire NG24 1WT
T: 01636 677711
F: 01636 670001
E: enquiry@wildlifetrusts.org
www.wildlifetrusts.org
CEO: Stephanie Hilborne
Aims to protect wildlife for the future and to educate the public in the understanding and appreciation of nature and the need for its conservation.
Employees: 2000
Volunteers: 43000
Regional offices: 47

## Theatres Trust

22 Charing Cross Road,
London WC2H 0QL
T: 020 7836 8591
E: info@theatrestrust.org.uk
www.theatrestrust.org.uk
We are the national advisory public body for
theatres. We champion the past, present and
future of live theatre, by protecting the
buildings and what goes on inside. We do this
through providing advice on planning and
development, supplying resources and advice
to make theatres sustainable and offering
financial assistance through grants. We help
people discover more about theatres and
campaign for theatres at risk.
**Employees: 8**
**Volunteers: 5**

## Thera Trust

The West House, Alpha Court,
Swingbridge Road, Grantham,
Lincolnshire NG31 7XT
T: 01476 562777
F: 01476 565677
E: sarah.frost@thera.co.uk
www.thera.co.uk
Thera Trust offers those with a learning
disability support and is thereby helping them
to get the most out of life.
**Employees: 650**

## Think Global

CAN Mezzanine, 32–36 Loman Street,
London SE1 0EH
T: 020 3751 3000
F: 020 7922 7929
E: info@think-global.org.uk
www.think-global.org.uk
**Chief Executive: Tom Franklin**
Think Global promotes education for a just
and sustainable world. We have a network of
200 member organisations that share this
commitment and we work with them to
change UK education for the better. Our
mission is to promote: education that puts
learning in a global context, fostering critical
and creative thinking; self-awareness and
open-mindedness towards difference;
understanding of global issues and power
relationships; optimism and action for a
better world.
**Employees: 10**
**Income: £400,000 (2010–11)**

## Third Age Trust (National Office U3A)

The Old Municipal Buildings, 19 East Street,
Bromley, Kent BR1 1QE
T: 020 8466 6139
E: national.office@u3a.org.uk
www.u3a.org.uk
**Chairman: Pam Jones**
The Third Age Trust is the national
representative body for the Universities of the
Third Age in the UK. U3As are democratic
self-funded, self-managed, later-life learning
organisations providing daytime education
activities for people no longer in full-time
employment.
**Employees: 10**

## This Way Up Youth Project

The Bethany Centre,
155a Kineton Green Road, Olton,
Solihull B92 7EG
Helpline: 0121 439 9181
E: info@twup.org.uk
www.twup.org.uk
**CEO: Pete English**
Our team works in local Solihull schools
supporting young people affected by loss
through family breakdown or bereavement.
We offer help to those trying to come to
terms with this difficult life-changing event
through our Lost and Found Course. We also
train Christian youth and community workers
across the country to deliver our course so
that more young people can be helped to
turn their lives the right way up.
**Employees: 6**
**Volunteers: 5**
**Regional offices: 1**

## Thomas Pocklington Trust

5 Castle Row, Horticultural Place,
London W4 4JQ
T: 020 8995 0880
F: 020 8987 9965
E: info@pocklington-trust.org.uk
www.pocklington-trust.org.uk
Provides quality housing care and support
services for adult people with sight loss.
Sponsors social and public health research
in the field of visual impairment.
**Employees: 19**
**Volunteers: 116**
**Regional offices: 10**

## Thrive

The Geoffrey Udall Centre, Beech Hill Road,
Beech Hill, Reading, Berkshire RG7 2AT
T: 0118 988 5688
F: 0118 988 5677
E: info@thrive.org.uk
www.thrive.org.uk or www.
carryongardening.org.uk
**Chief Executive: Kathryn Rossiter**
Thrive is a national charity whose mission is to
research, educate and promote the use and
advantages of gardening for people with a
disability. It is the only national charity of its
kind working to bring change to disabled
people through gardening. This is done by
offering advice and information, supporting
health and education professionals, carrying
out research and running local gardening
projects in Battersea, Reading, Birmingham
and Gateshead.
**Employees: 50**
**Volunteers: 110**
**Regional offices: 4**

## Through the Roof

PO Box 353, Epsom, Surrey KT18 5WS
T: 01372 749955
E: info@throughtheroof.org
www.throughtheroof.org
**CEO: Tim Wood**
Mission: Transforming lives through disabled
people. Our work: Providing life-changing
opportunities and equipping churches,
communities and individuals. Our vision: A
world where people live interdependently,
mutually giving and receiving as God intended.

## Tibet Relief Fund

2 Baltic Place, 287 Kingsland Road,
London N1 5AQ
T: 020 3119 0041
E: info@tibetrelieffund.co.uk
www.tibetrelieffund.co.uk
**Chief Executive: Philippa Carrick**
Tibet Relief Fund was set up to respond to
the needs of Tibetan refugees, following the
Chinese invasion of Tibet in 1950. Today, we
provide vital support to Tibetans in exile in
India and Nepal and inside Tibet, including
emergency aid to newly arrived refugees
and education, healthcare and income-
generating projects for the long-term.
Tibet Relief Fund also runs a sponsorship
programme to support children, university
students, elderly people, monks and nuns.
**Employees: 6**
**Volunteers: 3**

## Time Banking UK

The Exchange, Brick Row, Stroud,
Gloucestershire GL5 1DF
T: 01453 750952
E: info@timebanks.co.uk
www.timebanking.org
Chief Executive: Sarah Bird
We provide information, practical support,
inspiration and training to anyone wanting to
use time banking as a tool to build community
and encourage active citizenship.
Employees: 4
Regional offices: 1
Income: £116,636 (2013–14)

## Time For God

Community House, 46–50 East Parade,
Harrogate, North Yorkshire HG1 5RR
T: 01423 536248
F: 05602 053964
E: office@timeforgod.org
www.timeforgod.org
Director: Paul Webster
TfG is a faith-based organisation which
matches volunteers with long-term
volunteering placements. It is supported by all
the major Christian denominations in the UK.
With over 40 years' experience, our projects
are based in areas of social need. The majority
of our work involves placing international
volunteers in placements in the UK, however
we also have opportunities for UK volunteers
to travel abroad.
Employees: 6
Volunteers: 100
Regional offices: 1

## TimeBank

One KX, 120 Cromer Street,
London WC1H 8BS
T: 020 3111 0700
E: helpdesk@timebank.org.uk
www.timebank.org.uk
Chief Executive: Helen Walker
TimeBank is a national volunteering charity.
We recruit and train volunteers to deliver
mentoring projects to tackle complex social
problems. We also work with businesses to
engage their staff in volunteering. We believe
that great volunteering can transform the
lives of both volunteers and beneficiaries by
building stronger, happier and more inclusive
communities.

## Tiny Tickers

76 Chiswick Lane, London, 4 Fennel Court,
Methley W4 2LA
T: 07733 034533
Helpline: 07793 093181
E: jon@tinytickers.org
www.tinytickers.org
Chief Executive: Jon Arnold

Around 1,000 newborn babies will leave UK
hospitals this year with no one realising they
are suffering from a major heart condition.
Tiny Tickers is the only national charity with
the sole aim of improving the early detection,
diagnosis and care for babies with serious
heart problems and their families.
Employees: 5
Volunteers: 10
Income: £290,000 (2015–16)

## Toc H

PO Box 15824, Birmingham,
West Midlands B13 3JU
T: 0121 443 3552
E: info@toch.org.uk
www.toch.org.uk
Chair of Trustees: Terry Drummond
Striving to eliminate social exclusion, Toc H
is a charity committed to building a fairer
society. Toc H provides alternative education,
self-development and mentoring programmes
for young people, in partnership with schools,
local authorities and youth agencies. The
charity also offers community centres. Toc H
has a 20-bed outdoor pursuits center in
Langdale in the Lake District.
Volunteers: 300
Income: £121,000 (2014–15)

## Together for Short Lives

4th Floor, Bridge House,
48–52 Baldwin Street, Bristol,
Avon BS1 1QB
T: 0117 989 7820
Helpline: 0845 108 2201
E: info@togetherforshortlives.org.uk
www.togetherforshortlives.org.uk
Chief Executive: Barbara Gelb
We estimate that there are 23,500 children
and young people across the UK unlikely to
reach adulthood. Together for Short Lives
is the only charity working across the UK
representing all these children and their
families as well as the organisations and
people that support them. We want to help
ensure that all of these children and their
families get the best possible care and support
whenever and wherever they need it.
Employees: 30
Volunteers: 2

## Together Trust

Together Trust Centre, Schools Hill,
Cheadle, Cheshire SK8 1JE
T: 0161 283 4848
F: 0161 283 4747
E: enquiries@togethertrust.org.uk
www.togethertrust.org.uk
Chief Executive: Mark Lee
We provide a range of social care, special
education, community support and
consultancy services in the North West of
England and surrounding areas. In addition to
local authority funded places, Together Trust
services can be purchased by families, carers
and service users over the age of 18 or their
brokers via a direct payment, individual
budget, individual service fund or personal/
private funds.
Employees: 770
Volunteers: 50
Income: £22,980,000 (2014–15)

## Together Working for Wellbeing

12 Old Street, London EC1V 9BE
T: 020 7780 7300
F: 020 7780 7301
E: contactus@together-uk.org
www.together-uk.org
MACA is a leading national charity providing
high-quality services in the community and
hospitals and prisons for people with mental-
health needs and their carers.
Employees: 800
Regional offices: 3

## Tommy's

Nicholas House, 3 Laurence Pountney Hill,
London EC4R 0BB
T: 020 7398 3400
Helpline: 0800 014 7800
F: 020 7398 3479
E: mailbox@tommys.org
www.tommys.org
Chief Executive: Jane Brewin
Tommy's is dedicated to funding research
into the cause and prevention of miscarriage,
stillbirth and premature birth, as well as
promoting pregnancy health through a
national information programme.
Employees: 22
Volunteers: 1

## Tomorrow's People Trust

1st Floor, Minster House,
York Road, Eastbourne,
East Sussex BN21 4ST
T: 01323 418143
E: alevitt@tomorrows-people.co.uk
www.tomorrows-people.org.uk
Chief Executive: Debbie Scott
Tomorrow's People is a national employment charity helping long-term unemployed people out of welfare dependency and into jobs and self-sufficiency. Advisers work with individuals directly in their communities helping them to overcome their barriers to work, and develop the confidence, motivation and skills they need to move forward in their lives. Since 1984 we have helped more than 440,000 people on their journey back to work.
Employees: 135
Regional offices: 15

## Tools for Self Reliance

Netley Marsh Workshops, Ringwood Road,
Netley Marsh, Southampton,
Hampshire SO40 7GY
T: 023 8086 9697
E: jemma@tfsr.org
www.tfsr.org
Chief Executive: Sarah Ingleby
Tools for Self Reliance works with partners in Ghana, Malawi, Sierra Leone, Tanzania, Uganda and Zambia. Our mission is to reduce poverty in Africa by helping people build sustainable livelihoods through the provision of tools and training. We aim to empower men and women to gain meaningful employment through our vocational, business and life skills training and the provision of tool kits for their trade.
Employees: 10
Volunteers: 800

## Topps – Training Opportunities

Hanover House, Wolverhampton,
West Midlands WV2 3BY
T: 01902 877920
E: info@toppstraining.co.uk
www.topps.org.uk
Provides information, support and training to women returning to the workplace and young people and women who wish to set up a small business or social enterprise.

## Torch Trust for the Blind

Torch House, Torch Way,
Northampton Road, Market Harborough,
Leicestershire LE16 9HL
T: 01858 438260
F: 01858 438275
E: volunteers@torchtrust.org
www.torchtrust.org
Chief Executive: Gordon Temple
The principal aim of the Torch Trust is to meet the spiritual needs of blind and partially sighted people through producing Christian literature in accessible media and promoting Christian fellowship across the UK and around the world.
Employees: 40
Volunteers: 81

## Torridge Community Transport Association

E: john.conniss@torridge-cta.org.uk

## Tourette's Action (Tourette Syndrome (UK) Association)

The Meads Business Centre, 19 Kingsmead,
Farnborough, Hampshire GU14 7SR
T: 01252 362638
Helpline: 0300 777 8427
E: help@tourettes-action.org.uk
www.tourettes-action.org.uk
Chief Executive: Suzanne Dobson
Tourette's Action is the UK's leading support and research charity for people with Tourette Syndrome (TS) and their families. We want people with TS to receive the practical support and social acceptance they need to help them live their lives to the full. We deal with all forms of TS including the most challenging.
Employees: 8
Volunteers: 8

## Tourism for All UK

7A Pixel Mill, 44 Appleby Road, Kendal,
Cumbria LA9 6ES
T: 0845 124 9971
E: info@tourismforall.org.uk
www.tourismforall.org.uk
Chief Executive: Ray Veal
Tourism for All UK is an independent charity supporting leisure and tourism opportunities for all, operating an information service to older and disabled people, and working with the industry and government to raise the standards of welcome to all guests.
Employees: 1
Volunteers: 2
Regional offices: 1

## Tower Hamlets CVS

E: khadiru.mahdi@thcvs.org.uk

## Town and Country Planning Association

17 Carlton House Terrace,
London SW1Y 5AS
T: 020 7930 8903
F: 020 7930 3280
E: tcpa@tcpa.org.uk
www.tcpa.org.uk
Provides an informed and independent voice on national, regional and environmental planning policies and legislation, and campaigns for more local initiatives and decentralisation of decision-making.
Employees: 7
Volunteers: 40

## Townswomen's Guilds

Tomlinson House, 329 Tyburn Road,
Birmingham B24 8HJ
T: 0121 326 0400
F: 0121 326 1976
E: tghq@townswomen.org.uk
www.the-tg.com
National Chair: Pauline Meyers
Aims to advance the social awareness of all women, irrespective of race, creed or political affiliation.

## Toynbee Hall

28 Commercial Street, London E1 6LS
T: 020 7247 6943
F: 020 7377 5964
E: info@toynbeehall.org.uk
www.toynbeehall.org.uk
Chief Executive: Graham Fisher
Toynbee Hall is a community organisation that pioneers ways to reduce poverty and disadvantage. Based in East London, we provide free legal, debt and general support service advice; as well as elderly and youth programmes. We have been a catalyst for social reform in the UK for 130 years, and continue to bring together communities, organisations and policy makers to create new ways to help those who find themselves in poverty today.
Employees: 75
Volunteers: 100+
Income: £6,000,000 (2013–14)

## Tpas England

Suite 4B, Paragon House,
48 Seymour Grove, Manchester,
Greater Manchester M16 0LN
T: 0161 868 3500
E: info@tpas.org.uk
www.tpas.org.uk
Acting Chief Executive: Jenny Osbourne

Tpas exists to promote resident and community empowerment. We are a membership organisation of housing associations, local authorities and tenants groups. We provide training, conferences, advice and consultancy services.
**Employees: 12**
**Volunteers: 50**
**Regional offices: 1**

## Tracheo-Oesophageal Fistula Support Group

**St George's Centre, 91 Victoria Road, Netherfield, Nottingham NG4 2NN**
**T: 0115 961 3092**
**F: 0115 961 3097**
**E: info@tofs.org.uk**
**www.tofs.org.uk**
Supports the families and carers of children born unable to swallow because of oesophagael atresia, tracheo-oesophageal atresia, tracheo-oesophageal fistula and associated conditions.
**Employees: 3**
**Volunteers: 45**

## Trafford Carers Centre

**E: info@traffordcarerscentre.org.uk**
**www.traffordcarerscentre.org.uk**

## Transaid

**137 Euston Road, London NW1 2AA**
**T: 020 7387 8136**
**F: 020 7387 2669**
**E: info@transaid.org**
**www.transaid.org**
**Chief Executive: Gary Forster**
Transaid is an international NGO working through the application of best practice in transport and logistics to alleviate poverty, facilitating access to basic services such as healthcare, and encouraging economic growth and development.
**Employees: 6**
**Volunteers: 10**
**Regional offices: 3**

## Transform Africa

**GQ Leroy House, 436 Essex Road, London N1 3QP**
**T: 020 7354 5455**
**F: 020 7354 5499**
**E: charles@transformafrica.org**
**www.transformafrica.org**
**Chief Executive Officer: Charles Kazibwe**
Transform Africa aims to strengthen and empower African organisations and their communities to more effectively tackle poverty and its causes. We offer training

services and work in partnership with local organisations to support local communities.
**Employees: 3**

## Transparency International (UK)

**32–36 Loman Street, London SE1 0EH**
**T: 020 7922 7906**
**F: 020 7785 6355**
**E: info@transparency.org.uk**
**www.transparency.org.uk**
We are the UK national chapter of the global anti-corruption non-governmental organisation, Transparency International (TI). TI, which is co-ordinated by an international secretariat in Berlin, is a coalition of more than 90 autonomous national chapters who are committed to fighting corruption using transparency as a major tool. TI is dedicated to combating corruption at the national and international levels through constructive partnerships with governments, the private sector, civil society and international organisations.
**Volunteers: 20**
**Regional offices: 1**

## Transplant Sport UK

**Basepoint Business Centre, Winnall Valley Road, Winchester, Hampshire SO23 0LD**
**T: 0115 837 0878**
**E: office@transplantsport.org.uk**
**www.transplantsport.org.uk**
**CEO: Kevin Kibble**
We are a registered charity whose main aim is to raise awareness of the need for organ donation in the UK and worldwide. Through organising sports and social events for transplant recipients Transplant Sport UK shows the benefits of organ donation and proves that you can lead a normal and active life again after transplantation.
**Employees: 3**
**Volunteers: 100**
**Regional offices: 1**

## Transport Trust

**202 Lambeth Road, London SE1 7JY**
**T: 020 7928 6464**
**E: info@thetransporttrust.org.uk**
**www.transporttrust.com**
Promotes and encourages the permanent preservation, for the benefit of the nation, of transport items of historical or technical interest and books, drawings, films, photographs and recordings of all forms of transport by rail, air and water.

## Travelling Light Theatre Company

**Barton Hill Settlement, 43 Ducie Road, Barton Hill, Bristol, Avon BS5 0AX**
**T: 0117 377 3166**
**E: info@travellinglighttheatre.org.uk**
**www.travellinglighttheatre.org.uk**
**General Manager: Dienka Hines**
Travelling Light Theatre Company creates exciting and inspiring theatre for and with young people from its base in Barton Hill, Bristol. We are world renowned for our innovative devised productions which tour locally and nationally to venues and schools. Our participation programme works with young people from babies to age 25s, including projects for children with additional needs. We work closely with our local community, showcasing our work with free performances, storytelling sessions and school theatre workshops.
**Employees: 8**
**Volunteers: 7**
**Regional offices: 1**

## Tree Council

**71 Newcomen Street, London SE1 1YT**
**T: 020 7407 9992**
**F: 020 7407 9908**
**E: info@treecouncil.org.uk**
**www.treecouncil.org.uk**
**Director General: Pauline Buchanan Black**
Promotes for the public benefit, the improvement and development of the environment through the planting, care, nurture and cultivation of trees in town and country.
**Employees: 5**
**Volunteers: 8000**

## Trees for Cities

**Prince Consort Lodge, Kennington Park, Kennington Park Place, London SE11 4AS**
**T: 020 7587 1320**
**F: 020 7793 9042**
**E: david@treesforcities.org**
**www.treesforcities.org**
**Chief Executive: David Eliott**
Planting trees and greening cities worldwide.
**Employees: 24**
**Volunteers: 50**
**Income: £1,140,000 (2014–15)**

## Treloar Trust

Powell Drive, Holybourne, Alton,
Hampshire GU34 4GL
T: 01420 547400
E: info@treloar.org.uk
www.treloar.org.uk
CEO: Tony Reid
The Treloar Trust exists to provide education,
independence training and care for physically
disabled young people from all over the UK.
It aims to provide support and opportunities
and to develop each individual student's
confidence and abilities in all aspects of his
or her life.

## Trigeminal Neuralgia Association

PO Box 234, Oxted, Surrey RH8 8BE
Helpline: 01883 370214
E: admin@tna.org.uk
www.tna.org.uk
Chairman: Jillie Abbott
We exist to reach those affected by trigeminal
neuralgia (TN) (sufferers, carers, healthcare
professionals and the wider public); to provide
evidence-based information, support and
encouragement: with opportunities for
people to express their feelings and concerns
with those who understand their situation,
and encouragement to actively self-manage
their TN and to add to the body of knowledge
about TN by increasing the level of knowledge
about TN and TNA UK amongst healthcare
professionals, policy-makers and others.
Employees: 1
Volunteers: 20
Income: £69,929 (2013–14)

## Tropical Health and Education Trust

5th Floor, 1 Wimpole Street,
London W1G 0AE
T: 020 7290 3892
F: 020 7290 3890
E: info@thet.org
www.thet.org
Chief Executive: Andrew Purkis
THET is committed to improving access to
and the quality of health services in
developing countries. We believe that the
most effective way of doing this is to work in
partnership with those delivering and running
healthcare, helping to strengthen and extend
existing services.
Employees: 12
Volunteers: 4

## Trust for Urban Ecology

T: 020 8293 1904
E: information@tcv.org.uk
www.urbanecology.org.uk

Supports the conservation of the natural
elements of the urban landscape; promotes
the use of urban nature areas for the health,
enjoyment and education of all sections of
the community; provides information, advice
and expertise on the design, creation and
management of urban greenspaces.

## Tuberous Sclerosis Association

PO Box 8001, Derby DE1 0YA
T: 01332 290734 (also fax)
E: admin@tuberous-sclerosis.org
www.tuberous-sclerosis.org
Chief Executive: Jayne Spink
Offers support to people with tuberous
sclerosis complex and their families or carers.
Promoting education, publicity and
information to increase awareness and
understanding. There are specialist advisers to
advise on any problems relating to TSC.
Employees: 11 P/T

## Turning Point

Standon House, 21 Mansell Street,
London E1 8AA
T: 020 7481 7600
F: 020 7480 6288
E: info@turning-point.co.uk
www.turning-point.co.uk
Turning Point is the UK's leading social care
organisation. We provide services for people
with complex needs, including those affected
by drug and alcohol misuse, mental health
problems and those with a learning disability.
We provide services in 200 locations and
worked with around 130,000 people last
year.
Employees: 1800
Regional offices: 200

## Tutu Foundation UK

Tutu Foundation UK,
18 Victoria Park Square, London E2 9PF
T: 020 8980 9737
E: info@tutufoundationuk.org
tutufoundationul.org
The Tutu Foundation UK builds peace in
fractured communities in the UK using
Ubuntu, a model inspired by Archbishop
Desmond Tutu's peace and reconciliation
work all over the world. To successfully tackle
the anti-social behaviour and violence in
our communities, underlying attitudes and
behaviours must first be addressed in order
to build a lasting peace.
Employees: 2
Volunteers: 70
Regional offices: 1

## Twin Ltd

3rd Floor, 1 Curtain Road,
London EC2A 3LT
T: 020 7375 1221
E: info@twin.org.uk
www.twin.org.uk
Uses trade positively to redress the imbalance
between north and south, to build better
livelihoods for the poorest and weakest in the
trading chain and to provoke development
and longer term shifts in the political and
economic environment.

## Twins and Multiple Births Association

Manor House, Church Hill, Aldershot,
Hampshire GU12 4JU
T: 01252 332344
Helpline: 0800 138 0509
E: enquiries@tamba.org.uk
www.tamba.org.uk
CEO: Keith Reed
Tamba exists to enable the families of twins,
triplets and more to meet the challenge of
their unique experience.
Employees: 12
Volunteers: 100
Regional offices: 2

# U

## UCCF

5 Blue Boar Street, Oxford OX1 4EE
T: 01865 253678
F: 0116 255 5672
E: reception@uccf.org.uk
www.uccf.org.uk
IT Manager: David Holland
Employees: 106
Volunteers: 50

## UK Acquired Brain Injury Forum

c/o Royal Hospital for Neuro Disability,
West Hill, Putney, London SW15 3SW
T: 020 8780 4500
E: info@rhn.org.uk
www.ukabif.org.uk
The UK Acquired Brain Injury Forum
(UKABIF) is a not-for-profit coalition of
organisations and individuals that seeks to

promote understanding of all aspects of acquired brain injury and to provide information and expert input to policy makers, service providers and the general public to promote the interests of brain injured people and their families.
Employees: 1

## UK Community Foundations

12 Angel Gate, 320–326 City Road, Angel, London EC1V 2PT
T: 020 7713 9326
F: 020 7713 9327
E: lkarban@ukcommunityfoundations.org
ukcommunityfoundations.org
Chief Executive: Stephen Hammersley
UKCF is the UK-wide organisation supporting and promoting UK community foundations. Community foundations are charities dedicated to strengthening local communities. They manage funds donated by individuals and organisations, building endowment and acting as the vital link between donors and local needs.
Employees: 10
Income: £11,400,000 (2013–14)

## UK Council for International Student Affairs

9–17 St Albans Place, London N1 0NX
T: 020 7288 4330
Helpline: 020 7107 9922
F: 020 7288 4360
E: membership@ukcisa.org.uk
www.ukcisa.org.uk
Chief Executive: Dominic Scott
The UK Council for International Student Affairs (UKCISA) is the UK's national advisory body serving the interests of international students and those who work with them. It aims to encourage best practice, professional development and the highest quality of institutional support for international students throughout the education sector, increase support for international education and raise awareness of its values and benefits, and promote opportunities for greater student mobility.
Employees: 17

## UK Council for Psychotherapy

2nd Floor, Edward House,
2 Wakley Street EC1V 7LT
T: 020 7014 9955
F: 020 7014 9977
E: info@ukcp.org.uk
www.psychotherapy.org.uk
UKCP is recognised as the leading professional body for the education, training and accreditation of psychotherapists and psychotherapeutic counsellors. We represent member organisations and over 7,000 individual therapists.
Employees: 20

## UK Council on Deafness

Westwood Park, London Road,
Little Horkesley, Colchester C06 4BS
T: 01206 274075
F: 01206 274077
E: c.long@deafcouncil.org.uk
www.deafcouncil.org.uk
The national infrastructure organisation for voluntary sector organisations working with deaf people. Our mission is to create an environment in which voluntary sector organisations working with deaf people can flourish. We aim to support members in their work with deaf people and to encourage cooperation between members in promoting and representing the diverse interests of deaf people.
Employees: 3

## UK Health Forum

Fleetbank House, 2–6 Salisbury Square,
London EC4Y 8JX
T: 020 7832 6920
F: 020 7832 6921
E: dan.french@ukhealthforum.org.uk
www.ukhealthforum.org.uk
Chief Executive: Paul Lincoln
Aims to preserve and protect the health of the public and to advance public education about all matters concerning avoidable chronic disease and its prevention.
Employees: 20

## UK Overseas Territories Conservation Forum

Icknield Court, Back Street, Wendover,
Buckinghamshire HP22 6EB
T: 01733 569325
E: cwensink@ukotcf.org
www.ukotcf.org
Honorary Executive Director :
Dr Mike Pienkowski
UKOTCF exists to protect and promote the diverse and increasingly threatened plant and animal species and natural habitats of UK's Overseas Territories (UKOTs) and Crown Dependencies. It aims to do this by providing assistance in the form of expertise, information and liaison between non-governmental organisations and governments, both in the UK and in the Territories themselves. UKOTCF has over 30 years' experience of working with partners in the UKOTs on various projects.
Employees: 1
Volunteers: 14
Income: £371,155 (2015–16)

## UK Public Health Association

2nd Floor, 28 Portland Place,
London W1B 1DE
T: 0870 010 1932
F: 020 7061 3393
E: info@ukpha.org.uk
www.ukpha.org.uk
Promotes and defends public health in the UK; brings together local and national statutory and non-governmental organisations, professional associations, trade unions, voluntary and community groups and individuals; promotes the development of healthy public policy at all levels of government, including the European Union, in order to ensure that the health needs of the UK become a permanent feature of national policy and spending decisions.
Employees: 7
Volunteers: 20

## UK Thalassaemia Society

19 The Broadway, Southgate Circus,
London N14 6PH
T: 020 8882 0011
F: 020 8882 8618
E: office@ukts.org
www.ukts.org
Campaigns on behalf of people suffering from thalassaemia; promotes and coordinates research; educates people on the problems of thalassaemia; offers counselling to sufferers and carriers.
Employees: 2

## UK Youth

Avon Tyrrell, Bransgore,
Hampshire BH23 8EE
T: 01425 672347
F: 01425 673883
E: info@ukyouth.org
www.ukyouth.org
UK Youth exists to develop and promote innovative non-formal education programmes for and with young people
Employees: 59
Volunteers: 40000

## Unique – Rare Chromosome Disorder Support Group

The Stables, Station Rd West, Oxted,
Surrey RH8 9EE
T: 01883 723306
Helpline: 01883 723356
E: craig@rarechromo.org
www.rarechromo.org
Chief Executive Officer: Beverly Searle
Unique provides specialist information and
support to anyone born, often sick and
disabled, with a rare chromosome disorder
and their families. Our aim is to alleviate
feelings of isolation by linking families whose
children have similar clinical and/or practical
problems caused by rare chromosome
disorders. Unique provides family support
services to more than 6,000 UK families.
Employees: 8
Volunteers: 200
Income: £300,000 (2015–16)

## United Kingdom Homecare Association

Group House, 2nd Floor,
52 Sutton Court Road, Sutton,
Surrey SM1 4SL
T: 020 8288 1551
F: 020 8288 1550
E: enquiries@ukhca.co.uk
www.ukhca.co.uk
The professional association of home care
providers from the independent, voluntary,
not-for-profit and statutory sectors.
UKHCA helps organisations that provide
social care, which may include nursing
services, to people in their own homes,
promoting high standards of care and
providing representation with national and
regional policy makers and regulators. The
association represents over 1,500 members
across the UK.
Employees: 10
Volunteers: 14

## United Kingdom Sports Association for People with Learning Disability

2E Leroy House, 436 Essex Road,
London N1 3QP
T: 020 7490 3057
F: 020 7251 8861
E: info@uksportsassociation.org
www.uksportsassociation.org
Chief Executive: Tracey McCillen
The UK Sports Association (UKSA)
promotes, facilitates and supports talented
sports people with learning disability in the
UK to train, compete and excel in national
and international sport. UKSA leads eligibility
and classification, is recognised by UK Sport,
is a member of the British Paralympic
Association and is the official GB member of

the International Sports Federation for Para
Athletes with Intellectual Disability (INAS),
a member of the International Paralympic
Committee.
Employees: 3
Volunteers: 30

## United Kingdom's Disabled People's Council

Litchurch Plaza, Litchurch Lane,
Derby DE24 8AA
T: 01332 295551
F: 01332 295580
E: info@ukdpc.net
www.bcodp.org.uk
Aims to relieve the disability of people with
physical, mental or sensory impairments
and to further their independence and full
participation in the community.
Employees: 10
Volunteers: 50
Regional offices: 1

## United Nations Association

3 Whitehall Court, London SW1A 2EL
T: 020 7930 2931
F: 020 7930 5893
E: woods@una.org.uk
www.una-uk.org
Campaigns for fuller implementation of the
UN Charter in British policy decisions. It aims
to educate government and as wide a cross-
section of the British public as possible in
understanding the principles and purposes
of the UN. Particular interests include:
UN and conflict; international security
and disarmament; human rights; refugee
issues; economic and social, sustainable
development; environmental protection,
culture of peace.
Employees: 20
Regional offices: 130

## United Response

Vantage House, 1 Weir Road,
Wimbledon Park, London SW19 8UX
T: 020 8246 5200
F: 020 8780 9538
E: su.sayer@unitedresponse.org.uk
www.unitedresponse.org.uk
Chief Executive: Su Sayer
United Response is a national charity that
works with people with learning disabilities,
mental health needs and physical disabilities
in over 200 localities across England and
Wales. Our mission is to enable people to
take control of their lives and our vision is of
a society where people with disabilities or
mental health needs are equal participants

and have access to the same rights and
opportunities as everyone else.
Employees: 2900
Volunteers: 300
Regional offices: 4

## United Trusts

PO Box 14, 8 Nelson Road, Edge Hill,
Liverpool L69 7AA
T: 0151 709 8252
F: 0151 708 5621
E: information@unitedtrusts.org.uk
www.unitedtrusts.org.uk
Fundraising to support the relief of poverty,
the advancement of education and such
other purposes beneficial to the community.
United Trust endorses the Workplace
Charity Fund.
Employees: 4
Volunteers: 20

## Universities Federation for Animal Welfare

The Old School, Brewhouse Hill,
Wheathampstead, Hertfordshire AL4 8AN
T: 01582 831818
F: 01582 831414
E: ufaw@ufaw.org.uk
www.ufaw.org.uk
Promotes humane behaviour towards animals
by enlisting the energies of members of the
universities and professional people. Obtains
and disseminates accurate information
relating to the welfare of animals.
Employees: 8

## Universities UK

Woburn House, 20 Tavistock Square,
London WC1H 9HQ
T: 020 7419 4111
Helpline: 020 7419 5523
F: 020 7388 8649
E: info@universitiesuk.ac.uk
www.universitiesuk.ac.uk
Chief Executive: Nicola Dandridge
Universities UK is the major representative
body and membership organisation for the
higher education sector. Its members are the
executive heads of UK universities. Within it
are the England and Northern Ireland
Council, Universities Scotland and Higher
Education Wales. Our mission is to be the
essential voice and best support for a vibrant,
successful and diverse university sector, to
influence and create policy for HE and to
provide an environment where the sector
can flourish.
Employees: 81
Regional offices: 2

## University Association for Contemporary European Studies

School of Public Policy,
University College London,
29–30 Tavistock Square,
London WC1H 9QU
T: 020 7679 4975
F: 020 7679 4973
E: admin@uaces.org
www.uaces.org
The academic association for contemporary European Studies.
Employees: 3

## UNLOCK – for people with convictions

Maidstone Community Support Centre,
39–48 Marsham Street, Maidstone,
Kent ME14 1HH
T: 01622 230705
Helpline: 01634 247350
E: admin@unlock.org.uk
www.unlock.org.uk
Co-directors: Julie Harmsworth / ChristopherStacey
Unlock is an independent, award-winning charity which provides information, advice and advocacy for people with convictions. Our staff and volunteers combine professional training with personal experience to help others overcome the long-term problems that having a conviction can bring. Our knowledge and insight helps us to work with government, employers and others to change policies and practices to create a fairer and more inclusive society so that people with convictions can move on in their lives.
Employees: 6
Volunteers: 6

## UnLtd – the Foundation for Social Entrepreneurs

123 Whitecross Street, Islington,
London EC1Y 8JJ
T: 020 7566 1100
E: pa@unltd.org.uk
www.unltd.org.uk
Chief Executive: Mark Norbury
UnLtd is a charity that supports social entrepreneurs – people with vision, drive, commitment and passion who want to change the world for the better. We do this by providing a complete package of funding and support to help these individuals make their ideas a reality.
Employees: 76
Volunteers: 3
Regional offices: 3
Income: £12,854,579 (2014–15)

## Upkeep

2 The Courtyard, 48 New North Road,
Exeter BX4 4EP
T: 020 7256 7646
E: info@upkeep.org.uk
www.upkeep.org.uk
Director: Sarah Bentley
Upkeep promotes good practice in building care. We deliver short courses on building repair, maintenance and improvement. We believe that good maintenance of existing buildings is key to a sustainable future. Upkeep also runs the Charities Facilities Management Group, the network for people who look after buildings and facilities issues in the voluntary sector. The CFM Group was set up in 2000 and has 250 member-charities nationwide.
Employees: 1
Volunteers: 2
Regional offices: 1

## Urban Forum

33 Corsham Street, London N1 6DR
T: 020 7253 4816
F: 020 7253 4817
E: info@urbanforum.org.uk
www.urbanforum.org.uk
Urban Forum is an umbrella body for community and voluntary groups with interests in urban and regional policy, especially regeneration.
Employees: 5
Volunteers: 15

## Urostomy Association

4 Demontfort Way, Uttoxeter,
Staffordshire ST14 8XY
T: 01889 563191
E: secretary.ua@classmail.co.uk
www.urostomyassocation.org.uk
National Secretary: Hazel Pixley
Charity set up in 1971 to provide support for people having a urinary diversion (e.g. urostomy, mitrofanoff, neo-bladder, bladder reconstruction). Sixteen local branches; magazine published three times a year; leaflets and other publications available.
Employees: 2
Volunteers: 100
Income: £125,000 (2013–14)

## Us in a Bus

Queens House, Philanthropic Road,
Redhill RH1 4DZ
T: 01737 764774
E: info@usinabus.org.uk
www.usinabus.org.uk
Chief Executive: Janet Gurney
Us in a Bus delivers services to people with profound learning disabilities and/or complex needs, in their own home and in the community, across Surrey and the surrounding areas. We also provide training in Intensive Interaction for families, carers, support staff and other professionals nationwide. Us in a Bus enables people with profound learning disabilities and/or complex needs to connect with others through interaction, play and self expression.
Employees: 14
Volunteers: 2
Regional offices: 1

## Variety

E: stuart.rogers@variety.org.uk

## Vegetarian Society UK Ltd

Parkdale, Dunham Road, Altrincham,
Cheshire WA14 4QG
T: 0161 925 2000
F: 0161 926 9182
E: info@vegsoc.org
www.vegsoc.org
Chief Executive: Lynne Elliot
The Vegetarian Society influences, inspires and supports people to embrace and maintain a vegetarian lifestyle. We organise National Vegetarian Week each year and we run the Cordon Vert Vegetarian Cookery School in Altrincham, Cheshire.
Employees: 28
Volunteers: 150
Regional offices: 1
Income: £1,306,000 (2013–14)

## Victta Children Ltd

Silverstone House, 46 Newport Road,
Woolstone, Milton Keynes,
Buckinghamshire MK15 0AA
T: 01908 240831
F: 01908 668868
E: admin@victa.org.uk
www.victa.org.uk
**Chief Executive: Tracie Tappenden**
VICTA supports blind and partially sighted
children, young people and their families
by providing: grants; two annual family
weekends; family days; international youth
trips for ages 18+; youth weekends for ages
18+; youth weekends for ages 14–17;
multi European camps for ages 16+; early
years weekends; family support. For more
information please visit our website
www.victa.org.uk.
Employees: 8
Volunteers: 40
Regional offices: 1

## Victim Support

Hallam House, 56–60 Hallam Street,
London W1W 6JL
T: 020 7268 0200
E: contact@victimsupport.org.uk
www.victimsupport.org.uk
**Chief Executive: Mark Castle**
Victim Support is the independent national
charity for people affected by crime. Staff
and volunteers offer free and confidential
information and support for victims of any
crime, whether or not it has been reported
and regardless of when it happened. The
organisation operates via a network of
affiliated local charities, the Witness Service
and the Victim Supportline.
Employees: 1000
Volunteers: 3000
Regional offices: 5

## Viewpoint

Viewpoint, Weltech Business Centre,
Ridgeway, Welwyn Garden City,
Hertfordshire AL7 2AA
T: 01707 386136
E: leslie@hertsviewpoint.co.uk
www.hertsviewpoint.co.uk
**Chief Executive: Leslie Billy**
Viewpoint is a user-involvement charity in
Hertfordshire for people with mental health
or drug and alcohol problems. It is essential
that the people who use or who have used
mental health or drug and alcohol services are
enabled to help make positive changes. The
experience and expertise which can be gained

can help commissioners and providers to
make the biggest difference in people's lives.
Employees: 7
Volunteers: 5
Regional offices: 1
Income: £250,000 (2015–16)

## Village Aid

Suite 1, Fearnehough House,
Riverside Business Park, Buxton Road,
Bakewell, Derbyshire DE45 1GJ
T: 01629 814434
F: 01629 812272
E: info@villageaid.org
www.villageaid.org
We work with the most marginalised rural
communities in West Africa, establishing
partnerships with African communities and
local organisations to enhance sustainable
development and find solutions using African
resources and experience. In the UK we aim
to raise awareness of development issues and
present positive images of African people and
their abilities.
Employees: 3
Volunteers: 3

## Vine Centre, The

PO Box 442, 33 Station Road, Aldershot,
Aldershot, Hampshire GU11 9FQ
T: 01252 400196
E: mags.mercer@thevinecentre.org.uk
thevinecentre.org.uk
**Chief Executive Officer: Mags Mercer**
The Vine Centre has been established in
the community of Aldershot, north east
Hampshire since 1987, supporting vulnerable
and homeless adults since inception and
registered as a charity in February 2003. Our
primary aims are to reduce social isolation, to
facilitate and enable change and to improve
the quality of life for homeless and vulnerable
men and women aged 21 years and over
including training and employment services.
Employees: 9
Volunteers: 25
Regional offices: 1
Income: £228,000 (2015–16)

## VISION 2020 UK

PO Box 70172, London WC1A 9HH
T: 07837 692026
E: m.broom@vision2020uk.org.uk
www.vision2020uk.org.uk
**CEO: Mercy Jeyasingham**
VISION 2020 UK is the umbrella
organisation which facilitates greater
collaboration and co-operation between
organisations within the UK which focus on

vision impairment and operate on a national,
regional or international basis.
Employees: 5
Income: £110,000 (2015–16)

## Vision Aid Overseas

12 The Bell Centre, Newton Road,
Manor Royal, Crawley,
West Sussex RH10 2FZ
T: 01293 535016
F: 01293 535026
E: info@visionaidoverseas.org
www.vao.org.uk
**Director: Dr Natalie Briggs**
Vision Aid Overseas is a charity dedicated to
people in the developing world whose lives
are blighted by poor eyesight.
Employees: 7
Volunteers: 1200

## Vision Homes Association

Trigate, 210–222 Hagley Road West,
Oldbury B68 0NP
T: 0121 434 4644
F: 0121 434 5655
E: caroline@visionhomes.org
www.visionhomes.org.uk
**Chief Executive: Ewa Stefanowska**
Pursues ways of improving facilities and
services for adults who have vision impairments
and/or additional disabilities. Promotes the
provisions of residential accommodation
and home support throughout the UK.
Employees: 110
Volunteers: 2
Regional offices: 1

## Visionary – Linking local sight loss charities

5/14 Western Harbour View, Leith,
Edinburgh, Leith, Edinburgh EH6 6PF
T: 020 8417 0942
E: visionary@visionary.org.uk
www.visionary.org.uk
**Chief Executive: Angela Tinker**
Visionary supports local independent
charities that support blind and partially
sighted people across the UK. Our core aims:
to connect: bringing the network of local
societies together and learning from best
practices; to influence: consulting members
on issues that affect them, representing them
on the national stage; to develop: offering
direct support to members, providing advice,
learning opportunities, guidance and funding
to facilitate the development of new local
societies and services from existing local
societies.
Employees: 2
Volunteers: 12

## Vista

**Viata House, 1a Salisbury Road, Leicester, Leicestershire LE1 7QR**
T: 0116 249 0909
Helpline: 0116 249 8839
E: info@vistablind.org.uk
www.vistablind.org.uk
**Chief Executive: Paul Bott**
Vista is the leading provider of services to blind and partially sighted people in Leicester, Leicestershire and Rutland. Vista runs four residential care homes, providing care to older people and to adults with learning disability and sight loss. It also runs community services including social groups, rehabilitation and deaf/blind services.
**Employees: 250**
**Volunteers: 100**
**Regional offices: 2**

## Vita Nova

**11 Roumelia Lane, Boscombe, Dorset BH5 1EU**
T: 01202 309999
E: office@vitanova.co.uk
www.vitanova.co.uk
**Chief Executive: Simon Bull**
Vita Nova is an arts organisation that supports those who have been through drug/alcohol addiction and those with mental health issues. Vita Nova also provides awareness education to primary and secondary schools, colleges and universities.
**Employees: 4**
**Volunteers: 10**
**Income: £100,000 (2013–14)**

## Vitalise

**12 City Forum, 250 City Road, London EC1V 8AF**
T: 0845 345 1972
F: 0845 345 1978
E: info@vitalise.org.uk
www.vitalise.org.uk
Aims to enable visually impaired and disabled people to exercise choice, and to provide vital breaks for carers and inspirational opportunities for volunteers.
**Employees: 290**
**Volunteers: 6000**

## Vitiligo Society

**24 Greencoat Place, London SW1P 1RD**
T: 020 7840 0855
Helpline: 0800 018 2631
E: general@vitiligosociety.org.uk
www.vitiligosociety.org.uk
Promotes a positive approach to living with vitiligo. Offers support and understanding to people with vitiligo and their families and advice on how to cope with the condition. Funds research to establish the causes of vitiligo and finding safe and effective treatments.
**Employees: 1**
**Volunteers: 4**

## Voice Care Network UK

**25 The Square, Kenilworth, Warwickshire CV8 1EF**
T: 01926 864000 (also fax)
E: info@voicecare.org.uk
www.voicecare.org.uk
**Chair: Jeremy Stoke**
VCN provides information and practical help for people to keep their voices healthy, to avoid voice loss, to communicate skillfully and with confidence through its professional members who are: teachers and coaches of speaking voice; speech and language therapists experienced in clinical treatment for voice disorders.
**Employees: 1**
**Volunteers: 230**

## Voluntary Action Calderdale

**Resource Centre, Hall Street, Halifax, West Yorkshire HX1 5AY**
T: 01422 348777
E: info@cvac.org.uk
www.cvac.org.uk
**Chief Officer: Soo Nevison**
We are established as a local infrastructure organisation supporting the VCS in Calderdale. We also run small projects that support the local communities in our borough with an aim to improve life chances for anyone living in Calderdale.
**Employees: 12**
**Volunteers: 45**

## Voluntary Action History Society

**WC1H 0AL**
E: georginabrewis@yahoo.co.uk
www.vahs.org.uk
**Chair: Dr Peter Grant**
The Voluntary Action History Society (VAHS) aims to advance the historical understanding and analysis of voluntary action. VAHS is a network of postgraduate students, academics and voluntary sector practitioners. Activities include: a seminar series at the Institute of Historical Research; conferences and workshops; New Researchers group for postgraduates and early-career scholars; an edited blog.
**Volunteers: 15**

## Voluntary Action Islington

**200a Pentonville Road, London N1 9JP**
T: 020 7832 5800
F: 020 7832 5835
E: mike.sherriff@vai.org.uk
www.vai.org.uk
**Chief Executive: Mike Sherriff**
Voluntary Action Islington provides services to community groups in Islington, including the accredited volunteer centre for the borough. We have a resource centre with training and meeting rooms available for hire.
**Employees: 6**
**Volunteers: 15**
**Income: £539,000 (2013–14)**

## Voluntary Action South West Surrey

**39 Castle Street, Guildford GU1 3UQ**
T: 01483 504626
E: c.dunnett@vasws.org.uk
voluntaryactionsws.org.uk
**Chief Officer: Carol Dunnett**
We provide information, advice and support for voluntary and community organisations in the Boroughs of Guildford and Waverley. We run a volunteer brokerage service both online and through our volunteer centres. We have a supported volunteer programme and a project that supports older people to volunteer.
**Employees: 10**
**Volunteers: 20**
**Regional offices: 1**

## Voluntary Arts

**121 Cathedral Road, Pontcanna, Cardiff CF11 9PH**
T: 029 2039 5395
E: info@voluntaryarts.org
www.voluntaryarts.org
**Chief Executive: Robin Simpson**
Voluntary Arts promotes active participation in creative cultural activities across the UK and Republic of Ireland. We recognise that they are a key part of our culture and are vital to our health and to our social and economic development. Over half the UK adult population already takes part in arts and crafts activity for self-improvement, social networking and leisure. Activities include folk, dance, drama, literature, music, visual arts, crafts, applied arts and festivals.
**Employees: 18**
**Regional offices: 5**

## Voluntary Norfolk

St Clements House, 2–16 Colegate,
Norwich, Norfolk NR3 1BQ
T: 01603 614474
F: 01603 764109
E: admin@voluntarynorfolk.org.uk
www.voluntarynorfolk.org.uk
CEO: Alan Hopley
Voluntary Norfolk supports volunteers and
voluntary organisations, recruiting, training
and deploying many hundreds of volunteers
each year. We deliver projects including
a volunteering website, befriending,
employability services and neighbourhood
development programmes. Via our social
enterprise, Charity BackRoom, we offer a
wide range of individually tailored back-office
services including HR and employment law,
DBS checks and payroll. We provide support
for charities to raise funds through grant
applications and appeals via our subsidiary,
Blue Tree Fundraising.
Employees: 50
Volunteers: 500
Regional offices: 3
Income: £1,500,000 (2013–14)

## Voluntary Sector Training

45 Stortford Road, Great Dunmow,
Essex CM6 1DQ
T: 01371 876747
E: maddy@voluntarysectortraining.org.uk
www.voluntarysectortraining.org.uk
Director: Linda Riley
We are an independent charity providing
affordable, relevant and accessible training
for charities and community groups in
Essex and beyond. We want to support the
development of a strong, effective and
diverse voluntary and community sector.
We run a programme of regular one-day
courses all over Essex for staff, volunteers,
trustees and committee members. We also
offer bespoke in-house training tailored to
your charity's needs, wherever you are based.
Employees: 5
Volunteers: 3
Regional offices: 1
Income: £172,000 (2014–15)

## Voluntary Services Lewisham

300 Stanstead Road, London SE23 1DE
T: 020 8291 1747
E: evelyn@vslonline.org.uk
www.vslonline.org.uk
CEO: Evelyn Brady
To provide direct voluntary services to
Lewisham residents including: befriending,
gardening transport projects plus drop-ins
and wellbeing workshops for people
experiencing mental health difficulties. To

recruit, train, place and support volunteers in
roles that develop skills and build confidence
and enhance the lives of our service users. To
liaise with other groups and agencies with the
aim to build partnerships that enable the
delivery of quality effective services.
Employees: 9
Volunteers: 200
Income: £275,000 (2014–15)

## Volunteer Centre Greenwich

E: annie@volunteersgreenwich.co.uk

## Volunteering Matters

18–24 Lower Clapton Rd, Hackney,
London E5 0PD
T: 020 3780 5870
E: information@volunteeringmatters.org.uk
www.volunteeringmatters.org.uk
Chief Executive: Oonagh Aitken
Volunteering Matters is a national charity
leading UK volunteering in policy and
practice. We focus on the needs of four
distinct communities: older and retired
people, disabled people, vulnerable families
and young people.
Employees: 200
Volunteers: 30000

## Volunteers for Rural India

56 Homecross House, 21 Fishers Lane,
London W4 1YA
T: 020 8013 7314
Helpline: 07786 570377
E: enquiries@vri-online.org.uk
www.vri-online.org.uk
Chair: Shobhana Snow
VRI aims to relieve poverty in India by
undertaking voluntary work, raising funds
to assist village development schemes and
educating the public in the UK about Indian
culture and traditions and other aspects of
Indian life.
Volunteers: 15
Regional offices: 1
Income: £1,000 (2015–16)

## Voscur

Royal Oak House, Royal Oak Avenue,
Bristol BS1 4GB
T: 0117 909 9949
E: info@voscur.org
www.voscur.org
Chief Executive: Wendy Stephenson
Voscur supports, develops and represents
Bristol's voluntary and community sector.
It strengthens and advocates for local
organisations so they can improve the quality
of life of individuals and communities. As the
city's volunteering hub, it also supports

individuals to create positive social change,
particularly those often excluded from such
opportunities. It facilitates partnerships within
and between the public, private and voluntary
sectors to create social impact, add value to
public spending and increase social inclusion.
Volunteers: 46
Income: £738,988 (2013–14)

## VSO

317 Putney Bridge Road,
London SW15 2PN
T: 020 8780 7200
F: 020 8780 7300
E: david.son@vso.org.uk
www.vso.org.uk
VSO is an international development agency
working through international volunteering.
VSO's purpose is to build reciprocal local and
global partnerships that bring people together
to share skills, creativity and learning to build a
fairer world.
Employees: 700
Volunteers: 1450
Regional offices: 5

## Wales Council for Voluntary Action

Baltic House, Mount Stuart Square,
Cardiff Bay, Cardiff CF10 5FH
T: 0800 288 8329
F: 029 2043 1701
E: help@wcva.org.uk
www.wcva.org.uk
Chief Executive: Ruth Marks
Supports working relationships between the
voluntary sector and government and public
bodies; supports and promotes the work of
voluntary and community groups at national
and local level; supports and promotes
volunteering and the interest of volunteers;
promotes community cohesion and inclusion
and builds social capital; develops and
supports new initiatives; enhances resources
available to the voluntary sector; improves its
performance and effectiveness.
Employees: 99
Regional offices: 3
Income: £20,855,366 (2013–14)

## Walsall Society for the Blind

Hawley House, 11 Hatherton Road, Walsall,
West Midlands WS1 1XS
T: 01922 627683
E: areed@wsftb.co.uk
www.walsallblind.org
CEO: Amanda Reed
Our mission is to provide information,
support and friendship to those affected by
sight loss within the Borough of Walsall. Our
services include: a community officer; a
community engagement officer; talking
newspaper and magazine service; a social
activity centre; an eye clinic liaison officer;
transcription service.
Employees: 12
Volunteers: 30
Regional offices: 1
Income: £183,679 (2015–16)

## Walsingham Support

Walsingham House, 1331–1337 High Road,
Whetstone, London N20 9HR
T: 020 8343 5600
F: 020 8446 9156
E: enquiries@walsingham.com
www.walsingham.com
Chief Executive: Paul Snell
Walsingham Support is a leading national
charity providing highly personalised services
for over 420 people with learning disabilities,
autism, brain injuries and complex needs.
Employees: 900

## War on Want

44–48 Shepherdess Walk, London N1 7JP
T: 020 7324 5040
F: 020 7324 5041
E: drudkin@waronwant.org
www.waronwant.org
Executive Director: John Hilary
War on Want fights poverty in developing
countries in partnership and solidarity with
people affected by globalisation. We
campaign for human rights and against the
root causes of global poverty, inequality
and injustice.
Employees: 19
Volunteers: 5

## War Widows Association of Great Britain and Northern Ireland

C/O 199 Borough High Street,
London SE1 1AA
T: 0845 241 2189
E: info@warwidows.org.uk
www.warwidows.org.uk/
The Association seeks to improve the
conditions of war widows in Great Britain. This
is done by engaging with government ministers
and relevant influential individuals, We hold
regular national and local events, publish a
newsletter three times a year and ensure that
widows are represented at significant national
and local remembrance events.

## Water for Africa

12 The Midway, Newcastle-under-Lyme,
Staffordshire ST5 1QG
T: 01782 593289
E: info@waterforafrica.org.uk
www.waterforafrica.org.uk
We believe that water, sanitation and health
are basic human rights and the key to
emerging long-term from poverty. We
have set up and successfully run a UK-led
organisation over the last four years managed
by local professionals. Its service has provided
a fast, professional, targeted service directly
to benefit the people of Africa who need
it most at a fraction of the cost of traditional
methods.
Volunteers: 3

## WaterAid

Second floor, 47–49 Durham Street,
London SE11 5JD
T: 0845 600 0433
F: 020 7793 4545
E: wateraid@wateraid.org
www.wateraid.org
Chief Executive: Barbara Frost
WaterAid is a leading independent
organisation that enables the world's poorest
people to gain access to safe water, sanitation
and hygiene education. We work in Africa,
Asia and the Pacific region and campaign
globally with our partners to realise our vision
of a world where everyone has access to
these basic human rights.
Employees: 518
Volunteers: 600
Regional offices: 20

## WAY Widowed and Young

Suite 17, The College Business Centre,
Uttoxeter New Road, Derby,
Derbyshire DE22 3WZ
E: enquiries@widowedandyoung.org.uk
www.widowedandyoung.org.uk
Chairperson: Georgia Elms
WAY Widowed and Young helps men and
women widowed when aged 50 or under to
rebuild their lives, whether or not they have
children. We offer support and friendship
through a national network of groups,
message board and chatroom, newsletter,
book loan service and weekend trips for
members.
Employees: 2
Volunteers: 50

## WDC, Whale and Dolphin Conservation

Brookfield House, 38 St Paul Street,
Chippenham, Wiltshire SN15 1LY
T: 01249 449500
E: info@whales.org
www.whales.org
Raises public awareness of all the threats
facing whales, dolphins and porpoises. The
society funds, throughout the world, research
and conservation methods concerning
whales, dolphins and porpoises and their
habitats, and campaigns for their protection
from all threats.

## Weight Concern

1–19 Torrington Place, London WC1E 7HB
T: 020 7679 1853
F: 020 7679 8354
E: enquiries@weightconcern.org.uk
www.weightconcern.org.uk
Executive Director: Dr Laura McGowan
Weight Concern exists to tackle the issue
of obesity in the UK. Our vision is to support
and empower people to live a healthy
lifestyle, and our mission is to increase the
understanding of both health professionals
and the public about the causes,
consequences and treatments of overweight
and obesity. We aim to provide clear,
evidence-based information on obesity and
weight-management to provide a 'voice
' for those who have first-hand experience of
being overweight.
Employees: 4
Volunteers: 3

## Wellbeing of Women

27 Sussex Place, London NW1 4SP
T: 020 7772 6400
F: 020 7724 7725
E: hello@wellbeingofwomen.org.uk
www.wellbeingofwomen.org.uk
Director: Liz Campbell
Wellbeing of Women is a charity dedicated to
improving the health of women and babies, to
make a difference to everybody's lives today
and tomorrow. We provide information, to
raise awareness of health issues to keep
women and babies well today. We fund
medical research and training grants, which
have and will continue to develop better
treatments and outcomes for tomorrow.
Employees: 10

## WellChild

16 Royal Crescent, Cheltenham,
Gloucestershire GL50 3DA
T: 01242 530007
E: info@wellchild.org.uk
www.wellchild.org.uk
Chief Executive: Colin Dyer
WellChild is the national charity for sick
children. We provide essential practical and
emotional support for seriously ill children,
young people and those who care for them
across the UK to ensure they receive the best
possible quality of care.
Employees: 26
Volunteers: 250
Regional offices: 1

## Wellcome Trust

Gibbs Building, 215 Euston Road,
London NW1 2BE
T: 020 7611 7210
F: 020 7611 8800
E: s.wallcraft@wellcome.ac.uk
www.wellcome.ac.uk
Aims to protect, preserve and advance all or
any aspects of the health and welfare of
humankind and to advance and promote
knowledge and education by engaging in,
encouraging and supporting research into any
of the biosciences.
Employees: 500

## Wells for India

The Winchester Centre,
68 St George's Street, Winchester,
Hampshire SO23 8AH
T: 01962 848043
F: 01962 848029
E: office@wellsforindia.org
www.wellsforindia.org
Employees: 2
Volunteers: 27

## Welwitschia Welfare Centre

Imperial House, 64 Willoughby Lane,
Tottenham, London N17 0SP
T: 020 8808 1255
F: 020 8885 3471
E: info@wwcuk.org
www.wwcuk.org
Chief Executive: Pedro Lunguela
The WWC is a voluntary community charity
organisation. It was set up to help Angolan
community and other Portuguese-speaking
migrants, refugees access the mainstream
services, not to suffer in silence through lack
of knowledge of their rights and entitlements
in their host country. It also combats poverty
and helps the community integrate into

British society. WWC services are now also
offered to other minority ethnic groups.
Employees: 2
Volunteers: 8
Income: £13,100 (2014–15)

## WESC Foundation

E: kgaulton@wescfoundation.ac.uk

## West Harton Churches Action Station Ltd

Boldon Lane, South Shields,
Tyne and Wear NE34 0LZ
T: 0191 455 8122
E: ceo@actionstation.org.uk
actionstation.org.uk
Manager: Keith Hardy
To reduce social isolation, increase job
readiness of the community, increase the
overall health of the community and promote
individuals working together for the benefit
of the local community. To provide a one-
stop shop.
Employees: 4
Volunteers: 50
Income: £140,000 (2015–16)

## Western Lodge

Western Lodge, 85 Trinity Road, Tooting,
London SW17 7SQ
T: 020 8696 1564
F: 020 8672 6232
E: info@westernlodge.org.uk
westernlodge.org.uk
Chair of the Board of Trustee's: Mr R
Plummer
Western Lodge is a 10-bed medium support
hostel for male clients over the age of
30 years. All clients need to have support
needs in addition to being homeless and
priority is given to Wandsworth clients. The
project is staffed 24/7 and full support is given
to all clients.
Employees: 5
Regional offices: 1

## Westminster Drug Project

7th Floor, Kingsway House, 103 Kingsway,
Holborn, London WC2B 6QX
T: 020 7421 3100
F: 020 7421 3199
E: communications@wdp-drugs.org.uk
www.wdp-drugs.org.uk
Chief Executive Officer: Stuart Campbell
WDP is a vibrant and innovative charity
committed to helping all those who are
affected by drug and alcohol use. We believe
that with the right support, people can make
long-lasting change in their lives to improve

health, wellbeing and social integration.
We provide drug and alcohol services across
London and the south east of England.
We work with individuals, families and
communities to help people recover from
drug dependency and to reduce crime.
Employees: 360
Volunteers: 100
Regional offices: 24

## Weston Park Hospital Development Fund Ltd

23 Northumberland Road, Sheffield,
South Yorkshire S10 2TX
T: 0114 226 5391
Helpline: 0114 226 5666
E: karen.holmes@cancersupportcentre.co.uk
www.cancersupportcentre.co.uk
Centre Manager: Karen Holmes
Providing information, support and advice for
cancer patients and their families and friends,
via a drop-in centre. Healthcare professionals
are available to take enquiries.
Employees: 10
Volunteers: 12
Regional offices: 1
Income: £398,200 (2015–16)

## WheelPower

Stoke Mandeville Stadium, Guttmann Road,
Stoke Mandeville, Buckinghamshire,
Buckinghamshire HP21 9PP
T: 01296 395995
F: 01296 424171
E: nigel.roberts@wheelpower.org.uk
www.wheelpower.org.uk
Chief Executive: Martin McElhatton
WheelPower – British Wheelchair Sport
provides, promotes and develops
opportunities for men, women and children
with disabilities to participate in recreational
and competitive wheelchair sport from
grass roots to international level throughout
the UK.
Employees: 10
Volunteers: 250
Regional offices: 1

## Whitehall and Industry Group

80 Petty France, London SW1H 9EX
T: 020 7222 1166
F: 020 7222 1167
E: charitynext@wig.co.uk
www.wig.co.uk
Chief Executive: Mark Gibson
The Whitehall and Industry Group is an
independent, not-for-profit and non-
lobbying membership organisation.

Established in 1984, we have a charitable purpose to build understanding and cooperation between the public, private and voluntary sectors for the greater public good – a nation better governed, business better managed and society better served.
**Employees: 23**

## Whizz-Kidz

Bressenden Place, Victoria,
London SW1E 5BH
T: 020 7233 6600
E: info@whizz-kidz.org.uk
www.whizz-kidz.org.uk
Whizz-Kidz improves the quality of life of young disabled people under 18 in the UK through the provision of customised mobility equipment such as powered and manual wheelchairs and tricycles. The charity provides help and advice to children and their families and raises awareness of mobility-related issues through national campaigning.

## Wigan and Leigh CVS

E: sue.barrett@gmcvo.org.uk

## Wildfowl and Wetlands Trust

Slimbridge, Gloucestershire GL2 7BT
T: 01453 891900
F: 01453 890827
E: enquiries@wwt.org.uk
www.wwt.org.uk
**Chief Executive: Martin Spray**
The Wildfowl and Wetlands Trust (WWT) is the largest international wetland conservation charity in the UK. Its mission is to promote, protect and develop wetlands and their wildlife. WWT operates nine visitor centres in the UK aimed at bringing people closer to wetland wildlife.
**Employees: 420**
**Volunteers: 520**
**Regional offices: 9**

## Wildlife Aid

Randalls Farm House, Randalls Road,
Leatherhead, Surrey KT22 0AL
T: 01372 377332
Helpline: 0906 180 0132
F: 01372 375183
E: becky@wildlifeaid.org.uk
www.wildlifeaid.com
**Managing Trustee: Simon Cowell**
Wildlife Aid is a registered charity dedicated to the rescue, care and rehabilitation of sick, injured and orphaned British wildlife. Based in Leatherhead, Surrey, since its opening over 25 years ago the centre has grown to be one of the largest wildlife rehabilitation hospitals in

the country, dealing with more than 20,000 incidents each year.
**Employees: 3**
**Volunteers: 300**
**Regional offices: 1**

## Wildlife and Countryside Link

89 Albert Embankment, London SE1 7TP
T: 020 7820 8600
F: 020 7820 8620
E: enquiry@wcl.org.uk
www.wcl.org.uk
Wildlife and Countryside Link brings together environmental voluntary organisations in the UK united by their common interest in the conservation and enjoyment of the natural and historic environment. Our aim is to maximise the efficiency and effectiveness of the voluntary sector through collaboration. Through Link, groups of people from different organisations get together to exchange information, develop and promote policies and work to effect change.
**Employees: 5**
**Volunteers: 2**

## William Sutton Trust

William Sutton Housing Association,
Sutton Court, Tring,
Hertfordshire HP23 5BB
T: 01442 891100
E: customerservice@affinitysutton.com
www.affinitysutton.com
A registered charity and a housing association registered with The Housing Corporation, which provides affordable housing and associated community support for people in housing need in 44 local authority areas throughout England, including London.

## Williams Syndrome Foundation Ltd

161 High Street, Tonbridge, Kent TN9 1BX
T: 01732 365152
E: enquiries@williams-syndrome.org.uk
www.williams-syndrome.org.uk
**CEO: Elizabeth Hurst**
Provides support and expert research backed information to those with WS and those who care for and educate them. Fundraises and supports research and exchanges information on William's syndrome, a rare disorder caused by an abnormality in chromosomes. Puts parents in touch through a national contact network. Stimulates interest, particularly among the medical profession, in the condition. Runs social and information events. Subsidises respite breaks and supported holidays.

## Wincanton Community Venture

E: sueplace@balsamcentre.org.uk

## Windle Trust International

37A Oxford Road, Cowley,
Oxford OX4 2EN
T: 01865 712900
E: cathryn@windle.org.uk
www.windle.org.uk
Windle Trust International provides access to education and training for those affected by conflict in Africa. We equip talented young Africans to meet the challenges of development in their own countries.

## Windsor Leadership Trust

Adair House, Madeira Walk, Windsor,
Berkshire SL4 1EU
T: 01753 830202
F: 01753 842775
E: jonathan.story@windsorleadership.org.uk
www.windsorleadershiptrust.org.uk
**Chief Executive: Dr James McCalman**
For 15 years, the Windsor Leadership Trust has been bringing together top leaders from every sector to reflect on how they can use their influence, decisions and actions to benefit their organisations and wider society. Through our programmes we enable leaders to explore for themselves the responsibilities of leadership. The different programme levels reflect the increasingly complex challenges leaders face as their roles become more strategic and their leadership responsibilities grow.
**Employees: 10**

## Winston's Wish

16 Royal Crescent, Cheltenham,
Gloucestershire GL50 3DA
T: 01242 515157
Helpline: 0845 203 0405
E: info@winstonswish.org.uk
www.winstonswish.org.uk
**Chief Executive: Fergus Crow**
Winston's Wish helps children rebuild their lives after the death of a parent or sibling, enabling them to face the future with confidence and hope. We offer practical support and guidance to families, professionals and anyone concerned about a grieving child. We want children to avoid the problems that can occur in later life if they are unable to express their grief.

## Wish – A voice for women's mental health

15 Old Ford Road, London  E2 9PL
T: 020 8980 3618
F: 020 8980 1596
E: info@womenatwish.org.uk
www.womenatwish.org.uk
**Director: Joyce Kallevik**
Wish is the only national, user-led charity working with women with mental health needs in prison, hospital and the community. It provides independent advocacy, emotional support and practical guidance at all stages of a woman's journey through the mental health and criminal justice systems. Wish acts to increase women's participation in the services they receive and campaigns to get their voice heard at a policy level.
**Employees: 15**
**Volunteers: 25**
**Regional offices: 2**

## Wishing Well

4 Laurel Avenue, Fleetwood, Lancashire  FY7 7PT
T: 01253 773546
E: wishingwellappeal@yahoo.co.uk
www.wishingwellcharity.org
**Lead Trustee: Jason O'Flaherty**
Wishing Well is a small international development charity. We work with children and families, promote volunteering and support community development initiatives. Wishing Well is currently working in Romania and in the UK. Our projects include: providing educational support to young Roma children; advocacy; work with children with HIV and special needs; delivering a schools' NGO community development training programme and promoting volunteering, including coordinating National Volunteering Week.
**Employees: 2**
**Volunteers: 20**
**Regional offices: 1**

## Woking Association of Voluntary Service

E: sylvie@wavs.org.uk

## Wolverhampton Domestic Violence Forum

PO Box 4984, Wolverhampton, West Midlands  WV1 9GE
T: 01902 555643
E: wdvf@wolverhampton.gov.uk
**Strategy Co-ordinator: Kathy Cole-Evans**
WDVF aims to work in partnership to stop domestic violence and abuse, to ensure the safety and empowerment of victims and their children and to bring perpetrators to justice. Integrated partnership working is key to achieving our aims. We work closely with a number of local partnerships, and collectively develop and implement multi-agency strategies and action plans towards meeting these aims.
**Employees: 8**

## Womankind Worldwide

Womankind Worldwide, Wenlock Studios, 50–52 Wharf Road, London  N1 7EU
T: 020 7549 0360
F: 020 7549 0361
E: info@womankind.org.uk
www.womankind.org.uk
**Chief Executive: Caroline Haworth**
Womankind is an international women's rights charity. We work with women's rights organisations and movements in Africa, Asia and Latin America to end violence against women, give women a voice and improve women's economic rights.
**Employees: 22**
**Volunteers: 6**
**Income: £3,600,000 (2014–15)**

## Women and Girls' Network

PO Box 13095, London  W14 0FE
T: 020 7610 4678
E: info@wgn.org.uk
www.wgn.org.uk
Offers counselling to women and girls who have experienced any form of violence, whether physical, sexual or emotional.

## Women and Manual Trades

Tindlemanor, 52–54 Featherstone Street, London  EC1Y 8RT
T: 020 7251 9192
F: 020 7251 9193
E: info@wamt.org
www.wamt.org
Info and support for women training and working in the manual building trades. Campaigns to make women 'on the tools' the norm rather than the exception.
**Employees: 6**

## Women's Aid Federation of England

PO Box 3245, Bristol  BS2 2EH
Helpline: 0808 200 0247
E: info@womensaid.org.uk
www.womensaid.org.uk
**Chief Executive: Polly Neate**
Women's Aid is the national charity working to end domestic abuse against women and children. Our three key aims: to improve the protection available to abused women and children by ensuring that their needs and experiences inform developments in law, policy and practice; to work towards the prevention of gender-based violence through public awareness and education; to ensure the provision of high-quality services for abused women and children.
**Employees: 63**
**Volunteers: 1**
**Regional offices: 2**
**Income: £2,572,485 (2014–15)**

## Women's Engineering Society (WES)

Michael Faraday House, Six Hills Way, Stevenage, Herts  SG1 2AY
T: 01438 765506
E: info@wes.org.uk
www.wes.org.uk
The Women's Engineering Society aims to: support members of WES and women in general to achieve their potential as engineers, scientists and technologists; encourage the study and application of engineering; help engineering companies to promote gender diversity and equality in the workplace; lobby government, organisations and policy makers to strive for equality, both in the workplace and in the promotion of engineering as a career.
**Employees: 1**
**Volunteers: 100+**
**Regional offices: 1**

## Women's Environmental Network

PO Box 30626, London  E2 7EY
T: 020 7481 9004
F: 020 7481 9144
E: info@wen.org.uk
www.wen.org.uk
Campaigns on environmental and health issues from a woman's perspective, and informs and empowers women and men who care about the environment.
**Employees: 11**
**Volunteers: 2**
**Regional offices: 100**

## Women's Farm and Garden Association

175 Gloucester Street, Cirencester,
Gloucestershire GL7 2DP
T: 01285 658339
E: admin@wfga.org.uk
www.wfga.org.uk
Creates interest in and promotes the study
and practice of agriculture and horticulture
among women throughout the UK. Trains
returners through the Women Returners to
Amenity Gardening Scheme (WRAGS).
Offers a programme of specialist workshops,
tours and visits to its membership. Offers
grants to the membership through the
Christine Ladley Fund for education and
work-related funding.
**Employees: 15**

## Women's Health Advice Centre

1 Council Road, Ashington, Ashington,
Northumberland NE63 8RZ
T: 01670 853977
E: cathhale@whac.uk.com
www.whac-online.co.uk
**Manager: Cath Hale**
Incorporated charity aiming to provide people
(14+) in Northumberland with quality
counselling, personal development, education
and information on issues contributing to
their general health and wellbeing.
Specialising in domestic and sexual abuse,
bereavement, mental health, relationship
problems, self esteem and suicide.
**Employees: 6**
**Volunteers: 25**
**Regional offices: 1**

## Women's Resource Centre

Ground Floor East, 33–41 Dallington Street,
London EC1V 0BB
T: 020 7324 3030
F: 020 7324 3050
E: info@wrc.org.uk
www.wrc.org.uk
**Chief Executive: Vivienne Hayes**
The Women's Resource Centre is a charity
that supports women's organisations to be
more effective and sustainable. We provide
training, information, resources and one-to-
one support on a range of organisational
development issues. We also lobby decision-
makers on behalf of the women's not-for-
profit sector for improved representation
and funding. Our members work in a wide
range of fields delivering services to and
campaigning on behalf of some of the most
marginalised communities of women.
**Employees: 18**

## Women's Royal Naval Service Benevolent Trust

311 Twyford Avenue, Stamshaw,
Portsmouth, Hampshire PO2 8RN
T: 023 9265 5301
F: 023 9267 9040
E: generalsecretary@wrnsbt.org.uk
www.wrnsbt.org.uk
**General Secretary: Sarah Ayton**
The primary aim of the Trust is to provide
relief in cases of necessity or distress amongst
its members and their dependants. The Trust
is also empowered, in suitable cases, to make
grants for the education of dependants.
**Employees: 2**
**Volunteers: 20**
**Regional offices: 1**

## Women's Technology and Education Centre

Blackburne House Centre For Women,
Blackburne Place, Liverpool L8 7PE
T: 0151 709 4356
E: bh.wtec@blackburnehouse.co.uk
www.blackburnehouse.co.uk
Promotes education and training for women;
establishes and promotes equal opportunities
in education and training. Encourages women
into non-traditional jobs.

## Women's Therapy Centre

10 Manor Gardens, London N7 6JS
T: 020 7263 7860
Helpline: 020 7263 6200
F: 020 7272 4222
E: enquiries@womenstherapycentre.co.uk
www.womenstherapycentre.co.uk
**Chief Executive: Monika Schwartz**
We offer both group and individual
psychoanalytic psychotherapy for women.
Therapy is offered on a sliding scale according
to financial means. Please see website for
up-to-date information on making an
appointment.
**Employees: 10**
**Volunteers: 10**
**Regional offices: 1**

## Woodcraft Folk

13 Ritherdon Road, London SW17 8QE
T: 020 7703 4173
F: 020 8767 2457
E: info@woodcraft.org.uk
www.woodcraft.org.uk
Unites children, young people and all who
are young in spirit. Directs the energy
and enthusiasm of youth towards the
transformation of society, educating

members in the principles of universal
tolerance, equality and friendship.
**Volunteers: 3500**
**Regional offices: 500**

## Wooden Spoon Society

115–117 Fleet Road, Fleet,
Hampshire GU51 3PD
T: 01252 773720
F: 01276 502134
E: idoorbar@woodenspoon.com
www.woodenspoon.com
Enhances the quality and prospect of life
for children and young persons in the UK
and Ireland who are disadvantaged, either
physically, mentally or socially.
**Employees: 23**
**Volunteers: 400**
**Regional offices: 1**

## Woodgreen The Animal Charity

King's Bush Farm, London Road,
Godmanchester,
Cambridgeshire PE29 2NH
T: 0844 248 8181
F: 01480 832815
E: paula.loveday-smith@woodgreen.org.uk
woodgreen.org.uk
**Chief Executive : Paula Loveday-Smith**
Animal welfare and rehoming charity.
**Employees: 270**
**Regional offices: 3**

## Woodland Trust

Kempton Way, Grantham,
Lincolnshire NG31 6LL
T: 01476 581111
F: 01476 590808
E: hilaryallison@woodlandtrust.org.uk
www.woodlandtrust.org.uk
The Trust is the UK's leading charity
dedicated to protecting, restoring and
expanding our native woods. Our long-term
aims are to enable the creation of more new
native woods, to protect native woods, trees
and their wildlife for the future and to restore
our native woodland heritage.
**Employees: 320**
**Volunteers: 1000+**
**Regional offices: 4**

## Worcester Volunteer Centre

33 The Tything, Worcester,
Worcestershire  WR1 1JL
T: 01905 24741
F: 01907 23688
E: sally@wvc.org.uk
www.worcestervolunteercentre.org.uk
Chief Officer: Sally Ellison
Local infrastructure organisation and
volunteer recruitment centre. Aims to
promote volunteering, community action
and deliver community services through
volunteers.
Employees: 15
Volunteers: 110

## Work Foundation

21 Palmer Street, London  SW1Y 0AD
T: 020 7976 3500
E: partnership@theworkfoundation.com
www.theworkfoundation.com
The Work Foundation aims to improve
productivity and performance of all British
organisations by enriching the quality and
integrity of working life. Our unique
understanding of the importance and
developing human capital enables us to work
with our clients to bring about in-depth
sustainable change, through our distinctive
brand of research, consultancy, advocacy,
leadership and coaching programmes.

## Workaid

The Old Boot Factory, 71 Townsend Road,
Chesham, Buckinghamshire  HP5 2AA
T: 01494 775220
E: publicity@workaid.org
www.workaid.org
General Manager: John Fox
Supplying refurbished donated tools, sewing/
knitting machines and horticultural
equipment to vocational training projects in
East Africa and the UK.
Employees: 4
Volunteers: 280
Income: £220,000 (2014–15)

## Workers' Educational Association

4 Loop Sreet, London  EC2A 4XW
T: 020 7426 3450
F: 020 7426 3451
E: london@wea.org.uk
www.wea.org.uk
General Secretary: Ruth Spellman
The WEA creates and delivers around
14,000 courses for adults each year in
response to local need across England and
Scotland, often in partnership with
community groups and local charities. We
believe that education is lifelong and should
continue beyond school, college and

university in order to help people develop
their full human potential in society.
Employees: 3500
Volunteers: 4000
Regional offices: 10

## Working Families

1–3 Berry Street, London  EC1V 0AA
T: 020 7253 7243
Helpline: 0300 012 0312
F: 020 7253 6253
E: office@workingfamilies.org.uk
www.workingfamilies.org.uk
Supports and acts as a voice for working
parents and carers, especially those who are
disadvantaged; promotes workplace cultures
that support work
Employees: 12
Volunteers: 10

## Working with Words

Carlton Centre, Carlton Road, Sidcup,
Kent  DA14 6AH
T: 020 8302 4619
E: words@mcch.org.uk
www.mcch.org.uk/workingwithwords/index.
aspx
Design and Contracts Manager:
Colin Thomas
There are 1.2 million people with learning
disabilities and 1.7 million adults with low
literacy in the UK. Working with Words can
help you reach this audience. We produce
accessible information and easy read
documents, making it easy to understand for
people with learning disabilities and low
literacy. All of our documents are created
using government and European guidelines
and are proof read by our target audience.

## World Association of Girl Guides and Girl Scouts

World Bureau, Olave Centre,
12C Lyndhurst Road, London  NW3 5PQ
T: 020 7794 1181
F: 020 7431 3764
E: wagggs@wagggsworld.org
www.wagggs.org/en
Provides a dynamic, flexible, values-based
educational programme that is relevant to
girls' needs. Strives for excellence by
providing opportunities to enable girls to
make informed decisions. The largest
voluntary organisation for girls and young
women in the world, WAGGGS bases its work
on spiritual values and has a commitment to
peace and world citizenship.
Employees: 51
Volunteers: 1000000
Regional offices: 1

## World Society for the Protection of Animals

5th Floor, 222 Gray's Inn Road,
London  WC1X 8HB
T: 020 7587 5000
F: 020 7587 5057
E: wspa@wspa.org.uk
www.wspa.org.uk
For 25 years, WSPA has aimed to promote
the concept of animal welfare in regions of
the world where there are few, if any,
measures to protect animals. Politically, we
have campaigned to convince governments
and key decision-makers to change practices
and introduce new laws to protect or improve
the welfare of animals.
Employees: 50
Volunteers: 4
Regional offices: 10

## World Vision UK

World Vision House, Opal Drive, Fox Milne,
Milton Keynes  MK15 0ZR
T: 01908 841000
F: 01908 841001
E: info@worldvision.org.uk
www.worldvision.org.uk
Chief Executive Officer: Justin Byworth
World Vision is a Christian relief,
development and advocacy organisation
dedicated to working with children, families
and communities to overcome poverty
and injustice.

## Worshipful Company of Information Technologists

39A Bartholomew Close,
London  EC1A 7JN
T: 020 7600 1992
F: 020 7600 1991
E: caroline@wcit.org.uk
www.wcit.org.uk Getting the maximum
benefit from IT is now a prerequisite, not just
for commercial organisations but also for the
charity sector. We work with a wide range of
not-for-profit organisations with the aim of
helping them to gain the maximum benefit
from their IT. Our members give their time
and expertise to provide pro bono IT advice
(usually at a strategic level).
Employees: 4
Volunteers: 200

## Worster-Drought Syndrome Support Group

10 St Vincent Chase, Braintree,
Essex  CM7 9UJ
Helpline: 01376 348948
E: j.leech@btopenworld.com
www.wdssg.org.uk
Chair: Jacqueline Leech

Helps support those with WDS, a rare form of cerebral palsy, and their families.
Volunteers: 6

## Worthing Women's Aid Trading as Safe in Sussex

Safe in Sussex, PO Box 4127, Worthing, West Sussex BN11 1AF
T: 01903 219994
Helpline: 01903 231939
E: louise@safeinsussex.org.uk
www.safeinsussex.org
**Services Manager: Sharon Howard**
Providing domestic abuse awareness through freedom and education. The provision of a refuge service for women and their children. Facilitation of the Freedom Programme for women and educational programmes for young people.
Employees: 15
Volunteers: 18
Regional offices: 1

## WPF Therapy

23 Magdalen Street, London SE1 2EN
T: 020 7378 2000
F: 020 7378 2010
E: counselling@wpf.org.uk
www.wpf.org.uk
**Chief Executive: Joan Baxter**
WPF Therapy works to broaden access to good psychological therapies. It provides therapy to a high standard tailored for each individual as well as training for counsellors and psychotherapists with a wide range of accredited training programmes. The organisation's clinical services and training cover ongoing psychodynamic counselling, psychodynamic psychotherapy, time-limited psychodynamic counselling, group analytic psychotherapy and CBT (cognitive behavioural therapy).
Employees: 150
Volunteers: 100
Regional offices: 27

## WRVS

Garden House, Milton Hill, Steventon, Abingdon, Oxfordshire OX13 6AD
T: 01235 442900
Helpline: 0845 600 5885
F: 01235 861166
E: enquiries@royalvoluntaryservice.org.uk
www.wrvs.org.uk
**Chief Executive: Lynne Berry**
Works independently and in partnership with government departments, local authorities and the private sector in carrying out welfare and emergency work through a nationwide network based on local authority areas in England, Scotland and Wales. WRVS is the largest active voluntary organisation in the UK.
Employees: 1600
Volunteers: 65000

## Wycombe Women's Aid Ltd

PO Box 1477, High Wycombe, Buckinghamshire HP11 9HP
T: 01494 461367
F: 01494 452622
E: wwal@btconnect.com
www.wycombewomensaid.org.uk
**Director: Lisbeth Harvey**
Wycombe Women's Aid provides support to women and children experiencing the effects of domestic violence by offering safe, temporary and emergency accommodation as well as practical and emotional support within the refuge and through outreach in the Wycombe, South Bucks and Chiltern Districts of Bucks. This is achieved using an equal opportunities approach incorporated in a women-centred philosophy.
Employees: 17
Volunteers: 1
Income: £546,648 (2013–14)

# Y

## Y Care International

3rd Floor, 67–69 Cowcross Street, London EC1M 6BP
T: 020 7549 3150
F: 020 7549 3151
E: enq@ycareinternational.org
www.ycareinternational.org
**Chief Executive: Adam Leach**
Y Care International creates opportunities for vulnerable young people across the globe to change their lives for the better. Inspired by and faithful to our Christian values, we work with people of all faiths and none to build a more just world, free from poverty.
Employees: 35
Volunteers: 2
Income: £5,572,896 (2015–16)

## YHA (England and Wales) Ltd

Trevelyan House, Dimple Road, Matlock, Derbyshire DE4 3YH
T: 01629 592654
F: 01629 592702
E: customerservices@yha.org.uk
www.ywcagb.org.uk
YHA operates a network of more than 200 youth hostels across England and Wales. Our accommodation is open to all and everyone can experience a warm welcome, comfortable accommodation, good food and affordable prices. We also have more than 230,000 members, who receive many additional benefits, most notably an exemption from paying a non-member supplement each time they stay with YHA.
Employees: 1150
Volunteers: 5250
Regional offices: 80

## YMCA England

29–35 Farringdon Road, London EC1M 3JF
T: 0845 873 6633
E: enquiries@england.ymca.org.uk
www.ymca.org.uk
The YMCA is a leading Christian charity committed to supporting all young people, particularly in times of need. YMCA England supports and represents the work of over 140 YMCAs providing professional and relevant services that make a difference to the lives of young people in over 250 communities.
Employees: 884
Volunteers: 250
Regional offices: 7

## YMCA Indian Student Hostel

41 Fitzroy Square, London, W1T 6AQ W1T 6AQ
T: 020 7387 0411
F: 020 7383 4735
E: gs@indianymca.org
www.indianymca.org
**General Secretary/CEO: Thomas Abraham**
YMCA stands for worldwide fellowship based on the equal value of all persons, respect and freedom for all, tolerance and understanding between people of different opinions and concern of the needs. YMCA Indian Student Hostel is a project of the National Council of YMCAs of India (NCYI), for the mental, spiritual and physical wellbeing of the youth in accordance with the YMCA worldwide. It provides a home for the youth and helps new arrivals.
Employees: 30
Volunteers: 9

## Yorkshire Cat Rescue

The Farm, Lower Pierce Close, Cross Roads,
Keighley, West Yorkshire BD22 9AQ
T: 01535 647184
E: mail@yorkshirecatrescue.org
yorkshirecatrescue.org
**Founder and Chief Executive Officer:**
**Sara Atkinson**
A half-way home for unwanted and stray cats
and kittens in Yorkshire. All cats are neutered,
microchipped, vaccinated and treated for
worms and fleas. Volunteers are needed for
cat care, fundraising, admin and to help out in
our charity shops in Keighley and Halifax.
**Employees:** 8
**Volunteers:** 75
**Regional offices:** 1
**Income:** £250,000 (2013–14)

## Yorkshire Coast Enterprise Ltd

E: jennifer.crowther@yce.org.uk

## Young Christian Workers

St. Antony's House, Eleventh Street,
Trafford Park, Manchester M17 1JF
T: 0161 872 6017
E: info@ycwimpact.com
www.ycwimpact.com
**National President: Phil Callaghan**
The Young Christian Workers (YCW) is an
organisation for 16–30 year olds (YCW)
and Impact 13–17 years; it is for young people
and run by young people. Our purpose is to
help all young people live life to the full and
realise their potential. The mission of the
YCW is lived out among young people in the
working world, paid or unpaid work, or those
studying. YCW encourages them to grow in
confidence and responsibility.
**Employees:** 2
**Volunteers:** 50
**Income:** £44,492 (2014–15)

## Young Enterprise

Peterley House, Peterley Road, Cowley,
Oxford OX4 2TZ
T: 01865 776845
E: info@young-enterprise.org.uk
www.young-enterprise.org.uk
With direct practical experience, the
organisation introduces young people to
the world of commerce and industry. It gives
school and college students the opportunity
to acquire a basic understanding of the world
of work and wealth creation.

## Young Epilepsy

St Piers Lane, Lingfield, Surrey RH7 6PW
T: 01342 832243
Helpline: 01342 831342
F: 01342 834639
E: info@youngepilepsy.org.uk
www.youngepilepsy.org.uk
**Chief Executive: Carol Long**
Young Epilepsy is the national charity working
exclusively on behalf of children and young
people with epilepsy. With over 100 years of
experience we are a leading provider of
specialist health and education services.
The charity offers support, information,
training for health, social care and education
professionals and campaigns to improve
access to, and quality of, health and
education services.
**Employees:** 750
**Volunteers:** 50
**Regional offices:** 1

## Young Explorers Trust

Stretton Cottage, Wellow Road, Ollerton,
Newark, Nottinghamshire NG22 9AX
T: 01623 861027
E: info@theyet.org
www.theyet.org
**Chairman of Trustees: Graham Derrick**
YET is a registered charity promoting safe
and responsible expeditions. It aims to give
young people the opportunity to take part
in exploration, discovery and challenging
adventure to help foster the qualities of
service, self-sufficiency and leadership. By
giving advice to youth expeditions it aims to
help schools, youth organisations and peer
groups to run their own expeditions in a safe
and responsible manner. It can also give grant
aid to individuals and expeditions.
**Volunteers:** 20

## Young Lancashire

Preston's College, Fulwood Campus,
St Vincent's Road, Preston,
Lancashire PR2 8UR
T: 01772 556127
F: 01772 251334
E: grahamw@younglancashire.org.uk
www.younglancashire.org.uk
**CEO: Graham Whalley**
Young Lancashire is a local infrastructure
organisation which offers support to all
front-line, voluntary children, young people
and family based organisations to achieve
the highest standards of practice and

effectiveness in their work by building their
capacity to deliver quality services.
**Employees:** 3
**Volunteers:** 12
**Income:** £442,741 (2014–15)

## Young People Matter

The Old Laundry, 20 Eastcote Street,
London SW9 9BY
T: 020 7274 4503
E: m.dawes@youngpeoplematter.org
youngpeoplematter.org
**MD: Ms Kemi Folarin**
Young People Matter is a local Lambeth
Community Anchor Group and charity based
at The Old Laundry, Stockwell, with satellite
sites located within the borough's primary
schools providing after-school and holiday
club services at the behest of local parents.
Since 2007 the charity has created and
facilitated programmes that respond to what
families want and need. A social heart and
business mind govern the core curriculum of
programmes and services based on the
community's needs.
**Employees:** 22
**Volunteers:** 4
**Regional offices:** 1
**Income:** £270,000 (2015–16)

## Young People's Support Foundation

E: k.roberts@ypsf.co.uk

## Young People's Trust for the Environment and Nature Conservation

43 South Street, South Petherton,
Somerset TA13 5AE
T: 01935 385962
E: peter.littlewood@ypte.org.uk
www.yptenc.org.uk
Encourages young people's understanding
of the environment and the need for
sustainability.

## Young Women's Trust

New Barkley House, 234 Botley Road,
Oxford OX2 0HP
T: 01865 304209
F: 01865 204805
E: joe.levenson@youngwomenstrust.org
www.youngwomenstrust.org
YWCA is the leading charity working with
the most disadvantaged young women in
England and Wales. Young women face
unique problems in today's society. They are
largely unheard and lack influence. We want a
future where they can overcome prejudice
and take charge of their own lives. We run

services to support them and campaign with them to combat the discrimination they face.
**Employees: 250**
**Regional offices: 19**

## YoungMinds

**Suite 11, Baden Place, Crosby Row,**
**London  SE1 1YW**
**T: 020 7089 5050**
**Helpline: 0808 802 5544**
**E: ymenquiries@youngminds.org.uk**
**www.youngminds.org.uk**
**Chief Executive: Sarah Brennan**
YoungMinds is the UK's leading charity committed to improving the emotional wellbeing and mental health of children and young people. Driven by their experiences we campaign, research and influence policy and practice.
**Employees: 35**
**Volunteers: 15**

## Youth Access

**1–2 Taylors Yard, 67 Alderbrook Road,**
**London  SW12 8AD**
**T: 020 8772 9900**
**E: admin@youthaccess.org.uk**
**www.youthaccess.org.uk**
**Director: Barbara Rayment**
Youth Access is the national membership organisation for young people's information, advice, counselling and support services (YIACS). It: promotes and encourages the growth of young people's counselling and advisory services; promotes good practice in these services; provides a forum for individuals and agencies; promotes public recognition of the importance of these services.
**Employees: 5**

## Youth at Risk

**The Old Warehouse, 31 Upper King Street,**
**Royston, Hertfordshire  SG8 9AZ**
**T: 01763 241120**
**F: 01763 244735**
**E: clare@youthatrisk.org.uk**
**www.youthatrisk.org.uk**
**Chief Executive Officer: Sue Handly**
Our mission is to enable society's most disadvantaged, difficult and damaged young people to transform their lives and build a future beyond their present expectations; the main activity is to advance the social education of young people at risk either from physical, mental or sexual abuse, drug or other substance abuse, criminal activity,

poverty, homelessness, unemployment or illiteracy.
**Employees: 11**
**Volunteers: 800**

## Youth Sport Trust

**SportPark, Loughborough University,**
**3 Oakwood Drive, Loughborough,**
**Leicestershire  LE11 3QF**
**T: 01509 226600**
**E: info@youthsporttrust.org**
**www.youthsporttrust.org**
Our charity is passionate about helping all young people to achieve their potential by delivering high-quality physical education and sport.
**Regional offices: 1**

## YouthNet

**1st Floor, 50 Featherstone Street,**
**London  EC1Y 8RT**
**T: 020 7250 5700**
**F: 020 7250 3695**
**E: media@youthnet.org**
**www.youthnet.org**
**Chief Executive: Emma Thomas**
YouthNet helps young people make choices today for a brighter tomorrow, by providing impartial information and support about anything and everything for 16 to 25 year olds, whenever and wherever they need it, inspiring them to get involved. YouthNet do this primarily through their three websites: TheSite.org, do-it.org and Lifetracks.com.
**Employees: 50**
**Regional offices: 1**

## Youthscape

**3A Upper George Street, Luton,**
**Bedfordshire  LU1 2QX**
**T: 01582 877220**
**E: chris.curtis@youthscape.co.uk**
**CEO: Chris Curtis**

## Zoological Society of London

**Regent's Park, London  NW1 4RY**
**T: 020 7449 6253**
**F: 020 7586 5743**
**E: ian.meyrick@zsl.org**
**www.zsl.org**
**Director General: Ralph Armond**
By conducting scientific research, we promote zoology and the conservation of biological diversity, the welfare of animals and care and breeding of endangered species. We foster public interest and participation in conservation worldwide.
**Employees: 725**
**Volunteers: 300**
**Regional offices: 1**

## Zurich Community Trust (UK) Limited

**PO Box 1288, Swindon, Wiltshire  SN1 1FL**
**T: 01793 511227**
**F: 01793 506982**
**E: kate.hodges@zct.org.uk**
**www.zct.org.uk**
**Head of Zurich Community Trust:**
**Pam Webb**
The umbrella for all Zurich's community involvement in the UK and supports the most disadvantaged people. A registered charity in its own right, Zurich Community Trust gives time, money and skills donated by Zurich and its employees in the UK. The Zurich Community Trust has a long history of pioneering grant-making to support less popular issues, works in genuine partnership with charities and supports around 600 local, national and overseas charities each year.
**Employees: 18**
**Volunteers: 2600**

INDEX

THE VOLUNTARY
AGENCIES DIRECTORY

## ABUSE & VIOLENCE – VICTIMS' & SURVIVORS' SUPPORT SERVICES

Breaking Free – Primarily Supporting Women survivors of sexual abuse
Breastcancer Haven
Broken Rainbow LGBT Domestic Violence Service UK
CARA (Centre for Action on Rape and Abuse)
Jewish Women's Aid International
Internet Watch Foundation
Mankind
Murdered Abroad
NAPAC
National Organisation for the Treatment of Abusers
Phoenix Domestic Abuse & Support Services Ltd
Rape and Sexual Abuse Support Centre – Rape Crisis South London
Refuge
RESPECT
RoSA
Safe Partnership Limited
Safer Places
SafeLives
Savana
Stop Abuse for Everyone
Support After Murder and Manslaughter
Survivors Trust
Victim Support
Wolverhampton Domestic Violence Forum
Women and Girls' Network
Women's Aid Federation of England
Women Survivors of Child Sexual Abuse
Wycombe Women's Aid Ltd

## ACCOMMODATION & HOUSING

**See also HOMELESSNESS SUPPORT; HOSPICES; RESIDENTIAL & CARE HOMES**
Building and Social Housing Foundation
Chartered Institute of Housing
Christian Camping International
City South Manchester
Empty Homes Agency
Federation of Private Residents Associations Ltd
Field Lane Foundation
Fylde Coast YMCA
Habitat for Humanity Great Britain
Housing Associations' Charitable Trust (hact)
Housing Justice
Journalists' Charity
National Housing Federation
Newcastle Tenants and Residents Federation
Notts Housing Advice
Raglan Housing Association
Royal Masonic Benevolent Institution
Rural Housing Trust
SITRA (Services)
Staying First

Stonewall Housing
William Sutton Trust

### EX-OFFENDERS
Langley House Trust

### EX-SERVICEMEN & WOMEN
Douglas Haig Memorial Homes (Haig Homes)
The Royal Star and Garter Homes

### HOLIDAY & HOSTEL ACCOMMODATION
International Youth Hostel Federation
Lin Berwick Trust
YHA (England and Wales) Ltd
YMCA Indian Student Hostel

### HOSPITAL / NEAR HOSPITAL ACCOMMODATION
The Sick Children's Trust

### FOR OLDER PEOPLE
Abbeyfield Society
AgeCare
Almshouse Association
Anchor Trust
Care and Repair England Ltd
Elderly Accommodation Counsel
KeyChange Charity
MHA Care Group
Relatives and Residents Association
Sons of Divine Providence
The Brendoncare Foundation

### VULNERABLE ADULTS
Adullam Homes Housing Association
ARP
Stonham

### WOMEN
Chapter 1
Christian Family Concern
Eaves Housing for Women Limited
House of Saint Barnabas in Soho
LIFE
Women's Aid Federation of England

### YOUNG PEOPLE & CHILDREN
Centrepoint
Foyer Federation
KeyChange Charity
Reedham Children's Trust

## ADDICTION SUPPORT SERVICES

**See also ALCOHOL AWARENESS & SUPPORT GROUPS; ARTS & CULTURE DRUG AWARENESS & SUPPORT GROUPS; GAMBLING SUPPORT GROUPS; SMOKING 'STOP SMOKING' SUPPORT GROUPS**
Action on Addiction
Addiction Recovery Agency
EDP Drug and Alcohol Service

Foundation66
Gordon Moody Association
Odyssey Trust (UK)
Streetscene
Vita Nova

## ADMINISTRATION

**See GOVERNANCE & ADMINISTRATION**

## ADOPTION & FOSTERING SERVICES

Adoption UK
After Adoption
British Association for Adoption and Fostering
CCS Adoption
Childlink
Consortium of Voluntary Adoption Agencies
Faith in Families
Families for Children
Intercountry Adoption Centre
PAC-UK Ltd
PACT (Parents and Children together)
The Adolescent and Children's Trust (TACT)
The Fostering Network

## ADULT EDUCATION & TRAINING

**See also LITERACY & NUMERACY**
African and Caribbean Voices Association
Apex Charitable Trust Ltd
Aurora Health Foundation
Creative and Supportive Trust
Deafax
Educational Centres Association
European Extension College
Find a Future
FOCUS
Inter-Action Associated Charitable Trusts and Companies
Learning and Work Institute
Learning for Life
Linkage Community Trust
National Extension College
PEYTU
Prisoners Education Trust
Rathbone
Shannon Trust
Skills for Communities
Spadework Ltd
Third Age Trust (National Office U3A)
Topps – Training Opportunities
Women and Manual Trades
Women's Technology and Education Centre
Workers' Educational Association

## ADVISORY SERVICES

**see also ADVOCACY SERVICES; ALBANIAN COMMUNITY GROUPS; ANGOLAN COMMUNITY GROUPS; BENGALI COMMUNITY GROUPS; CHINESE COMMUNITY GROUPS;**

**CONGOLESE COMMUNITY GROUPS; ETHIOPIAN COMMUNITY GROUPS; FINANCIAL ADVICE SERVICES; IMMIGRATION ADVICE & SUPPORT GROUPS; IRANIAN COMMUNITY GROUPS; LEGAL ADVISORY & SUPPORT SERVICES; PHILIPPINE COMMUNITY GROUPS; TRAVELLER GROUPS; WEST INDIAN COMMUNITY GROUPS**

Advice Services Alliance
Advice UK
Cass Centre for Charity Effectiveness
Christians Abroa
Citizens Advice
Cult Information Centre
Direct Help & Advice (DHA)
Enterprising Futures
Family Lives
Federation of Private Residents
    Associations Ltd
Gharweg Advice Training and Careers Centre
INQUEST
LASA
Olmec
Prisoners Advice Service
The Royal Society for the Prevention of
    Accidents (RoSPA)
Sahara Communities Abroad (SACOMA)
SWAN Advice Network
WAY Widowed and Young

**DISABILITIES**
ADD International (Action on Disability
    and Development)
Asian Peoples Disability Alliance Ltd
Change People
DIAL UK
Disability Alliance
Disability Awareness in Action
Disability Law Service
Disabled Living Foundation
RICABILITY Incorporating RICA (Research
    Institute for Consumer Affairs)

**ADVOCACY SERVICES**

**see also ADVISORY SERVICES; LEGAL ADVISORY & SUPPORT SERVICES; PEACE CAMPAIGNS; POLITICAL ENGAGEMENT**
Campaign for Freedom of Information
Citizens Income Trust
Conscience the Peace Tax Campaign
Consumers' Association
Direct Help & Advice (DHA)
Democratic Progress Institute
Fraud Advisory Panel
Henry George Foundation of Great
    Britain Ltd
Joint Council for the Welfare of Immigrants
Library Campaign
Minority Rights Group International
National Council for Voluntary Organisations
National Youth Advocacy Service
Onside
SEAP

Transparency International (UK)
United Nations Association
Vegetarian Society UK Ltd

**MEDICAL**
Action Against Medical Accidents
Bladder and Bowel Foundation
Medact

**AFRICAN & AFRO-CARIBBEAN COMMUNITY SUPPORT GROUPS**

1990 Trust
Africa Development Network
African and Caribbean Voices Association
African Community Partnership
Angolan Civic Communities Alliance
Black Training and Enterprise Group
Community Action Project
Community of Congolese Refugees in
    Great Britain
Dudley Caribbean and Friends Association
Embrace
Ethiopian Community in Britain
Nubian Life Resource Centre Ltd
Sahara Communities Abroad (SACOMA)
Welwitschia Welfare Centre

**HEALTH**
African Caribbean Leukaemia Trust
African HIV Policy Network
AMREF Health Africa
Black and Ethnic Minority
    Diabetes Association
Black Health Agency
Innovative Vision Organisation
The Forum for Health and Wellbeing

**AIDS & HIV**

African Community Involvement
    Association
African HIV Policy Network
AVERT
Body and Soul
British HIV Association
Cara Trust
Children of Africa
Ernest Foundation
Food Chain (UK) Ltd
Innovative Vision Organisation
JAT (formerly Jewish AIDS Trust)
Macfarlane Trust
National AIDS Trust
Positively UK
St Peters House Project
Terrence Higgins Trust

**ALBANIAN COMMUNITY GROUPS**

British Albanian Kosovar Council
Shpresa Programme (Albanian for Hope)

**ALCOHOL AWARENESS & SUPPORT GROUPS**

Addaction
ADFAM
Al-Anon Family Groups UK and Eire
Alcohol Concern
Alcohol Research UK
Alcoholics Anonymous
ARP
British National Temperance League
Campaign Against Drinking and Driving
Drug and Alcohol Action Programme
Hope UK
Institute of Alcohol Studies
Kenward Trust
Life For The World
Medical Council on Alcohol
Phoenix Futures
Portman Group Trust
The Drinkaware Trust
The Matthew Project

**ALLERGIES**

Action Against Allergy
Allergy UK
Anaphylaxis Campaign
The MedicAlert Foundation

**ALTERNATIVE MEDICINE**

**See COMPLEMENTARY MEDICINE**

**ANGOLAN COMMUNITY GROUPS**

Angolan Civic Communities Alliance
Welwitschia Welfare Centre

**ANIMALS**

**See also BIRD PROTECTION; CAT WELFARE; DOG WELFARE & SERVICES FOR THE DISABLED; HORSE WELFARE; MARINE LIFE & WATERWAYS; WILDLIFE CONSERVATION**
Animal Rescue Charity
Amphibian and Reptile Conservation
Animal Welfare Foundation
Blue Cross
Booktrust
Born Free Foundation
British Union for the Abolition of Vivisection
Buglife – the Invertebrate Conservation Trust
Catholic Concern for Animals
Community Hygiene Concern
Compassion in World Farming
Donkey Sanctuary
Environmental Investigation Agency Trust
Farm Animal Welfare Network
Humane Slaughter Association
International Fund for Animal Welfare
League Against Cruel Sports
Mammal Society
National Animal Welfare Trust

PDSA for Pets in Need of Vets
People's Trust for Endangered Species
Rare Breeds Survival Trust
Royal Society for the Prevention of Cruelty
to Animals
Society for the Protection of Animals Abroad
The Brooke
Universities Federation for Animal Welfare
Woodgreen The Animal Charity
World Society for the Protection of Animals

## ANXIETY DISORDERS

See STRESS & ANXIETY DISORDERS

## ARMED FORCES WELFARE AND SUPPORT SERVICES

See also EX-SERVICEMEN & WOMEN
SUPPORT SERVICES
RAF Association
Royal Air Forces Association
Royal Air Force Benevolent Fund
Royal Air Force Music Charitable Trust
Royal British Legion
Royal British Legion Industries Ltd
Royal Naval Benevolent Society for Officers
Royal Naval Benevolent Trust
Soldiers, Sailors, Airmen and Families
Association (SSAFA)
Women's Royal Naval Service
Benevolent Trust

## ARTHRITIC CONDITIONS

Arthritic Action
Arthritis and Musculoskeletal Alliance
Arthritis Care
Adoption
Horder Centre for Arthritis
National Ankylosing Spondylitis
Society (NASS)
National Rheumatoid Arthritis Society

## ARTISTS & PERFORMERS SUPPORT GROUPS

Equity Trust Fund
Federation of British Artists
Royal Literary Fund
Royal Theatrical Fund
Society of Authors

## ARTS & CULTURE

See also ADDICTION SUPPORT
SERVICES; ARTISTS & PERFORMERS,
SUPPORT GROUPS; ARTS
EDUCATION; DANCE; MUSEUMS;
MUSIC; THEATRES
Arts Council England
Artswork
British Council
British and International Federation
of Festivals
Cinema For All (British Federation of
Film Societies)

Collage Arts
Comic Relief
Common Ground
Free Form Arts Trust
Guernsey Arts Commission
National Association of Decorative and Fine
Arts Societies
National Campaign for the Arts
National Operatic and Dramatic Association
Paintings in Hospitals
Royal Television Society
Southbank Mosaics CIC
Template Foundation
Voluntary Arts

## ADDICTION RECOVERY

Vita Nova

## COMMUNITY GROUPS

darts (Doncaster Community Arts)
Finn-Guild
Kurdish Cultural Centre

## FOR DISABILITIES & SPECIAL NEEDS

Conquest Art – Enriching the Lives of
People with Disabilities and long term
health issues
Dark Horse Theatre
Disabled Photographers' Society
EPIC Arts
Living Paintings
Mind the Gap

## REHABILITATION OF OFFENDERS

Clean Break

## ARTS EDUCATION

Associated Board of the Royal Schools
of Music
Council for Dance Education and Training
Dark Horse Theatre
Music Education Council
Raw Material Music and Media Education
Royal Academy of Dance

## ASIAN COMMUNITY SUPPORT GROUPS

1990 Trust
Adhar Project
Alternative for India Development
Asha Projects
Asia House
Asian Family Counselling Service
Black Health Agency
Chinese in Britain Forum
Chinese Information and Advice Centre
Consortium of Bengali Associations
Council of British Pakistanis
Imkaan
India Welfare Society
Indian Volunteers for Community Service
QED-UK
The Forum for Health and Wellbeing

## ASYLUM SEEKERS

See REFUGEE & ASYLUM SEEKERS,
SUPPORT GROUPS

## AUTISM

Autism Independent UK
Autism Plus
Autism Research Ltd
Autistic Research Organisation
Education and Services for People with
Autism Ltd
Hillingdon Autistic Care and Support
Resources for Autism
The National Autistic Society

## AUTOIMMUNE DISORDERS

Behcet's Syndrome Society
British Society for Immunology
Coeliac UK
Guillain Barre & Associated Inflammatory
Neuropathies

## BEHAVIOURAL DIFFICULTIES – SUPPORT FOR PARENTS & CARERS

See also FAMILY SUPPORT
Caspari Foundation for Educational Therapy
and Therapeutic Teaching
Centre for Fun and Families
Glebe House
Home-Start UK
Home-Start Canterbury and Coastal
Home-Start Haringey
Home-Start International
Home-Start South Hams, Plymouth
and Tavistock
Home-Start Stoke-on-Trent
Home-Start Worthing and Adur
Place2Be
Right From the Start
Social Emotional and Behavioural
Difficulties Association
The Respite Association

## BEHAVIOURAL TRAINING

Alternatives to Violence Project, Britain

## BELIEF SYSTEMS

See also BUDDHIST FAITH; CHRISTIAN
FAITH GROUPS; HUMANISM; JEWISH
FAITH; MUSLIM FAITH
Alliance of Healing Associations
Faith Based Regeneration Network UK
Guild of Pastoral Psychology
Inter Faith Network for the United Kingdom
Isbourne Foundation
Krishnamurti Foundation Trust
Maharishi Foundation

## BENEVOLENT SOCIETIES

Actors Benevolent Fund

Architects Benevolent Society
Cavell Nurses' Trust
Journalists Charity
LionHeart
National Benevolent Fund for the Aged
National Benevolent Institution
Rainy Day Trust
Royal Agricultural Benevolent Institution
Royal Air Force Benevolent Fund
Royal Literary Fund
Royal Medical Benevolent Fund
Royal Naval Benevolent Society for Officers
Royal Naval Benevolent Trust
Royal Navy and Royal Marine
    Children's Fund
Royal Theatrical Fund
Royal UK Beneficent Association (Rukba)
Sailors' Families' Society
Shipwrecked Fishermen and Mariners' Royal
    Benevolent Society
Society for the Assistance of Ladies in
    Reduced Circumstances
SBA The Solicitors' Charity
Women's Royal Naval Service
    Benevolent Trust

## BENGALI COMMUNITY GROUPS

Consortium of Bengali Associations

## BEREAVEMENT SUPPORT GROUPS

Aftermath Support
Child Bereavement UK
Child Death Helpline
Cruse Bereavement Care
Jewish Bereavement Counselling Service
Jigsaw 4ULtd
Murdered Abroad
Rainbow Centre for Children affected by
    Life-Threatening Illnesses or Bereavement
Support after Murder and Manslaughter
Survivors of Bereavement by Suicide
The Compassionate Friends
Winston's Wish

## BIPOLAR DISORDERS

Bipolar UK

## BIRD PROTECTION

British Ornithologists' Union
British Trust for Ornithology
Royal Society for the Protection of Birds

## BISEXUAL SUPPORT GROUPS

**See GAY/LESBIAN/BISEXUAL/
TRANSGENDER SUPPORT GROUPS**

## BLINDNESS & SIGHT IMPAIRMENT

Action for Blind People

Association of Blind and Partially Sighted
    Teachers and Students
Association of Blind Piano Tuners
Blind Veterans UK
British Blind Sport
British Retinitis Pigmentosa Society
British Wireless for the Blind Fund
International Glaucoma Association
Keratoconus Self-Help and
    Support Association
Look National Office
Macular Society
National Federation of the Blind of the UK
National Music for the Blind
Nystagmus Network
Partially Sighted Society
Queen Alexandra College
Royal Blind Society for the UK
Royal London Society for the Blind
Royal National Institute of the Blind
RP Fighting Blindness
SeeAbility
The Royal National College for the Blind
Victa Children Ltd
VISION 2020 UK
Vista
Vitalise
Walsall Society for the Blind
WESC Foundation

## OVERSEAS AID

Blindaid Africa
ORBIS Charitable Trust
Sight Savers International
Vision Aid Overseas

## RESOURCES FOR

CALIBRE Audio Library
International Guide Dog Federation
Listening Books
Living Paintings
RNIB National Library Service
Telephones for the Blind Fund
The Seeing Dogs Alliance
Thomas Pocklington Trust
Torch Trust for the Blind
Vision Homes Association

## BLOOD DISORDERS

Haemophilia Society
Macfarlane Trust
UK Thalassaemia Society

## BUDDHIST FAITH

Friends of the Western Buddhist Order
Golden Buddha Centre
Karuna Trust
New Kadampa Tradition – International
    Kadampa Buddhist Union

## BUILDINGS & OPEN SPACE PROVISION

**See also ACCOMMODATION &
HOUSING**

CAN
CRASH
Ethical Property Foundation
Learning Through Landscapes
Open Spaces Society
Upkeep

## BUSINESS & ENTERPRISE DEVELOPMENT

Association of Community Based Business
    Advice
BCS
Black Training and Enterprise Group
Business in the Community
CAN
Co-operatives UK
Enterprising Futures
Ethical Trading Initiative
Industry and Parliament Trust
Institute of Business Ethics
Novas-Ouvertures Group Ltd
School for Social Entrepreneurs
Social Enterprise Coalition
Social Market Foundation
Social Partnership
Social Venture Network UK
Society for Co-operative Studies
Strategic Planning Society
Supporters Direct
Topps – Training Opportunities
Twin Ltd
UnLtd – the Foundation for
    Social Entrepreneurs
Yorkshire Coast Enterprise Ltd

## BUSINESS & INDUSTRY TRAINING

Association for Project Management
Association of Charity
    Independent Examiners
British Psychological Society
CASE Kent
Enterprising Futures
IGD
Institute for War and Peace Reporting
Inter-Action Associated Charitable Trusts
    and Companies
IVAR
Mathematics in Education and Industry
Royal Institute of British Architects
School for Social Entrepreneurs
Skillset Sector Skills Council
Social Emotional and Behavioural
    Difficulties Association
Stephen Lawrence Charitable Trust
Voluntary Sector Training
Women's Engineering Society (WES)

## CANCER RESEARCH & SUPPORT GROUPS

African Caribbean Leukaemia Trust
Angel Foundation
Bowel Cancer UK

Breast Cancer Now
Breast Cancer Care
Breast Cancer Research Trust
Breastcancer Haven
British Association for Cancer Research
British Colostomy Association
British Dental Health Foundation
British Voice Association
Cancer Care Society
Cancer Laryngectomee Trust
Cancer Research UK
CancerBACKUP
Cancerkin
Challenge Fund – the Fight against Cancer
   in the Emerging World
Childhood Eye Cancer Trust
Dimbleby Cancer Care
Elimination of Leukaemia Fund
Free Access Cancer Therapy Database
Gorlin Syndrome Group
Institute of Cancer Research
Leukaemia Care
Lymphoma Association
Macmillan Cancer Support
Neuroblastoma UK
Ovacome
Ovarian Cancer Action
Prostate Cancer Charity
Roy Castle Lung Cancer Foundation
Teenage Cancer Trust
Weston Park Hospital Development
   Fund Ltd

**CARDIAC CONDITIONS & RESEARCH**

British Cardiac Patients Association
British Cardiovascular Society
British Heart Foundation
Cardiomyopathy UK
Children's Heart Federation (CHF)
Circulation Foundation
Coronary Artery Disease
   Research Association
Little Hearts Matter
Magdi Yacoub Institute
The Somerville Foundation

**CAREERS GUIDANCE & ADVICE**

Careers Research and Advisory Centre Ltd
Medway Youth Trust

**CARERS**

Carers Association Southern Staffordshire
Carers Centre (Leicestershire & Rutland)
Carers Network
Carers Trust
Carers UK
Carers' Support – Canterbury, Dover
   & Thanet
Carer Support Wiltshire
Enfield Carers Centre
Hambleton and Richmondshire
   Carers Centre

Solihull Carers Centre
The Respite Association
Trafford Carers Centre

**CAT WELFARE**

Cats Protection
International Cat Care
Yorkshire Cat Rescue

**CEREBRAL PALSY**

Scope
Worster-Drought Syndrome Support Group

**CHILD PROTECTION**

Ann Craft Trust
ChildLine
Churches Child Protection Advisory Service
ECPAT UK
Kidscape Campaign for Children's Safety
NAPAC
NSPCC
Rape and Sexual Abuse Support Centre –
   Rape Crisis South London
Youth at Risk

**CHILDBIRTH SUPPORT SERVICES**
**See also POST-NATAL SUPPORT GROUPS; PREGNANCY; STILLBIRTH & NEONATAL DEATH**
Association of Radical Midwives
Birth Companions
Group B Strep Support
Royal College of Midwives

**MULTIPLE BIRTHS**
Multiple Births Foundation
Twins and Multiple Births Association

**CHILDCARE PROVISION**

4Children
Caldecott Foundation
Christian Family Concern
Children England
Children's Hope Foundation
National Day Nurseries Association
Professional Association for Childcare and
   Early Years (PACEY)
Young Lancashire

**CHILDREN & YOUNG PEOPLE**
**See also BEHAVIOURAL DIFFICULTIES – SUPPORT FOR PARENTS & CARERS; CHILD PROTECTION; CHILDCARE PROVISION, CHILDREN'S ACTIVITY SCHEMES & CLUBS; COUNSELLING & PSYCHOTHERAPY SERVICES; EXCHANGE AND OVERSEAS PROGRAMMES; FURTHER & HIGHER EDUCATION; HELPLINES; INFANT & CHILDREN HEALTH SUPPORT GROUPS; INFANT, PRIMARY &**

**SECONDARY SCHOOL EDUCATION; INFANT DEATH; OUTDOOR EDUCATION & RESIDENTIAL COURSES; PRE-SCHOOL EDUCATION**
4Children
Action for Children
Albert Kennedy Trust
Attlee Foundation
Barnardo's
British Youth Council
Buttle UK
Diagrama Foundation
Centre for Youth and
   Community Development
Child Accident Prevention Trust (CAPT)
Child Migrants Trust
Child Poverty Action Group
Children and Families Across Borders
   (Formerly ISS UK)
Children's Family Trust
Children's Society
City Year London
Coram Family
Coram Voice
Council for Awards in Children's Care
   and Education
CXK
Dorset Youth Association
End Child Poverty
Friendship Works
Learning Plus UK
Life Education Centres
Missing People
National Association of Child
   Contact Centres
National Children's Centre
National Youth Advocacy Service
National Youth Agency
NCB
New Choices for Youth
Potential Plus UK
Prince's Trust
Roald Dahl's Marvellous Children's Charity
School-Home Support (SHS)
Skill: National Bureau for Students
   with Disabilities
Skill Force
The Eikon Charity
The IARS International Institute
Variety
Young Enterprise
Young People's Support Foundation
Youthscape

**ACCOMMODATION & HOUSING**
BYHP
Centrepoint
Foyer Federation
KeyChange Charity
Reedham Children's Trust
Together for Short Lives

**ADVICE & INFORMATION SERVICES**
Children's Legal Centre
Kidsaid
National Association of Children's
   Information Services

Off Centre Hackney
Youth Access
YouthNet

## ALCOHOL & DRUG EDUCATION
Hope UK
Kenward Trust
National Association for Children
   of Alcoholics
The Matthew Project

## ARTS & MUSIC
Artswork
Creative Youth Network
Live Music Now!
National Association of Youth Theatres
National Youth Orchestra of Great Britain

## BEREAVEMENT SUPPORT
Child Bereavement UK
Child Death Helpline
Cruse Bereavement Care
Jigsaw 4 U Ltd
This Way Up Youth Project
Winston's Wish

## CARE SERVICES
NAGALRO
Shaftesbury Young People
Spurgeon's Child Care
TACT
The Who Cares? Trust

## COMMUNITY GROUPS
British Albanian Kosovar Council
Centre for Youth and
   Community Development

## DISABILITIES
3H Fund (Helping hands for Holidays)
Bexley Snap
BIBIC
Blind Children UK
CALIBRE Audio Library
Care Co-ordination Network UK
Children's Trust
Dame Hannah Rogers School
Deaf Education through Listening and
   Talking (DELTA)
Deaf Ex-Mainstreamers Group
Down's Syndrome Educational Trust
Dreamflight
Elizabeth Foundation
Fledglings Family Services
KIDS
Kids Can Achieve
Lifeworks
Medical Engineering Resource Unit
National Deaf Children's Society (NDCS)
Newlife
Parents for Inclusion
Parents in Partnership
Reach- Association for Children with Upper
   Limb Deficiency
The Log Cabin
Treolar Trust
Victa Children Ltd

Whizz-Kidz

## GRANTS
Attlee Foundation
BBC Children in Need Appeal
Buttle UK
Children's Country Holidays Fund
Dreamflight
Dreams Come True Charity
Help a Poor Child
Make-A-Wish Foundation UK
Prince's Trust
Promise Dreams
Royal Navy and Royal Marine
   Children's Fund
Sailors' Families' Society

## OVERSEAS AID
AbleChildAfrica
Blindaid Africa
Children of Africa
Child Soldiers International
EveryChild
Global Care
Hope and Homes for Children
Hope for Children
Humanity at Heart
International Children's Trust
Orphans In Need
Orphans Relief Fund and Charitable Trust
Plan International
Railway Children
Save the Children UK
SOS Children's Villages UK
Street Child Africa
Wishing Well

## PERSONAL DEVELOPMENT
Chance UK
Children and Young People's
Diversity Role Models
Empowerment Project
Endeavour Training Ltd
Explore
Headliners (formerly known as
   Children's Express)
Inspire!
Nell Bank
TOC H
Woodcraft Folk
Wooden Spoon Society

## RESEARCH
Anna Freud Centre
Caspari Foundation for Educational Therapy
   and Therapeutic Teaching
ChildNet International
Dartington Social Research Unit

## SPEECH & COMMUNICATION
## SUPPORT
AFASIC
I CAN

## SPORT & RECREATION
Children's Links
Construction Industry Trust for Youth

Fair Play for Children Association/
   Charitable Trust
Get Hooked on Fishing Charitable Trust
Happy Days Children's Charity
Horse Rangers Association (Hampton
   Court) Ltd
International Youth Hostel Federation
Kidsout UK
Youth Sport Trust

## CHILDREN'S ACTIVITY
## SCHEMES & CLUBS
See also OUTDOOR EDUCATION &
RESIDENTIAL COURSES
3 Villages Youth Project
Adventure Service Challenge Scheme
Air Cadets
Amal Trust
Ambition
Army Cadet Force Association
Be Your Best Foundation
Boys' Brigade
Camberwell After School Project
CLCBG – Church Lads and Church
   Girls Brigade
Farms for City Children
Girlguiding UK
Girls' Brigade England and Wales
Girls' Venture Corps Air Cadets
Grail
Hi8us Projects Ltd
HOST UK
Jewish Lads and Girls Brigade including
   Outreach/Kiruv and Hand-in-Hand
   Young Volunteers
National Federation of Young Farmers' Clubs
National Youthbike
Salmon Youth Centre
Sea Cadets
Tall Ships Youth Trust
The Duke of Edinburgh's Award
The Scout Association
World Association of Girl Guides and
   Girl Scouts
Young Christian Workers
Young Explorers Trust
Young People Matter

## CHILDREN'S HEALTH
See INFANT & CHILDREN'S HEALTH
SUPPORT GROUPS

## CHINESE COMMUNITY
## GROUPS
Chinese in Britain Forum
Chinese Information and Advice Centre

## CHRISTIAN FAITH GROUPS
A Rocha UK
Apostleship of the Sea
Arthur Rank Centre
Association of Interchurch Families
Bible Society

BMS World Mission
British and International Sailors' Society
Brothers of Charity Services
Canterbury Diocesan Board of Finance
Caritas Social Action Network (CSAN)
Catholic Association for Racial Justice
Catholic Clothing Guild
Catholic Concern for Animals
Catholic Truth Society
Catholic Women's League
Chapter 1
Christian Aid
Christian Camping International
Christian Education
Christian Family Concern
Church Action on Poverty
Church Army
Church Housing Trust
Church of England: Archbishops' Council
Church Pastoral Aid Society
College of St Barnabas
Evangelical Alliance
Field Lane Foundation
General Assembly of Unitarian and Free
    Christian Churches
Gideons International in the British Isles
Glebe House
Grail
Greater World Christian
    Spiritualist Association
Grubb Institute
Guild of Health Ltd
Guild of St Raphael
Institute for Community and
    Development Studies
Kenward Trust
KeyChange Charity
Kingham Hill Trust
Kingsway International Christian Centre
Langley House Trust
League of Mercy
Leeds Church Institute
Lesbian and Gay Christian Movement
Lutheran Council of Great Britain
Maroa Christian Counselling International
MHA Care Group
Mission Care
Mothers Union
Oasis Charitable Trust
Pax Christi
People of God Trust
Pilgrim Hearts Trust
Prison Fellowship England and Wales
Prospects for People with
    Learning Disabilities
Queen Victoria Seamen's Rest
Salvation Army
Scripture Union
Society for Promoting Christian Knowledge
The Anscombe Bioethics Centre
The Lodge Trust
Time For God
Torch Trust for the Blind
UCCF

**CHILDREN & YOUNG PEOPLE**
Bethany Children's Trust

Boys' Brigade
Centre for Youth and
    Community Development
Friendship Works
GFS Platform for Young Women
Girls' Brigade England and Wales
Ormiston Families
Student Christian Movement
YMCA England
Young Christian Workers

**OVERSEAS AID**
African Pastors' Fellowship
BMS World Mission
Catholic Agency for Overseas Development
Christians Abroad
Global Care
Global Connections
HCPT (Hosanna House and Children's
    Pilgrimage Trust)
Intercontinental Church Society
InterHealth Worldwide
Learning Plus UK
Lightforce International
Mission Aviation Fellowship UK
Pontifical Mission Societies
Roald Dahl's Marvellous Children's Charity
Tearfund
Youthscape

**CHROMOSOMAL DISORDERS**
Fragile X Society
Unique – Rare Chromosome Disorder
    Support Group
Williams Syndrome Foundation Ltd

**CHRONIC FATIGUE
SYNDROME**
**See ME**

**CIRCULATORY DISORDERS**
Raynaud's and Scleroderma Association

**CIRCUMCISION**
Norm UK

**CITIZENSHIP**
Anne Frank Trust UK
Beacon Awards
British Future
Citizens UK
Citizenship Foundation
Common Purpose
Nell Bank
Operation Black Vote OPUS
Royal Humane Society
Royal Life Saving Society UK

**COMMUNICATIONS & MEDIA
HANDLING**
Community Media Association

Community Network
Institute for War and Peace Reporting
Inter-Action Associated Charitable Trusts
    and Companies
International Institute of Communications
Media Trust
Media Wise Trust
PublicMedia CIC
Raw Material Music and Media Education
Royal Television Society
Royal Theatrical Fund
Rural Media Company
Telephone Helplines Association
Television Trust for the Environment
The Radio Amateurs' Emergency Network

**COMMUNITY DEVELOPMENT
& RESOURCES**
**See also HOMELESSNESS; UMBRELLA
& RESOURCE BODIES; VOLUNTARY
ACTION AND VOLUNTEER CENTRES**
Access Community Trust
Alington House Community Association
Andover Neighbourcare
ARVAC Association for Research in the
    Voluntary and Community Sector
Be Your Best Foundation
Bore Place
Centre for Volunteering and
    Community Leadership
Churches Community Work Alliance
Citizens UK
Civic Trust
Community Action Project
Community Action Network
Community Action Wyre Forest
Community Development Agency Limited
Community Development
    Finance Association
Community Development Foundation
Community First
Community Foundation for Lancashire
    & Merseyside
Community Links
Community Links Bromley
Community Matters
Develop Enhancing Community Support
Empowering West Berkshire
Faith Based Regeneration Network UK
Federation for Community
    Development Learning
Groundwork UK
Highbury Vale Blackstock Trust
Institute for Community and
    Development Studies
John Huntingdon's Charity
Maidstone Community Support Centre
Mark Hall and Netteswell
    Community Association
Middlesbrough Voluntary
    Development Agency
National Association for Voluntary and
    Community Associations
National Communities Resource Centre
National Community Safety Network

North Taunton Partnership
Number One Community Trust (TW) Ltd
Peel Institute
Portchester Community Association
Quaker Social Action
Renaisi Limited
Selby Trust Ltd
Student Hubs
The Cambridge Centre
The Vince Hines Foundation
Toynbee Hall
TPAS England
UK Community Foundations
Urban Forum
West Harton Churches Action Station Ltd
Wigan and Leigh CVS

## COMPLEMENTARY MEDICINE

Association of Reflexologists
British Acupuncture Council
British Homeopathic Association
British Medical Acupuncture Society
General Council and Register of Naturopaths
Get Well UK
Homeopathy Action Trust
Institute for Complementary Medicine
National Institute of Medical Herbalists
Society of Homeopaths

## COMPUTERS & THE INTERNET

AbilityNet
British Computer Society
ChildNet International
Citizens Online
Computers for Charities
Deafax
DoBe.org
GreenNet Educational Trust
Online Centres Foundation

## CONGENITAL DISORDERS

HemiHelp
The Arthrogryposis Group (TAG)

## CONGOLESE COMMUNITY GROUPS

Community of Congolese Refugees in
 Great Britain

## CONSERVATION GROUPS

**See also HERITAGE & HISTORY
GROUPS**
Conservation Foundation
CSV Cathedral Camps
Friends of Friendless Churches
Game & Wildlife Conservation Trust
Institute for Conservation
National Churches Trust
Pilgrim Trust
Plant Heritage
The Churches Conservation Trust
UK Overseas Territories Conservation Forum

## CONTINENCE (INCONTINENCE) ADVICE & SUPPORT

Association for Continence Advice
Bladder and Bowel Foundation
ERIC – Education and Resources for
 Improving Childhood Continence

## COUNSELLING & PSYCHOTHERAPY SERVICES

**See also CHILDREN AND YOUNG
PEOPLE; PSYCHOLOGY**
Albany Trust
Arbours Association Limited
Asian Family Counselling Service
British Association for Counselling
 and Psychotherapy
Bromley Y
Counselling
Counselling and Support For Young People
Crisis Counselling for Alleged Shoplifters
Immigrant Counselling and Psychotherapy
Institute of Group Analysis
Institute of Psychoanalysis
Institute of Transactional Analysis
Kidsaid
Maroa Christian Counselling International
Metanoia Institute
Off Centre Hackney
Psychosynthesis and Education Trust
Refugee Therapy Centre
Research Society of Process Orientated
 Psychology UK
Samaritans
Step Together Volunteering
TASHA Foundation
The Prebend Day Centre
UK Council for Psychotherapy
WPF Therapy
Youth Access

## CRIME & JUSTICE

Centre for Crime and Justice Studies
Circles UK
Clinks
Crime Reduction Initiatives
Crimestoppers Trust
Fellowship of Reconciliation
Howard League for Penal Reform
National Community Safety Network
National Justice and Peace Network
Restorative Justice Council
SOVA
Suzy Lamplugh Trust
The Federation

## DANCE

Council for Dance Education and Training
Dance UK
Foundation for Community Dance
Royal Academy of Dance

## DEAFNESS & HEARING IMPAIRMENTS

Action on Hearing Loss (the new name
 for RNID)
British Deaf Association
British Tinnitus Association
Cued Speech Association UK
Deafconnect
Deaf Education through Listening and
 Talking (DELTA)
Deaf Ex-Mainstreamers Group
Deaf PLUS
Deafblind UK
Deafway
Elizabeth Foundation
Foley House Trust
Hearing Link
Hearing Dogs for Deaf People
Meniere's Society
National Association of Deafened People
National Deaf Children's Society (NDCS)
Royal Association for Deaf People
Sense
Shape London
Signature
SignHealth
Sound Seekers
The Ear Foundation
The Makaton Charity
UK Council on Deafness

## DEMENTIA SUPPORT GROUPS

Alzheimer's Society
Lewy Body Society

## DENTAL HEALTH

British Dental Health Foundation
British Endodontic Society
British Society of Disability and Oral Health

## DERMATOLOGY & SKIN DISORDERS

British Association of Dermatologists
National Eczema Society
Psoriasis and Psoriatic Arthritis Alliance
Psoriasis Association
Vitiligo Society

## DIABETE S RESEARCH & SUPPORT

Black and Ethnic Minority
 Diabetes Association
Diabetes Foundation
Diabetes UK
InDependent Diabetes Trust (IDDT)

## DISABILITIES

**See also BLINDNESS & SIGHT
IMPAIRMENT; DEAFNESS & HEARING
IMPAIRMENTS; DOG WELFARE &**

## SERVICES FOR THE DISABLED; LEARNING DISABILITIES
ACCURO (Care Services)
ADD International (Action on Disability and Development)
Aurora Health Foundation
Asian Peoples Disability Alliance Ltd
Assist UK
Breakthrough UK Ltd
Blesma, The Limbless Veterans
Disability Foundation
Disability Partnership and MOVE
Disability Pregnancy and Parenthood
Disability Rights UK
Disabled Motorists' Federation
Disabled Parents Network
Enham
Handicap International UK
Impact Foundation
Lifeworks
Linkage Community Trust
Livability
Motivation
Optua
Outsiders
PHAB
Queen Elizabeth's Foundation for Disabled People
Realife Trust
Regard
The Grange
United Kingdom's Disabled People's Council

## ACCESS TO ENVIRONMENTS
Centre for Accessible Environments
Disabled Motoring UK
Ealing Centre for Independent Living
Fieldfare Trust Ltd
Kingston Centre for Independent Living
Leicestershire Centre for Integrated Living
Mobilise Organisation
Mobility Information Service
Mobility Trust
National Federation of Shopmobility
Norwich Door To Door
Remap
Through the Roof

## ACCOMMODATION
Anchor Trust
British Home and Hospital for Incurables
Care and Repair England Ltd
Chaseley Trust
Disabilities Trust
Foley House Trust
Hollybank Trust
Independent Living Alternatives
Leonard Cheshire Disability

## ADVICE & INFORMATION
Action on Disability & Development
Centre 404
Change People
DIAL Basildon and South Essex
DIAL West Cheshire
DIAL UK
Disability Alliance

Disability Awareness in Action
Disability Law Service
Disabled Living Foundation
RICABILITY Incorporating RICA (Research Institute for Consumer Affairs)

## CHILDREN
3H Fund (Helping hands for Holidays)
BIBIC
Blind Children UK
CALIBRE Audio Library
Care Co-ordination Network UK
Children's Trust
Dame Hannah Rogers Trust
Deaf Ex-Mainstreamers Group
Down's Syndrome Educational Trust
Dreamflight
Elizabeth Foundation
Fledglings Family Services
KIDS
Lifeworks
Medical Engineering Resource Unit
National Deaf Children's Society (NDCS)
Newlife
Parents for Inclusion
Reach – Association for Children with Upper Limb Deficiency
Skill: National Bureau for Students with Disabilities
Treloar Trust
Whizz-Kidz

## DEAFBLINDNESS
Deafblind UK
Sense
Signature

## EDUCATION & VOCATIONAL TRAINING SUPPORT
Hannahs (formerly Dame Hannah Rogers Trust)
Skill: National Bureau for Students with Disabilities
St Loye's Foundation
The Emily Jordan Foundation
The Hextol Foundation
The Orpheus Centre

## EMPLOYMENT & PROGRESSION SERVICES
Action on Disability and Work UK
Association of Disabled Professionals
Lifeline Community Projects
Papworth Trust
Progress Recruitment Shaw Trust Ltd
Spadework Ltd
TAEN – The Age and Employment Network

## OVERSEAS AID RECREATION
Albrighton Moat & Gardens
Conquest Art – Enriching the Lives of People with Disabilities and long term health issues
Disabled Photographers' Society
Disaway Trust
Drake Music Project
EPIC Arts

EXTEND Exercise Training Ltd
Gardening for Disabled Trust
Jubilee Sailing Trust
Lin Berwick Trust
Mind the Gap
Peter le Marchant Trust
Thrive
Tourism for All UK

## REHABILITATION SERVICES
ASPIRE

## RESOURCES FOR
AbilityNet
British Society of Disability and Oral Health
CALIBRE Audio Library
Clothing Solutions for Disabled People
Dog AID (assistance in Disability)
Dogs for Good
Independent Home Solutions CIC
International Guide Dog Federation
Listening Books
National Music for the Blind
Remap
Sequal Trust
Talking Newspaper Association of the UK
The Seeing Dogs Alliance

## RESPITE CARE & SHORT BREAKS
3H Fund (Helping hands for Holidays)
Adventist Special Needs Association (ASNA)
HCPT (Hosanna House and Children's Pilgrimage Trust)
Shared Care Network
Take a Break Warwickshire

## SPORT
Disability Snowsport UK (Bromley)
Disability Sport England
English Federation of Disability Sport
National Association of Swimming Clubs for the Handicapped
Riding for the Disabled Association
Rounders England
RYA Sailability
United Kingdom Sports Association for People with Learning Disabilities
WheelPower

# DIVORCE & SEPARATION
National Association of Child Contact Centres

# DOG WELFARE & SERVICES FOR THE DISABLED
Dog AID (assistance in Disability)
Dogs for Good
Dogs Trust
Forever Hounds Trust
International Guide Dog Federation
The Seeing Dogs Alliance

## DOMESTIC VIOLENCE

**See ABUSE & VIOLENCE – VICTIMS' & SURVIVORS' SUPPORT SERVICES**

## DRUG AWARENESS & SUPPORT GROUPS

Addaction
ADFAM
Adverse Psychiatric Reactions Information Link (APRIL)
ARP
Cranstoun
Drug and Alcohol Action Programme
Foundation66
Hope UK
Inside Out TrustKenward Trust
Life For The World
Lifeline Project Ltd
Mentor Foundation (International)
Phoenix Futures
Re-Solv
Release
SOLVE IT
Streetscene
The Matthew Project
Westminster Drug Project

## DYSLEXIA SUPPORT

Adult Dyslexia Organisation
British Dyslexia Association
Dyslexia Action
Helen Arkell Dyslexia Centre

## EATING DISORDERS

beat
Foundations UK
Overeaters Anonymous

## EDUCATION

**See also ADULT EDUCATION; ARTS EDUCATION; EDUCATION & TRAINING SERVICES FOR OVERSEAS RELIEF; ENVIRONMENTAL EDUCATION; FURTHER & HIGHER EDUCATION; HOME SCHOOLING; INFANT, JUNIOR & SENIOR EDUCATION; LITERACY & NUMERACY; OUTDOOR EDUCATION & RESIDENTIAL COURSES; PRE-SCHOOL EDUCATION; SPECIAL EDUCATIONAL NEEDS; TEACHING STANDARDS & SUPPORT**
Academy of Youth
ASDAN
Association for Language Learning
British Association for Early Childhood Education
British Council
Caldecott Foundation
Campaign for Learning
CapeUK

Centre for Youth and Community Development
Christian Education
Council for Awards in Children's Care and Education
DEA
Down's Syndrome Educational Trust
Foundation for Conductive Education
High/Scope UK
Human Scale Education
Learning from Experience Trust
Learning plus UK
National Association for Able Children in Education
National Association for Gifted Children
Open Doors International Language School
Pestalozzi International Village Trust
Rathbone
School-Home Support (SHS)
Treloar Trust
UK Youth

## EDUCATION & TRAINING SERVICES FOR OVERSEAS RELIEF

CAMFED International
Corona Worldwide
Filipino International Emergency Services Training
International Network for the Availability of Scientific Publications
INTRAC
Skillshare International
Think Global
Tools for Self Reliance
Windle Trust International

## EMERGENCY SERVICES

Dorset and Somerset Air Ambulance
East Anglian Air Ambulance

## EMPLOYMENT & JOB SEARCH SUPPORT SERVICES

Black Training and Enterprise Group
Enham
First Step Trust
Involvement and Participation Association (IPA)
Medway Youth Trust
Pay and Employment Rights Service (Yorkshire) Ltd
Public Concern at Work
Royal London Society for the Blind
Social Partnership
TAEN – The Age and Employment Network
Tomorrow's People Trust
Workaid
Work Foundation
WRN (Women Returners' Network) in Association with the Grow Trust

## END OF LIFE ISSUES

Dignity in Dying

Hospice UK
Hospice Information Service
Prospect Hospice

## ENDOCRINE DISORDERS

Association for Multiple Endocrine Neoplasia Disorder

## ENERGY CONSERVATION

Centre for Sustainable Energy
National Energy Action (NEA)
National Energy Foundation

## ENVIRONMENTAL EDUCATION

10:10
Fieldfare Trust Ltd
Nakuru Environmental and Conservation Trust
National Association for Environmental Education (UK)

## ENVIRONMENTAL HEALTH & POLLUTION

Chartered Institute of Environmental Health
Environmental Protection
Keep Britain Tidy
Noise Abatement Society

## ENVIRONMENTAL SUPPORT GROUPS

**See also CONSERVATION; ENERGY CONSERVATION; ENVIRONMENTAL EDUCATION; GARDENS & GARDENING; MARINE LIFE & WATERWAYS; TREE PRESERVATION**
10:10
Association of Natural Burial Grounds
Aviation Environment Federation
BirdLife International
Black Environment Network
British Cave Research Association
British Ecological Society
British Naturalists' Association
British Waterways
Centre for Accessible Environments
Common Ground
Earthwatch (Europe)
Environmental Law Foundation
Environmental Vision
Eye on the Wild
Friends of the Earth
Galapagos Conservation Trust
Game Conservancy Trust
Global Action Plan
Global Witness Limited
Green Alliance
Greenpeace UK
Groundwork North East
ICA:UK
Institute for European Environmental Policy London

International Tree Foundation
Keep Britain Tidy
Landlife
Landscape Institute
Living Streets
National Flood Forum
Nakuru Environmental and
    Conservation Trust
New Economics Foundation
People and Planet
Rainforest Foundation UK
Royal Geographical Society
Television Trust for the Environment
Trust for Urban Ecology
Wildfowl and Wetlands Trust
Women's Environmental Network
Young People's Trust for the Environment
    and Nature Conservation

## ENZYME DEFICIENCY DISORDERS

Gauchers Association Ltd

## EPILEPSY

David Lewis Centre
Epilepsy Action
Epilepsy Research UK
Fable Charity
National Centre for Young People
    with Epilepsy
Epilepsy Society

## EQUAL OPPORTUNITIES & DIVERSITY

**See also AFRICAN & AFRO-CARIBBEAN SUPPORT GROUPS; OLDER PEOPLE; WOMEN**
British Future
Catholic Association for Racial Justice
Diversity Hub
Inclusion London
Jewish Council for Racial Equality (JCORE)
Lifeworks
MOSAIC Black and Mixed Parentage
    Family Group
Overseas Development Institute
Parity
Runnymede Trust

## ETHIOPIAN COMMUNITY GROUPS

Embrace
Ethiopian Community in Britain

## EX-SERVICEMEN & WOMEN SUPPORT SERVICES

Blind Veterans UK
Blesma, The Limbless Veterans
Combat Stress
Douglas Haig Memorial Homes
    (Haig Homes)
Fire Fighters Charity

Joint Committee of the Order of St John and
    British Red Cross
League of Remembrance
National Gulf Veterans and
    Families Association
Officers' Association
Royal British Legion Women's Section
Royal Corps of Signals Benevolent Fund
The Not Forgotten Association
The Royal Star and Garter Homes

## EXCHANGE & OVERSEAS PROGRAMMES

AIESEC (UK) Ltd
Concordia (Youth Service Volunteers) Ltd
Gap Activity Projects (GAP) Ltd
International Youth Hostel Federation
Nakuru Environmental and
    Conservation Trust
Outreach International
Raleigh International

## FACIAL DISFIGUREMENT

Changing Faces
Headlines, the Craniofacial Support Group
Let's Face it Support Network for the
    Facially Disfigured

## FAMILY SUPPORT

**See also GRANDPARENTS; PARENTING; BEHAVIOURAL DIFFICULTIES – SUPPORT FOR PARENTS & CARERS**
Asian Family Counselling Service
Association for Family Therapy
Aylesham Neighbourhood Project
Catholic Children's Society
Contact a Family
Direct Help & Advice (DHA)
Family Action
Family and Childcare Trust
Family Education Trust (Family and
    Youth Concern)
Family Holiday Association
Family Links
Family Lives
Family Matters Institute
Family Rights Group
Furzedown Family Centre
Gingerbread
Home-Start UK
Home-Start Canterbury and Coastal
Home-Start Haringey
Home-Start International
Home-Start South Hams, Plymouth
    and Tavistock
Home-Start Stoke-on-Trent
Home-Start Worthing and Adur
Kith and Kids
MOSAIC Black and Mixed Parentage
    Family Group
Mothers Union
National Association of Children's
    Information Services

Opportunity Links
Parents for Inclusion
Relatives and Residents Association
Single Parent Action Network
Surrey Nurturing Links
Working Families

## (DEALING WITH) ADDICTIONS

ADFAM
Al-Anon Family Groups UK and Eire

## (DEALING WITH) BEHAVIOURAL PROBLEMS

Centre for Fun and Families

## FORCES FAMILIES

Army Families Federation
National Gulf Veterans and
    Families Association
Royal British Legion
Royal British Legion International
Royal British Legion Women's Section
Royal Corps of Signals Benevolent Fund
Soldiers, Sailors, Airmen and Families
    Association (SSAFA)
War Widows Association of Great Britain and
    Northern Ireland

## HEALTH

Duchenne Family Support Group
Fledglings Family Services
Look National Office
Primary Ciliary Dyskinesia Family
    Support Group

## PRISONER SUPPORT

Action for Prisoners' Families
Partners of Prisoners and Families
    Support Group
Prison Advice and Care Trust
Prison Chat UK
Prisoners Abroad
Prisoners' Families and Friends Service

## FINANCIAL ADVICE SERVICES

Big Society Capital
Chartered Institute of Taxation
Community Accountancy Self-Help
Elizabeth Finn Care
Money Advice Trust
Pensions Advisory Service
ShareAction
TaxAid UK

## FOSTERING

**See ADOPTION & FOSTERING SERVICES**

## FURTHER & HIGHER EDUCATION

AGCAS
British Accreditation Council for
    Independent Further and Higher
Business and Education London South

East London Advanced Technology Training
Education and Services for People with
    Autism Ltd
Fellowship of Postgraduate Medicine
Fellowship of the School of
    Economic Science
GuildHE Limited
Hammersmith Management College
International Students House
Open College Network YHR
PFEG (Personal Finance Education Group)
Royal Society of Medicine
Sutton Trust
UK Council for International Student Affairs
Universities UK
University Association for Contemporary
    European Studies
UCCF

## GAMBLING SUPPORT GROUPS

GamCare

## GARDENS & GARDENING

Garden Organic
Garden History Society, The
Gardening for Disabled Trust
Good Gardeners' Association
National Council for the Conservation of
    Plants and Gardens
National Gardens Scheme
National Society of Allotments and
    Leisure Gardeners
Painswick Rococo Garden Trust
Thrive
Women's Farm and Garden Association

## GASTRO-INTESTINAL
## DISORDERS

CORE
National Association for Colitis and
    Crohn's Disease

## GAY/ LESBIAN /BISEXUAL/
## TRANSGENDER SUPPORT
## GROUPS

Albert Kennedy Trust
Broken Rainbow LGBT Domestic Violence
    Service UK
Consortium of Lesbian, Gay and Bisexual
    Voluntary and Community Organisations
Lesbian and Gay Christian Movement
Naz Foundation International
PACE
Positively UK
Regard
Stonewall
Stonewall Housing
The Lesbian and Gay Foundation

## GENETIC DISORDERS

Cornelia de Lange Syndrome Foundation
DebRA Ehlers-Danlos Support Group

Genetic Disorders UK
Genetic Interest Group
Haemochromatosis Society
Marfan Association UK
Prader-Willi Syndrome Association (UK)
Primary Ciliary Dyskinesia Family
    Support Group
Stickler Syndrome Support Group
The National Society for Phenylketonuria
    (UK) Ltd
The Neuro Foundation
Tuberous Sclerosis Association

## GIVING

JustGiving
Localgiving
London Funders
PayPal Giving Fund
The Giving Machine

## GOVERNANCE &
## ADMINISTRATION

Association of Charity
    Independent Examiners
Association of Chief Executives of
    Voluntary Organisations
Association of Volunteer Managers
Cards for Good Causes Ltd
Centre for Charity Effectiveness
Centre for Innovation in Voluntary Action
Charities Advisory Trust
Charities Aid Foundation
Charities HR Network
Charity Administration, Resourcing
    and Accountability
Charity Bank
Cranfield Trust
Directory of Social Change – London
Ecumenical Council for
    Corporate Responsibility
EIRIS Foundation
Ethical Property Foundation
Examination Officers' Association (EOA)
Fit4Funding (The Charities
    Information Bureau)
Impetus– The Private Equity Foundation
    (Impetus-PEF)
Institute of Fundraising
IVAR
Legislation Monitoring Service for Charities,
    Voluntary Organisations and their Advisors
Locality
Local Investment Fund
Media Trust
National Council for Voluntary Organisations
New Philanthropy Capital
NCVO Charities Evaluation Services (CES)
Northern Ireland Council for
    Voluntary Action
Pilotlight
Public Concern at Work
Public Fundraising Regulatory Association
The Philanthropy Workshop
Scottish Council for Voluntary Organisations
Wales Council for Voluntary Action

## GRANDPARENTS

The Grandparents' Association

## GRANT-MAKING TRUSTS &
## FOUNDATIONS

**See also BENEVOLENT SOCIETIES**
3H Fund (Helping hands for Holidays)
AFTAID – Aid for the Aged in Distress
Alexandra Rose Day
Almshouse Association
Architectural Heritage Fund
Association of Charitable Foundations
Association of Charitable Organisations
Beacon Awards
Body Shop Foundation
Buttle UK
CAF Philanthropy Services
Charity Bank
Church Urban Fund
Cicely Northcote Trust
City Bridge Trust
Comic Relief
Elimination of Leukaemia Fund
Elizabeth Finn Care
Elmham Charitable Trust
Emerge poverty free
Equity Trust Fund
Eritrean Relief Association (UK)
Esmee Fairbairn Foundation
Family Action
Family Holiday Association
Grantscape
Guild of Aid
Henry Smith Charity
Hospitality Action
International Fund for Animal Welfare
Islamic Relief Worldwide
J P Morgan Chase
John Ellerman Foundation
Joseph Levy Foundation
League of Remembrance
Lions Clubs International National
Local Trust Association of Round Tables of
    Great Britain and Ireland
Nurse Aid – Edith Cavell and Nation's Fund
    for Nurses
Rainy Day Trust
Rotary International in Great Britain
    and Ireland
Royal Air Force Music Charitable Trust
Royal Blind Society
Royal British Legion
Royal British Legion Industries Ltd
Royal Literary Fund
Royal Theatrical Fund
The Harland Trust
The Nationwide Foundation
Zurich Trust Limited

## FOR CHILDREN

Attlee Foundation
BBC Children in Need Appeal
Children's Country Holidays Fund
Dreamflight
Dreams Come True Charity

Help a Poor Child
Make-A-Wish Foundation UK
Prince's Trust
Promise Dreams
Royal Navy and Royal Marine
   Children's Fund
Sailors' Families' Society

## GYNAECOLOGICAL CONDITIONS

Daisy Network
Endometriosis SHE Trust (UK)
Endometriosis UK
Foundation for Women's Health Research
   and Development
Hysterectomy Association
National Association for
   Premenstrual Syndrome
Norm UK
Royal College of Obstetricians
   and Gynaecologists
Wellbeing of Women

## HAIR LOSS

Alopecia UK

## HEALTH & WELLBEING SUPPORT SERVICES

See also AIDS & HIV; ALLERGIES;
ARTHRITIC CONDITIONS;
AUTOIMMUNE DISORDERS;
BIPOLAR DISORDERS; BLOOD
DISORDERS; CANCER RESEARCH &
SUPPORT GROUPS; CARDIAC
CONDITIONS & RESEARCH;
CEREBRAL PALSY; CHILDBIRTH
SUPPORT SERVICES; CHROMOSOMAL
DISORDERS; CIRCULATORY
DISORDERS; CIRCUMCISION;
COMPLEMENTARY MEDICINE;
CONGENITAL DISORDERS;
CONTINENCE (INCONTINENCE)
ADVICE & SUPPORT; COUNSELLING
& PSYCHOTHERAPY SERVICES;
DEMENTIA SUPPORT GROUPS;
DENTAL HEALTH; DERMATOLOGY
AND SKIN DISORDERS; DIABETES
RESEARCH & SUPPORT; EATING
DISORDERS; ENDOCRINE
DISORDERS; ENZYME DEFICIENCY
DISORDERS; EPILEPSY; FACIAL
DISFIGUREMENT; GASTRO-
INTESTINAL DISORDERS; GENETIC
DISORDERS; GYNAECOLOGICAL
CONDITIONS; HAIR LOSS;
HYPERACTIVITY DISORDERS;
IMMUNE SYSTEM DEFICIENCIES;
INFANT & CHILDREN HEALTH
SUPPORT GROUPS; INFANT DEATH;
KIDNEY DISORDERS; LIVER
DISORDERS; ME (MYALGIC
ENCEPHALOMYELITIS) (CHRONIC
FATIGUE SYNDROME); MEDICAL
RESEARCH; MENTAL HEALTH; MET

ABOLIC DEFICIENCY DISORDERS;
MULTIPLE SCLEROSIS; MUSCULAR
DISORDERS;
NEURODEVELOPMENTAL
DISORDERS; NEUROLOGICAL
DISORDERS; NUTRITION; OBESITY;
ORGAN DONATION & REGISTERS;
PAIN MANAGEMENT; PALLIATIVE
CARE; PATIENT CARE &
ENVIRONMENT; PHOBIAS & PANIC
ATTACKS; PREGNANCY;
REPRODUCTIVE & SEXUAL HEALTH
CARE; SPINAL CARE; STILLBIRTH &
NEONATAL DEATH; STRESS &
ANXIETY DISORDERS; STROKE
ADHD Solutions cic
African Community Involvement Association
AMREF Health Africa
Alliance of Healing Associations
Aquaterra Leisure
Black Health Agency
British Medical Acupuncture Society
Cicely Northcote Trust
DIPEx Charity
Freedom from Torture
Healing Foundation
Health Foundation
Medical Women's Foundation
Men's Health Forum
Metamorphic Association
NHS Confederation
PACE
Pituitary Foundation
Royal College of General Practitioners
Royal Society for Public Health
Self management uk
St John Ambulance
The Forum for Health and Wellbeing
The NFSH Charitable Trust Limited
UK Public Health Association

## ADVOCACY

Action Against Medical Accidents
Bladder and Bowel Foundation
Medact

## ANGELMAN SYNDROME

ASSERT

## ASTHMA

Asthma UK

## BLOOD PRESSURE

Blood Pressure UK

## CONGENITAL DIAPHRAGMATIC HERNIA

Freshwinds

## CARE FOR LIFELIMITING ILLNESSES

CDH UK
Rainy Day Trust

## CYSTIC FIBROSIS

Cystic Fibrosis Trust

## DEPRESSION

Fellowship of Depressives Anonymous

## DOWN'S SYNDROME

Down's Heart Group
Down's Syndrome Association
Down's Syndrome Educational Trust

## DRUGS & REACTIONS

Information Link

## GLYCOGEN STORAGE

Association for Glycogen Storage
   Diseases (UK)

## HERPES

Herpes Viruses Association

## HOLISITIC MEDICINE

British Holistic Medical Association

## HUNTINGON'S DISEASE

Huntingdon's Disease Association

## HYGIENE

Community Hygiene Concern

## INFERTIILTY

Infertility Network UK

## LARYNGECTOMY

Cancer Laryngectomee Trust
National Association of Laryngectomy Clubs

## LEG ULCERATION

The Lindsay Leg Club Foundation

## LEPROSY

St Francis Leprosy Guild
The Leprosy Mission

## LUNG DISORDERS

British Lung Foundation

## LUPUS

Lupus Patients Understanding and
   Support (LUPUS)
LUPUS UK

## LYME DISEASE

Lyme Disease Action

## MENINGITIS

Meningitis Research Foundation
Meningitis Now
Meningitis UK

## MIGRAINE

Migraine Action
The Migraine Trust

## MUCOPOLYSACCHARIDE DISEASES

Society for Mucopolysaccharide Diseases

## NARCOLEPSY

Narcolepsy Association UK (UKAN)

**OEDEMAS**
British Lymphology Society
Lymphoedema Support Network

**OSTEOARTHRITIS**
Paget's Association (AKA National
    Association for the Relief of
    Paget's Disease)

**OSTEOPOROSIS**
National Osteoporosis Society

**OVERSEAS AID**
AMREF Health Africa
Asian Foundation for Help
Blindaid Africa
Health Unlimited
Healthlink Worldwide
HealthProm
InterHealth Worldwide
Tropical Health and Education Trust
Y Care International

**PARKINSON'S DISEASE**
Parkinson's Disease Society of the UK

**POLIO**
British Polio Fellowship

**RARE DISORDERS**
Rare Disease UK

**RESOURCES**
IA (The Ileostomy and Internal Pouch
    Support Group)

**RESTRICTED GROWTH DISORDERS**
Restricted Growth Association

**SEASONAL AFFECTIVE DISORDER
(SAD)**
SAD Association

**SEIZURES**
STARS – Syncope Trust and Reflex
    Anoxic Seizures

**SICKLE CELL**
The Sickle Cell Society

**SPINA BIFIDA & HYDROCEPHALUS**
SHINE

**THYROID DISORDERS**
British Thyroid Foundation

**TOURETTE SYNDROME**
Tourette's Action (Tourette Syndrome
    (UK) Association)

**TRACHEO-OESOPHAGEAL SUPPORT**
Tracheo-Oesophageal Fistula Support Group

**TUBERCULOSIS**
Target Tuberculosis

**UNNAMED SYNDROMES**
SWAN UK (Syndromes Without a Name)

**URINARY SYSTEM**
Urostomy Association

**VOMITING**
Cyclical Vomiting Syndrome Association UK

**HEALTH PROFESSIONALS,
ORGANISATIONS FOR**
AMSPAR
Association for Perioperative Practice
Association for the Study of Obesity
British Association for Immediate Care
British Homeopathic Association
British Institute of Radiology
British Medical Acupuncture Society
British Psychological Society
British School of Osteopathy
Cavell Nurses' Trust
Centre for the Advancement of
    Interprofessional Education
Chiropractic Patients' Association
Foundation of Nursing Studies (FoNS)
Metanoia Institute
PRIMHE
Psychosynthesis and Education Trust
Research Society of Process Orientated
    Psychology UK
Royal College of Midwives
Royal Medical Benevolent Fund
Social Emotional and Behavioural
    Difficulties Association
Society for Endocrinology
Society for General Microbiology
Society of Homeopaths
The Queen's Nursing Institute

**HEALTHCARE & MEDICAL
TRAINING**
AMSPAR
Animal Welfare Foundation
Association for Perioperative Practice
British Acupuncture Council
British Association for Counselling
    and Psychotherapy
British Association for Immediate Care
British Association of Dermatologists
British Medical Acupuncture Society
Fellowship of Postgraduate Medicine
Foundation of Nursing Studies (FoNS)
Metanoia Institute
Response International
Royal College of Midwives
Royal College of Paediatrics and Child Health
Royal Society of Medicine

**HEARING IMPAIRMENTS**
See **DEAFNESS & HEARING
IMPAIRMENTS**

**HEART DISEASE**
See **CARDIAC CONDITIONS**

**HELPLINES**
ChildLine
Get Connected Helpline
Helplines Partnership
Message Home Helpline
SupportLine
The Cry-sis Helpline

**HERITAGE & HISTORY
GROUPS**
See also **CONSERVATION GROUPS**
Ancient Monuments Society
Antiquarian Horological Society
Architectural Heritage Fund
Arts Council England
British Archaeological Association
British Association for Local History
British Association of Friends of Museums
Council for British Archeology
CSV Cathedral Camps
Heritage Link
Historical Association
National Association of Decorative and Fine
    Arts Societies
National Churches Trust
National Trust
Pilgrim Trust
Rescue: the British Archaeological Trust
SAVE Britain's Heritage
Society for the Protection of
    Ancient Buildings
Society of Antiquaries of London
The British Evacuees Association
The Churches Conservation Trust
The Heritage Alliance
Theatres Trust
Transport Trust

**HIGHER EDUCATION**
See **FURTHER & HIGHER EDUCATION**

**HISTORY**
See **HERITAGE & HISTORY GROUPS**

**HOME SCHOOLING**
The Otherwise Club

**HOMELESSNESS SUPPORT**
Access Community Trust
Alone in London
Big Issue Foundation
Centrepoint
Chapter 1
Church Housing Trust
CRASH
Crisis
Direct Help & Advice (DHA)
Emmaus UK

Foyer Federation
Habitat for Humanity Great Britain
Homeless International
Homeless Link
HOPE
House of Saint Barnabas in Soho
Kairos Community Trust
New Horizon Youth Centre
People Potential Possibilities (P3)
Salvation Army
Shelter
The Prebend Day Centre
Vine Centre, The
Western Lodge

## HORSE WELFARE

British Horse Society
International League for the Protection
   of Horses
The Mare and Foal Sanctuary

## HOSPICES

**See also LIFE-LIMITING ILLNESS
SUPPORT**
Barnsley Hospice
Claire House – Hospice for Children
Greenwich & Bexley Community Hospice
Hospice UK
Hospice Information Service
St Joseph's Hospice Association

## HUMAN & PERSONAL RIGHTS

Advice on Individual Rights in Europe
Airey Neave Trust
Amnesty International Secretariat
Amnesty International United Kingdom
Anti-Slavery International
Article 19
British Institute of Human Rights
Democratic Progress Institute
Equality and Diversity Forum
Fair Trials International
Global Witness Limited
Interights
JUSTICE
Liberty
Minority Rights Group International
People and Planet
The IARS International Institute

## HUMAN RESOURCES

**See STAFF & VOLUNTEERS**

## HUMANISM

Association for Humanistic Psychology
British Humanist Association
Conway Hall Ethical Society

## HYPERACTIVITY DISORDERS

ADD Information Services
Hyperactive Children's Support Group

## IMMIGRATION ADVICE & SUPPORT GROUPS

AVID (Association of Visitors to
   Immigration Detainees)
Child Migrants Trust
Immigrant Counselling and Psychotherapy
Immigration Advisory Service
Joint Council for the Welfare of Immigrants
Migrant Helpline
Migrants Resource Centre

## IMMUNE SYSTEM DEFICIENCIES

British Society for Immunology
Chronic Granulomatous Disorder

## INCONTINENCE

**See CONTINENCE (INCONTINENCE)
ADVICE & SUPPORT**

## INFANT & CHILDREN HEALTH SUPPORT GROUPS

ACT (The Association for Children's
   Palliative Care)
Action for Sick Children
ADD Information Services
Association for Child and Adolescent
   Mental Health
Association of Young People with ME
Ataxia-Telangiectasia Society (A–T Society)
BLISS
Bobath Centre for Children with
   Cerebral Palsy
Brook
CDH UK
Challenge Fund – the Fight against Cancer
   in the Emerging World
Changing Faces
Cherubs UK
Child Brain Injury Trust
Child Growth Foundation
Childhood Eye Cancer Trust
Children's Burns Trust
Children's Heart Federation (CHF)
Children's Trust
Crohn's in Childhood Research Association
Diabetes Foundation
Different Strokes
Down's Heart Group
Down's Syndrome Association
Edward's Trust
ERIC – Education and Resources for
   Improving Childhood Continence
Great Ormond Street Hospital
   Children's Charity
HemiHelp
Hyperactive Children's Support Group
Information Point for Centronuclear and
   Myotubular Myopathy
Matthew Trust
National Centre for Young People
   with Epilepsy
Neuroblastoma UK

Perthes Association
Peter Rigby Trust
Rainbow Centre for Children affected by
   Life-Threatening Illnesses or Bereavement
Rainbow Trust Children's Charity
Rapid Effective Assistance for Children with
   Potentially Terminal Illness
Reach – Association for Children with Hand
   or Arm Deficiency
Roald Dahl's Marvellous Children's Charity
Royal College of Paediatrics and Child Health
Teenage Cancer Trust
The Cry-sis Helpline
The Ear Foundation
The National Autistic Society
The Sick Children's Trust
The Somerville Foundation
Tiny Tickers
Together for Short Lives
WellChild
YoungMinds

## CANCER SUPPORT

Childhood Eye Cancer Trust
Neuroblastoma UK
Teenage Cancer Trust

## MENTAL HEALTH

Association for Child and Adolescent
   Mental Health
Matthew Trust
YoungMinds

## INFANT, PRIMARY & SECONDARY SCHOOL EDUCATION

**See also CHILDREN AND YOUNG
PEOPLE; SPECIAL EDUCATIONAL
NEEDS**
Advisory Centre for Education Ltd (ACE)
Association for Physical Education
Association for Science Education
Association of Governing Bodies of
   Independent Schools
Beanstalk
British Centre for Science Education
Commonwealth Education Trust
Dame Hannah Rogers Trust
Deaf Ex-Mainstreamers Group
Inspire!
Learning Plus UK
Muntham House School Ltd
National Association for the Teaching
   of English
National Association for Small Schools
National Association of Independent Schools
   and Non Maintained Special Schools
National Confederation of Parent
   Teacher Associations
Newcastle Action for Parent and Toddler
   Groups Initiative
Peacemakers
PFEG (Personal Finance Education Group)
School Governors' One-Stop Shop
School Home Support Service (UK)

School Library Association
SciDevNet
Sutton Trust
Teacher Support Network
The Cry-sis Helpline

## INFANT DEATH

The Lullaby Trust
Together for Short Lives

## INTERNET

**See COMPUTERS AND THE INTERNET**

## IRANIAN COMMUNITY GROUPS

Iranian Association

## JEWISH FAITH

Anglo Jewish Association
Association of Jewish Ex-Servicemen
    and Women
Association of Jewish Refugees in
    Great Britain
Board of Deputies of British Jews
British ORT
Community Security Trust (CST)
Council of Christians and Jews
Institute for Jewish Policy Research
Interlink Foundation
Jewish Association for the Mentally Ill
Jewish Bereavement Counselling Service
Jewish Council for Racial Equality (JCORE)
Jewish Lads and Girls Brigade including
    Outreach/Kiruv and Hand-in-Hand Young
    Volunteers Projects
Jewish Marriage Council
Jewish Women's Aid
Liberal Judaism
League of Jewish Women
Leo Baeck College
Lubavitch Youth
Norwood
Merseyside Jewish Community Care

## KIDNEY DISORDERS

Africa Resource for Kidney Diseases
British Kidney Patient Association
National Kidney Federation
Polycystic Kidney Disease Charity

## LEADERSHIP SKILLS TRAINING

Ashoka (UK) Trust
Diversity Hub
Ella Forums CIC
Institute for Community and
    Development Studies
Leadership Trust Foundation
Sports Leaders UK
Windsor Leadership Trust

## LEARNING DISABILITIES SUPPORT

**See also AUTISM; DYSLEXIA SUPPORT**

Ann Craft Trust
ARC
Aurora Health Foundation
British Institute of Learning Disabilities
Brothers of Charity Services
Canterbury Oast Trust
Care Co-ordination Network Cymru
Change People
Circles Network
Dark Horse Theatre
Elfrida Society
Elizabeth Fitzroy Support
Education and Services for People with
    Autism Ltd
First Step Trust
HFT the Home Farm Trust
Judith Trust
Kingwood Trust
L'Arche
Leo Trust
Life Opportunities Trust
Lifeworks
MacIntyre Care
Mencap
Powerhouse
Prospects for People with
    Learning Disabilities
Reading Mencap
Real Life Options
Realife Trust
Rescare
RESPOND
Sequal Trust
Shaping Our Lives – National User Network
Signalong Group
Spadework Ltd
St Albans Mencap
The Grace Eyre Foundation
The Lodge Trust
Thera Trust
United Kingdom Sports Association for
    People with Learning Disability
United Response
Us in a Bus
Walsingham Support
Working with Words

## CHILDREN'S SUPPORT SERVICES

Children's Trust
Norwood

## LEGAL ADVISORY & SUPPORT SERVICES

Action Against Medical Accidents
Bar Pro Bono Unit
CANS Legal Information
Children's Legal Centre
Coram Children's Legal Centre
Disability Law Service
Environmental Law Foundation
Fair Trials International
International Action Network on Small Arms

International Alert
LASA
Law Centres Network
LawWorks
Legal Action Group
Norfolk Community Law Service Ltd
Public Law Project
RCJ Advice Bureau
Refugee Legal Centre
Release
Rights of Women
Sangat Advice Centre

## LESBIAN SUPPORT GROUPS

**See GAY/LESBIAN/BISEXUAL/
TRANSGENDER SUPPORT GROUPS**

## LIFE-LIMITING ILLNESS SUPPORT

Edward's Trust
Rainbow Centre for Children affected by
    Life-Threatening Illnesses or Bereavement
Rainbow Trust Children's Charity
Rapid Effective Assistance for Children with
    Potentially Terminal Illness

## LITERACY & NUMERACY

Caxton Trust (working name Catch Up)
National Literacy Trust
Reading Matters
Working with Words

## LIVER DISORDERS

British Liver Trust
Primary Sclerosing Cholangitis Trust

## MARINE LIFE & WATERWAYS

Advisory Committee on the Protection of
    the Sea
Association of River Trusts
British Waterways
CIWEM
Inland Waterways Association
Marine Conservation Society
Marine Stewardship Council
Sea Watch Foundation
WDC, Whale and Dolphin Conservation

## MARRIAGE & RELATIONSHIP COUNSELLING

Explore
Family Links
Family Matters Institute
Jewish Marriage Council
Marriage Care
National Family Mediation
One Plus One Marriage and Partnership
    Research
Relate Brighton, Hove, Worthing
    and Districts
Relate Central Office

Relate Lincolnshire
The Tavistock Centre for
Couple Relationships

## ME (MYALGIC ENCEPHALOMYELITIS) (CHRONIC FATIGUE SYNDROME)

25% ME Group – Support for Severe
ME Sufferers
Action for ME
Association of Young People with ME
ME Association

## MEDIA

See COMMUNICATIONS AND MEDIA
HANDLING

## MEDIATION SERVICES

Centre for Effective Dispute Resolution
Mediation Works Milton Keynes

## MEDICAL RESEARCH

Action Medical Research
Alcohol Research UK
Arthritis Research Campaign
Association of Medical Research Charities
Association of Research Ethics Committees
Autism Research Ltd
Blond McIndoe Research Foundation
Bloodwise
Brain and Spine Foundation
Brain Research Trust
Breast Cancer Now
Breast Cancer Research Trust
British Association for Cancer Research
British Cardiovascular Society
Cancer Research UK
Challenge Fund – the Fight against Cancer
in the Emerging World
Coronary Artery Disease
Research Association
Crohn's in Childhood Research Association
Diving Diseases Research Centre
Dr Hadwen Trust for Humane Research
Epilepsy Research UK
Foundation for Women's Health Research
and Development
Fund for the Replacement of Animals in
Medical Experiments
Humane Research Trust
Institute of Cancer Research
Judith Trust
Keratec
King's Medical Research Trust
LDN Research Trust
LEPRA
Lewy Body Society
LUPUS UK
Magdi Yacoub Institute
ME Association
Meningitis Research Foundation
Mental Health Foundation

National AIDS Trust
Nuffield Trust
Progress Educational Trust
Research Society of Process Oriented
Psychology UK
Royal Society of Medicine
Royal Society for Public Health
Sir Halley Stewart Trust
Society for General Microbiology
The Anscombe Bioethics Centre
The King's Fund
UK Health Forum
Wellcome Trust

## MEDICAL TRAINING

See HEALTHCARE & MEDICAL
TRAINING

## MEN'S SUPPORT GROUPS

British Society of Psychosomatic Obstetrics
Gynaecology and Andrology
Men's Health Forum
Regard

## MENTAL HEALTH

See also COUNSELLING &
PSYCHOTHERAPY SERVICES

Adverse Psychiatric Reactions Information
Link (APRIL)
BasicNeeds UK
Capital Project
Chinese Mental Health Association
Combat Stress
Community Housing and Therapy
Consortium of Lesbian, Gay and Bisexual
Voluntary and Community Organisations
Fellowship of Depressives Anonymous
First Step Trust
Gaia House
Guideposts Trust Ltd
Guild of Aid
Hamlet Trust
Havering Mind
Human Givens Foundation
Jewish Association for the Mentally Ill
Judith Trust
Lyme Trust
Making Space
Mary Frances Trust
Matthew Trust
Mental Health Foundation
Mental Health Matters
Mental Health Providers Forum
Mind
Mind in Camden
Mind in Tower Hamlets and Newham
Mosaic Clubhouse
Oakleaf Enterprise
Philadelphia Association
PRIMHE
Psychiatric Rehabilitation Association
Revolving Doors Agency
Richmond Fellowship
SANE

Sesame Institute (UK)
SignHealth
Social Perspectives Network
St Andrew's Healthcare
Together Working for Wellbeing
United Response
Viewpoint
WISH – a voice for women's mental health

### CHILDREN & YOUNG PEOPLE

Association for Child and Adolescent
Mental Health
YoungMinds

### WOMEN'S MENTAL HEALTH

Creative and Supportive Trust

## METABOLIC DEFICIENCY DISORDERS

Alkaptonuria Society
Climb
Niemann-Pick Disease Group UK

## MULTIPLE SCLEROSIS

LDN Research Trust
MS Trust
Multiple Sclerosis International Federation
Multiple Sclerosis National Therapy Centres
Multiple Sclerosis Society of Great Britain
and Northern Ireland

## MUSCULAR DISORDERS

Duchenne Family Support Group
Information Point for Centronuclear and
Myotubular Myopathy
Muscular Dystrophy Campaign
Myaware
Myositis Support Group
Myotonic Dystrophy Support Group

## MUSEUMS

Julia Margaret Cameron Trust
Museums Association

## MUSIC

Associated Board of the Royal Schools
of Music
Council for Music in Hospitals
Drake Music Project
Friends of Cathedral Music
Live Music Now!
More Music
Music Education Council
National Music for the Blind
National Youth Orchestra of Great Britain
Nordoff-Robbins Music Therapy
Raw Material Music and Media Education
Sound and Music

## MUSLIM FAITH

Amal Trust
Europe Trust

Islamic Relief Worldwide
League of British Muslims
Muslim Aid

## MYALGIC ENCEPHALOMYELITIS (CHRONIC FATIGUE SYNDROME)

See ME

## NEONATAL DEATH

See STILLBIRTH & NEONATAL DEATH

## NEURODEVELOPMENTAL DISORDERS

Rett Syndrome Association UK
Williams Syndrome Foundation Ltd

## NEUROLOGICAL DISORDERS

See also SPINAL DISORDERS
Ataxia UK
Ataxia-Telangiectasia Society (A-T Society)
BASIC
Brain and Spine Foundation
Brain Research Trust
Brainwave Centre Ltd
British Acoustic Neuroma Association
Child Brain Injury Trust
CMT United Kingdom
Dystonia Society
Headway Devon
Headway – the Brain Injury Association
Hypothalamic Hamartoma Uncontrolled
    Gelastic Seizures UK
Neurological Alliance
Sturge Weber Foundation (UK)
Sue Ryder
TBPI Group
The Association for Post-Natal Illness
The Encephalitis Society
Trigeminal Neuralgia Association
UK Acquired Brain Injury Forum

## OBESITY

British Obesity Surgery Patient
    Association Trust
Weight Concern

## OLDER PEOPLE ADVISORY & SUPPORT GROUPS

Action on Elder Abuse
Age Concern Central Lancashire
Age Concern Eastbourne
Age Concern Hassocks and District
Age UK
Age UK Portsmouth
Assist UK
Beth Johnson Foundation
Centre for Policy on Ageing
Contact the Elderly Counsel and Care

Crowthorne Old Age To Teen
    Society (COATS)
Friends of the Elderly
Guideposts Trust Limited
Help Age International
International Longevity Centre – UK
Little Sisters of the Poor
National Pensioners Convention
Nubian Life Resource Centre Ltd
RICABILITY Incorporating RICA (Research
    Institute for Consumer Affairs)
Tapestry Care UK

## EDUCATION & TRAINING

Third Age Trust (National Office U3A)

## GRANTS & LOANS

AFTAID – Aid for the Aged in Distress
National Benevolent Fund for the Aged
National Benevolent Institution
Royal UK Beneficent Association (Rukba)

## HOUSING & CARE PROVISION

Abbeyfield Society
AgeCare
Almshouse Association
Anchor Trust
Care and Repair England Ltd
Elderly Accommodation Counsel
KeyChange Charity
MHA Care Group
Relatives and Residents Association
Sons of Divine Providence
The Brendoncare Foundation

## HEALTH CARE

British Geriatrics Society

## RECREATION

Albrighton Moat & Gardens
EPIC Arts
EXTEND Exercise Training Ltd

## RETIREMENT

Civil Service Retirement Fellowship
Retirement Trust

## ORGAN DONATION & REGISTERS

Anthony Nolan Trust
Transplant Sport UK

## OUTDOOR EDUCATION & RESIDENTIAL COURSES

See also CHILDREN'S ACTIVITY SCHEMES & CLUBS
Active Training and Education Trust
Adventure Unlimited
Institute for Outdoor Learning

## OVERSEAS AID & DEVELOPMENT

Action Against Hunger UK

Action to Regenerate Community Trust
ActionAid
African Pastors' Fellowship
Alternative for India Development
Asian Foundation for Help
Association of Dance Therapists
ATD Fourth World UK Ltd
Book Aid International
Bond
British Red Cross
Build Africa
Catholic Agency for Overseas Development
Christians Abroad
Child Soldiers International
CHS Alliance
CORD
Environment Africa Trust
Emerge poverty free
Eritrean Relief Association (UK)
FARM – Africa
Generation for Change and Development
Global Justice Now
Green Life UK
Hamlet Trust
Harvest Help
Help Age International
HOPE Worldwide
Human Relief Foundation
IDE-UK
International Community Assist
International Development Partnerships
International Service
Islamic Relief Worldwide
Landmine Action
Management Strategies for Africa
Mission Aviation Fellowship UK
Mission Care
MOC Foundation
Muslim Aid
One World Action
Oxfam
Overseas Development Institute
Pontifical Mission Societies
Progressio
Rainforest Foundation UK
Refugee Action
Refugee Council
Self Help Africa
Survival International
Tearfund
Tibet Relief Fund
Transaid
Transform Africa
Village Aid
World Vision UK

## CHILDREN & YOUNG PEOPLE

AbleChildAfrica
Blindaid Africa
Children of Africa
Child Soldiers International
EveryChild
Global Care
Home-Start International
Hope and Homes for Children
Hope for Children
Humanity at Heart

International Children's Trust
Merlin
Orphans in Need
Orphans Relief Fund and Charitable Trust
Plan International
Railway Children
Save the Children UK
SOS Children's Villages UK
Street Child Africa
Wishing Well
Y Care International

## EDUCATION & TRAINING
Ashoka (UK) Trust
CAMFED International
Children of Africa
Corona Worldwide
Filipino International Emergency
    Services Training
Harvest Fields Commissioning International
International Network for the Availability of
    Scientific Publications
Practical Action
Skillshare International
Tools for Self Reliance
Windle Trust International

## EQUIPMENT
Operation Florian

## HEALTH
AMREF Health Africa
AVERT
BasicNeeds UK
Blindaid Africa
Britain-Nepal Medical Trust
Children of Africa
Ernest Foundation
Health Unlimited
Healthlink Worldwide
HealthProm
Interact Worldwide
InterHealth Worldwide
Lifeline International
Merlin
Naz Foundation International
ORBIS Charitable Trust
Response International
Sight Savers International
Vision Aid Overseas

## HOMELESSNESS
Big Issue Foundation
Homeless International
Shelterbox Trust

## VOLUNTEERS
AVIF (ABLe Volunteers International Fund)
Indian Volunteers for Community Service
International Voluntary Service
RedR UK
VSO

## WATER AID
Just a Drop
Water for Africa
WaterAid

Wells for India

## PAIN MANAGEMENT
British Pain Society
Pain Relief Foundation
Pelvic Pain Support Network

## PALLIATIVE CARE
ACT (The Association for Children's
    Palliative Care)
Earl Mountbatten Hospice
Helen & Douglas House

## PARENTING
Disabled Parents Network
Families Need Fathers
Family and Childcare Trust
Family Lives
Gingerbread

## PATIENT CARE & ENVIRONMENT
ATTEND
Expert Patients Programme Community
Hull Churches Home from Hospital Service
Long-Term Conditions Alliance
National Association for Patient Participation
National Confidential Enquiry into Patient
    Outcome and Death
National Patients Support Trust
National Voices
Paintings in Hospitals
Patients Association
Patients Forum

## PEACE CAMPAIGNS
See also POLITICAL ENGAGEMENT
Campaign for Nuclear Disarmament (CND)
Fellowship of Reconciliation
Network for Peace
Peace Brigades International: UK Section
Peace Direct
Peace Pledge Union

## PHOBIAS & PANIC ATTACKS
Anxiety Care UK
Anxiety UK
No Panic
OCD Action

## POLITICAL ENGAGEMENT
See also PEACE CAMPAIGNS
European Atlantic Movement
Hansard Society
Industry and Parliament Trust
International Action Network on Small Arms
International Alert
Operation Black Vote
Transparency International (UK)
United Nations Association

## POST-NATAL SUPPORT GROUPS
See also CHILDBIRTH; PREGNANCY;
STILLBIRTH & NEONATAL DEATH
Association of Breastfeeding Mothers
La Leche League Great Britain
LIFE
The Association for Post-Natal Illness

## POVERTY RELIEF
Cambridge House
CARE International UK
Child Poverty Action Group
Christian Aid
Church Action on Poverty
Comic Relief
Concern Universal
Concern Worldwide UK
End Child Poverty
Engineers Against Poverty
Evidence For Development
Fairtrade Foundation
Habitat for Humanity Great Britain
Karuna Trust
Livability
One World Action
People and Planet
Smile International
St Vincent de Paul Society (England
    and Wales)
United Trusts
Volunteers for Rural India
War on Want

## PRE-SCHOOL EDUCATION
British Association for Early
    Childhood Education
National Portage Association
Pre-School Learning Alliance

## PREGNANCY
See also CHILDBIRTH; POST-NATAL
SUPPORT GROUPS; STILLBIRTH &
NEONATAL DEATH
ARC (Antenatal Results and Choices)
British Pregnancy Advisory Service
Disability Pregnancy and Parenthood
FAS Aware UK
Foresight the Association for the Promotion
    of Preconceptual Care
Maternity Action
National Childbirth Trust
Royal College of Obstetricians
    and Gynaecologists
Society for the Protection of
    Unborn Children

## PRISON & PROBATION SERVICES
Action for Prisoners' Families
Adullam Homes Housing Association
Apex Charitable Trust Limited

ATTEND
AVID (Association of Visitors to
    Immigration Detainees)
Birth Companions
Bridging the Gap
Butler Trust
Clean Break
Creative and Supportive Trust
Female Prisoners Welfare Project and
Hibiscus
Independent Custody Visiting Association
Koestler Trust
Langley House Trust
NACRO
New Bridge Foundation
Prison Fellowship England and Wales
Prison Reform Trust
Prisoners Abroad
Prisoners Advice Service
Prisoners Education Trust
Re-Start
Revolving Doors Agency
Royal London Society
Shannon Trust
SOVA
UNLOCK – for people with convictions

**PROFESSIONAL BODIES'
INFORMATION SERVICES**

Bank Workers Charity
Charity Retail Association
Chartered Institute of Library and
    Information Professionals
Equity Trust Fund
Hospitality Action
LionHeart
National Association of Local Councils
Pharmacist Support
Registry Trust Limited
Royal Society of Medicine
Society of Authors
Textile Institute International
The Printing Charity

**PSYCHOLOGY**

**See also COUNSELLING &
PSYCHOTHERAPY**
Association for Humanistic Psychology
Society of Analytical Psychology

**RECYCLING & WASTE
MANAGEMENT**

Composting Association
Furniture Re-use Network
International Institute for Environment
    and Development
Keep Britain Tidy

**REFUGEE & ASYLUM SEEKERS,
SUPPORT GROUPS**

Association of Visitors to
    Immigration Detainees
Asylum Aid

Boaz Trust
Community of Congolese Refugees in
    Great Britain
Embrace
Ethiopian Community in Britain
Gateway Community Action
Imkaan
Ockenden International
Olmec
Refugee Action
Refugee Council
Refugee Legal Centre
Refugee Therapy Centre
Sangat Advice Centre
Southampton and Winchester Visitors Group
STAR (Student Action for Refugees)
Tibet Relief Fund

**REHABILITATION**

**ADDICTIONS**
Action on Addiction
Independence Initiative
Kairos Community Trust
Phoenix Futures
Salvation Army

**PHYSICAL**
ASPIRE
Back-Up (transforming lives after spinal
    cord injury)
Brainwave Centre Ltd
Headway Devon
Hearing Link
Psychiatric Rehabilitation Association
St Loye's Foundation

**REPRODUCTIVE & SEXUAL
HEALTH CARE**

Brook
Education for Choice
FPA
Interact Worldwide
JAT (formerly Jewish AIDS Trust)
Marie Stopes International
Naz Foundation International
Progress Educational Trust
Safehands for Mothers Charitable Trust
Terrence Higgins Trust

**RESEARCH SUPPORT &
POLICY DEVELOPMENT**

**See also MEDICAL RESEARCH:
PROFESSIONAL BODIES'
INFORMATION SERVICES**
Arthur McDougall Fund
British Future
Careers Research and Advisory Centre Ltd
Cass Centre for Charity Effectiveness
Centre for Crime and Justice Studies
Centre for Effective Dispute Resolution
Centris
Charity Retail Association
Conway Hall Ethical Society
Evidence For Development

Historical Association
Inclusion London
Institute for Jewish Policy Research
Institute of Biology
National Centre for Social Research
New Economics Foundation
Police Foundation
Policy Studies Institute
Regional Studies Association
Rowntree Society
Royal Commonwealth Society
SABRE Research UK
Saferworld
Strategic Planning Society
The Clinic for Boundaries Studies

**CITIZENSHIP**
Operation Black Vote
OPUS

**COMMUNITY DEVELOPMENT**
ARVAC Association for Research in the
    Voluntary and Community Sector
Lifeline Community Projects

**EDUCATION**
Federal Trust for Education and Research

**ENVIRONMENT**
British Cave Research Association
British Ecological Society
Royal Geographical Society
Town and Country Planning Association

**HERITAGE**
British Archaeological Association
British Association for Local History
Society of Antiquaries of London

**SOCIAL POLICY & CHANGE**
British Future
Centris
Joseph Rowntree Foundation
Rowntree Society
Social Care Institute for Excellence
Social Research Association

**RESIDENTIAL & CARE HOMES**

British Home and Hospital for Incurables
Elizabeth Finn Care
Journalists Charity
Mission Care

**EX-SERVICEMEN/WOMEN**
Douglas Haig Memorial Homes
    (Haig Homes)
The Royal Star and Garter Homes

**FOR PEOPLE WITH DISABILITIES,
LEARNING DISABILITIES & MENTAL
HEALTH PROBLEMS**
Aurora Charity
Autism Plus
Canterbury Oast Trust
Chaseley Trust
Community Housing and Therapy

Disabilities Trust
Education and Services for People with
    Autism Ltd
Foley House Trust
Hollybank Trust
Independent Living Alternatives
Leo Trust
Leonard Cheshire Disability
Life Opportunities Trust
Orione Care
Real Life Options
Richmond Fellowship
Sons of Divine Providence
St John of God Care Services
Thomas Pocklington Trust

## RESPITE CARE

3H Fund (Helping hands for Holidays)
Adventist Special Needs
    Association (ASNA)
Learning Through Landscapes
Rainbow Trust Children's Charity
Vitalise

## RHEUMATISM

British Sjogren's Syndrome
British Society for Rheumatology

## RURAL & FARMING COMMUNITIES

Action with Communities in Rural England
Arthur Rank Centre
Associated Country Women of the World
Campaign to Protect Rural England
Camphill Village Trust Ltd
Composting Association
Countryside Restoration Trust
Farms for City Children
Federation of City Farms and
    Community Gardens
National Federation of Young Farmers' Clubs
Penwith Community Development Trust
Permaculture Association (Britain)
Pesticide Action Network UK
Plunkett Foundation
Ramblers' Association
Royal Agricultural Benevolent Institution
Rural Action Yorkshire
Rural Community Action Nottinghamshire
Rural Housing Trust
Rural Stress Helpline
Soil Association
Sustain: the Alliance for Better Food
    and Farming
Spitalfields City Farm
Television Trust for the Environment
The Farming Community Network
Wildlife and Countryside Link
Wincanton Community Venture
Women's Farm and Garden Association

## SEAFARERS & MARITIME WORKERS

Apostleship of the Sea
Federation of Merchant Mariners
International Committee on
    Seafarers Welfare
International Seafarers' Assistance Network
Merchant Navy Welfare Board
National Coastwatch Institute
Nautilus UK
Queen Victoria Seamen's Rest
Royal Alfred Seafarers Society
Royal National Lifeboat Institution
Royal National Mission to Deep
    Sea Fishermen
Sailors' Families' Society
Sea Cadets
Seafarers' Advice and Information Line
Seafarers UK
Shipwrecked Fishermen and Mariners' Royal
    Benevolent Society

## SEXUAL ABUSE

See ABUSE & VIOLENCE – VICTIMS' &
SURVIVORS' SUPPORT SERVICES

## SIGHT IMPAIRMENT

See BLINDNESS & SIGHT IMPAIRMENT

## SMOKING 'STOP SMOKING' SUPPORT GROUPS

Action on Smoking and Health

## SOCIAL CARE & WELFARE

ATTEND
Avocet Trust
British Association of Social Workers
British Sociological Association
Caritas Social Action Network (CSAN)
Catholic Clothing Guild
Clothing Solutions for Disabled People
Community of Reconciliation and Fellowship
Community Resilience
Council of Voluntary Welfare Work
Diagrama Foundation
Disaster Action
Disasters Emergency Committee
Ethiopian Community Integrated Care
Field Lane Foundation
Food Chain (UK) Ltd
Foundation for Public Service Interpreting
Heritage Care
Home from Hospital Care after Treatment
In Kind Direct
International Social Service (UK)
Lifeline Community Projects
Mary Ward Centre
NAGALRO
Rowntree Society
SCA Group
Skills for Care Ltd
Smile Support & Care

Social Care Institute for Excellence
Stonham
Turning Point
Tutu Foundation UK
United Kingdom Homecare Association

## CHILDREN & YOUNG PEOPLE

Child Migrant Trust
National Playbus Association

## FAMILY SUPPORT

Family Action
Family Rights Group
Home Start
Home-Start International

## RESEARCH

Cicely Northcote Trust
Joseph Rowntree Foundation
Social Research Association

## SPECIAL EDUCATIONAL NEEDS

See also CHILDREN AND YOUNG
PEOPLE; INFANT, PRIMARY AND
SECONDARY EDUCATION
Adventist Special Needs
    Association (ASNA)
Adventure Service Challenge Scheme
Centre for Studies on Inclusive Education
Choices 4 All
Dyslexia Action
Dyspraxia Foundation
Happy Days Children's Charity
Kidsout UK
Muntham House School Ltd
National Association for Special
    Educational Needs
National Association of Independent Schools
    and Non Maintained Special Schools
Network 81
Nurture Group Network
Parents for Inclusion
Special Kids In the UK
South Lancashire Learning Disability
    Training Consortium
Together Trust

## SPEECH & COMMUNICATION SUPPORT

AFASIC
British Stammering Association
British Voice Association
CONNECT – the Communication
    Disability Network
European League of Stuttering Associations
I CAN
Speakability (Action for Dysphasic Adults)
Voice Care Network UK

## SPINAL CARE

See also NEUROLOGICAL DISORDERS
BackCare
Scoliosis Association (UK)

Spinal Injuries Association
Spinal Muscular Atrophy Support UK
Steps Charity Worldwide
The SMA Trust

## SPORT & RECREATION

Achieve Lifestyle
Association for Physical Education
CTC – UK's National Cycling Organisation
EXTEND Exercise Training Ltd
Fair Play for Children Association/
    Charitable Trust
Federation Of English Karate
    Organisations (international)
FIA Foundation for the Automobile
    and Society
Fields In Trust
Fulham Football Club Foundation
Get Hooked on Fishing Charitable Trust
Iyengar Yoga Institute
Keep Fit Association
League Against Cruel Sports
Ramblers' Association
Rugby Football Foundation
Sea Cadets
Sport and Recreation Alliance
Sports Leaders UK
Supporters Direct
Surf Life Saving Association of Great Britain
The INSPIRE Foundation
Transplant Sport UK
Youth Sport Trust

## DISABILITIES

ADD International (Action on Disability
    and Development)
Albrighton Moat & Gardens
Amal Trust
Back-Up (Transforming lives after spinal
    cord injury)
British Blind Sport
Conquest Art – Enriching the Lives of
    People with Disabilities and long term
    health issues
Disability Snowsport UK (Bromley)
Disability Sport England
Disabled Photographers' Society
Disaway Trust
Drake Music Project
English Federation of Disability Sport
EPIC Arts
EXTEND Exercise Training Ltd
Gardening for the Disabled
Jubilee Sailing Trust
Lin Berwick Trust
National Association of Swimming Clubs for
    the Handicapped
Peter le Marchant Trust
Riding for the Disabled Association
RYA Sailability
Tourism for All UK
United Kingdom Sports Association for
    People with Learning Disability
WheelPower

## STAFF & VOLUNTEERS

Beanstalk
Charities HR Network
HOPE Worldwide
Indian Volunteers for Community Service
REACH
RedR Register of Engineers for
    Disaster Relief
Returned Volunteer Action
Roots HR CIC
SAGGA
School Governors' One-Stop Shop
TimeBank
Time Banking UK
Time for God
Volunteers for Rural India
Volunteering Matters
VSO
WorldWide Volunteering
WRVS

## STILLBIRTH & NEONATAL DEATH

Miscarriage Association
Stillbirth and Neonatal Death Society
Tommy's, the Baby Charity

## STRESS & ANXIETY DISORDERS

Anxiety Care UK
International Stress Management
    Association UK

## STROKE

ARNI Institute
Different Strokes
HemiHelp
Stroke Association

## STUDENTS

UCCF

## SUBSTANCE ABUSE

See ADDICTION SUPPORT SERVICES;
ALCOHOL AWARENESS & SUPPORT
GROUPS; DRUG AWARENESS &
SUPPORT GROUPS

## TEACHING STANDARDS & SUPPORT

Association for Language Learning
Association of Blind and Partially Sighted
    Teachers and Students
British Sociological Association
CfBT Education Trust
Commonwealth Education Trust
National Association for Pastoral Care
    in Education

## TECHNOLOGY

See also COMPUTERS & THE INTERNET
Association for Learning Technology
Charity IT Leaders (CITL)
Freeplay Foundation
Millipedia
Online Centres Foundation
Practical Action
Remap
Royal Television Society
Sonic Arts Network
STAGETEXT
Talking Newspaper Association of the UK
The Radio Amateurs' Emergency Network
The Sequal Trust
Women's Technology and Education Centre
Worshipful Company of
    Information Technologists
YouthNet

## THEATRES

Independent Theatre Council
National Association of Youth Theatres
Spare Tyre Theatre Company
STAGETEXT
Travelling Light Theatre Company
Theatres Trust

## THERAPY SERVICES AND CENTRES

Association of Dance
    Therapists (International)
Association of Therapeutic Communities
British False Memory Society
Community Housing and Therapy
Refugee Therapy Centre
The Therapy Database

## EDUCATIONAL & SPECIAL NEEDS

Caldecott Foundation
Caspari Foundation for Educational Therapy
    and Therapeutic Teaching
Foundation66
Nordoff-Robbins Music Therapy
RESPOND

## MEDICAL & HEALTH BENEFITS

Bobath Centre for Children with
    Cerebral Palsy
British Association and College of
    Occupational Therapists
Free Access Cancer Therapy Database
Freshwinds
Gaia House
Iyengar Yoga Institute
Multiple Sclerosis National Therapy Centres
Rainbow Centre for Children affected by
    Life-Threatening Illnesses or Bereavement

## WOMEN

Women's Therapy Centre

## TOWN PLANNING

Town and Country Planning Association

## TRAINING

**See ADULT EDUCATION & TRAINING; BEHAVIOURAL TRAINING; BUSINESS & INDUSTRY TRAINING; HEALTHCARE & MEDICAL TRAINING; LEADERSHIP SKILLS TRAINING**

## TRANSGENDER SUPPORT GROUPS

**See GAY/LESBIAN/BISEXUAL/ TRANSGENDER SUPPORT GROUPS**

## TRANSPORT

Aftermath Support
Arun Co-ordinated Community Transport
Campaign Against Drinking and Driving
Campaign for Better Transport
    Charitable Trust
Carplus
Chartered Institution of Highways
    and Transportation
Community Transport
Community Transport Association
Ealing Community Transport
FIA Foundation for the Automobile
    and Society
Institution of Highways and Transportation
Parliamentary Advisory Council for
    Transport Safety
RoadPeace
Sustrans
The Royal Society for the Prevention of
    Accidents (RoSPA)
Torridge Community Transport Association
Transport Trust

## TRAVELLER GROUPS

Advisory Council for the Education of
    Romany and Other Travellers
London Gypsy and Traveller Unit
The Traveller Movement

## TREE PRESERVATION

Tree Council
Trees for Cities
Woodland Trust

## UMBRELLA & RESOURCE BODIES

**See also COMMUNITY DEVELOPMENT & RESOURCES, VOLUNTARY ACTION**
Association of British Credit
Association of Charitable Organisations
Association of Chief Executives of
    Voluntary Organisations
AVID (Association of Visitors to
    Immigration Detainees)
Braintree District Voluntary Support Agency

British Spiritualist Federation
Castle Point Association of Voluntary
    Services (CAVS)
Centre for Effective Dispute Resolution
Charities HR Network
Charity Administration, Resourcing
    and Accountability
Charity Finance Group
Churches Together in Britain and Ireland
Confederation of Indian Organisations (UK)
Co-operatives UK
Cumbria CVS
Enfield Voluntary Action (EVA)
Federation of Irish Societies
Gateshead Voluntary Organisations Council
Gosport Voluntary Action
Greater London Volunteering
Greater Manchester Centre for
    Voluntary Organisation
Hambleton Community Action
Horsham and Mid Sussex Voluntary Action
Institute of Money Advisers
Joint Epilepsy Council
Locality
Magistrates' Association
National Council for Palliative Care
National Council for Voluntary Organisations
National Development Team for Inclusion
Newcastle Council for Voluntary Service
Nova Wakefield District Limited
Northern Ireland Council for
    Voluntary Action
Redbridge Council for Voluntary Service
REMA
Scottish Council for Voluntary Organisations
Small Charities Coalition
Southend Association of Voluntary Services
Sport and Recreation Alliance
Sustain: the Alliance for Better Food
    and Farming
Telephone Helplines Association
Textile Institute International
The Electrical Safety Council
Tower Hamlets CVS
Voluntary Action History Society
Voluntary Norfolk
VOSCUR
Wales Council for Voluntary Action
Woking Association of Voluntary Service
Worcester Volunteer Centre
World Society for the Protection of Animals
WorldWide Volunteering

## ADVICE & INFORMATION

Advice Services Alliance
Advice UK
Citizens Advice
Consortium of Bengali Associations
Direct Help & Advice (DHA)
Enterprising Futures
Evelyn 190 Centre
Helplines Partnership
SWAN Advice Network

## ARTS & CULTURE

British Federation of Film Societies
British & International Federation of Festivals

Federation of British Artists
National Association of Decorative and Fine
    Arts Societies

## CHILDREN & YOUNG PEOPLE

Ambition
British Youth Council
Care Co-ordination Network Cymru
Churches Child Protection Advisory Service
Consortium of Voluntary Adoption Agencies
Direct Help & Advice (DHA)
National Association of Child
    Contact Centres
National Association of Youth Theatres
National Day Nurseries Association
National Playbus Association
Professional Association for Childcare and
    Early Years (PACEY)
Staffordshire Council of Voluntary
    Youth Services

## COMMNUITY DEVELOPMENT

Action with Communities in Rural
    England (ACRE)
Civic Trust
Community Matters
Consortium of Lesbian, Gay, Bisexual and
    Transgender Voluntary and
    Community Organisations
Federation of City Farms and
    Community Gardens
National Association for Voluntary and
    Community Associations
Shared Lives Plus

## DISABILITIES

ARC
Care Co-ordination Network UK
National Association of Swimming Clubs for
    the Handicapped
UK Council on Deafness
United Kingdom Sports Association for
    People with Learning Disability
United Kingdom's Disabled People's Council

## EDUCATION

British Council
National Association of Independent Schools
    and Non Maintained Special Schools
National Confederation of Parent
    Teacher Associations
Universities UK
University Association for Contemporary
    European Studies

## ENVIRONMENT

The Rivers Trust
Town and Country Planning Association

## HEALTHCARE

Alliance of Healing Associations
Hospice UK
National Patients Support Trust
UK Public Health Association
United Kingdom Homecare Association
Visionary – linking local sight loss charities

**HERITAGE & HISTORY**
British Association for Local History
The Heritage Alliance

**OVERSEAS AID & DEVELOPMENT**
Bond
Overseas Development Institute

**PERSONAL DEVELOPMENT**
Mentoring and Befriending Foundation

**RESEARCH ORGANISATIONS**
Association of Medical Research Charities
British Association for the Advancement
   of Science

**SEAFARERS & MARITIME WORKERS**
Federation of Merchants Mariners

**SOCIAL CARE**
British Association of Social Workers

**WOMEN'S GROUPS**
National Alliance of Women's Organisations
National Association of Women's Clubs
National Council of Women of Great Britain
National Federation of Women's Institutes
Townswomen's Guilds
Women's Aid Federation of England
Women's Resource Centre
World Association of Girl Guides and
   Girl Scouts

## VISUAL IMPAIRMENT
**See BLINDNESS & SIGHT IMPAIRMENT**

## VOLUNTARY ACTION AND VOLUNTEER CENTRES
**See also UMBRELLA AND RESOURCE BODIES, COMMUNITY DEVELOPMENT & RESOURCES**
Enfield Voluntary Action (EVA)
Gateshead Voluntary Organisations Council
Gosport Voluntary Action
Horsham and Mid Sussex Voluntary Action
involve Community Services
Kent Volunteers
Step Together Volunteering
Voluntary Action Calderdale
Voluntary Action Islington
Voluntary Action South West Surrey
Voluntary Norfolk
Voluntary Services Lewisham
Volunteer Centre Greenwich
Wigan and Leigh CVS
Worcester Volunteer Centre

## WILDLIFE CONSERVATION
**See also MARINE LIFE & WATERWAYS**
Born Free Foundation
Care for the Wild International
Durrell Wildlife Conservation Trust
Game Conservancy Trust
The Wildlife Trusts
Wildfowl and Wetlands Trust
Wildlife Aid
Wildlife and Countryside Link
World Society for the Protection of Animals
Zoological Society of London

## WOMEN'S SUPPORT GROUPS
Asha Projects
Association of Breastfeeding Mothers
Breaking Free – Primarily Supporting
   Women Survivors of Child Sexual Abuse
Catholic Women's League
Clean Break
Eva Women's Aid
FATIMA Women's Network
Fawcett Society
Female Prisoners Welfare Project and
Hibiscus
GFS Platform for Young Women
Jewish Women's Aid
Mothers Apart from their Children
Mothers Union
National Alliance of Women's Organisations
National Association of Women's Clubs
National Council of Women of Great Britain
National Federation of Women's Institutes
National Women's Register
Positive Body Image
Positively UK
Powerhouse
Rape and Sexual Abuse Support Centre
   – Rape Crisis South London
Refuge
Rights of Women
Self Injury Support
Society for the Assistance of Ladies in
   Reduced Circumstances
The Fairlight Trust
Townswomen's Guilds
War Widows Association of Great Britain and
   Northern Ireland
WOMANKIND Worldwide
Women and Girls' Network
Women and Manual Trades
Women's Environmental Network
Women's Farm and Garden Association
Women's Health Advice Centre
Women's Resource Centre
Women's Royal Naval Service
   Benevolent Trust
Women's Therapy Centre
Worthing Women's Aid Trading as Safe
   in Sussex
WRVS
Young Women's Trust

## ACCOMMODATION
Chapter 1
Christian Family Concern
Eaves Housing for Women Limited
House of Saint Barnabas in Soho
LIFE
Women's Aid Federation of England

## EDUCATION
CAMFED International
Creative and Supportive Trust
Josephine Butler Educational Trust
Topps – Training Opportunities
Women's Technology and Education Centre

## HEALTH
Birth Companions
Daisy Network
Disability Pregnancy and Parenthood
Endometriosis SHE Trust (UK)
Endometriosis UK
FAS Aware UK
Foundation for Women's Health Research
   and Development
LIFE
Medical Women's Federation
Positive Body Image
Positively UK
The Association for Post-Natal Illness
WISH – a voice for women's mental health